HELL

ON THE BORDER

HE HANGED EIGHTY-EIGHT MEN

A HISTORY OF THE GREAT UNITED STATES CRIMINAL COURT AT FORT
SMITH, ARKANSAS, AND OF CRIME AND CRIMINALS IN THE INDIAN
TERRITORY, AND THE TRIAL AND PUNISHMENT THEREOF BEFORE HIS HONOR

JUDGE ISAAC C. PARKER

"THE TERROR OF LAW-BREAKERS,"

BY S. W. HARMAN

COMPILED BY C. P. STERNS

FORT SMITH, ARK.

1898

Contents

PUBLISHER'S NOTES

More than one hundred years after its first publication, there is still no more comprehensive and exciting published work on one of the most famous courts in history: the Parker Court. There is something here for everyone from True Crime aficionado to law professor. Here is frontier justice as it played out in the courts, as opposed to how it plays out in Hollywood. The cases are detailed and riveting and even Parker's instructions to a grand jury makes fine reading for anyone interested in courtroom proceedings.

Justice in Indian Territory at the end of the nineteenth century was sometimes as brutal as the crimes it was punishing. However, in Judge Isaac Charles Parker, one finds an erudite, articulate, even eloquent and impassioned advocate for the rule of law. Though the appellation of "the hanging judge" was hung on him you will not find a rough, mean-spirited, fire-breathing magistrate here. He will surprise and often amuse you.

Judy Galonska, author of the introduction for the 2001 print version of this classic, cautions that the author, Samuel Harman, and his assistants, J. Warren Reed and C.P. Stearns, were not detached observers of Judge Parker's court. They knew him and loved him. But they drew extensively on court records, newspaper accounts, and interviews when writing this exhaustive compilation of Parker's two decades on the bench in Indian Territory.

During Parker's service, non-Native Americans were flooding into the territory. Crime was really rampant and much of it was shocking. Many outlaws believed they would not face justice in the wild and open spaces. Most Americans and certainly most citizens of the territory approved of Parker's severe sentencing. Many felt that the relative stability at the end of Parker's service was largely a result of that severity, ignoring other factors that settlement of the territory brought with it.

There are some inaccuracies in the book but they appear minor. One more egregious one is the section on Belle Star, which is enormously entertaining but pretty much cribbed from the dime novel, *The Bandit Queen*.

You'll find more than just murder and robbery in these pages, although many of the cases involved those crimes. In the end, there is a mountain of entertaining reading.

AUTHOR'S PREFACE.

In preparing and putting before the reading public a History of the Federal Court of Fort Smith, Arkansas, the most famous court in the world's annals, the greatest distinctive criminal court ever known, than which none ever existed with jurisdiction over so great an expanse of territory, and the only trial court in the civilized world from whose decisions there was—for many years—no right of appeal, I am governed by mingled emotions of sympathy and triumph: Sympathy for the unfortunate thousands in our land, who, under our present system of civilization, are brought into the world criminals at birth, with the mark of Cain already set upon their brows, practically irresponsible for their acts because of a lack of proper opportunities for cultivating the virtues, lacking discipline in childhood and allowed to grow up like a bramble—untended and untutored; their vices encouraged and their natural good— that lying dormant—was smothered for lack of nutriment: Of triumph at the achievements of our courts, and of this especial court, whose duty it was to run down and ferret out those of the criminal classes in the Indian Territory who were too much hardened, too old in sin to be susceptible of reforming influence, and whose inevitable and certain punishment for crimes committed may serve as a warning to others who, not having yet entered the whirling vortex leading to a criminal career, may be induced to direct their footsteps in another direction.

In 1888 I moved to Bentonville, Arkansas, and continued to reside there and at Rogers for a period of nearly ten years. During that time I was frequently summoned to serve on the

Federal Jury at Fort Smith and this, with other private business affairs, took me to that city so frequently that I became conversant with the peculiarities of the court and its environments as well as becoming intimately acquainted with Judge I. C. Parker and all the leading attorneys who practiced at his world famous bar. as well as with many of the deputy marshals and other court attaches.

Very early in my experience with the court I decided that a book which should give a carefully compiled list of the leading criminals who were there convicted would be of value to moralists, and as time grew apace I concluded that such a book to be valuable should contain as well descriptions of the more noted trials, stories of the crimes committed and sketches of the criminals themselves, as well as a biography of Judge Parker, also of the executioner and other officers of the court, and many bits of information and data of curious facts which might be considered worthy of being handed down in history.

This information, on account of my intimate acquaintance with Judge Parker and the leading attorneys, I was enabled to obtain, and being of a naturally observing turn of mind I picked up many things that, placed together, makes a whole that is of undeniable interest.

Looking about for a title for the book, I remembered standing one evening at the entrance to the United States Jail, when an old Arkansas gentleman passed and, looking in, for a moment, paused and listened to the ribald songs and coarse, brutal jests that fell from the lips of the prisoners; he heard the demoniacal yells, saw the prisoners, Indians, whites and negroes, all mingled together in a heterogeneous mass, and turning to me, with a look that spoke the anguish he felt, remarked:

"If this is not hell, I do not know where hell is."

"Yes," replied a bystander. "And it is right on the border."

I was deeply impressed, and I shudder now as I think of the emotions which filled my soul as I listened to their words, and by a species of analytical digression cogitated upon the present, past and possible future of the unfortunate beings within that veritable hell.

Then there came to me like an inspiration: "Teach the youth; instill correct principles into their hearts, crowding out the seeds of crime and there'll be none to fill a hell like this."

At a point in the Indian Territory where the trail leading from "No Man's Land" crosses the north fork of the Canadian River stands a sign bearing the legend:

FORT SMITH

FIVE HUNDRED MILES

In the fall of 1882, after the Federal Court under Judge Parker had gained a reputation which mad: it a terror to the red-handed Territory outlaws, a posse of deputy marshals were in the vicinity in search of a well-known bandit gang, composed of six of the most desperate characters in the Indian country. The officers were close upon them; the outlaws hastening to reach No Man's Land which offered better opportunities for defense than the broad expanse of prairie to the east. Finally, with the marshals in full sight, not more than two miles away, the bandits reached the borders of the stream when, as if by common impulse, they stopped, turned their horses and raising their Winchesters each fired several volleys at the innocent guide board as if to show their contempt for Fort Smith and the Federal Court, and then wheeling about rode away to safety. A few days later one of them, having something of the wag in his make up, returned, and glancing up at the words, whose typography was well-nigh destroyed by the bullets, was struck with the humor of the situation, and standing high in his saddle he cut with his dirk in rude characters underneath, this legend: "To Hell."

It told of the profound fear rather than contempt which the Territory outlaws had for the Fort Smith Court, and the new emblem was a mighty sermon in itself. More than that, it assisted me in making a title to my book.

In closing, I wish to say to the reader: Should you be of an esthetic mind and find sketches herein which appear to be too real do not criticize the author harshly. This is not fiction, and I did not make the characters which the book reveals. I present to you a history of events as they occurred without "fixing over," as a writer of fiction might do.

It is truth, and if at times it is even stranger than fiction, then is a well-known proverb proven.

In preparing the contents of this work I have entirely-ignored the advice of Byron:

"Truth's fountains may be clear—her streams are muddy.

And cut through such canals of contradiction

That she must often navigate o'er fiction."

And have rather trusted to the chances of there being no truth in these lines by Churchill:

"When fiction rises pleasing to the eye,

Men will believe, because they love the lie;

But truth herself, if clouded with a frown,

Must have some solemn proof to pass her down."

The Author.

INTRODUCTION

"Thou shalt not kill" was handed down to Moses, repeated on Sinai and thundered down the ages until the present, when it has become a part of the organic laws of every civilized nation on the globe.

Stringent laws have been enacted, severe punishment has been prescribed, awful vengeance has been visited upon the slayer of his fellow man, but the red hand of murder is no stayed. In the dawn of creation, we are told, the first born, ere he reached man's prime estate, became a murderer, was branded in the sight of God and banished from his home. We read the history of the two brothers filling out over their sacrifices. Cain through jealousy slays his brother, Abel.

Here we find a history of the first murder trial. God accuses, condemns and punishes Cain, Josephus tells us that the death penalty was withheld because Cain had offered sacrifice, but the punishment meted out, branded for life before men, the mark upon him so that all should know, must have been even more terrible than death.

When we consider that the first child born into the world became the slayer of his own brother, just outside the garden of Eden, little need we wonder that so many misguided persons in the nineteenth century, burdened with the hereditary' taint of crime handed down from generation to generation, should follow the precedent established by the first prince of the universe, and become slayers of men.

Beginning with the earliest account of man, trace his footsteps down the ages, and the bloody trail leads us to the present. This we prove, not only by the Mosaic account of early humanity, but the records left by ancient Egypt and China paint primitive man in the same crimson hue.

The enlightenment of these latter days is calling loudly for a change. Who will point out a remedy? Who can tell us how to staunch this useless flow of human blood? It has been suggested that the law of "a life for a life" or "an eye for an eye," the punishment by death of him who takes life, does not lessen the number of murders. For example; the state of Kansas, where capital punishment has been practically abolished, is cited as having very few such crimes within its borders. On the other hand, the Creek Nation in the Indian Territory, where the death penalty was prescribed oftener and for more trivial offenses than anywhere on the American continent, furnished more candidates for the jail and gibbet at Fort Smith than all the other districts under the jurisdiction of that famous court. An eminent authority on crime and its causes has said," it is not the severity of punishment that deters men from crime, but the certainty of being apprehended and punished."

However that may be, it is certain that unless more effective means be adopted for the suppression of the flagrant and ever increasing violation of law in our land, checking the mighty volume of wickedness in country and cities, large and small, the future of our nation will indeed be black.

It is a matter of grave doubt with many prominent writers and speakers if, after all, we have not all this time been working at the wrong end. We have been endeavoring to suppress crime by perpetrating what some term" legalized crime," for getting that love alone is capable of ruling the universe, while force but antagonizes. It may seem perfectly natural that we should attempt to offset terrible crimes by severe punishment; yet, when one comes to think seriously of it, this but places the law in the position of seeking revenge; the voice of a mighty people, backed by the force of the law, all raised against one poor unfortunate, who, held in the law's clutches as in a vice, is unable to help himself.

"But," says one," would you allow a system of lawlessness with no punishment for him who stains his hands with his brother's blood?" Certainly not. I would invoke the strong arm of the law to gather in and withhold the hands of the lawbreaker, but I would at the same time work at the other end, seek the prime cause; for if we but stud)', there is no action without a cause.

The histories of all criminal courts, of jails, penitentiaries and alms houses have proven that the prime and imminent cause of the downfall of nine tenths of those who commit crime is alcohol in one form or another; it may be in the shape of the sparkling glass of wine which the charming young lady unthoughtedly urges upon her sweetheart, carelessly leading him on, like the siren, to certain destruction; or the fateful sip of fermented grape juice taken by the penitent while kneeling at the communion table; it may be in the shape of the barrel of hard cider in father's cellar in which "there is no harm because we were raised with it," or in the small doses dealt out by order of a short-sighted physician. Never believe it is the first glass of ardent spirits taken over the bar of a grog shop that in the majority of cases leads to the excessive use of intoxicant. Were our children taught the physiological effects of the poison as they are taught to walk or converse; were the same diligence exercised in pointing out to them the evil that exists in the ruby wine, that we use in teaching them the first lessons in morals, the time would far sooner come when our people would do right, when our voters would vote right and our law makers legislate right, and we should seethe commencement of the banishment of King Alcohol from our land. Then, when our young men could start in the world free from the insidious temptations of the viper, should we see the commencement of a new era, a new generation, free from the influences which drag men down to crime.

And then the church. Ah! there must we look for influences for good, far stronger than any we have yet experienced. To the church belongs the sacred duty of lifting up the fallen, aye more, of teaching by example and precept that which shall prevent the commission of crime, by preventing the making of criminals.

Listen! In New York City, eight thousand saloons, brothels of hell, their doors open day and night, three hundred and sixty-five days in the year; four hundred churches, too, their doors open a few hours of fifty-two days in the year, which think you is doing the most missionary work, at home our churches pass the hat, our mothers sew, and bibles and preachers are sent to save the heathens who never heard of a hell, but in the majority of these self-same churches, the seats are too clean, their precincts altogether too sacred to permit of entrance to a poor tramp without a friend on earth. No wonder that to him the bright lights, the sparkling glasses, the sounds of reveling and laughter of the saloons seem so inviting. There his dime, while it lasts, is as good as the gentleman's dollar, and a few kind words at least are vouchsafed him. Had the church during the century just passing, put forth as much energy as the saloons, our prisons today would be empty; our alms houses, jails and penitentiaries would stand as so many monuments of a degenerate age. What fond parent, could he but lift the veil of the future and gazing upon the scenes of coming years see his idolized son in the role of a criminal, a murderer perhaps, the result of the "harmless" glass of wine drank while sitting at his father's table, would not banish the terrible drug from his home forever?

Let me quote from a recent sermon by a noted Baptist divine, Rev. Stephen A. Northrop, in a leading western city, from the text, "Thou Shalt not Kill:"

"The two greatest tragedies of history, the murder of Abel and the crucification [*sic*] of Christ, plainly emphasize the necessity of this commandment. There is another text, however, which confirms this one: 'The voice of thy brother's blood crieth out unto me from the ground,' says Almighty God in the face of guilty Cain. And it has always been thus. You cannot wash out human blood. There is no fuller's soap, no chemical mixture strong enough to cleanse the crimson marks wherever they may fall.

"We may hush many voices, but the voice of blood eloquently cries out from the ground for redress. The brand of Cain may appear not only on the face, but it is most surely written in letters of blood on the conscience. 'Murder, though it has no tongue, will speak with most miraculous organ.' Historians, poets, reformers and moralists most familiar with humanity have chronicled repeated tragical illustration-^ to prove that crime cannot escape from its shadow or from its awful forebodings.

"How heart rendering has been the experience of thousands of murderers after the crime has been committed! Blood stains forever! His steps dogged to the day of doom or the day of the scaffold. No angel's efforts can remove the weight of guilt. The sullen lips pour forth no cry for pardon! The fountain of tears are dried up! No contrition asks for mercy! He stands before his friends an icy pillar of despair. Hope offers no support. He must go forth at last to reap what he has sown. He has learned the sad lesson, 'The way of the transgressor is hard.'

"'Other sins speak; murder shrieks out. The element of water moistens the earth, but blood mounts upward.'

"Driven away from God, ostracized from home, cast out of society, like Cain of old, he is a wanderer up and down the earth. He can only cry aloud for the rocks to fall on him and hide him from the face of Him who sitteth upon the throne.' O God, save the murderer! With thine atoning blood wash out the crimson stain and prepare him for an entrance into the paradise of God! As he falls from the trap of the spectral scaffold, receive his soul, in the name of a pardoning God!

"A criminal who was condemned to hang for homicide, and awaiting execution in prison, drew upon the walls of his cell the sketch of a man upon the gallows, with five steps leading to the platform on which he stood. On the first step he wrote: 'Disobedience to parents;' on the second, 'Sabbath breaking;' on the third, 'gambling and drunkenness;' on the fourth, 'Murder,' and on the fifth, 'the fatal platform.' How true a picture of the experience of thousands of criminals about us. Men do not go into crime with a single leap; step by step, step by step, till they are led up to the heights of criminal practice, and at last to the scaffold.

"A hundred thousand graves are filled every year in the United States. The funeral procession reaches mile after mile, the mourners are the millions. Who are digging these graves? Who are cutting the hearts out of our fathers, mothers and sisters? The saloonist! God have mercy on his blood-stained soul! Of the seven thousand three hundred and eighty-six murderers in this country in one year, five thousand one hundred and nine traced the cause to strong drink. Fearful facts! Bloody statistics! They are homicidal facts given out by the bureau of statistics. They are, therefore, not mine, and are given without prejudice. They are enough, however, to compel us to bestir ourselves. Let us plead with Almighty God to revolutionize our country and purify its halls of justice! Let us pledge high heaven that we will do our part in bringing this to pass lest the voice of human blood cry out to us in the great day of judgment.

I have dealt with this subject at some length, with a view to preparing the reader for what is to come, reminding him that while it is right to abhor evil doing, to hate the acts of evil men, it is humane to have sympathy for those who have been lead to crime by unseen and evil influence.

Here let me state a truth. Over 30 per cent, of the criminals indicted and sentenced from the Fort Smith Court were orphans, who had not known a fostering mother's care, had never kneeled at her side and in childhood's innocence lisped the "Now I lay me down to sleep," had never received the wise counsel of a doting father whose example should stand through life a monument to right doing, the memory of whose precepts should serve as a bulwark of strength to guard against the temptations of chance evil companions.

Nearly one-third were orphans, thrown upon a heartless world at a susceptible age without a reliable guide, placed in a condition similar to the fated mariner who, without chart or compass, drifted with the waves, never knowing, sometimes scarcely caring wither he was going except when buffeted by the winds, when he would have sought refuge upon a barren island or have accepted the hospitality of a bandit band as readily as he would have hailed the captain of a passing ocean greyhound, little caring how or where, so he escaped the roughness of an unruly sea.

The rugged determination resulting from a life of self dependence, added to the careless, lawless disposition that becomes second nature to the child without a home, forms a combination easily influenced for good if met at the right time by the hand of kindness, the voice of love. It is a combination too, which, turned in the direction of vice, led on by the voice that seems so alluring (because none other voice e'er spake so kindly) becomes at last the very counterpart of vicious, unscrupulous cunning, bringing the subject to a state where he fears neither God nor man, with the propensity for love lying dormant, never more capable of experiencing a real fondness for members of the human family except—ah yes, such a one sometimes finds his idol, and to her his whole heart goes out, and he loves, passionately, fondly, madly, with all the strength of rugged character; for her he would descend to the lowest grades of crime, would even murder, and sleep peacefully thereafter unmindful of his act, providing it met with her approval. And why? By what means could a woman, so lost to a sense of true womanliness, gain such an influence over a being whom all others seemed unable to impress? Very simple; the kind word rightly spoken and at the right time; the one thing more than all others the human soul yearns for, the first, perhaps, he had heard in years, and it casts a spell; he is a child again when in her presence; nothing she may ask will be refused, he is as a lamb or a tartar as she wills.

There are those who will doubt the truth of the above, call it imagination, but if they will search in the outskirts of civilization they will come to believe, as did the writer. It is a fact, that our worst outlaws are m ide up of a class whose recklessness, and boldness, is but the result of a nature cramped, trod upon, crowded to the wall at a time when the good born in them should have been carefully nurtured, until at last having broken loose, freed from their cramped environments they go out to the world free, free as the air they breathe and ready to adopt whatever course points to a continuance of that freedom.

The nature that is too retiring or too indolent to escape from uncomfortable conditions, bids the boy grow to manhood still kicked about, believing he is the scum of humanity and fulfilling the belief; he becomes a vagabond, it may, be but never a great criminal, nor would he have been great had he been reared in influence and provided with the finest education.

Just so, the one who, having fought his way to manhood, maintaining and believing that as one of God's creatures he had the same right to live as any of the others, and backing his belief with courage sufficient to sustain it, becomes successful in his undertakings, and if, because of neglect, from want of proper instructions in his tender years he becomes a bad rather than a good citizen it is the fault rather of our social system than of the individual.

Such a nature, if properly guided, properly nurtured, the twig inclined" in the right direction is capable of becoming a leader in all things right, an example, and a worthy one, to mankind. A child with such a nature, provided with kind but wise parents to teach him the proper distinction between right and wrong, may become a power for good; left to his own devices, his susceptible nature a prey to the temptations of whatever evil companions chance throws in his way, he becomes a power for evil.

An eminent student of the causes which lead to crime, none other than Rev. W. D. Morrison, editor of the Criminology Series, and for years chaplain of an English prison, whose long experience enables him to speak with a voice of authority on questions of fact and matters of detail regarding this subject, says that the proportion of habitual criminals in the criminal population is steadily increasing. He maintains that "society is suffering from crime and criminals largely as a result of having neglected its boys."

Bad company and bad literature has set the standard of thousands of misguided youths. Some of them, it is true, had parents, but how much more likely is the orphan child to be led away by undue influences! The devil has little difficulty in alluring the boy "without a home," who, without the protection of a home, is easily led down the incline that ends in outlawry. Verily the opportunities for missionary work are great within our own borders. We are indeed a sympathetic people. We weep for benighted souls in foreign lands, but pass by those of our own land who every day are taking their first steps in the broad road that seems so easy, but leads to a felon's cell. A land of plenty, washed with nine thousand miles of seashore, boasting of over seventy millions of people and seventy billions of wealth supports a social system that drives to unlawful deeds the homeless and friendless; makes tramps and criminals where it should lend a hand and secure instead splendid citizens.

I well remember pleading with an old man to just let me, an orphan, work for a home and clothes. He was a father and should have had a father's heart, but he turned a deaf ear to my supplications, and at last I said: "Well, old man, you have boys of your own. Suppose you were to die and leave them to be turned out to the cold world, would you not rise up in your grave and cure the man who, having plenty, would turn one of them out into the road hungry, tired and cold?" His answer was: "I would not be afraid to turn all my children out to take care of themselves at any time. They would seek their level and find good homes in less than a year,"

"In less than a year "the old man died; he was shortly followed by the mother, and in less than three years one of the sons was sentenced to three years in a state penitentiary for burglary. So much for the level he sought. Like thousands, he fell in with evil associations.

Before closing this chapter let me state the objects of this book. They are three fold. It is hoped that the lessons to be taught within its covers may tend to forewarn, and thus forearm those of its readers who might be led astray by the glittering promises of the tempter, and if it shall cause one young man or young woman to shun evil associates and continue in the path of rectitude, or cause one who is already started on a downward course to stop and consider, to look ahead and shudder and turn again to the right, then shall I have been well repaid for my labor. Forty thousand young women in America, a majority of them born under the brightest auspices, are each year laid away in dishonored graves; as great a number of young men each year start upon the path that leads to a felon's cell. Each year as they disappear from their usual haunts the places occupied for a brief period by these thousands of both sexes are supplied regularly by recruits from among our brightest and best. We are living in an age when all possible influences for good should be assisted and encouraged; on these depends the coming social structure, the welfare of posterity.

Again, I have long desired to see established a home where orphan children, denied the protection intended by nature, may be kept from the hard knocks of the outside world and given a chance for education, an opportunity to determine for what particular vocation or niche he or she is best adapted. I would take a different course than have the managers of ordinary institutions of this character. I would select for a location a suitable tract among the broad acres of our productive western plains and there, far out from the enervating and soul-destroying influence of the cities, would I erect suitable buildings, properly equipped for the purpose in view. The work of tiding the soil, of keeping the buildings and grounds in repair and the gradual improvements necessary, as well as the task of teaching the youthful minds, bending them in the right direction, should be performed, as they arrived at the proper age, by the beneficiaries themselves, who should be held responsible for the divisions under their charge and report to a board of managers; thus would they by the time they arrived at maturity have bet n disciplined to correct business methods and be in a position to go out into the world a benefit to society, rather than a detriment to it. Should the influences exerted in this book become the means of establishing a fund to be used for the laudable purpose here detailed, then is the second object accomplished.

Finally, but by no means least, as the labor of gathering and preparing the data within these covers progressed, its subject matter expanded until it entirely outgrew the original intentions of the author; the pages have multiplied as research extended until in its present form it is a connecting link between a period of savagery, in a portion of our country, and of civilization. It fills a gap in the history of our nation, covering a space of over a quarter of a century, which would otherwise have become a blank. Ten years more and much of the data here given would have been lost, and indeed many important historical facts here recorded cannot, even now, be found elsewhere, except in the memories of a few early settlers, who will soon be, too, "of the forgotten past." This book is destined to become of importance to the student of the future and writers of the nation's history will yet turn to these pages for authority on matters concerning that portion of our country hitherto untouched by writers other than the fictionist. Thus have the two original objects expanded into a whole that, while it does not detract from the others, yet gives to the book a character that carries it further down the path of time, increasing its influence and broadening its field of usefulness.

In closing, let me urge upon the reader to keep sacred the lessons taught as you peruse the coming pages and so live that in after years, when your journey across life's meadows leads you close to the river that marks the unknown shore, your page in the great book in Heaven shall be filled with a record of deeds of charity, the golden keys that open the pearly gates standing before the palace of eternity.

FORT SMITH AND THE FAMOUS COURT

"O, yes! O, yes! The Honorable District and Circuit-Courts of the United States for the Western District of Arkansas, HWING CRIMINAL JURISDICTION OF THE INDIAN TERRITORY, are now adjourned. God bless the United States and these honorable courts," rang out the voice of Court Caller J. G. Hammersly.

Thus ended, on the first day of September, 1896. the criminal jurisdiction over the Indian Territory of the most famous court the world has ever known, which for more than twenty-five years presided over the Western District of Arkansas, the United States Criminal Court at Fort Smith, Arkansas.

Fort Smith, Arkansas, is a city of 20,000 population, located at the confluence of the Poteau with the Arkansas River, in the western part of the State, and on the line dividing Arkansas from the Indian Territory. Its early history dates back to 1816, when the United States government established there a military post giving it the name which the city still bears, in honor of Gen. Thomas A. Smith, under whose direction the site was selected. A stockade of squared logs driven closely together deep into the ground, and with two wooden block houses and other necessary buildings, constituting the first fort, was erected in 1817, at Belle Point, a high sand-stone bluff overlooking the mouth of the Poteau. This fort was in the Choctaw Nation, about 100 yards west of the Arkansas line,* and its northern and southern boundaries were at points between what would be Garland Avenue and High Street, where these extended to the Poteau. It was first occupied by Maj. William Bradford with a company of infantry in November, 1817. In 1824 the troops were withdrawn for a season, were again-returned, and in 1830 the fort was abandoned, the garrison having been ordered to Fort Coffee in the Indian Territory, later to Fort Wayne in the Indian Territory, and still later to-Fort Gibson, where a fort had been established In 1822.

At the time of the location of Fort Smith, the land now known as the "Choctaw Strip," was claimed and occupied by a Choctaw Indian named Thomas Wall. The government purchased the improvements from Wall and the latter gave up possession. After the abandonment of Fort Smith by the removal of the Garrison, as stated, in 1830, the Indian returned and again occupied the Choctaw Strip, and after his death another Choctaw Indian, Campbell LeFlore, a noted attorney, purchased of the heirs of Tom Wall their interests in the improvements, and thus secured the possession of the "Strip." The heirs of Campbell LeFlore still claim this property.

The protection and sense of security given to the Indian Territory by the Stars and Stripes attracted settlers to the western portion of Arkansas, where the new fort was located, and on October 30, 1829, the first entry of government I md was made by one Hugh Tygert, who on that day entered the southeast quarter of section 8, township 8, range 32 west, and the west fractional half of section 17. On January 31, 1832, the northeast quarter of section 17, lying south and east of the two tracts above noted, was entered by David McKee. The southwest quarter of section 9 had been entered by one

John Rogers, January 10th of the same year, and on August 1, 1832, Rogers purchased of Tygert the above noted southeast quarter of section 8, adjoining his original entry on the west. The records in regard to the southeast quarter of section 17, together with the transfer of the northeast quarter of section 17, by Rogers by McKee and of the west fractional half of section 17 by Tygert, were destroyed by fire in 1861, but it is known that the three tracts subsequently came into possession of and that portions of the east half of 17, all of the fractional west half of the same section and a small portion of the southeast quarter of section 8, were sold later by Rogers to the United States government for a reservation, at an increased price, as will be noted later.

By act of Congress, approved June 15, 1836, the Territory of Arkansas was admitted to the Union as a State (U. S. St. at L, Vol. 5, Chap. 490. p. 397). About this time the remnants of the Cherokee Indian tribe were being removed from the State of Georgia to the Cherokee Nation, in the northeast corner of the Indian Territory, their reservation extending south to the Arkansas River, opposite Fort Smith. There proved to be three parties, or clans, of the Cherokees; those previously removed to the Indian Territory and who were friendly to the whites, those who had been lately removed from the State of Georgia, known as the "Treaty Party," who were also friendly and in favor of their new possession*, and a third clan, known as the "Ross Party," who strongly opposed being removed to a new country, but were compelled by the government to acquiesce in its ultimatum. Between these three parties difficulties arose and, with them, fears for the safety of the whites in the then sparsely settled State of Arkansas. Indeed, before the admission of the Territory as a State wise counsel had advised the re-establishment of Fort Smith, and a month before the passage of the act of admission, on May 14, 1836 (Laws of United States, Vol. 9, 23d Cong., Sess. I1, Chap. 452, p. 337) an act was passed authorizing the removal of the garrison at Fort Gibson to some feasible point for the better accommodation of the troops and for better defense of the Arkansas frontier, and appropriating $50,000 [about $1,282,051 in 2015] for a fort to be built at a point to be selected on or near the frontier line of Arkansas.

By act of July 2, 1836 (Laws of the U. S., Vol. 9, Chap. 658, p. 459), there was appropriated $42,000 for the purchase of sites and causing to be built arsenals for the deposit of arms in Arkansas, Missouri, and at Memphis, Tennessee, none of the arsenals, including sites, to cost more than $14,000 each. The Arkansas arsenal provided by this account was built at Little Rock. In the autumn of that year the government called upon the Governor of Arkansas for a regiment of volunteers, which, as soon as organized, was stationed for several months, in 1837, at Fort Towsen, southwest of Fort Smith, forty miles west of the Arkansas line in the Choctaw Nation, to oppose a possible outbreak of the red men. On April 4, 1838 (Laws of U. S., Vol. 9, 25th Cong., Sess. I1, Chap. 1125, p. 838), a resolution was passed by which the Secretary of War was authorized to take not to exceed $15,000 from the sum appropriated by act of May 14, 1836, and purchase a site for a fort at or near the western border of Arkansas. The money thus appropriated was used in purchasing from John Rogers the west fractional half of section 17 and portions of the other quarter sections above mentioned. See plat of city. The portion enclosed by heavy black lines and named "Roger's Purchase" indicates the quarter section originally entered by him (less a triangular tract in the southeast corner which he disposed of at an early date), the greater part of the quarter section purchased by him from Hugh Tygert in August, 1832, and a small triangular portion of the northeast quarter of section 17. This tract was finally sold by Rogers to private individuals for building lots. The tract enclosed by lighter black lines, lying close along the "Choctaw Strip," indicates the land sold by Rogers to the government under the act of April 4, 1838, for a site for the new fort and for a reservation about the same. It will be observed that the fort itself was located in the southeast corner of the southwest quarter of section 8, first entered by Hugh Tygert in 1829. This reservation comprised three hundred and nine acres. The site chosen for the fort was in the shape of a pentagon with its western corner projecting some forty feet or more across the line into the "Choctaw Strip." The fort thus located was about a quarter of a mile from the original stockade.

On March 12, 1885, the land within the reservation was ceded by the government to the City of Fort Smith, with the exception of certain tracts which were reserved for purposes as follows: National cemetery, city park and sites for two court houses; there were built, later, a new government court house on one of the sites, and on the other a fine edifice for use of the Fort Smith District, Sebastian County Circuit; the land within the fort wall was also reserved at this time. The land thus ceded to the city was held for the specific use of the schools of the Fort Smith School District. It was provided that it must be sold within ten years succeeding March, 1885, the money derived therefrom to be devoted to erecting school buildings, the interest arising from the in id to be devoted to plying salaries of teachers. In 1885, the land sold brought to the school fund the handsome sum of $126, 254.27 In 1887, the sales amounted to $116,390.50; in 1890. to $83,792.40; in 1891, $3,365, and in 1894, $3,760.08, a total of $333 662.25. From this fund has been built eight fine school buildings, and there remains in the fund $1 14,297.05. The real estate occupied by the several school buildings is valued at $46,500; the buildings are valued at $179,900; furniture, $8,000, and office fixtures and library at $1,750. In 1895 there remained unsold a considerable portion of the grant, and this was purchased by the school board; it is valued at $187,600.

In 1839 the government set about enclosing the site, (the same as is now known in memory to the people of Fort Smith as the old barracks or jail yard), with a heavy stone wall, originally intended to be made thirteen feet high and surmounted by a heavy coping. (The material was secured by blasting out the sandstone bluff on which stood the old stockade or first fort.) It was provided with loopholes for the use of muskets, and gateways were built at the north western, north-eastern, eastern and south-western sides. All were afterwards closed except at the north-east and east, and the latter, a massive affair with heavy stone posts, continued in use until the wall was razed in 1897. Bastions were built out from the corners at the north-east, south-east and south. This latter was used as a powder magazine, and it was just inside the wall at this precise spot that, in 1873, after the property was given over to occupancy by the United States District Court, was erected the great gallows that afterward became famous as having taken the lives of more than four score of convicted felons. Two large two-story brick buildings (see cut on page 23) were built for officers and a barracks building of brick (where now stands the building known as the old court house) for use of the privates. Another smaller building, also of brick, was erected near the wall on the north-east side of the enclosure for use as a guard house. This was afterwards used, subsequent to 1872, as a grand jury room. Four block houses of stone, intended to be mounted with heavy artillery, were commenced, as it was the purpose to garrison the new fort with one thousand armed men. The work moved slowly as is usual with government construction, and ere the fort was completed the Indian scare had ceased, and in the summer of 1842 the work was stopped by General Taylor, who was then in charge. The cut shows the condition of the wall, only half built on the north-east side of the enclosure, just as it was left when orders were given to cease work. At most other points the wall had been completed to its full height. Two of the block houses were abandoned at their very foundations, one at the southern corner and the other near the south-east bastion. The other two, one at the corner of the enclosure pointing north and the other at the west (a greater portion of its foundation being over the line in the "Choctaw Strip") had progressed too far to be judiciously abandoned and they were completed as ordinary stone buildings without the intended accommodations for heavy ordnance and were turned over to the use of the quartermaster, the one at the north being used as a commissary. Both stone buildings are still standing.

The fort was garrisoned with a small force of two companies and on April 23, 1861, was captured by a detachment of the Arkansas state troops under Captain Sturgis.* Later, after the state had joined the ranks of the secessionists, it was turned over to the war department of the Confederacy and held until September 3, 1863, when it was re-possessed for the United States government by the Federal troops under Gen. Blount. Previous to 1867 the brick building erected as a barracks for the use of privates was destroyed by fire. It was rebuilt on the original foundation and made only one and one-half stories high. Of the other two brick buildings, the officers' quarters, shown in the cut, the one to the left was burned in 1866 and the remaining one was destroyed by fire in 1871. These buildings were never rebuilt. The cut is from an old and faded photograph, taken in 1865, and retouched for use of the engraver by R. H. Mohler, a skillful artist formerly residing in Fort Smith, now of New York city.

*Samuel Davis Sturgis (1822–1889) fought in the Mexican-American War and the Civil War. During the Indian Wars, he was the nominal commander of the 7th United States Cavalry, made famous by its Lieutenant-Colonel, George Armstrong Custer. As Sturgis was frequently on detached duty, Custer was the actual commander of the 7th. Custer and five *companies (over 200 men) of the 7th were killed on June 25th, 1876 at the Battle of the Little Bighorn.—Ed. 2015*

In September 1871 the fort was again abandoned, the soldiers being removed to Fort Gibson, up the river in the Indian Territory, and the property was taken from the control of the War department, transferred to the department of the Interior and placed in charge of the Marshal for the Western District of Arkansas. In 1886 the "Frisco" railway, coming from Paris, Texas, to Van Buren, gained permission to run its line across the southwestern corner of the old enclosure and east of the LeFlore building, located at that corner of the fort. To obtain the proper grade it was necessary to make a cut some ten feet deep. The famous old building was thus left standing alone, as it is at present, on an embankment between two lines of railway, the "Frisco" and Missouri Pacific, the wall being rebuilt by the former company along the line of their acquired right of way to a connecting point with the wall running along the south-west side of the enclosure (see plat). This building, cut off from the rest of the fort by the construction of the road noted, was entered by Campbell LeFlore at the time of the abandonment of the fort in 1870, and there he resided with his family in undisputed possession until the above mentioned "Frisco" construction, when, owing to its inconvenience of access, he removed to other quarters. Later he died, and his heirs still claim ownership of the historic old building. Its companion, the stone building still standing at the extreme north corner of the old enclosure, formerly occupied as the regimental commissary, was made use of, after 1873, for a number of years by Judge I. C. Parker, who established there his chambers.

At the time of the final abandonment of Fort Smith as a military post, the town had become firmly established and it soon became an important commercial point, the Arkansas river being navigable for boats of light draught, having served prior to the advent of railroads as a means of furthering its mercantile interests and as an outlet for staple products of the country round about. In 1880 it had risen to the dimensions of a city of 3,000 inhabitants. Since then it has several times doubled in size and importance and has become a manufacturing center.

It has four trunk lines of railroad with more building. It has paved and macadamized streets, good sidewalks, electric lights and street cars, a good public library, fine business houses and public buildings of which any larger city might well be proud, and a perfect sewerage system, costing over $500,000. Its commercial business is stated at $13,000,000 annually; the annual output of its manufacturing industries is valued at $4,000,-OOO, and its coal shipment yearly is over 5,000,000 tons, while its shipments of lumber are extensive. As a cotton center it is increasing, and in early fruits and vegetables it is one of the leading points in the south.

THE FAMOUS COURT

The famous United States Criminal Court at Fort Smith was established as office of the judge of the Western District of Arkansas on the second Monday in May, 1871. The court had previously been held at Van Buren, the county seat of Crawford County,

Arkansas, five miles from Fort Smith, on the opposite of and down the Arkansas River, but prior to the admission of the Territory of Arkansas to statehood, on June 30, 1834, the last day of the twenty-third congress, an act was passed which was in after years to have an important bearing upon the country and courts of which this work treats. It was entitled (Laws of U. S., vol. 9, 23rd Cong. Chap. 161, p. 128), "An act to regulate trade and intercourse with the Indian tribes and preserve peace on the frontiers." Much of the act related to similar conditions in other parts of the country; we will pay attention only to those sections which have to do with the future of the great court soon to be discussed.*

Section 1, of the act above noted, provides "that all that part of the United States west of the Mississippi and not within the States of Missouri or Louisiana or the territory of Arkansas, also that part of the United States east of the Mississippi and not within any state, to which the Indian title has not been extinguished, for the purposes of this act be taken and deemed to be the Indian Country." Section 20 named as the penalty for selling, exchanging, giving, bartering or disposing of any ardent spirits or wine to an Indian, "(in the Indian Country y" $500, and for introducing or attempting to introduce the same, "except such supplies as shall be necessary for officers of the United States troops of the service under the direction of the War department," $300, and (§ 22), for setting up or continuing any distillery for the manufacture of any ardent spirits, $1,000.

A feature of this act that may interest most readers, was the provision against any person not an Indian member of the tribes in the Indian Territory nor possessed of a right on account of having married into one of the tribes, being allowed to engage in trade or traffic in the Indian Territory without a license granted by the Indian Council. As none of the councils ever issued such a license, this provision for many years gave to the squaw men (whites who had married Indian women, often times for the purpose of gaining commercial or financial advantage) held a monopoly of the mercantile business within the Indian Territory, profiting greatly thereby.—note in original

Section 22 reads as follows: "That in all trials about the right of property in which an Indian may be a party on one side and a white man on the other, the burden of proof shall rest upon the white person whenever the Indian shall make out a presumption of title in himself from the fact of previous possession or ownership." (There was an evident attempt at this time to be fair with "Lo" the poor Indian. Observe the change as time draws on). It was also provided (§ 24), "that for the sole purpose of carrying this act into effect, all of that part of the Indian country west of the Mississippi River that is bounded north by the north line of the lands assigned to the Osage Indians, produced (or continued) east to the State of Missouri; west by the Mexican possessions; south by the Red River; and east by the west line of the Territory of Arkansas and the State of Missouri, shall be and hereby is, annexed to the Territory of Arkansas; and that for the purpose aforesaid, the residue of the Indian Country west of the Mississippi River shall be and hereby is annexed to the judicial district of Missouri; and for the purpose aforesaid, the several portions of the Indian

Country east of the said river shall be, and are hereby severally annexed to the (judicial) Territory in which they are situate."

The above will correct the erroneous impression that seems to be quite prevalent, to the effect that it was not until the removal of the Court to Fort Smith, or at least until after the civil war that the Indian Territory was made subject to the Western District of Arkansas for judicial purposes.

Section 25 of the above, provides: "That so much of the laws of the United States as provides for punishment of crimes committed within any place within the sole or exclusive jurisdiction of the United States shall be in force in the Indian Country. Provided, That the same shall not extend to crimes committed by one Indian against the person or property of another Indian."

It is here observed that by the treaty of 1866, between the United States and the Indian tribes in the Indian Territory the trial and punishment of Indians charged with offenses against the person or property of another Indian in the Indian Territory was left to the tribal courts, and that this right of tribal courts should not be disturbed in the Cherokee, Choctaw nor Chickasaw Nations. It is interesting to observe the gradual encroachment by Congress upon the treaty rights of the Indians until at last the tribal courts and the privilege guaranteed to them of punishing in their own way (consistent with the constitution and laws of the United States) Indian offenders against Indian laws and against the person or property of other Indians, was taken away altogether.

Section 4 of the act of Congress, approved June 15, 1836 (U. S. St. at L., vol. 5, chap. 490, p. 3/9), admitting the Territory to Statehood, made of the new state one judicial district" and a District Court shall be held therein to consist of one judge. He shall hold at the seat of government of the State (Little Rock) two sessions annually on the first Monday of April and November, * and he shall, in all things, have and exercise the same jurisdiction and powers which were by law given to the judge of the Kentucky f District, under an act of September 24, 1789, entitled "An act to establish the Judicial Courts of the United States."

The judge was empowered to appoint a clerk, who should receive the same fees as the clerk for the Kentucky District for similar services. The salary of the judge (§ 5), was fixed at $2,000 per annum to be paid "quarter yearly." Provision (§ 6), was made for the appointment of a district attorney, who was to be paid, in addition to his stated fees, $200 yearly as a full compensation for extra services and (§ 7), for the appointment of a marshal "to perform the same duties, be subject to the same regulations and penalties and be entitled to the same fees as are prescribed to the marshal in other districts, and he shall be entitled to $200 annually as compensation for extra services."

By act of Congress approved March 1, 1837, (U. S. St. at L., 24th Cong., Sess. 1, Vol. 6, Chap. 783, p. 594) the Court of the United States for the District of Arkansas, was given "the same jurisdiction and power in all respects, whatever, that was given to the several districts courts of the United States by an act of Congress entitled, 'an act to regulate trade and intercourse with the Indian tribes and preserve peace on the frontiers.'"

The act quoted in the act of March 1, 1837, as above, was that one approved June 30, 1834, and on June 17, 1844 an act (U. S. St. at L., Vol. 5, 28th Congress. 1, Chap. 103, p. 680), supplementary to it was approved as here quoted: "That the courts for the United States in and for the district of Arkansas be and hereby are vested with the same power and jurisdiction to hear, try, determine and punish all crimes committed within that Indian country designated in the twenty-fourth section of the act to which this is a supplement, and therein and thereby annexed to the Territory of Arkansas as were vested in the courts of the United States for said territory before the same became a state. And for the sole purpose of carrying this act into effect ail that Indian country hereunto annexed by the said twenty-fourth section of the act aforesaid to the Territory of Arkansas be, and the same hereby is, annexed to the State of Arkansas."

By an act approved March 3, 1851 (U. S. St. at L., 32d Congresses, I1, vol. 9, chap 24, p. 594) it was enacted that the seven counties of Benton, Washington, Crawford, Franklin, Johnson, Madison and Carroll, situated in the northwest corner of the state of Arkansas; the counties of Scott and Polk, south of the Arkansas river, and one county removed from the counties named above, "and all that part of the Indian Territory within the present judicial district of Arkansas shall constitute a new judicial district to be styled the Western District of Arkansas, and the residue of the state shall be styled the Eastern District of Arkansas. "It was further enacted (§2), that the judge of the District of Arkansas should hold "two terms of said court at the town of Van Buren, the county seat of Crawford county, on the second Mondays of May and November in etch and every year;" and (§3), that "the district court for the Western District, hereby established, in addition to the ordinary jurisdiction and power of a district court shall within the limits of its respective district have jurisdiction of all causes, civil or criminal, except appeals and writs of error, which now or hereafter may by law be made cognizable in a circuit court and an appeal or writ of error shall be prosecuted from the final decree or judgment of said district court to the Supreme Court of the United States in the same manner that appeals and writs of. error now are, by law, from a Circuit Court of the United States." And it was further enacted (§4), that the president should appoint a district attorney and marshal for the said new district "who respectively shall receive the same salary and perquisites as the present district attorney and marshal of the State of Arkansas have by law: and the judge of said court shall appoint a clerk of said court hereby established." (It is here observed that at this time Sebastian county, of which Fort Smith was the county seat. formed a put of tine Eastern District of Arkansas). By act of Congress approved March 27, 1854 (U. S. St. at L., 33d Cong., sess. 1, vol. 10, chap. 24, p. 269) the act of March 3, 1851 dividing the state of Arkansas into two judicial districts was so amended as to provide that offenders convicted in the Western District of Arkansas and punishable by confinement at hard labor in the penitentiary "may be sentenced by the Court to the Penitentiary House in the Eastern District of Arkansas the same as if the Penitentiary House was in the Western District of Arkansas" and by the same act the Arkansas counties of Sevier and Sebastian, in the western portion of the state, were added to the territory comprising the Western District of Arkansas; it also provided (§4), that any white person setting fire to, or attempting to fire, any buildings in the Indian Territory belonging to an Indian, or any Indian setting fire to, or attempting to fire, any buildings belonging to or in lawful possession of a white person, should on conviction thereof be deemed guilty of a felony and be sentenced to hard labor for a term of from two to twenty-one years, and that (§5). any white person assaulting an Indian or other person in the Indian Territory, or any Indian assaulting a white person, with deadly weapons, with intent to kill or maim, should on conviction thereof be deemed guilty of felony and sentenced to imprisonment at hard labor for a term of not less than one year nor more than five years,

The new court at Van Buren was held in the Sebastian county circuit court room with Daniel Ringo judge, who by virtue of the act of March 3, 1851, above noted, (§2), had jurisdiction of both the Eastern and Western Districts of Arkansas. George W. Knox was marshal and Hon. Jesse Turner district attorney, appointees of President Millard Filmore. Alexander McLain was the first district clerk. The first entry in the records now in a state of preservation is dated December 1, 1855. It was styled: vs.

The United States vs. William England, Forfeiture on Bond.

The first trial of which any record is to be found was:

The United States vs. Thomas Burkhardt, Larceny.

This case came on for trial at the May term 1855. Alfred Wilson was district attorney and Samuel Mays marshal, both appointees of President Franklin Pierce. Judge Ringo continued as judge until 1865, when Henry C. Caldwell was appointed by President Andrew Johnson. He occupied the position when the office was removed to Fort Smith and for a year thereafter. Marshal Hays was succeeded by Benjamin Jacoway, an appointee of President James Buchanan, and he by Luther C. White, appointed by President Johnson, followed by Joseph S. C. Rowland, appointed September 7, 1868. On April 16, 1869, President Grant appointed William Britton to the place and on March 31, 1871, just before the removal of the court to Fort Smith, he appointed Logan H. Roots to fill the vacancy resulting from the retirement of Marshal Britton. Succeeding Allred Wilson as district attorney came E. D. Ham, James H. Huckleberry appointed in 1869, and Newton J. Temple, all appointees of President Grant, the latter being in office when the court was removed to Fort Smith.

In the winter of 1871 Hon. Thomas Boles, the present clerk of the United States Circuit Court at Fort Smith, then a representative in congress, drafted and introduced a bill whose object was to cause the transfer of the United States District Courts for the Western District of Arkansas from Van Buren to Fort Smith. The bill was approved March 3, 1871, but the act as passed was scarcely recognizable as the bill prepared by Congressman Boles. True, it attained the original object aimed at by his bill, but it also performed much else that was undesirable and wrong. It provided (U. S. St. at L , 41st Cong., sess. Ill, vol. 16, chap. 106, p. 47) that in addition to the terms of court for the Western District of Arkansas, held under existing laws at Van Buren, two terms of said court should be held at Helena, Phillips county, Arkansas, (a town at the extreme eastern limits of the state, more than three hundred miles from Van Buren), on the second Mondays in March and September, but (§4), no court was to be held at Helena until an instrument in writing be duly executed by the proper authorities of Phillips county agreeing to furnish suitable rooms for holding court for a term of ten years without expense to the government be filed with the office of the clerk of the United States District Court at Little Rock. It also provided (§5), that the counties of Phillips, Crittenden and Mississippi, at the eastern border of the state along the Mississippi river; Craighead and Green, in the north-eastern part of the state; Randolph, Marion, Fulton and Boone, lying along the northern border of the state and east of that portion of the state first included in the Western District of Arkansas, and three interior counties, Jackson, Independence and Izard, lying far to the north-east of the center of the state, be made a part of the Western District of Arkansas. The original purpose of the bill was left appended to section 5 in these words: "And that the two terms of court now held each year at Van Buren shall be held hereafter at Fort Smith" and (§6), that "so much of the act of March 3, 1851, entitled 'An act to divide the District of Arkansas into two judicial districts,' as gives to the judge of the Eastern District of Arkansas jurisdiction over the Western District of said state, be and hereby is repealed." The act as approved was considered by many as a gerrymander of the very worst kind. Congressman Boles opposed the riders annexing the far distant counties to the Western District and the establishment of a place of holding court at Helena with all the power at his command. He saw in them a scheme to injure and cripple the jurisdiction of his friend, Judge Caldwell, who was then also judge of the Eastern District at Little Rock. He also foresaw that a soft place was being prepared for the prospective son-in-law (William Story), of Senator Aleck McDonald of Arkansas, (McDonald was an eastern man who came to Arkansas in "carpet bag" times and located at Little Rock, establishing there the Merchants' National Bank. In 1868, with the state under "carpet bag" rule, he and Ben F. Rice were elected to represent the state in the United States Senate), and being shrewd enough to discover what all the world after wards learned at the expense of the government, that Story was a rascal, he refused to endorse his application for appointment for judge of the Western District. By a strange line of circumstances, however, Congressman Boles' friends in Washington favored Story's appointment, and the gerrymandering bill was therefore put through and became a law, and Story was appointed as hereafter noted.

In accordance with the provisions of the act the offices of the judge, marshal, district attorney and clerk of the court were removed to Fort Smith and, as previously stated, the first session of the court in its new location was opened the second

Monday in May, 1871. Previous to its removal it had been a small institution to what it afterwards became, although the records show that in addition to quite a large business done in antagonism to the traffic of liquor in the Indian Territory and in handling many larceny cases, it also tried and sentenced nine men to hang for murder, not to mention a period from December IS, 1860, to August 31, 1865, the records for which period are missing, having been, it is supposed, destroyed by fire at the time of the burning of the building in which the court was held, in 1872. Of the nine men who were sentenced to death at Van Buren, six were executed, one was commuted to life imprisonment, one was commuted to fifteen years imprisonment and later was pardoned, and one escaped and after scouting* nine years was again captured and was resentenced by the court at Fort Smith, and was there executed. During the latter years of the court's existence at Van Buren, a large part of its time was taken up with cases styled" treason" and "confiscation of enemy's property." These were cases growing out of the Civil War, and the records for several years teem with them, and are of much interest to a present-day curiosity seeker; it is observed that very many of the treason cases were *nollied* [sic] on account of a general pardon issued by the President.

Nolle prosequi = "we shall no longer prosecute."—Ed. 2015

Scouting.—A. term applied in the Indian Territory to any person who. having committed a breach of law, or having escaped from the clutches of the law, took up a transient or nomadic existence, remaining only a brief time in any one locality, in a strenuous endeavor to evade the officers and arrest. Such persons were said to be "On the scout." It usually occurred that men who were on the scout continued to break the law, becoming highwaymen and outlaws.—note in original

In 1872, Judge Caldwell was succeeded by William Story, on appointment by President Grant. He was a flippant young man of little character who had drifted into the country during the reconstruction period. Under his administration many disorders existed and the expenses of the court during fourteen months reached the enormous sum of $400,000. Marshal Roots was removed, but Marshal John Sarber, who was appointed his successor March 18, 1873, was no improvement. He issued certificates to witnesses and jurors for their services some of which have never been paid. Witnesses were of necessity subpoenaed from distant points in the district, and being unable to collect their pay were in some instances compelled to sell their ponies and walk home. Charges of receiving bribes and other misconduct were preferred against Judge Story and in April, 1874, Col. Ben. T. DuVal, Judge John T. Humphrey and District Attorney Newton J Temple were summoned to Washington as witnesses before the Judiciary Committee. In June, 1874. Story, finding that a strong case was being made against him, resigned to escape impeachment; and, it is remarked in passing, he did not become the Senator's son-in-law. Col. DuVal was employed by the government as attorney, to prosecute a vigorous investigation of the court and all its attaches, but he came near being employed instead by Marshal Roots to defend the case brought against him by the government in the general overhauling. While still in

Washington, after giving in his testimony and before he had been retained by the government, Col. DuVal was approached by Roots and asked to defend him. Col. DuVal was in need of ready money and he named $500 as the required retainer fee, at the same time warning Roots that the government had spoken of employing him. The marshal replied, "I'll see you in the morning." That evening when Col. DuVal retired to his lodgings he found a letter from the Attorney General requesting immediate audience; a few hours later he hid been paid $250 ca-h as a first retainer, and by the time his task as special government attorney was concluded his fees had amounted to over $5,000, During the investigation, although no charges were made against District Attorney Temple, yet as the government desired to make a clean sweep and start over (there being quite a strong inclination on the part of Congress to abolish the court for the western district altogether') Col. DuVal was instructed to request him to resign, and in July, 1874, the vacancy thus caused was filled by President Grant appointing Judge Wm. H. H. Clayton. After the resignation of Judge Story the office of judge for the Western District of Arkansas remained vacant until March, 1875, but on instructions from Washington, Judge Caldwell, from the Eastern District of Arkansas, came to Fort Smith and presided over the November term of court. The instructions from Washington to Judge Caldwell were as follows:

"Department of Justice, Washington, June 27, 1874.

"Hon. H. C. Caldwell,

United States District Judge,

Little Rock, Ark.

"Sir.—There is a vacancy in the office of District Judge in the Western District of Arkansas, occasioned by the resignation of Judge Story. I refer you to the act of August 6, 1861 {12, Stats. 318) and have to request that under and by virtue of the provisions of that act you will hold the courts and discharge the other duties of the district judge for said western district until the vacancy is filled.

"This is in accordance with the wishes of the President, the members of the Judiciary Committee of the Senate and other Senators, and it was the understanding when the bill abolishing that district failed to pass the Senate.

"'Very respectfully,

George H. Williams,

Attorney General.

If so much of the act of March 3, 1871, as annexed eastern territory to the Western District of Arkansas was a "gerrymander" the redistricting act passed by the revising session (43rd Cong., 1873-74, Rev. St., Chap. 1, § 533) was one of the most iniquitous measures ever brought to the attention of a deliberative body. When the members of that session of Congress ceased their manipulations the district was found to consist of, besides the Indian Territory, thirteen counties, (Benton, Washington, Crawford, Scott, Polk, Franklin, Johnson, Madison, Carroll, Sevier, Sebastian, Fulton, and

Boone,) in the western and north-western part of the State of Arkansas, and seventeen counties, (Phillips, Crittenden, Mississippi, Craighead, Green, Randolph, Cross, St. Francis, Monroe, Woodruff, Jackson, Independence and Izard), occupying the eastern and north-eastern portions of the State, leaving Clay County in the extreme north-eastern corner and Lee county on the Mississippi River, in the central east, (surrounded on three sides by some of the seventeen counties named), to the Eastern District of Arkansas. The spectacle of counties away in the east being made to constitute a portion of the western district while other counties in the western part of the state, one of them actually bordering the Indian Territory, were retained in the eastern district, was a fraud so palpable it smelled to Heaven and was the cause of much deserved censure being heaped upon the heads of the statesmen (?) who secured the passage of the act by means best known to themselves and their tools.

In furtherance of the scheme above noted it was enacted (Rev. St., 43rd Cong. 1873-'74, Chap. I1, § 556, p. 93) "In the Western District of Arkansas there shall be appointed two clerks of the district court thereof; one of whom shall reside and keep office at Fort Smith and the other shall reside and keep office at Helena, (§ 571 and 97), Provided. The district courts for the Western District of Arkansas, Northern District of Mississippi, Western District of South Carolina, and the District of West Virginia shall have, in addition to the ordinary jurisdiction of district courts, jurisdiction of all cases, except appeals and writs of error, which are cognizable in a circuit court and shall proceed therein in the same manner as a circuit court." The time for holding court in the eastern district and in the two divisions of the western district was named as follows: (Rev. St , 43d Cong. 1873-'74, Chap. 4,§ 572i P-98). "In the Eastern District of Arkansas, on the first Mondays in April and October. In the Western District of Arkansas, at Fort Smith on the second Mondays in May and November and at Helena on the second Mondays in March and September."

A revulsion of feeling or a stroke of conscience inducive of reform seems to have affected the next Congress, however, for sweeping changes were made, which, although they reduced the jurisdiction of the court for the Western District of Arkansas, yet gave evidence of common sense in the manner of the changes wrought as commended them to all fair minded people. Reference is made to the act approved January 3 1, 1877, (44th Cong., Sess. I1, Vol, 19, Chap. 41, p. 230) amending section 533 of the revised statutes to read, "The Western District of Arkansas shall consist of counties (in Arkansas) of Benton, Washington, Crawford, Sebastian, Scott, Polk, Sevier, Little River, Howard, Montgomery, Yell, Logan, Franklin, Johnson, Madison, Newton, Carroll, Boone and Marion, and the country lying west of Missouri and Arkansas known as the Indian Territory. The Eastern District of Arkansas includes the residue of the state." By this act, the territory of Arkansas attached to the western district was composed of nineteen counties in compact form reaching from the north across the state to a line even with the southern boundary of the Indian Territory, and the work of the gerrymanders was destroyed.

Section 556 of the revised statutes were by the same act amended to read, "In the Eastern District of Arkansas there shall be two clerks of the district court thereof, one of whom shall reside and keep office at Little Rock and the other shall reside and hold office at Helena." Section 571 was so amended as to include the district court for the Eastern District of Arkansas at Helena in the list of courts whose jurisdiction was increased to include "all causes, except appeals and writs of error which are cognizable in the circuit court," and section 5 72 of the revised statutes was so amended as to provide for holding the regular terms of court as follows: "In the Eastern district of Arkansas at Little Rock on the first Mondays in April and October and at Helena on the second Mondays in March and October; in the Western District of Arkansas at Fort Smith on the first Mondays in February, May, August and November.

In July, 1874, Judge W. H. H. Clayton was appointed by President Grant to the office of district attorney for the Western District of Arkansas; he was succeeded in 1885 by M. H. Sandel, an appointee of President Cleveland, but in 1890, Judge Clayton was again given the position, by appointment from President Harrison. In 1893, James H. Read was appointed his successor by Grover Cleveland, in his second term as President, and in 1897, President McKinley appointed Thomas H. Barnes, a noted criminal attorney of Fort Smith, to the place; after his removal by death, April 13, 1898, his brother, Ex-Postmaster James K. Barnes, of Fort Smith, was appointed to fill the vacancy.

On the 10th day of May, 1875, Judge Isaac C. Parker presided for the first time over the court that was destined to attract, under him, universal attention as the greatest criminal court on earth.

From the time of its incipiency, in 1851, until the close of its jurisdiction over the Indian Territory, September 1, 1896, over 28,000 criminals and suspects stood before its bar, including those who were discharged before the Commissioner's

Courts and those against whom bills of indictment were issued, and ignored by the grand jury. Under Judge Parker, in a little more than twenty-one years, 13,490 cases were docketed, not to mention the numerous and petty cases that got no farther than the Commissioner's Courts, and of this number 9,454 persons were either convicted by a jury trial or entered pleas of guilty. During the twenty-five years, after the court was removed to Fort Smith, 344 were tried for offenses punishable by death, 174 were convicted and 168 were sentenced to die on the scaffold; eighty-eight of the convicted ones were hanged, one was killed while attempting to escape, five died in prison, two were pardoned, forty-three were commuted by the President to terms of from ten years to life imprisonment; four were granted new trials and were finally discharged on acquittal or *nolle prosequi*; twenty three were given new trials on appeal to the Supreme Court—under a new law—and, of these, nine were acquitted, thirteen were convicted on charges of lesser degree and their grade of punishment reduced to terms of imprisonment of from one year to life, and one was returned to the Choctaw Nation and turned over to the Indian courts. One of the 174, not heretofore specifically mentioned, was adjudged insane and was placed in an asylum, and another was released on a bond of $5,000 on an order granting a new trial, he failed to return, and his bond was forfeited. A draft of the official records for a period of ten years ending December 31, 1894, shows 7,419 criminal cases convicted; 305 of that number were for murder and manslaughter; 466 for assault with intent to kill; 1,910 for selling liquor to Indians; 2,860 for introducing liquor into the Indian Territory; 97 for illicit distilling; 124 for violating the internal revenue laws; 65 for violating the postal laws; 50 for counterfeiting; 24 for arson; 48 for perjury; 32 for bigamy; 27 for conspiracy to commit crime; 59 for stealing government timber; 24 for resisting arrest, and 149 for other crimes not here enumerated; and added to this, be it known, that the years 1895 and 1896 placed more than 2,000 additional cases on the docket, and the reader commences to gather somewhat of an idea of the immense amount of work performed by this famous court. Let it be understood, however, that of the large number of executions occurring at Fort Smith, and at which the whole civilized world stood aghast, (People at a distance remarking, with bated breath, one to another, "What manner of place is this terrible Fort Smith, where they hang a man nearly every week?") not one was for crimes committed in Fort Smith, nor, for that matter, in the State of Arkansas. This court had no jurisdiction of capital crimes committed in that portion of its district which rested within the State of Arkansas, except, as in one instance hereinafter described, where the crime was committed upon land included within the original Fort Smith military reservation.

The court had exclusive, original and final jurisdiction of all crimes committed in the Indian Territory and No Man's Land, as well as having the usual jurisdiction of a portion of the State of Arkansas, excepting offenses committed against the person or property of a member of Indian tribes in the Indian Territory by other members of Indian tribes in said Territory, and so energetic was the court and its officers that it came to be known as the court in whose jurisdiction there was a certainty of arrest and a surety of punishment for law breakers.

But the great court was not to continue unhampered in the enjoyment of its magnificent jurisdiction, indefinitely. Less than ten years after Judge Parker's reign opened, the United States Congress commenced tampering with its territory, passing laws to reduce the burdens laid upon it, burdens which it was carrying without a murmur, like a huge monolith supporting the temple of justice.

The first act of Congress tending to reduce the jurisdiction in the Indian Territory, of the Federal Court for the Western District of Arkansas, was approved January 6, 1883 (U. S. St. at L, 47th Cong. Sess. 2, Vol. 22, Chap. 13, pp. 383-390).

It provided (§ 2) that "AH that part of the Indian Territory lying north of the Canadian River and east of Texas and the one hundredth meridian not set apart and occupied by the Cherokee, Creek and Seminole Indian tribes" be annexed to and form a part of the United States Judicial District of Kansas and giving the United States

District Courts at Wichita and Fort Scott, Kansas, exclusive original jurisdiction of all offenses committed within the limit of said territory against the laws of the United States, and (§3) that all that portion of the Indian Territory not so annexed to the district of Kansas for judicial purposes and not set apart and occupied by the Cherokee, Creek, Choctaw, Chickasaw and Seminole Indian tribes be annexed to and constitute a part of the judicial district, known as the Northern District of Texas, the United States Court at Graham in said district to have exclusive original jurisdiction of all offenses committed in said territory against any of the laws of the United States; it was, however, specifically provided (§4) that the act should not in any way effect whatever cases in such territory were already commenced and then pending in the Fort Smith Court, nor were said district courts of Kansas or Texas given any greater jurisdiction in the territory annexed than was previously held by the court for the Western District of Arkansas.

This act had no noticeable effect upon the volume of work coming before the great court at Fort Smith, in fact, the burden laid before Judge Parker was rather increasing month by month and on July 4, 1884, two other bills were approved by Congress which, though their effect was little noticed, yet could they be considered a direct blow at the court at Fort Smith. The acts noted (U. S. St. at L., 48th Cong. Sess. 1, Vol. 23, Chap. *77, PP. 69-72, and Chap. 179, ,pp. 73-76) granted rights of way through the Indian Territory to the Southern Kansas and the Gulf, Colorado & Santa Fe railroads and (§8) gave the United States Circuit and District Courts for the Northern District of Texas, the Western District of Arkansas and the District of Kansas, 11 and such other courts as may be authorised by Congress concurrent jurisdiction of all controversies arising between the said railroads and the nations and tribes through whose territory they should be constructed, also between the inhabitants of said nations or tribes and the said railways, without reference to the amount in controversy, and the civil jurisdiction of said courts was also extended within the limits of said Indian Territory without distinction as to the citizenship of the parties so far as was necessary to carry out said acts.

As stated, these acts had little effect on the court at Fort Smith, and were so little noticed that some of the deputy marshals were unaware of their provisions for several years thereafter. Congress would not down, however, but seemed determined to keep haggling away and the next movement was one which was the beginning of the breaking down of the barriers protecting the Indians in the Indian Territory in the right to punish the members of their own tribes for offenses committed against each other (U. S. St. at L., 48th Cong., 1885, March 3, vol. 23, chap. 341, § 9, p. 482). "Any Indian committing against the person or property of another Indian any of the crimes, as follows: murder, manslaughter, rape, assault with intent to kill, arson, burglary and larceny, in any Territory of the United States and within or without an Indian reservation, shall be subject therefor to the laws of such Territory relative to such crimes, and shall be tried in the same courts and in the same manner and be subject to the same penalties as are all other persons charged with the commission of said crimes, and said courts shall govern and have jurisdiction in all such cases.'*

By act of Congress, approved June 19, 1886 (U. S. St. at L., 49th Cong., Sess. 1, vol, 24, chap. 422, p. 83), the counties of Howard, Little River and Sevier, lying close to the southeast corner of the Indian Territory, were detached from the Western District of Arkansas and made to constitute a part of the Eastern District of Arkansas. Here again was a blow directed against the court at Fort Smith.

By act of 1887, March 2 it was enacted, that any Indian committing against the person of any Indian policeman, appointed under the laws of the United States, or any Indian' United States deputy marshal, while lawfully engaged in executing any United State; process or other duty imposed by the laws of the United States, the crimes of murder, manslaughter, or assault with intent to kill,. in the Indian Territory, should be subject to the laws of the United States relating thereto, and be tried by the United States district court exercising criminal jurisdiction of the territory where such offense was committed, and be subject to the same penalties as all other persons charged with said crimes, and said courts were thereby given jurisdiction thereof.

By act of 1888, February 15 (U. S. St. at L., 50th Cong., Sess. 1, vol. 25, chap. IQ, p. 5/8), any person convicted of horse stealing in the Indian Territory was made subject to a fine of $1,000 or fifteen years' imprisonment at hard labor, or both such fine and imprisonment, and (§2) any person convicted of robbery or burglary in the Indian Territory was made subject to the same penalty or penalties; "Provided, that this act shall not be construed to apply to an Indian committing offenses against the property of another Indian." Nor was it to repeal any former act in relation to robbing the United States mails. Congressional conscience seems to have held a place in the passage of this act and to have insisted upon the above quoted proviso:

By act of June 4, 1888 (U. S. St, at L., 50th Cong., Sess. 1, vol. 25, chap. 343, p. 588), any United States marshal was authorized, when necessary to execute any process out of a circuit or district court of the United States for the district for which he was the marshal, or any commissioner of circuit, to enter the Indian Territory and execute the same as if it was within his own district.

By act of 1888, June 9 (U. S. St. at L., 50th Cong., Sess. 1, vol. 25, chap. 373, p. 583, repealing the act of March 2, 1887), any Indian committing against the person or property of any Indian agent or police appointed under the laws of the United States, or against any Indian United States deputy marshal, *posse comitatus* or guard, while lawfully engaged in such execution or other duties imposed by the laws of the United States: murder, manslaughter, assault with intent to murder, assault, or assault and battery, or who shall, in any manner, obstruct, by threats or violence, any person who is engaged in the service of the United States in the discharge of his duties as agent, police or other officer within the Indian Territory, or who shall commit any of these crimes in the Indian Territory against any person who at the time, or at any time previous belonged to either of the classes of officials noted, "shall be subject to the laws of the United States relating to such crimes, and shall be tried by the District Court of the United States exercising jurisdiction where such offense was committed, and shall be subject to the same penalties as all other persons in said cases, and the said courts are hereby given jurisdiction." This was an act most sweeping in its provisions, made necessary, no doubt, by the difficulties experienced by the officers of the various United States courts exercising jurisdiction of the Indian Territory. Its results were easily noticed, and officers were greatly assisted in performing their duties thereby.

A few months later (1889, February 6th; 50th Cong., Sess. I1, U. S. St. at L., vol. 5, chap. 113, pp. 655-666), Congress again interfered with the jurisdiction of the great court, leaving it shorn of its rights as a court of last resort; there were established by this act (§ 1) a Circuit Court of the United States in and for the Western District of Arkansas, the Northern District of Mississippi and the Western District of South Carolina, terms of circuit court to be held at such times and places in the said districts as were previously provided for holding district courts, and also provided that terms of circuit court should be "hereafter held at Helena, in the Eastern District of Arkansas, at the same time and place that the district court is now required by law to be held, also at the time and place in West Virginia where district court is now required by law to be held. The said circuit courts created by this act were given (§ 2) "the same original and appellate jurisdiction as is now conferred by law on other circuit courts of the United States;" and all cases then pending in the said district courts were ordered transferred to the said circuit courts (§3). The marshals and district attorneys of the ' aid district courts were authorized to discharge the duties of such offices in said circuit courts, and it was also ordered that, in the future, all clerks of circuit courts should be appointed by the judges of the respective circuit courts (§ 5). The provisions of act of January 3 1, 1877, amending sections 533, 556, 571 and 572, relating to courts in Arkansas and certain other states, conferring on district courts therein named (including that for the Western District of Arkansas) circuit court powers, and section 570, as amended by the last mentioned act, were repealed. On the passage of this act, the work in the office of clerk of the court for the Western District of Arkansas was divided, making two offices in the place of one, as had so long been in vogue, and thenceforth all capital cases coming for trial in the Western District of Arkansas were tried in the circuit court. Of vast importance and far reaching in its effects, were the provisions of a briefly worded portion of this act (§6), which ordered that, hereafter, the right of appeal to the Supreme Court of the United States should be allowed in all cases of conviction of crime where the punishment provided is death. This provision was given full effect on and after May 1, 1889, and resulted, eventually, in very many reversals of decisions given by this famous court, with new trials and, in some instances, supreme court reversals were returned the second and third time in a single case.

(The act above referred to and quoted was given to the-President for his signature January 25, 1889, and not being returned within the time required by the Constitution, it became a law, February 6, without his approval.)

THE FIRST WHITE MAN'S COURT IN THE INDIAN TERRITORY

By act of 1889, March I (U. S. St. at L., 50th Congress I1, vol. 25, chap. 333, § 1), the first white man's court in the Indian Territory was created, and given jurisdiction over all the Territory, It was principally a court of civil jurisdiction, putting in force the civil laws of the State of Arkansas, and in no way interfering with the criminal jurisdiction of the United States Courts at Fort Smith. A judge was appointed by the President, at a salary of $3,500 a year, for a term of four years.

(§ 2)-, a district attorney and marshal to serve four years with fees and salary, the same as was received by the district attorney and marshal of the Western District of Arkansas, their terms to be of four years' duration, and a clerk, to receive the same fees and compensation as was paid to the clerk of the United States Court for the Western District of Arkansas, was appointed by the judge.

The first judge of this court was Gen. James Shackleford; the first marshal, T. B. Needles; the first district attorney, Z. T. Waldroud, and the first clerk, Maj. William Nelson, appointed during the administration of President Benjamin Harrison.

The court was given (§5) exclusive, original jurisdiction of all offenses against the laws of the United States, committed in the Indian Territory, not punishable by death or imprisonment at hard labor, and civil jurisdiction (§6) in all cases between citizens of the United States who were residents of the Indian Territory, or between citizens of the United States, or of any State or Territory, and any citizen of, or any person or persons residing in or found in the Indian Territory, where the value of the thing in controversy or damages or money claimed amounted to $100 or more, but this section did not apply to controversies between persons of Indian blood only.

Now, for practically the first time in the history of the Indian Territory, was it possible to collect debts contracted within its borders. Previously there had been in none of the Indian Nations in that Territory any laws for the collection of debts and mortgages. Chattel mortgages and bills of sale were worth only the paper they were written on. This act was regarded as a material advance along the lines of civilization, except by a class of theorists who reason that the inability to collect debts on the part of the creditor prevents the making of debts, and, therefore, reverts beneficially to a class who would always be a debtor class. This theory may bear more of logic than most people are willing to confess.

This section also repealed all previous laws having the effect to prevent the Indians from entering into leases or contracts for mining coal for a period of more than ten years, and the court so created was given jurisdiction over all controversies originating with said mining leases and contracts, and all questions of mining rights, or invasions thereof, where the amount involved exceeded the sum of $100. Two terms of court (§7) were authorized to be held each year, at Muscogee, on the first Mondays in April and September; all the court's proceedings (§ 8) to be conducted in English, and all bona fide residents of the Indian Territory, over twenty-one years of age, who had a sufficient understanding of English to comprehend the proceedings were made competent to serve as jurors, subject to the exceptions and challenges as provided in the rules governing the district court for the Western District of Arkansas, providing (§ 15) "that in all criminal trials where a jury is demanded and in which the defendant or defendants are citizens of the United States, none but citizens of the United States shall be competent as jurors."

By the passage of this act, apparently repealing the act of January 6, 1883, annexing certain portions of the Indian Territory to the Northern District of Texas, another "most un-kindest cut of all" was dealt the court at Fort Smith (§ 17). This was affected by annexing the Chickasaw Nation and a greater portion of the Choctaw Nation, bounded thus: From the southeast corner of the Indian Territory north to where Big Creek, a tributary of Black Fork of Kiamisha River, crosses the line between the Indian Territory and the State of Arkansas, thence west with Big Creek and Black Fork to the junction of Black Fork with Buffalo Creek and to a point where the latter is crossed by the old military road from Fort Smith to Boggy Depot in the Chickasaw Nation, thence southwest along the road as fir as Perryville Creek, then northwest up said creek to its crossing by the Missouri, Kansas & Texas Railroad, thence north, up the center of the main track, to the South Canadian River, then up the center of the main channel* to the west boundary line of the Choctaw Nation at the northwest corner of said nation, thence south to the boundary line between said nation and the Wichita Indian reservation; thence south with the boundary line of the Choctaw Nation and the reservation of the Kiowa, Comanche and Apache Indian tribes to Red River, and then down Red River to place of beginning; also all that part of the Indian Territory not annexed to the District of Kansas and not set apart and occupied by the Five Civilized Tribes of Indians; to constitute a part of the Eastern Judicial District of Texas for judicial purposes, the Texas counties of Lamar, Fannin, Red River and Delta constituting the balance of the said Eastern District of Texas. Two terms of district and circuit court were authorized, annually, at Paris, Texas, on the third Monday in April and the second Monday in October, and the court was given exclusive, original jurisdiction of all offenses committed against the laws of the United States within that portion of the Indian Territory so annexed, of which jurisdiction was not given by this act to the new court established at Muscogee.

Another important feature of the act of March 1, 1889, was the penalties prescribed for certain offenses committed in the Indian Territory, to-wit: (§ 20) Obstructing railroads, imprisonment at hard labor for not to exceed twenty years, "Provided, that if any person is killed as the result of said obstruction, the person or persons placing said obstruction shall be deemed guilty of murder;" (§21) wilful injury to telegraph or telephone lines, not to exceed $500 fine nor more than one year's imprisonment; (§ 22) disturbing religious meeting, sixty days' imprisonment or $100 fine or both such fine and imprisonment; (§23) assault with intent to rob, one to fifteen years' imprisonment; (§25) malicious injury to animal property, six months imprisonment or $100 fine or both, "Provided, that if the animal be killed the court shall render judgment in favor of the injured party for three-fold the amount of damages assessed;" (§25) assault with a deadly weapon with intent to injure, $50 to $1,000 fine and one year's imprisonment; (§ 26) setting fire to any woods, marsh or prairie in the

Indian Territory with the intention of destroying fences or other improvements, $500 line or six months' imprisonment or both; (§27) sections 5, 23, 24 and 23 not to be applied to offenses committed by one Indian on the person or property of another Indian.

The act creating the Muscogee court was in line with the treaty of 1866 between the government and the Five Civilized Tribes, and was especially favored by many of the more intelligent Indians, who objected to seeing citizens dragged to an adjoining State for trial before a jury composed of residents of said State and not of the Territory.

On May 2, 1890 (U. S. St. at L., 51st Cong , Sess. 1, vol. 26, chap. 182, p 720) an act was approved creating the Territory of Oklahoma, comprising all that part oi the Indian Territory not actually occupied by the Five Civilized Tribes of Indians and the Indian tribes within the Quapaw Agency and except the unoccupied part of the Cherokee outlet, together with that portion of the United States known as the Public Land Strip (No Man's Land). A full, independent territorial judicial system (§ 9), with three judicial districts, was established and given full and original jurisdiction of all cases originating under certain laws of the United States, the same as is vested in the circuit and district courts of the United States, and, in addition, exclusive, original jurisdiction over that portion of the Cherokee outlet not included in Oklahoma Territory. Thirty-four (§11) chapters of the revised laws of Nebraska, in force November 1, 1889, were, so far as locally applicable and not in conflict with the laws of the United States, put in force until the adjournment of the first session of the Territorial Legislature. Jurisdiction was conferred (§ 12) upon the Oklahoma district courts of all controversies between citizens of one tribe of Indians and citizens of another tribe in Oklahoma, the same as if both were citizens of the United States, and Indian citizens of Oklahoma were given the same rights to invoke the courts to protect their persons or property as if they were citizens of the United States. The boundaries of the Indian Territory were by this act thus described: (§29) "All that portion of the

United States, bounded on the north by Kansas, east by Arkansas and Missouri, south by Texas, and west and north by Oklahoma shall, for the purposes of this act, be known as the Indian Territory." The jurisdiction of the new court at Muscogee was, by this act, restricted as to territory more than one-half its area, but it was given increased jurisdiction and powers over the domain remaining as the Indian Territory, jurisdiction over all civil cases except those over which the tribal courts had exclusive jurisdiction. Another feature (§ 30) was the division of the Indian Territory into three divisions, with terms of court to be held twice annually at Muscogee, South McAlester and Ardmore. Fifty-six chapters (§ 3 1) of certain "general laws" of Arkansas, in force in 1883 and published in 1884 and known as "Mansfield's Digest of the Statutes of Arkansas," so far as locally applicable and not in conflict with any Federal statute, were put in force in the Indian Territory; and (§ 33) certain laws of Arkansas (chapters 45 and 46) were, as far as applicable, put in force to govern certain crimes known as misdemeanors, the Federal statutes to govern in all cases of conflict With said laws of Arkansas. Another provision of this act gave the United States circuit courts, respectively, for the Western District of Arkansas and the Eastern District of Texas, continued exclusive jurisdiction in the Indian Territory over all crimes and misdemeanors punishable by death or imprisonment at hard labor, except as in the following sections: It conferred (§ 34) upon the United States courts in the Indian Territory original jurisdiction in the protection of Indians, and also conferred concurrent jurisdiction with the courts for the Western District of Arkansas and the Eastern District of Texas in violations of the intercourse law by introducing ardent liquors into the Indian Territory. This provision of the act of 1890 was practically the first to interfere with the criminal jurisdiction of the Fort Smith Federal Court in the territory of which it had, at the same time, jurisdiction; it was a species of Congressional short-sightedness that resulted in great confusion. Warrants were often issued from two or more courts for the same offense and men were frequently arrested for introducing into the Indian Territory after having been already tried by one or another of the three courts. This act also (§ 36) conferred upon the Federal court in the Indian Territory jurisdiction of all controversies arising between the members of different tribes of Indians, and empowered the court to inflict the same punishments, as if both parties to the controversy were citizens of the United States, and any member of an Indian tribe was given the right to invoke the said court's protection to his property or person as against any person not a member of some tribe or nation, the same as if he were a citizen of the United States. By this act (§ 37) the operating of a lottery in the Indian Territory was made a misdemeanor, and punishable for the first offense by a fine of $500 and for the second offense $500 to $5,000 and, in the discretion of the court, one year or less imprisonment. Jurisdiction of this offense was given to the Federal court in the Indian Territory, and all persons, Indians or others, were made subject to the provisions and penalties. Another provision (§ 38) was the power conferred upon the clerk and deputy clerks of said court to issue marriage licenses and solemnize marriage. Another (§ 41), gave the judge of the said court the same power to extradite persons who have taken refuge in the Indian Territory charged with crimes in the States or other Territories of the United States, as was before given to the Governor of Arkansas, in that State, and empowered him to issue requisitions upon the governors of other States or Territories for persons who have committed offenses in the Indian Territory and taken refuge in any of the States or Territories. Another (§ 42), granted the right of appeal and writs of error from the decisions of the said court to the Supreme Court of the United

States, and, finally (§ 43), gave the judge of the said court the right to hear and determine applications presented by a member of any Indian tribe in the Indian Territory to become a citizen of the United States. It will be seen that certain provisions made the judge of the Federal court under discussion next to a monarch, and made the Indian Territory more than ever a court governed country, probably the only one on earth in which the judiciary is also, to a great degree, the governing power.

Thus, step by step, did Congress encroach upon the Fort Smith Federal Court, gradually taking away its criminal jurisdiction over the Indian Territory; by degrees, like the slow bleeding to death of an unfortunate patient under the knife of the bungling surgeon, the restriction was continued. By act of May 3, 1892, (U. S. St. at L., 52nd Cong., Sess. 1, vol. 27, chap. 59, p. 12) another court was created and given certain jurisdiction in the Indian Territory. This act created a third division of the District of Kansas from portions of the First District. For judicial purposes, the counties of Miami, Linn, Bourbon, Crawford, Cherokee, Labette, Neosho, Allen, Anderson, Coffey, Woodson, Elk and Greenwood were established as the Third District of Kansas, and (§3) all crimes and offenses thereafter committed against the laws of the United States in the counties named and within the limits of the Quapaw Agency in the Indian Territory, of which the courts of Kansas had previously had jurisdiction, were held to be amenable to trial at the court for the Third Kansas District at Fort Scott.

But of all the acts antagonistic to the Fort Smith court none were so vicious, nor had such depressing effect, as it swooped down upon its victim like some monster bird of prey, as the act of March 1, 1895, which practically demolished the greatest court on earth, signaling the ending of its career as such, and sweeping it, almost, from its very foundations. This act (U. S. St. at L., 53rd Cong., Sess. Ill, vol. 28, chap. 145, p. 693), by its first section, divided the Indian Territory into three judicial districts, to be known as the "Northern," "Central" and "Southern" districts. Four places were appointed for holding court (two terms annually at each place); in the Northern District, comprising all of the Creek Nation, all of the Cherokee and Seminole Nations, all of the country occupied by Indian tribes in the Quapaw Indian Agency and the town-site of the Maimi Town-site Company; the places appointed for holding court were Vinita, Maima, Tahlequah and Muscogee. The Central District comprised all of the Choctaw country, and South McAlester, Antlers, Atoka and Cameron were appointed as places for court to be held, two terms annually at each place. The Southern District comprised all of the Chickasaw country, and two terms of court were authorized to be held annually at Ardmore, Purcell, Paul's Valley, Ryan and Chickasha. The President was authorized (§ 2) to appoint, with the advice and consent of the Senate, two additional judges for the Northern and Southern districts, respectively, to terms of four years each; the judge of the Federal court, heretofore appointed to preside over the Indian Territory being made judge of the Central District, and the salary of each was placed at $5,000 annually, the judge of the former

Federal court having been paid a salary of $3,500. The judge of each district was qualified to hold court in either of the other districts for the trial of any case which the judge of said district should be disqualified from trying, "and in the case of sickness or for other reasons either of the judges should be unable to sit in judgment, either of the remaining judges may sit in his stead." Provision was made for the appointment of a district attorney and marshal for said courts, in each of the four districts, the terms of office to be four years, the district attorneys to be paid annually as salaries $4,000 each, and the marshals the same, and each of the deputies, to be appointed by each of the three marshals, to be paid $1,200 per year and necessary expenses while on duty. The clerk (§3) of the former Federal court at Muskogee vas made clerk of the Southern District, and the judges of the Central and Northern Districts were authorized to appoint clerks for their respective courts; the clerks to be paid $3,000 each yearly salary, and their deputies $1,200. Each of the three judges (§4) were given power to appoint commissioners in their respective districts, who should have original jurisdiction as justices of the peace in civil cases, according to the Arkansas code, "where the value of the thing in controversy does not exceed $100;" appeals to. be submitted from the commissioner's courts where the amount of judgment exceeds $20; the commissioners to draw $ 1, 500 yearly salary. Very stringent were the provisions of this act in girding the traffic in intoxicants in the Indian Territory. It provided (§8) that any person, Indian or otherwise, who shall make, sell or give away, or in any way furnish to anyone, either to himself or others, any vinous, malt or fermented liquors or intoxicating drinks, whether medicated or not, or who shall carry into said Territory any such drinks, or who shall be interested in such making, giving away or furnishing any of the liquors described above, shall be liable to a fine of $500 and imprisonment of from one month to five years. The act further provided (§9) and gave to the United States courts thereby established in the Indian Territory exclusive, original jurisdiction of all offenses committed in the Indian Territory, of which the court then had jurisdiction, and after September 1, 1896, to have exclusive, original jurisdiction of all offenses against the laws of the United States committed in the Indian Territory, except such cases as the Federal courts at Paris, Texas, Fort Smith, Arkansas, or Fort Scott, Kansas, may have already proceeded against, and all laws previously enacted conferring jurisdiction on United States courts held in Arkansas, Kansas, Texas, outside of the limits of the Indian Territory, as to offenses committed in the Indian Territory, were repealed, to take effect September 1, 1896, and the jurisdiction previously given to those courts, to be given after that date to the Federal courts newly established in the Indian Territory, except in cases already commenced and on the dockets of said courts. Section 10 empowered the several marshals in the Indian Territory to provide suitable places for holding court in their respective districts, and (§ I 1) the judges-of the said courts were constituted a court of appeals, to be presided over by the judge oldest in commission as chief justice of said court; said court of appeals to have the same jurisdiction! and powers in the Indian Territory as was conferred on the Supreme Court of Arkansas over the decisions of the State courts, provided by chapter 40 of Mansfield's Digest of the Laws of Arkansas.

As shown by the several sections of the act just quoted, its slaughter of the famous old court at Fort Smith, so far as it related to the Indian Territory, was complete, although eighteen months' lease of life was given it; but on September 1, *896, as stated, that portion of the act went into effect which stripped from the courts for the Western District of Arkansas, the Eastern District of Texas and the Third District of Kansas all jurisdiction over any portion of the Indian Territory. It was a matter of grave doubt in the minds of many whether the act was a wise one, and many petitions were sent to Congress during the session of 1896 praying for a repeal and the rein-instatement of the Fort Smith Federal Court, but to no avail, and the court which had borne so important a part in the criminal annals of that portion of the country, where were gathered the worst and most desperate of the criminal classes from all parts of the country and from nearly every country on earth, shrunk to the dimensions of a petty tribunal with a pitiful jurisdiction over a few Arkansas counties. Well said Col. Ben T. DuVal, in an able address delivered at a meeting of the Fort Smith bar, held in the autumn of 1896, in honor of Judge Parker, soon after his death, "How great has the mighty fallen.

The annual practice of passing bills relating to the Indian Territory had become a penchant with Congress, and on May 25, 1896, an act was approved naming penalties for special crimes, as follows: (U. S. St. at L., 54th Cong., Sess. 1, vol.

29, chap. 242, pp. 136-137) Any person shooting at a locomotive or any kind of car of a train in the Indian Territory, or who throws at the same or at any person thereon any dangerous missil [sic], or attempts to derail any locomotive or car of a railroad train, is deemed guilty of a felony and on conviction thereof is liable to not more than twenty years' imprisonment at hard 'labor, provided that if any person be killed, directly or indirectly, by reason of said shooting, throwing or attempt to derail, the person guilty of said felony shall be deemed guilty of murder and shall be tried and punished accordingly; and it was further provided (§2) that any person in the Indian Territory shooting willfully at any car of any train, whether attached to a locomotive or not, or who shall throw any missil at such car, shall be deemed guilty of a misdemeanor and subject to a term of ninety days' imprisonment or a fine of $300 or both such fine and imprisonment.

On May 28, 1896 (U. S. St. at L., 54th Cong., Sess. 1, vol. 29, chap. 252, p. 180, § 7), a change was made in the manner of remunerating the district attorneys and marshals of the several judicial districts in the United States, from the fee to the salary system, the salary of district attorney and marshal for the Western District of Arkansas being placed at $5,000 each per annum. The same act (§ 19, p. 184) provided that the terms of office of ail United States commissioners of circuit courts should expire on June 30, 1897, the offices to be abolished on that date, and for the appointment by the judge of the district court of each judicial district such number of persons as should be deemed necessary, to be known as United States district court commissioners, to have the same privileges and duties as were formerly held by the commissioners of circuit courts.

A little later, June 10, of the same year (U. S. St. at L, 54th Cong., Sess, 1, vol. 29, chap, 398, p. 340), with great pomp, a resolution passed both houses of Congress, declaring it to be "the duty of the United States to establish a government in the Indian Territory which would rectify the many inequalities, irregularities and discriminations now existing in said Territory and afford needful protection to the lives and property of all citizens and residents thereof." This resolution paved the way for the Curtis Bill, which was finally approved a little more than two years later.

On February 20, 1897 (U, S. St. at L, 54th Cong., Sess. I1, vol. 29, chap. 269, pp. 59-91), Congress again began tampering with the judicial districts of Arkansas, this time slightly increasing the territory comprising the Western District. By its provisions the counties of Benton, Washington, Carroll, Boone, Madison. Newton, Crawford, Franklin, Johnson, Logan, Sebastian, Scott, Yell, Polk, Sevier, Howard. Pike, Little River, Hempstead, Miller, Lafayette, Nevada, Columbia, Union, Ouchita and Calhoun, twenty-six counties in the western portion of the State, were made to constitute the Western District, the residue of the State to constitute the Eastern District. Two divisions were created, known as the Fort Smith and Texarkana divisions of the Western District of Arkansas, and all civil and criminal cases issued thereafter against persons in any of the first named fourteen counties were made returnable to the Fort Smith division; those in the remaining twelve to be returnable to the Texarkana division, and two terms of United States circuit and district court were provided to be held annually at Fort Smith and at Texarkana. Fort Smith was continued as office of the judge, marshal and district attorney; the jail at Fort Smith was made to do service for the entire district, but each division was supplied with separate clerks.

On June 7, 1897, an act was approved which, although expressed in few words, was far reaching in effect and made useless the tribal courts of the Indian Territory (U. S. St. at L., 55th Cong., Sess. 1, vol. 30, chap. 3, p. 83). The act provided that on and after January 1, 1898. the United States courts in the Indian Territory should have original and exclusive jurisdiction and authority to try and determine all civil cases in law and equity, and all criminal cases for the punishment of offenses committed, after the said date, by any person in the Indian Territory, giving United States commissioners in the Indian Territory the power and jurisdiction already conferred by existing laws of the United States as respects all persons and property in said Territory, and the laws of the United States and of Arkansas, in force therein, to apply to all persons therein, irrespective of race, said courts to exercise jurisdiction thereof, as now conferred upon them in the trial of like cases, and any citizen of an)one of said tribes in the said Territory otherwise qualified, who can speak and understand the English language, to be competent to serve as juror in any of the said courts; also that after January 1, 1898, all acts, ordinances and resolutions of the councils of either of the Five Civilized Tribes shall be immediately certified, on their passage, to the President of the United

States and shall not take effect, if dis approved by him, or until after thirty days have passed. Provision was also made for the appointment by the President of an additional judge for the said Territory, the appellate court in said Territory to designate the time and place in the several judicial districts, at which such judge shall hold court, and the courts shall be held at the town of Wagoner, and at such other places as the appellate court shall determine; said court to have all the authority, exercise all the powers, perform like duties, and receive the same salary as other judges of said courts. Well might one have believed that Congress was becoming Indian Territory court mad.

On June 30, 1897 (U. S. St. at L., 54th Cong., Sess. I1, vol. 30, chap. 109, pp. 506-507), an act was approved by Congress enlarging the scope of the laws against introducing liquor into the Indian territory to conform with the ingenuity of that class of studious criminals who strive, where there are results to be gained thereby, to circumvent by cunning schemes whatever laws may be passed tending to restrict them in law-breaking. The list of prohibited liquors was, by this act, made to include "beer, ale and wine, or any ardent or other intoxicating liquor whatever, or any essence, extract, bitters, preparation, compound, composition or any article whatever, under any name, label or brand, which produces intoxication," but providing for cases wherein the person so introducing had been authorized in writing from the War Department, or by any officer authorized by the War Department. There is opportunity here for those who believe that prohibition can be made effective by legislation alone, to determine whether their theories are correct.

On June 28, 1898, the Curtis Bill (U. S. St. at L., 55th Cong. Sess. I1, vol. 30, chap. 517, p. 495) was approved. It was entitled "An act tor the protection of the people of the Indian Territory and for other purposes," Section 9 gave to the City of Fort Smith police jurisdiction over the Choctaw Strip, previously noted, and putting in force the Fort Smith city ordinances for the preservation of peace and health, as far 35; practical; "Provided that no charge or tax shall ever be levied against said tribe or nation to which it belongs." Section it increased the number of chapters of the Arkansas laws in force in the Indian Territory and gave the United States power to enforce the same. City and town councils were allowed thereby to pass ordinances, and If consisting of two hundred or more inhabitants said towns may become incorporated, but they must make careful provisions against allowing the sale or introduction of intoxicants. Section 26 provided that the laws of the various Indian tribes in the Indian Territory "shall no longer be enforced at law or equity by the Federal courts in the Indian Territory;" (§27) that on July 1, 1898, all tribal courts in the Indian Territory shall be abolished, the authority of all officers of such courts to cease and all civil and criminal cases pending in such courts to be transferred, to the United States courts in the Indian Territory, "Provided that this section is not to be enforced as to the Chickasaw, Choctaw and Creek tribes until October 1, 1898;" (§ 29) for the allotment of all lands in the several Indian nations, the United States courts in the Indian Territory to have exclusive jurisdiction of all controversies growing out of titles or the use of real estate; provided also for the members of the Choctaw and Creek tribes indicted for certain crimes, if fearing an unfair trial, to file affidavit so stating, and authorizing the judges of said court to order a change of venue to the United States courts for the Western District of Arkansas or the Eastern District of Texas, whichever is the nearest and most convenient; also providing for the tribal courts of the Choctaw and Chickasaw Nations to continue for eight years after March 4, 1898.

In September, 1898, a test case was brought before Judge Thomas, of the Indian Territory, in the Northern United States Judicial District, at Muscogee, to decide the constitutionality of the act of Congress approved June 7, 1897, already noted, which act went into effect January 1, 1898, depriving the courts of the Five Civilized Tribes in the Indian Territory of exercising jurisdiction over their own citizens, Judge Yancy Lewis and William T. Hutchings, attorneys for the Creek and Cherokee Nations, began the proceeding by petitioning Judge Thomas for a writ of habeas corpus for Bount Martin, a Cherokee Indian who was indicted in the Federal court at Muscogee far the theft of a horse from another Cherokee Indian. Martin acknowledged the crime, but claimed that the United States court had no jurisdiction, both parties being Cherokee Indians, and on that account his attorneys asked for his release. On September 20th, Judge Thomas rendered an opinion in the matter, in which he held that the act of Congress approved June 7, 1897, giving the United States courts in the Indian Territory original, exclusive jurisdiction over all crimes committed in the Indian Territory, irrespective of race, after January 1, 1898, is constitutional, and Martin was remanded to jail to await trial. An attempt was made to bring a similar proceeding before the Supreme Court of the United States, for immediate and final settlement, but the Supreme Court refused to entertain the matter except it be brought upon appeal from a lower court. The Supreme Court is reported far behind in its work, and it is said that on this account it will be several years before a test case can be brought to its notice. It would seem to matter but little, however, for is the creature greater than its maker? Congress creates and demolishes courts and mikes laws for the courts of its creation to be guided by and act upon. Let us remember the fate of the man, who, while sitting upon a lofty branch of a tall tree, foolishly severed it between himself and the trunk, and have mercy on the court, the creature of Congress.

THE INDIAN ALLOTMENT

Just at this point, having discussed, briefly, the "Curtis Bill.-' which provides for an allotment of the land in the Indian Territory in severalty, to the members of the Five Civilized Tribes, it may be of interest to note the following statement concerning four Indian nations, vis: Creek, Cherokee, Choctaw and Chickasaw, showing the amount of land, number of Indian inhabitants and those who have been adopted into the different tribes, along with the apportionment each will receive:

CHOCTAW AND CHICKASAW.

Total number of acres in Chickasaw Nation................. 4,650.935

Total number of acres in Choctaw Nation................... 6,6.88,000

Total, both Nations...................................... 11.338,935

8,700 freedmen at 40 acres each........................ 348,000

Estimated reservations for town-sites, railroad rights-of-way. school, church, court house, cemetery grounds, etc. 100,000

Total.. 448.000

Net acreage to be allotted to citizens, excepting' freedmen 10.890.935 This number of acres divided equally among the 19,754 citizens of the two nations, exclusive of freedmen, would make a per capita allotment of (acres)........................ 551

CKEEK NATION.

Creek Indians by blood.................................. 10,014

Freedmen.. 4,757

Total population... 14,771

Total number of acres in Creek Nation................. 3,040,000

Less estimated reservations for town-sites, railroad rights-of-way, schools, churches, court houses, cemetery grounds, etc.. 30,000

Leaves net amount (estimated) number of acres to be allotted among the 14,771 citizens at.................. 3,010,000

Which, if divided per capita, would give each citizen (acres) 203

CHEROKEE NATION.

Cherokees by blood..................................... 26,500

Adopted intermarried whites............................. 2,300

Freedmen.. 4,000

Delawares... 871

Shawnees.. 790

Total... 34,461

Total area of the Cherokee Nation (in acres)................. 5,031,351

Less estimated amount of land to be reserved for town-sites, railroad rights-of way, schools, churches, cemetery grounds, etc.. 60,000

Leaves the net (estimated) number of acres to be allotted among the 34,461 citizens at............................ 4,971,351

Which, if divided per capita, would give each (acres)........ 144

THE JAIL AND COURT HOUSE

A description of the court house, in which this famous court was held, and the jail, in which were incarcerated the many hundreds of men held for trial and while awaiting execution or transmission to the penitentiary to serve out their sentences, may be of interest.

The first session of the court in Fort Smith was held in the second story of a brick building that stood near the west corner of Second and A streets, on ground now occupied by several wholesale houses. The post-office was, at that time, in a leased building, standing on the corner noted, and the next building adjoining it on the southwest was known locally as "The Hole in the Wall," from a saloon which, before the war, had been kept in a back room and was reached by a long and narrow hallway running back to it between the two buildings. It was in the back part of the second story, and above the room formerly occupied by this saloon, that Judge Henry C. Caldwell first opened up court, after its removal from Van Buren, on the second Monday in May, 1871. As a further reminiscence, it is given that Col. Ben T. Duval occupied the second story of the next adjoining building southwest, towards Garrison Avenue. This building only extended back as far as the front wall of the court room, and from a rear balcony, or second story veranda, Col. DuVal was wont to enter the court room by means of a low window, and thus avoid going down to the street and up again by the regular entrance.

For jail purposes, the marshal made use of the old military prison, of hewed logs, standing on the Poteau bluffs above its mouth, a short distance from where the block houses in the old stockade had formerly stood, near the spot now occupied by the office of Ketcham's foundry. Charles Burns was made jailer, and he continued to hold the position, with the exception of one period of four years, until February, 1882.

With the incoming of Judge Story, in the spring of 1872, the court room over the "The Hole in the Wall" and the jail of hewed logs were still in service. At this term of court the trial of John Childers, who was indicted for murder, May 15, 1871, was begun, and continued to the November term, and was one of the first cases on the November docket. The case came on for trial Wednesday morning, November 6th, and continued to Monday, November 18th, when the jury returned a verdict of guilty. This case enjoyed the distinction of its trial having been conducted in three different court rooms. On the night of November 13th, after the close of a day hard spent by the attorneys in examining witnesses, the building in which the court was held was burned, and at the usual time for convening court the next morning an adjournment was taken to November 13th at the Sebastian County Circuit Court room, then situated in the first story of the Kennedy block, erected in 1870 (now occupied as the Hotel LeFlore), where a two days' session was held, the examination of witnesses in the Childers case being still under consideration when court adjourned on Saturday evening. By that time Marshal Roots had received permission from the Department of the Interior at Washington to open up the large brick building (heretofore mentioned) inside the garrison walls, which had been built for use as a soldier's barracks and was now standing idle. To this building the court and its effects were removed and the trial of John Childers was continued to its close. His was the only capital offense sentenced at that term, and the first since the court's removal from Van Buren; but the musty old brick building, where sentence was pronounced on him, was destined to become famous as a court house and infamous as a jail.

The building, as constructed, stood with its sides to the northwest and southeast, its gables pointing to the northeast and southwest. The northeast half of the first floor was the portion used as a court room, while the other half was appropriated by the marshal, clerk and other court attaches. Underneath the building was a musty basement or dungeon, with the ceiling scarcely eight feet above the rough, damp, stone floor. It was divided into two compartments, each thirty by sixty feet area, separated by a heavy stone wall which continued above the foundation and acted also as a partition between the two departments above; the building having been designed to accommodate two companies of infantry. The entrances to the basements noted were from the outside, fronting southeast, at either side of the high porch, seen in the full page cut showing the old court house and present jail. Both of these basements were made use of for jail purposes, and the log jail up the Poteau was abandoned. Inside of each of the basement entrances were constructed small vestibules or corridors of rough lumber and eight by ten feet area. It was here that the prisoners, during sessions of court, were permitted to come from their bunks on the floor of the foul smelling dungeons to hold conference with their attorneys.

But very little attention was given to the comfort of the prisoners; they were left to shift for themselves as best tiny could with a blanket apiece, but it is quite evident that there was no cutting short of rations, for it is related by one of the early court bailiffs that he used to raise and fatten several hogs each year, their sole food being taken from the barrel into which was thrown the refuse bread, meat, etc., left over by the prisoners. The cooking was done in a couple of old building, since destroyed by fire, which stood under the shelter of the barracks wall southeast of the jail building. As time advanced and the number of prisoners crowded into the dungeons increased they became so very filthy from lack of any kind of sanitation as to become a national disgrace. A book could be written concerning the horrors of the place that almost rivaled the famous "Black Hole" of Calcutta, but let one tale suffice: Early in the seventies a member of the grand jury, who had heard much about its unfitness as a habitation, even for hogs, declared his intention of going below and examining the jail by himself—without an escort. Other members of the jury attempted to withhold him, telling him "they are not ready for the inspection yet." He replied, "that's just what I want—to go and inspect the rotten hole before they have a chance to get ready." He went; the jailer, unthinkingly, allowed him to enter. The stench that met his nostrils nearly knocked him down. He persisted in his examination; when he returned to the court room he carried a piece of bread and another of meat, both alive with vermin.

These he laid on the judge's desk, saying: "I'm going to send these to Washington." It required all the eloquence of the judge, who was then on the bench, assisted by the district attorney and members of the bar present to dissuade him from making good his threats of exposure. It is probable that had such a disclosure been made at that time, such an uproar would have resulted as would have caused the court to be abolished. That state of affairs continued, however, until 1877, when a new three story brick jail (see cut), adjoining the court house at the southwest end, at a cost of $75,000, with easy accommodations for 144 prisoners, although at one time, February 2, 1896, the records prove there were 244 prisoners confined within its walls, and it is even asserted that on an occasion there were 300; this is not vouched for, however.

Previous to the erection of the new jail, the half story attic of the court house had been devoted to rubbish of all kinds, old guns and other weapons taken from prisoners, bloody garments and other gruesome articles brought for submission as evidence in court, and the place was a veritable museum. With the spirit of humanity and enterprise that caused the construction of a new jail, however, the court house walls were raised and a full second story was added. For a time it was used as a place of detention for female prisoners, but later was given over to hospital purposes. The new jail contains a large three story steel cage, with a seven foot open space between it and the walls of the building at the two sides and the southwest end, while at the other end, adjoining the old court house, is sufficient space (or stairways and an area way. The cells are in size five by eight feet, each supplied with two iron cots, one above the other; each cell closes with an iron door, which opens into a four foot aisle that extends along the entire length of both sides of the cage, inside the steel lattice and across the southwest end. On each floor are twenty-four cells, twelve on each side, and numbered alternately, those looking to the southeast bearing the odd and the others the even numbers, making seventy-two cells entire. The lower twenty-four cells—being those on the first floor—were designated "Murderers' Row," and were used to confine persons charged with murder while awaiting trial, sentence or execution, as well as for the detention of the more desperate class of men charged with various severe crimes. The second floor was used for confining men charged with burglary, robbery, larceny, assaults, etc.: and in the cells of the top floor were confined persons charged with selling or introducing whiskey into the Indian Territory, which acts were direct violations against the United States laws, and for which on conviction severe punishments were dealt out. Since the restriction of the famous court's jurisdiction to twenty-six counties in Arkansas, the cells formerly composing "Murderers' Row" are used for the confinement of all prisoners held for trial in the Fort Smith and Texarkana divisions of the new Western District of Arkansas; the second and, when necessary, third floor cells are used as a penitentiary for all Federal prisoners convicted by the United States courts in the Indian Territory and sentenced to imprisonment for one year or less.

In 1889 a new court house was built, three blocks away, southeast of the old court house and close to the heart of the city, on the site reserved by the government in 1885, originally purchased from John Rogers; and the former court house, or first floor of the old barracks, has since been devoted to jailer's quarters, etc. That portion of the old court room where used to stand Judge Parker's desk and the space within the railing, for the accommodation of attorneys, juries and prisoners on trial, is now the jail kitchen, and the other part, now separated by a partition, where used to sit the throngs of spectators watching the court proceedings, is now used for the detention of female United States prisoners, pending trial at Fort Smith or Texarkana, and as well is a penitentiary for women sentenced by the Federal courts in the Indian Territory to terms of imprisonment for twelve months or less. The basement, beneath, where so many thousand prisoners were confined, is now given over to rubbish of all kinds, and at one side, where used to lay some of the unfortunate beings he sentenced, is Judge Parker's old, high paneled cherry de.-k, covered with old, musty jail records, slowly rotting away and keeping company with the roaches and the rats and the industrious spiders, that now spin their webs across the desk from which, for fourteen years, Judge Parkes dispensed justice with no uncertain hand.

The new government building on South Sixth Street, one square from Garrison Avenue, the city's main thoroughfare, is a fine three story brick structure, with basement and a large attic. The first floor is occupied by the post-office and the Federal revenue department. On the second floor are the offices of the district attorney, marshal, the court stenographer, the grand jury and witness rooms and ladies' toilet. The third floor devotes space to the offices of the circuit and district clerks; here, too, are the chambers of the judge, and here the famous court room; made famous during Judge Parker's jurisdiction, where so many murderers were tried and sentenced in the latter third of his reign. The petit jury room is on the fourth floor. The building is the pride and glory of Fort Smith. I had the distinction of serving on the petit jury in the last case ever tried in the old court house, and was also he'd as juryman in the first case tried in the new building.

The old wall enclosing the fort, a solid work of masonry that had stood the test of over half a century, has now nearly all disappeared; the result of an act of Congress, approved February 26, 1897 (U. S. St. at L., 54th Cong., Sess. I1, vol. 29, chap. 332, pp. 596-597), authorizing the extension of Rogers and Parker avenues in a northwest direction on a straight line to the right-of-way to the "Frisco" Railroad through the barracks grounds, and the extension of South

Second and Third streets southwest across the barracks grounds and reserving the block within the square bounded by the said extension, three hundred feet by two hundred and ninety feet, two and three-fourths inches, on which stands the Federal jail and hospital, for the sole use of said jail and hospital. The city was authorized to remove the old fort walls and the stone building at the north corner of the enclosure and dispose of the material for its own use. The Secretary of the Interior was authorized to have the land, outside of the said jail and hospital reserve, surveyed into lots and blocks and cause the same to be sold at public auction to the highest bidder, the money thus received being conveyed to the United States Treasury.

The accompanying full page illustration, from a photograph taken before the wall was destroyed, gives a fair view of the fort, minus the buildings destroyed by fire, and of the great gateway near the right. To the extreme left is seen the bastion which was used as a magazine, and just inside the wall, at this point, the roof of the old gallows and the whitewashed fence enclosing it. Beyond, looking to the west, is the sandy shore of the Arkansas on the opposite side of the river. At the left of the jail building rises one of the two block houses, previously mentioned, and claimed by the LeFlore estate, and to the right is the ruins of one of the old brick officers' quarters—the guard house is also shown—while the old stone building in which Judge Parker for several years maintained his chambers, and which is now the property of the city, is partially hidden by the trees, The Missouri Pacific Railroad bridge, crossing the Arkansas, and which appears in the foreground of a preceding cut showing a bird's eye view of the city, is directly back of the jail, therefore is not shown here.

It was a grievous mistake—the removal of the old fort walls and the conversion of the barracks grounds into city lots. It was done at the instance of a class of beings who regarded the rare old landmark as only so much rubbish covering valuable real estate, and Congressman "Bass" Little was urged to push the bill through Congress. There are some, however, who are competent to understand that the government should have retained the wall and buildings forever, establishing a museum in the latter for the benefit of pupils half a century hence, to whom the works now destroyed would have been of inestimable value. The grounds within the fortress would have become most attractive for park purposes and would have been the means of bringing tourists to the city, and already many of the citizens of Fort Smith, who urged Congress to commit the sacrilege, have discovered their mistake now that it is too late, and are computing the dollars that might have been spent in the city, in years to come, by the thousands who would have traveled long distances to view the evidences of frontier life which have been so ruthlessly destroyed, only remaining in the memory of those who looked upon it before its destruction, and preserved to posterity only through the medium of photography. At this writing, October, 1898, the government has in hand a proposition to establish grades and erect a fine iron fence enclosing all that is left of the old frontier fortress.

A few readers will enquire regarding the old scaffold. That, too, was destroyed, burned by order of the Fort Smith City Council, with the consent of the government, in the autumn of 1896, soon after the death of Judge Parker. This was the result of a morbid sentiment of certain citizens who feared that if allowed to stand and become a source of interest to sight-seers it would, in some inconceivable manner, reflect upon the city to its discredit, and a sigh of relief arose on high when the last vestige of the old death machine had been reduced to smoke and ashes.

A SKETCH OF JUDGE PARKER'S LIFE

Judge Isaac Charles Parker was born in Belmont County, Ohio, in 1838. In 1859, he removed to St. Joseph, Missouri, and engaged in the practice of law, and in 1860 was chosen city attorney, filling the office acceptably until 1864, when he was elected prosecuting attorney of Buchanan County.

He entered into politics soon after his arrival at St, Joseph and was president of the first Stephen A. Douglass Club organized in Missouri, but early in 1861 he espoused the principles of the Republican party, continuing under its banner until his death. In 1864 he was chosen presidential elector and, as such, assisted in casting Missouri's vote for Abraham Lincoln. In 1868 he was made judge of the Twelfth Judicial Circuit of Missouri, and two years later was elected a member of Congress from the Sixth Missouri District. in 1872 he was reelected and during the second term served on the Committee on Territories, of which James A. Garfield was chairman.

More than one of the members of this committee became famous; Garfield, as president of the United States; William Wheeler, as vice-president; William Hale, of Maine, who declined the appointment as postmaster-general under President Grant; James N. Tyner, who accepted the place, and later rose to the office of assistant attorney general for the United States Post-office Department, and I. C. Parker, who became world-renowned as judge for the Western District of Arkansas.

In 1875, Judge Parker was appointed chief justice of Utah. It is more than probable that he would have made a name for himself there, but two weeks later President Grant withdrew the appointment, and at the request of Senators Dorsey and Clayton and for the sake of putting an end to the fierce Brooks-Baxter War that was making the Western District of Arkansas a place unfit to live in, established the strange precedent of appointing a judge from outside of the State and Kimmon, of Massachusetts, a nephew of [Civil War General] Benjamin F. Butler, having failed of confirmation by the senate, judge Barker was chosen to the post, being at that time the youngest member on the judicial bench.

On page 118, Common Law Record 5, 1874, lying in the vault of the circuit clerk's office in the United States Courthouse at Fort Smith, appears a copy of the appointment as follows:

Ulysses S. Grant, President of the United States.

To all who shall see these Presents, Greeting:

Know ye, that reposing special confidence in the wisdom, uprightness and learning of Isaac C. Parker, I have nominated and by and with the advice and consent of the Senate, do appoint him to be judge of the United States Court for the Western District of Arkansas, and do authorize and empower him to execute and fulfill the duties of that office according to the constitution and laws of the said United States, and to have and to hold the said office, with all the powers, privileges and evolutions to the same of right appertaining, unto the said Isaac C. Parker, during his good behavior.

In testimony whereof I have caused these letters to be made patent and the seal of the United States to be hereunto affixed.

[seal] Given under my hand in the City of Washington, the nineteenth day of March, in the year of our Lord the eighteen hundred and seventy-five, and of the independence of the United States the ninety-ninth.

By the President: U. S. GRANT.

Hamilton Fish, Secretary of State.

It was on the 10th day of May, 1875, that Judge Parker fir.-t entered upon his duties as judge of the Fort Smith court As stated in the preceding chapter, it had but recently been removed from Van Buren, and from that time until June, 189^ over twenty-one years, Judge Parker held court almost continuously, without losing a day on account of sickness.

On the day named, Judge Parker was given the oath of office a second time (he was formally sworn into office in March previous and had, before going to Fort Smith, issued certain orders necessary for the proper conduct of matters pertaining to the court) before James C. Churchill, the veteran clerk for the district court for the Western District of Arkansas, appointed December 4, 1867. Immediately thereafter he opened court, and the first case to which his attention was called was styled:

United States vs. Henry Knowles: Indicted for assault with intent to kill.

"Now comes the United States of America, by Wm. H. H. Clayton, Esq., attorney for the Western District of Arkansas, and said defendant, by his attorneys, Messrs. DuVal & Cravens, whereupon the defendant, by his attorneys, filed his written motion for a continuation of this cause, for reasons therein given."

This case was continued to May 25, then to the November term, and on November 11, 1875, the defendant was discharged on a *nolle prosequi* entered by the district attorney.

Eleven cases were considered by the new judge on that day, all of them being minor ones except one, the consideration of which was that of:

United States VS. Oscar Snow: Indicted for murder

On motion of defendant, by his attorney, Campbell Le Flore, Wm. M. Cravens, was appointed to assist in defending the case, and here, on page 122, Common Law Record No. 5, 1874, appears for the first time Judge Parker's signature appended to an order adjourning court till the following day.

When he entered upon the discharge of his duties he encountered difficulties such as most men would have quailed before. Judge Story had been a weakling, wholly incompetent, and was but a puppet in the hands of unscrupulous and stronger men. The court had fallen into disrepute with the people over whom it had jurisdiction. The extravagant and fraudulent expenditures with but few convictions had made the guardians of the United States Treasury suspicious, and it had come to be almost an impossibility to get money to pay the expenses of the court. It was also extremely difficult to procure witnesses, and there was a strong undercurrent of antagonism to the court and its officers throughout the district. The bar of the court was able, but far from harmonious, and a general demoralization and distrust prevailed. Meanwhile the jail was crowded with prisoners awaiting trial.

Judge Parker entered upon his duties fearlessly, and he soon won the respect and confidence of the bar and the people. All came soon to feel the wonderful effect of his masterful nature. The court was without precedent. It was an anomaly. It can have no successor. It would be impossible for the conditions which environed it to be repeated. Here was a pure and upright judge administering the law under apparently insuperable difficulties. History contains nothing like this court and its judge.

The opening of the railroads in the Territory was followed by a horde of lawless and desperate criminals, who, banded together to defy the laws, terrified the country by their terrible crimes. These crimes were not subject to the courts of the Indian tribes, and this was the only tribunal having jurisdiction over them. The class of ruffians who infested the territory were a refuse humanity, to whom Judge Parker gave the title of "criminal intruders." They were renegades, refugees from other states, and even from other countries, who had left behind them, often, more tangible records than mere reputation for vice. They had perpetrated murders or other crimes, some of them were several times murderers. They had come to the new country with a tigerish appetite for blood, keenly whetted by their past experience. Often they came from a race of criminals, and it was with their foul heredity, as well as with their acquired thirst for crime, that the court had to contend. They were bold and fearless. A large number of deputy marshals (sixty-five during Judge Parker's administration) were slain by them—murdered in the discharge of their duty, and when arrested and placed on trial it was a difficult matter to convict them because of their numbers and influence.

When the Territory was set apart for the Indians, in 1828, the government promised them protection; the promise was always ignored, the only protection having been offered them being through the courts.

To Judge Parker and his deputies, located on the borderland, fell the task of acting as protectors. It was necessary for the judge to be stern and inflexible on the bench and to bring all the strength of his nature to the enforcement of the law. His judicial career cannot be fairly comparisoned [sic] with that of other judges because of the difference in their environments.

The court under Judge Parker came to be known throughout the world as having convicted and sentenced to the gallows more murderers than any court had ever done in the same length of time; and Judge Parker was looked upon by the people who did not know him as being harsh and cruel. He was feared by the criminal classes, but the representative Indians, generally, loved and respected him, for they knew him to be their true friend and protector. They knew that many, high in authority, censured them for the lawlessness of their country and made it a pretext for depriving them of their tribal governments. He knew that the Indians furnished a very small percentage of the criminals in his court, and that, under treaty stipulations, the persons who made their country a pandemonium—a veritable hell—were beyond their jurisdiction, and he was their defender on all occasions, and they appreciated him. To this day, in many households, the heart of the Red Man mourns his loss as that of a friend and brother.

For many years it was with the ruffians of an immense tract of country, 74,000 square miles, stretching away to the Colorado line, that Judge Parker had to cope. Criminals were taken to Fort Smith for trial where they could be tried by a disinterested jury, which conditions made impossible in the Territory. They were brutes, or rather demons, in human form, and their crimes were deliberately planned and fiendishly executed. Robbery was the chief incentive, and the victims were usually men with whom the murderers traveled on long, lonely rides across the country.

A man less resolute than Judge Parker would have failed in the task set before him. Failure would have meant bloodshed and a fierce domination of the lawless class in the district. A great work was to be performed and a man equal to the emergency sat upon the bench, who was fearless amid disorders, powerful in his grand individuality.

Gradually but slowly the opposition to the law's enforcement was weakened. Juries, strengthened by his splendid courage, upheld the law. The officers of the court, including the 200 deputy United States marshals, were inspired to heroic efforts, and the days of chivalry never produced a body of men more courageous and fearless than the deputies who executed the process of the court of the Western District of Arkansas. It was bringing order out of chaos, and, whereas, as already stated, the costs of the court, while yet a small affair, had footed $400,000 in little more than a year, they settled down under Judge Parker, while doing many times the amount of work, to $300,000 annually.

In Judge Parker his friends found two distinct characters. On the bench he was stern, impartial, inflexible; off the bench he was gentle, kind, familiar and easily approached. To the person on trial he appeared harsh and sometimes invective, but he was generally impersonal. He did not see the man on trial, his thoughts were on what laid beyond. He saw the reckless desperadoes, riding red-handed over the fair Indian Territory, debauching women and regardless oi the rights of property; the raided trains, where many lives were imperiled and some were destroyed; the homes desolated by the burning torch, after the husband, father or brother had been laid low by the assassins; he saw, too, the widow and her helpless children, fleeing from danger by the light of the flames which licked up their home; he saw the defenseless wife, during the absence of her husband, or the innocent maiden, dragged from their beds and subjected to the most unspeakable indignities, their virtue despoiled by these beastly marauders. He came to know, too, that in the trials of these cases before him, the defense was often—very often—sustained by the most glaring perjury, and that the lives and character of those who assisted in the enforcement of law were forfeited to the vengeance of the accomplices of the criminals.

Small wonder, then, that his charges to the jury sounded pitiless when he presented to them the law as a terrible and sublime avenger. To us, who were actors in those trials, it is not difficult to find good reason for all that appeared harsh in his language. There was an irrepressible, almost uninterrupted, conflict between the law and the lawbreaker, and the victory was not always on the side of the law; naturally, therefore, victory for the prosecution was not always on the side of real justice.

Strange to say, this just judge, who had sentenced 172 criminals to death, believed in the abolition of capital punishment, with the proviso, using his own words, "provided that there was a certainty of punishment, whatever that punishment may be. In the uncertainty of punishment following crime, lies the weakness of our halting justice." On this subject he was wont to say: "The trouble is with the bench, and behind it the maudlin sentiment that condones a crime upon which the blood stains have dried. The bench is indifferent and careless. Avarice, which is the curse of this age, has so poisoned the people that civil law, for the protection of property rights, concerns it more than criminal law, for the protection of life, limb and virtue. Practically, the bench asks the people: 'Which is of greater value, your house, your life or the sanctity of your women?' And the people, by their attitude in specific cases, answer: 'My house.' Little wonder then that the bench comes to take the same view and adjudges accordingly.

"The fault does not lie with juries," said Judge Parker to me one day when we were discussing the apparent inability of certain courts to convict. "The fault does not lie with juries, the persons who constitute them are usually honest men. We have had as fine juries here in Fort Smith as could be found in the land. They have seldom failed me. Juries are willing to do their duty, but they must be led. They must know that the judge wants the enforcement of the law."

Judge Parker's first term was indicative of what was to follow. Eighteen murder cases came before him; convictions were secured in fifteen of them. Never will those who were in the court room when Judge Parker pronounced his first death sentence forget the scene. It was at the opening of court on the morning of June 26, 1875. Eight men, convicted of murder, had been brought up for sentence. They were: Daniel Evins, John Whittington, Edmund Campbell, James Moore, Smoker Man-Killer, Samuel Fooy, Frank Butler and Oscar Snow. Evins was the first man called up. Judge Parker spoke the fatal words with a clear voice and in measured terms, but as soon as he had finished he bowed his head and wept. The sixth on the list of the convicted men sentenced that day was Sam Fooy; he had murdered and robbed a character known by the sobriquet "The Barefooted School Teacher." The young school teacher had been known to possess a roll of money and Fooy shot him to secure it. He hid the body of his victim, and no trace of the young man was discovered for a year, an Indian boy afterwards finding the skeleton, among the bones of which was a flyleaf of a teacher's manual bearing the name of the murdered teacher, still legible. Another of those early cases was that of Martin, better known as "Bully," Joseph, a negro, who, with a colored companion, murdered a Texan and his pretty young wife in the Arbuckle mountains. They shot and killed the Texan and left him to rot. Then they went to the wife at the camp and told her that her husband had fallen from his horse and was badly injured. They offered to guide her to the spot. She mounted a horse which they had provided and went to shame and death; both of the brutes ravished her, then threw her body into an old well sixty feet deep. Months afterward her skeleton was found in what had become a den of rattlesnakes. A searching party discovered the poor girl's burial place, their attention being attracted by a piece of her dress which had caught upon the rocks in the fall. One of the murderers, Martin Joseph, lived to be apprehended and convicted by a strange chain of circumstances. His comrade in crime had boasted to his brothers of their double crime and they kept the secret until the fellow was murdered by Joseph. Then they captured the remaining criminal and turned him over to the marshals.

Another cold blooded crime was that of a half-breed desperado who murdered a camper and followed the little son of the murdered man into the brush and killed him, even while the little fellow was begging for mercy. The brute confessed. "I killed big white man and little white man," he said.

John Pointer, who killed two young men who left Eureka Springs with him for a trip across the Territory in a wagon, was another of the murderers who was convicted during Judge Parker's reign. With an axe Pointer cleft open the head of one of them while he was mixing a pan of dough for their evening meal; the other, who was a lame boy, fled to the woods for shelter, but was struck down by the relentless demon in full pursuit.

It did not seem to Judge Parker to be an act of cruelty to sentence such blood-thirsty men to die. "I never hanged a man," he said when lying on his death bed, "I never hanged a man. It is the law. The good ladies who carry flowers and jellies to criminals mean well. There is no doubt of that, but what mistaken goodness! Back of the sentimentality are the motives of sincere pity and charity, sadly misdirected. They see the convict alone, perhaps chained in his cell; they forget the crime he perpetrated and the family he made husbandless and fatherless by his assassin work."

A short time before his death he said to me. "Crime in a general way has decreased considerably in the last twenty years, but murder is largely on the increase. Why, do you know, that in the past five years 43,000 persons, more than are in the regular army, have been murdered in this country? Parallel with these have been 723 legal executions and 1, 118 lynchings. Think of an average of 7,317 murders a year! Last year 10,-500 persons were murdered; that is at the rate of 875 a month, while five years ago the number of murders in this country were, for the year, but 4,290. There is a doubling of the murder rate an five years. This fearful condition does not exist because of defective laws; we have the most magnificent legal system in the world. The trouble lies in the fact that the bench is not alive to its responsibilities. Courts of justice look to the shadow in the shape of technicalities instead of the substance in the form of crime. Everyone knows, too, that corrupt methods are used to defeat the administration of law. This is a dangerous condition, and the government cannot survive a demoralized people, swayed and dominated by the man of crime. We must have a remedy. Thinking persons are realizing this, but they are wrongfully looking toward the abolition of the jury system as a relief from these evils. I believe this is wrong. Not a jot or tittle of the dignity of the right of trial by jury should be abated. I have often told you that juries should be led. They have a right to expect that, and if guided they will render that justice which is the greatest pillar of society. Without it, with the bench weak and hesitating, even with the terrible penalty of death as the punishment for murder, that branch of crime will not diminish. It is the uncertainty of punishment that causes a lack of fear in the man about to commit a terrible crime. With a milder form of punishment, say imprisonment for life, and courts that have the strength to ensure conviction, without chance of the criminal being released after a few years on a technicality or by executive clemency, even murderers would come to fear the law."

When it is considered that all the cases of murder, assault with intent to kill and larceny tried in this great court came from the Indian Territory, wherein the population numbered only 60,000 souls, some idea of the vastness of crime per capita may be conceived, especially when we also consider that during Judge Parker's reign this court had no jurisdiction in cases where both parties were Indians, except in the case of the Ottawas and a few other small tribes whose members were citizens of the United States, having given up their tribal relations.

At the first term of the court over which Judge Parker presided eight men were convicted of murder. At the November term of that year eleven were tried on that charge and six were convicted, while it was estimated that near half a hundred murders were committed in the Indian Territory that first six months of the judicial year of 1875 where no arrests were made, some of the murderers being Indian slayers of their own blood. The records of the November term of court, 1875, for the Western District of Arkansas shows the following trials, acquittals and convictions:

TRIALS.

Criminal cases, 91; found guilty, 60: not guilty, 31; pleaded guilty, 18; sent to the penitentiary, 61; convicted of murder, 6; acquitted of murder, 5; sent to the garrison jail, 4; number of indictments returned, 150.

CONVICTIONS.

Larceny, 48; murder, 6; selling tobacco contrary to law, 1; assault, 6; whiskey trade, 6; obstructing process, 1; resisting officer. 1; violating internal revenue laws, 7; manslaughter, 1.

ACQUITTALS.

Larceny, 13; murder, 5; assault, 6; whiskey, 4; internal revenue, 2; forgery, 1; fraudulent voucher, 1; *nolle prosequi*, 16; mistrial, 3.

CONTINUED.

Larceny, 7; murder, 3; assault, 5 I resisting officer, 3; by default, 20.

Appalling as was this record, it was asserted by good and reliable authority to show less than one-fourth of the murders and other crimes committed within the confines of the Indian Territory.

During Judge Parker's reign, he was often misrepresented by the press, notably regarding his attitude towards the courts of appeal: he was placed by the newspapers in the position of being opposed to the right of appeal. This was untrue. He did not dream of destroying the appellate courts; he would have remodeled them. He was desirous of seeing organized in the States and in the Indian Territory, courts of criminal appeal made up of judges learned in criminal law and desirous of its speedy enforcement. To these courts Judge Parker would have seen sent full records of the trials and would have had the cases passed upon according to their merits as quickly as possible. He would have brushed aside all technicalities that did not effect the guilt or innocence of the accused, would have had law provide against the reversal of judgments unless innocence was manifest. He believed the establishment of such courts would restore public confidence in the law and its administrators. The party convicted, he admitted, should have the right of having his case reviewed upon a writ of error, but the review, he believed, should take place at once and the case passed upon according to its merits.

People generalized in regard to Judge Parker's administration. He was called heartless and bloodthirsty; but no man ever pointed to a case of undue severity. A common saying was: "Judge Parker is too rigid;" but no one case could be pointed to with the words: "He was too hard in this," or "He should have been more lenient in that." He had ever the single aim of justice in view. He reasoned that no judge who is influenced by any other consideration is fit for the bench. "Do equal and exact justice" was his motto, and he once said to the grand jury, "Permit no innocent man to be punished, but let no guilty man escape." The judge often bewailed the disposition of certain judges to engage actively in politics. In his twenty-one years of judgeship he attended but one political meeting and that was when he accidentally drifted into a Democratic street meeting. He had another motto for his court, "No politics shall enter here," and stringently did he enforce it.

Judge Parker was a true friend of the public school system. He manifested unusual interest in the schools for a man whose mind was so heavily engrossed in other important matters. During the four years and over, just prior to his death, in which he was a member of the Fort Smith Hoard of Education, he never failed to attend the meetings of the board, although the distance from his home made it necessary to employ a carriage for the trip. Owing to the pressure of his official duties he was unable to give much time to committee work, but as a counselor, on account of his wonderful mental resources, he was of untold value to his colleagues on the board. During all the time he was a member of the Board Judge John Rogers, who succeeded him on the bench, was president. In the published report of the Fort Smith School Board for 1896-'97, President Rogers, in his address to the patrons, spoke of Judge Parker, as follows:

"During, the year 1896 the public schools of Fort Smith suffered great loss in the death of Hon. I. C. Parker, one of the members of the Board of Directors. He may be said to have been one of the pillars of the schools in the city. He was their ardent supporter and in them he had abiding faith. From the time he went on the Board until his last illness, although a hard worked man all the time, he scarcely missed a meeting of the Board; and while his duties on the bench of the United States Court precluded his doing any work in the matter of looking after the properties of the district, his counsel on committee work and on the Board was valuable and always timely. In the Board meetings he had the courage of conviction, and in the many embarrassing and perplexing questions presented he stood, always, for the integrity, purity and efficiency of the schools and the sacred preservation of the property of the district. He looked forward to the time when night schools could be organized for indigent young men and women, whose conditions imposed upon them labor during the day, and he cherished and often spoke of adding several industrial features to the system, so that young men and women might not only be trained morally and mentally but also given some means of earning a livelihood when they were through with their school course. The Board feels deeply his loss and gladly pays tribute to his memory."

During the twenty-one years and more that Judge Barker reigned as judge of the court for the Western District of Arkansas, a court that was characteristic both for the large number of cases tried and for the fact that it was always open, he was at all times robust both in body and mind. The daily session was from 8 o'clock in the morning until dark, and when others grew weary he was still fresh and strong. the district over which the court presided was from time to time shorn of its proportions by the establishment of other courts, without visible diminution of the work of Judge Parker's court. Its perennial term went on, and the administration of the law was vigorously enforced, and the judge grew more robust as the years rolled by.

At last, Congress, with ruthless hand, took from the court its jurisdiction over the Indian country, passing a law, March C 1895, providing that such jurisdiction should cease after September 1, 1896. Congress, no doubt, thought it had done wisely, but Judge Parker thought differently. That court was hi: idol; with its destruction his mission ended. It was impossible for so great a man to dwarf his magnificent proportions to the dimensions of a petty court. Belittled as it was, it was his no longer; nature revolted; and as the day grew near for the great catastrophe, it was reported for the first time—early in July, 1896—that Judge Parker was too sick to hold court. He had performed his duty nobly; he had fought a good fight for the enforcement of law and for the preservation of the lives and property of those within his jurisdiction. He had taught the lawless to respect the rights and property of peaceful citizens, and had assisted the Indians in the Territory to advance to a higher civilization.

As time diminished the period of the court's life, its honored judge lay upon a bed of suffering, his splendid physique succumbed to the ravages of disease. The perfect health and strength which had heretofore sustained him in his great labors departed, and his life and the life of his court passed away *pari passu*.

During the remainder of July and through the month of August, after the beginning of Judge Parker's illness, the court was opened each morning and closed each evening with the accustomed regularity, and though there was no Judge Parker there to preside in person, yet he may be said to have been present in the spirit, for he was kept in close touch with the matters of greater importance and the necessary orders were delivered by him from his sick bed. The grand jury met as usual and conducted its investigations, but withheld its reports, awaiting the return of the great judge to health and strength. At last it became evident that a judge must preside directly ever the court, for a short time at least, in order that some disposal be made of the vast number of cases on the docket, and on August 24, the following order was issued by Judge Caldwell, our former acquaintance, who had risen to a position as one of the judges of the Eighth Judicial Circuit:

"United States of America, Eighth Judicial Circuit.

"In my judgment, the public interests require the designation and appointment of a district judge of this circuit to hold the circuit and district courts of the United "States for the Western District of Arkansas in the place or in aid of the United States district judge for that district. It is, therefore, ordered that the Honorable Oliver P. Shiras, United States judge for the Western District of Iowa, be, and hereby is designated and appointed to hold the district and circuit courts for the Western District of Arkansas from the date hereof until the first day of December, 1896, in the place or in aid of the Honorable Isaac C. Parker, United States District Judge for the Western District of Arkansas.

"Given under my hand this 24th day of August, 1896. [Signed]

"Henry C. Caldwell,

United States Circuit Judge,

Eighth Judicial Circuit."

In obedience to the order Judge Shiras proceeded to Fort Smith and presided over the court for two days, August 27 and 28. On the first of these two days, the grand jury reported and were discharged from further duty. Of the 210 bills of indictment they had investigated, 54 were ignored and 156 were returned as true. On the next day thirty-three of the prisoners indicted entered pleas of guilty, and on that day eighty-seven criminal cases were set for trial during the coming term, leaving sixty-nine cases to be set a week later. The last case considered on that memorable 28th day of August, 1896, being the last actual work of the great court before its jurisdiction over the Indian Territory ceased; as to new cases, was styled:

United States vs. Robert Wilson: Indicted for violating revenue laws.

It was still the hope with all who were connected with the court, in any way, that Judge Parker's health would soon permit his occupying the bench again, and for two months the work was allowed to accumulate, waiting for his master-mind to dispose of it. Once or twice he was of sufficient strength to issue orders from his bed of sickness, but on Monday, November 2, the day for opening the November term of court, he was too ill to leave his home, and adjournment was taken to Monday, November 9. Hon. John E. Carland, United States Judge for the District of South Dakotah, in obedience to orders from Judge Walter Sanborn, one of the circuit judges of the Eighth Judicial Circuit, went to Fort Smith and held court during the remainder of Judge Parker's life, and until the close of December 7. On November 27, Hon. John H. Rogers, a prominent attorney of Fort Smith, was appointed to the vacancy caused by Judge Parker's demise; he was given the oath of office December 5, and three days later he took formal charge, twenty-one days after the death of his friend and predecessor, to whom he had been bound, during his life, by many kindly ties that neither death nor time could break.

Returning to our subject: No higher tribute to Judge Parker's gentle nature was ever paid him than that given by a lady newspaper writer, Miss Ada Patterson, then employed on the staff of the Si. Louis (Mo.) Republic, one of the greatest of American newspapers. Miss Patterson was sent to interview him as he lay on his deathbed, on the first day of September, the day of "The departure of the scepter from the judicial Judah." She had been told that he was stern and cruel and she had experienced an uncontrollable dread of the meeting. She persevered, however, mastered her fears and secured the interview; her private opinion of him was given in these words: "He is the gentlest of men, this alleged sternest of judges. He is courtly of manner and kind of voice and face, the man who has passed the death sentence on more criminals than has any other judge in the land. The features that have in them the horror of the Madusa [sic] to desperadoes are benevolent to all other humankind." After quoting a prominent member of the Fort Smith Bar, thus: "'Judge Parker is learned in the law; he is conscientious in the administration of it. He has a kind heart and a big soul. He is absolutely faithful to his home ties. All I could say of him for days would be summed up in this: He is a good man;'" she concluded thus:

"'He is a good man!' What a tribute is that by one man of the world to another! What music in the ears of the woman who loves him! I am glad to have the honor of knowing this alleged cruel judge. It is darkly, indeed, the press and people view him through the glass of distance. He is a twentieth century hero, worthy of the fame of the most just of Romans. More than all, as the old lawyer said to me, while a moisture he was not ashamed of made the office belongings and the face of the visitor look misty and far away, more than all, 'He is a good man.'"

His physician said his illness was the result of overwork. "Dropsy" and "an affectation of the heart," was the way the town gossips described it. He was an invalid long enough to know and feel how the people over whom he had presided, and among whom he had lived, loved and honored him. From all parts of his old district came anxious inquiry concerning his condition, with prayerful pathos for his recovery; from all parts of the Indian Territory came eager questioning in regard to the condition of their friend and brother. He lingered, surrounded by friends and family who, with loving hearts and gentle hands, soothed the agony of his pain. The dread monster, death, assailed the citadel of his life and the contest continued for months. With such patience as only a great nature is capable of, he bore his sufferings; to his friends and family he was ever kind and gentle.

The people of Fort Smith and many from all parts of the district, even from four hundred miles away, assembled to escort his remains to their last resting place. The immense cortege, the largest in the city's history, attested the universality of sorrow for his departure ana respect for the Honored dead.

Thus, in the autumn of 1896, expired the great court and its greater judge.

The day of Judge Parker's death, November 17, 1896, was hailed as a gala day by the prisoners in the old jail, awaiting trial. These were those whose cases had been listed on the docket before the arrival of the time for the finale of the court's jurisdiction over the Indian Territory, but it was well-known that all such cases remaining on the docket would be taken up in their regular order the same as if the court's jurisdiction had not been reduced. Those who were awaiting trial had hoped, during the months Judge Parker was too ill to attend court, that he might continue confined to his bed until their cases were disposed of, hoping that with some other judge upon the bench they would stand better chances of light sentences or of possible acquittal. The announcement of Judge Parker's death was, therefore, the signal for a jubilee. Word was quickly passed from cell to cell. "The devil's shore got de ole cuss dis time!" sang out a negro criminal "Is he dead? Whoopee!" yelled another, and, almost in a twinkling, those prisoners nearest the ones first learning of Judge Parker's demise, took up the refrain, and for a brief period it looked as if pandemonium was about to break loose, but "Uncle Dick" Berry, the astute jailer, was on the ground and by prompt action and energetic measures he quelled the disturbance, and the offenders were brought to understand that open contempt for Judge Parker, even when dead, would not be tolerated in the Federal jail. However, if ever there was an acknowledgement of the impartiality of a court, surely it was plainly expressed by a few prisoners in this instance.

I cannot bring this chapter on the life of a man who occupied one of the most prominent, if unique, places in the world's history without relating a few anecdotes, that fell within my knowledge, tending to show that, with all that has been said of him, he was one of the most companionable of men, and that no one loved a harmless joke better than he.

My first acquaintance with him was in November, 1889, when 1, having in the previous year removed from Kansas, was empanelled on the United States petit jury, from Bentonville, Arkansas. One of the first cases tried at that term was one charging assault with intent to kill. The testimony adduced brought out that a quarrel had occurred between two men over some pine knots, with which the country abounds, and which are considered very valuable for fuel. In the vernacular of the country people of that section, a man named Flanagan was running a "saw mill" and a man named John Monday was hauling "pi'nots" for his use as fuel. They were hauled from piles which had been gathered by Flanagan. Monday was to have his pay in "pi'nots." After performing his work, Monday found that Flanagan had burned all the "pi nots" he had hauled and his pay was not forthcoming. The men quarreled. Flanagan struck Monday with a "pi'not with a handle to it," and was in turn stabbed with a knife. I listened patiently to the evidence, wondering what in all creation was a "pi'not;" and at last I rose and said: "Your honor, please, I would like to ask a question," "Why, certainly," replied the Judge. I said, "This transaction started over pi'nots,' 'pi'nots' were legal tender, the fight started with 'pi'nots,' and wound up by one of the men taking a 'pi'not' by the handle and knocking the other in the head; now, what I want to know is, what is a "pi'not?' "Judge Parker removed his spectacles, his features diffused with smiles, he laughed outright, and calling his private bailiff, he said, "George, go and get a 'pi'not.'" Then, as I sat down, the jury and audience joined with the judge in a hearty laugh at my expense. When George returned bearing a pine knot, that had been found where a pine tree had rotted away, I knew what a 'pi'not' was.

After court adjourned Judge Parker walked with me to the elevator and as we were going down he took hold of my arm and. with merriment twinkling in his eyes, he asked: "Young man, where were you raised?" I replied, "In Iowa." "I knew you were not a native of Arkansas," he said, "for you didn't know a 'pi'not.' "

During the same term of court, one Peter House was up for bigamy, and Lee Galcatcher was under charge of perjury. House was a fine specimen of physical manhood and possessed excellent features, while the other was of ugly mein and very unpleasant to look upon. I remember thinking, as I cast a momentary glance at him, that his face must have spells of aching, his look was so painful.

The bigamy case was called on for trial and by some error on the part of a bailiff Galcatcher was brought up.

"Who is that?" asked the judge, as the pinched and weazened [*sic*] features appeared in the doorway.

"Lee Galcatcher," answered the bailiff.

"Take him back," said the judge; "He's not the man. This is a bigamy case. He never caught a 'gal' in his life; he's too ugly to catch anything."

House was then brought in, was convicted and sentenced to five years' imprisonment.

At another time an old Irishman was up for selling whiskey in the Territory. When the case was called Pat asked Judge Parker:

"Plaze, yer honor, an' may I plade me own case?"

"Certainly," answered the judge.

"Then," said Pat. "I plade guilty;" which brought forth a hearty laugh from the court, and gained for Pat the lowest possible sentence under the law.

One day another son of Erin's Isle was up on the same charge—whiskey selling. He answered to the name of Mike, and he annoyed the court not a little by frequently interrupting the prosecuting witnesses, and by his attempts to correct their statements to his liking. Judge Parker rapped him down numerous times, but to no effect. Finally, as Mike became unusually exasperating, Judge Parker brought his gavel down with thundering force, and commanded:

"Mike, sit down; you will get justice."

"Be Jazzes, an' that's what I'm afraid of," said Mike, earnestly; and business was temporarily suspended while judge and attorneys enjoyed a fit of laughter

Once, during the trial of an important case, Hon. Dan W. Voorhees, of Indiana, was present as counsel for defendant. After the case had been given to the jury, a nondescript negro was brought up to answer to a petty charge. He was too poor to employ an attorney and Judge Parker appointed Mr. Voorhees and George A. Grace, Esq., to defend him. The attention of the great attorney was directed to the honor conferred upon him; he asked to see his client and looking critically at the negro, who was pointed out, he first frowned, then, as he caught the look of merriment in Judge Parker's eyes and noted the evidences of suppressed laughter on the part of the other attorneys, he took in the situation and enjoyed the joke as well as the rest. Mr. Grace took charge of the case and the negro was acquitted.

One day, during the last year of my residence in Arkansas, a white man, residing in the Indian Territory, was being tried for assault and battery. His attorney, a shrewd lawyer, was cross-examining a witness, brought by the government to testify to the reputation of the complaining witness as a law abiding, peaceful citizen. The witness, on direct examination, had sworn to the angelic character and disposition of the complainant.

"Now," said the attorney for defense, "Don't you know that this complainant frequently gets into trouble with his neighbors?"

"Yes," assented the witness.

"Don't you know, sir, that he gets drunk and whips his wife, and that he was arrested last spring for badly beating a boy, and that he gets into quarrels nearly every time he goes to town?"

"Yes," again admitted the witness.

"What, sir! You know all this, and yet you come here and state on your oath that his reputation is good in the neighborhood where he resides? "

"Oh!" replied the witness without the least sign of discomfiture, "It takes more than that to give a man a bad reputation up where I live."

An instant and hearty chuckle from the lips of Judge Parker caused me to glance quickly in his direction, and the next moment his face had taken on its severest lines and he remarked, sternly: "That indicates the class of civilization this court has to contend with."

I well remember a young Indian boy, who was among the government witnesses in a case wherein a number of Indians were being tried for larceny. At first the boy failed to respond to the questions asked of him by the district attorney, appearing as if he did not understand questions asked in the English language. It was known, however, that the boy could speak English, and the attorney became not a little vexed at the stoical indifference affected by the boy. At last, Judge Parker turned towards the witness stand and, in his kindest tone, enquired: "Why is it you do not answer the questions?" "Well, me tell you, judge," answered the boy. "He no un'erstan' all words in Inglis,"n sometimes me know Indians come here make mistake 'cause they no un'erstan' good'n then they get in trouble—get locked up. He no care nothing'bout these people; they bad Indians-; me good Indian. He tell all me know'bout'em, only me 'fraid make mistake—get in trouble—get locked up." "Very well," said the judge, kindly; "You shall have everything explained to you. Don't you answer any questions till you understand them fully. If the lawyers ask you anything you don't understand, just ask me, and I will see that it is made plain to you before you shall answer it."

It was a picture worthy an effort of a master in oil. The great jurist and the untutored savage; the former bending over, watching against pitfalls, for his charge, the latter with the trustful expression in his eyes as he turned ever now and then to his protector, whenever the question asked him was in words which he failed to comprehend; then would Judge Parker, quick to note the need of assistance, make the meaning clear to the unschooled mind, receiving therefor looks of gratitude from the Indian. Who will believe the latter did not, from that time forward, consider Judge Parker the friend of the Red Men?

GEORGE MALEDON, THE PRINCE OF HANGMEN

George Maledon was born June 10, 1830, at Landau, Bavaria. He came to America in the next year with his parents, who settled at Detroit, Michigan. Here he received an education at the city schools, in both German and English branches. He was of an adventurous turn of mind, and on reaching the age of manhood, he bid adieu to his friends in Detroit and started out to seek his fortune in the great West.

After a few months, he found himself in the Choctaw Nation, in the southeastern part of the Indian Territory, where he took charge of a small lumber mill for Chief Allen and Councilor Riley. Not long after, he went to Fort Smith and secured a position on the police force, serving for several years under Chiefs Christopher Doff, Robinson and Wheeler. At the breaking out of the civil war he enlisted in the First Arkansas Federal Battery and served to the close of hostilities. In 1865, soon after he was mustered out, he was appointed deputy

When the United States Criminal Court was moved from Van Buren to Fort Smith, he was offered and he accepted a commission as Deputy United States Marshal under Logan S, Roots, noted in a preceding chapter, and was appointed turnkey. A year later he was appointed special deputy and given charge of the execution of condemned prisoners. This position he held until 1894, and during the twenty-two years he is said to have performed the uncanny task of executing over sixty* criminals and shooting two to death, gaining the unenviable reputation of having executed several times as many men as any officer in America, more than any known legal executioner of modern times, with the exception of the famous Deibler, of Paris, France, who is reported to have decapitated 437 persons.

The scaffold, where the executions were held, was built with a trap thirty inches wide and twenty feet in length, giving room for twelve men to stand thereon, side by side, at one time. Six men were executed at once on two occasions, three times five were hanged together, as many times four were executed at once, and on four occasions three men were dropped off together, while double executions became too numerous, finally, to excite comment.

Maledon preserved and took away, when he ceased the gruesome occupation, a hempen rope with which he had launched twenty-seven men into eternity; another which had served in a like capacity eleven times, and another nine.

In 1894, Maledon tired of the business of killing men and tried the grocery business in Fort Smith, afterwards removing to Fayetteville, Arkansas, to take charge of an eighty acre farm.

Maledon is small of stature, five feet, five inches in height. He is a quiet, inoffensive man, loved by his family and respected by all who know him. From the expression of his eyes, one would think him wholly indifferent to human feeling, and it is doubtful if a smile has crossed his features in many years. He has said he has hanged few truthful men, for nearly all he has ever hanged persisted in declarations of innocence, even with their last breath. Just before he left Fort Smith, an old lady, who visited the prison and was escorted through it by him, asked him if he ever had any qualms of conscience or feared the spirits of the departed. He replied: "No; I have never hanged a man who came back to have the job done over. The ghosts of men hanged at Fort Smith never hang around the old gibbet."

While he has often expressed regrets that it ever became necessary to execute a human being he has always felt that he only performed his duty as an officer of the law.

Besides the large number of men he has hanged, fate willed that while he occupied the position of legal executioner at Fort Smith, he should shoot five prisoners. The first was Frank Butler, a negro, who had been convicted of murder and was being brought out for sentence at a night session of the court, which Judge Parker had convened at the request of Butler's attorney. Just as the negro stepped from the old basement jail, noted in a preceding chapter, he threw out both arms and, knocking back the guards on either side, sprang forward in the darkness. Mr. Maledon, whose aim is unerring, quickly turned to the door of the jail, locked it to prevent the escape of other prisoners, then turning his attention to the fleeing negro, who was swiftly making for the east wall, leveled his pistol and fired. The stone which, for years, marked the spot where the prisoner fell dead is just seventy-five yards from the door where he made his break for liberty. His mother and father were discovered just over the wall waiting to receive the body; knowing that the attempted escape had been nicely planned, knowing, too, the deadly aim of the jailer, they had preferred that their son be shot dead to seeing him hanged.

Frank Wilson was a desperate character, brought in for horse stealing. On arriving at the jail he knocked the marshal down and ran. The night was dark and rainy, and Wilson took a zigzaz course, dodging from side to side, hoping thus to miss Maledon's fire. He was mistaken in the man, for at the first shot the prisoner fell, pierced through the hip. He died two days later, a victim of his own foolhardiness.

Ellis McGee attempted to escape and was shot by Maledon, re-captured and sentenced to fifteen years at Little Rock, from where he again escaped. He was finally killed by George Hawkins at Skully Valley, Indian Territory.

His brother, Orpheus McGee, tried and convicted at the same time and sentenced to hang, attempted to escape with Ellis, but was shot and crippled by Jailer Charlie Hums and was afterwards executed.

John Werthington was a cell-mate of McGee's. They secured exit from the Fort Smith jail, together, by lifting the stone mantle from the fire place and using it as a battering ram to free the outer door of its fastenings. While Werthington was climbing the gates, a shot from the fatal left hand of the old hangman brought him to the ground, writhing in agony.

He was a preacher horse thief. His mode of procedure was to go from place to place among the Indians preaching the gospel of a merciful Savior. Having gained their confidence, by long and eloquent prayers, he would borrow a horse to ride to his next rendezvous. The horse thus borrowed (?) would never be returned, as his pals, whom he would meet in ambush, would dispose of it while he played the same trick on other unsuspecting ones.

Mr. Maledon is now past sixty eight years old. His head is silvered o'er with gray; deep lines upon his face mark the passing years. His frame shows the ravages of time, yet he is still hale and hearty, and the burden of his years rests lightly upon him. He comes before the reader believing that the history of his life may assist in teaching the great moral lesson which is one of the objects of this book, causing the busy world to pause and consider whether a proper estimate is being placed upon human life; he has consented to the publication of this sketch, given by his own lips. Let us exercise the benignity we would ask for ourselves and draw the mantle of charity about the executioner and the executed.

In the spring of 1897, after the great-court's jurisdiction over the Indian Territory had ceased, when it was known that no more executions would ever be performed by order of the United States court for the Western District of Arkansas (except it might be for a capital crime committed on a government reservation within the said district), after Congress had ordered the removal of the garrison wall and the gallows that had borne so important a part in the history of the court; with my mind more than ever intent upon publishing a book relating to the court, but desiring to secure some expression of public opinion before giving the necessary time and expense to preparing the manuscript, of ascertaining to my own satisfaction how the people in general would regard such a work, I made arrangements with Mr. Maledon and, after securing for him some of the ropes and other gruesome relics of his late vocation, as well as numerous photographs of the most noted desperadoes with whom the court had dealt, made a summer's tour of some of the country towns and smaller cities within a radius of, perhaps, five hundred miles from Fort Smith, exhibiting the famous hangman and the instruments of his office, in a tent, pitched in convenient localities in the places visited.

The success of the venture far exceeded my most sanguine expectations. At every stopping place people of all classes flocked to the show ground, stood about the tent entrance to listen to the lecturer (who never failed, in addition to detailing and describing what was to be seen within, to make a statement concerning the book then in contemplation), and eagerly crowded the interior to look upon the famed executioner and view the evidences of his craft, while he told of the various criminals whose lives had, in die name of the law, been strangled out by this and that of the various ropes, the instruments in his hands of an avenging people.

Again and again, during this tour, was I assured of the demand already existing for the book I had in view, and when I would address the listening hundreds upon the great moral lessons to be learned from a close scrutiny of the records of crime and criminals punished by the court that stood at the head, in America, in the number of capital punishments it had administered, many were the gray-haired fathers and earnest spoken mothers, who grasped my hand and in thrilling accents bade me God-speed in the work I had in mind and which, in their 'belief, would be a mighty agent in saving the girls and the boys of our land.

The accompanying full page illustration is from a photograph showing the interior of the tent where the exhibition was given; some of the more important articles in the collection are seen to bear distinguishing marks, allowing of the following brief description:

The dark object marked by the numeral "4" is a piece of the main beam of the old gallows, from which were suspended the ropes used in the executions. This beam was first brought into use August 15, 1873. On that day John Childers was executed, and the large beam, of which this a piece, bore his weight as his body suddenly dropped through the trap to almost instant death. The rope used on this occasion was the one bearing the figure "6;" ten other convicted murderers were also hanged by this same piece of "hemp." The beam mentioned continued in use for many years and from it were from time to time suspended the ropes used in executing eighty-two of the eighty-eight men hanged on the noted scaffold, The last time it was brought into use was April 30, 1896, at which time occurred the execution of the two brothers, George and John Pierce. At that time it was noticed that the old beam, that had been the silent witness to legal tragedies that had precipitated more than four score souls before their Maker, was becoming weak from age and the effects of weather, and just previous to June 1, of that year, the date named for the execution of the infamous Buck gang for their horrible crime, it was removed and a new and sound piece of timber placed in its stead. The new beam also served at the execution of James Casharago, alias George Wilson, elsewhere noted, and then the history of the old gallows closed forever. It will be observed that in the collection there are shown seven ropes.

All of these, with the exception of No. 2, were used on September 3, 1873, in executing the first sextet, elsewhere described. Number 2 is the rope by which the life of Cherokee Bill was destroyed; the noose was given by the hangman, George Lawson, to a Pinkerton detective. Number 3 saw more service than any of the others, being used in the execution of twenty-seven men. Number 5 was used to drop nine men to death, and the rope marked "X" is one by which poor Bood Crumpton and George Wilson were executed. The padlock and chain, seen lying on the tarpaulin covered box in the center, was the one used in securing the old military prison during John Childers' detention. The heavy iron bar, standing on end, with the hasp and staple attached, were attachments of the old gallows, and the round object, to the right of the padlock, is one of the two cast iron weights, whose office was to hold open the trap doors after having "dropped" their victim to death. The two revolvers, seen at the top, were the guns carried by Maledon while officiating as hangman. The ropes here pictured were formerly one and one-eighth inches in diameter, but were oiled and stretched before using till only one-inch in diameter; they were twenty-seven feet in length.

It may interest certain readers to learn of the circumstances which finally resulted in the old scaffold being burned by the order of the mayor and council of Fort Smith:

After I had completed arrangements with Hangman Maledon and we were preparing for our tour, he expressed to me a desire to secure the old trap doors, the last thing on earth pressed by the feet of the eighty-eight men executed, saying that if made into trinkets they would bring fabulous sums. The idea was not a pleasant one to me, but I accompanied him to a meeting with several of the city officers and we were promised the trap doors, provided all of the members of the council should consent to the arrangement. I attended the next meeting of the city council and our request was promptly refused.

Very soon after, Mr. Maledon told me that he had learned from the best of sources that two men were offering the council a large sum for the privilege of removing the gallows intact and taking it about the country for exhibition purposes. I at once determined that if we could not have the trap doors no others should have the gallows. It came to me that the proposed secret sale was already partially consummated. I at once sought the leading newspaper offices of Fort Smith and caused them to believe that I was about to procure the old death trap and exhibit it about the country, and the press was suddenly stricken with a holy horror and, imbued with the idea that such an act would reflect great discredit upon Fort Smith, their columns teemed with denunciations of the proposed sale; then the people began to antagonize the supposed plan most bitterly, and a howl of opposition went up, so strong as to compel the city council to forego any intentions it may have had regarding the alleged sale, and by a special act, approved by the mayor, the gallows was ordered torn down and burned.

It is to be regretted that the city fathers could not have shown better diplomacy and, while wisely refusing to sell the gallows, have preserved it intact as one of the greatest of object lessons and a rare historical relic.

GEN. STEPHEN WHEELER

BIOGRAPHICAL SKETCHES

PRINCIPAL COURT OFFICERS AND A FEW LEADING ATTORNEYS

Brief sketches of the lives of some of the more noted officers connected with this famous-court, with biographies of a few of the leading attorneys who practiced before its bar, are here given:

GENERAL STEPHEN WHEELER

General Stephen Wheeler, who served as clerk of the United States Court for the Western District of Arkansas during all the time that Judge Parker reigned as judge of that district, and who was at the same time clerk of the Federal circuit court at Fort Smith, a division of the Eighth judicial circuit, was a native of Hammondsport, Steuben county, New York. He was born February 28, 1839. His paternal great grandfather was a native of England; he settled in Vermont and there the grandfather of the subject of our sketch was born, subsequently removing to Pennsylvania, where he married, and later, in 1806, at the age of twenty-five years, was drowned in the Ohio river. General Wheeler's father, Daniel Wheeler, was born in Lycoming county, Pennsylvania, in 1804. His mother dying soon after the drowning of her husband, the young son was taken to New York and adopted by a man named Sorrney; here he grew to manhood and married, the fruits of the union being the subject of this sketch. When he was nine years old his mother died, and two years later he removed with his father to Wisconsin. At sixteen years of age he was apprenticed to a druggist, continuing three years, when he returned to New York and secured a position as salesman in a wholesale dry goods house. After a few months, in the latter part of the year 1858, he again went west, and settled in southern Michigan. He was one of the early volunteers in the Federal army, enlisting as a private September 1, 1861, at Battle Creek, Michigan. He continued until the close of the civil war, serving alternately as private, sergeant, first lieutenant and captain in the engineer, infantry and cavalry branches of the service; was attached to the seventh army corps; took part in the battles of Pea Ridge, Prairie Grove and Newtonia and performed his duties valiantly in Arkansas, Missouri and Louisiana under Generals Freemont, Blunt and Steel. From April 1864 until he received an honorable discharge, in April 1866, he served on the staff of General Charles Morgan as assistant adjutant general with the rank of captain.

After his discharge he settled at Powhattan, Arkansas, where he was appointed assistant assessor of internal revenue; then was made assessor and later collector. He afterwards removed to Searcy, retaining the office last named, and while in the discharge of his duties, going from the state capitol to his home, August 1, 1868, he was waylaid by two would-be assassins who opened fire, one of the bullets going through his right arm. In 1868 he was elected as a republican to the first state senate under the reconstruction act; he resigned in June 1869 and removed to DeVall's Bluff, where for some time he edited the White River Journal, the leading republican organ

68

of the first congressional district. In July 1869 he was appointed quartermaster general of militia with rank of brigadier general, holding this office until January 1, 1873. In 1872 he was again nominated by the republican convention of the counties of Arkansas and Prairie as state senator, but declined to run. At the republican state convention of the same year he was nominated for auditor of state and elected. This office he held until May 1874, when he was taken out of office by the adoption of the new constitution.

In April 1875 he removed to Fort Smith, and May 24 he was appointed clerk of the United States Criminal Court for the Western District of Arkansas and also clerk at Fort Smith of the Federal Circuit Court for the Eighth Judicial Circuit.

This latter office he held until his death; he continued as clerk of the district court, after Judge Parker's death, until

June 4, 1897, when Judge John Rogers, who came after Judge Parker as judge of the Western District of Arkansas and acting judge of the Fort Smith Federal Circuit Court for the Eighth Judicial Circuit, appointed Gen. Wheeler's former deputy circuit clerk, Gen. FI. B. Armistead, to the position of clerk of the district court, where Gen. Wheeler had held position for more than twenty-two years.

Less than a month later, June 30, his term of office as United States circuit court commissioner (which office he had held continuously since receiving appointment, June 29, 1875,) expired, according to one of the provisions of an act of Congress, previously noted.

During the twenty-two years that he held the office of United States Commissioner for the circuit court, Gen. Wheeler, as shown by his docket, issued 18,877 writs for the arrest of persons charged with nearly every crime named in the decalogue, including both those who were released after examination and those who were held with or without bail to await action by the grand jury.

After retiring from the offices of district clerk and of United States commissioner, Gen. Wheeler looked about for a position more in keeping with his abilities than that of clerk of the circuit court, and he was an applicant for the position of clerk of the new United States court just established in the Southern District, Indian Territory, at Ardmore, in the Chickasaw Nation. It was on this account that he took the train on the afternoon of Thursday, August 19, 1897, bound for Ardmore, going by way of Gainesville, Texas.

At Gainesville he stepped from the train, at 1 o'clock on the morning of August 20, to purchase a lunch, and while he was making change the train started. Not realizing the speed attained by the cars, he ran to the train and while attempting to board one of the coaches was knocked down and the heavy wheels of one truck passed over his face just below the mouth. His shrill cry attracted immediate attention and the train was stopped in time to prevent further mutilation of his dead body. The remains were forwarded to his family at

Fort Smith. The citizens of his home city were greatly shocked at his sudden taking off, and the funeral pageant testified to their universal sorrow. The funeral services were conducted under Masonic auspices and were attended in a body by the local G. A. R. post, and by those of several other fraternal societies of which he was a member. He had been prominent in lodge work, and had served as department commander of the Grand Army for three successive terms. Of him, one of the Fort Smith newspapers said: "General Wheeler was a man of modest, retiring nature; he was a man of few words and he made very little outward show of whatever he saw, felt or did, but a kinder, more generous heart never beat in a human bosom." The paragraph was universally commented upon by those who knew him as truly representing the man they had loved and respected.

JAMES BRIZZOLARA

James Brizzolara, one of the leading citizens of Fort Smith and who was for over twenty years prominently identified with the Federal Court for the Western District of Arkansas, was born in Richmond, Virginia, January 9, 1848, the son of James and Osa Brizzolara, natives of Italy, the father, at the time of the birth of our subject, being engaged in mercantile business at 329 Market Street, in the city named.

When he was six months old his parents removed to Pittsburg, Pennsylvania, where his boyhood was passed and his early education achieved, being as a child sent to board with a school teacher named James Cavenaugh, from whom he obtained the rudiments of learning, preparatory to higher courses.

In 1858, young Brizzolara made a trip to Italy and entered the Don Basco College and a year later he left the school room and drifted into the insurgent army under the patriot, Gen. Garabaldi. Here he served for three years, meeting with many narrow escapes, receiving more than thirty wounds, and, on one occasion, being captured by the enemy and coming very near being shot as a spy. For meritorious service he was rapidly advanced to the rank of colonel, which position he held at fourteen years of age when he left the revolutionary service. During the seven years he was in Italy his intrepid and forceful nature led him into many heated discussions and he fought several duels in consequence.

In 1865, he returned to his home in Pittsburg and a little later removed to Memphis, Tennessee, where he began the study of law in the offices of Gen. Albert Pike and James R. Chalmers. He was an apt student and after two years, while in his nineteenth year, was admitted to the bar.

In 1869, as the result of a political quarrel, he fought a duel, at Memphis, with George R. Phelan. His antagonist had the choice of weapons and the duel was with navy revolvers, Col. Brizzolara receiving a slight wound. Soon after this "little affair" he went to Little Rock, and in November, 1869, he settled in Fort Smith and entered the practice of law.

Here he soon attracted attention on account of his energetic qualities and was made city attorney, which office he held for several years, and on May 8, 1875, he was appointed assistant to District Attorney William H. H. Clayton, of the Federal Court for the Western District of Arkansas, continuing in this office for three terms. In 1878 he was elected mayor of Fort Smith, then an incorporated town. He took the oath of office on April 8, and continued as the city's chief executive by virtue of successive re-elections until 1883. About this time he was chosen colonel of a regiment of 750 volunteers to participate in the fierce Brooks-Baxter War, in which it was sought by the people of the State to supersede "carpet-bag" rule. Col Brizzolara was for several months stationed with his men at Little Rock, until the difficulty was brought to a close upon orders from President Grant, recognizing the Baxter element.

On June 12, 1878, he was appointed United States Circuit Court Commissioner for the Western District of Arkansas. From that time until the close of his several terms as mayor of Fort Smith, he not only held commissioner's court, sitting as a Federal justice of the peace, but under the State statutes was also, by virtue of his office as mayor, ex-officio justice of the peace, and as such was judge of the city police court, it being one of the few cases on record where two separate and distinct judgeships were held by one man at the same time. He continued to hold office as United States commissioner until June 30, 1897, when his term was brought to a close and the office abolished by an act of Congress, noted in a previous chapter.

An idea of the volume of business transacted by the Federal court may be gained from the fact that Col. Brizzolara's docket alone, from July 1, 1888, to December 30, 1890, shows a total of 2,801 persons examined, given preliminary hearings in his court, charged with all the various crimes known to the code; from January 2, 1891, to February 8, 1896, the number of persons examined in his court was 2,861, and from February 9, 1896, to March 17, 1897, 495, a total for the nine years, less 105 days, of 5, 158 persons. This number includes those who were held on bonds or were remanded to jail to await investigation by the grand jury and those released as not guilty, after examination by the commissioner.

No examinations appear to have been conducted by his court during the three closing months of its existence, the last case on the docket being styled:

UNITED STATES vs. Eli Vandruff: Contempt

The case was continued from March 17 to March 22, at which time the defendant was discharged.

In the summer of 1897 Col. Brizzolara again took up the practice of law, associating himself with a brilliant young attorney who was already well and favorably known about the State, J. M. Hill, the firm name being Hill & Brizzolara.

Col. Brizzolara has been prominently identified in politics in later years, and is a stalwart Republican. At the State Convention of his party, in 1898, he was chosen candidate for the office of associate justice of the State Supreme Court. He failed of election since the opposing party was the dominant one in the State, but he had the satisfaction of leading his ticket by a handsome margin.

Col. Brizzolara served for several years a member of the Arkansas Republican State Central Committee.

On May 27, 1898, he was appointed by President McKinley as postmaster of Fort Smith.

IRVING M. DODGE

Irving M. Dodge, deputy clerk of the United States District and Circuit Courts at Fort Smith, Arkansas, during ten years of the most important portion of their history, was born at Lindenburg, Vermont, July 15, 1862. His parents were of Puritan extraction and were good Yankee stock. He was born on the farm where his boyhood days were spent, and as a child was given such education as was afforded by the village school. He was ambitious, however, and he made such progress in his studies that at the age of sixteen he was sufficiently advanced to enter Dartmouth College, at Hanover, New Hampshire.

After two years' study, in the year 1880, he bade adieu to his friends in the Green Mountain State, accepted Horace Greeley's advice and emigrated west; he has grown up with the country. Until 1884 his time was spent in different parts of the West, principally in Iowa, Idaho and Kansas. He finally went to the Cherokee Nation, in the Indian Territory, and engaged extensively in stock raising, to use his own words, "as long as his money lasted." In 1885 he removed to Chicago and later to Fort Smith, and in October, 1887, was appointed deputy United States clerk of the Court for the Western District of Arkansas, where he had full charge of the clerk's office until June, 1897, when he resigned, and was immediately appointed deputy United States clerk for the Central District, Indian Territory, with office at South McAlester.

MISS FLORENCE HAMMERSLY

Miss Florence Hammersly, the present charming and efficient deputy clerk of the United States District court at Fort Smith, was born in Arkansas, the daughter of J. A. Hammersley. She was a student of the Fort Smith High School and on the occasion of commencement exercises. June 7, 1888, she delivered an essay on the subject, "Should the Indian Territory Be Opened," discussing the affirmative. The effort was highly complimented by the local press, and by Judge Parker a special letter to the press, as presenting a much discussed question in a lucid form that would have honored Miss Florence Hammersly a much older head.

When the bridge was built across the Arkansas River at Fort Smith, an important event in the history of the city and State, a prize was offered for the best poem suitable for a place on the program, arranged for the celebration accompanying the opening; the prize was won by Miss Hammersly. She has written numerous other poems which were honored by publication in the Louisville Courier-Journal and other papers of note.

As a complement to her already fine schooling she decided to add the stenographic art and entered the short-hand department of the Fort Smith Commercial College; her superior knowledge of the English language and her versatility enabled her to thoroughly master the work and graduate with distinction. On that occasion she was awarded a diploma, and her rendition of a vocal solo, which charmed the large and intelligent audience, only proved the extent of her accomplishments.

She has had many years' experience in the work attending the clerk's office, dating almost from her childhood, and the books of record, over which she has charge, are a model of neatness, which many another clerk might follow to advantage, both to themselves and to those who have occasion to refer to them.

Miss Hammersly is most beautiful in face, figure and deportment; in her official capacity she is kind and obliging, her sweet and amiable disposition winning for her many friends from among those who have business with the department. The Author has occasion to acknowledge many courtesies extended, without which the task of compiling this work would have been multiplied. Her abilities and her refinement mark her as a sample of American womanhood to which the land of her birth may point with pride.

JUDGE WILLIAM H. H. CLAYTON

Judge William H. H. Clayton, for fourteen years prosecutor at the Fort Smith Federal Court, first saw the light of day in Delaware County, Pennsylvania, near Delaware Bay, October 13, 1840, just before the national election of that year, and he was named in honor of William Henry Harrison, the successful candidate for president. Judge Clayton's father was John Clayton, a farmer, and a native of Delaware County, whose ancestors came to America with William Penn in 1664; the ancestral line ascending from John Clayton being, Powell Clayton, grandfather of the subject of this sketch, his progenitors being Richard Clayton and William Clayton.

John Clayton married Miss Ann Clark, daughter of a captain in the English army; the home in which William H. H. Clayton was born was settled by the earlier Claytons about the time William Penn laid off the City of Philadelphia.

His ancestors were unknown in public life, but in later days the Claytons have been remarkable men. They have made history, have battled for the maintenance of right; they have great executive ability and unyielding perseverance. Of this family, Hon. John M. Clayton, who served with credit as United States Senator from Delaware, was a member. Another, Thomas H. Clayton, brother of William H. H, Clayton, served as judge of the Court of Common Pleas of Delaware County, Pennsylvania. Another brother, Powell Clayton, entered the army as captain, rose to the rank of brigadier-general, was mustered out at the close of the war, was elected Governor of Arkansas and served in that capacity four years, from 1868 to 1872; served six years in the

United States Senate, from 1872 to 1878, and was appointed minister to Mexico by President McKinley in 1897.

His twin brother, John M. Clayton, served with distinction in both houses of the Arkansas Legislature; served three terms as sheriff of Jefferson County, Arkansas, and In 1888 he was elected member of Congress from his district; he did not live to take his seat, however, as he became the victim of a foul political murder in the autumn of that year.

W. H. H. Clayton received a liberal education, completing his three years' course of study at Village Green Seminary in his native county. Reared on a farm, yet not taking easily to humdrum existence, he formed no settled purpose until after the close of the Civil War. He has a military record brief but brilliant. In 1862, in three days' time, he raised a company at his home, but as he had no military knowledge he took the position of second lieutenant in Company H, One Hundred and Twenty-fourth Pennsylvania Infantry, under Colonel Hawley, and took part in the battles of South Mountain, Antietam, Burnside's defeat at Fredericksburg and Hooker's battle of the Wilderness. Retiring from the service he took a position as teacher of military tactics and other branches in Village Green Seminary, holding the position from the spring of 1863 till autumn, 1864. In the following winter he removed to Pine Bluff, Arkansas, and the next spring rented from the government an abandoned plantation and raised a fine crop of cotton, which he disposed of with profit. In the winter of 1865-66, he and his brothers, Powell and John M. Clayton, purchased a plantation of two thousand acres on the Arkansas River below Pine Bluff, and there engaged in agricultural pursuits until the spring of 1868, when he sold his one-third interest and has since been in public life.

In 1867, while yet on the farm, he began the study of law and in 1868, soon after leaving the plantation, he joined the law class of Judge Stevenson, at Huntsville. In the same year he was appointed assistant assessor of internal revenue, a position he held for several months, and in August he was appointed circuit superintendent of public instruction for the Seventh Judicial Circuit of Arkansas, embracing seven counties At that time there were no public schools in the district and very few of any kind. The grossest illiteracy and prejudice against public schools, the outgrowth of the slave system, prevailed throughout, and the task set before him would have seemed superhuman to anyone with less indomitability of purpose. Nothing daunted, however, young Clayton, then in his twenty-eighth year, set about his duties; he lectured throughout the district, following the courts, and such an influence did he bring to bear upon the people that when he left the office there were from thirty to forty free public schools in each of the seven counties, with thirty to fifty pupils in each school. In the words of a former biographer, "He built school houses and organized districts, having by indefatigable labor created a sentiment in favor of public instruction in communities where previously not one child in forty could read or write, even up to the age of twenty." In 1870 he was appointed by the governor a trustee of the Arkansas Industrial Seminary, mentioned elsewhere in this work. In

1871 he was admitted to the bar by Judge Stevenson, and on March 23, of the same year, he received the appointment of prosecuting attorney for the First Judicial Circuit of Arkansas. Two years and one month later he was appointed by Governor Baxter to the position of judge of the same district. In July, 1874, he resigned the office to accept the appointment, offered by President Grant, as district attorney for the Western District of Arkansas, embracing the Indian Territory and the western portion of the State of Arkansas; he was reappointed by President Hayes, January 20, 1879, and with the exception of the four years during which Grover Cleveland was president he continued to hold the position until the spring of 1868, when he sold his one-third interest and has since been in public life.

He was a vigorous prosecutor, and during the fourteen years he was in the service at the old Federal court he had charge of over 10,000 cases tried before its bar, not to mention the large number of criminals who pleaded guilty, making no defense; and during that time he convicted eighty men of murder, a number greater than that to the record of any other prosecutor in the United States; forty of the number were executed. At one term of court, out of eighteen murder cases, he convicted fifteen. His success in this, as in the other walks in which he has engaged, is attributable to close application, indomitable energy and tireless perseverance. Judge Parker said of him: "As a lawyer, he is a very close, shrewd, prudent examiner of witnesses." As a man, he has fine social qualities; he is openhearted to all; he is energetic, industrious, devoted to his profession; he is a good neighbor, a most excellent husband and parent.

On May 18, 1897, he was appointed by President McKinley, judge of the Central District, Indian Territory, with office at South McAlester, a position he still holds.

JAMES F. READ

James F. Read, during the closing three years of Judge Parker's reign and for a year thereafter, United States district attorney for the Western District of Arkansas, and during which time he prosecuted an average of 1,000 cases a year, was born in Columbia, Adair County, Kentucky, in 1853.

He gained a good education in the common schools of his native city, graduating from the high school in 1870. He then entered and graduated from Center College at Danville, Kentucky. He commenced the study of law in Louisville, Kentucky, under his uncle, Judge T. F. Alexander, and was admitted to the bar in Louisville; he immediately commenced the practice of law, being admitted as a partner with his uncle.

After two years, he went to Fort Smith and shortly afterwards formed a partnership with Hon. John H. Rogers. Following this partnership he was a member of the law firms of Read & Luce and Clendening & Read, and in 1890 he again formed a partnership with Mr. Rogers, which existed until he was appointed district attorney in 1893.

Mr. Read is an able lawyer, an easy and fluent speaker, and during his term he successfully prosecuted some of the most desperate criminals ever before the bar of justice.

He is a prominent member of the Masonic order and is a Knight Templar.

THOMAS H. BARNES

One of the prominent members of the Fort Smith bar, during the time when important. history was being made at and around the Federal Criminal Court, was Thomas H. Barnes, born at Irvine, Kentucky, August 29, 1842, and died April 13, 1898. Major Barnes as a boy was apt to learn and at an early age showed marked ability. After passing through the several preparatory grades he entered Center College at Danville, Kentucky, and would have graduated in 1862 had not the college suspended on account of the Civil War. In 1861 he enlisted in the Kentucky home guards, and before he was twenty years of age was actively engaged in organizing the Forty-seventh Regiment Kentucky Union Volunteers, in which service by his enthusiasm and eloquence, he did as much or more than any one man towards raising the regiment. In its organization he was commissioned regimental adjutant; his soldierly ability was soon recognized and for meritorious service he was advanced to the rank of major, which position he held when the regiment was mustered out in 1865. At the close of the war he entered upon the study of law under his father, Col. Sidney M. Barnes, one of the foremost lawyers of Kentucky. He was duly admitted to the bar, in the circuit in which he was born and reared, and there he continued the practice of his profession until the spring of 1871, when he removed to Fort Smith. He soon took rank among the most prominent criminal lawyers of the State, and was connected with many of the principal criminal cases tried before the United States Court for the Western District of Arkansas. Politically he was a Republican, as staunch as he was prominent, and was repeatedly honored by his party. In 1872 he was chosen presidential elector; in April, 1873, he was appointed prosecuting attorney for the Fifth Judicial Circuit, which then embraced Sebastian, Crawford and Washington counties, holding the office until the adoption of the new State Constitution, October, 1874; in 1876 he was Republican candidate, on the State ticket, for attorney-general, and in 1888 he was a candidate for presidential elector.

Soon after going to Fort Smith he associated himself with William M. Mellette, a rising young attorney, and Cornelius E. Boudinot, and for a term of years the law firm of Barnes, Mellette & Boudinot maintained a profitable business. In 1889 Mr. Mellette was appointed first assistant district attorney for the Federal court at Fort Smith, under W. H. H. Clayton, and the vacancy thus caused in the law firm mentioned was taken by J. Warren Reed, an energetic attorney, who had lately removed from Parkersburg, West Virginia, the style of the firm being Barnes, Boudinott & Reed. Col. Boudinott died about a year later, and Messrs. Barnes and Reed continued together until the close of President Harrison's administration, when Mr. Mellette found it necessary to retire from the office of assistant district attorney;

the firm of Barnes & Reed was dissolved and that of Barnes & Mellette was re-established.

On April 14, 1897, Mr. Barnes was appointed United States district attorney for the Western District of Arkansas, continuing in that office until his death, April 13, 1898, as stated, from hemorrhage of the lungs. The remains were buried under the auspices of the Grand Army of the Republic, and were followed to their last resting place by a large concourse of citizens and government employees; his brother, Postmaster James K. Baines, having secured permission from the authorities at Washington to allow the clerks and carriers to attend the services in a body, and the flag on the Federal building was placed at half mast, out of respect to the dead man's memory. The body was interred in the National Cemetery at Fort Smith, beside that of his father, who, in his life, as did his son. towered high above the heads of ordinary men.

J. A. HAMMERSLY

Among the officials of the famous court, none knew Judge Parker better nor stood as close to him as Court Crier J. A. Hammersly. He occupied the position for over sixteen years continuously, and was still in office when the act of Congress cut down the jurisdiction of the court. With the death of Judge Parker and the incoming of a new judge, Mr. Hammersly found it necessary to retire to private life.

He was stern in discipline, but on account of his genial nature he was liked by all who ever had business with the court.

GEORGE S. WINSTON

One of the old time land marks, prominent in the eyes of the historian in search of data concerning the old Federal court at Fort Smith, and whose history is justly a part of the court's history, is G. S. Winston, who, for many years, enjoyed the position of special private bailiff to the judge.

Mr. Winston was born February 5, 1846, near West Point, Georgia, but on the west side of the Chattahoochee River, which, beginning at West Point, forms the dividing line between Georgia and Alabama to the Gulf of Mexico. He was the slave of George Winston, son of "Capt." Tom Winston. Both father and son owned large plantations on both sides of the river. Another son, Tom Winston, had a large tract on the Alabama side, and the three, the father and the two sons, were the possessors of from three hundred to four hundred slaves. The Winstons were kind to their negroes, if we compare their treatment of them with that dealt out by many Southern planters, and the progress of the war had but little effect upon the Winston slaves, nor caused them to take advantage of the troublous times and run off; doubtless it was well for them that they stayed. Even the knowledge that President Lincoln had issued a proclamation on January 1, 1863, declaring all slaves free, which began to be circulated among the Winston slaves, a year later, made but little impression upon them,* and our subject, whose mother had died in the first year of the war, and who was past eighteen years old before he ever heard of freedom, continued at the work assigned him about the home of "Massa" George Winston in West Point, wither he and his mother had been removed during his childhood.

At least not an impression they were willing to share with people who held them in bondage.—Ed. 2015

On a bright Sunday morning in June, 1864, a detachment of Federal troops, from Montgomery, opened fire on the retrenchments in the southwestern part of West Point, overlooking the river, and "Massa" George, who had been keeping a close eye on the movements of the Yankees, repaired to his Georgia plantation, a mile and a half north of the town, and with a score of his negro men and boys, among them our subject, prepared his teams and wagons for instant flight, loading the wagons with the boxes containing his money, jewelry, plate and other movable, valuable articles, and headed away for Macon. The country was full of Yankees and the fleeing party had no sooner reached a piece of timbered country, near Griffin, Georgia, than they were captured by a squad of Federals under Lieutenant Burch. They, too, were moving towards Macon and as there was need of some of the negroes to ride the mules and horses they were told by the officer that they could either go with him or return to their toil in the cotton fields. The boy, Winston, had now tasted his first breath of freedom, and the effect was so exhilarating that he decided, with some of the others, to "go along," and he was given a gray pony to ride. The trip to Macon was completed without incident, but after two days he grew nervous at the many strange faces and stranger sights and decided that he would prefer to go "home." Permission was granted and he was again given the gray pony; he returned alone to Griffin, fifty miles, where he stopped for two days at the home of Judge Warner and was very kindly treated, as was sure to be the case with a slave returning to his master. Continuing to West Point, he was sent to a merchant relative of "Massa" Winston, where he was to receive $to per month. Although he did not receive the money, he continued at odd jobs about the store until the following spring, 1865, when, after Lee's surrender, he went to Atlanta and secured a place as waiter in a hotel; it was his first experience at making wages, contracting his own labor, and having entire charge of the proceeds of his toil. On May 15, 1867, he, with about two hundred other freedmen, enlisted with Sergeant Yates, a government recruiting officer, as a private in the regular army. With the other recruits he was taken to Jefferson Barracks, near St. Louis, Missouri, and after two weeks to Fort Riley, Kansas, and thence to Junction City, on the new Kansas Pacific Railroad, and from there was marched to Fort Marker, where he was assigned to Company B, Thirty-eighth Infantry. Here he remained nearly a year at garrison duty, with the exception of three months during the spring of 1868, when, on account of cholera having invaded the fort, he was assigned to hospital service at the fort, and later was detailed as quartermaster's orderly, for four months. For the next year he served with his company as escort to government trains going and coming between Fort Harker and the several posts on the Mexican frontier. In the summer of 1869 his command marched to Fort Griffin, Texas, which was garrisoned and squads were detailed to escort the government mail wagons passing between Forts Griffin and Concho. He continued here until the expiration of his term of enlistment, and was honorably discharged May 15, 1870, by Major John W. Clouse, from Company E, Twenty-fourth Infantry, the consolidation of the Thirty-eighth, in 1869, with the Twenty-fourth, having caused his transfer to the latter.

Our subject now found himself past twenty three years old, with slightly more than $1,000 cash, including $250 which was due him from the reserve, and, better than all, he had, during the three years he was in the service, learned himself to read and write, as well as having become quite proficient in mathematics. He had made good use of his first years of freedom. He now desired to visit his relatives at Atlanta, and must go by way of Fort Smith to collect the balance of his pay; he paid $60 for stage ride, and at Boggy Depot, in the Choctaw Nation, met the government paymaster, Major Kennedy, on his return from having discharged his duties at Fort Sill. He arrived at Fort Smith on Sunday, June 5. and in company with a comrade, Private Rufus Jones, drew his money, and looked about for employment. He found it at the old Flemming

Hotel, still standing at the corner of North A street and the "Frisco" Railroad track. He continued at this place until the spring of 1871 and then worked in a local brick yard until autumn, when he made one trip to New Orleans on the steamboat "Importer" as second cook.

On his return he applied to United States Marshal Roots' chief clerk, J. W. Donnolley, and was given charge of a large stock of dry goods, groceries and liquors, the contents of the Hill & DuVal general store, which was held for execution under an attachment by the Federal court. He was in charge of this stock night and day until it was sold in the spring of 1872, when he was appointed one of the six bailiffs to serve in the Federal court room under Judge Story.

During the winter, while guarding the bankrupt stock, he detected a negro bailiff, Albert Hamilton, and his two sons in the act of burglarizing the store and at their second visit effected their capture and the return of the goods they had stolen. For this he was commended by Marshal Roots, but for some reason the burglars were allowed to go scott free, without a trial.

During his first year as bailiff, Winston gained favor with the court by his diligence and close attention to details, and in 1873 Judge Story appointed him as his private bailiff. He was not molested by Judge Caldwell, in the autumn of 1874, after Judge Story had resigned, and when the new appointee, Judge Parker, took his seat, the following May, he appointed Winston as his private bailiff, on the recommendation of all the court officers.

In March, 1872, he married and purchased a house and lot, where he still resides, at 701 North Eleventh Street, then well out in the suburbs. He remained with Judge Parker, with the exception of eight months, until the incoming of George J. Crump, appointed by President Cleveland to succeed Marshal Jacob Voes, when Judge Parker, to please the new marshal, appointed as his private bailiff, John Bloomburg, a Democrat.

Mr. Winston had, meanwhile, been saving and investing his earnings, and he now enjoys a comfortable income, sufficient for the support of himself and wife. He has been a lifelong Republican; he cast his first ballot in 1872, voting for Grant and Wilson electors.

COL. BENJAMIN T. DUVAL

Col. Ben T. DuVal was one of the conspicuous figures about the Fort Smith court in its palmy days and until the close of Judge Parker's criminal jurisdiction over the Indian Territory. He was the oldest attorney at the Fort Smith bar, and his acts are a part of the famous court's history. He came to Fort Smith as a boy, in 1829 (his father having emigrated from Virginia in 1825 and prepared the way for his family to follow), at a time when the greater part of the land on which the city now stands was covered with a heavy growth of hardwood timber. He grew up with the town, studied law, proved to be an apt pupil, and before 1850 had been admitted to the bar of the Supreme Court of the State, at Little Rock. He began practicing law in 1851, and was thereafter, and to the end of the great court, successfully identified with very many of the leading cases tried in the Federal court for the Western District of Arkansas. In March, 1853, Col. DuVal was admitted to the bar of the United States Supreme Court, at Washington, D. C. In the autumn, previous, he had been chosen a presidential elector on the Pierce ticket, and, while in Washington in the following spring, attending the inaugural ceremonies, he visited, among other places of interest, in company with Captain (afterwards General) Albert Pike, the Supreme court room, court being then in session, and Col. DuVal was admitted to its practice on motion of Hon. Beverly Johnson, of Maryland. He was the first and for many years the only member of the Fort Smith bar to achieve this distinction.

Col. DuVal was always, since an early day, considered an authority on matters of history concerning the struggling days of Fort Smith and the early history of the court that made the city famous, and the writer is deeply indebted to him for many points of interest that appear in this work. At the trial of Cherokee Bill, for the murder of Lawrance Keating, the defense entered the claim that Judge Parker had no jurisdiction in the case because of the crime having been committed by an Indian in Arkansas. Col. DuVal was called as a witness to prove that the land on which the jail stood was government property.

As an orator, Col. DuVal is easy and dignified, and at a meeting of the bar, called soon after Judge Parker's death, to draft resolutions of respect for the dead jurist, it was he who was called to deliver the oration; it was given in a manner most respectful, and showing how deeply he felt the loss of his honored and intimate friend.

Since the summer of 1896, Col. DuVal has devoted a greater portion of his time to the Creek citizenship cases. These were the result of claims to an interest in the property of the tribe by those who had been cut off by the Creek enrollment officers or by the Dawes Commission. In this work Col. DuVal has been eminently successful. Of fifty-four cases taken by him before the United States court at Muscogee, on appeal, he won fifty-one.

In December, 1898, he was appointed by the Creek Indian Council, as attorney, to look after contested claims, at a salary of $2,500. He accepted the office but its duties do not interfere with his regular practice.

E. C. BOUDINOT

The subject of this sketch, Col. E. C. Boudinot, was well termed "A remarkable man," excelled by few ever produced in this country; as a representative of the higher type of the American Indian he had few equals; as a specimen of pure and noble manhood he stood high above the average of his fellows, either Indian or white.

Col. Boudinot was the product of rare breeding, the son of a high born and educated Indian, a prince of the Cherokee tribe, descended from a long line of tribal chiefs, dating back to the first settlement by the white race on the James River in 1607, and of a white mother, a cultivated and refined woman, born and reared in New England.

In the days when Col Boudinot's father was a boy about his father's wigwam in the State of Georgia, surnames were unknown among the Cherokee Indians, and at his birth, about 1795, he was given his father's name, Kill-ke-nah, about which, meaning in English "male deer;" he had an elder brother named Major Ridge, who had two sons about the age of Kil-ke-nah, named John Ridge and Stand Waitie.* All of these latter became noted for their superior abilities and statesman-like qualities, as their progenitors had been distinguished among the Cherokees for their prowess in war and their sagacity and eloquence in the councils of their nation.

*Stand Watie (1806–1871) Cherokee: "stand firm," was a leader of the Cherokee Nation and a brigadier general of the Confederate States Army during the American Civil War.— Ed. 2015

About the year 1805, these Indian boys were sent to Cornwall, Connecticut, under the auspices of New England missionaries, to acquire an education. Soon after, a gentleman of high attainments, an old French Huguenot named Elias Boudinot, visited the school and was attracted by the bright and vivacious Kill-ke-nah, and an intimacy sprang up which resulted in the Huguenot prevailing upon the young aborigine to take his name, and thereafter he was called Elias Boudinot.

During his school days he became acquainted with Harriet Gould, the daughter of a clergyman, and they were afterwards married, the subject of this sketch and two brothers, William P. and Frank Boudinot, resulting from the union.

At the completion of their studies at Cornwall, these Indian boys returned to the Cherokee Nation, in Georgia, and, with the Yankee wife of Boudinot, assumed their tribal relations. Here the second Boudinot, our Elias C., was born in 1835, at New Echola, not far from what is now the city of Rome, Georgia.

Just previous to this time, the United States government was treating with those of the Cherokees (a majority) still in the State of Georgia, and with all the Indian tribes east of the Mississippi River, for their removal west, to reservations in the Indian Territory, a small portion of the Cherokees having already taken up their abode there. The celebrated and notorious John Ross was then the principal chief of the Cherokees. Ross was only about one-eighth of Indian blood and his personal appearance gave no indication that he was other than of white parentage. He was possessed of the peculiar shrewdness and cunning so often resulting from a mixture of races; he had little or no conscience, was as blood-thirsty as the renowned but vicious Simon Girty, and no man ever excelled him in knowledge of Indian character; he subordinated it to the promotion of his personal success, crushing opposition where persuasion failed.

A division arose among the members of the Cherokee tribe and two parties, known as the Ross and Ridge parties, were finally established, between whom great bitterness existed. Boudinot and his brother, Major Ridge, with the latter's sons, John Ridge and Stand Waitie, had fought against the British and the Creek Indians in the East, on the side of the United States, and they now, in a true spirit of diplomacy and statesmanship, advocated the exchange of their possessions in Georgia for land in the Indian Territory, and their influence lent aid to the treaty to that end which was consummated in 1835.

The removal to the Indian Territory was finally effected, the adherents of Ross settling in the northern part of the Cherokee Nation and the Ridge party, the followers of Boudinot and the others, settling the southern part along the Arkansas River. An ancient Cherokee law had provided death as the punishment of any chief or prominent member of the tribe who should sign a treaty for the disposal or sale of tribal lands, and the bitterness of the feud increased and resulted, in 1839, in the brutal assassination, by the Ross party, with tomahawks, at their homes, of Elias Boudinot and his brother, Major Ridge, and a son of the latter, John Ridge; Boudinot's dead body, almost hacked to pieces, falling before the door of the home of his sister, Mrs. J. E. Wheeler. By a miscarriage, Stand Waitie, Boudinot's nephew, was left the sole great survivor of the noted quartette and leader of the Southern Cherokees, the adherents of Ross being at that time known as the Northern Cherokees. The bloody scenes here narrated made an impression upon the young son, Elias C. Boudinot, which time could not erase and which marked his course in after years.

Immediately after the assassination of his kinsmen, Stand Waitie sent all the children to New England, Boudinot's widow going with them to her home in

Connecticut, where the eldest and youngest sons, William and Frank, were reared and educated. Elias C. Boudinot was left at Manchester, Vermont, where he mastered a fine education. William P. Boudinot studied law, and at the age of manhood returned to his own country, took up his abode at Tahlequah, capital of the Cherokee Nation, was successful In the practice of his profession, and for over a quarter of a century he edited the Cherokee Advocate the official organ of the Cherokees. In the autumn of 1897 he disappeared very mysteriously; he was traced to Chicago, but nothing further has been heard of him.

Frank Boudinott remained in the land of his mother, and took up with the ways of the North, imbibing their political faith. He chose the dramatic profession and became a successful actor, his stage patronymic being Frank Starr. At the outbreak of the Civil War he enlisted in the Union army and served with credit, rising to the rank of a commissioned officer, and was wounded in one of the very last battles before Richmond, from the effects of which he died. He left a widow, an actress, whose name was Brinsmaid; their son, Frank Boudinot, adopted his father's profession, but he lacked the physical strength of his parent, and early in the '90's he succumbed to disease, dying in New York.

Elias C. Boudinot at first chose engineering as his profession and, at the age of seventeen, he spent one year as civil engineer to railroad interests in Ohio, but on account of physical injuries to one of his ankles, existing from early infancy, he abandoned that profession for law and entered the law office of Hon. A. M. Wilson, at Fayetteville, Arkansas, and there, in 1856, was admitted to the bar. Then began a career which gave every promise of brilliant success. He was soon admitted to the bar of the Federal court for the Western District of Arkansas, and from the start his wonderful elocutionary powers and oratorical ability marked him as a man before whom was a magnificent future. One of his first cases was in defense of his cousin, Stand Waitie, charged in the Federal court at Van Buren with murder, as junior to the celebrated Alfred W. Arlington and Wilbur D. Reagan.

Boudinot led off in the arguments for defense, following his old preceptor, Hon. A. M. Wilson, then United States district attorney, in one of the most effective and polished orations ever delivered by a man of his age.

"After hearing an account of this trial from persons who witnessed it," writes a former biographer, "I asked Col. Boudinot about the chief incidents attending it, and he made this memorable remark: 'All the innocent blood and sufferings of my race came in panoramic procession before my mind as vivid as the lightning's flash, and determined me to make an effort worthy of my lineage or ruin my brain in the attempt.'"

While at Fayetteville he was offered and, for a time, occupied a position as editor of the Arkansan, a weekly paper published in the interest of Democracy; here his abilities were given full sway and his editorial writings attracted signal attention. This position, as one of the great leaders of Democracy, led him into editorial charge of the

True Democrat, the leading organ of the party in the State, published at Little Rock. The editorials in both these papers bespoke him as a man of more than ordinary ability and, for one so young, indicated extraordinary mental vigor, a combination which soon won for him a national reputation.

In 1860 the Democratic State Convention had made him Chairman of the State Central Committee, a distinguished compliment for a young man, only twenty-five years of age, and in 1861 he was elected, by acclamation, secretary of the Secession Convention, which took Arkansas out of the Union. At the adjournment of this convention he embraced the cause of the South and repaired to the Cherokee Nation, where John Ross was still the principal chief, and assisted his cousin, Stand Waitie, in raising a Cherokee regiment for the Confederate service, under a commission from the Confederate Government, issued to General Albert Pike, then stationed at Montgomery. Alabama. Stand Waitie was elected colonel of the regiment; young Boudinot was elected major, and soon after was made lieutenant-colonel, Stand Waitie finally becoming brigadier-general by appointment from President Jefferson Davis.

In October, 1861, John Ross, then at Tahlequah, the capital of the Cherokee Nation, concluded a treaty with the Confederate States, espousing their cause, issued a stirring proclamation, penned by the hand of Gen. Pike, to the Cherokees, and he was personally engaged in the bloody battles of Oak Hills and Elkhorn.

In 1863, under a provision of the Cherokee treaty with the Confederate States, Col. Boudinott was elected to the Confederate Congress, serving in that capacity until the closing scenes of the war. With the conclusion of the great civil conflict, the members of the Five Civilized Tribes were in an unenviable position; they had broken all former treaties in which they had solemnly pledged against taking up arms against the United States Government, and now that the Confederacy had fallen to pieces they had no place they could call their own. The representative Indians were eager for a new treaty which should place them right before the authorities at Washington, and in September, 1865, the largest Indian council ever held in this country convened at Fort Smith, to determine the terms of the treaty then under consideration.*

*A peculiar condition existed at this time between the Indians and the negroes in the Indian Territory which, in spite of the digression, it is best to briefly explain here: Before the removal of the Indians to the reservations in the Indian Territory, many of them had patterned after the white aristocracy and being of a naturally indolent disposition had taken to the custom of bartering in human flesh, and many individual members of the several tribes had and held human chattels, the same as did the whites. When they removed to their new homes in the West they took their slaves with them and at the time of the breaking out of the Civil War these Indians were building an aboriginal aristocracy similar to that holding forth among the whites of the South, but without its culture, education and refinement. Some of the Indians, moreover, had married negroes and, besides, many illegitimate offspring of slave mothers, by slave holding Indians, had been born, and the Federal Government found itself facing a perplexing situation. It found the Indians, however. ready and willing to treat;

and, finally, as a compensation to the slave negro, be he of full African birth or a mixture of the negro, white and Indian, or whatever mixture or cross, who had been born of a slave mother in the Indian Territory, or who had been a slave of any of the individual Indians of any of the tribes in the Indian Territory, was, by the terms of the treaty of July, 1866, given the same rights to have and to hold land in the Indian Territory, to make homes there, remain and acquire and hold property, as the Indians themselves; and that condition, with certain slight variations, exists at present.—note in original

Chief Ross had been guilty of treason, not only against the Federal Government but to the Confederate States as well. Shrewdly foreseeing that the rebellion would most certainly be crushed, in 1863 he deserted the South and proceeded to Washington to sue for peace and pardon, on the ground that he had been morally overawed and forced to join the rebellion against his will, and that Elias C. Boudinot and Stand Waitie were responsible for his having taken up arms in behalf of the Seceding States.

When, therefore, Boudinot appeared at the council, representing the Southern Cherokees, and made a manly and able defense of the course pursued by them during the war, John Ross was on hand to cry "traitor and treason" against the Southern Cherokees for aiding in the rebellion, forgetting or being shameless of his double act of treason to both sides» When Boudinot came to answer these charges he brought documentary evidence that was irresistible, "pursuing now the patient, deliberate methods of the trained logician, then rising to the highest offices of the impassioned orator, he covered the name of John Ross with the brand of both assassin and traitor and overwhelmed it with an all-consuming fire which will burn in lurid light as long as the history of the Cherokee Nation is preserved. He followed Ross to Washington and foiled all his machinations and combinations to inflict flagrant injustice on the Southern Cherokees. John Ross died before the final ratification of the treaty in July, 1866, and his faction tried to perpetuate their power in the person of another and younger Ross but signally failed. John Ross had survived his usefulness and fame— had lived too long. He saw the son of the murdered Kil-ke-nah, with the force of powerful logic and polished oratory, carrying senates against him. He lived to see the murdered martyr triumphant in the person of his noble son, as he himself sank beneath a cloud of shame in a dishonored grave."

Soon after the consummation of the treaty of 1866, under the provisions of article 10 of that instrument, with the Cherokees, Col. Boudinot established a tobacco factory in the Cherokee Nation. This solemn treaty especially exempted the Cherokees from taxation of any kind. A year after Boudinot erected his tobacco factory, on July 20, 1868, a revenue law was passed by Congress, one section of which imposed the revenues provided by law upon the several articles so taxed "anywhere within the exterior boundaries of the United States." Immediately upon the passage of this act Col. Boudinot entered into a correspondence with Secretary of the Interior Delano, and from that high officer he received an official construction of the treaty of 1866, exempting him from the payment of revenue on the product of his factory, but, soon after, his factory was seized and confiscated and over $60,000 worth of property destroyed, the government claiming it forfeited on account of his failure to pay the revenue tax. The question was taken before Judge H. C. Caldwell, of the United States Circuit Court at Van Buren; he rendered a decision upholding the seizure of the factory; this decision was afterwards sustained by the Supreme Court of the United States. Colonel Boudinot then appealed to Congress for compensation and for nearly twenty years he urged his claim, at last being awarded nominal damages in the sum of a little more than $3,000.

During nearly the whole of this period Col. Boudinot remained in Washington, becoming intimately acquainted with and well-liked by all of the leading men of the country. His accomplished and dignified manners, coupled with a heart overflowing with kindness for every creature, made him a general favorite. In every household at the national capital he was always a welcome guest. In the art of elocution he was a master, yet his mastery of it was without artifice; his charming delivery and his fine vocal powers placed him in demand and no social function was complete without his presence. As a story teller he was always most entertaining, yet he never, even in a company composed exclusively of "Then, repeated aught that smacked of vulgarity, nor were his fund of stories other than could be told in the presence of the most daintily reared lady without causing a blush to mantle her cheek. He might justly be termed a pure minded man, for he was, on all occasions, a man of pure words, using the same choice distillation of choice expression to all listeners, whether to his own wife, to a company of male acquaintances or in the presence of the most dignified and stately women.

During this time he took advanced views on the Indian question He was enabled to foresee the inevitable, and he early advocated the division of their lands in severalty to individual members of the tribe and the establishment of United States courts in the Indian Territory, with the dissolving of the Indian courts and of the tribal relations. For this he became unpopular and on account of a strong address, delivered at Vinita, September 21, 1871, in advocacy of his views, he was obliged to flee for his life and not until about 1884 could he again safely tread the soil of his nation.

As a sample of the earnest eloquence with which he pleaded the cause of advancement for the Indians, is here given his closing of a famous address delivered by him before the House Committee on Territories, February 7, 1882, in behalf of a territorial government for the Indian Territory:

"I appeal to this Congress to give us an absolute individual title to our lands, as it is proven beyond question that our title in common is insincere. I have been moved to take the position I advocate because our national house is tottering to its fall. I see the rains descending and the floods coming.

"I know the rains and floods and winds are beating upon our house, and that it will fall, because it is founded upon the sand of a title in common. If we ever shall hold a tide to any portion of our lands which we can defend and maintain, it must be a title in individuals, and not in common.

"Make us citizens of the United States; clothe us with prerogatives of such; arm us with the power and rights of American citizens. Depend upon it, the Indian will bless you, if he but understands that he is elevated from the degrading rank of a subject to the proud position of an American citizen. You struck the shackles from the limbs of font million slaves; and, while still dazzled by the full blaze of liberty, you girded them with the armor of American citizenship., and bade them protect their new-born rights. You transformed the ignorant slave into an American citizen, without waiting for him to graduate in that school of guile which my Indian friends imagine to be necessary. Do as much for the Indian.

"His title in common is insecure. Give him a better one in severalty. He is subject to your laws and your courts. Give him a voice in making the laws which are to govern him, and the right to sit upon a jury which is to try his own countrymen.

"He is subject to your revenue laws, and pays taxes to the support of your government. Give him that representation which should go hand in hand with taxation.

"Give the Indian those equal rights before the law which are conceded to all other people. Arm him with the powers and privileges of an American citizen. Give him that title to his land which he can protect and defend. Then, and not till then, will he have a country which he can call his own; then will he be possessed of land which is his indefeasible property; then will he have a home where he can rest his weary feet, with no dark forebodings of the future."

Many striking and beautiful passages are to be found in Col. Boudinot's speeches. Of his native language he said: "The Cherokee language seems to be distinct and independent of all other tongues; it is smooth and soft and when spoken, by females, especially, sounds most musical. There are but two words in the language which require the touching of the lips to pronounce; these words mean water and salt, and have the sound of M.

"The Cherokees are the only Indians who have an original alphabet for their language. The Creeks and Choctaws use the English characters, but the Cherokees have an alphabet of their own, invented by a Cherokee who could not speak a word of English; his name was Sequoyah.* He was the Cadmus of his race; he had none of the lights of science or civilization to guide him, but conceiving the idea of enabling the Indian to talk on paper, as he one day saw an agent of the United States doing, he shut himself in his cabin for one year, and endured, like many reformers and inventors, the jibes and jeers of the ignorant and thoughtless, who pronounced him crazy, until he came forth with a perfect alphabet, and established his claim to be ranked among the first inventive minds of the century of wonderful inventions. This alphabet was invented in 1822 and consists of seventy-eight characters and, strange to say, is most easily learned by children."

Sequoyah, otherwise known to the early settlers of Fort Smith as "Old George Guess" or Guest, lived across the Arkansas River, about six miles from the fort. He was of a taciturn mind, usually wore moccasins, a blue hunting shirt, and on his head a turban. In the early days, it is said, that he and his wife were frequent visitors to the fort for the purpose of selling chickens and eggs. Sequoyah was a native of North Carolina, son of a Scotch Tory named Gist and a full-blood Cherokee mother. After having invented the alphabet, now in use by the Cherokees, he tired of even the evidences of advancing civilization and with a friend he went West and took habitation with the wild tribes of red men. During an illness he sought shelter in a cave near the banks of the Rio Grande; he died in the arms of his friend, and was by him given a rude burial.—note in original

In April, 1885, about the time of the close of his celebrated contest before Congress for a settlement of his claim against the United States Government, Col. Boudinot married an estimable and highly educated lady of Washington, Miss Clara Minear, possessed of splendid connections and excellent accomplishments. Each seemed to be peculiarly suited to the other and, during the five years that remained to him of life, it proved a very happy union. In the fall of 1885 they removed to Fort Smith and Col. Boudinot again took up his law practice. He had always claimed the Cherokee Nation as his home, and he had maintained a ranch of about 2,000 acres two and one-half miles south of Chetopa, Kansas. He rented out the residence thereon, but always retained a room for his own use when at home, and there he locked his private belongings when preparing for a trip away. Now, however, that he was planning to again enter vigorously the practice of law in the Federal courts having jurisdiction over the Indian Territory, he purchased the improvements on a ranch of three hundred acres at Pawpaw, six miles up the Arkansas River from Fort Smith, and there he made his home, principally, driving into town every morning during the sessions of court. He was associated at different times with attorneys Thomas H. Barnes, William M. Mellette and J Warren Reed, all successful practitioners, as law partners, and he was accredited by all as a worthy and able member of the profession. He was one of the three members of the Fort Smith bar to be admitted to the bar of the Supreme Court of the United States, receiving his certificate April 2, 1867, and he was the third (Col. Ben T. DuVal and William M. Cravens being the others) to achieve that distinction.

Colonel Boudinot was of fine physique and classic features. Regarding the latter was a peculiarity, in that his profile was so entirely different to the casual observer than was the full front view. The two half-tone reproductions of photographs, showing him at forty and at fifty years old, prove this. As stated, his fine abilities as an elocutionist and his wonderful musical talent, with one of the most charming voices ever given to men, made him greatly in demand at social functions and his appearance in the doorway, his face wreathed in smiles, was enough to cause a flutter in the hearts of everyone within sight, both male and female. After his death, at a meeting of the bar, called to draft resolutions of respect, a distinguished attorney and jurist said of him, "Men loved him, not as men love men, but as men love women." The first cut given, shows him as he appeared among his friends, having laid aside for the present the cares of business; the second shows him the lawyer student, investigating deeply a case before the bar, his turn soon to address the jury, when he will thrill all listeners with the logic of eloquence, touch deeply their hearts by the pathos with which he pleads for his client.

For several years before he died the members of the Cherokee tribe became reconciled to his views, came to learn of his worth and of his honesty, to know that he was not the traitor to his natural ties that they had been led by the unscrupulous, to believe but that he was, in fact, their best friend, wise in all his plans and honest in every movement.

He died just before 9 o'clock on the morning of September 27, 1890, surrounded by loving friends, after an illness of eighteen days. He was first taken ill in St. Louis, Missouri, while conveying to the East a cousin, George Gould, who had become insane while living at the Colonel's home at Pawpaw; the attack was so severe he was compelled to deliver his charge to other hands and he returned to Fort Smith. After his decease the body was viewed from the residence of a cousin, Mr. W. W. Wheeler; the remains were interred under Masonic honors at Oak Cemetery.

From many points came letters and telegrams to the bereaved wife and the friends of the deceased, and the press teemed with articles expressive of sincere condolence. Let us quote from two, the Gazette, of Little Rock, Arkansas, and the Phoenix, of Muscogee, Indian Territory—from the former.

"The announcement of the death of Col. E. C. Boudinot, in Sunday's issue, was read with deep regret by all who knew the deceased in life. For many years Col. Boudinot was prominent in Arkansas affairs; was known by all classes of our citizens, and possessed qualities which rendered him a prime social favorite everywhere. He was the soul of honor; brave and chivalric. He wore his heart on his sleeve, that all might see it, for he had nothing to conceal from friend or foe. His long and varied career, if properly written, would make one of the most interesting contributions to the history of life in the Southwest."

From the Phoenix: "One by one the notable Indian statesmen, who have played a conspicuous part in the history of this country before and after the reconstruction period, which began in 1865, are passing away. The ranks of the old chiefs and warriors are being thinned and the rising generation of modernized Indians are taking their places. Within the past twelve months a score or more of Indian men, every one of whom had, for a quarter of a century, been prominent in the councils of their nations, have died. Within the past few days two men, Boudinot, of the Cherokees, and Whistler, of the Sac and Fox tribe, have passed over the river. The memory of the lives and deeds of these two men, each of whom had for twenty years been prominently identified with the best interests of their country, will long remain fresh in the minds of their people It is to be hoped that the biographies of these men, as well as of many other stalwart Indian statesmen, will be written and preserved for coming generations. It will be of inestimable value to the world of letters one hundred years hence to know who were the star actors in the Indian federations of the latter part of the nineteenth century."

JUDGE THOMAS BOLES

Judge Thomas Boles, appointed clerk of the Fort Smith court under President McKinley's administration, was born in Johnson County, Arkansas, July 16, 1837. In 1865 he was elected judge of the Fifth Judicial District of his native State. He filled the office with credit and, in 1868, was elected to serve in the Fortieth United States Congress, and was again elected to serve in the Forty-first and Forty-second. During the second year of his first term he secured an appropriation of $150,000 with which to erect the Arkansas Industrial University of Fayetteville; it is one of the finest educational institutions of its kind in the country.

In 1878 Judge Boles was appointed, by President Hayes, receiver of the land office at Dardanelle, Arkansas. In 1882 he was appointed, by President Arthur, United States marshal of the Western District of Arkansas; he was succeeded by John Carroll, appointed under Cleveland's first administration. In 1889 he was candidate for reappointment and a petition circulated in his behalf secured 16,000 signatures; for the sake of party harmony he withdrew from the race and Jacob Voes was given the place. He was appointed clerk of the United States circuit court at Fort Smith October 1, 1897.

In private and public life he is kind and sociable, and is familiarly known by all as "Uncle Tom." He is an able lawyer and a reliable friend. In spite of his three-score years he is straight as an arrow and as light of step as a man of thirty-five. His magnificent bearing has caused his intimate acquaintances to give him the title," The Old Roman."

J. WARREN REED

Of all the attorneys who practiced at the Fort Smith bar, none worked so energetically nor won as much fame as J. Warren Reed, who fought harder for his clients and secured more reversals in criminal cases by the Supreme Court than any attorney in that court.

Mr. Reed was born in Parkersburg, West Virginia, December 9, 1849. Like many other famous attorneys, he spent his childhood on a farm and there laid the foundation for a strength of character that marked him in after years. In early life he chose the law as a profession, and though he met many difficulties in equipping himself for his life work, yet the same energy and perseverance which distinguished and made him successful before the courts in after years enabled him to overcome all obstacles, and after many hard struggles he secured a fair education, studied law and was admitted to the bar in 1879—his thirtieth year.

He at once commenced the practice of law in Wood! County, West Virginia, and in southeastern Ohio, being successful from the start, soon gaining the name of "That

Lawyer Who Always Wins His Cases." In 1886 he was admitted to practice in the Supreme Court of West Virginia and in the United States District and Circuit Courts for the District of West Virginia. In April, of the same year, he went to California, and was admitted to the bar of that State by the Supreme Court, in full session in San Francisco. While in California he practiced with his cousin, ex-Judge Ira H. Reed, of San Andrea, and successfully conducted many important mining, land and criminal cases; after which, making a tour over Mexico, the United States and Canada, he returned to his native State and resumed his practice there. In 1889 he went to Fort Smith to defend a noted case, and being attracted by the outlook and magnitude of business attending the United States court he settled down to permanent practice. He was the only member of the Fort Smith bar who had practiced law on both sides of the continent. He associated himself with Thomas II. Barnes, afterwards United States district attorney, and Col. E. C. Boudinot; the firm name was Barnes, Boudinot & Reed. On the death of Col. Boudinot, about a year later, his two associates continued, under the firm name of Barnes & Reed, for three years, since when the latter has practiced alone.

Mr. Reed soon became noted for his untiring labors in behalf of his clients, and his unparalleled energy and enterprise marked him as a criminal attorney of vast resources and great reserve power. The record he justly gained created a demand for his services, and during the first seven years after he began practice in Fort Smith he defended and assisted in the defense of 134 persons charged with murder and other capital offences in the United States court before Judge Parker and in the various commissioner's courts, besides over one thousand other cases of minor importance, such as assault with intent to kill, robbery, larceny, etc. Of the 134 persons noted, but two were hanged; the others were either discharged by commissioners on examination trials, acquitted by juries, or the grade of their crimes reduced to manslaughter. It can be truthfully said and shown from the records of the Fort Smith court that he secured the acquittal of more persons charged with crime in that court than any attorney who practiced at its bar during that period.

He was connected with many of the most important murder cases tried in this court, some of which are as follows: Alexander Lewis, Charles Bullard, William Alexander, Sam Hickory, Ed Alberty, Buss Luckey, Cherokee Bill, Frank Carver, Jake Harles, et al, Isaac M. Yustler, John Allison, A. H. Craig, Berry Foreman, Rufus Brown, Jess Miller, Tom Thornton, Frank Perry and four others; and numerous other cases. He was connected with the famous Bland-McElroy case as prosecutor, and in his address to the jury he made what

Judge Parker pronounced the most eloquent, logical and effective argument he had ever heard in a court room.

In private life J. Warren Reed exhibits remarkable social qualities; his is a disposition that is at once noble, generous, magnificent; he is loyal to his friends and magnanimous to a foe; he is sympathetic to a high degree, and is as energetic in his labors for a penniless client as for those whose wealth is unstinted.

He has traveled extensively; he is an ardent seeker after information, his love for the curious leading him into many nooks and ways that are unobserved by ordinary sight seers; he is an apt student of human nature and is fortunate in his ability to retain an intimate knowledge of what he has seen and heard. He is a very fluent and eloquent speaker, courageous in his convictions, and is ever ready to draw upon his fund of information for the benefit of any assemblage. In 1877, just after he commenced the study of law, Mr. Reed married the cultured Miss Viola C. Sheppard, a proficient and experienced school teacher, resident of Marietta, Ohio. During all the years of his early struggles, and since he has become noted as practitioner at the bar, she has been to him truly a help-mate, ably assisting him in his labors and glorying in his every success. She also studied law with a view to applying for admission to the bar, but on account of a lack of provisions in the West Virginia statutes for the admission of women to practice in its courts her application was never made.

In January, 1897, after the reduction of the jurisdiction of the Federal court at Fort Smith, foreseeing the coming importance of the newly established Federal courts in the Indian Territory and their increase of business resulting from the restriction noted, Mr. Reed opened a law office at Muscogee, and he now practices in all the United States courts in the Indian Territory, as well as in both divisions of the courts for the Western and Eastern Districts of Arkansas.

In the spring of 1898 he was called to Chicago by legal duties and while there he applied for and was admitted to the bar of the United States district and circuit courts in that city.

The attention of the reader is called to the various cases described in this work, with which Mr. Reed was connected, cither as prosecutor or as attorney for defense.

Lack of space prevents the insertion of biographies of all the members of the Fort Smith bar; suffice to say, they stand among the best in the land, and their success, whenever it becomes their fortune to attend to matters pertaining to the profession in other cities and other States, has been phenomenal. Fort Smith may well be proud of her attorneys.

EX-JAILER J. D. BERRY

J. D. Berry, the last jailer at the United States jail at Fort Smith prior to the restriction of the court's jurisdiction, a brother of United States Senator James H. Berry, of Bentonville, Arkansas, was a native of Alabama. He went to Carroll County, Arkansas, when nine years old and lived there until the Civil War broke out when he enlisted in the Confederate army, serving until the close of hostilities. He was in all of the principal battles west of the Mississippi River. After the war he was appointed deputy sheriff of Franklin County, Arkansas, by a Union sheriff, on the recommendation of Governor Murphy. He retained the position under two succeeding sheriffs and was appointed postmaster during President Cleveland's first administration. In 1894 he was appointed United States jailer at Fort Smith. He took charge of the jail November 1, of that year. There were then 209 prisoners in the jail; the number increased during his term to 244, on February 2, 1896. During the two years that he occupied the position of jailer there were more desperate characters confined behind the bars than at any time in the jail's history. There were seventy men in murderer's row when he took charge, and among the desperate characters he had to deal with were Cherokee Bill, Bill Cook, Henry Starr, the Pierce brothers and their ilk. There was scarcely a day that some scheme was not on foot for a wholesale delivery.

The five members of the Buck gang attempted to disarm Jailer Berry and two guards as they were being taken down on the elevator from the court room, after their conviction for rape; prompt and judicious action on Berry's part prevented their escaping to repeat their acts of horror.

During Jailer Berry's term the visitors numbered many thousands; curiosity seekers from all parts of the country, from every State and Territory and from foreign countries, eager to view the interior of the place where were confined the prisoners convicted by the famous court, as well as to get a peep at the prisoners themselves. On Sunday, July 25, 1895, the second day after the murder of Guard Lawrence Keating, the number of visitors exceeded 1800 and hundreds, besides, were unable to gain entrance.

Mr. Berry is by nature kind and accommodating; he had many friends, even among the prisoners over whom he had charge.

Campbell Hoff, who had a very interesting experience at the time Guard Lawrence Keating was killed, is the proprietor of a hotel at Clarksville, Arkansas; he has a fund of stories With which he sometimes regales traveling men.

Clarence Owensby, the squarely built man standing directly in front of the open door leading into the jailer's office, is a well-known hack driver of Fort Smith; one of the best known, in fact, in the State of Arkansas, having spent fifteen years of his life on the box. He is said to have been the only guard who ever served as death-guard. He sat in that capacity in front of the cell occupied by Cherokee Bill for eight days prior to that felon's execution, and was death-guard for the Buck gang for four days. It is not uncommon for condemned murderers to entrust secrets to their death-guards, and if Mr. Owensby could be induced to divulge some of the facts thus revealed to him it would make interesting reading.

W. H. Lawson was a victim of the tornado which swept across Fort Smith on the night of January 11, 1898, filling the city with sorrow and lamentation. He was seriously injured, but recovered, and volunteered in the service of the United States, in the following spring, on account of the Spanish-American war. His fate overtook him at Chattanooga; while working in the pit during target practice, he raised his head at an unfortunate moment and he was killed by a bullet fired by one of his comrades.

Ex-Jailer Berry resides on his farm, three-fourths of a mile east of Fort Smith, on the Little Rock road.

"Brass" Parker lives at Harrison, Boone County, where he is chief deputy sheriff under his brother, Sheriff Ceph Parker.

Tom Parker's home is with his widowed mother in Benton County. His place was given a few months prior to the "dissolution" to Capt. Steel, a veteran of the Civil War.

William Franklin worked for a time in the liquor store of Reynolds & Danner, in Fort Smith, and later removed to Texas; and E. A. Berry is a farmer, living at Charleston, Arkansas.

THE CAPITAL CASES TRIED AND CONVICTED

In this chapter are given tabulated lists, compiled at great expense, of the persons convicted of capital crimes and sentenced to death, both at Van Buren and after the court was removed to Fort Smith. The number of persons arraigned before the bar of the famous court runs away into the thousands, and space only for those convicted of crimes for which death by hanging was the punishment provided by law, can be given in these tables.

The total number of convictions for capital crimes, both at Van Buren and Fort Smith, as shown by the records now in a state of preservation, was 181, all but nine of the number being convicted after the court's removal to Fort Smith. Of the nine known to have been convicted of murder while the court was at Van Buren, one escaped after being sentenced, and after scouting nine years was recaptured, brought before Judge Parker, resentenced and executed at Fort Smith; two were executed at Van Buren; one was commuted to life imprisonment at Little Rock and was afterwards released by Confederate soldiers; one was commuted to life imprisonment , and was afterwards pardoned, and the remaining four* were commuted to terms of imprisonment of various lengths.

Tabulated list number 1 gives the names of those convicted of capital offenses at Van Buren, giving the dates of conviction and sentence and the dates set for execution in each case, with a column showing the final disposition of each.

Tabulated list number 2 gives the names of those who were executed at Fort Smith, with columns showing the names of the victims of each murderer or rapist (except in a few of the early cases), the nations in the Indian Territory in which each of the crimes were committed, the dates of conviction, sentence and execution, and the race to which the prisoners belonged, whether whites, Indians or negroes.

This corrects a statement, in error, appearing on page 41, line 22 of this work, to the effect that six executions were held at Van Buren.

Tabulated list number 3 gives the names of those convicted at Fort Smith and sentenced to die on the scaffold, but who, for reasons shown, were not finally-executed, with the dates of conviction and sentence, and the dates they were to have suffered death, and a column stating final disposition of each case.

Tabulated list number 4 gives the names of those who were charged with murder (one of whom was convicted) and who forfeited their bonds and thus escaped punishment for their offenses. Separate columns show the date upon which each of them were indicted or arraigned, so far as the records show, the dates on which the forfeitures were taken and the amount of bond in each case. In two cases it will be seen the order of forfeiture was rescinded on proof of the death of the subjects being established to the satisfaction of the court.

Three more cases complete the list: In October, 1883.

Sparing Harjo, a Seminole Indian, was indicted by the grand jury under a charge of murder. On October 4 the jury, while ready to declare the prisoner guilty as charged in the indictment, yet found that his victim also was an Indian, this fact releasing the prisoner from the Federal court's jurisdiction, and Harjo was turned over to the Seminole authorities for punishment. In March, 1886, Morris Green and Timber Reed, two Choctaw Indians, were indicted and tried for killing Hardy Henderson. The case was given to the jury March 20, and after deliberating, the jury, while believing in the guilt of the prisoners, found that Henderson was an Indian and that the court had therefore no jurisdiction in the case and the prisoners were turned over to the Choctaw authorities for punishment. The third was that of Leander Dixon, arraigned July 7, 1887, on an indictment charging murder. The case was set for trial, was continued from term to term, and on August 23, 1888, Dixon was reported dead, having taken his case before a higher tribunal, and the case against him on earth was dismissed.

Previous to the date heretofore mentioned, at which the earliest preserved records appear, during a period of about four years after the court was established at Van Buren, it is said, on good authority, there were no convictions for capital crimes; from December 15, 1860, to August 31, 1865, the records are missing, if any were kept during the troublous war times, and it will be noted that while tabulated list No. I mentions one James Buchanan, who was twice tried on a charge of murder just previous to December 15, 1860, both trials resulting in a "hung" jury, yet there is no stroke of a pen to indicate the final outcome of the case.

The attention of the reader is called to the fact that in addition to the lists here given, a vast number, especially after the removal of the court to Fort Smith, were tried for murder and were convicted of manslaughter and sentenced to terms in the penitentiary; also, that a great number of murder trials at Fort Smith, and nearly a score at Van Buren, resulted in acquittal at the first and only trial. Of these no list is attempted.

TABULATED LIST NO. 1.

NAME OF MURDERER.	WHEN CONVICTED.	WHEN SENTENCED.	DATE SET FOR EXECUTION.	REMARKS.
Thomas Beard	November 19, 1856	October 8 1856	May 29, 1857	The first execution at Van Buren.
George White	June 25, 1858	June 30, 1858	October 1, 1858	Commuted.
William Shannon	October 1, 1858	December 2, 1858	May 6, 1859	Commuted.
John Wolford	May 25, 1859	May 27, 1859	September 30, 1859	Commuted.
John Raper	December 1, 1859	December 2, 1859	April 27, 1860	Commuted to life imprisonment, March 2, 1860
Jas. Buchanan	(Two mistrials Dec. 3 and Dec. 10, 1860)			Records from December 15, 1860 to August 31, 1865, missing.
Blakey Wilson, alias Piper Wilson, alias Brown	December 1, 1867	December 30, 1867	February 7, 1868	Execution wounded 9 victims; executed September 8, 1876 at Fort Smith.
Ta Ka Ne Ger, alias Wilson	December 1, 1867	December 30, 1869	February 7, 1868	Commuted.
David Ross	May 18, 1869	May 22, 1869	September 3, 1869	Commuted to fifteen years at Little Rock—afterwards pardoned.
Amos McCurtain	November 20, 1869	May 14, 1870	June 24, 1870	Executed at Van Buren.

TABULATED LIST NO. 2.

Name of Murderer	Name of Victim	Nation where Crime was Committed	Date of Conviction	Date of Sentence	Date Set for Execution	Race
John Childers	Reyborn Wedding	Cherokee	November 18, 1872	May 19, 1873	August 15, 1873	Indian
Young Wolf		Creek	January 23, 1873	August 1, 1873	October 15, 1873	Indian
Sin Killer	Two trappers on Grand River	Creek	June 25, 1873	August 4, 1873	October 10, 1873	Indian
Tuneeger, alias Tusi		Creek	June 25, 1873	August 4, 1873	October 10, 1873	Indian
John Billee	Perry DaVal	Creek	December 19, 1873	January 5, 1874	April 3, 1874	Indian
John Pointer	a cattle drover	Choctaw	December 19, 1873	January 5, 1874	April 3, 1874	White
Isaac Filmore	Unknown white men	Creek	December 17, 1873	January 5, 1874	April 3, 1874	Indian
McClish Impson	Unknown white man	Creek	November 10, 1873	November 14, 1874	January 15, 1875	Indian
Daniel Evans	Seabolt	Creek	May 10, 1875	June 26, 1875	September 3, 1875	White
John Whittington	John J Turner	Chickasaw	June 16, 1875	June 26, 1875	September 3, 1875	White
James Moore	William Spivey	Cherokee	May 25, 1875	June 26, 1875	September 3, 1875	White
Edmund Campbell	Lawson Ross	Choctaw	May 27, 1875	June 26, 1875	September 3, 1875	Negro
Smoker Man Killer	William Short	Creek	June 2, 1875	June 26, 1875	September 3, 1875	Indian
Samuel Fooy	R Neff	Cherokee	June 25, 1875	June 26, 1875	September 3, 1875	Indian
Ollie McGee	Robert Alexander	Choctaw	December 11, 1875	February 5, 1876	April 21, 1876	White
William Leach	John Watkins	Cherokee	December 10, 1875	February 5, 1876	April 21, 1876	White
Isham Seeley	Mrs. Mason	Chickasaw	December 20, 1875	February 5, 1876	April 21, 1876	Indian
Gibson Ishtonubbee	Dr. Pussy	Chickasaw	December 31, 1875	February 5, 1876	April 21, 1876	Indian
Aaron Wilson	James and John Harvis	Chickasaw	January 1, 1876	February 5, 1876	April 21, 1876	White
*Osey Sanders	Thomas H Carlile	Cherokee	January 5, 1876	February 5, 1876	April 20, 1876	Indian

* Respited; executed September 8, 1876.

TABULATED LIST NO. 2.—Continued.

Name of Murderer	Name of Victim	Nation where Crime was Committed	Date of Conviction	Date of Sentence	Date Set for Execution	Race
John Valley	Bill Hackett	Cherokee	May 10, 1878	June 21, 1878	September 6, 1878	White
*Shaker Wilson	Datus Cowan		December 2, 1878	June 12, 1879	September 5, 1879	Indian
Samuel Peters	Charity Hansom	Choctaw	June 21, 1879	June 21, 1879	September 5, 1879	Negro
John Postoak	John Ingley and wife	Creek	August 11, 1878	October 14, 1879	December 19, 1879	Indian
James Diggs	J C Gould	Cherokee	November 8, 1878	November 3, 1879	December 19, 1879	Negro
Wiley, alias Colorado Bill	David J Ropex	Choctaw	May 28, 1879	June 10, 1879	August 29, 1879	White
William Miller	David J Brown		May 28, 1879	June 10, 1879	August 29, 1879	White
Dr. Henri Stewart	Dr J B Jones		May 28, 1879	June 10, 1879	August 29, 1879	Black
George W Padgett	W B Stevens	Cherokee	February 17, 1881	June 10, 1881	September 6, 1881	White
William Brown	Ralph C Tate	Ind. Ter.	March 3, 1881	June 10, 1881	September 6, 1881	White
Patrick McGowan	Sam Loftis	Chickasaw	May 17, 1881	June 10, 1881	September 6, 1881	White
Amos Manley	Ellis McVay	Choctaw	June 3, 1881	June 16, 1881	September 6, 1881	Indian
Abler Manley	Ellis McVay		June 3, 1881	June 16, 1881	September 6, 1881	Indian
Edward Fulsom	John Stewart, William Massingill		March 11, 1882	April 21, 1882	June 30, 1882	Indian
Robert Massey	H P Clark	Chickasaw	December 11, 1882	February 1, 1883	April 13, 1883	Negro
William H Finch	Mash Johnson, Wash Grimsky	Choctaw	February 23, 1883	May 5, 1883	June 10, 1883	Negro
Te-ta-lo-ta	Emanuel M Cochran		March 10, 1883	May 5, 1883	June 29, 1883	Indian
Martin Joseph, alias Bullyjoseph	Bud Stephens and wife	Chickasaw	April 8, 1883	May 5, 1883	June 29, 1883	Indian
Thomas L Thompson	James O Holderen		February 19, 1884	April 28, 1884	July 11, 1884	White

* Twice sentenced—escaped after being sentenced in 1867.

TABULATED LIST NO. 2.—Continued.

Name of Murderer	Name of Victim	Nation where Crime was Committed	Date of Conviction	Date of Sentence	Date Set for Execution	Race
Lewis Holder	George Bickford	Choctaw	Sept. 18, 1895	Sept. 18, 1895	November 5, 1895	White
Crawford Goldsby alias Cherokee Bill	Ernest Merton	Cherokee	Feb. 17, 1896	April 13, 1896	March 17, 1896	Indian
Webber Isaacs	Mike F Cushing		Feb. 21, 1896	April 25, 1896	April 30, 1896	
George Pearce	William Vandever	Creek	March 1, 1896	June 5, 1896	April 30, 1896	White
John Pearce	William Vandever			June 5, 1896		
Rufus Buck						Indian
Lewis Davis						
Luckey Davis	Committed Rape on Mrs. Rosetta Hassan	Creek	Sept. 18, 1896	Sept. 18, 1896	July 17, 1896	Negro
Sam Sampson						Indian
Maoma July						
Jan Cumberage, alias Geo Wilson	Zacharia W Thatch	Creek	Dec. 18, 1895	Feb. 14, 1896	July 30, 1896	Indian

TABULATED LIST NO. 3.

Name of Convict	Date of Conviction	Date of Sentence	When to be Executed	Remarks
George LeFlore	Dec. 21, 1871			Died in jail while awaiting sentence, October 27, 1872.
John Broaderick	Dec. 4, 1872	January 3, 1874	April 2, 1874	Commuted to five years.
Robert T Booker	Jan. 2, 1873	Nov. 10, 1874	(Manslaughter)	Three years in penitentiary at Little Rock.
Frank Butler	May 27, 1875	June 26, 1875	Sept. 3, 1875	Killed while escaping.
Osee Snow	June 1, 1875	June 26, 1875	Sept. 3, 1875	Commuted to life at Joliet, Ill. Afterwards pardoned.
Black Crow	Dec. 11, 1876	Feb. 26, 1877	April 27, 1877	Commuted to life at Moundsville, Va.
Irving Perkins	Dec. 16, 1876	Feb. 26, 1877	April 27, 1877	Commuted to life at Moundsville, Va.
Charles Thomas	Dec. 27, 1876	Feb. 26, 1877	April 27, 1877	Commuted to life at Moundsville, Va.—Pardoned after six years.
William A Meadows	Sept. 18, 1877	October 12, 1877	Jan. 18, 1878	Commuted to life imprisonment at Detroit, Mich.
*Joshua Wade	Sept. 29, 1877	October 12, 1877	Jan. 18, 1878	Commuted to life at Moundsville, Va.
Thomas Robinson	Sept. 29, 1877	October 12, 1877	Jan. 18, 1878	Commuted to life imprisonment at Detroit, Mich.
Carolina Grayson	Dec. 13, 1877	Feb. 25, 1878	June 21, 1878	Commuted to life imprisonment at Detroit, Mich.
Peter Grayson	Dec. 13, 1877	Feb. 25, 1878	June 21, 1878	Commuted to life at Detroit, Mich.
Mat Louis	Dec. 13, 1877	Feb. 25, 1878	June 21, 1878	Commuted to life at Detroit, Mich.
Robert Love	Dec. 13, 1877	Feb. 25, 1878	June 21, 1878	Commuted to life at Detroit, Mich.
Urban M Guosse	Dec. 12, 1879	March 29, 1880	June 18, 1880	Commuted to life at Detroit, Mich.
Jackson Marshal	Dec. 19, 1879	March 29, 1880	June 18, 1880	Died in jail before date of execution.
James N Heazier	Feb. 18, 1880	March 29, 1880	June 18, 1880	Commuted to life at Detroit, Mich.
Lun Smith	Sept. 23, 1880	Oct. 12, 1880	Dec. 17, 1880	Commuted to life at Detroit, Mich.

* Convicted at rape.

TABULATED LIST NO. 3.—Continued.

Name of Convict	Date of Conviction	Date of Sentence	When to be Executed	Remarks
Alexander Lewis	Oct. 26, 1891	Jan. 12, 1892	April 27, 1892	New trial granted and acquitted
*John Brown	March 22, 1892	April 30, 1892	June 28, 1892	Reversed—served one year in penitentiary
Fannie Smith	Jan. 8, 1894	August 9, 1894	Sept. 28, 1894	Reversed and not prosecuted
John Hicks	March 7, 1894	Oct. 29, 1894	Dec. 27, 1894	Reversed, new trial and acquitted
Willie Johnson alias Willie Overton	March 7, 1894	May 3, 1894	July 25, 1894	Reversed, new trial sent up for life
Marshall Turner	March 17, 1894	Oct. 29, 1894	Dec. 27, 1894	Reversed and commuted to 10 yrs Brooklyn, N. Y.
John Gourke	May 22, 1894	Oct. 29, 1894	Dec. 27, 1894	Reversed and pleaded guilty to manslaughter and given five years at Columbus, O
John Graves	July 29, 1894	Sept. 19, 1894	Nov. 2, 1894	Reversed and acquitted
Frank Carline	Aug. 11, 1894	Sept. 19, 1894	Nov. 2, 1894	Commuted to life imprisonment at Columbus
Robert M Hall	Aug. 17, 1894	Sept. 19, 1894	Nov. 2, 1894	Commuted by Supreme Court—new trial and acquitted
Sam Hickory	Aug. 25, 1894	Sept. 19, 1894	Nov. 2, 1894	Reversed, new trial sent to penitentiary for five years
Alexander Allen	Oct. 11, 1894	Oct. 29, 1894	Dec. 27, 1894	Reversed, new trial and sent up for life
Harry Starr	Oct. 30, 1894	Nov. 6, 1894	Feb. 20, 1895	Reversed, new trial, and sent to penitentiary for fifteen years
Patrick Pewis	Nov. 17, 1894	Feb. 2, 1895	April 3, 1895	Adjudged insane and placed in an asylum
Thomas Thompson	Dec. 4, 1894	Jan. 19, 1894	April 24, 1895	Reversed
Charles Smith	Feb. 20, 1895	April 18, 1895	June 23, 1895	Reversed, new trial and given two years for manslaughter
John Kilson	May 28, 1895	July 9, 1895	Oct. 1, 1895	Reversed, new trial, and sent up for seven years for murder
Mollie King	Feb. 24, 1894	March 4, 1896	Aug. 30, 1896	Appealed, new trial sent up for life
Eli Lucas	June 11, 1896	July 9, 1896	Oct. 1, 1895	Reversed, and rejected by the Choctaw Nation

* John Brown was sentenced to hang, the case was reversed; a new trial, again sentenced, again reversed, and a third trial resulted in life being served in one year in the penitentiary.

97

TABULATED LIST NO. 3.—Continued.

Name of Convict	Date of Conviction	Date of Sentence	When to be Executed	Remarks
John Parvin	March 11, 1886.	Oct. 30, 1886	Jan 14, 1887	Commuted to five years at Newark, N.
Jeff Hilderbrand	Aug. 2, 1887	Feb. 9, 1888	April 27, 1888	Died in jail while awaiting execution.
Richard Sutherland	Sept. 14, 1887	Feb. 9, 1888	April 27, 1888	Commuted to twenty-one years at Little Rock
* William Alexander	Sept. 14, 1887	Feb. 9, 1888	April 27, 1888	Commuted to life imprisonment at Little Rock.
Emanuel Patterson	Oct. 30, 1887	Feb. 9, 1888	April 27, 1888	Commuted to life imprisonment.
Lewis Barrow	Sept. 15, 1888	Nov. 3, 1888	Jan. 25, 1889	Commuted to ten years at Little Rock.
Steve Buxom	Sept. 27, 1888	Nov. 2, 1889	April 19, 1889	Commuted to life at Little Rock.
William G. Border	Oct. 12, 1888	Nov. 2, 1888	Jan. 23, 1889	Commuted to life at Little Rock.
George Brashears	Nov. 2, 1888	Feb. 2, 1889	April 19, 1889	Commuted to life at Columbus.
William Woods	Nov. 20, 1888	Feb. 2, 1888	April 19, 1889	Pardoned.
Henry Miller	Nov. 20, 1888	Feb. 2, 1889	April 19, 1889	Commuted to life at Columbus.
Frank Carel	March 1, 1889	March 29, 1889	April 19, 1889	Commuted to life at Columbus.
Elvin James	March 22, 1889	April 29, 1889	July 17, 1889	Commuted to life at Columbus.
Jo Martin	April 6, 1889	April 29, 1889	July 17, 1889	Commuted August 9, 1889, to life imprisonment at Columbus.
Madison James	Sept. 4, 1889	Nov. 1, 1889	Jan. 16, 1890	Commuted to fifteen years at Detroit.
Charles Bullard	Oct. 16, 1889	Nov. 1, 1889	Jan. 16, 1890	Commuted to life at Columbus, pardoned after one year.
William Alexander	Jun. 21, 1890	Aug. 2, 1890	Oct. 1, 1890	Reversed, two acquittals and nol. pros.
† John Boyd	Oct. 29, 1890	Jan. 12, 1891	April 21, 1891	See foot note.
† Eugene Stanley	Oct. 29, 1890	Jan. 12, 1891	April 21, 1891	See foot note.

* Convicted of rape.
† John Boyd and Eugene Stanley were found guilty of murder, but on appeal to the Supreme Court the case was reversed, new trial granted and they were convicted of manslaughter. Boyd was sent to the penitentiary for ten years. Stanley was found guilty of killing and of robbery in three counts and was sentenced to fifteen years for each robbery, and ten years for the murder case, making fifty-five years in all.

TABULATED LIST NO. 3.—Concluded.

Name of Convict	Date of Conviction	Date of Sentence	When to be Executed	Remarks
Frank Carre	June 29, 1893	July 9, 1895	Oct. 1, 1895	Reversed, new trial, and sent to Columbus, Ohio, for life.
Thomas J. Thornton	August 14, 1895	August 31, 1895	October 9, 1895	Ten years at Columbus. Sent to insane asylum at Washington, 1898.
Ben Lockey	Aug. 24, 1895	Sept. 7, 1895	Oct. 28, 1895	New trial, acquitted, and sent to Columbus, O. for fifteen years for trials robbery.
* Ed Witley, alias One Davis	Sept. 25, 1895	Oct. 9, 1895	Dec. 19, 1895	Commuted
Ed Alberty, alias Charles Boots	Nov. 15, 1895	Dec. 4, 1895	Jan. 29, 1896	Reversed, new trial, and acquitted
Mary A. Kettering	June 24, 1895	July 13, 1895	Oct. 1, 1895	Reversed, new trial, and acquitted April 3, 1896.
George Washington Fraziler	June 24, 1895	July 13, 1895	Oct. 1, 1895	Reversed, new trial, and acquitted April 3, 1896.
Richard Calhoun	June 24, 1895	July 13, 1895	Oct. 1, 1895	Reversed, new trial, and acquitted April 3, 1896.
† James Mills	March 3, 1896	April 1, 1896	June 23, 1896	Reversed, new trial, jury disagreed, and finally acquitted October 27, 1898.

* Convicted of rape.
† Indicted for rape.

TABULATED LIST NO. 4.—Bonds Forfeited in Murder Charges.

Name of Prisoner	Date of Indictment	Date of Conviction	Date Bond Forfeit Declared	Amount of Bond
Samuel Smith	November 22, '71	May 22, '72	July 19, '72	$ 5,000*
Charles Robertson, alias Rich Cowan	November 22, '71	Not tried	May 24, '72	1,000
Mark McLaughlin	(Arraigned Nov. 29, '71)	" "	May 23, '72	1,000
James Frater	January 22, '73	" "	May 30, '72	1,000
Ira Amey	(Records lacking)	" "	May 31, '72	1,000
Joel Denton		" "	June 7, '72	1,000
John Hoyle	May 2, '73	" "	November 18, '72	2,000
Johnathan Anthony	May 15, '73	" "	July 6, '72	1,000
Charles Covert	May 24, '72	" "	June 7, '72	1,000
Alex Cheatham	May 23, '72	" "	November 8, '72	2,500
Johnathan Offel	(Records lacking)	" "	January 16, '73	3,000
Charles Jaycox	June 23, '73	" "	November 24, '73 (Again forfeited)	10,000
Charles Jaycox	(Recaptured Dec. 4, '79)	" "	November 8, '74	10,000
Tetaka	(Same as lacking)	" "	November 12, '74	12,000
Jarratt Love		" "	May 15, '76	400
James Brashears	(Arraigned Nov. 23, '76)	" "	November 8, '77	1,000
William Carney		" "	November 8, '77	4,000
Jack Hartgraves	Aug. 2, '89	" "	September 12, '89	500†

Total amount of bonds forfeited, less bonds revoked $ 62,400

* Bond allowed on order granting new trial.
† Order of forfeiture rescinded November 16, 1875, on proof being established of the defendant's death.
‡ Order of forfeiture rescinded April 30, 1890, on proof being established of defendant's death.

THE FIRST EXECUTION

THOMAS BEARD PAYS THE PENALTY FOR A TERRIBLE CRIME

For several years after the establishment of the judicial district known as the Western District of Arkansas, with court at Van Buren, although there were several trials of men charged with the crime of murder, no convictions were secured. The very first man convicted of the awful crime before this court was Thomas Beard, a white man, who had married a daughter of Jack McKing, a squaw man,* and he lived fourteen miles from Fort Smith in the Cherokee Notion, where he operated a blacksmith shop.

A term used in the 19th century for white men who had married Native American women.—Ed. 2015

In the spring of 1856, an old man, a stranger, apparently a returned "forty-niner," appeared in Fort Smith, having come up the Arkansas river in a little steamboat, the closing of a long voyage from the California gold fields "via the Horn" to New Orleans and up the Mississippi. The stranger said he was on his way to Kansas to visit a son and purchase a farm. He was suffering from scurvy, and he said to several persons with whom he conversed that he desired to find a place in the country where he could live through the summer and where he could be provided with plenty of good milk and vegetables. Beard, who chanced to be in town, overheard the remark, and he said to him: "Go with me; you can get plenty of milk and vegetables at my place." Arrangements were completed between the two and they crossed the river together and went to Beard's house. That they crossed together was proved by the merchant with whom they both traded and by the boatman in the merchant's employ. At that time the Fort Smith merchants made a practice of keeping large row-boats in constant readiness with which to convey their customers, free of charge, from the west to the east bank of the river whenever they wished to visit Fort Smith, returning them again to the west bank after they had completed their purchases.

Near neighbors of Beard saw the old man about the house during the next week, and often saw them on short fishing excursions. One day Beard sent his wife to Fort Smith for coffee, and he surprised the woman almost out of her wits by giving her additional money with which to purchase calico for dresses for herself and little daughter. No sooner had she departed than Beard and his guest started up the creek. Beard carrying a shotgun and his guest a fishing pole and line. That was the last seen of the old man alive. When the wife returned she was told that he had proceeded on his way to Kansas. Nothing more was thought of him until a few months later, when the bones of a man, their flesh having been devoured by wolves and buzzards, were found in a gulch, partially covered by brush, by a negro boy who was searching for estrayed cows. The alarm was given, and the neighbors who flocked to the scene identified the remains as those of the old man who had stopped at Beard's house. The authorities at Van Buren were notified, and Beard suddenly disappeared. He was followed to Fort Smith and was finally overtaken by Sheriff William Porter near Lavaca, twelve miles from Fort Smith on the Little Rock road. In his possession was a canvas belt containing $2,000 in California $20 gold pieces. He first said that he was on his way to Clarksville to enter land, then, as he was asked concerning the large amount of gold, he said that he had earned the money several years before while in California and that, having tired of life in the West, he had decided to return to his former home in the state of Georgia.

He was turned over to the Federal officers and a search of his house discovered many personal articles that the stranger would scarcely have left behind, such as a razor, pocket knife, comb and brush. At the trial it developed that the marks by which the neighbors had identified the remains were a pair of heavy brogan shoes and a small piece of the trousers he had worn. The stranger had purchased a pair of shoes just before leaving Fort Smith of the same make as those found with the body, and had also purchased pantaloons of the same kind and color of cloth as the pieces now found, but both articles of wear were of the commonest kind, exactly the same as were being sold to country customers every day, hence they were not considered the best possible means of identification. Another feature of the trial was the date stamped on the gold coins, all of which were the same, the date being two years later than that which Beard gave as the year he had left California. The indictment was for murder, and he was convicted as charged.

His attorneys were Messrs. Vandever and Ben T. DuVal. A motion for new trial was argued and denied. Judge Ringo said he could see no good in setting aside the verdict unless more evidence could be produced by the defense; yet he hesitated at pronouncing sentence, and the clerk of the court was instructed to send notices to such newspapers as were then printed within a few hundred miles of Fort Smith, as well as in a few of the eastern cities, describing the man who had come up the river in the little steamboat, and calling on him, if alive, to return, and save a human life and claim his gold. The case created a good deal of attention, but no response was ever received from the published notices, and on the last of May, 1857, Beard suffered death by the rope. He was said to be the first man ever convicted of murder on circumstantial evidence within the State of Arkansas. The gallows stood near where the Crawford county fair grounds were afterwards located, and it was kept in order and utilized in executing the one other man convicted of murder while the court remained at Van Buren.

THE JOHN RAPER CASE

One other very interesting murder case tried at Van Buren was that charged against John Raper for the murder of John Rogers, a Cherokee Indian. It was believed by the majority of people who knew of the facts that the killing, if not wholly justifiable, was, under the circumstances, excusable, and that Raper should have been acquitted.

Raper was a farmer who lived in Arkansas, not far from the Indian Territory line. In the summer of 1859, his young son, while visiting the home of a supposed friendly

Indian in the Cherokee Nation, was set upon by several Indians and brutally murdered. The murder was committed at night, and early the next morning the father was informed of the untimely killing of his son, and was also told that the deed was performed by the Indian, John Rogers. He at once hastened to the house where lay the ghastly remains of his boy, and while he was there, "exhibiting emotions of the deepest grief,"* the Indian, Rogers, rode to the vicinity, emitting whoops and howls, and, dismounting, started for the house. Raper, hearing the noise, went to the door of the cabin and looked out just as the Indian had started towards him, and raising his rifle he slew Rogers in his tracks.

The trial resulted in a conviction by the jury, December 1, 1859, and eight days later sentence was pronounced, naming April 27, 1860, for his execution. Immediately thereafter, a petition signed by a large number of the leading citizens of Arkansas, including the judge before whom Raper was tried, was forwarded to President James Buchanan, setting forth the facts relating to the killing of the Indian, and on March 22, about a month before the day named for his execution, an order from the President was received commuting Raper's sentence to life imprisonment at Little Rock.

During the following year Raper, with all other prisoners incarcerated in Little Rock, was released by the Confederate soldiery, and it is supposed that he entered the service of the South and that he was killed in battle.

AN EXPOSITION OF INDIAN CHARACTER

The second and last man to die on the scaffold at Van Buren was Amos McCurtain, a Choctaw Indian, executed June 24, 1870, for the murder of Jim McLain, a Choctaw peddler, and his negro driver, in 1868. The story of his crime exposes a strange trait of character that would scarcely be found in the Anglo-Saxon. McCurtain lived five miles from Boggy Depot. He followed the occupation of teamster, kept several yoke of oxen, and was often employed by the merchants at Boggy Depot to haul goods from Fort Smith, their nearest and most accessible city. On the occasion of the crime he had been sent for a load of merchandise, and had been intrusted by several merchants with sums aggregating $1,000 with which he was to liquidate certain bills due to Fort Smith wholesale houses. The Indian faithfully carried out his instructions, paid the money to the proper persons, loaded up his wagon and started back with the goods, drawn by three yoke of oxen. At a point on Buffalo Creek, about ninety miles southwest of Fort Smith, he encountered McLain and the negro as they were camped for the night. They had a small stock of goods and one yoke of oxen. While they slept McCurtain slew the two men, piled their goods on top of those he was hauling for the merchants, piled the bleeding corpses on top of all, hitched their oxen in the lead of his own, and about three miles further on he dumped the bodies of his victims into a creek and proceeded on his way.

His progress, was slow, about fifteen miles a day, and as he was passed by frequent men on horseback, the news of his crime preceded him. Arriving at Boggy Depot after dark, he calmly removed his plunder from the wagon, piling it on the ground, then, after unloading the goods he had been hired to haul, placed the peddler's property, smeared with the blood of the two men, again in the wagon and drove home. Knowledge of the crime spread rapidly and finally reached the ears of the Federal authorities, and a few days later William Faulkner was detailed especially to go and bring McCurtain to court. Faulkner made the trip, 150 miles, on horseback, arrested McCurtain, handcuffed him and roped his arms securely, then mounted and led the Indian all the way to Van Buren, where he was tried, found guilty, sentenced, and executed nearly two years after the commission of the crime.

Concerning the other convictions for murder at Van Buren, the reader will find, in "Tabulated List No. 1," all the information the compiler has been able to obtain.

SOME OF THE FAMOUS CASES

CRIME AND EXECUTION OF JOHN CHILDERS

The first legal murder committed at Fort Smith by this famous court was the execution of John Childers, a half-blood Cherokee Indian, charged with killing a peddler named Rayburn Wedding.

The crime was particularly vicious and cold-blooded, and the events concerning it created so great an impression upon the minds of the people of Fort Smith and Van Buren that they are still fresh in the memories of many citizens there.

Childers was the son of John Childers, a white man, and Katy Vanne his Cherokee wife. He was born on Cowskin Creek, in the Cherokee Nation, May 3, 1848, being a little past 25 years old on August 15, 1873, his last day on earth. He was strongly built, muscular and an athlete; he was 5 feet 11 inches in height and weighed 160 pounds. The greater part of his life had been spent in the Cherokee and Creek Nations, and all obtainable information indicates that he was a very wicked young man, a member of an organization composed of Indians and whites, whose object was murder and plunder, and whose obligations bound them closely to each other, right or wrong, in all their transactions. Previous to committing the crime for which he was executed he had been mixed up in a personal difficulty with Deputy Marshal Vennoy, and he stated just before his execution that he killed a man from Vennoy's state, Kansas, to get even. It appears, however, that Reyburn Wedding, the peddler, who made his living by traveling through the Indian Territory with a team and wagon trading flour and bacon for hides and farm products, had a very fine black horse which, as soon as he saw it, struck Childers' fancy, and, coming up with the peddler while riding in the north part of the Cherokee Nation near the Kansas Line, on Caney Creek, he began bantering for a trade. It was in the autumn of 1870, October 14. Wedding informed Childers that he had no desire to part with the animal. The Indian's brow darkened; the sin of covetousness had entered his heart and would not be stilled He dropped behind for a short distance, studying plans by which to obtain the horse which he had now determined to secure at any cost. Finally, having decided upon a plan, he spurred his pony ahead, overtook the peddler, who was driving along unconcernedly, at peace with all the world. Tying his own animal to the rear of the peddler's wagon he climbed into the seat beside him. Together they rode on until they reached Caney Creek, at a point near Childer's Station, when, suddenly drawing a big knife, he forced the peddler back and cut his throat from ear to ear. He then dumped the dead body out into the water and drove the team out upon the prairie, where he found not the least difficulty in trading upon his own terms. Stripping the harness from the horse he coveted so madly, he saddled it and rode proudly away leaving the other horse, the wagon and his late mount standing without a claimant.

At the trial of his case it developed that twenty-seven times he had bargained to part with the horse which he had secured by committing a heinous crime, and that as many times fate had intervened to prevent. The animal was finally the means of his destruction, for it was so well-known that it led to his arrest soon after at Klo Kotchka, or Broken Arrowtown, in the Creek Nation, by Deputy Marshal Vennoy and a posse of men from Kansas, who started towards Kansas with him. Dreading to go to the Sunflower State, and fearing that he would not be taken to Van Buren (the court had not made itself the terror to murderers that it afterwards became), he effected his escape with irons on.

About the first of February following he was arrested at the same place by the same party and taken to Kansas, kept there a week in chains (for what reason does not appear), and was then conveyed to Van Buren and was examined before United States Commissioner J. A. Churchill, and held to await the action of the next grand jury.

No court was then in session; at the close of the day, December 2, 1870, Judge Caldwell, then the Federal judge for the Western District of Arkansas (by virtue of his office as judge for the eastern district), adjourned court in course, and on the 8th day of the following May, the second Monday of the month, the court was re-convened at Fort Smith, with William Story as the newly appointed judge,

Childers did not remain long in jail; he and six others broke out and took to the woods (to get something to eat is the way they expressed it), and it is possible he would never have been recaptured nor Reyburn Wedding's death have been avenged but for a circumstance such as has lured thousands of other men to disgrace and destruction. There was a woman of the town residing in Fort Smith of whom Childers was enamored. She was like the majority of her class; she induced Childers to believe that she had for him a true affection, while secretly planning at all times to secure money from him by various pretexts. Learning of this, Deputy Marshal Vennoy visited the woman and easily made arrangements by which on a promise of $10, she agreed to aid in Childers' capture. In her own way she communicated with him after he had visited her for the last time and bade her adieu, intending to quit the country. With all the seductiveness only a harlot could employ, she pleaded for just one more meeting before he should leave her forever. Childers listened, hesitated, yielded and was lost. He allowed himself to be enticed once more to her den, which to him was a palace and of which she was the queen. That night, while he was reveling in her embrace, intoxicated with her charms (?), his brain befogged with passion and oblivious to danger, the house was quietly entered by Vennoy and Deputy Joe Peevy through a door which the harlot had purposely left unfastened, and Childers was suddenly apprised of the fact that he was in the clutches of the law by the cold touch and the stern click of the handcuffs as they encircled first one wrist and then the other. Dragging him from the arms of his seducer, who eagerly clutched the promised reward, the officers led him back to the jail.

On May 15, 1871, the beginning of the second week of the first term of Federal court ever held in Fort Smith, the grand jury made a report, returning eleven true bills of indictment, naming sixteen persons charged with various crimes. At the foot of the list stands the name of John Childers, charged with murder. Childers was arraigned on Thursday, May 18; he pleaded not guilty, trial of his case was continued till the next term of court, and he was admitted to bail in the sum of $1,500. The records show that on November 16 following, his attorney, J. S. Robinson, filed Childers' affidavit and application for witnesses, asking that Cowito, Mico and William Sevier be subpoenaed as witnesses for defendant, and brought to court at government expense. A little later, Messrs. Campbell and DuVal & Cravens appear as additional attorneys for defense, and on December 5 they applied in the open court asking that the trial of Childers be continued; two days later the application was granted, trial was set for May, 1872, and the court issued an order transferring Childers to the penitentiary house at Little Rock for safe keeping, pending trial. The court was evidently thinking of the former escapes. To this order Childers' attorneys appear to have made vigorous protest, for on January 18, 1872, the order was set aside, and on January 29 the defendant was admitted to $2,000 bond, Capt. E. M. Adair and Mark Bean being his sureties. On May 30, 1872, continuance was again asked for and for lack of witnesses was allowed; the case was finally opened for trial on the sixth day of November following. The trial lasted until November 18, one day being lost (besides Sundays) on account of the burning of the building wherein the court room was located. The case was stoutly defended, at least one of Childers' attorneys, Col. B. T. DuVal, believing firmly in his client's innocence. The arguments of council occupied two and one-half days. After being out a short time the jury returned a verdict of guilty. The case for the prosecution was prepared by Hon. John H. Rogers, the present judge of the Federal court for the Western District of Arkansas. He was then a young attorney recently from Kentucky; he had defended a case of assault in the court at Van Buren and had practiced slightly in the state courts. He was employed by friends of Wedding to assist District Attorney Newton J. Temple.

Childers, for a year before his trial, had felt certain of ultimate acquittal, as he depended on the members of the gang of which he was a member, to clear him, and he had been warned by his attorneys that for a man charged with crime to break jail or attempt to escape was an act calculated to prejudice the minds of the jury. This warning and his belief that he would be acquitted may or may not have influenced him in honoring his bond; however, just before the day set for his trial, early in November, 1872, Jailer Burns, while sitting outside the door of the jail on the banks of the Poteau, was surprised to see Childers approaching, his clothing dripping wet. He had swam the Arkansas river in his eagerness to return in compliance with the terms of his bond. He asked to be locked up; the jailer refused, telling him he must first report to the United States Marshal, and a few hours later, on an order from Marshal Sarber, Mr. Burns had Childers under lock and key.

After his conviction Childers was kept in confinement (in the garrison dungeon) until May 19, 1873, when he was brought out and sentenced, August 15 being set for his execution. Just prior to that date the gallows which was destined to serve for twenty-three years, and in that time to take the lives of eighty-eight human beings, was erected, and John Childers was the first to stand upon its fatal trap. Until a few days previous to his execution, Childers had great hopes of a pardon or of commutation, as strong petitions for executive clemency had been sent to Washington. These hopes were dispelled by a telegram from the attorney-general informing his attorneys that he believed Childers guilty and declining to interfere. Strong influence had been brought to bear on the case from Southern Kansas urging that the law take its course, and this may have had something to do with the attorney-general's decision.

A REMARKABLE OCCURRENCE

A remarkable occurrence, witnessed by hundreds of people, many of whom live to testify to it, to this day, took place at the moment of Childers' execution. The day was as bright and clear as a brilliant sun and cloudless skies could make it. An immense crowd was present, some 2,000, of all shades, colors and of both sexes, from the prattling infant in arms to the old and gray-bearded, were gathered about the gibbet, drawn' by a desire to witness, calmly, the killing of a human being. People had driven many miles, with the same eagerness as is often manifested at the coming of a widely advertised circus. As the hour arrived the crowd, with the harlot in the front rank, grew restless at what seemed like delay, so anxious were they to witness the spectacle of a life being snuffed out in a moment. Finally, at precisely 1 o'clock, there came a signal from one of the company who had stationed himself a hundred feet or so east of the gallows, where he had a view of the jail door. The signal informed the waiting crowd that the victim, 'under guard of six deputy marshals, headed by Marshal Sarber and Jailer Burns, had left the jail and had started him on his last earthly march and eager faces were turned in that direction.

Slowly the march proceeded, and at the same time a small black cloud was seen approaching from the southwest. It crossed the Poteau, came nearer, and as the party with the condemned man reached the scaffold it seemed to pause and hover over them; a few drops of rain fell as if a benediction or a curse upon the proceedings about to take place, or as if nature was shedding tears over the terrible punishment about to be inflicted.

Childers kept up the same cool indifference he had maintained from the first, and smoked his cigar with as much nonchalance as if the affair was none of his. He was given an opportunity to speak, and he talked for sixteen minutes. It had been reported that he had made a full confession in the jail and the onlookers watched his words eagerly. He quibbled at first, but finally admitted that he was the murderer of Wedding, but he claimed that he should not have been convicted, as the time named in the indictment and in the testimony at the trial by Witnesses Vennoy and Erkhart, as the date on which the crime was committed, was not correct. He cautioned young and old to beware of bad company and bad practices. He said this was the only murder he had ever committed by himself; he regretted it, he said, and he now forgave all who had ever injured him, and he hoped to be forgiven. He said that those witnesses who had sworn that he was sixty miles away when the crime was committed had sworn lies, and he hoped God would forgive them for it. He had no regrets, except that he must leave his sister and friends, and asked that his body be not given for dissection, but that his sister be permitted to give it burial in the Cherokee Nation. Finally, looking out on the crowd that was drinking in every word, he remarked that he saw a dozen of his pals, all of whom had sworn to aid each other, no matter what the conditions; "But they seem to be doing nothing for me now," he added.

"If you will give me their names I pledge you not to hang you now," said the marshal. "What is your answer?"

"Didn't you say you was going to hang me?" asked Childers.

"Yes," said the marshal.

"Then why in h—l don't you do it," coldly responded Childers.

His sense of honor—as he understood the term—had been insulted; though he could commit a cold blooded murder, deliberately planned, and though he himself had been betrayed, he could not betray his pals—would not even to save his neck from the halter.

"Greater love hath no man than this, that he gave up his life for his friends," says the Scripture, The reader should learn from this strong point of character, developed from so unexpected a source, that the most degraded criminal may have redeeming qualities; and that it is the duty of mankind to probe down and find those qualities, hoping for an opportunity to say a kind word which may perchance save a soul.

Childers was followed by Rev. Mr. Harrell in a few eloquent remarks, closing with a prayer that brought tears to many eyes.

Jailer Burns read the death sentence, Childers meanwhile retaining remarkable control of his muscles.

The rope was adjusted by Jailer Burns and Deputy Marshal Messier (who had volunteered to serve as executioner), the prisoner offered a short prayer, the black cap was adjusted, and at 2 o'clock Marshal Messier pulled the lever that sprung the trap, dropping the murderer to the rope's end, and at the same instant the forked tongues of thousands of tiny bolts of lightning shot through the frame work of the scaffold, accompanied by a tremendous clap of thunder which reverberated through the enclosure, completely drowning the appalling noise of the cumbrous death messenger as it unfolded its treacherous arms and withdrew the last prop that sustained the sinking soul. A moment later the ghastly work was done, the cloud had vanished and all that was mortal of John Childers hung limp and quivering. The entire proceeding, the grim service of the law, the terrifying effects of the thunder and the flashes of lightning, as if a vigorous protest of nature against the destruction of one of her children filled the spectators with awe; those who were believers in the supernatural bowed their heads in fear, and the scoffers never attempted to explain the strange visitation; or was it a coincidence?

One negro woman in the crowd cried out, "John Childers' soul has gone to hell; I done heerd de chains clankin'." Other superstitious negroes believed that Childers was never executed but that the form appearing on the scaffold that day was the devil in human disguise.

Sometime afterwards a story gained credence, and was current for several years, to the effect that the fall did not kill Childers, and that after being cut down he returned to consciousness and climbed over the wall near the gallows and escaped. Some even went to the extent, several years after the execution, of saying that they had seen Childers, alive and well.

It is known, however, that the body of Childers, dead, was given over to his sister, and by her removed to the Indian Territory and given burial.

In his last moments Childers had referred to a statement made to Jailer Burns. This statement was published later in one of the Fort Smith papers. It proved to be a repetition of his verbal statements, reaffirming the confession given on the scaffold.

THE NEXT EXECUTION

October to, 1873, witnessed once more a legal destruction of human life. This time Young Wolf, Six Killer and Tunagee alias Tuni, Cherokee Indians, climbed the twelve steps to the ghastly scaffold to pay the death penalty for the murder of two trappers, on Grand River, in the Cherokee Nation. The object of their crime was robbery, but they only secured a trapper's outfit for their deed—a few steel traps and other plunder of little value. It is not known whether they confessed; after the ropes were adjusted they each made a speech in their native language, but as none present understood the language it will never be known on earth what manner of sentiments they expressed. The execution passed off quietly and without incident. The press and the better class of citizens had begun to realize the blot upon the fair name of their city, caused by the erection in their midst of a perpetual engine of death, to see the evil effect upon the young which must result from its proximity; there came a desire to keep the acts of the court, and the announcement of the many executions that were sure to take place, as quiet as possible. This determination, upon the part of the people of Fort Smith, the result of a pardonable pride in their home city, makes it difficult for the historian to procure, in some instances, complete records of famous cases. Try as they would, however, to offset the bad influences of the court and its acts, its effects upon certain classes were very marked. It bred in the minds of many a carelessness regarding the value of human life, and a hanging, or even the killing of a man in a street broil, came to be regarded as of little consequence; a stranger in the city on "killing day" would wonder at the uncanny, thunderous crash and thump coming from the direction of the fiver, but if he knew aught of the court and its workings he would soon be informed of the strange sounds by hearing street urchins shouting to their fellows, "O, Bill! There's another'n gone to hell with his boots on." This applies, however, more to later years, after hangings had become of common occurrence. As stated, hitherto, though it was, undoubtedly, an unwise act of Congress that so narrowed the jurisdiction of this greatest court on earth, yet there can be no doubt that if corporal punishment must continue to be employed as a penalty for murder, the removal of the court and its gibbet was a blessing to Fort Smith.

The effect of the removal of the gallows is nearly, if not quite, as noticeable as was that of its continual use, and the Fort Smith of to-day is not the same as was that of a decade or even five years back; on the streets of no city in the land is more evident the quiet, unassuming marks of culture and refinement, and the new Fort Smith seems to have fairly outlived and thrown off its stain. Equally true is this: that but for the court and its inflexible judge, the old Fort Smith could not have given away to the new, and it would still be as it once was—a "Veritable Hell on the Border."

OTHER EARLY CASES

The third day of April, 1874, was the day recorded as the last in the lives of John Bille, John Pointer and Isaac Filmore, Convicted and sentenced in November, previous, for murders committed in the Indian country. Billee, an Indian, was of a ferocious temperament, and it was necessary to keep him chained to a corner of the old basement. Like all Indians, he had a special aversion to being hanged. The manner of death inflicted by the Indian courts was by the bullet. This form of death an Indian will face bravely, with stoical indifference, but to die by hanging is considered by the red man the most ignoble of all forms of death; possibly because that was the Style of punishment dealt out by the whites to horse thieves, the most ignoble of criminals in the eyes of the frontiersman.

One day as Maledon, the hangman, chanced to be in the basement where Billee was confined, the latter rose to his feet and pointing to a black spot which he had made just over his heart begged the hangman to kill him with his pistol, saying: "You shoot me; I no tell. Shoot me right here," pointing to the place where the black indicated the location of his heart. "I no like this," accompanied by a motion of his hand about his neck, indicating the noose. "Shoot me right here," he begged; "I no tell." The hangman shook his head and walked away. A few months later, as the deputies went to the jail to bring Billee and the others out for execution, they found Billee in a terrible state of excitement and a terrific struggle ensued before he was sufficiently shackled to be safely taken to the scaffold. "Shoot me! Shoot me!" he kept begging, piteously. "I no tell; I no want to hang."

The victim of Billee's crime was Perry DuVal, a guard, one of the posse of Deputy Marshals James Wilkerson and Will Ayers. They were in charge of four prisoners, and had camped one mile from the Creek Indian Agency at Muscogee, in a deserted building, on the night of November 2, 1873. Marshal Ayers and three of the prisoners were chained together. Perry DuVal slept alongside of Ayers and had a pistol in his belt. During the night Billee slipped one of his handcuffs and securing DuVal's pistol shot him through the head, killing him. He next fired at Ayers, who lay on his back with his right hand across his breast; the bullet went through the hand and cut away the right nipple. Wilkerson, who was asleep in another room with the fourth prisoner and a guard, rose to his side and was shot through the back, the bullet passing through the kidneys. Ayers then seized the prisoner, and while the scuffle was in progress the guard who had slept with Wilkerson raised and shot Billee in the head and body, causing dangerous wounds. He was taken to Fort Smith, cured and then tried and hanged. Billee knew no fear. Previous to shooting the guards, an adversary had attempted to assassinate him, firing on him as he passed a clump of bushes.

At the first fire Billee wheeled his horse and rode straight into the brush and shot his assailant dead.

John Pointer was a young Seminole, convicted as accessory to the murder of a cattle drover, in the autumn of 1873, on the Canadian River in the Chickasaw Nation.

Isaac Filmore was a Chickasaw Indian, seventeen years old; he was hanged for the murder of an unknown white man near Fishertown in the Creek Nation, in June, 1873, the object being robbery.

McClish Impson, a young and ignorant Indian, was the next to be hurled into eternity in the name of the law; he was hanged January 15, 1875, for killing an unknown white man in 1873. On the scaffold he confessed the crime and said his father's teachings had brought him to the gallows.

THE FAMOUS SEXTETTE

The scaffold which swung John Childers to his death, and which was built large enough to launch twelve men into eternity "all in a bunch," was destined twenty-five months later, September 3, 1875, to be tested to just half its capacity. The event, looked upon as such, is notable as being the first time on record at which six human beings were legally executed in America at one time; that many were hanged there upon another occasion, years after. The scaffold was strongly built, and it bore its fated burden without a tremor. The victims of this execution were Daniel Evans, a white man twenty years old, with respectable connections in Missouri, Tennessee and Texas, convicted May 19, 1875, of the cold-blooded murder of a young Texan named Seabolt; John Whittington, white, thirty years, convicted June 16 of the same year of the murder of John J. Turner, a white man; Edmund Campbell, a negro, convicted May 27* of the murder of one Lawson Ross and a young negress; James Moore, white, twenty eight years, convicted May 25, of the murder of William Spivey in the Cherokee Nation; Smoker Man-killer, a Cherokee Indian, nineteen years old, convicted June 2, of the murder of William Short, a neighbor; and Samuel Fooy, a Cherokee Indian, twenty-six years old, convicted June 25, of killing in cold blood a man named J. E Neff, a school teacher.

The trial of the first of these, Daniel Evans, was a very interesting case, and was remarkable as showing upon how slight a thread often depend the chances of escape to a vicious criminal.

A dead body, that of a boy about nineteen years old, name unknown, had been found in a strip of timber land skirting a small stream in the Creek Nation; a few miles away, with a bullet through its brain, was the body of a small gray pony, and at another place, hidden away in a clump of bushes, was a well-worn saddle. The feet of the dead boy were without boots or shoes, while hidden beneath a stone were an old pair of coarse heavy shoes. In one of the pockets of his clothing was a pocket book bearing the name, "Seabolt."

The finding of the body and articles named started an investigation by the officers; persons living in the vicinity were soon found who remembered seeing, a few days previously, a man and a boy, the latter wearing a pair of new boots with high heels and fancy tops, and riding a large bay horse with a fine new saddle, while the man with him was riding a small gray pony with an old saddle, and had his feet incased in a pair of heavy shoes, old and considerably worn. A little later, a man about twenty years old, answering the description of the man who had been seen riding the gray pony, was arrested near Eufaula, where resided a. brother of Evans. He was in possession of a large and beautiful bay, with a fine new saddle; he also had on his feet a pair of high heeled and fancy topped boots nearly new. The circumstances seemed clearly to warrant the stranger's arrest, although he told a very plausible story of his connections and the circumstances concerning the property found in his possession, saying he had traded with the boy and that they had afterwards parted company by common consent. Despite his protests he was conveyed to Fort Smith; he was given a hearing before one of the United States commissioners, was held in jail to await the investigation of his case by the United States grand jury, and later that body returned a true bill of indictment against him, charging him with the murder of a boy to them unknown; the indictment bears date of November 2 7, 1874.

Evans, for so his name proved to be, was arraigned the next day before Judge Caldwell, who was then holding court temporarily by reason of Judge Story's resignation, Evans pleading not guilty as charged in the indictment and employing H.

A. Rogers and William M. Cravens to defend him, the case being set for trial December 8, following. The trial lasted two days and the jury stood for sixty hours, unable to agree, standing eleven to one for conviction, the lone juryman, who had probably never seen eleven others so contrary, being P. T. Devaney of Fort Smith.

On December 10, the jurors were discharged, Evans was returned to jail and the case was again set to be tried May 14, of the following year. At the appointed time Hon. Isaac C. Parker had just recently been installed as judge of the Federal Court for the Western District of Arkansas, and this was the first murder case tried before him. William H. H. Clayton, the vigorous young prosecutor, was then just becoming fairly accustomed to the work to which he was appointed in July, 1874, and he prepared for the prosecution of Evans, full of determination to convict, believing him to be guilty of the crime, but the evidence he had thus far been able to produce was purely circumstantial, and remembering the failure of the former jury to arrive at a verdict, it was not without a degree of nervousness that he went into the trial, which came on Monday, May 17, On the previous Friday the counsel for defense had appeared in court and on their motion Messrs. Bond and Robinson were appointed to assist in the defense, the motion for a continuance of the case being overruled.

On Monday, as stated, the trial commenced, and a greater portion of the evidence was taken. That evening as District Attorney Clayton sat in his office thinking deeply on the case and fearing an acquittal, without more evidence for the prosecution, his reverie was disturbed by the entrance of a stranger, a man of about forty years. He introduced himself:

"My name is Seabolt. My home is near McKinney, Texas. I am the father of the boy murdered by Dan Evans now on trial for murder"

This startling announcement nearly caused the young prosecutor to fall off his chair, but he retained his composure and asked the stranger for his story.

"I live near McKinney," he repeated. "My son and Dan Evans, whose parents live in Bosque county, twenty-five miles from Waco, Texas, left Texas, next October is a year ago. In November was the last I heard from him, as they were leaving Denison, Texas, for the Territory. The horse my son rode was a large bay that I had given him, and Evans rode a gray pony and an old saddle, while my son's saddle was a good and new one. Just before they left home I gave my son a new pair of boots; I bought myself a pair at the same time; they were exactly alike," and he raised one foot to the level of the table in order that Clayton could have a good view of the boot incasing it.

The prosecutor's heart began to beat faster. That boot, with its high heel and fancy top, was an exact mate, to all appearances, to the ones now worn by Evans.

"One of the heels came off," continued the speaker, "just before my boy left home, and he put it back and drove three horse-shoe nails into it to hold it in place. I think it was the left boot, and I remember that he did not get it back on quite as it was before and you could see the place where it had been joined anew; and, if I remember rightly, he also drove three horse-shoe nails into the heel of the other boot to keep it from coming off, too."

Prosecutor Clayton was now in ecstacy. What a strange coincidence that the father of the victim, of whom the government had hitherto known nothing, should come just at this time, prepared to furnish just the missing evidence needed to-insure a conviction. After a few words of council, the father went to a quiet boarding house, designated by the attorney, with instructions to remain there until he should send for him.

The next morning the attorneys for defense submitted their closing testimony and rested, and to the query of the judge, the district attorney answered, "Call Mr. Seabolt." As he said this, Evans was seen to turn nervously, and a look of keen inquiry came into the faces of his counsel. The father went to the stand and related the facts concerning his son as he had previously told them to the prosecutor, and at the close of the story all eyes, including those of the judge and jury, and even of the attorneys for defense, were cast upon Evans, who sat a little back, his feet thrust beneath one of the attorney's chairs. He was at once called up and made to raise his feet in full view of the jury, and, during breathless silence, Clayton pointed to the heads of the three hor.-e shoe nails in the heels of each boot and to the unmistakable indications of the heel from the left boot having been at some time removed and replaced. A comparison of the boots with those worn by the witness completed the testimony. Arguments by counsel were made the next day, and, after being out but a few minutes, the jury returned with a verdict of guilty of murder, as charged in the indictment. A short time later, June 26, the death sentence, the first in Judge Parker's experience, was pronounced upon him.

During his confinement, Evans had exhibited a gay and careless demeanor, and as his sentence was pronounced he cheerfully thanked the judge, and his face took on a scornful smile as, tears filling Judge Parker's eyes, he bowed his head and wept. According to Evans' statements, he had been a long time associated with outlaws. He told of riding with various scouts, and claimed to have assisted Jim Reed (noted elsewhere in this work) and his pal, Wilder, on November 19, 1873, in robbing Watt Grayson, in the Cherokee Nation, of $30,000 in gold coin (Wilder was arrested for this and given a penitentiary sentence). Evans claimed to have held burning pine torches to the bare feet of old man Grayson to make him divulge the hiding place of his money. He also claimed to have been nearby at the time Jim Reed was killed, near McKinney, Texas. This was untrue, as at the time Reed was killed Evans was in the toils.

For the statements concerning the remaining five who were executed with Evans, I am indebted to J, W. Weaver, a veteran newspaper man, one of the few remaining pioneers of Western Arkansas, now past eighty years old, and who was then a writer for the Fort Smith Independent and a valued correspondent of the New York Herald and several other of the big Eastern dailies. I have also to acknowledge having the kind permission of Mr. Weaver to glean much information of value concerning the early cases from a series of copyrighted reminiscences, published from his pen in recent years, in the Fort Smith Weekly Elevator, the files of which publication have been of great assistance to the compiler.

James Moore was a native of Johnson County, Missouri, but while he was but a babe his parents removed to Grayson County, Texas, and there they resided at the time their son was executed. Before he had attained his majority he, had become a member of a daring band of Indian Territory outlaws, whose field of operations reached from the Missouri and Kansas lines to the western counties of Texas.

On the night of August 6, 1874, he and an outlaw named Hunton robbed a crippled farmer, named Cox, residing in Washington County, near the site of the old Federal barracks known as "Fort Wayne." Hunton stood guard while Moore took the old man's two horses. A citizens posse followed them to Fort Gibson and thence to Eufaula, where one of the pursuers boarded a train while the others followed the trail. At Atoka the lone pursuer saw them as he was leaving the train and he hastily gathered a fresh posse, and Moore and his associate were followed a hot chase for over one hundred miles, finally being overtaken at the Little Blue, near Red River. Brought to bay, the bandits opened a desperate fight and one of the pursuers, William Spivey, fell dead, a bullet in his brain. It was at night, and the two bandits lost their horses and became lost to each other, both escaping from the posse. Hunton, for some reason, turned back over the route they had come and was met and captured by the posse on horseback, previously mentioned; they returned with him to Washington County, where he was allowed to plead guilty to horse stealing, being let off easily on account of valuable information furnished to his captors. He was placed in the Federal jail at Fort Smith; soon after he escaped, was pursued to the Indian country and killed by the officers who attempted to arrest him.

After the killing of Spivey, Moore had made his way back to Caddo, a station on the Missouri, Kansas & Texas Railroad, about seven miles from the Blue River, and taking a train went to Eufaula, where he hired a negro to convey him to the camp of a drover with a bunch of cattle enroute from Texas to Missouri. From there he sent a confederate named Nowlin, to Fort Wayne to ascertain the lay of the land and also to make arrangements to sell the cattle, the intention being, as the officers had been informed by Hunton, to murder the drover, then sell the cattle as their own. Nowlin proceeded to a cattle distributing point near the Arkansas line, in the State, bargained for feed, representing the cattle as his own, and began negotiating for their sale. To his surprise, he was quickly recognized and, after being arrested, he confessed to the intended plot and stated, as had Hunton, that Moore would be found in the drover's camp hid in the wagon. Possessed of the clew, two officers started out and on September 10, 1874, stopped at the camp of the drover, one mile east of Fort Gibson, near the National Cemetery. Moore was found lying on his back in a ravine, his clothing saturated with perspiration, the result of fear. He had seen the officers and had attempted to escape, but being very lame from a bullet received in the leg during the fight on Blue River, he could go no farther, and when arrested he begged the officers not to shoot him. He talked freely of his past, told of his birth-place and of his having been a cow-herder on the Texas plains from boyhood; he had fought Indians and had been twice before shot in the leg that stopped the bullet on the Blue, and until his capture he had supposed that fight to be with a party of Texans. He was curious to know how the officers learned of his presence with the drover; he suspected the infidelity of Hunton, but declined to tell of that which concerned others than himself. He did not express sorrow nor surprise when informed of Spivey's death, but said, boastfully, that, "If I have killed Spivey he was the eighth man I've killed— niggers and Indians I don't count." He stated that if he ever got out of "this scrape" he would go back to the old life; that he never intended to work for a living; that the world owed him a living and, "I'll have it if I have to war on civilization to get it."

The capture of Hunton, Moore and Nowlin was the winding up of an organized band of horse and cattle thieves that had been thriving for three years; several men who had not been suspected of outlawry disappeared soon after the three had been captured, probably fearing treachery on their part, Nowlin was turned over to a Texas sheriff and returned to the Lone Star State for trial on a serious charge. At Moore's trial he denied being present at the killing of Spivey, claiming to have been one hundred miles away. He acknowledged at the last, that he had been a wayward boy and that his parents had never been able to control him.

Samuel Fooy was less than half of Cherokee blood and was nearly white. He has a son still living in the Indian Territory. He had a fair education, but in his confession to Mr. Weaver, published after his execution, he admitted that even as a boy he had preferred the company of bad boys to properly spending his time in the school room. His father, James C. Fooy, and uncle, Benjamin Fooy, from Memphis, Tennessee, had both lived in Fort Smith, where the boy, Sam, was born in 1849, and both had later removed to the Cherokee Nation, where they died, the mother of Sam afterwards remarrying. By his own statements, the step-father tried to train him rightly and his good Christian mother often prayed with him to leave off his evil ways and companions but to no avail. He loved intoxicants and the interiors of the rough dives, by courtesy called saloons, in Fort Smith were frequent witnesses to his debaucheries; nearly every Saturday he would go to town, with others of his ilk, and indulge in the wildest kind of sprees. He had several difficulties with the authorities, always escaping conviction, but the crime of murder brought him down. In his confession and statement he said, "I have broken all of the Ten Commandments." The story of his last crime is gleaned from the Fort Smith Independent:

A young white man, John Emmit Neff, employed to teach school at Tahlequah, had received as his recompense $250, and started to tramp to the Illinois River. He was known as "The Barefooted School Teacher." Night overtook him at the home of a Mrs. Stevenson, a sister of Sam Fooy. The following morning Neff tendered a five dollar bill in payment of the fifty cents he owed the woman and as she had no change he promised to leave the money he owed at a certain store several miles distant. He started off, accompanied by Sam Fooy, and was never again seen in life. About a year later a skeleton was found lying by the Illinois River, at the foot of a high bluff; in the skull was imbedded a leaden bullet. Sometime later, an Indian boy, while exploring the fatal spot, found a partially bound book and on the fly leaf the name of the missing school teacher, his late residence and other memoranda, also a quotation in Latin from Horace, book 1, ode 4, which reads, in English, "Pale death treads with even step the hovels of the poor and the palaces of kings;" other articles found nearby were identified as having been the property of the school teacher. Only a few weeks after the murder, Fooy had confessed the crime to Stevenson, his brother-in-law, begging him to keep the terrible secret, and later told of the deed to a young woman of whom he was enamored. The confessions afterwards assisted in his conviction. He left a wife and three children, at Webbers Falls, in the Cherokee Nation; one of the latter, a young man about twenty-eight years old, walked into the office of the Fort Smith Elevator one day in December, 1898, and seeing a piece of the old gallows beam hanging on the wall requested a piece from it, saying, "My father was hanged from that beam.'"

John Whittington, also known as William Jackson Whittington, was a native of Reynolds, Taylor County, Georgia, but was reared in Upshur County, Texas. In 1870 he removed to the Chickasaw N Hon, where, at the time of his execution, his wife and mother with his two children resided. A letter written by him under the caption "How I Came TO THE Gallows," was read to the crowd of sight-seers by Rev. H. M. Granade just before the drop fell. It was published by Mr. Weaver. It is given in full, and is truly a sermon worthy of heed.

"My father taught me to be honest and avoid those great sins that disgrace the world, but he did not teach me to be religious. If he had I would have been a Christian from my boyhood. I was just what my father taught me to be." He showed me how to drink whiskey, and set me the example of getting drunk. I took to this practice and this is what has brought me to the gallows. When I got drunk I knew not what I was doing and so I killed my best friend. If it had been my brother it would have been the same. If I had been blessed with the good instruction I have had since I have been in prison I would be a good and happy man to-day with my family. Oh! what will become of my poor wife and two dear little boys, who are away out on Red River? I fear that people will slight them, and compel them to go into low, bad company, on account of the disgrace that I have brought upon them. But I leave them in the hands of that gracious God in whom I have learned to trust * * * Oh! that men would leave off drinking altogether. And, O, parents, I send forth this dying warning to you to-day, standing on the gallows: 'Train tip your children in the way they should go.' My father's example brought me to ruin. God save us all! Farewell! Farewell!

"William Jackson Whittington. "Fort Smith, Arkansas, September 3, 1875."

On the Texas side of Red River, not far from Whittington's home in the Chickasaw Nation, where he was operating a farm for a citizen by the name of Simon James, was a vile rum shop, conducted by one Ottery, a man who lacked the courage to defy the law and operate in the Indian country, but who was so mean as to conduct his place as near as possible to the line, where it might serve as a bait to tempt the appetites of the red men and lure their money to his till. It was a bad place and murders there were of frequent occurrence, one man being killed there soon after Whittington's arrest. To this place Whittington had gone one Sabbath day, in company with a friend and neighbor, an old man named Turner, who, most unfortunately, had about $100 on his person. After freely indulging in the poison they had purchased they started for home. While yet a short distance away, Whittington became possessed of evil and seizing a club he struck the old man from his horse and in frenzy leaped to the ground and cut his victim's throat, but not forgetting, even though crazy drunk, to secure possession of the money. An eighteen-year-old son of Turner's had ridden out to meet his father and, while crossing a small opening in the timber, he discovered Whittington in the distance in the act of cutting the fatal gash. Not perceiving clearly, for the distance, what was taking place, only noticing that a man with two horses was busily engaged with something on the ground, the boy rode forward and finally recognized Whittington, who instantly fled, leaving the boy beside the bleeding corpse of his own father. The brave youngster gave chase and captured Whittington at the river'; the money was in his pockets and was identified as Turner's, and Whittington's knife, red with his victim's blood, was found on the ground close by the body.

Smoker Man-killer was from the Flint district, Cherokee Nation. He had a wife and a child. His mother, wife and two sisters visited him at the jail; they wept silently, evincing great grief and, the greatest possible proof of sincerity, made no noisy demonstration of sorrow. Smoker sat through it with the usual Indian stoicism, in moody silence. He denied the crime for which he was convicted; he denied being acquainted with William Short, although a neighbor; he claimed that John and Dick Welch killed Short. The man had been murdered on September 1, 1874. It was claimed at the trial that while Short was out hunting wild game he was met by Man-killer who greeted him pleasantly, speaking in Cherokee, then borrowed his gun and shot him dead. No cause was assigned for the cruel act. It was sworn on the stand that he afterwards openly boasted of his treachery, and other evidence satisfied the court and jury of his guilt. Man-killer could speak no word of English but he was fairly educated in his native tongue. To Mr. Weaver he said, a short while before the execution, that he was not guilty as charged, but he believed his punishment was a judgment of God upon him for killing a Cherokee Indian in self-defense, for which he was tried in a tribal court and acquitted.

Edmund Campbell (nicknamed "Heck"), the last of this noted sextette, was born on the old "Ring" farm in the Choctaw Nation about nine miles from Fort Smith. He could read, and he had a wife and two children. In company with his brother, Samuel Campbell, and Frank Butler, he went to the house of a colored neighbor, Lawson Ross, and in revenge for some real or fancied insult, he slew Ross and a young colored woman; he claimed to be guiltless of the charge against him

On the day named, the entire lot of six convicted felons were lined up with their feet squarely across the line where met the two planks forming the death-trap, and after prayer and the singing of gospel hymns the last farewells were spoken, the black caps were drawn and at the word all were shuffled off together; their necks were broken and all died without a struggle.

The event was the means more than any previously enacted, perhaps, in its entire history, of calling the attention of the world at large to the court, and its alleged cruel judge. Strangers from abroad, hearing of the unusual attraction, were observed to be centering at Fort Smith during the entire week preceding the execution. The announcement went out and many of the great Eastern and Northern daily newspapers sent representatives to report the scene. People from nearby towns, even from forty and fifty miles distant, began pouring into the city at daybreak, and by 10 o'clock it was estimated that 5,000 strangers were in town to witness the hanging. The reports given by the press acted as a shock to the people throughout Christendom, and no wonder. The cool destruction of six human lives by legal process is no small matter, and to the mind not conversant with the atrocity of the crimes committed, a feeling of human sympathy might naturally enough cause the belief that none but a heartless judge could be so lacking in compassion as to decree killing by wholesale. Let us criticise the system, not the man whose duty lay under it.

In his report of the execution, Mr. Weaver closed as follows: "Now that these desperadoes are gone, many will breath freely who have been active in their arrest and prosecution. On the growing youth of our country these terrible scenes should make a lasting impression. All these men were young and in the full prime of strength, and should have been active and useful members of society, the pride of their friends, the staff of their aged parents. And why does society, through the stern mandates of the law, thus consign these men to death and exterminate them from the earth? Because they are preying wolves upon the lives and property of their fellow beings, unfit to live and unsafe to remain at large. The moral should not be lost in the excitement and glare of the terrible exhibition, nor forgotten in the morbid curiosity which absorbs the mind in witnessing an event so rare and tragical.

"Cuniculi peltri ne reynard ecce assinus comerandum; ('More hides of foxes than of asses come to the tanners')."

A CARNIVAL OF HANGING

The following spring, April 21, 1876, less than a year from the time that Judge Parker took charge of the tribunal, Aaron Wilson and William Leach, white, with Isham Seely, Gibson Ishtonubbee (sometimes spelled Gibson Stone-Nubbee), and Orpheus (often called "Office") Magee, Indians, five victims of their own unlawful acts, were marched up to the gallows together, and in the presence of a few officers and representatives of the press, were sent to eternity, as evidence that outraged law knows no mercy. They completed the even dozen who were executed during the first year of Judge Parker's reign, one of the number, McClish Impson, having been convicted and sentenced in 1874 by Judge Caldwell.

On the day of this execution of five, the *Western Independent* of Fort Smith, published twelve columns concerning the men and their crimes under the caption: "A Carnival of Hanging!" Mr. Weaver, whose ready pen produced the copy for the two page article, began with these words:

"A little over seven months ago we laid before our readers the details of the execution of six men on the gallows in the prison yard of the United States Court. Today the same prison yard and the same gallows have again been the scene, and we are called upon to chronicle the hanging of five other men, sentenced at the last term of the United States Court, to be hanged for murders committed in the Indian Territory, to-wit: (Here follows the names as given above.) Osee Sanders was also to have been hanged today but on yesterday the following telegram was received:"

Washington City. D. C., April 19, 1876.

To J. F. Fagan:—I have this day granted a reprieve to Osee Sanders, sentenced to be hanged on the 21st inst. Suspend his execution. Acknowledge receipt. U. S. Grant.

"It might have been expected that, with the number of previous hanging', the morbid appetite would have been satiated and but few would be present on this occasion, but the crowd was as great, if not greater, than at any previous execution. Since yesterday people have been coming from all quarters, and the roads thronged with comers until the town was crowded, and early this morning they hastened to take positions as near the gallows as possible to make sure of being present at the first act of the drama. The number present must have been between six and seven thousand.

Then followed a description of the execution, which passed off quietly and orderly, concluding with long sketches of the lives of the men hanged, together with stories of the crimes for which they were executed. From the columns of matter the following is principally gleaned: William Leach was forty-four years old, a native of Georgia but a long time resident in the Cherokee Nation, where he had married a Cherokee woman; his home was about twenty-five miles west of Fayetteville, Arkansas. From facts brought out at the trial it seems that John Wadkins, for whose murder Leach was hanged, a neighbor of Leach, left the latter's house on Monday, March 8, 1875, between 9 and 10 o'clock, intending to go to Fayetteville. He was accompanied by Leach, who had been requested by Wadkins to conduct him to the Fayetteville road. An hour later they were seen at Foreman's blacksmith shop, three miles from Leach's house, where the latter's horses were shod; they left together, Wadkins riding the horse, carrying a fiddle under his arm, and Leach walking, carrying a gun. Wadkins had been expected at Fayetteville; he did not appear, and soon word of inquiry was passed back over the road and Leach was questioned, only to give vague and unsatisfactory answers. Just a month after Wadkins was last seen alive, a man while hunting wild turkeys, was attracted to a spot about which a lot of buzzards were hovered and there he discovered a human skeleton.

Evidences of a brutal murder abounded; a fire had been made in the dry leaves as if with the intention of burning the corpse and thus destroying all traces of the crime or chances for identification; the larger bones were charred and most of the smaller ones burned. The skull, lying several yards away, had been punctured by a bullet, and one of the ribs showed what appeared to be the marks of a bullet, the conditions indicating that the shot had been fired from the rear and had punctured the rib in passing out of the body. At a point seventy-five yards away were the embers from a fire that had been built with small sticks and on scraping away the ashes clotted blood was discovered. A few steps from this place there were indications of a heavy body having been dragged (here also had been a fire and blood was found beneath the embers), the trail continuing to the spot where the bones were found. Among the latter were found a piece of cat-gut, a knife, pieces of the clothing worn by Wadkins, a screwdriver and close by a glove, all articles known to have been in Wadkins' possession.

United States Commissioner Harrison, at Fayetteville, issued a warrant; Leach was arrested, examined and committed for trial at the Federal court at Fort Smith. Leach had several times attempted to sell a pair of boots, which were produced on the stand and proven to be the ones worn by Wadkins when last seen. On December 20, 1875, Leach was convicted of murder and was sentenced to pay the penalty for shedding man's blood by the forfeiture of his own life on the gallows. Leach wrote a lengthy statement of his life, containing much of little real interest, but neither affirming nor denying his guilt. He admitted having been a very profane and wicked man and a gambler. Near the close of the statement he said:

"A life of such dissipation I now feel has had a blighting influence and has brought me to my present condition. I therefore warn all young men not to engage in such a life. I had early impressions that ought to have made me a religious man, but I stoutly resisted. Again and again I resisted. Oh! had I yielded, I had been saved all the sorrow and remorse I have since endured on account of my sins. I earnestly pray that all who read these lines may take warning and not resist the spirit of God. My resistance had well-nigh proved my eternal rum."

Isham Seely, twenty-one years old, and his uncle, Gibson Ishtonubbee, twenty-four, both Chickasaws, were convicted of the murder of a Mrs. Mason and a white man named Funny (called "Squirrel" in the Chickasaw tongue). Funny resided eight miles from Stonewall; he employed a colored woman Mrs. Mason, as cook. Sometime previous to the killing, Isham and Gibson had threatened the life of the man, for no given cause, although the former, in his ante mortem statement, said that the white man had attempted to kill his brother three days before the murder. Some grudge, at least, rankled in the hearts of the Indians, and on the night of May 10, 1873, they proceeded, fifteen miles, to the white man's house, about midnight. Seely first killed Funny's horse, and then the two called up the occupants, asked permission to stay all night, and the permission was granted. Just before day-break they both arose. Gibson went into the yard and procured an axe, while Seely procured a gun-barrel with which he struck the colored woman on the head, killing her; then the uncle knocked Funny on the head with the axe and Seely took the victim's knife and finished the job by cutting the man's throat. The Indians then took from the house a pair of boots, pantaloons and a dress. Before being arrested they traded off the boots, burned the pantaloons and hid the dress in a hollow log back of the field, to rot. Who can tell why they took these garments from the house at all? Both men made full and free confession of the crime.

Orpheus (corrupted to Office), McGee, a Choctaw Indian, was executed for the murder of Robert Alexander. His conviction was the result, purely, of circumstantial evidence. His victim was last seen alive by his friends on April 20, 1874. Two days later his corpse was found sixty yards back from an old road in the timber, within two miles of the home of his brother, "Red" Alexander. In the confession made by McGee, just before his execution, he contended that the Alexander brothers had not long before killed a Choctaw Indian, and for which they were not tried. McGee seems to have brooded over the said killing, and to have killed one of the said brothers for revenge. On the day noted, Alexander had called at the home of one Conrad Miller about 3 o'clock in the afternoon, and, after an hour or more, hearing a wild turkey gobble not far away, he took his gun and started out to shoot it. Half an hour later the report of two gun shots were heard. Miller had expected Alexander to return for supper and as he did not,a horn was blown for him, and as he was still absent the next morning, Miller notified the brother, and the two searched the entire day without success. The next day they were accompanied by a negro boy who at last discovered the man's dead body; one of the bullets had entered the front part of the neck, glanced downwards and come out of the center of the back. The gun carried by the murdered man was found in McGee's possession. McGee was convicted in December following. In his confession he said there was another man with him when he met Alexander. He said: "I took his gun from him and shot him down, then took his pistol and shot him with it. It was about sundown." At the close of his statement he said: "Try and do right. My mother tried to teach me right, but I would not listen to her. The Choctaws have bad laws that make men do wrong. There ought to be preachers all over the nation to teach them right."

Aaron Wilson, the fifth of the lot hanged at this time, was a big, burly negro, twenty-five years old. About the middle of August, 1875, James Harris, an old man of fifty-six years, and his little son, John F. Harris, twelve years old, started from Beatty, Kansas, with a wagon and three horses, the wagon loaded with the remnant of a stock of goods taken from a store James Harris had operated in the Sunflower State. They had, also, a double and a single barreled shotgun, and a dog. They started for Texas, and their route led them by Fort Sill, in the Indian Territory, then in command of Gen. McKenzie. Not far from the fort the travelers passed a camp of Comanche Indians, among whom was Aaron Wilson. An hour later the negro mounted an old gray horse and left the camp, going in the direction taken by the wagon. He followed on for two days, and finally stopped at their camp and partook of their hospitality, ate a hearty supper and laid down to sleep by their fire, wrapped in a proffered blanket. At midnight he awoke and killed the old man by a blow with an axe; the dying agonies of the father awoke the son. The frightened boy begged, pleaded for mercy, promised to do anything for the ruffian, to love him, work for him—all in vain. After amusing himself with the boy's fears and prayers, the brute pulled the double barreled weapon from the wagon, and, after shooting the poor little fellow, at close range, full in the center of the breast, tearing a fearful hole through the body, pointed the gun at the dead father and planted the contents of the second barrel in the right breast; he then removed the clothing from the old man's body, searched the pockets thoroughly, wrapped the body in the quilt under which he had slept, and carried it about twenty-five yards, dropping it behind the roots of an upturned tree; the body of the boy he carried 175 yards in an opposite direction and left it uncovered. He then removed a soldier's old uniform he had been wearing and clothed himself in a new suit taken from the old man's stock. Next he secured the three horses belonging to his victims, left his own to care for itself, and four days from the time the father and son had passed the Comanche village, he returned just at dark with one of the shotguns and the three horses. The barking of a dog aroused the attention of the chief, and going out he saw a man with his head wrapped in a blanket. The chief pulled the blanket away and discovered it was Wilson. He said he had taken the gun from the wagon of two white men he had killed, "beyond, on the other side of the post." The chief recognized the horses as belonging to the old man who passed a few days before, and borrowing one of them he went to the post to notify the Indian agent. Wilson took fright and ran away, but was arrested next day by Lieut. Leeper, who had been detailed with a squad to search for the bodies of some men who had been murdered. The prisoner, under duress, conducted the officer and his men to the scene of his double crime, where all was found as described. In the left boot of the old man was near $350 in government money which the negro had missed.

Osee Sanders, a Cherokee Indian, twenty-nine years old, who was reprieved on this occasion only to be again brought out and executed with three others early in

September following, was convicted of killing Thomas S. Carlyle, a white man, on August 6, 1875. Carlyle had a Cherokee wife; he resided on a farm twelve miles from Tahlequah. About dark on the day stated Carlyle and his wife were seated in the passage that separated their double house (a style of architecture frequently seen in that country), when Osee Sanders and a stranger rode to the gate and spoke pleasantly. Carlyle invited them in and sent his little boy to open the gate, which was fastened on the inside. As the men approached the house they each carried their pistols in their hands. The stranger at once commenced a struggle with Carlyle, and Sanders covered the wife with his weapon; taking fright, she called her children and they ran 150 yards from the house, hiding in the tall grass. As they ran they heard three shots fired, and when they returned an hour later they found the husband and father lying in a pool of his own blood, dead. A pocketbook containing a small sum of money was gone, as was also a trunk containing $1,200 in money and Cherokee warrants, which had been kept in the house. Sanders lived three miles away. He was arrested the next day.

The story given above was told by Mrs. Carlyle on the stand during the trial. Sanders maintained his innocence; and produced evidence to prove that in the afternoon of the day on which Carlyle was murdered, Sanders was taken violently ill, being obliged to go to his bed, where he remained till the next morning. Sanders' alleged confederate nor the man who really killed Carlyle (if Sanders was innocent) were ever apprehended. Sanders died protesting that Carlyle was his best friend and that he had never harmed a hair of the white man's head.

In closing his report of the execution that day. Mr. Weaver said:

"This is a fearful commentary on the morals of the Indian country, and terrible as such scenes are, and shocking as they must be to the finer feelings of humanity, it must be admitted that such crimes as these men were found guilty of, merit the severe punishment meted out to them. The certainty of punishment is the only sure preventative of crime and the administration of the laws by Judge I. C. Parker, since his advent as judge of the United States Court for the Western District of Arkansas, has made him a terror to all evil doers in the Indian country. The determination shown by the judge that the laws shall be faithfully and fearlessly administered, and the firmness he has displayed during the less than twelve months he has sat on the bench, has won for him the confidence and respect of the members of the bar and our citizens, as well as of the law-abiding men of all races in the Indian Territory, and it will soon remove from the Western District of Arkansas the odium under which he found it."

NEARLY FOURTEEN YEARS OF CRIME

During the period following the second great execution, narrated in the last chapter, and previous to the sixteenth day of January, 1890, nearly fourteen years, the appalling number of ninety-three men were convicted of murder (or rape) committed in the Indian Territory, and ninety-two were sentenced to hang. Of the ninety-three noted, forty-six died on the scaffold, one died in jail while awaiting sentence, two died in jail after receiving sentence, while awaiting the day of execution, forty were commuted by the president to terms of from four years to life imprisonment in the penitentiaries at Detroit, Michigan, Columbus, Ohio, Albany, New York, Little Rock, Arkansas, Joliet and Menard, Illinois, and at Moundsville, West Virginia; two were granted new trials before Judge Parker and were discharged and two were granted executive clemency—were pardoned by the president—one of these having already served one year of the life sentence that had been pronounced upon him. Surely this was an evidence of swift retribution and a warning to law breakers. Little wonder is it, the guide board on the Canadian River, pointing towards Fort Smith, was a target for the apparently fearless outlaws, who yet had a wholesome fear of Judge Parker's court; little wonder that the spot where the sign board stood was said to be only "Five hundred miles from hell." It was a much shorter distance than five hundred miles for some of them.

A TOUGH QUARTETTE

Less than five months after the famous execution just detailed, on September 8, 1876, four men convicted of murder committed in the Indian Territory, Osee Sanders and three others, John Valley, white; Sinker Wilson, Indian, and Samuel Peters, negro, formed a quartette on the trap that was becoming noteworthy, and had been named by Federal prisoners "The gates of hell."

Valley was executed for killing Eli Hackett, in the Cherokee Nation. Sinker Wilson died for the murder of Datus Cowan, in the Cherokee Nation in 1867; he was arrested, convicted and sentenced the same year, by the court at Van Buren, but afterwards escaped and prolonged his life nine years, but, at last, the fate which hung over all criminals within the jurisdiction of the Fort Smith court, and which was as inexorable as the law of the Medes and Persians, overtook him and he was re-sentenced June 24, 1876. Samuel Peters killed Charity Hanson, in the Choctaw Nation; he was convicted June 2 1, 1876.

In the following year, 1877, six convictions of murder and one of rape were secured, making, with the murder convictions secured in December, 1876, ten malefactors who were sentenced to die by the rope. The first three, Black Crow, Irving Perkins and Charles Thomas were to have hanged April 26, 1877, and the rest, William J. Meadows, Joshua Wade (rapist), Thomas Robinson, Carolina Grayson, Peter Grayson and Man Lewis were to have made the fatal plunge January 21, 1878; the entire ten were fortunate in gaining the assistance of able counsel and the ear of the president and their sentences were commuted to terms in the penitentiaries.

Irving murdered his illegitimate babe, the offspring of his step-daughter. Black Crow was convicted of the murder of a son of Dr. Holloway at Fort Sill, in 1875. Joshua Wade's victim was Miss Elizabeth Hale. Thomas Robinson was convicted of the murder of Pat Common, July 10, 1877.

The two Graysons, Man Lewis and Robert Love were four negroes out of nine who were tried for the murder of a negro named Perry Ross, in the Creek Nation, May 15, 1877. They were sent to Detroit, Michigan. On July 1, 1887, word came to the officers at Fort Smith that Carolina Grayson had died, leaving a confession, stating that he alone was guilty of the murder. He said that although, the others, were all at the house of Ross and all knew there was likely to be trouble; he was the only man-who fired a shot.

The next year two, one negro and one Indian, were tried, convicted and hanged, execution being given December 20, of that year. The Indian, bearing the euphonious name of John Postoak, was convicted of the murder of John Ingley and his wife, in the Creek Nation. The negro, James Diggs, was convicted of the deliberately planned and cold blooded murder of J. C. Gould, in 1873. The crime was most dastardly and the details leading up to the conviction were very interesting, reflecting great credit upon the skill arid determination of Deputy United States Marshal James C. Wilkinson, whose home is on a farm near Fort Smith, and who is now one of the guards at the Federal jail at Muscogee, who worked up the case after all others had abandoned it.

In the summer of 1873, a cattle-drover, J. C. Gould, with his employes, Hiram Mann, a white man, and James Diggs were traveling through the northern part of the Indian Territory, near the Kansas line. On the fourth day of August, at the close of the day, they arrived at a deserted cabin and camped for the night. Early the following morning Diggs startled some people living in the vicinity by the fearful intelligence that Gould and Mann had been murdered by two mounted Texans who came just before daylight and killed his companions, chasing him into the woods where he lay concealed under a log until the pursuers departed. A number of citizens hastened to the scene of the tragedy and discovered the victims lying side by side in a pool of their own blood. Gould was cold in death's embrace; Mann was unconscious and apparently gasping his last. Both their skulls were fractured, and a bloody axe nearby proclaimed itself the instrument by which the horrible deed had been committed. An examination of the premises failed to find any evidences of horses having been near, neither was there found the log to whose shelter Diggs claimed he had fled. Suspicion pointed to the negro as the murderer and he was rigidly questioned. He claimed to have no money, but $27 in greenbacks were found under the lining of his coat; it was ascertained that Gould had recently been paid that amount of money in corresponding bills.

Diggs was arrested and taken to Fort Smith, where he was held in jail for awhile, but no Judge Parker then sat upon the bench and, as no witnesses put in an appearance, he was released. Deputy Wilkinson heard of the case after being sworn in as an officer of the court and he succeeded at that late day in obtaining some clues and followed them with such intelligence and energy that he soon discovered Diggs and took him into custody. The witnesses were scattered to different parts of the country, in the long interval that had elapsed since the crime. One had gone to Michigan, one to Ohio and others were in Kansas, Missouri and in various parts of the Indian Territory. The man who was supposed to have been killed with Gould had continued unconscious for thirty days and had not recovered from the effects of his wounds until after Diggs' release and he had then emigrated to Michigan.

The trial lasted three days and the evidence was so direct that the jury returned a verdict of guilty after only a brief deliberation.

The year 1879, also, was noted for the small number of convictions for capital offenses. The criminal business was light throughout the year and Judge Parker was able to give time to a large number of civil cases, in which he handed down opinions that have since been widely quoted. Of those convicted of murder during 1879, one died in jail while awaiting his turn to tread the fatal plank; another was commuted. The cases of William Elliott and Dr. Henri Stewart, who were executed, and Uriah M. Cooper, commuted, were interesting cases and are thus briefly outlined:

Dr. Stewart was a man thirty-five years old, of good address and good education. He was born in the Choctaw Nation. His father was white and his mother part Indian. He was educated at Yale and Harvard, taking up the study of medicine. After graduating he held positions as ship physician and in this capacity had been in Cuba and along the coast of South America and California. He had returned to the

Indian Territory a short time before the murder and had at once begun a career of recklessness. He was, for a time, a member of the notorious Sam Bass gang of train robbers which created so much excitement in Texas in 1877 and '78. Stewart left a wife and four children and step-mother in Illinois; he had a brother in Kansas. In early May, 1879, at Caddo, a station on the Missouri, Kansas & Texas Railroad, in the Choctaw Nation, thirty-five miles from Denison, Texas, Stewart, in company with Wiley Stewart, his cousin, rode to the railroad depot and accosted Dr. J. B. Jones, who stood on the ground near the depot platform, and Henri fired from a six-shooter, the bullet doing no harm; the cousin, who was very drunk, thereupon fired, killing Jones instantly. Both men escaped and Henri Stewart was subsequently captured in Missouri; Wiley Stewart was never caught. Twenty-three witnesses were placed on the stand in the trial of Dr. Stewart and the testimony of the prisoner was the same as all the rest, except that he claimed he only shot into the ground to call the attention of his cousin and induce him "To come on home." He explained as his reasons for fleeing to Missouri, that he was afraid of the people, knowing that his previous bad record would be against him and he thought he would be lynched if he stayed about home. He was convicted May 16, 1879, little more than a year after the killing of Dr. Jones.

William Elliott was hanged for the murder of David J. Brown, sometimes called "Cooke" Brown, February 23, 1879, at Muskogee. He was a native of Ohio. He went South with the Union army during the civil war, after which he drifted West and led a reckless life. He was a very bad man and was wanted in four different states for murder. He was convicted May 28, 1879, and a local paper said of him, speaking of the number of murder charges still hanging over him elsewhere: "He will hardly be wanted by any other state after they get through with him here."

Uriah M. Cooper killed Robert A. Donnelly at Caddo. Cooper was a photographer, well educated, but a physical wreck, the result of dissipation. Donnelly was an employe of the railroad company. While in discharge of his duties, at night, four or five men induced another employe, by threats, to go to the car where Donnelly was at work, and call him out, when Cooper shot him. It was sworn at the trial that he had previously threatened Donnelly's life. His friends made extra efforts to clear him; twenty-five witnesses were examined' the defendant tried hard to prove an alibi. Thos. Barnes, J. K. Barnes and C V. Buckley were counsel for defense, and District Attorney Clayton with George Grace conducted the prosecution. The fight was hard on both sides. The trial commenced December 3, 1879, and the testimony closed December 9. Two days were taken up by the arguments. When the jury returned the verdict, guilty, December 12, Cooper broke down; he cried like a child. March 29 he was brought before Judge Parker, and when asked if he had aught to say why sentence should not be pronounced upon him, he solemnly raised his right hand and with faltering voice, invoked Heaven to strengthen him while he made a few remarks. He said he had never threatened the life of Donnelly; that he was not dressed as was stated by the witnesses, and that he did not have a shotgun at the time and place stated. He said he fled the country to escape from Scott and Magee, who did the killing, and who had threatened to kill him. Then he excitedly exclaimed: "While my body stands before the court a wrecked vessel, my soul rides the waves of life perfectly free from all stain of the blood of Robert A. Donnelly;" in conclusion, he invoked the court to let the bitter cup pass.

Previous to June 18, 1880, the day named for his execution, his attorneys had gained the sympathy of the president and his sentence was commuted to life imprisonment.

The year 1880 goes down in the history of the court as being entirely free from judicial murders. Nine murder cases were tried at the August term but only one was convicted, Lum Smith, for the murder of Mike Allison, in the Indian country, in 1875. His sentence was commuted to life imprisonment, as was that of James Heaslet, convicted of murder February 18, 1880. Through the entire year the gallows stood idle and during the summer it was given a coat of white-wash. The good people of Fort Smith began to breathe freer, and reasoned that crime was on the decrease; they congratulated themselves that the days of what they considered to be Fort Smith's disgrace were passing away, but this thought was dispelled by the year following the year 1881, noted especially for the execution of no less than five men at one time, on September 9. The names of the men executed that day were: George Padgett, white; William Brown, white; Patrick McGowan, white; Amos Manley, Indian, and Abler Manley, Indian. The names of the victims of the first three, named in regular order, were: W. H. Stephens, Ralph C. Tate and Sam Latta. The two Indians. brothers, were convicted of the vicious killing of Ellis McVay in the Choctaw Nation, and with the other three mentioned, they paid the penalty for the dastardly act by being in turn robbed of their own lives. The three first named waited anxiously during President James A. Garfield's illness, hoping against hope that he would recover from the bullets sent hissing into his body by a murderer like themselves, believing that if returned to health and given opportunity to review their cases, he would extend to them either pardons or commutations. The martyred President was still lying upon his death-bed when their last hour arrived.

STORIES OF THE CRIMES

George W. Padgett was born in Smith County, Texas, November 20, 1858. His parents were farmers. His father died while he was a child, and his mother married again, and after that moved several times, to various Texas counties. Left largely to himself the boy grew up an admirer of the reckless, and as soon as he attained sufficient years he took up the occupation of "cow-puncher," learned to ride the fiercest and wildest bronchos, to leap the widest ditches and to "split a hair at forty yards" with his six-shooter. There was little intentionally wrong in his make-up, but he was full of daring and had much of bravado. In 1880 he left home and worked for W. T. Wagoner, a cattle man in Wichita county, Texas, bordering the Indian Territory. In 1881 he left Wagoner to assist W. H. Stephens drive a "bunch" of cattle to the Kansas market. On July 26, while in camp at the north fork of the Canadian river, at the mouth of Pond Creek, thirty-five miles south of Caldwell, Kansas, he discovered some cattle in Stephens' herd that he thought belonged to Wagoner. Before his leaving Texas, Wagoner had told him he thought some of his cattle, bearing a certain brand, were in Stephens' herd, and asked him to look out for them. He accosted Stephens about certain cattle, bearing a certain brand, and hot words ensued, during which Padgett whipped out his revolver and shot the other, who was unarmed, killing him. Padgett was unmarried.

William Brown was born in Davis county, Missouri, March, 1854. He went to Grayson county, Texas, with his parents and grew up as a cowboy. In 1878 he went to the Chickasaw Nation and married a Miss Love at White Bead Hill. In 1880 he went to Fort Sill, leaving his wife at home, and assisted in putting up hay for the use of the military post under a contractor named McGarvey. On the evening of August 19, all the men were sitting around pissing away the time till bed time; Brown and one Moore arranged a foot race on a wager of fifty cents on a side. Brown won the race, and Moore, being dissatisfied with the decision, the two disputed bitterly, Moore finally giving Brown a severe beating. Brown rushed to the house, and, when near there, someone handed him a gun. At once he stepped aside, and in the gathering darkness waited for Moore. A moment later someone rushed by his place of ambush and to the house, looked in at the window, and, turning, came back straight towards Brown, who shot and fled; the man whom he had taken for Moore, but who was Brown's best friend and room-mate, Ralph C. Tate, fell dead in his tracks. Brown went to his home at White Bead Hill, where he was horrified to learn whom he had killed. He immediately left for Texas, and soon after Tate's father came to his rendezvous, captured him and returned with him to Fort Sill, from where he was conveyed to Fort Smith, tried and convicted.

Patrick McGowan was born in Ireland March 17, 1846, and because of his having first seen the light on St. Patrick's Day, he was named Patrick. His father died and the mother, with her three sons and four daughters, removed to Burlington, New Jersey. In 1858 Patrick went to Philadelphia and engaged as clerk in a business house, continuing until 1862, when he went to Illinois, and while there enlisted from Rockport in the 12th Illinois Cavalry, rising to the rank of sergeant. In 1865 he went to Texas, and after two years returned to Illinois. In 1870 he returned to the Chickasaw Nation, and soon after married Mary Boutwell, daughter of a citizen, taking up the occupation of farming. In 1880 he leased twenty acres of farming land to Sam Latta. During the summer he accused Latta of trying to induce his young brother-in-law to steal some horses, and he tried to induce Latta to leave the farm. Latta sold his interests to William Boutwell, a brother of McGowan's wife. On July 13 Latta was at the house of the elder Boutwell, where his widowed sister lived. Latta went to the orchard for some purpose, and as he was returning he was shot in the right side; he screamed and fell dead. His sister saw McGowan run away. He was soon captured and taken to Fort Smith, was indicted and placed on trial. He claimed that Latta had threatened his life and claimed that he thought he had a right to put him out of the way in self-defense. He was ably defended by Thomas H. Barnes, James K. Barnes and William M. Mellette, but the jury could not see logic in the theories put forth by the defense and McGowan was convicted of murder.

The crime for which Amos and Abler Manley, Creek Indian boys, nineteen and seventeen years old, respectively, was perhaps one of the most dastardly of any ever planned or perpetrated in the Indian country. Murders are always foul and brutal, but this was a crime so unprovoked and so wholly unnecessary as to make almost any kind of punishment seem totally inadequate.

The Manly boys were born near Eufaula; their parents being farmers. On the night of December 3, 1880, between 10 and 11 o'clock, they went to the house of Ellis McVay, a white man, living on the line between the Creek and Choctaw nations, six miles from Eufaula. The family had retired and the brothers asked permission to enter and warm, the weather being very cold. McVay opened the door and stirred up the fire, returning to his bed. The brothers said they were going to a place ten or fifteen miles farther to engage at picking cotton. William Burnett, a young man from

St. Clair County, Missouri, had recently come to the Territory and had worked for McVay one month; he occupied a bed in one corner of the room. The Indians were given a pallet by the fire.

About 3 o'clock in the morning McVay arose and sat by the fire with one of his children who was sick. The Indians also rose and dressed, and asking for tobacco stood by the fireplace and smoked, passing McVay's pipe from one to the other. They talked to each other in the Creek language for a little while, and suddenly the older brother drew a pistol and fired; the younger brother also fired and McVay fell dead, shot once in the head and once or twice lower in the body. As he fell, he exclaimed, "O, Lord!" Burnett awoke and the Indians fired at him; the first shot missed and the second struck him in the side and he fell, As he went down he grappled with his assailants and while thus engaged, the elder one grabbed a double-edged axe and cut a fearful gash in Burnett's neck, and cut off his right hand at a single blow, the hand flying under the table. Burnett also received severe cuts on both legs and on the back, and was supposed to be dead. The fiends next started to attack Mrs. McVay, but before they reached her a big dog bounded up and standing in the door with his head towards the outside barked and barked loudly. Believing that men were approaching the house the murderers took fright and fled. Mrs. McVay looked out and, in the bright moonlight, she saw them reloading their pistols, and hastily taking her two children she ran in her night-clothes, with bare feet upon the frozen ground, three-fourths of a mile to the home of a neighbor, Dr. Tenants, crying out that some Indians had murdered her husband and Burnett, and were chasing her. Burnett soon followed her, bleeding profusely. He said the first he knew of his hand being gone, as he recovered consciousness, was when he reached for his Winchester and the bloody stump came in contact with the weapon. He recovered and, with the blood-stained axe, was a witness in court.

On the way to the scaffold William Brown fainted, after walking about one-third of the distance and the party halted while ice water was thrown on his head. He soon rose and remarked that he had been sick and that his nerves were not strong. On the scaffold-, Padgett said he was not guilty of murder in his heart; he said his life had been threatened by Latta. Brown spoke briefly, saying he did not kill the man he intended to, but an innocent man, his best friend; if he had killed the man he intended to he did not believe any jury would have convicted him for it. The Manly boys also confessed to their crime, but did not tell why they committed it.

Two others were convicted of murder in 1881, Tul-wa-har-jo, June 24, and Sah-quah-nee, August 9; the former was sentenced to be hanged at the same time as the quintet just noted, but, on application of his attorneys, a new trial was granted and Tul-wa-har-jo was discharged. This case was interesting from the fact that two while men were murdered, without the shadow of an excuse, by some members of a party of five, and the one above named was the only one ever captured.

The crimes were committed on the line between the Chickasaw and Seminole Nations, in May, 1880. The party of malefactors comprised Charley Bowlegs, colored (son of Billy Bowlegs of Florida notoriety), as leader, Tul-wa-har-jo and three others, Indians. Bowlegs afterwards committed suicide, another was killed in a quarrel and the others kept themselves out of reach of the officers.

The five men crossed the Canadian River into the Chickasaw Nation, in the neighborhood of where the white men, Scott Davis and one Bateman, lived, on the night before the murder, on pretense of gathering cattle. It must have been known to them that Scott Davis would also be out hunting cattle on the next day, and they posted themselves on a sand t; bar where they could see some distance about them. They soon saw Davis, in company with Thomas Factor, approach. Bowlegs and his party at once crossed over and secreted themselves in a ravine, commanding a view of the trail traversed by Davis and Factor. The two men came leisurely along, Factor being just in advance; as Davis came within range Bowlegs gave the order to fire and Davis fell from his horse, still alive, and one of the attacking party ran up to him and placing the muzzle of his gun to the head of the prostrate man, blew out his brains. They told Factor to "go on home;" and after concealing the body in a hollow tree near the scene of the murder, they went to the field, several miles distant, where Davis' partner, Bateman, was at work plowing. They crept to within a short distance of Bateman and Bowlegs again gave the order to fire, but the others refused, saying, "We killed one, you kill this one." Accordingly Bowlegs crept to the fence, and raising his Henry rifle to his shoulder, brought it to bear on the unsuspecting victim, shooting him through the body.

At the trial, Harjo admitted having fired one shot, but he said he did not know what the party were intending to do; that he was with them as interpreter, supposing they were looking for estrayed cattle; he said he was not with the others when Bateman was killed. Factor was arrested on the supposition that he conspired with the murderers to lead Davis into a trap, but he produced evidence to cause doubt in the minds of the jury and he was acquitted.

Se-quah-nee was convicted for the murder of an unknown white man in the Indian Territory in the summer of 1879. Se-quah-nee was a full-blood Indian of the Sac and Fox tribe. He was a man of powerful build and determined look, and coarse, heavy features; he was dressed a la mode Indian, hickory shirt, blue blanket, fringed leggins, beaded moccasins—all the paraphernalia of the wild Indian. This nurseling of the woods maintained before the court and jury the blank, absent countenance of the aboriginee. His tribe for many years had been looked upon as almost equal to the Five Civilized Tribes, yet we find from the records of the case the following story of genuine wild Indian practices:

Se-quah-nee and his friends went on a visit to their neighbors, the Pawnees; they had their jollification and were returning home; they went into a camp and a white man went to them and requested food. They fed him and he departed, going north;

132

someone of the Indians (claimed by the government to have been Se-quah-nee) followed, shot and scalped him and brought back the scalp as a trophy. The Indians rejoiced over the trophy but pledged each other to secrecy. However, it came out through Wah-su-quah, daughter of Se-quah-nee. She was a fair sample of the wild Indian maiden of whom the early American poets sang; she attracted no end of attention from the visitors to the court room during her father's trial, and she did all she could to save her father. Learning of the crime, she doubtless thought, in her ignorance, that her father would be justified in killing a horse thief, as the Indians claimed the man to be, and she reported the affair to the Indian Agent.

The scene at the time the death sentence was imposed was interesting. The conversation between the court and prisoner was conducted through an interpreter. Se-quah-nee was asked if he had aught to say why sentence should not be passed in his case and he replied:

"I want to tell the truth, I did not kill the man I am accused of killing; it was an Indian I killed; he was a horse-thief."

Asked if he believed in a hereafter or a Divine being, he answered:

"Indians never hear 'bout such things. I no believe anything only there be God somewhere." His voice trembled with emotion at times and he presented an aspect of pity rather than the Ideal brave of the wilderness.

The date set for Se-quah-nee's execution was October 14, 1881. On Monday night previous, October 10, he dreamed that he would see the corn grow again, sprout from the kernel tassel out, and yield its fruitage of yellow ears and the dream whispered hope to his saddened heart, and told him he would escape the death by hanging—that was but a few hours ahead. The keepers thought differently, and on Thursday they had just returned from trying a new rope and the working of the scaffold, in order that death should be sure and speedy, when news came flashing over the wires that Se-quah-nee's death sentence had been changed to life imprisonment at Detroit, Michigan, and the strange but true dream of Se-quah-nee proved to be a puzzling fact. Se-quah-nee, on being told of his good fortune, said, "Mighty glad." Just before he left, in charge of an officer, for Detroit, he was visited by his brother, Keo-kuk, a chief of the Sac and Fox tribe.

The year 1882 was not noted for a large number of murderers convicted. A good many were tried and acquitted by the assistance of able counsel, and seven were convicted of manslaughter. Three were convicted of murder; one of these was commuted, the others were executed.

The two who were executed were: Edward Fulsom, on June 30, 1882, and Robert Massey, April 13, 1883, just ten years and ten days after the execution of the famous sextette.

Edward Fulsom was a little Choctaw Indian of good stock; he was the son of Judge Fulsom of Scullyville county. He was educated and cultured. On his mother's side he was connected with the McCurtains and Page's, highly respected people of the Choctaw Nation. After he left school he became a rover and a cattle-herder. He had served one term in the penitentiary previous to the year 1880, and in February, 1881, he was tried for horse-stealing in the State court and barely escaped. He rode into Fort Smith early one morning, began drinking, and finally sold his horse for money to buy more whiskey. Later in the day he concluded to return to his home, and seeing the horse still saddled, tied to an awning post on Garrison Avenue, he mounted and rode away. The purchaser saw him as he turned the corner of Sixth street going towards the Reserve and gave chase. Fulsom was overtaken before he reached the city limits and arrested, tried and acquitted. About this time he made the acquaintance of one Hobbs and engaged with him in catching horses for Dock Woods. On August 12, 1881, they went to a saloon run by a man named John Stewart, on the line between Arkansas and the Indian Territory, so situated that a part of the building stood in the Choctaw Nation, part in Scott county, Arkansas, and part in Sebastian county. It was claimed that Hobbs had planned to destroy the life of Stewart, but Fulsom always denied having been made a party to such plans. After filling up with whiskey a game of cards was proposed and during its progress a dispute arose and Stewart was shot. Fulsom claimed the shot was fired by Hobbs, but he admitted shooting several times into Stewart's body after he fell and as he lay on the floor unarmed and helpless. At this juncture William Massingill, a stranger to all, appeared on the scene, and he was shot. While Hobbs finished Stewart by beating him, Fulsom approached the recumbent Massingill, who was still alive, and beat him on the head with a pistol until he was dead. Then they mounted their horses and rode away "yelling for two miles." They stopped five miles from the place of their crime, at the home of Jesse M. Wiight, and asked for cartridges to reload their pistols, saying they had killed two men. The story given here is taken largely from the testimony of Mrs. Stewart, the only eye witness, at the trial. Hubbs was never captured. Fulsom was of so slight build that his fall was not heavy and his neck was not broken. He turned his head in the noose just as the drop fell and the knot caught in such a manner as to prevent his sudden death. His pulse beat for an hour and three minutes.

Robert Massey was charged with the willful murder of his traveling companion and associate, Edmond P. Clark. Massey's home was in Grayson county, Texas, and Clark's in Comanche, County, Texas; both were unmarried, and when not away at work resided with their parents. They were each about twenty years old.

In the summer of 1881 they left Dodge City, Kansas, with a herd of cattle, bound for Dakota Territory. They completed the trip successfully and started to return to Texas. At a point on the South Canadian, 225 miles west of Fort Smith) on December 1, 1881, Massey killed Clark, in camp, by shooting him in the back of the head. He concealed the body of his late companion in a hole fifty yards from their camp, burned his saddle, coat and other clothing, with the exception of two articles—which afterwards aided in his conviction—but took his six-shooter and horse, leaving his own jaded animal to care for itself and proceeded on his way.

Clark had written to his parents telling them he would be at home about Christmas; the letter was mailed at Abilene, Kansas. The time arrived but no sign of the son. A week passed and still no tidings from the loved one reached the humble Comanche County home. The father began to make inquiries and inserted advertisements in certain Kansas papers. Time rolled on, and the body of an unknown man was found in the Indian Territory. One of the discoverers had read the notice placed by the elder Clark and he wrote to him, telling of the body and suggesting that the unknown might be the lost son. The father at once proceeded North, carrying a photograph of his boy. He continued his investigations on the back trail; he found that his boy and Massey had left Kansas together, and many persons who had seen them together recognized the photograph. At the camp, where the murder was committed, the irons of the burned saddle were found, one spur, and the boots that had been worn by the murdered man. All the connecting links of the chain were carefully gathered and the father began his search for Massey. He found him in April, twenty-five miles from Fort Sill, and turned him over to the proper officers. His victim's pistol was found in the possession of a young man to whom Massey had traded it; the letter "E" on the handle and the name "Clark" cut in the nickel mounting, apparently with a pin, proved its former owner; the horse Massey had traded to his brother-in-law in Texas. The chain of evidence was perfect. The travelers had stopped thirty-five miles from the place of the killing with two cowboys, remaining with them two days, and the boots and the spur were identified by them.

Strange as it may seem to residents of certain States I need not name, no desire was evidenced for a lynching, the father and his friends seeming to have absolute confidence in. the tribunal which had jurisdiction of the crime. It is a fact, proven by the history of this court, that sure and speedy justice meted out by law, is not only a barrier against primary crime, but it also acts as a preventative of that which may be styled secondary crime, wholesale lynching. During Judge Parker's reign, prisoners were safely conducted hundreds of miles to his court and during the twenty-one years that he sat upon the bench there were but three examples of mob violence in his jurisdiction. One man, old and gray, followed the murderer of his own son for months, continuing the trail through the Rocky Mountains, and when at last he overtook the murderer he arrested him, and with chains and rivets securely fastened him to his own body and conducted him to Judge Parker's court, where he listened to the trial and witnessed the execution.

In the words of the noted jurist: "If people expect justice, they prefer that the courts should mete it."

Massey surprised everybody in the court room, with the possible exception of his attorneys, by pleading guilty to the killing, but he claimed it was done in self-defense. He said that Clark owed him and that they had quarreled over the debt and that Clark had shot at him three times and then he had fired, killing Clark. He said he had kept the horse for what his victim owed him; he was asked why he had not burned the boots and he replied that he must have become excited and overlooked them. He was ably defended by William M. Cravens and Thomas H. Barnes. The arguments for defense were closed by Mr. Barnes, who made one of the best and most touching appeals ever heard in the court in behalf of a prisoner. Mr. Clayton made an able argument in behalf of law and justice. Massey's conduct after the killing wholly discredited the theory of self-defense. The prisoner's aged mother and his brother, George Massey, attended the trial. They left for their homes immediately after its close, the former a picture of despair.

John Jacobs, who was convicted in November, 1882, and sentenced to die on the fatal thirteenth day of April, following, but who was so fortunate as to receive a commutation, oi his sentence to life imprisonment, was a full-blood Choctaw Indian. He and another Indian killed Lee Morrales, a Mexican, who had been sent to Detroit, Michigan, one year for larceny, from the Fort Smith Court. He had completed his term, had been provided with a railroad pass, carrying him to Atoka in the Choctaw Nation, from where he intended to go to Fort Worth, Texas. He left Detroit, December 15, 1881. He was a stranger in the Choctaw Nation, and while traveling on foot he stopped at the home of Jacobs for rest and food, and, on leaving, he stole a pair of boots and other articles. Jacobs and: another man pursued him on foot; at Caddo they gave up the-chase, but on their return they stumbled on his camp for the night, having in some way passed him while on the chase. They arrested him and started to take him back, but concluded it was too much trouble, and so they killed him then and there and took the stolen boots from off his dead feet. The body was discovered and identified as that of the man whom Jacobs was pursuing; Jacobs was arrested and the jury returned a verdict of guilty alter being out but a short time. His partner in crime was never apprehended.

On June 29, 1883, William H. Finch, a negro, was executed for the murder of Wash Grimkey in the Choctaw Nation; Tu-al-is-to, an Indian, was executed for the murder of Emanuel M. Cochran, in the Choctaw Nation, and Martin Joseph paid the death penalty for killing Bud Stephens and his pretty wife, in the Chickasaw Nation. In the same year, from March 29 to December 22, two men and a woman were convicted of murder and one man of rape. All four were sentenced to hang July 11, 1884. Mat Music, the rapist, was pardoned; Barua Maha was granted a new trial and discharged, and the others, Dan Jones and Fanny Echols, were commuted.

Had these four been executed on the day named, the old gibbet would have gained the reputation of destroying the lives of seven at one time, for in the winter and early spring of 1884. three men were convicted of murder and were hanged on the same day, July 11. These were: Thomas L. Thompson, white, who killed James O'Holleren in the Chickasaw Nation; John Davis, Indian, who killed William Bullock, in the Chickasaw Nation, and Jack Woman Killer, Indian, who was convicted of killing Nathanial Wyatt in the Cherokee Nation.

The execution of July 29, 1883, released from earthly existence three as sinful men as it seldom falls to the lot of a court to sentence.

The first one convicted was William H. Finch, a mulatto, thirty years old, well-educated and a fluent writer. On the twenty-third day of July, 1882, he stole a horse, at Fort Sill, from an Indian named Quinette. About August 10 he was arrested at Decatur, Texas, by the civil authorities, on information received from Fort Sill, and three colored soldiers were sent after him. While returning, with their journey nearly done, they camped for the night within eighteen miles of Fort Sill. They had slept little the night before on account of mosquitos. Sergeant Bush Johnson and Private Wash Grimke laid down and at once were locked in a blissful slumber; Private Jerry McCarty took their canteens and went down an incline to a spring, a short distance, for water, not thinking Finch would attempt to escape. No sooner had McCarty disappeared than the prisoner took a gun and shot both sleeping guards, killing Grimke instantly; Johnson died later. McCarty heard the first shot and rushed up the hill and saw Finch fire the second shot, but as he was unarmed he feared to approach from cover. Finch took a key from Johnson's pocket and unlocked his shackles, then picked up two of the carbines and hid them in the tall grass near the camp. He took the other carbine and a pistol, provided himself with provisions and saddling a horse belonging to one of his victims rode away.

Then McCarty hurried to the side of his comrades, and was told by Johnson that Finch had killed Grimke and shot him, and instructed him to ride at once to Fort Sill for assistance. McCarty did as directed, and started back with a squad and a surgeon, but because of his losing his way in the timber he did not reach the camp till 9 o'clock the next morning. Johnson had died during the night.

Finch was arrested by a deputy United States marshal in Texas and taken to Fort Smith. The defense was an ingenious invention of the imagination. Finch swore that he did not kill the two men; that the deed was done by McCarty who told him he had nothing against him and he would let him go if he would keep out of the way, giving him a horse and provisions, after loosening his shackles. The jury believed his story false and returned a verdict of guilty.

Tu-al-is-to was a Creek Indian. On July 6, 1881, he saw Emanuel M. Cochran passing through the Choctaw Nation, near the Creek line, on foot. Tu-al-is-to wanted money to attend a green corn dance soon to come off in the neighborhood, and he decided to kill and rob the white man. He borrowed a pony and followed Cochran to a secluded spot, then rode up behind and shot him through the back of the head causing instant death. He rifled the dead man's pockets, securing $7 40. For some time the murder was shrouded in mystery and the brothers of Cochran offered a reward of $200 for information leading to the detection of the murderer. Deputy United States Marshal Beck began work on the case, assisted by the citizens and soon traced the crime to Tu-al-is-to. He employed John Sumner, a full blood Creek, to gain the confidence of the murderer, and he succeeded in getting the story as above, from his own lips. Beck then swore out a writ for him, before one of the United States Commissioners at Fort Smith Tu-al-is-to had been tried in the Indian Courts for larceny, and convicted; he was sentenced to be whipped and was sent home without bond. Knowing that the Indian would return at the appointed time, early in August, 1882, to receive his punishment, Marshal Beck arranged to be on hand the same day. He arrived just in time to witness the first blow from the whip and waited till the Indian was released from the post, when he stepped forward and arrested him and conveyed him to Fort Smith. Tu-al is-to was a fair sample of the uneducated Indian, uncouth and only half civilized. He was ably defended but the evidence was too overwhelming to admit of acquittal. He confessed his crime on the scaffold, also to having killed other men; he had four buttons sewed to his hat and he said each of the buttons was in honor of a man he had killed.

THE CELEBRATED RATTLESNAKE STORY

The trial of Martin Joseph, above noted, was one of the most interesting, developing the most curious chain of circumstances of any in the history of the court. It was known as "Clayton's rattlesnake story."

A few years previous, a Texas horse thief, named Bud Stephens, fleeing from justice, came to the Chickasaw Nation, accompanied by a pretty young woman of sixteen years, twenty years or more younger than himself, whom he claimed to be his wife. She was the daughter of poor parents and having fallen deeply in love with Stephens had left her home for him, despite parental protest. For the purpose of better avoiding the Texas officers, Stephens took up his habitation in the fastness of the Arbuckle mountains. There seemed to cling to him a fascination for the avocation for which he had risked his life in the Lone Star State, and he had not been long in the mountains till he once more began taking unlawful possession of whatever horses chanced to stray in the direction of his cabin.

In the vicinity lived a colored family named Loftus. One of the sons, Henry Loftus, was a bad negro, of a roving disposition and without regard for law or the rights of others. The other son, William Loftus, was a good man, with the respect and confidence of all his acquaintances. Henry Loftus had fallen in with Martin Joseph, sometimes called "Bully" Joseph, and they had committed many unlawful deeds, in spite of the prayers of his aged mother and father, and of his brother William. On April 20, 1882, Joseph went to the home of Stephens and asked him to go with him to help steal some horses, which he had that morning discovered grazing, in one of the deep ravines at the foot of the mountains. Stephens readily consented and accompanied by the beautiful wife and a basket of provisions, set out on the task. They left Mrs. Stephens alone, and went down the mountain and stretched a rope around some trees, making a circular enclosure, for a corral into which they drove the horses. While they were roping the animals, Loftus slipped behind Stephens and shot him and left his body to rot; then Joseph rode back to the camp and told the girl that her husband had fallen from his horse, receiving severe injuries and that he had desired her to come to him. She readily consented, little, thinking of what was in store for her, and accepting the negro's proposition to "mount up behind," rode to degradation and death. The proposition to Stephens to assist in stealing horses, and his murder, were but parts of a plan to the fulfillment of a desire the two negroes had long cherished. The physical charms of the beautiful white woman had so aroused their passions they could think of little else and they were ready to commit any crime to possess her. Up the mountain they went and as they continued were joined by Loftus. When near the top of the mountain the girl, who had begun to suspect treachery, from some base, insinuating remarks made to her by Joseph, spoke of the distance and inquired, in tremulous tones, if they were not "almost there." The black fiend answered; "we are there now," and leaping from his horse he seized her in his arms and threw her to the ground and there, in the seclusion of the forest, far away from any human habitation, both of the negroes committed the foul crime they had planned, after which, as she sat crying, with her apron thrown over her face, they shot and killed her. She struggled with all her weak strength for life and honor, and called in vain for husband but the unpitying monsters knew not mercy; a bullet was sent to her vitals, and carrying the body to the top of the mountain they conducted it into a narrow cave like place, the result of an upheaval of the rocks by some mighty interior force. At the terminus of this room or cave was a fissure which descended with a slant for some distance, ending with an abrupt drop of sixty feet into the bowels of the earth. Into this "well" as it was afterwards called, they threw the body of their second victim and her saddle-bags filled with clothes, a bed-quilt and other articles, and hurriedly left the place.

Not long after, Loftus, while intoxicated, told of the triple crimes to his brother, William Loftus, and this caused a row between himself and Joseph, and Loftus was killed. After his brother's death, William being afraid of the bully, kept the terrible secret for awhile, until Joseph left the country. Then he, with his father and mother, visited the cave in the mountains and guided by a piece of the poor girl's dress, that had caught on the rocks in her fall, found the spot, and made sure that her remains and clothing were there. They then searched for the body of Bud Stephens and found it at the place described by Henry. The old man Loftus next went to a Mr. Henderson, a merchant, and guided him to where the bones of Stephens lay and Henderson called the attention of Deputy Un ted States Marshal J. H. Mershon and a thorough investigation of the case was made, resulting in his ferreting the hiding place of Martin Joseph and placing him in the federal jail at Fort Smith. He then walked into the office of District Attorney Clayton, and lifting a grain sack from his shoulder dropped it to the floor with the remark "here's the bones of the horse-thief."

To many it would have been a remark most startling, but to one situated as was Judge Clayton it only meant another possible murder case to be tried, and glancing up he carelessly inquired, "What horse-thief?" In a few words the officer explained the details of the story just related, and Clayton remarked that the officer ought to get the bones of the woman.

"Great God," said the marshal, "that well is full of rattlesnakes;" adding, after a momentary pause, 'But I'll get them. One of my men," naming a gaunt Pennsylvanian, "wanted to be let down there with a rope but I didn't think it was necessary; but if you want the woman's bones I'll get them."

True enough, the deep hole in the mountain where the negroes had thrown the body of their victim, thinking thus to hide their crime, had been pre-empted by rattlesnakes and was a veritable den of the slimy creatures. The officer at once started back with the posse, and provided with a strong rope of sufficient length, they went to the cave in the mountains. The brave Pennsylvanian, John Spencer, without a tremor, allowed the rope to be placed about his body and the men slowly lowered him to the di mal and foul smelling sepulcher. No sooner had his feet touched the bottom of the well than numbers of huge snakes stuck their heads through the interstices in the rocks and in the dim light our hero could see the gleaming eyes of the reptiles as their heads swayed to and fro or darted in and out, hissing betimes their anger at this unwonted and unwelcomed intruder, and for a moment he lost his nerve and delivered a mighty yell.

"Lift me out for God's sake," he cried, and in a few moments he stood on the floor of the cave, his face as white as chalk. The officer was about to arrange some plan for the destruction of the snakes, but before he could utter a word, Spencer, after drawing a few deep breaths to calm himself, said sternly, between his tightly closed teeth: "Gi'me that lantern," and without another word he was again lowered into the depths.

This time, taking advantage of the blinding effects of the lantern, upon the reptiles, he held the light beside the head of the largest and nearest snake, and with his other hand placed his pistol to its eye and fired. The result is left to the reader's imagination; the hair raising conditions of the next minute cannot be described. The explosion put out the light in Spencer's lantern and, to his mind, snakes by the hundreds were crawling, darting their heads and hissing in every direction and all about him. The snake he had shot threw about wildly in its dying throes, wrapping its form about one of his arms, and Spencer, with grim determination, took a string from his pocket and tying it about the throat attached it to his wrist; then commenced calmly but swiftly to gather the human bones in the pit, together with the saddle-bags and clothing, and place them in the sack he carried, and not until the last piece was secured did he give the signal to be lifted from as nerve-racking a spot as was ever visited by a human being; the report of the pistol shot had frightened the remaining snakes and he was not again molested. When he appeared above the mouth of the well with one end of the great rattler attached to his wrist and the other wrapped about his neck, he presented an appearance that nearly caused a stampede among the posse, but the trophy had been secured, the tell-tale bones were in the sack and they were returned to Fort Smith to be used finally in the trial of the negro and on the verdict of the jury "Bully" Joseph was sentenced; he was hanged as stated, and the pretty Texan was avenged.

At the trial the bones of both Stephens and his wife were produced in evidence, with the aid of expert testimony. The teeth in the skull of the former were in that condition indicating a man of the age Stephens was said to be, while those of the skull of the girl were sound and even, their pearly whiteness gleaming forth rarely beautiful in their gruesome setting, and the facial lines, the curves pertaining to the cheek, forehead and the lower jaw and chin betokened the beauty in life of the being of whom the well-bleached bones were a part.

The jury was composed of five white men and seven negroes. Allen Bubo, colored, was chosen foreman. Tt e defense was conducted by W. M. Cravens and J. K. Barnes and an able fight was made for his acquittal, but the negroes on the jury laid aside all race prejudices and the verdict of guilty was returned after brief deliberation.

Before his execution Joseph made a full confession.

Thomas L. Thompson, the first one convicted of the trio executed, July 11, 1884, killed his sick and feeble partner, James O'Holeren, near Johnsonville, Chickasaw Nation, September 20, 1883 Both men were unmarried. They had resorted to this secluded spot presumably for the purpose of dealing in whisky in defiance of law. O'Holeren was in bad health, and his partner, on the day stated, stabbed him in the breast and dragged him into the yard where he beat him on the head with a club until dead, then threw his body into a dry well on the premises. O'Holeren was a stranger in the country, had been seen by few and would doubtless not have been missed, and it is probable Thompson's crime would not have been discovered but for his indiscretion. The details here given show additional proof of the truth of the proverb, "murder will out."

Not realizing the true state of affairs as regards his neighbor's knowledge of O'Holeren, and with a view to throwing them off the scent they had not picked up, Thompson proceeded in just the manner which ensured his being suspected and his crime discovered. He began making inquiries about his partner Jim, saying he had started for Texas for a lot of whiskey,* and was to be back in twenty days but the time was past and he had not returned. He had Jim's horse in the stable and he explained that he and Jim had traded horses just before the latter had started away Next he concluded that it was best to explain away the fact that he also had in his possession, the horse he claimed to have traded to Jim; he therefore told the people who lived in the vicinity that early one morning he was on the prairie and found the horse, saddled and bridled, but minus a rider, and he was afraid something terrible had befallen Jim, and urged that a searching party be formed. He continued in this strain for about ten days, until suspicion was aroused and a few men decided to investigate. They went to Thompson's home and discovered a stench; Thompson said it came from a dead hog that had fallen in the well, and tried to keep them away and go on a wide search for his missing partner. When he saw they were certain to descend into the well he confessed to having killed O'Holeren, but said that he had first attacked him with a knife and had run him out of the house with an axe and at last, in sheer self-defense he had, to save his own life, knocked O'Holeren on the head with a club, unexpectedly killing him. The club was found lying near where it had been used, and it was found to be *bloody on the small end*, showing that the person who had used it had blood on his hands when he picked it up. The remains of the murdered man were taken from the well and Thompson was confronted with the wound in the breast; he tried to explain it away but failed and the murder was clearly proven.

It was a custom of whiskey sellers in the Indian Territory to carry whiskey on horseback, in two kegs, each provided with a handle, like a valise, and fitted with a faucet. These kegs they would carry in a sack, swung across the saddle, allowing a keg to swing free on each side. With a good horse, an experienced man can carry ten to fifteen gallons of the drunk producer.—note in original

Thompson was born at Chambers, Alabama; his mother was living, at Mather's Post-office, near West Point, Georgia.

John Davis was a full-blood Choctaw Indian. His victim was William Bullock, white, and a respected citizen of Howard county, Arkansas; he had four motherless children dependent upon him. In June, 1883, he went to the Indian Territory with a drove of cattle and on June 27, while returning home, through Red River county on foot, he met Davis; they had some conversation and Bullock continued on his way to Arkansas. After he had passed from sight, the Indian decided to kill and rob him. He therefore made a detour through the woods, intending to strike the road ahead of the white man and waylay him as he came up, but when he reached the road again, tracks showed that the intended victim had already passed. The Indian took to the woods for another detour and again met with the same results; again he made the semi-circle and this time as he came into the road he found that he had gained the lead and he concealed himself behind a log and waited. When Bullock came along, thinking not of danger, the Indian slew him and obtained $16 for his crime. He buried the body by the roadside. Bullock was unknown in that part of the country and he was not missed. His friends, however, wondered at his absence, and about a month after the murder they began a search and the murder was discovered.

Meantime Davis had, during a period of intoxication, told his companions of the affair—Indian like—and how he had killed and disposed of a white man. He also told of his crime to a girl with whom he was living, but to whom he had never been married. There were no eye witnesses to the deed, but strong circumstantial evidence caused his arrest. When taken into custody he had on Bullock's boots and Bullock's pocket-book was found on his person. The jury returned a verdict within ten minutes after going out

Nathaniel Hyatt, the white man for whose murder Jack Woman Killer, alias Galcatcher, was hanged, resided in the Cherokee Nation, thirteen miles from Maysville, Arkansas. In May, 1883, he left home for a trip to Arkansas and never returned. His body was found by the roadside pierced with two bullets. Inquiry brought out the fact that he was seen with Woman Killer on May 7, on foot; the Indian was mounted and carrying two kegs of whiskey; he was also drunk. Arriving at the home of a Mr. Tehee, four miles from Hyatt's home, Woman Killer stopped for dinner. He was asked why the white man had not stopped and he replied, "Oh, I sent him along," adding, "It don't make no difference; I intend to kill him and you can look out for buzzards up that way." After dinner he followed the old man, who was never seen again alive.

It was not until May 10, that the body was found and the buzzards had mutilated the features past recognition, but the coat, vest and cane were identified by Mrs. Hyatt. The body was found two miles from the Tehee home. The old man had stopped and lay down to sleep with his coat under his head; he was shot in the left side and one eye. Davis was soon after arrested at Tahlequah; he had confessed to a girlfriend, named Ida Jones, and had later told all about the crime to a crowd of Indians, while drunk as a lord, boasting of what he had done. The strong circumstantial evidence resulted in a quick conviction.

Mat Music, one of the four who was named for execution on the same day as the last three noted, was convicted of perpetrating an outrage on a little colored girl, six or seven years old, about July 14, 1881, at his own home on Caddo Creek, Chickasaw Nation. The child lived with him and his wife, they having no children of their own, In his beastly assault he had communicated to the child a loathsome di-ease. When on trial, Music said that the outrage had been committed by others in the neighborhood who had the same opportunities as himself. Strange to say, he was granted a full and free pardon.

A brief, but exciting, scene was witnessed by the few persons who were sitting in the court room during his trial. It was in the second week in July and the weather was torrid. All the windows and doors in the old barracks court room were wide open to admit of possible, but unlikely, breezes. The case was proceeding, languidly, and outside the bees hummed lazily. Nature seemed almost to be at a standstill, as the sun, in all its fierceness, beat down upon the sweltering earth. The negro, a big and powerful creature but quick as a cat, conceived a plan to escape. Behind him, to the right, were open windows, but a few deputy marshals sat conveniently near. In front, but with Judge Parker's desk, over five feet high, between him and them, was a door and a window, both wide open. Close in front of the desk was a table, covered with a mass of books and papers. The table might serve as a stepping stone to the top of the desk, and from there to the open door was but a flying leap, thought Music. Judge Parker sat before the window with his right hand in line between the prisoner and the door. While one of the attorneys indolently argued a law point, Music suddenly darted to the table, then to the top of Judge Parker's desk, and almost over his head, and was in the very act of taking a header for the outside, through the doorway, when the judge darted out his right arm and following the negro's body with his own the two fell in a heap at the threshold. Before either could rise half a dozen officers were at the spot and Music was securely shackled, after which the trial proceeded.

Fanny Echols was an unfortunate negro girl, who reaped the sad results of improper relations between herself and her victim. For a long time previous to the murder, which occurred in July, 1883, she had been the mistress of a colored man, John Williams. He was jealous of her and they frequently quarreled. On the night of the killing, in Fanny's room, they had quarreled, and during the early part of the evening persons in the same building heard a pistol shot and heard Fanny say, "There! I've killed him." On rushing in they saw Williams lying on a pallet, shot through the body, the bullet being imbedded in the floor. Appearances indicated that he had either been killed as he slept or while he was lying on his back, unsuspectingly. Fanny stoutly maintained that she had shot in self-defense, She said another colored man had come in and hung the pistol on the bed post. Williams was then in an angry mood and as the man went out he said he was going to kill her with the weapon. Both made a dash for it and in a scuffle, caused by Williams' attempt to wrest the revolver from her, she pulled the trigger while the barrel was pointed towards Williams' body, fearing he was about to overpower her and secure the weapon. This story did not explain the bullet being found in the floor underneath the dead body, and the girl was convicted and afterwards commuted to life imprisonment at Detroit, Michigan.

The Dan Jones case closes the list for the year. He was convicted, December 22, 1883, of killing his cousin, Bill Jones, August 6, 1879, in the Chickasaw Nation, seventy-five miles from Fort Smith.

Both were outlaws; both had fled from Scott County, Arkansas, to escape arrest. They resided in an old shanty.

On the night in question, Bill's mistress was awakened by a pistol shot to find Bill dead by her side, the bullet having struck the cheek and ranged upward into the head, and Dan standing near the bed with a lighted candle in his left hand. Bill's pistol lay near the head of the bed with one chamber empty. It was clearly proven that no one from the outside could have performed the deed, and that it could only have been done by someone on the interior. The only other occupants of the house were Dan, his wife and children and the woman who was sleeping beside Bill. The defense stated that Bill was in the habit of flourishing his pistol in his sleep, but this theory did not account for the appearance of Dan, close by his side, light in hand, immediately after the shot.

The inquisitive reader will ask why the cousin would seek to kill Bill Jones. This is why:

During the year 1876 Dan was sent to the Texas penitentiary for two years, for embezzlement. He had a wife and two children in Scott county who were kindly looked after by his cousin. When Dan had served his time and returned, he found there a third child whose presence he could not account for. Bill acknowledged the parentage but the family trouble was fixed up, and the two cousins were afterwards constant companions. It is supposed that Dan brooded over the wrong and that revenge rankled in his heart, causing him to rise from his bed and slay his wife's traducer.

Dan was not arrested for this crime, but nine months later he was brought in on a larceny charge and convicted. The court suspended sentence, and while he was in jail he was indicted by the grand jury and was brought in and tried for murder and convicted. A motion for a new trial was argued by his attorneys, Thomas H. Barnes and William M. Cravens. The motion was overruled, but he was finally commuted.

Still another conviction may be charged to the year 1884, but the sentence was not pronounced till January 31 following, and the day named for execution was April 17, 1885, the day on which four others were to have been executed. Of the entire five, only one was convicted, the others being commuted to penitentiary sentences. The conviction noted, the last in 1884, was that of William Dickson for the murder of Sam Laster, on the night of December 10, 1883. Laster was a merchant in the Indian Territory. In an unoccupied store-room he had allowed the colored people of the vicinity to hold a dance, and at their request, Laster was present to prevent disturbances.

While the dance was in progress, Dickson and Mat Brown came, uninvited and fully armed. Dickson mounted the counter on one side of the room and he and Brown disturbed the dance in various ways. Laster objected to their conduct and remonstrated with the men; Dickson drew a pistol and shot him dead. Both were given trial but Brown was acquitted.

William Phillips, the only victim of the gallows, April 17, 1885, was convicted of the murder of his father-in-law, William Hill, in the early summer of 1884, at his home in the Cherokee Nation, one and a half miles from Fort Smith. Bad feeling had prevailed between the two and Phillips had shot at Hill on a previous occasion, wounding him in the ankle, and had repeatedly threatened his life.

One Saturday night Hill was assassinated as he lay in bed asleep, by someone on the outside firing through a crack in the wall. Phillips, Bob Hill, a son, and one Lackey were arrested, but the two latter were discharged by the commissioner. Phillips denied being guilty of the crime with his last breath, and in a last written statement to Col. Thomas Boles, then the United States Marshal for the district, he said the killing was done by Bob Hill with Lacky's gun. With the denial fresh on his lips, his soul was wafted to its reward on the seventh of April, just when new life was budding into bright promises and all nature seemed to be saying: "It is good to live."

Two others were executed in the year 1885, on June 26. They were: James Arcene and William Parchmeal, a negro, and an Indian, for the murder of William Feigel, thirteen years before, November 25, 1872.

Feigel was a Swede. He had worked around Tahlequah, the capital of the Cherokee Nation, and on the day he was murdered he had passed through town on foot and stopped at a cobbler's and had his boots half soled, proceeding in the direction of Fort Gibson. The next day his dead body was found on the Gibson road, two miles from Tahlequah. He had been shot and his skull crushed with a stone. His boots, hat, coat and overshirt were gone and no money remained about his person. The discovery was a mystery and a sensation for a time. Feigel had no relatives in the country, and although suspicion rested on Arcene and Parchmeal, it finally died away as no one cared to file a complaint.

In 1883, Deputy Marshal Andrews rode that portion of the country; he interested himself in the case and secured evidence and a warrant, and on March 30, 1884, he arrested the negro, and soon after, Parchmeal, who confessed to a knowledge of the crime, but said it was committed by Arcene; he had witnessed the act.

At the trial in the following November the men prosecuted each other. It was a ten days' trial but the jury failed to agree on a verdict and were discharged. At the February, 1885, term, they were again tried and found guilty, and both finally confessed in their cells, and on the scaffold Parchmeal confessed that he planned the murder and induced Arcene to do the shooting. Parchmeal then smashing the old man's skull with a stone. They found 25 cents as payment for their terrible deed.

The others who would have been hanged April 17, 1885, but for becoming the glad beneficiaries of executive clemency, were: Fred M. Ray, William Meadows and Mason Halcomb.

Ray and Meadows were convicted jointly of killing an old negro, named Fenn Morgan, 80 years old. Ray was a man of 40, and Meadows a lad of 16. Ray's twelve year old son, Joel Ray, was tried on the same charge and acquitted.

The murder was committed on the first day of August, 1883. The old negro was employed by George Alberti, a citizen of the Cherokee Nation, to feed hogs and perform other light services, on a firm which he rented to Henry Meadows, father of William Meadows.

Fenn was supposed to have $800 or $900. On the day stated, Fred Ray, who lived at the house of Henry Meadows, returned from a farm of George Alberti, where he had been at work two weeks. After leaving the supper table he asked Meadows if he wanted to make some money and on receiving an affirmative reply, he said, "get your pistol and follow me." The boy at first demurred, but finally went, and the two were followed by little Joe Ray, to a corn crib where the negro, Fenn, was in the act of taking a basket of corn to feed some hogs. Fred Ray demanded money and the old negro assured him he had none; then Ray punched Fenn in the side with the muzzle of his revolver and Fenn drew from his pocket a ten cent piece, and a knife. Ray refused to take the bit of money and cursed the negro. While this was taking place, little Joe ran back to the Meadows' house and rushed into the kitchen; a moment later, Mrs. Meadows heard a shot and the child cried out in terror, "there! they've killed old Fenn."

As Ray refused the dime offered him by Fenn he fired, and as the old negro fell dead, he cut away the outside trousers and obtained some money from the pockets of the inside pair: how much cannot be stated, but he gave the Meadows boy $8 for his share of the plunder. Joel returned to the scene and was sent for a hoe with which was dug a shallow pit in which to bury Fenn. In a day or two some hogs resurrected the body and Ray, with assistance of the two boys, dragged the body to a lake, some 400 yards away and threw it in. This was on Friday, and on Monday next, Ray went to a negro barbecue and told of Fenn's disappearance; he arranged for a searching party to come the next day and hunt for the body, as he maintained that Fenn, being old and feeble, must have come to some harm. On his return that night he induced the Meadows boy to take the two pistols, the knife and the $8 and go to Clare-more, take the train and leave the country.

When the searching party arrived he told them he had found the body of the dead man, in the edge of the lake, and suggested that the sudden disappearance of Meadows, just after he was informed of the intention to make an organized search, pointed to his having fired the fatal shot. Meadows was accordingly followed and arrested and he at once confessed to the whole affair as is given above. Ray denied all knowledge of the crime. Both the man who planned and committed the foul murder and his ignorant accomplice, were commuted to life imprisonment.

Mason Holcomb, the last in the list of these who were sentenced to hang April 17, 1885, and whose sentences were commuted, was convicted of the murder of his friend, Seigel Fisher.

Holcomb was a native of Kentucky. He was a Union soldier in the late war and after being mustered out he emigrated to Missouri, and married a Miss Bridgeman, whose brother, at the time Holcomb was tried for murder, resided near Hopkins, Missouri. From Missouri Holcomb removed with his family to Arkansas, living for a while near Jasper, in Newton county, and from there to Franklin, living about five years, six miles west of Ozark. He removed to the Indian Territory about the close of 1882, and had, for seven months prior to the killing, been living near McAlester's store, on the Canadian river.

On July 23, following, Holcomb and Fisher were working together in a hayfield; both became intoxicated:

"Oh, that men should put an enemy in their mouths to steal away their brains!"

They started home together at evening and on the way Holcomb killed Fisher, leaving the body uncovered; there was no human witness to the deed. Halcomb fled to his native state and in March, 1884, he was arrested at Mount Vernon, Kentucky, by a brother of the man he had murdered, and taken to Fort Smith (or trial.

Holcomb entered a plea of not guilty, claiming to have killed Fisher in self-defense. He said that Fisher had a pistol, that they had a difficulty and Fisher drew the weapon, threatening to kill him; in the struggle that followed. Holcomb secured the pistol and shot him in the back. There was no evidence of a struggle at the place where the body was found, although the grass was knee high and very thick, and the fact that Fisher was shot in the back was considered by the jury, ample evidence, together with other circumstances, to warrant a verdict of guilty, alter a trial which lasted over a week.

Holcomb had a wife and three little children living.

Two convictions not heretofore mentioned, secured in 1885, resulted in a double execution, April 23, 1886. The chief actors in this legal tragedy, were James Wasson, a double murderer, and Joseph Jackson. Wasson participated in the murder of Henry Martin in 1872, but was not captured till he took a hand in killing Almarine Watkins in 1884, and he might never have been captured for this crime, but the widow Watkins offered a large reward for his arrest. He was indicted jointly with John McLaughlin for the murder of Watkins and was tried and convicted July 30, 1885. After Wasson's conviction, McLaughlin was arrested, and a few days prior to the execution of Wasson, in April, 1886, McLaughlin was tried and the jury failed to agree. The defense was conducted by Col. Ben T. DuVal, Thomas H. Barnes, William M. Cravens and James K. Barnes. All of the attorneys made most impressive pleas in behalf of the young man, setting up an alibi, claiming their client was a great distance from the scene of Martin's murder. The claim was not well enough sustained by the evidence however to prevent a doubt in the minds of a portion of the jury. Three or four witnesses were sworn who were not present at Wasson's trial, among them a sister of Wasson, who testified that herself and McLaughlin were intimate and that he told her on the day following the murder, that himself and her brother would have to leave the country as they had killed Martin, and further, that they did leave right away after. McLaughlin's case came up again in August, 1886, resulted in another disagreement, and the case was set down for November first. On Monday, November 8, the case was given to the jury and after occupying the time till Thursday afternoon they returned a verdict of acquittal. McLaughlin had been in jail fifteen months. He was known as a kind and peaceful man at all times, except when drunk; then he was wild and reckless. His uncles, Ben C. and Wesley B. Burney and J. J. McAlester, prominent citizens in the Territory, believed him innocent and they used all honorable means in his behalf.

It was believed that had James Wasson's friends secured a continuance of his case until after McLaughlin was arrested and insisted on a joint trial, he too would have been acquitted of the charge of killing Henry Martin, when he would have stood a chance of winning out on the charge of killing Almerine Watkins.

Joseph Jackson brutally murdered his wife, Mary Jackson, at Oak Lodge, in the Choctaw Nation, March 9, 1885. He was a negro. The evidence against him was very conclusive and the jury returned a verdict after being out only a few minutes, September 15, following.

Seven others still, were convicted of murder in the year 1885, and all but one were sentenced to give their lives for their crimes on April 23, in the following year. That one died in jail while awaiting sentence by Judge Parker. A higher Judge than he called him to his last account and William Hamilton, murderer, was ushered into the presence of his Maker, without the assistance of man's devices. Of the others, five, Robert Wolf, Meredith Crow, Luce Hammond, Newah-na-cke and one Wiley, were sentenced January 30, 1886; the sixth, Robinson Kemp was sentenced February 27. Before the time for execution came, all were commuted, and the gallows was cheated of its second set of six victims; seven rather, (or another, a white man, who flourished under the name, "Blue Duck," who was convicted January 30, 1886, and was sentenced April 30, to be hanged July 23, following, was also commuted. An execution occurred on that day, however, and Calvin James, and Lincoln Sprole received the extreme sentence for murder. Kit Ross, who was sentenced to be hanged at the same time, was respited and was finally executed August 6, following.

BRIEF STORIES OF THE CRIMES

Robert Wolf was a negro, twenty-five years old. He was raised in the Cherokee Nation by Mrs. Lucy Watkins, mentioned in the James Wasson case. Wolf killed Frank Stock-bridge, also a negro.

Wolf and his wife had separated and he accused Stock-bridge of being the cause of it. He rode to a house in the neighborhood where the other was seen sitting in the front yard talking with some colored girls, dismounted and going through the gate, began teasing one of the girls. Suddenly he drew a pistol and turning to Stockbridge said: "I am going to kill you." Stockbridge grappled with the assailant and during the struggle the weapon was discharged in his breast, causing a mortal wound.

At the trial Wolf denied having had any intention of killing, claiming that he made the threat in sport and for the purpose of frightening Stockbridge; that although he had accused, him of having caused the separation in his family yet there was no enmity in his heart and they were the best of friends.

He was ably defended by William M. Cravens, and Mrs. Watkins was said to have paid $600 fees to the attorney in Wolf's behalf. She assisted in sending counsel to Washington to seek to save him from the gallows.

Robinson Kemp was a wealthy Indian, sixty-five years old, though he did not look to be over fifty. He was convicted of killing a well-to-do white man, Henry Rich, May 15, 1880.

Rich was shot from ambush near Fort Washita, in the Chickasaw Nation.

Rich drove home and told his friends that he had met Kemp and his stepson, Edmund Jefferson, in the road, a short time before the shot rang out that spilled his life blood, from the loss of which he died soon after. It was supposed that the two Indians had taken a circle through the woods, entering the road ahead of Rich and awaited his coming.

It was also thought by some that the shooting was done by a Mexican named Martinas and a white man by the name of Thurman. They were arrested at Denison, Texas, and taken to Fort Smith. On the day set for the trial of the Mexican the jury was called, but as there were no witnesses he was released. Sam Munn and Peter Robinson were also arrested and were discharged for want of evidence. Kemp and Jefferson were arrested and held a few weeks and released on bond. At the August, 1884, term both men appeared, but when the case was called Kemp was missing and his bond was forfeited. On October, 13, 1884, Kemp surrendered and the case was set for trial in November. Both men were tried and the jury disagreed. In August, 1885, they were again brought out; Kemp was convicted and Jefferson was acquitted. It was regarded as a most extraordinary verdict as one was as guilty as the other. Kemp's attorney, William M. Cravens, fought hard for a new trial and when he failed in that he made a trip to Washington and succeeded in securing a commutation of the sentence to life imprisonment.

Meredith Crow was a white man, thirty-five years old.

He was arrested for the murder of Cub Courtney, June 8, 1875, in the Chickasaw Nation. He fled to Texas and remained at large till January 14, 1885, when he was arrested by James H. Guy, afterwards murdered by the Lee boys.

Cub Courtney was a suitor for the hand of the dashing Widow Thurman, and was jealous of Thurman Pitts, whom Mrs. Thurman preferred. Crow was at the house of one Carsons, a near neighbor of Mrs. Thurman, when Courtney, a wild, reckless boy, rode up to her house, and Mrs. Thurman, leaving Pitts in her house, went across to Carsons' to avoid meeting her unwelcome admirer, Courtney.

As the boy approached the widow's house he sat on his horse and fired into a window, probably either with the intention of killing or frightening Pitts, having no doubt seen Mrs. Thurman go away from the house. After shooting, the boy cursed loudly, and Crow stepped from the Carson house and sent a bullet into his brain. An attempt was made to convince the jury that Crow left the house for the purpose of going away peaceably, and that as soon as he passed into sight of Courtney, the latter raised his gun to fire, at which Crow, being quicker than the other, killed in self-defense. The attempt failed and Crow was convicted, and later his sentence was commuted and he was shut up at Detroit, Michigan, for life.

Luce Hammond, Newah-na-cke, and one Wiley, three half-civilized Creek boys were tried for the murder of a white man named Owens, March 8, 1883, in the Creek Nation, near the Seminole line.

Owens traveled alone, and while camped at night he was visited by the boys and asked by each for a chew of tobacco. He gave each of them a chew and they left, but returning soon after he had fallen asleep, they shot him for the purpose of robbery; they secured a few dimes.

Owens lived three or four days in a house nearby; he made a dying statement but did not identify the murderers, and they remained at large. Indian like, they boasted of their crime, and told of killing a white man; they were arrested soon after and convicted. They were from seventeen to twenty years old.

After their conviction by the jury they were recommended for commutation by Judge Parker and District Attorney Sandels, on account of their youth and ignorance, and they were finally sent to the penitentiary for life.

Blue Duck and William Christie were tried together for the murder of a young man named Wyrick, who was assassinated while at work, in the field, June 23, 1884

The officers were somewhat slow in working up the case, for Martin Hopper, a relative of Blue Duck, was suspected of having participated in the crime, and as Blue Duck went on the scout soon after Wyrick was killed, they believed that to arrest Christie and Hopper would only make it the more difficult to apprehend Blue Duck.

Martin Hopper was the man for whom young Wyrick was at work, at the time of the murder, and he was finally arrested, but was released by the commissioner, for want of sufficient evidence to hold him. A writ was then issued against Christie, for introducing whiskey into the Indian Territory, and the deputy making the arrest made him a proposition that if he would arrest Blue Duck the charge against himself would be annulled, on their arrival at Fort Smith. Accordingly he arrested Blue Duck and turned him over to the marshal. During the examination circumstances were brought to light implicating Christie in the murder of Wyrick and he was kept in jail, but the grand jury ignored his case and he returned home; he was soon after arrested on a whiskey charge and while serving a jail sentence he was again investigated by the grand jury and he was indicted with Blue Duck. The trial was another of those interesting three-cornered affairs where each respondent prosecuted the other, with the government prosecuting each.

Christie stated on the stand, that on the day Wyrick was killed, he and Blue Duck and several others were at the house of one Ross, about three miles from Hopper's, all on a drunken spree. Blue Duck and Christie went to Hopper's but he was not at home, and Christie proposed that they wait for his return. Mrs. Hopper went to a spring for a bucket of water, and during her absence five pistol shots were heard in rapid succession in a field not far away, and immediately the horse Wyrick had been working came dashing toward the house, still attached to the plow. Christie claimed that he was lying on the porch, Blue Duck having stepped away somewhere, and hearing the shots he aroused and saw the horse running towards the house, and that he went out and caught the animal and tied it to the fence. Soon Blue Duck came up, with Martin Hopper's revolver in his hand, empty, but Mrs. Hopper testified that when she appeared on the scene, soon after the shooting, Christie had the pistol. This was used as evidence against Hopper, for the mystery was, how did Blue Duck or Christie get possession of Hopper's pistol unless Hopper had a hand in instigating the crime, as it was clearly proven that neither had a pistol when they left the house of Ross. Christie had a belt filled with cartridges and he gave Blue Duck six of them with which to reload the weapon. Blue Duck then mounted his horse and started off, firing one shot at a little boy named Willie Wolf. He then went to the house of Hawky Wolf and shot at him three times, without 'injury. He told Hawky that he had killed Wyrick and he substantially made the same statement to others, all of which was brought out at the trial. The statements of Christie were pretty well corroborated, except in the matter of the pistol, as stated by Mrs. Hopper.

Blue Duck denied in toto all the evidence against him, even denying having told anyone he had killed the boy, Wyrick. Many who attended the trial believed Christie was as guilty as Blue Duck, but he was acquitted. Hopper dodged the officers and was not present at the trial and many believed he was the instigator of the murder, though what his object could have been was not intimated.

Blue Duck's neck was saved by the assistance of his dashing friend, Belle Starr, who employed able counsel, after he had been sentenced to die and he was finally commuted to life imprisonment at Menard, Illinois, and after a year, through the agency of unseen influences, of which Belle Starr was said to have wielded the directing hand, his pardon was secured and he was set free.

An interesting case that was tried in March following the conviction of Blue Duck, was that wherein Henry Woods was charged with the murder of Henry Milks, August 10, 1887

The case was given to the jury on Friday evening, March 5 at 5.30 o'clock; all night the deliberations continued and at the next morning session they came in with a verdict, not guilty. Woods never denied the killing but he claimed the act was done in self-defense. His attorneys were W. H. H Clayton,

Thomas H. and James K. Barnes and an attorney from Tahlequah, named Walker. The government side of the case was conducted by M. H. Sandels, Col. E. C. Boudinot and Thomas Marcum. It was proven that Milks had made frequent and violent threats against Woods, and that he was advancing on Woods with a heavy rock, otherwise unarmed, at the time Woods shot him. The prosecution was most ably represented and great credit was due to Woods' attorneys for the manner in which they carried their client through to liberty.

ANOTHER BAD TRIO

Calvin James was a negro, a Territory whiskey peddler. He associated with violators of the whiskey laws and was a leader in their crimes. On August 1, 1885 he, with Tony Love, Henry Roby and Albert Kemp, all negroes, went to Texas from the Chickasaw Nation and each purchased four gallons of whiskey. On their return, while riding along a secluded spot, James killed Love for no other purpose than to obtain the four gallons of whiskey he carried.

When the crime was committed, Roby and Kemp were in advance of the others, and James carried the body 200 yards off the road and concealed it in the brush, then unsaddled the dead man's horse and turned it loose. He told Kemp and Roby he would kill them if they told of his crime. Lane was missed and all three were arrested, at which Kemp and Roby confessed to all they knew. They were acquitted.

Kit Ross was part Cherokee Indian, 25 years old. He was wild and reckless when in his cups. He was convicted of murdering Johnathan Davis. Sometime in 1883, Ross visited the home of Davis while Mrs. Davis was sick. Ross was drunk; he rode his horse into the house and was roughly ejected by Davis. They met frequently after that and were apparently on good terms but a spirit of revenge still lurked in Ross' treacherous heart.

On December 20, 1885, while Davis was in a store at Chocteau trading, Ross entered, in an intoxicated condition. He stood around the store until Davis started out, when he followed closely; as they passed the door Davis remarked:

"Kit, I believe we will have some snow."

Ross replied; "Yes I believe we will," and with the words he fired, shooting Davis in the back, and fled, dropping his hat and pistol. Davis chased the coward for seventy-five yards and wounded him twice; then he began to weaken from loss of blood, and was assisted back to the store; he died that night.

The citizens made up a purse of $150 and offered it as a reward for the capture of Ross, and six weeks after he was arrested at Shawneetown by Wiley Beavard.

Lincoln Sprole was a white man. He murdered Ben Clark and his son, Alexander Clark, eighteen years old, May 30, 1885, in Paul's Valley in the Chickasaw Nation. Sprole and the Clark's were white renters on the Sam Paul farm,* and previous to the killing they had personal disputes about watering stock at a certain well on the premises. On the day of the murder Clark and his son went to White Bead Hill to trade and on their return, Sprole, who was concealed in a thicket by the roadside, fired upon them, but missed. Clark turned in his seat to ascertain whence came the shot, and the Winchester cracked again and Clark tumbled over mortally wounded, the bullet striking him in the breast. The horses took fright and started to run, at which the boy jumped from the wagon and, disabled in the knee by a shot from Sprole, fell by the road. Sprole came up for the purpose of finishing his fiendish work, but the boy begged pitifully for his life and the murderer's hand was stayed for a moment; then he raised his gun, held it to his face and fired, the shot striking the boy's right breast and going through the shoulder. Sprole then fled the country. Clark, senior, died six hours after the shooting but the boy lived seventeen days, in great agony. Deputy United States Marshal John Williams arrived in the valley soon after the boy's death, and learning of the facts he set to work on the case and soon had

Sprole located. He arrested him and brought him to trial. His defense was that the Clarks were bad and dangerous men and that he had great fear of them; he, therefore, waylaid them to get them out of his way.

Another "Carnival of hanging" occurred January 14, 1887, when four convicted murderers, James Lamb, Albert O'Dell, John T. Echols, all white, and John Stephen's, negro, were executed. Patrick McCarty and John Parrott were to have paid the death penalty at the same time, but the latter was commuted and McCarty was granted a respite and was finally hanged on the eighth of the following April.

The crime, or crimes, of James Lamb and Albert O'Dell were most revolting and heinous. These men were not only murderers but were adulterers, bigamists, thieves and burglars as well; little doubt that they, too, had "broken all the ten commandments,"

Lamb was twenty-three years old, a native of Crawford County, Arkansas; O'Dell was twenty-six years old, born in Alabama. In the autumn of 1885 Edward Pollard and George Brassfield were tenants on some farming land near Lebanon, in the Chickasaw Nation. Lamb and O'Dell worked for them, picking cotton. Mrs. Pollard conceived an ardent passion for Lamb and Mrs. Brassfield nursed a growing fancy for O'Dell. Their open conduct caused great scandal in the neighborhood but they seemed rather to enjoy it. The two disreputable scamps took great pleasure in boasting of their amours and they grew so bold as to even threaten the lawful husbands of the women, at which Brassfield left home, and O'Dell at once most obligingly, took possession of his family, to the delight of the faithless wife. Pollard was not so easily intimidated and he continued in charge of his chattels, if not of his wife, until December 26. On that day, Mrs. Pollard sent him to Lebanon for coffee and coal oil and while he was gone Lamb went to engage a preacher to come and marry Mrs. Brassfield and O'Dell. That night Pollard was killed and the two usurpers at once circulated the story that he had deserted his family. The next morning the preacher came and performed the marriage service for O'Dell and the Brassfield woman, and Lamb tried to induce him to do the same for himself and Mrs. Pollard, telling him the husband had deserted her (At this time no one had missed Pollard, but those most interested in his remaining away). The preacher refused to perform so glaring an act and went away, and the next day the entire outfit left for more remote territory.

Two months later Pollard's body was found, less than a mile from home. He had been waylaid while returning home with his package of coffee and the can of oil; a bullet hole in the head showed how he had met his death. Deputy Marshal Mershon was camped with his posse near where the body was found, and he at once began work on the new mystery. He followed up the clews so rapidly and intelligently that he soon located O'Dell and Mrs. Brassfield on Buck Horn Creek, fifty miles from the scene of their late crime. Lamb and Mrs. Pollard had grown wary and left, the day before, for a still more secluded place.

Mershon secured a confession from Mrs. Brassfield by telling her that O'Dell had confessed, and after arresting O'Dell in a field nearby, secured a confession by acquainting him of the trap into which the woman had fallen. He denied having shot Pollard, laying that to Lamb, but he admitted having assisted in dragging the body to a place of concealment. He also showed the officer where they had concealed the can of oil; the coffee they had consumed. Lamb and his paramour were trailed and arrested, and all were taken to the marshal's camp. Mrs. Brassfield had three children; Mrs. Pollard had one. While at the camp, Brassfield came and took away his two eldest, and a brother of the other woman, from Texas, came and took away her child. The wicked quartette were lodged in jail. Mrs. Pollard gave bond and went to her childhood's home in Livingston County, Missouri, and before her return to court she gave birth to a child of which Lamb was the author. Just before the trial Mrs. Brassfield gave birth to twins, fruits of her debauchery with O'Dell; God was merciful and they lived only a few hours. At the trial both men had separate attorneys and each prosecuted the other while the government prosecuted both. The women were held as witnesses and their testimony was a curious conglomeration. Lamb laid the responsibility for Pollard's death to O'Dell's door and vice versa, though both told the same story as regards Lamb firing the fatal shot, and O'Dell aiding him in secreting the body.

As the day for the execution drew near, Lamb became gentler, and said that O'Dell should go free as he had not assisted in the killing, only helping to hide the body. Application for a commutation of the death sentences were made and it was the general belief that O'Dell was not present at the killing of Pollard. After the application for commutation was refused, Lamb said he thought the President ought to pardon O'Dell, as he was not present at the murder, "my life is enough to pay for Pollard's. Hang me and let O'Dell go," he said "for he does not deserve to be hanged." This created sympathy for O'Dell and the fact came to the ears of Attorney General Garland, at Washington; he wired District Attorney Sandels to interview Lamb and report his opinion of any statement he might make In behalf of O'Dell. Lamb was brought out, but nothing was obtained that had not appeared at the trial, that O'Dell did not have a hand in the killing and that he helped conceal the body.

On the scaffold, both men expressed sorrow for their many crimes and died in a gentler frame of mind than they exhibited when they were first put in jail.

'Poor Lamb," remarked, after the execution, Patrick McCarty, who was in a happy state, having been respited that morning by order of President Cleveland; "The last thing he asked for was a chew of tobacco. When the guard gave him a chew he cut off enough for two and put a piece in his pocket. Nothing like being prepared when going off on a long journey."

John T. Echols was a white man, 35 years old. He was born in Fulton county, Georgia. He had a wife and five children; they resided with him near White Bead Hill, Chickasaw Nation. They had emigrated from Georgia to Sebastian county, Arkansas,

155

in 1870, and in 1873 they removed to the Indian Territory. He had a father, step-mother and several brothers and sisters in Sebastian county, all respectable, law-abiding farmers. John Echols was intelligent, and prior to the killing, he bore a good reputation as a peaceable, law-abiding man. In February, 1886, he traded a horse to a neighbor farmer, John Patten-ridge, for a pony, two yearlings and a Winchester rifle. The pony and gun were turned over to him, but the yearlings were on the range and Echols was to get them from there. He failed to find one of them and on February 16, 1886, he sent word to Pattenridge that he must find the missing animal or bring the horse back. Pattenridge sent reply that he was too busy at that time, as he was hauling logs to build a house, but he would attend to it as soon as possible. During the day, Echols and a brother-in-law went to the woods where Pattenridge was at work; he was sitting on a load of logs, just ready to start, as the men came up, and a few hot words passed, when Pattenridge (unarmed) made a movement as if to leave the wagon, at which Echols shot at him, the bullet going through the brim of his hat. The team became frightened and ran, and Pattenridge leaped to the ground, when Echols fired again and his victim fell, mortally wounded. Echols fired three shots into his body as he lay helpless on the ground, pleading for mercy,

On the stand, at the trial, Echols said that he did not go to the place where Pattenridge was purposely, but that they met by accident; that while they were quarreling, both stood upon the ground; that Pattenridge became enraged and drawing a large knife, sprang at him, and he shot at him in self-defense, knowing him to be a dangerous man who had more than once used a knife with fatal results; that he fired five shots in rapid succession, while Pattenridge was on his feet and not once after he fell. It was shown, however, by persons who examined the body soon after the killing, that the knife was in one of the pockets of the dead man, closed, and that as death must have been almost instant, it was hardly likely Pattenridge could have closed the knife and placed it in his pocket, even had he desired to do so. Echols prayed for executive clemency, without avail.

John Stephens was a fine looking mulatto, 28 years old born in Iroquois county, Illinois. He went to the Indian Territory in the spring of 1874. He had a wife and one child. His father and mother lived in Kansas. The crime for which he gave his life was committed in the Delaware Reservation, Chickasaw Nation. It was an unusually revolting murder, terrible in its inception. The evidence connecting him with it was wholly circumstantial, but, so strong and clear that he could not overcome it. On May 28, 1886, Stephens borrowed a horse and saddle blanket from an Indian named Whitefeather, and proceeded to the home of Mrs. Annie Carr, seven miles distant, arriving at a late hour, and finding the woman and her son sleeping on a pallet on the floor near the door, brained both with an axe. He left them weltering in their gore and proceeded to the residence of Dr. Pile, in the same neighborhood and attempted to murder the entire family. He struck both the Doctor and his wife on the head with an axe, severely injured a hired man who was asleep in the house, and dealt a little child a terrific blow with a board. Dr. Pile lived six days; Mrs. Pile recovered, by what seemed a miracle, and was in attendance at the trial as a witness, bearing the dreadful scars made by the axe on the back of her head, from where fourteen pieces of bone had been removed.

It was very dark when the crime was committed and the murderer was not recognized. When he left the Doctor's house, in haste to get away, he left the saddle blanket, which was afterwards identified by Whitefeather as the one he had loaned to Stephens that night, and a "foot rag," the mate to one found in Stephen's pocket, soon after, twelve miles from the scene of his crime. What prompted the terrible deed, no one knew. It was at first supposed that the killing of the Carrs was at the instigation of her husband, from whom she, Mrs. Carr, was separated, and with whom she was on very bad terms, and Carr and another son were arrested as accessories before the fact, but the charge was ignored by the grand jury. Pile was a witness against Stephens in a larceny case and this was, no doubt, what prompted the second part of his fiendish night's work.

THE FAITHFUL DOG

The story of the crime for which it was adjudged Patrick McCarty should die, brings out an instance where a foul murder was discovered through the affection of a dog.

Two young men, Thomas Mahoney and his brother, residing on a farm, near Fort Scott, Kansas, with their aged and widowed mother, decided to earn money, during a dull winter to assist in paying off the mortgage on their place, by working at railroad grading. They had two good teams and wagons, the opportunity offered in the Indian Territory, where the Atlantic and Pacific railroad was in course of construction, and they left home well prepared for the work, provided with plows, scrapers, shovels and a tent, expecting to be absent till spring.

They were quite successful and early in February, with about $200, they decided to return, that they might be in time to commence their spring work at home, and they started from Red Fork for the long drive to Fort Scott; they never completed the journey; their dead bodies were found in a drain from a coal bank, only partially covered, at a point in the Indian country between Coffeyville, Kansas, and Vinita. From Red Fork they were joined by two tramps, Patrick McCarty and Joe. Stutzer, and as a mere act of kindness they were allowed to travel with them, eat of their stores, and sleep by their camp fire at night. For several days they continued thus, and it seems that the brothers went almost direct to Coffeyville, from Red Fork, then veered south again in the direction of Vinita, taking this route to reach Fort Scott.

On the night of February 17, 1886, the tramps slew the brothers and the next day, McCarty and Stutzer, drove with their two mules, two mares and a wagon to a place in the timber, near to Vinita, and camped, McCarty represented the property to be his and said that he and Stutzer had been working on the railroad. He sold the mules for $125, about one-half their value and threw in a set of harness, then divided the money with Stutzer and the latter drove away with the mare and a big black dog, that, with a large yellow cur, had followed the brothers from the farm in Kansas. The cur remained at the camp where his masters were killed, where he laid on the newly made grave, whining by day and howling, betimes, at night. Neighbors passing the spot saw the poor brute and occasionally they carried food, pitying his famished condition; the dog ate, wagged his tail in mute expression of gratitude, returning always to the one place. His strange actions aroused curiosity and an investigation resulted in the discovery of the freshly mounded earth, which the dog guarded so zealously. The mound was opened and the bodies found. The discovery was given to the press and officers came and began an investigation. The poor old mother heard of the sad story and, hoping against her fears, she proceeded to the spot, where she recognized, not their bodies, which were past identification, but their clothing, and as well the bits of bed clothes, their boots and other articles they had taken from home, and which she knew only too well, although only small pieces remained from the fire the murderers had built to destroy traces of their crime. They had been sleeping on a feather-bed, and a neighbor remembered, having smelled the scent of burning feathers, leather and cotton, on the night the murder was committed; it was also remembered that on that night a slight wind blew in the direction of this neighbor's house, from the camp of the Mahoney's.

From the camp, where McCarty had sold the mules, and separated from Stutzer, he went to Springfield, Missouri, where he spent money freely. He also met persons at Springfield who knew him at Red Fork, and who knew, too, that he left there with two the brothers, and without money. He was arrested and on his person was found a watch that had been carried by his victims; it proved to be a watch that the mother had given to her now deceased husband, as a Christmas present, eighteen years before. McCarty was tried at Fort Smith, convicted and hanged.

The wagon and horses taken away by Stutzer, were discovered in the possession of a man near Fayetteville, Arkansas, who said that Stutzer had formerly lived in that neighborhood and in passing that way they had met and conversed. Stutzer told him he had come from Vinita. The wagon was bloody and when asked about it, he said he had picked up *two tramps* and allowed them to ride with him and one night he heard them plotting to kill him; he had kept quiet until they crawled into his wagon and then he killed them both. Stutzer had left suddenly, and the story coming to the ears of the Governor of Arkansas, he offered $500 reward for his capture. No results were obtained thereby, although one man was brought to Fort Smith, thought by nearly everyone to be the tramp described as McCarty's pal, in crime, but at last he was seen by men who had known Stutzer when he lived near Fayetteville and who had seen him there after the murder of the Mahoneys, and they failed to identify the man as Stutzer.

McCarty made a confession, shortly before his execution, in which he said that the murder was planned at Coffeyville.

He had suggested to the brothers, that as the route lay through such a dry country, where water to cook with, was scarce, it would be wise to cook several days' provisions ahead. The plan was accepted and they drove out seven miles from Coffeyville and camped, McCarty insisting that the brothers should sleep, while he and Stutzer were to remain up the greater portion of the night and perform the cooking. After the boys were asleep, McCarty took a 38 caliber revolver and Stutzer a shot gun, and approached the wagon, where their victims were sleeping peacefully on the feather bed they had brought from home. McCarty shot one of the boys in the eye, killing him; Stutzer's gun missed fire and as the uninjured one aroused, Stutzer killed him* with an axe. The blood rushing from the wounds, soaked into the feather bed, and they burned the bed and clothes, to avoid detection. After McCarty was respited, his attorneys made strenuous endeavors to secure a pardon for him. Judge Parker, learning of this, took a hand in the matter and he prepared a lengthy letter, giving a full statement of the facts, gleaned from the testimony at the trial, and as given here, and sent it for examination by the President and Attorney General, praying that justice might not be hampered.

One more execution, at which two men were hanged for murder, occurred in that year, October 7, 1887. The murderers were Silas Hampton and Seaborn Kalijah, alias Seaborn Green. Only nine convictions for murder were secured in that year. One of these died in jail while awaiting execution, three were commuted and three were executed, February 9, 1888. The wholesale slaughter and imprisonment by the Fort Smith court appears to have had a temporary wholesome effect upon the class of men who commit murder and to have caused many to think twice when tempted to strike a fatal blow. We will take up those who were executed, in the regular order:

THE FIVE MEN HANGED

Seaborn Kalijah, alias Green, was an ignorant, half-civilized Creek Indian, about eighteen years old. On January 17, 1887, Deputy United States Marshal Phillips, with Mark Kuykendall, Henry Smith and William Kelly as posse and guards, on duty in the Creek Nation, had, as a prisoner, Seaborn Green, who had surrendered for the purpose of going to Fort Smith to answer to an indictment for selling whiskey in the Indian Territory. Phillips went to Eufaula on business, leaving Green with the posse, in camp. He returned the next morning to find his comrades dead and the prisoner gone. Smith and Kuykendall had been killed with an axe as they slept. Kelly's dead body was found lying about twelve yards from the others; he had been shot and his body horribly mutilated with an axe. The murderer had pulled the bodies of Smith and Kuykendall close to the camp fire and piled burning faggots about their legs, and their extremities were completely roasted, from their waists down. Phillips buried the bodies and then hunted up Green and arrested him; he said some men had come in the night and killed the guards and he had escaped. A few days later, Dr. Walker and Joseph Ohoola, Creek Indians, were arrested as accessories, as some property taken from the camp was found under Walkers's house, said by Walker to have been placed there by O'Hoola, the evening before he was arrested. After they were arrested, Green confessed to having killed the three guards unaided, and on the witness stand, *t the trial, he gave as an excuse for the crime, that they had abused him. Walker was Green's uncle and Ohoola was also a relative and it was thought by some that Green was sacrificing himself. All three were tried by a jury and Walker and Ohoola were acquitted. A short time after the killing here narrated, Marshal Phillips was slain, at the same place, by the Bennett gang.

Silas Hampton, a full blood Cherokee, about eighteen years old, killed Abner N. Lloyd, sixty years old, December 9, 1886, for a small sum of money, near Tishomingo, capital of the Chickasaw Nation. Lloyd lived on the Washita River, thirty-five miles from where he was murdered, and he was on his way home with a load of hay. Alone, he camped at night and Hampton stealthily approached the sleeping man and shot him in the back, then robbed the body of $7.50 and a pocket knife. On the following day, about noon, the body was discovered by William Markham, and the next day Hampton was arrested by his uncle. He asked why he was arrested and was told it was for killing a white man; he at once said: "Don't take me to Fort Smith; kill me right now."

A man named Wolf, who lived nearby, had heard the shot, and soon after, Hampton came to his house and left his gun, then went to a store, three-fourths of a mile away, and paid $3.25 of the murdered man's money for trinkets, bright colored silk handkerchiefs, etc. He was tracked from the place of the murder to Wolf's house by a patch on the bottom of one of his boots; on his person were found Lloyd's knife and a portion of the money. The evidence was entirely circumstantial, but the jury returned a verdict on the first ballot.

Jackson Crow's father was a Creek Indian, his mother a negress; he was raised in the Choctaw Nation and was a bad citizen. On the morning of August 7, 1884, the dead body of Charles Wilson, a prominent citizen of the Choctaw Nation, was found in the road a few miles from Kully Chaha. The find created a great sensation, as Wilson was a well-known merchant. He had been assassinated while returning from an election, and the murder was charged to Jack Crow, Robert Benton, Peter Coinson, Ned McCaslin, John Alien, Dixon Perry, Charles Fisher, Jim Franklin, Corn McCurtain, Joe Jackson and John Slaughter. With the exception of Crow, all were Indians and could only be tried in the Choctaw courts. Crow had, up to this time, failed to take advantage of the Choctaw freedmen's registration law, which declared the ex-Indian slaves to be bona fide citizens, after having properly registered under the law. He was, therefore, amenable to the Fort Smith court for his crime and he "took to the woods." Some of the others were arrested by Indian officers but being prominent citizens they were released, the jury failing even to find an indictment. Crow was at large until the winter of 1886, and in the meantime his friends had registered him as a citizen. In December, 1885, Deputy Marshal Barnhill and posse struck his trail and brought him to bay in a log house in the Palean Mountains, where his family lived. He refused to surrender, and the marshal held the outside till one of his feet was frozen, when he set fire to the building, at which Crow surrendered and the flames were extinguished. When arrested he had Charles Wilson's pistol in his possession.

At the trial, in September, 1887, Crow tried to interpose his Choctaw citizenship between himself and justice, but the court held that as the crime was committed prior to his registration as a citizen his subsequent compliance with the registration law could not effect the Federal court's jurisdiction of his crime. Two of Crow's comrades in crime, Joe Jackson and John Slaughter were witnesses for the government. They said that the party of Indians met Wilson on the road and Robert Benton accosted him about a misunderstanding that arose between them at the election and Benton shot Wilson three times. Wilson fell, but quickly rose and grappled with Benton, at which Crow shot him in the back with a Winchester, killing, him, then beat his brains out and left the body where it was found. Crow testified in his own behalf to the effect that he was summoned as posse to assist Benton in arresting Wilson and Benton shot Wilson while he was resisting arrest and that it was Peter Coinson who shot Wilson in the back. During the trial he claimed he could not speak English, but after the president's refusal to grant him a pardon he could talk good English. Crow died as he had lived, a wicked, unrepentant man, at whose door was laid many other crimes. Only a few years prior to the killing of Wilson, a white man named Uriah Henderson, left a store on the line between the Indian Territory and Arkansas, in company with Crow and was never seen again.

"The only regret was that he could not suffer for some of his former crimes, also;" were the words of a Fort Smith paper, in detailing his crime and execution.

The crime committed by George Moss, who stood upon the fatal trap by the side of Jackson Crow and Owens D. Hill, on April 27, 1888, (all three having been sentenced together on February 9, previous) was, perhaps, the most diabolical of any that ever came within the jurisdiction of the Fort Smith Federal Court. On November 29, 1886, Moss, Sandy Smith, Foster Jones and Dick Butler, all negroes, conspired to steal a beef on the range in Red River county, Choctaw Nation. It was agreed among them that if anyone caught them in the act they would murder whoever he might be. They proceeded to the Red River bottoms and shot a fine steer, the property of George Taff, a citizen of the Choctaw Nation. Taff happened to be in the vicinity looking after his stock, and he came upon the thieving negroes just as the shot was fired. Moss shot him at once. The horse Moss had been riding, left him at the second shot, and leaving the beef and its owner where they had fallen, the guilty wretches hurriedly left the place, Moss going home on foot. Taff's absence called out an exploring party and the dead body was found, also the negro's horse, bearing saddle and bridle. Moss was arrested and he confessed, implicating his companions and with Sandy Smith he was conveyed to Fort Smith. Jones and Butler were registered citizens, and the Federal court had no jurisdiction of them. The infuriated citizens, knowing that no justice would be meted by the Indian courts, took them to the place where Taff was slain and riddled them-with bullets, their bodies being left as prey for buzzards and wolves.

Sandy Smith died before the trial, from wounds received while enroute to Fort Smith, while attempting to escape from the deputy marshal.

Owens D. Hill was the last one convicted in 1887, November 16. At one time, Hill was a resident of Fort Smith. In 1885, he married Viney D. Anderson, from just across the Poteau river, in the Choctaw Nation; both were colored; Hill had been raised in Cincinnati, Ohio. In the spring of 1887, he removed to the home of his wife's mother, on the Arkansas river, a few miles above Fort Gibson. From some unknown cause, he failed to live happily, in the same house, with his mother-in-law; she moved to another place nearby. In the following June, he became angered at his wife on account of her having given her mother a plug of tobacco and he slapped her face. The next day, as Owens was at work in the field, she took her child and went to the house occupied by her mother. Owens sought to persuade her to return to him but she refused all his entreaties, and he finally decided to kill both women and himself. Having so decided, he repaired to the house on the night of June 25, arrived with a shot gun and a razor. He met his wife's mother at the gate and immediately proceeded to beat her into insensibility, breaking his gun in the process and throwing it down. The wife had fled the scene and hid behind a bed in the house. After he had done with her mother he made a dash for his wife with the razor. He caught her in the yard and cut her throat. He afterwards said, that the reason he did not then kill himself was, that he had broken his gun on his mother-in-law and his razor on his wife and had no weapon with which to commit the act of self-destruction. He fled to Kansas City, Missouri, and was soon after arrested, as a result of his writing to an acquaintance, to inquire about his wife, not being certain whether she had died. The case was submitted to the jury without argument and the verdict was returned in a few hours.

One more execution occurred in 1888. It was a case of tardy justice, and quick execution after once the murder was placed on trial. Conviction was given May 10, sentence was pronounced May 26, and the execution July 6. The murderer who was thus summarily hustled off to the spiritual world, was Gus Bogles, a negro boot-black, who was raised in Dallas, Texas, where his mother and sister resided.

THE VICTIM

J. D. Morgan was a coal miner, employed at McAlester, Choctaw Nation. He went on a visit to Dennison, Texas, and late in the evening of June 27, 1887, with a bottle of whiskey, in his pocket, he boarded a freight train for McAlester, having sent his valise by express. At Blue Tank, in the Choctaw Nation, he and four negroes were put off by the train men, for not paying fare. Morgan was very drunk.

The next morning, Morgan's dead body was found, thirty yards from the section house, minus coat, trousers, shoes and, hat. He had apparently been garroted and beaten to death. Captain Charlie LeFlore, of the Indian police, was informed and: he soon "spotted" Bogles as one of the four negroes, and arrested him at Dennison, Texas, June 30; while in custody he told the officer they had killed Morgan by buckling a strap around his neck and beating him on the head with a gun; they secured $40, a watch and the clothing. At first, he told conflicting stories, but finally, William Netterby, Dennis Williams and Thomas Wright were arrested and all four were indicted by the Federal grand jury, at Fort Smith. At the trial no evidence was produced against the three last named; the conductor and brakeman of the freight train, failed to recognize them but did recognize Bogles as one of the four negroes they had put off the train, at Blue Tank. At the trial and to the time of his execution, Bogles denied ever having seen Morgan.

About ten minutes before he was taken out for execution, as John McNamee, one of the guards, was strolling up and down the area way of the jail on the side where was the cell occupied by the negro, he and two other guards had stopped to talk, standing carelessly opposite Bogles' cell, bringing his pistol-pocket close to the lattice. Quick as a flash, but noiseless as a cat, Bogles reached out and procured the revolver and dashed into his cell; his cell-mate, Emanuel Patterson, was lying on his bunk, as he came in; discovering in an instant the state of affairs, he grappled with Bogles, and, after a brief Juggle, succeeded in wresting the weapon from him and tossed it at the feet of the guard, making it slide into the area way beneath the lattice-work. The prisoners, and guards as well, breathed a sigh of relief as they saw the pistol once more in McNamee s possession. Only a few days before, Bogles had tried to induce a trusty to carry him out of the jail in an empty barrel, that had been brought in filled with sawdust, for filling the spittoons. The trusty failed to see where he would benefit by compliance with the proposition, and he refused.

EXECUTIONS OF A YEAR

The year 1889 witnessed the execution of five men, on three different occasions; two of them had been convicted in the latter part of the previous year. Eight others were under sentence to hang in that year, six of them having been convicted in 1888. The entire eight escaped the gallows, one of them being pardoned, the others commuted.

The first execution in 1889, was on January 25, when Richard Smith, colored, unwillingly gave up his life as a forfeit for that of Thomas W. Pringle; the conviction was secured under a perfectly clear but most peculiar chain of circumstantial evidence. The murder occurred during March, 1888. Pringle resided in Towson county, Choctaw Nation, near Wheelock. He had traded a rifle to Smith, and Smith had given him therefor, a bill of sale of a cow (claiming it as his own) belonging to Jerry Gardner, on whose premises Smith lived. On Sunday, March 25, Pringle went to Smith's house and procured his gun, telling him the cow was not good property. Smith agreed to go with Pringle to Gardner, the next Sunday, and fix the matter satisfactorily. On the following Wednesday Pringle was assassinated while at work in the woods. The murderer sneaked to within thirty yards and fired on him with a rifle. A young lady who was with Pringle heard the shot and saw the murdered man fall, but could discern nothing of the source of the bullet, on account of the heavy growth of brush. She alarmed the neighbors and men searched the vicinity. They discovered tracks behind a tree where the murderer had fired from ambush, and in the soft ground they were easily followed to a lake, across which he had waded, to ward off discovery. On the opposite side of the lake the track was found again; it led to a field back of Smith's house, and to the house. The tracks plainly showed that the boots worn by the man making them had round headed tacks in the heels, twenty-one tacks in one and fourteen in the other. A boy at Smith's house said that Smith had come home, wet to the waist, and had complained that his boots hurt his feet, then sat down and knocked off the heels, afterwards taking the tacks from one of them. Smith was arrested the next day by Deputy Marshal J. N. Ennis; on his feet were boots that fitted the tracks, but the heels were gone. A search revealed the heels in a brush pile, where he had thrown them; from one of them the tacks were gone but the holes remained, and their number, in each heel, corresponded with the number of tack marks in the tracks. The boots fitted the tracks perfectly, even to the print of a woolen sock, where the great toe protruded through a hole in one of the boots. Smith stated that Charley Mitchel had told him to take the Winchester and shoot Pringle; that he had known of that being done and it was never found out; Mitchell was arrested but was released by the commissioner. It was believed that Smith believed Pringle would have him arrested for larceny, for giving a bill of sale of another's property, and he thought to put a stop to the proceedings by killing him. He succeeded if this was his purpose, but he placed himself in a much greater difficulty, which cost him his life. He was hanged January 25, 1889.

The next execution was on April 19, 1889, when James Mills forfeited his life for the murder of another negro, and Malachi Allen was swung off at the same time for a murder committed less than a year before.

James Mills was a young negro, endowed with scarcely enough intelligence to, realize what murder meant. His victim, John Windham, was a resident of the Seminole Nation, and in December, 1887, Mills and Tom Robin, also a negro, were living or boarding at Windham's house. On the night of December 15, these three men, accompanied by Phillip Lincoln, a thirteen-year-old boy—step-son of Windham—went coon hunting, and during the night Windham was killed. According to the boy's statement, they were all walking through the woods, Windham in advance, when Robin shot him in the back; Windham fell and then Mills shot him twice, once in the mouth and once in the body. Then they returned to Windham's house, after telling the boy they would kill him if he told anything of what he had seen. They gave Mrs. Windham a plausible excuse for the failure of her husband to return, and they slept that night, as usual, at the home of their victim. The next day the boy told some of the neighbors of what had occurred and an investigation was made. Upon being questioned Mills said Robin had killed Windham, and m the afternoon he conducted a searching party to the spot where the murdered man lay. Both Mills and Robin remained in the neighborhood and a few days later a crowd of negro citizens, led by Ben and Mitchell Bruner, attempted to arrest them when they resisted, and in the fight Robin was wounded and captured, while Mills escaped. Robin was taken to Fort Smith, where he soon died of his wounds. Mills was arrested in January. He claimed Robin did the killing and that he had no more to do with it than the boy, but the evidence did not bear out this statement. Before his death, Robin claimed, that Mills did the killing. During the entire investigation of the case no motive for the murder was discovered, the three men having been, apparently, on the best of terms.

Malachi Allen was convicted of the murder of Shadrach Peters and Cy Love; all three were negroes. On July 15, 1888, at a religious meeting in the Chickasaw Nation, Peters, Love and two other negroes engaged in a dispute about a. saddle. Allen was sitting in a wagon, near enough to hear one of the disputants say: "I can prove it by Malachi Allen." At this, Allen approached the crowd, saying he did not want to mix up in their quarrel. The lie was passed between Allen and one of the four and Allen returned to the wagon and obtained his Winchester. Peters was leaning on the back of a. chair, and when Allen approached with the gun told him to "shoot," and Allen shot, killing Peters. He then began an indiscriminate fire, at which the others ran, and Love was killed. Allen then started away on foot, but soon, concluded he had best have a horse and returning he took possession of one and rode away. Deputy Marshal McAlester, happening to be in the vicinity, organized a posse and went in pursuit. The posse scattered and one of them, a man named Swain, soon overtook the fugitive and ordered him to halt. He did so, and turning his horse about came towards Swain as if to surrender, but instead, when within range, he slid from his horse and, taking a tree for ambush, opened fire, and a sharp fight ensued, several shots being exchanged. Finally the negro broke cover and started to run, when Swain shot him in the arm and he surrendered. The arm was so badly shattered that it was necessary that it be amputated before conveying him to. jail. Allen employed DuVal & Cravens to defend him but they had nothing on which to base a defense, except that Allen was of unsound mind, and that fact could not be established; his conviction naturally followed the presentation of testimony.

HIRED TO KILL FOR TEN DOLLARS

On the thirtieth day of the following August, William Walker and Jack Spaniard were hanged together, having been respited from July 7, 1889. Walker was a negro;' he had killed Calvin Church, also a negro, at Durant, in the Choctaw Nation, December 12, 1888, and was at once arrested and soon after tried. He was convicted February 12, 1889. He did not deny the killing but claimed he was employed to kill Church by a negro named Dick Gardner; he was to receive $10 and two quarts of whiskey; he had received the whiskey bet "never did see" the $10. Church was known to the Federal officers; he had been tried before Judge Parker for larceny and acquitted.

Jack Spaniard was a half-breed Cherokee, thirty-eight years old. He was hanged to atone for the life of Deputy Marshal William Irwin, one of the bravest and best officers in the history of the court. Spaniard claimed that his right name was Sevier. He said that his grandfather, on his father's side, was named Sevier, but that while living on Spaniard Creek, near Muscogee, he was called Spaniard and the name had clung to the descendants. Jack's father and mother died when he was a child and he, with three brothers, one older and two younger, was reared by his cousin, Andy Gourd; the three died and Jack was the last of his race.

Jack and a pal, Frank Palmer, slew Irwin, in April, 1886, for the purpose of releasing Felix Griffin, a horse-thief, who was in the custody of Irwin. They waited in ambush and killed the officer near Pheasant's Bluff, shooting him as soon as he rode within range. Palmer was never captured; it was believed that he left the country forever. After killing Irwin and releasing Griffin they rode hurriedly away, not noticing that Spaniard's dog, which had been seen with them previously, had stayed behind to serve as a mute but truthful witness to their crime The Government offered a reward of $500 for the arrest of each of the trio; Griffin was arrested and kept in jail till August, 1886, when the grand jury ignored the charge against him, but indicted Spaniard and Palmer; Griffin was indicted for robbery; he gave bond and went back to the Territory, where he was shot and killed while trying to steal a horse. Spaniard was arrested March 25, 1888, and brought to Fort Smith by Jailer James Petti-grew; his capture and conviction was the result of circumstantial evidence, strengthened by the aid of his dog, which remained with the dead body of the marshal, continuing its long vigil until the searching party discovered it there by the river. Spaniard and Palmer had been seen, soon after they left the scene, without the dog, and this fact, together with the appearance of the animal at the place of the killing, and the testimony of men who saw it in their company just previous to the murder, completed the chain that needed but the one link to convict. The dog was kept at the jail for months, held as a witness. There arose, during the trial, a doubt as to whether it was really Jack Spaniard's dog. The animal was accordingly brought into the court room and he immediately went to Spaniard, saying as plainly as if in words, that the half-breed was his master. It might have been supposed that these men would have been shrewd enough to take the dog away with them, but the fact that a murderer is always in haste to leave behind him the scene of his crime, and in his anxiety to avoid discovery, fails to do many things he might have thought of, but for the burden of guilt lying on his heart, has led to many a bad man's, undoing. Spaniard was a fine looking man, with black hair and mustache, and brown eyes.

A LIST OF CASES COMMUTED

It will be necessary to go back to March 11, 1886, and bring up a record of murder cases where convictions were secured, but in which the convicts were not executed. Of fourteen convictions between the date named and January 16, 1890, quoted at the beginning of this chapter, as the close of a period, twelve were commuted, one died in jail before the date set for his execution, and one was pardoned. The first of the fourteen was John W. Parrott, who was convicted March ii, 1886, of the murder of an old man named McAdams and his son, Louis McAdams, July 18, 1885. Parrott was 37 years old; he was a carpenter; he resided in Sherman, Texas, where he had two motherless children, but he had formerly come from Kentucky, where his mother, four sisters and a brother resided, and enjoyed the respect and confidence of a wide circle of highly cultured people. The mother was old and feeble and every endeavor was made to keep her son's trouble from coming to her knowledge lest the shock should shorten her life. The crime for which he nearly lost his life was committed at Alexander's store, in the Chickasaw Nation. He had formed a partnership with the two men whom he afterwards killed, and they had contracted to build a house upon which they were then working. On the morning of the day of the killing, Parrott and the elder McAdams quarreled about a division of profits and it was claimed, by the defense, that McAdams threatened the life of Parrott. As the latter left his boarding house to return to his work, after the noon hour, he placed a pistol in his pocket. There was no witness to the reopening of the trouble, but Parrott claimed that the elder McAdams threw a chisel at him and then advanced on him with a hand-axe, and Parrott fired, killing the other instantly. At this point, in the proceedings the son appeared, from an adjoining room and made an attack on Parrott with a knife and Parrott shot again, wounding him in a manner to cause death the next day. At the trial he claimed self-defense, in both counts; the jury went out at 5:30 p. m., remained under lock and key all night, and in the morning returned a verdict of guilty, in both counts, as charged in the indictment.

J. G. Cushman, one of the witnesses, was a native of northern Vermont. He did not see the conflict with the elder McAdams but was a witness to the killing of the son. He left for home soon after and was brought back at government expense, all the way from New England, to testify at the trial.

After his conviction, Parrott was placed in jail till October 30, following, when he was brought out and sentenced to be executed January 14, 1887. His brother in Kentucky, as soon as the motion for a new trial had been overruled, began putting forth all his energies towards securing his freedom. He obtained the influence of Governor McCleary of Kentucky, a friend of the Parrott family, in behalf of the brother, and long petitions were sent to the President asking for a pardon. At last, just a few days before the day set for the execution, a message came from President Cleveland to Marshal John Car-roll; it read as follows:

"I am not willing to pardon, absolutely, this convict, after his crime of murder, and after a denial of a motion for a new trial, based substantially upon all the papers now before me. I am entirely satisfied that he ought not suffer the extreme penalty of the law but I do not think that when he killed the elder McAdams, he was so driven to the wall by the attack of his assailants as to clearly define taking life. I do not believe the convict invited the attacks, but in considering an application for his pardon, I cannot overlook the fact that he armed himself and went to the place where the man was, who had threatened to kill him before night. In the belief that the prisoner should be punished for the part he took in the homicide, and that he is guilty of a crime much less than murder, I have determined to commute his sentence to imprisonment, at hard labor, for a term of five years."

On Monday, August 31, of that year, Judge Parker issued a writ of removal in the cases of Joel and Jake Tobler, murderers of Cass and Goodykuntz, of Vinita, and George W. Morris, charged with the murder of John W. Lake, in the Pottowatamie Nation, in March, 1884, and they were conveyed to Wichita, Kansas, for trial. Morris admitted killing Lake, but claimed self-defense. He had been in jail at Fort Smith, five months. The Toblers had been in jail more than a year; at Wichita, they were convicted of murder and were hanged.

Jeff Hilderbrand was a part Cherokee; he was a son of Judge Stephen Hilderbrand, a respected citizen of the Cherokee Nation, residing near Webbers Falls. He was convicted of the malicious killing of John Ridgeway, a negro, May 7, 1884, on Coon Creek in the Cherokee Nation Jeff and Jake Hilderbrand were charged with assault with intent to kill and Ridgeway was a witness against them. On May 9, 1884, the negro's dead body was found in the Cherokee Nation, near the Kansas line, lying under a tree. Mary Ridgeway, a white woman who was living with the negro (without being married) and by whom she had two children, said that Jeff Hilderbrand came to her house on the night of May 7, and represented to. Ridgeway that he was dodging the marshals and asked him to go to the woods with him and watch all night, while he slept. Ridgeway took a blanket and went with Hilderbrand and was not seen again till he was found dead, as stated. Her son, by a white husband, corroborated her statement, and it was the theory of the prosecution that the defendant wanted to get Ridgeway out of the way to prevent him testifying against himself and brother. The defendant claimed an alibi, his father and brother swearing that he was 125 miles away, at Webbers Falls, and their claim was supported by one or two-others. "The verdict was a great surprise to the defendant's attorneys, as they confidently expected an acquittal. Hilderbrand was twice respited by the president in order to give opportunity to investigate the papers filed in his behalf. He finally became very low with consumption and preparations-were on hand to ask the president for a pardon, in order that he might go home to die, when, just before the date last mentioned for his execution, he died of the disease that assailed him, thus cheating the gallows and the law.

HANGED IN SPITE OE BRIBERY

Richard Sutherland killed Jake Burris, August 25, 1885, near Fort Gibson, in the Cherokee Nation. Burris lived on land rented of Sutherland. A dispute arose over a load of corn that Burris had removed from a field without consulting Sutherland. The testimony tended to show, that on the evening preceding the murder they had hard words, and the discussion ended by Sutherland ordering Burris to keep out of the field. On the following morning, Burris went to the field and Sutherland followed, but before he found Burris he inquired of a neighbor whether Burris was there, remarking: "If he is here I intend to kill him;" then going to where Burris was at work he killed him as he had threatened to do. Burris was armed at the time, his weapon being a shot gun, and Sutherland claimed that Burris fired the first shot and that he (Sutherland) then fired, with fatal results, but in self-defense. There was but one eye witness, a man named Woods, who, soon after the killing, for a while, talked freely to the neighbors, saying that Sutherland came into the field and shot at Burris without warning, and that as the latter fell to the ground one barrel of his gun was discharged by the fall. After the killing Sutherland went on the scout for a while and finally surrendered, and, after examination before the commissioner, he was discharged, still claiming self-defense. In the meantime Woods had modified his version of the affair and in his testimony before the commissioner had sworn in a manner that did not verify his former statements. After Sutherland's discharge, the district attorney made an investigation in his own behalf, and the murderer was again arrested and convicted. Woods testified at the trial the same as he did before the commissioner, but witnesses were introduced to show that he not only contradicted his former statements, but also that he had accepted bribes from Sutherland.

William Alexander was a negro; he was convicted of committing rape on the person of a little colored girl, 13 years old, in July, 1886, in Red River county, Choctaw Nation. The victim was his step-daughter, Ella Whitefield. The little girl was at work in a cotton field and he met her at a safe distance from the other hands and accomplished his purpose. His was the second conviction for that crime before the court.

Emanuel Patterson killed Deputy Marshal Willard M. Ayers, August 11, 1880, near Cherokee town, Chickasaw Nation. Ayers had a writ for Patterson, charging larceny, and he went to his house, late at night, to serve it; while the officer was at the door demanding admittance, he was shot from within and killed. Patterson admitted firing the shot but he said he did not know it was an officer, as Ayers did not make his business known, but simply demanded admittance, in a rough manner and he thought it was an enemy seeking to do him great harm.

HIS BODY SPLIT WITH AN AXE

Lewis Burrows killed his father-in-law, William Morgan, September 10, 1886, at Oak Lodge, Choctaw Nation. The men had quarreled during the day. Morgan had abused Burrows on account of a boy who owed the defendant thirty-five cents. The same evening, Morgan went to Burrows' home and found him cutting wood. Burrows met him with an axe, and a second quarrel ensued, during which Morgan provoked Burrows into such a passion that he suddenly dealt Morgan a terrific blow with the sharp portion of the axe, driving it with such force as to split his heart in two, after cutting through the shoulder blade, killing him instantly. Burrows' wife (Morgan's daughter), was present, a witness to the entire proceedings; she was not allowed to testify at the trial but had she gone on the stand, she would have testified in her husband's favor. The father of the defendant was also present. Burrows set up a claim of self-defense, claiming that Morgan came at him with a knife, but he failed to prove this to the satisfaction of the jury, though several witnesses testified to it. Other witnesses testified that Morgan's knife was in his pocket when he was killed. Morgan was a minister and Burrows a deacon in the church. At the jail, the prisoner took great interest in the religious services and conducted himself with propriety; many thought the jury would reduce the crime to manslaughter and some of them were at first in favor of such a verdict but after due deliberation, they agreed on a verdict of murder. Burrows claimed that he tried to avoid having trouble with Morgan but was finally forced to kill him.

A MIXED UP AFFAIR

The crime for which Steve Bussel was convicted was the result of a personal enmity existing between his uncle, Alex Juzan, and James Christian, two extensive stock raisers in the Chickasaw Nation. Christian had accused Juzan and Dick Sacra of stealing cattle and had caused their arrest. One of the witnesses in the case, before the Choctaw courts, was a young man named Hamilton, who had gone to Texas. On April 10, 1887, James Christian, Dave Hardwick and Jim Bonds went to Texas and got Hamilton. On their return they fell in with a young man named Luttrell, who was given a seat in the buggy with Christian and Hamilton, while Hardwick and Bonds traveled on horseback; they were to go to Hardwick's house. Christian and his two companions were some distance ahead of the two horsemen when they met Juzan and Bussel, and Christian and Luttrell were both shot and killed, Hamilton being the only witness. Hardwick and Bonds soon came along and they immediately drew their guns on Hamilton and demanded a straight story. He told them that Juzan and Bussel had waylaid and shot his companions and rode away. Hardwick and Bonds followed a short distance, then gave up the chase and returned to attend to the dead. Three days later, Hardwick, who was then a member of the Indian police, summoned a posse and went in pursuit of Juzan and Bussell, and coming on them early one morning they ran and Juzan was killed, while Bussell received a shot and escaped. Hamilton was held for several days by Hardwick and several times he told the story of the crime as here given. A few days, later Bussel was arrested by Captain Charlie LeFlore. and bound over by the United States Commissioner at Muscogee and sent to Fort Smith, though Hamilton did not testify before the commissioner. Not long after, Mr. and Mrs. James Thompson, uncle and aunt of Bussel, went to Fort Smith and applied for bail, bringing Hamilton as a witness; he testified that Hardwick and his party were all drunk at the time of the killing; that they met Juzan and Bussell; that Christian, after addressing them very harshly, raised his Winchester to shoot, and Juzan shot and killed him; that Luttrell then started to leave the buggy and Juzan shot him also, but that Bussel did not fire. He also stated that the first story he told was incited by fear for his own safety. On this representation Judge Parker allowed Bussel released on a bond of $10,000, furnished by Mrs. Thompson. At the next term of court the prosecution had obtained new evidence and Bussel was sent to jail, but later was admitted to bail by the influence of Mrs. Thompson. In the meantime, Hamilton had left the country, and his statements before the court, also to private individuals, were ruled out, leaving the jury to judge of the circumstantial evidence that had been gathered by John Christian, brother of the deceased, and his friend Hardwick. The chain opposed the testimony of the defendant and conviction followed, much to the surprise of Bussel's friends. The government claimed that Juzan and Bussel waylaid Christian for the purpose of killing him, and Luttrell being in the buggy, he was killed also. The defense claimed that Juzan and Bussel had been to a pasture to look at some cattle and on the way home unexpectedly met Christian, who made an attack on Juzan's life and was killed in self-defense, and that the defendant was merely a spectator, having nothing to do with the killing.

William G. Sorder was convicted of the murder of a young man, Albert Lang, in June, 1887, in the Cherokee Nation It appeared from the testimony that Lang worked for Sorder at a coal bank, and having stopped work, asked Sorder for a settlement. Lang claimed $6 as his due; Sorder allowed him $2.30. A dispute arose and Lang told Sorder he proposed to have his full pay and if he attempted to move any coal from the pit before paying the debt, he would kill him. Whereupon Sorder grabbed up his shotgun, that stood nearby and ordered Lang to leave. Lang replied; "I don't have to," and Sorder shot and killed him. At the trial, Sorder claimed he was under the impression that he was justified in the act, because Lang had threatened him, but as the young man was wholly unarmed when killed, his claims had no grounds, under the law. The jury was out twenty-four hours. Both Sorder and his victim were white; Sorder had a family; Lang was single, and was but 19 years old.

George Brashears' conviction was largely the result of his voluntary confessions, as there was very little other evidence against him. From the testimony it appears that on the night pf September 26, 1883, the body of Jake Fouk, a freight brake-man, on the Missouri, Kansas & Texas railroad, was found near the depot, at Savanna, in the Choctaw Nation; death had evidently resulted from a shot in the breast. It was classed at the time as a mysterious murder, as the conductor nor any of the train-men could throw light upon it. In 1884, Brashears was arrested as the murderer and was indicted. When the case came to trial, however, the evidence against him was so meager that the district attorney entered a *nolle prosequi*, and Brashears was discharged. Sometime later, he was arrested and convicted of larceny, serving a sentence of one year, at Detroit, Michigan. After his return from Detroit, he told three different men, that he killed Fouk, but they appear to have kept the statements to themselves until Brashears was again arrested for larceny, in early March, 1888. While in jail, awaiting trial on the larceny charge, he was indicted a second time for the Fouk murder, and at the trial in November, 1888, which resulted in his conviction for murder, the three men to whom he had related the circumstances of the killing, Bragg, Stanton and Blansett, testified to the statements he had made to them, at different times. Blansett swore that Brashears told him he had five gallons of whiskey on the caboose; that after looking around the depot, and seeing no officers at hand, he went to get his liquor, but Fouk would not let him have it; that they had a few words, when Fouk kicked him in the mouth and he shot him off the caboose; that he would kill any man who would kick him. The testimony of these witnesses, coupled with the circumstantial evidence, brought forward by the government, made a fairly strong case and the jury was not long in agreeing on a verdict. The defendant, on the stand, denied ever having made any such statements. He had been convicted of larceny, a month prior to the trial for murder, but sentence was suspended, in order to allow for time to investigate the murder charge.

AN ACT OF TREACHERY

On November 20, 1888, Henry W. Miller and William Woods were convicted of the murder of John A. Hantz, just a year before, in the Cherokee Nation. The story of the crime, as it appeared from the testimony at the trial, is as follows:

On October 2, 1887, John A. Hantz and William Woods, two young men who had been close friends for years, left their homes at Kinsley, Kansas, for the purpose of making a tour through the Indian country and Arkansas, their object being to hunt and look at the country. They were provided with two good horses and a wagon, one extra saddle-horse and a good camping and hunting outfit. One of the horses belonged to John Hantz, one to his brother and one to a brother of Woods. The wagon they hired at a livery stable. At Caldwell, Kansas, they fell in with Henry Miller, a stranger to both, and upon learning of their intended trip, he expressed a desire to accompany them; he was permitted. They traveled through the Indian Territory, camping about a week, at what was known as Commodore Hollow, about twenty miles southwest of Choteau, then continued and visited the cities of Fayetteville, Van Buren and Fort Smith, Arkansas, and then went through the Choctaw Nation, via Oak Lodge and thence into the Cherokee Nation, again camping at Commodore Hollow. This, according to the prosecution, was about November 15 or 20, 1887. One afternoon, while in camp in the Hollow, according to the testimony of Miller, he and Hantz went out hunting and Hantz did not return. The next day, Miller and young Woods left the scene and Woods arrived at his home, at Kinsley, Kansas, on December 20, with the outfit, minus the horse owned by the missing man. He told the father of Hantz, that they had lost him in the Indian country, describing to him the place where they camped and where he had been last seen. Search was made by the brothers of Hantz, but no trace of him could be found, and the attempt was abandoned. On March 18, 1888, an old hunter found the body of a man, near where the young men had camped, a bullet hole in the skull, and he at once advised the old man Hantz of the fact. The father proceeded to the place and fully identified the body as that of his missing son. He then caused the arrest of Miller, who lived at Troy, Doniphan county, Kansas, and he was brought to Kinsley, where he was kept in jail until after a preliminary examination, then was turned over to a deputy marshal from the Western District of Arkansas, who had also arrested Woods, and both men were lodged in the Federal jail, at Fort Smith, on August 22, 1888.

At the trial, while the defense claimed that Hantz disappeared on or about November 27, the testimony introduced by the prosecution went to show that he must have been killed prior to November 20. The defendants did not deny that they broke camp and started for Kansas the next day after Hantz disappeared, without even looking for him or informing anyone that he was gone, though Woods wrote to a brother of Hantz about December 1, telling him he was lost. All this tended to strengthen the prosecution, and a chain of evidence was woven about the defendants that the best legal talent failed to break, although some of the most prominent citizens of Troy and Kinsley were at the trial and testified to the excellent character of both defendants. Besides Attorneys Grace and Edmiston, of Fort Smith, Col. Vandervert, of Kinsley, and Col. F. J. Close, of Troy, Kan., were employed for defense. Col. Close also testified to the good character of his client, Miller, whom he had known for nearly twenty years.

The theory of the government was that Hantz was killed by his companions for what little money he had. He had sold his horse at Fayetteville, and was the only one in the party who had money. Many believed that Miller was the chief offender, and that while the boy. Woods, knew what had become of his friend, he kept it a secret, partly through fear. In rendering its verdict the jury, in a polite note, asked the mercy of the court in behalf of the boy. An application for a new trial was argued and overruled. Later, a petition for executive clemency succeeded in obtaining for Woods a pardon, and for Miller a commutation of sentence to life imprisonment.

A feature of the case was the love of a dog, similar to others that have been connected with murder trials. Hantz owned a hound that had accompanied him through the entire trip. It refused to leave the camp, remaining for weeks, howling night and day, and trailing around from the camp to the stream where the body was found. Another feature was the murdered man's watch, which was found in Miller's possession when he was arrested, and which he accounted for by saying that he had been carrying it for some time on the trip, and had it in his possession when Hantz got lost from them.

THE BOUDINOT CASE

A celebrated case, the trial of which attracted, perhaps, more attention than any in the previous history of the court, was what was known far and wide as "The Boudinot Case," wherein Charles C. Boudinot, jr., was held for the murder of B. H. Stone, at Tahlequah, October 21, 1887. At the time Boudinot killed Stone, the latter was editing the Telephone, and the former, a nephew of the celebrated attorney-statesmen, and son of W. P. Boudinot, was editor of the Cherokee Advocate both papers being published at Tahlequah. Young Boudinot belonged to one political faction and Stone to another. Stone was a radical, an able writer, and his paper was often charged with vitriol. He criticised some public acts of Boudinot in connection with the Cherokee council, and later indulged in bitter personalities against Boudinot and others, making Boudinot a special target in his attack upon the National party, repeating the attack in several successive issues of his paper, bringing about very unfriendly relations between the two men.

On the day of the killing young Boudinot sent an employe of the Advocate office to collect a bill due the paper from Stone, for advertising, and Stone instructed the bearer to tell Boudinot to "come and collect it himself." Later in the day Boudinot called at the printing office and was told that Stone had gone to a photograph gallery which he was conducting in another part of town. Boudinot went out, and after sauntering into several business places, he finally entered a hardware store, and purchasing a pistol placed it in his waistband and proceeded to Stone's office, where he found Stone alone. After the passage of a few angry words between the two men, Boudinot fired the shot that sent Stone's soul to its Maker, and placed him on trial for his life. The affair created great excitement, and after quiet was restored Boudinot went to Fort Smith and surrendered to the Federal authorities, and requested permission to give bond. He was placed in custody of the marshal, and after examination by a commissioner, Judge Parker admitted him to bail in the sum of $10,000, which was readily given, and Boudinot was released from custody, notwithstanding Stone's friends made every possible effort to prevent his being allowed to give bond.

The trial of the case was a most interesting one, and none was ever fought with more energy and tact on both sides. There were twenty-five witnesses sworn by the prosecution and seventeen for defense. Senator Dan W. Voorhees, of Indiana, ex-District Attorney W. H. H. Clayton, F. P. Blair, of Kansas City, R. B. Rutherford and Col. E. C. Boudinot, uncle of the defendant, were engaged in the defense; Senator Voorhees volunteering his services, without regard to recompense, on account of his friendship for the family. The prosecution was conducted by District Attorney Sandels, assisted by O. L. Miles, a rising young attorney from Boonville, Logan County, Arkansas, who had already won fame as an eloquent speaker, and has since made a name for himself as an able attorney. The case was opened Wednesday morning, November 21, 1888, the taking of testimony beginning on Thursday. The theory of the government was that Boudinot went to Stone's office for the purpose of taking his life, and that Stone was wholly unarmed when killed. It was also held that Stone was never in the habit of carrying a pistol and did not possess a deadly weapon. The twenty-five witnesses summoned by the government supported this theory and testified to other circumstances connected with the killing. The respondent's attorneys, on the other hand, made their fight on the theory of self-defense, claiming that Stone had made repeated threats against Boudinot to different persons and at different times, and that when defendant shot him he was in the act of drawing a pistol from his right hip pocket. As no pistol was found in the room where the killing occurred this appeared a difficult circumstance to prove, yet the defense produced witnesses who swore they had seen a certain black handled pistol on the person of Stone, and two of them swore they saw him with it only an hour or so before the killing and in the very room where he was killed. It was also claimed that immediately after the killing a partisan friend of the deceased was in the room long enough to have taken the pistol and given it to Mrs. Stone, who was nearby. Of the many witnesses who testified that Stone had made threats against the life of the defendant, three of them swore they had communicated these threats to him only a day or two' before the killing. Three witnesses were produced, one of them a brother of the defendant, who swore they were near Stone's office when Boudinot entered and desiring to talk with him on a business matter, they were approaching the place—a small box house of 10x12 feet—when they heard Stone say, in an angry tone: "I won't pay it!"

Then they approached and, looking through a window, saw Boudinot standing, while Stone was sitting in an arm chair facing him; they heard Boudinot talking to Stone about the personal articles he had published in the Telephone and heard him tell Stone he must retract some statements he had published, at which Stone replied, with an oath: "I will publish what I please."

As he said this, these witnesses saw him place his right hand to his right side as if to draw a pistol, at the same time starting to rise from his chair, when Boudinot shot him, and as he fell the chair tumbled over with him, and Boudinot walked out of the office and across the street, where he met his brother, Frank Boudinot, told him he had shot Stone and asked him to do what he could for the wounded. Dr. Fite was immediately summoned, but the victim was past earthly assistance; he died within a short time.

In rebuttal the government introduced several witnesses who testified that the trousers worn by Stone when killed had no hip pockets, consequently he could not have carried a pistol in his hip pocket, as certified by the defense. Mrs. Bell, a sister-in-law of Stone, swore the trousers were not brought to Fort Smith during the examination before the commissioner in November, 1887, but were brought to the city in August, 1888, and then returned, since when she had not seen them. Her husband then took the stand and swore positively that the trousers were at the commissioner's trial; counsel had examined them and said they would not be needed, hence they were carried home, which the defense claimed to be evidence of the trousers being provided with hip pockets, or they would have been produced by the government at that time It being claimed by the government that Stone had no pistol, the defense offered a witness to prove that when the widow of Stone attended the commissioner's trial she had in her possession a black handled pistol, such as witness testified Stone carried, and showed it to him. Attorney Sandels objected to the admission of this testimony and, after some argument by Mr. Voorhees, the court ruled it out, on the ground that the circumstance was too remote from the killing to be admissible. Considerable testimony was introduced relative to the character and standing of the two men in the community where they resided. The reputation of Boudinot as a law-abiding, peaceful citizen was fully sustained, but the reputation of Stone was shown by the testimony to be of a very unsavory nature; he was shown to be a man well calculated to stir up strife in any community. A vast amount of evidence was introduced but all was similar to that here cited and many of the government witnesses gave testimony favorable to the defendant. On Monday noon, November 26, the taking of testimony by both sides was closed and the arguments begun. Mr. Miles opened for the prosecution, presenting the case in a clear and forcible argument, occupying the balance of the day. The time from opening court Tuesday morning until noon was taken by Mr. Clayton, for defense, in a speech replete with reason and sound argument.

He was followed, in the afternoon, by Mr. Voorhees and the knowledge that he would speak at that time having been circulated, the crowds began pouring into the court house early after dinner and by the time court was opened there was not even standing room for the multitude who were eager to listen to the words of the distinguished statesman-lawyer. The court officers found it impossible to seat all the women present, and the men were left to their own devices. The windows were crowded and the verandas at the front and rear of the court house were filled, many going away disappointed or standing out in the open air, as near to the court room as possible. Mr. Voorhees delivered a powerful argument in behalf of his client and it was listened to with marked attention. He was followed, Wednesday morning, by District Attorney Sandels who delivered the closing argument in his usual reasoning style, leaving no point untouched that might tend to the success of his cause. In the afternoon, Judge Parker charged the jury in a clear and elaborate manner and the case was given into their hands at 5 o'clock, p. m. About 8 o'clock, they agreed upon a verdict, and as soon as the Judge and Clerk could be sent for it was received and read.—"We, the jury, find the defendant not guilty, as charged in the within indictment." The defendant's wife, father, mother, brother, two sisters and uncle were present and the scene was one of great rejoicing. The members of the family, grasped each juror by the hand, with heartfelt expression of thanks, tears standing in their eyes. On their way from the court house to the city, the happy family met Mr. Voorhees, who appeared equally delighted with the verdict. The entire family accompanied the Senator to his hotel, where they remained for some time, bidding their friend and benefactor farewell.

THE RESULT OF AN ILLCIT LOVE

Frank Capel killed his mistress, Minnie O'Dell, November 7, 1888, at Purcell, Choctaw Nation. He was convicted of the crime, March 1, 1889. Capel and his victim had. been living; together for some time; he was jealous of her, objecting to her receiving attentions from others, She had formerly lived in Fort Smith and had gone to Purcell, at Capel's request. On the day before the murder, they quarreled and the girl left him, going to the house of a notorious prostitute, named Nell Singleton. The next day, Capel "got on a spree," and in the afternoon, while very drunk, went to the house where Minnie was. He fired his pistol in the house and knocked the girl down and kicked her. At first it was not thought that the injuries inflicted upon the frail creature were of a serious nature, but during the night her condition became alarming and she died the next morning. She told the doctor, just before she died, that Capel struck her with his six-shooter. A post-mortem examination revealed the fact that her skull was fractured. There were also bruises on the side from kicks, but death resulted from the blow upon the head. Capel claimed that when he entered the house the girl attacked him with a knife, and he struck her with his fist, knocking her down and that when falling, her head struck heavily against a stove, causing the fracture. He did not deny kicking her, but endeavored to justify his act by saying the girl tried to kill him on a previous occasion, while they were taking a buggy ride. Two inmates of the house saw Capel enter; they said Minnie was sitting on the floor; they saw the drunken man walk to her and deliver a brutal kick, then they hurriedly left the room and saw no more of the trouble. The case was given to the jury at noon, and a verdict of guilty was returned within an hour. Capel was 34 years old; he formerly lived at Marshfield, Missouri, where his parents and three sisters resided. His mother died soon after his incarceration at Fort Smith, her death being attributed to her son's disgrace. B. D. Capel, father of the murderer, was at Fort Smith to attend the trial but he became ill before the case was taken up, and was obliged to remain at his boarding house, dying the next evening after his son was convicted. Before he died, Frank was securely hand-cuffed and taken to his father's bed-side, under a strong guard. The old man had not been told of his son's conviction, and in a feeble tone, he asked the result of the trial. Frank replied:

"I cannot tell you a lie on your deathbed, father—I have been convicted of murder."

"It will kill me," moaned the poor father and he prayed God to have mercy on his son. The parting between the dying man and his condemned son was a touching scene. The old man sank rapidly after his boy was taken back to prison, dying within the hour. He was attended during his illness by a younger son, who resided at Huntington, in Sebastian county, Arkansas. The deceased was a poor but respected citizen of Marshfield, and a Mason, in good standing. He was buried under the auspices of the Masonic fraternity, of Fort Smith. The Fort Smith Elevator, in closing the account of the trial and details of the crime, said:

"The fate of Frank Capel is only another instance of ruin wrought by indulgence in strong drink, and cards. He was classed as a gambler, was the associate of gamblers, fast women, and toughs, and while indulging in one of the orgies common among men of his class, he committed a deed which will in due course of time, bring him to the gallows, has caused the death of his parents and brought misery and disgrace upon his young sisters, in their distant Missouri home. All this affliction, death, degradation and humiliation that has fallen upon this entire family, is simply the result of young Capel getting drunk on the 7th day of November, 1888, for had he been sober, he never would have taken the life of Minnie O'Dell. Let young men take warning by Frank's terrible experience and avoid fast women, wine and cards."

Elsie James and her daughter, Margaret James, with Zeno Colbert and Sampson Alexander, were charged with the murder of William Jones, at the home of Mrs. James, five miles from Stonewall, Chickasaw Nation, July 2, 1887. Jones cultivated a crop on Mrs. James' farm and, being unmarried, he boarded at her house. Soon after the date noted above, Jones was missed from his usual haunts and an investigation resulted in suspicion being turned against Mrs. James, who was the owner of a fine farm, well stocked with implements, teams and cattle; in the words of one of the witnesses, she was "well fixed." On being questioned, regarding the disappearance of

Jones,. Mrs. James at first denied all knowledge of his whereabouts but finally, being induced to make a statement, she said that Jones had attacked her with a butcher knife and she shot and killed him, and her daughter and herself buried him a short distance from the house. She instructed her daughter to show where the body lay. This confession was secured October 1, following the murder, but later she told a different story, to the effect that Zeno Colbert shot and killed Jones in her house because the latter had attacked him with a butcher knife; that the killing occurred in the afternoon and Colbert wanted to burn the remains but she would not allow it, and he left, telling her and her daughter to bury the body and say nothing about it or he would kill her; that the dead body lay in her hall all night, and the next morning she and her daughter carried it a short distance from the house and sent for Sampson Alexander to come and help bury it; that Sampson and his mother came and the body was buried. After Deputy Marshal Heck Thomas had arrested the two men and the women, the body was exhumed, and on examination it was found that the skull had been crushed with a blunt instrument. At the Commissioner's examination, the fractured skull was produced as evidence and the two women and Colbert were held to await the action of the grand jury. No evidence being found against Alexander, except that he simply knew of the killing, he was released. The grand jury ignored the cases of Colbert and Margaret James and Mrs. James was held for trial. She was a full Cherokee, and weighed over 200 pounds; the daughter was but a child. About two weeks after Colbert was released, having returned to his home, he was waylaid and murdered. The next grand jury indicted Margaret James, and the trial of herself and the mother was set down for January, 1889. At this trial the jury failed to agree. Mrs. James had sold her farm and all of her stock to secure counsel and was ably defended by Messrs DuVal & Cravens, Thomas Marcum and George A. Grace, Esq. The jury was discharged, and the case was remanded for trial at the February term of court, when the daughter was acquitted and the mother convicted, March 22, 1889. The government showed that Jones had received $65 through the post-office, on the day before the murder, and claimed Mrs. James shot him to secure the money, and that there were no others about the house, at the time the murder was committed, except the daughter Margaret, Mrs. James, only child. It was shown that Jones had expended $5 of the money for tobacco and a pair of shoes, having $60 remaining; that Mrs. James made a trip from home after the murder, that she was apparently well supplied with money, and that she sold a pair of shoes answering the description of the shoes purchased by Jones. It was also ascertained that Mrs. James sent the child to a spring for water, and while at the spring, she heard several shots and when she returned she saw Jones in the hall, dead. Sampson Alexander testified that Mrs. James said to him, "I have laid the murder on Zeno and I want you to swear you saw him with the $60." Sampson did not swear as the woman wanted him to, and she was convicted, as stated.

DEATH FOR A WATERMELON

Joe Martin, convicted April 6, 1889, of the murder of Ernest Adams, lived in the Choctaw Nation, near the home of his brother, Reed Martin, and not far from Red River. Adams, who was a married man, worked for Reed Martin. Adams had taken the liberty of pulling some melons from Joe Martin's patch without his permission, and on Sunday morning, July 15, 1888, Martin went to him and asked why he pulled the melons. Adams replied that he pulled them to eat, and some harsh words passed between them. Joe Martin went home and Adams went to a neighbor named Jones and borrowed a gun, saying he was going turkey hunting. About 10 o'clock in the morning he and Joe Martin passed by a house occupied by some negroes—Martin in advance—and while in sight of the negroes Martin suddenly grappled with Adams and took the gun from him. The two men continued around a bend in the road, and just after passing from sight a shot was heard by the negroes in the house, and soon Martin returned alone, saying the weapon had become accidentally discharged, and that Adams took fright and ran off through the brush. Adams failed to return, and on Monday morning a search was instituted. On the banks of Red River, about a mile from Martin's house, was found the tracks of a mule, where the animal had been tied to a sapling. The tracks of a man were also found, and evidence that something had been dragged down the steep bank to a sand bar. The tracks of the man led across the sand bar to the water and then back to the mule; from there the mule tracks led to Joe Martin's house. The search was continued, and the next day a comforter, recognized as having belonged to Adams, was found at the river, and a shoe that was supposed to have been worn by Adams. On Wednesday Martin was arrested, and on Thursday a bed-quilt was pulled out of a lot of driftwood; it was Martin's quilt. On Friday the body of Adams, minus the head, was found some distance down the river from where Martin's quilt was discovered. A thorough search failed to discover the dismembered portion of the body, and it was never found.

The body was identified by patches on the pantaloons. A piece of leather thong, with a rope attached, found at the river, was proven to have been in Martin's possession on the day before the murder. Reed Martin was arrested and taken to Fort Smith with his brother, but he was not indicted.

The defense tried to make it appear that Adams was seen alive several hours after the negroes at the house heard the shot, and that he said he was going to leave the country—as he and his wife could not agree—and tried to impress the jury with the idea that the dead body was not that of Adams at all. The theory of the prosecution was that adopted by the jury, to the effect that Martin killed Adams at the time the gun-shot was heard; then concealed the body until night, and under cover of darkness, carried it to the river on the mule; then, as the bank was too steep for the mule to descend, he tied the animal to a tree, and dragged the body down the bank and carried it across the sand bar to the water, having first removed the head to prevent identification; that he placed the head in a quilt before depositing it in the water, and that it rolled out, unnoticed, when the quilt was pulled from the drift. The evidence was all circumstantial, but very strong, and the verdict of guilty was returned in a very short time.

Martin's wife and four children were at the trial. When the verdict was announced Martin wept bitterly. The grief of the distressed wife was a most pitiful sight, and as the condemned man was conducted back to jail she followed him with her babe in arms, and her little ones clinging about her, all weeping as if their hearts were broken. She kept close to the prisoner until the iron doors of the prison hid him from view, after which she slowly walked from the jail yard, accompanied by her brother-in-law, a Mr. Stein, from Little Rock, who was also present at the trial, and who was very kind and attentive to the distressed family. The Martins formerly lived in Yell county, near Dardanelle, Ark. Reed Martin, who attended the trial of his brother, was arrested by an officer from Yell county and taken to Dardanelle, to answer to an offense charged to have been committed years before.

DANGERS BESETTING THE LIVES OF U. S. DEPUTY MARSHALS

RAPE OF PRETTY LEONA DEVERE

The life of a deputy United States marshal for the Western District of Arkansas, was one requiring a stout heart and the many dangers these men were compelled to face, begat an indifference to fear, that, at times, amounted to recklessness. Woe to the marshal, however, who became so careless, as to forget to take proper precautions, for it was necessary, on account of the nature of the criminal classes with which they had to deal, to be on the alert at every moment and to affect the capture of a noted criminal, a marshal was often obliged to "out Herod Herod." Not only must he hunt down the object of his search, ofttimes hidden in remote places where none but a criminal or a brave officer would dare intrude, but also must he study the methods of those with whom he was obliged to mingle, sometimes, for weeks together, before a favorable opportunity, for a successful arrest was presented. A United States deputy marshal was feared by the criminal classes in the Indian country, with that fear that begets the most dangerous hatred, for many of these men were there, because they had committed outlawry in civilized communities, and fled to the prairies and mountains of the Indian Territory, for the protection that the frontier gives to a desperate criminal. It naturally followed, that men who were there from a common cause, met upon an equal footing, and often they banded together to assist each other in avoiding the almost certain consequences of their acts, and finding so little opposition to a continuance of the style of conduct which had driven them beyond the bounds of civilization, with plenty of opportunities to satisfy their keen appetites for crime, they came to regard as a friend or an equal, any new corner whose record was shady, while one whose intent was to live a life of sobriety, in conformity with law was looked upon as an intruder and as either a victim or an enemy. These men, who hated, while they feared the officers of the law, had shrewd schemes, and even signals by which they connived together to prevent an officer from performing his assigned duty and it not infrequently happened that one was an accessary to murder, an aider and abettor of crime, while forty miles or more away from the precise spot where the act was committed. Throughout a large portion of the Indian Territory are located mountain peaks, or knobs, from whose heights one can see for many miles in that clear, unsullied atmosphere, enabling the operation of a perfect system of signals by the means of beacon lights at night. Often, this method was employed to warn of the approach of an officer, and the sentinel on the nearest knob would repeat the signal to the next and so on to the next, the inhabitants of the valleys meanwhile receiving full knowledge of the danger, so that within the space of a few minutes, the criminal classes in a tract, many miles in extent, could be warned of the approach of officers, their numbers, whether one or more, and sometimes their identity. It was not uncommon for an officer in search of a criminal, to enter the Indian Territory in the guise of a laborer and obtain employment among the squatters who were permitted by the Indian Nations to secure "rights" to till small tracts of land, using the position as a base of information from which to watch for a favorable opportunity to make a strike which should land a crafty outlaw in the clutches of the great court.

This was dangerous business for the deputy, for the faintest suspicion that he was an officer engaged in the role of a spy, was often sufficient to cause the gleam of a six-shooter and the crash of a bullet through the brain of a brave but too venturesome officer. At such times, the utmost secrecy of his plans and identity must be preserved if the officer would safely perform his duties, for though the knowledge that a marshal was in a neighborhood would cause the heart in many an outlaw's breast to quake with fear, that very fear was sufficient to make of the hunted criminal a most desperate foe when brought to bay. It mattered not, whom, of the many law breakers the officer might be in quest, each of his class in the vicinity of that officer's sojourn, once he was known to be present as a spy, made of it a common cause and considered it his duty to "society" to make way with the dangerous intruder. Because of this fact, more than one brave officer was taken by surprise and made to bite the dust, before he was aware that his identity was known.

As a sample of the serious position in which these brave men were often placed, and the difficulties they were sometimes obliged to surmount in order to secure a prisoner, the following experience of Deputy Marshal H. D. Fannin, in the Chickasaw Nation, in the summer of 1883, will illustrate:

Fannin went into the Indian Territory in search of one Jason Labreu, with several aliases, who was wanted for the murder of his sweetheart, Leona Devere, the beautiful daughter of a well-to-do farmer residing in western Arkansas.

Labreu had been a Texas cowboy, was of splendid physique and fine features, with chestnut curly hair, and eyes whose expression was capable of winning the heart of a Greek goddess in chiseled marble. His wild roving disposition, his reckless air, his laughing eyes and touch, tender and caressing as a woman's, had captivated the pretty little unsophisticated Arkansas maiden, and she had made him her hero, while she became to him a plaything. After a few short months, during which the poor girl reveled in the seventh heaven of happiness, the dastardly scoundrel tired of his toy and with honeyed words carefully selected, attempted to seduce her. Angered at his failure after repeated attempts, he one day, first pledging to her that he was only testing her and that he only loved her more devotedly because of her strength of character in resisting his enticements, induced her to go with him for a walk, in a stretch of timber land, in search of wild flowers. At a beautiful spot, just within the border of the Indian Territory, too far away from her home for her screams to be heard, in a sequestered nook close by a clear running stream, with bursting buds and spring flowers all about, he seated her while she innocently chatted away, unconscious oi her impending doom, and wove garlands from the flowers and ferns they had gathered. Here again he commenced his blandishments and finally, unable longer to control his passions, he seized her, crowded his handkerchief into her mouth and accomplished his brutal purpose; then he stood away, gazed for a moment upon the bent figure, whose shamed features were covered with heir pretty palms, her form shaken with convulsive sobs. In another instant he was as a maniac; with a savage oath he sprang upon her, dragged her to the stream and forcing her down, held her head beneath the waters until she was dead, then turned and fled. The dead body, horribly decomposed, was found a week later, and the poor mother went insane over the affair.

Fannin trailed the fiend for several months, and at last found him at work for a farmer in the Chickasaw Nation near the Red river, a few miles from Thackerville. Labreu was known to be a dead shot and Fannin realized, (when he discovered, after a reconnoiter of the field where he was at work, that Labreu carried his Winchester constantly, strapped to his back when working) that the task of arresting him, could be accomplished in no short order. Labreu had never known Fannin, and the officer hired to the farmer at three dollars a month "and found," and was sent into the field to assist the rapist and murderer.

For three long months the two worked together, slept in the same bunk at night, ate their meals at the same time, and in fact, were together almost constantly. Fannin was obliged to use the utmost discretion. He was heavily armed when he reached the farmer's house but he left all his weapons hanging in the kitchen to avoid arousing Labreu's suspicions. He gradually let drop the details of a story to the effect that he had slain a cattleman at Dallas, Texas, and that he was a fugitive from justice. This caused Labreu to have a fellow feeling for him and to become more sociable, and at last, having borne his-terrible secret until human endurance could stand no more, he told of his own crime, the one most horrible act of his life, which had made it necessary for him to flee to the fastness of the Indian Territory for protection.

Fannin bided his time; this confession was half of the battle and he could afford to Wait for the right opportunity to engage in the other. Often he would discover Labreu gazing upon him with those eyes, so terrible in their scrutiny, as if they would read his innermost soul. It was a hard strain upon even the experienced officer to maintain a cool composure under such conditions, with the knowledge full upon him that the slightest mistake, the tremor of an eye-lash, meant death. Study as he would, the officer could conceive of no plan by which he could throw Labreu off his guard long enough to arrest and shackle him. Once he walked up behind him in the field where they were at work, thinking: "If I only had my pistol now I could take him." The soft yielding earth gave fourth no sound from his footsteps, yet even the thought in the officer's mind seemed to have a magnetic effect upon Labreu, for when within twenty feet the latter suddenly turned about, at the same time slinging his rifle into position and bringing it to a full cock.

"Oh! It is you, is it?" Said Labreu, smiling, and then proceeded to his work.

Fannin had about given up all thought of ever winning the outlaw's confidence, or of being able to "get the drop," when Labreu, himself, gave the sudden opportunity, and it was seized by the officer just in the nick of time. They had answered the call to dinner. The day was hot and sultry and both men were fatigued from their half day's labor. A single wash basin, on a stool outside the kitchen door served for both. Labreu was the first to wash. He leaned his Winchester against the door casing, not noticing that Fannin, as he stood waiting his turn, occupied a position between himself and the weapon. He emptied the basin, reached a towel from a nail nearby, leaned forward and buried his face in it. Fannin saw the opportunity he had so long sought; noiselessly he picked up the weapon, leveled it upon the outlaw, but none too soon. It was only for the briefest possible space of time that the latter stood with his face so covered, and when he looked up, with that quick start, so often seen by Fannin, it was to find himself looking along a polished steel barrel with the determined right eye of the marshal gleaming at the other end. There was no foolishness about it, no attempt to laugh it off as a joke. Greek had met Turk; both understood the situation fully; each intuitively knew the other to be a desperate man, and without a word of explanation from either of them, Labreu threw up his hands, and calmly allowed the farmer, who was called from the house, to clasp the handcuffs about his wrists. He cheated the gallows, however, for before Fannin had reached Fort Smith with his prisoner he was obliged to leave him alone for but a moment, at a crossing of two railroads, when quick as a flash, as soon as he discovered he was unguarded, Labreu made a dash for liberty and the leaden messenger which the officer sent flying after him, brought him to the ground, dead.

THE TWENTY-EIGHTH EXECUTION

THE SECOND SEXTETTE, AND OTHER CASES

On January 16, 1890, for the second time in the history of the great court, six men were marched up the scaffold stairs, "The gates of Hell," to descend again suddenly, their bodies suspended between heaven and earth, their souls released for a flight to the unknown future. On several occasions more than six felons would have been executed together (at one time eleven) but for executive interference in the shape of respites or commutations of sentences to terms of imprisonment. Indeed, on this occasion also, seven murderers awaited the fatal day, having been sentenced to pay the death penalty on the date named, but just in the nick of time came a respite from the President for one, and his lease on life was extended, indefinitely, only to be terminated a few days later, January 30, 1890, on the same old scaffold.

This was George Tobler, a negro, who was convicted September 19, 1889, for the murder of Irvin Richmond at a dance, in Cache bottom, in the Choctaw Nation, April 30, 1889. The evidence on which Tobler was convicted was all circumstantial but of a nature so strong and clear that the jury were out but a short time. Richmond, the victim of Tobler's murderous passions, was also a negro; the men had previously quarreled about a woman to whom both were attached and Richmond had on this occasion escorted her to the dance, at which he was engaged as a musician. In the afterpart of the night, while the revelry was at its height, the dancers were suddenly startled by a shot from without and Richmond fell dead. The assassin had held the muzzle of his weapon close to a crack and sent the bullet into Richmond's body less than two feet away. The circumstances pointed to Tobler as the murderer and the defendant failed to rebut them. About a year before, two of Tobler's brothers, notice of whom has already appeared, were executed, at Wichita, Kansas. George Tobler denied being the murderer of Richmond, but on the morning of the execution he told Charles Bullard, his cell-mate, that he had dreamed during the night of the man he had killed. Bullard and another, Madison James, were to have been executed on the same day as were the sextette but were more fortunate and secured commutations.,

THE SECOND SEXTETTE

The six murderers above mentioned were Harris Austin, John Billy, Thomas Willis, Sam Goin, Jimmon Burris and, Jefferson Jones.

Harris Austin was a full Chickasaw; he was a splendid specimen of physical manhood, weighing 200 pounds. He lived on Red River. On May 25, 1883, he killed Thomas Elliott at Tishomingo, in the Chickasaw Nation. The crime was cold-blooded, unprovoked, atrocious and revolting in the extreme.

Elliott had only been in the Indian Territory two months. James Pearson, a half-brother of Austin, had been drinking and Elliott had accused him of stealing some whiskey from him. The two sat on the front porch of a store, talking, Pearson being armed. As they thus sat, Austin approached and. took Pearson's pistol and the two walked away a short distance, talked for a few minutes in their native tongue, and then Austin returned and shot Elliott in the breast, without giving a moment's warning. Elliott fell and the murderer shot a second time into the body, then, demon like, he walked close to the prostrate form, held the muzzle of his pistol close to the murdered man's forehead and fired, burning the skin badly. Austin escaped (murderers are cowards, for they always run) and went to his home, and, in spite of efforts to capture him, he was at large until April, 1889, when he was finally captured by Deputy Marshal Carr and his posse, through strategy. Austin would go home and sleep at night but would leave for the woods early in the morning and scout during the day. Carr and his posse went to the house towards morning and at a very early hour they saw him come from the house and go towards the river. They quietly watched him until he was well away from his door when they took positions between him and the house and surrounded him. He fought desperately but was shot down and was placed in the Fort Smith jail April 18, 1889, an(J cured, then tried and convicted. The jury were out only twenty minutes.

John Billy, Thomas Willis and Madison James were full Choctaw Indians. They were convicted jointly of the murder of William P. Williams. The principal witness against them was an Indian named Graham, who said that he and the three others named, fell in with Williams in the Kiamichi Mountains and he sold them whiskey. All of them became drunk. Williams had more whiskey but the Indians had no more money and he refused to trust them for anymore of his goods. Finally Williams accused them of stealing whiskey and Graham, foreseeing trouble, started to take Williams away and, as they were going, the others started up and Willis took deliberate aim at Williams with his Winchester, shooting him through the body. The three Indians ran to Williams as he fell and one of them drew the dying man's six-shooter and emptied its chambers into the prostrate form. Then they stripped the body of its clothing and Willis divided $12 with his companions and took possession of the six-fire, 45-calibre, nickel plated Colt's revolver and coat of the victim. They next buried the body in a shallow ravine, felled a tree across the place and piled brush over the tell-tale grave.

This crime was committed April 12, 1888, and the Indians had come to the conclusion that it was a secret with themselves alone, but on January 8, 1890, Deputy Marshal Ben Cantrail arrested Graham and he told the whole story and became a government witness. Williams' skull and coat, showing the marks of the seven bullets, were found and were produced as evidence at the trial, which was very short, lasting only a few hours.

Jefferson Jones was convicted of a most foul and disgusting murder, his victim being an old man of sixty years, named Henry Wilson. On March 12, 1889, Wilson started from near LeFlore, in the Choctaw Nation, for a trip to Polk County, Arkansas, his mission being to procure a horse and return within a week. His route lay through the Winding Stair Mountains. More than a week passed and he did not return and his sons began a search; they trailed him as far as Isaac Winton's, where he stopped the first night after leaving home, and from there all trace ceased. The mountains were scoured for the missing man and, finally, the Federal officers were informed of the matter. Deputy Marshal Barnhill picked up the thread and found Wilson's gun at the home of George Beams. He arrested Beams, who said Jefferson Jones had killed a white man and left the victim's gun at his house. The marshal then arrested Jones, who confessed and said he had hid Wilson's money, about $5, under the house of his brother, Jimson Jones. Jimson was arrested and he admitted the truth of his brother's statement, but said that he had spent the entire amount at Talihina. Jefferson Jones did not testify on the stand, but to others he said that the white man came to Beam's house to inquire the way to the big road and he had gone with him to give the desired information; a short distance from the house he had murdered the white man for his money and had thrown the body in a creek. The body was found, two months after the murder, badly decomposed. Jimson Jones and Beam were tried with the other and were acquitted. When pronouncing sentence on Jefferson Jones, Judge Parker requested him to make a truthful statement and he confessed he had committed the crime without the assistance or knowledge of anyone.

Sam Goin and Jimmon Burris became murderers through covetousness. On November 27, 1888, Houston Joyce, of Franklin, Texas, who was seeking to escape the results of some indiscretion at home, while traveling through the Indian Territory, stopped for dinner at the home of Jim Goin (uncle of Sam Goin) and in paying for his meal he displayed a considerable amount of money. Alter he had proceeded on his way, Jim Goin gave Burris and his nephew a pistol and told them to follow the stranger and kill him. They were soon in pursuit and overtaking him in an unfrequented spot they killed him, took his horse, money and other property and left the body to the mercy of wild beasts Two days later, at a dance in the vicinity, Sam Goin told of the horrible affair to Solomon Bacon, telling him also that the horse was then running loose on the prairie and asked him to post the animal as an estray. Bacon did not comply with Sam's request, but, instead, told of the crime to Deputy Marshal J. M. Ennis, who worked up the case and found the bones and pieces of clothing scattered about the scene of the killing and a letter addressed to "J. T. Babb, Smackover, Arkansas." Mr. Babb was then a member of the Arkansas Legislature and the find aroused not a little excitement. It was soon learned that Babb was alive and well and the mystery increased until it was learned that he had allowed young Joyce to use his name in writing home, and to receive mail in his name.

The execution of this second sextette was comparatively a quiet affair; very little announcement had been made by the press concerning it, executions at Fort Smith having become too common and trivial occurrences to waste much printer's ink over. The stockade about the gallows prevented crowds of sight seers from gloating their morbid passions at the sight and only the necessary officers, several newspaper men and a few others who had secured passes, were allowed within the enclosure. Very little was said on the scaffold; they had all made statements in their cells, acknowledging the crimes for 'which they were sentenced.

ANOTHER CRIME UNCOVERED

While preparing evidence to convict Goin and Burris. Marshal Ennis unearthed another dastardly crime, committed three months after the murder of Joyce. The victim of this murder was John Hyde, a white man. While traveling unarmed across the Indian country, riding one horse and leading another, he met G. D. Eastman, Battese and Toledo Cartubbee. They immediately halted him, tied his hands with a lariat, conducted him to the banks of Boggy River, three miles from where Joyce was killed, and calmly told him his time had come. They then, with great deliberation, placed him in position facing them and riddled his body with buck shot and Winchester bullets. Having fully satisfied their lust, they tied a heavy rock to the body and another to the saddle of the murdered man and dropped them into the river. Marshal Ennis arrested Cartubbee and the crafty Indian at once told the whole story and offered to conduct the officer to the place of the crime; he explained the details, pointing out the exact places where each of the men stood at the moment of the killing. Marshal Ennis divested himself of his clothing, went into the river and found the saddle with the rock still attached, but did not find the body. It was conjectured that the river being very high at the time the murder was committed, the ropes had slipped and the body thus freed from its encumbrance had been washed down the stream. Hyde's two brothers were present when the saddle was fished from the water and they identified it fully. Cartubbee, of course, claimed to have had no part in the killing. Battese remained at large, but Toledo Cartubbee was conveyed to Fort Smith. While awaiting execution, Goin and Burris confessed to having a hand in this crime also and told the same story as was given by Cartubbee to the officer. From all knowledge obtainable, however, the crime was never avenged. Just a few days after its commission the judicial district known as the Eastern District of Texas, with court at

Paris, Texas, had been established and the court there claimed jurisdiction in what came to be known as the Eastman case. United States Commissioner H. H. Kirkpatrick, of Paris, issued warrants for the murderers, as they had not been indicted at Fort Smith, but Judge Parker held that he had jurisdiction; the Supreme Court subsequently held the reverse, and from the records nothing tends to indicate that the men were tried at the Fort Smith Court and it seems likely that in the "shuffle" they escaped, for they were not tried at Paris.

THE HAND OF JUSTICE STAYED

Charles Bullard, who. would have been swung off at the same time as were the six murderers noted in this chapter, but for the energy and tenacity of his attorney, was an octoroon, about 24 years old, an orphan, who had been reared by an Eastern railroad magnate, and had gone West in search of conditions more to his liking than were the scenes of his childhood. He found his way into the Indian Territory, and at the time of the commission of his crime he was staying at Gibson Station, Cherokee

Nation. He had trouble with another man, Walker Bean, about a young woman to whom he was paying attention, and of whom Bean was also enamored. Bean was quarrelsome and overbearing, and was termed by his acquaintances as a "bull-dozer." On the evening of March 5, 1889, Bullard and Bean had a verbal encounter and threats were made by each of them. The next morning Ballard borrowed an old musket, ostensibly for the purpose of shooting wild game, and proceeded to where Bean was at work as a section hand on the Missouri, Kansas, & Texas Railroad. Bean was unarmed. The quarrel of the previous evening was renewed and both me* used very abusive language. Bean addressed a vile epithet to his enemy and was ordered to retract; he refused, and was instantly shot dead by Bullard, who surrendered to the authorities and was taken to Fort Smith and placed on trial for his life. He employed J. Warren Reed to defend him and entered a claim of self-defense, which was not sustained, nor was his action in killing Bean urged as being justifiable, and Bullard was convicted of murder. The only move which his attorney could make was in mitigation of punishment. By the aid of petitions, testimonials of previous good character and strong arguments for mercy, Mr. Reed, in behalf of his client, approached the throne of executive clemency at Washington, D.C., and by persistent appeal to Benjamin Harrison, secured the commutation of Bullard's death sentence to life imprisonment. Two years later Mr. Reed renewed the application for executive clemency and secured for his client full pardon and release, and he again returned to the civil walks of life, having learned a valuable lesson that should serve as a warning to all hot-headed youths. The trial in this case cost the government over $6,000.

THE FIRST APPEAL

The next murder case wherein conviction was secured was that of William Alexander, a Mexican, thirty-three years old, charged with killing David C. Steadman near Choska, in the Creek Nation, October 21, 1889. This case was a noteworthy one in the history of the Fort Smith Court; it attracted universal attention on account of its being the first murder case sent to the United States Supreme Court from the Federal court at Fort Smith on appeal. For near fifteen years Judge Parker had held full sway as Judge for the Western District of Arkansas, having full and final jurisdiction in all criminal cases under the Federal statutes, being, as legal history records it, the only trial court on earth from which there was no appeal, making it as well a court of last resort. In 1889, February 6, congress had passed an act, one of its provisions granting the right of appeal to the Supreme Court of the United States in all cases of conviction of crimes where the punishment provided was death, and the new law was made to take effect on May 1, of that year. Alexander was convicted of murder January 21, 1890, and his was the tenth conviction for murder in the Fort Smith court since the act here mentioned first took effect, but none of the attorneys practicing at the bar of Judge

Parker's court had shown the bravery to take advantage oi the new law, declining to do so, fearing to incur the displeasure of Judge Parker by reversing his decisions, as was so frequently done in latter years by the Supreme Court at Washington. The evidence against Alexander was circumstantial. With Steadman he had left Arizona with a drove of horses for Oklahoma, and afterwards they had gone to the Creek Nation and camped on the farm of Scott Gentry, near Choska; they still had with them several horses. On the afternoon of October 21, they were seen together some distance from their camp; late in the evening Alexander returned to camp leading the horse Steadman had been riding. Steadman did not return and the next day Alexander told Gentry that he had run off with a woman and taken all their money, leaving him penniless. Sixteen days later the remains of Steadman were found in a thicket seventy-five yards from where the two men were last seen together; the body was torn to pieces-and almost devoured by hogs, but was fully identified by the clothing, letters and papers found. Three days after the finding of the remains, Alexander was arrested, charged with murder, and he was found to be in possession of nearly $350. Steadman was supposed to have $700 or $800. R. B. Steadman, of San Diego, California, brother of the deceased, was immediately notified of the fact of his relative's death, and on December he arrived and began to assist in the investigation and in preparing evidence against Alexander. He said he had known Alexander for ten years and his brother had known him six years. He claimed that his brother was the owner of the horses the two men had possession of, and that when they left Arizona the Mexican had no money. Alexander was sentenced to be hanged October I following his conviction. One of his attorneys, J. Warren Reed, who had in the autumn of the previous year located at Fort Smith for the practice of criminal law, scorned the then prevailing notion regarding the displeasure of the court, and he maintained and urged that it was the duty of an attorney, under his oath, to avail himself of every right and advantage provided by law in the interest of a client, whether or not it should be displeasing to the court where conviction was secured. Mr. Reed, believing there were errors in the ruling of Judge Parker at the trial of Alexander, a writ of error was immediately taken to the Supreme Court of the United States at Washington, and the judgement of Judge Parker was reversed on the ground that R. G. Rawles, an attorney at Muskogee, with whom Alexander had consulted professionally a few days after the killing, in regard to some partnership horses owned by Steadman and Alexander, was permitted, over the objection of the defendant, Alexander, to testify to a confidential communication by Alexander, then his former client. Judge Parker had held that such communications were admissible as evidence in the interest of public policy, where it would tend to expose the commission of crime; the Supreme Court scouted the idea that Judge Parker should make any distinction in the long established rule that no confidential communication between attorney and client shall be exposed in a court of justice where objection is made by the person against whom it is used.

A new trial was granted Alexander some months later and Mr. Reed, by untiring and skillful efforts, succeeded in more plainly developing the circumstances of the case; the jury stood five to seven for acquittal. At a third trial about a year later, strange to say the jury again failed to agree, standing five to seven for acquittal, as before. Later, on the day before Christmas, 1892, Alexander having lain in jail nearly three years, District Attorney Clayton, who prosecuted the case, concluding he could not secure a conviction consented to a *nolle prosequi*, and Alexander was discharged, his liberty being given him as a Christmas gift. Thus was set in motion, in this court, the fundamental principal of law, providing for appeal, and Mr. Reed, by perseverance, saved the life of William Alexander, where a less skillful or less persevering attorney would have yielded him to the fate of his first trial and he would now be numbered among the subjects of the Fort Smith gallows.

THE ACTS OF A DEMON

John Stansberry was hanged, July 9, 1890, for the cruel murder of his wife; he had also killed his infant child. Stansberry was a native Missourian. He was born and reared near Granby, about six miles northeast of Neosho, Missouri. He subsequently married Miss Molly Ubank, of Newton county, Missouri, and settled in the Pottawatamie Nation, in the Indian Territory, where, after his wife had borne him a child, he forgot (or ignored) his marital ties, and fell in love with a Creek squaw, the owner of a lot of cattle, their commercial value, no doubt, assisting to influence his affections. So desirous was he of becoming husband of the squaw and possessor of the cattle, that he murdered his wife and babe, to be free from them. While his wife was temporarily absent from the house, on September 20, 1889, he killed the little one with a single blow, and to the agonized mother on her return, he stated that it had met its death by falling from the top of a bureau. His indifference to its fate aroused his wife's suspicions and she might well have sought safety in flight. Later they removed to the Creek Nation and squatted on a piece of land fourteen miles from Eufaula, not far from the home of the squaw. On October 13, 1889, Stansberry mounted a mule and rode away from home several miles, ostensibly on business, then made a detour through the fields, entered his enclosure by letting down a back fence, approached the house from the rear, his coming hidden by a stable, and entering the house unknown to the-woman he had sworn to protect, split her head open with an axe and with repeated blows from the murderous instrument, mutilated the body in a horrible manner. On the stand he maintained the utmost indifference concerning the outcome of his trial and died, protesting his innocence. He apparently cared nothing for life, even declining to ask for an attorney, but his father came from Missouri and employed Barnes & Reed to defend him; they had from the start, a hopeless case. The important bearing which little things often have in important cases, was shown by the circumstance which ensured his conviction. The mule which. he rode on the fatal trip that ended in murder, had a broken shoe, one-half of it being gone. Stansberry claimed that he had crossed the Canadian river at a certain place, and on returning home late at night had found his wife's mangled body, the crime, as he claimed, having been committed, while she slept, by Indians, who robbed him of $300. Logicians reasoned, that had he been away so late at night his wife would hardly have retired before his return; it was also gravely doubted that he had been possessed of cash to the amount of $300, and last and most important of all, the place where he claimed to have crossed the river while returning from a long ride, was carefully searched and no trace whatever of tracks such as were made by the mule with the broken shoe, could be discovered; moreover, its tracks for a portion of the distance he actually traveled while planning his wife's murder, were found, and the track made by the broken shoe led the investigators to the place where he had opened the fence, continuing to the outbuildings back of the house.

Stansberry was arrested immediately after his wife's funeral, while standing at her grave.

A MIGHTY TEMPERANCE LECTURE

Boudinot Crumpton, a beardless youth of nineteen, was hanged June 19, 1891, for the murder of Sam Morgan. His attorneys endeavored to save him on the theory that the killing was done by the victim's brother, Robert Morgan. Failing in this, they took a writ of error to the Supreme Court. The judgment of the lower court was sustained and Crumpton's execution was delayed only nine months.

Bood Crumpton's crime was the direct result of whiskey He was known as one of the best of boys when sober, but evil associations had led him to take his first drink, the demo* alcohol had stirred his vitals, the inevitable appetite had rendered him a slave to drink and it required only one glass to make of him a terror. On Sunday, November 3, 1889,

Crumpton and Morgan started on horseback to visit some young women several miles away. Late that evening Crumpton returned to his home greatly intoxicated, riding one of the horses and leading the other. He said they had met a man in a buggy who had employed Morgan to go with him to the Pawnee Indian Agency, and Morgan had instructed him to take care of his horse and other property until his return. A few days passed and Morgan's dead body was found in a hole at the base of an upturned tree. It was also learned that the two young men had obtained a quantity of whiskey before reaching this point and that both had indulged freely and were in a drunken state. It was claimed that Crumpton had lured Morgan to the hole mentioned by telling, him there was some whiskey hidden there, and while he was stooping over in search of the whiskey had struck him on the head with his pistol, and as he pitched headlong into the hole had finished his bloody deed with a bullet Crumpton had placed an enemy in his mouth to steal away his brains, and his persistent statement to the very last that he knew nothing of the deed which placed him in the laws clutches, and that if it was his hand that slew Sam Morgan it was guided solely by the demon drink, was generally believed, On the scaffold, just as he had stepped upon the fatal trap, the noose which was so soon to end his misspent life swinging idly by, Crumpton delivered a considerable talk upon the evils of intemperance, closing thus: "To all present, and especially to young men: when you are about to drink a glass of whiskey look closely in the bottom and see if you cannot observe therein a hangman's noose. There is where I first saw the one which now breaks my neck." Those were his last words; his arms were pinioned to his sides, the cap was drawn, the order given, and one more mighty lecture on the evils of intemperance had been given.

This was the only execution in the year 1891, but its influence upon those who witnessed it was a sermon greater, more potent, than all others which had preceded it. That influence has held many a young man from taking his first glass, perhaps saved others from Crumpton's sad fate.

MORE CASES APPEALED

The next capital cases wherein appeals were taken from the ruling of Judge Parker, were those of John Boyd and Eugene Stanley, both of whom were convicted of murder, October 29, 1890, and sentenced, January 12, to be executed April 21, 1891.

Stanley was a fair haired, light complexioned youth of 20 years. Boyd was 26 years old; he had a wife and a child, who were in the court-room during the trial, which lasted five days. The child was 2 years old and it kept up its baby prattle while the sword of justice was suspended over its father's head. Stanley and Boyd were charged with the murder of John Dansby, a negro, at Cache Creek, Choctaw Nation, 35 miles from Fort Smith, in the spring of 1890. They had engaged in a number of lawless acts previous to this, had become a terror to a large range of country. Their trial developed a record of crimes, which in their variety and frequency, cast in the shade the deeds of Dick Turpin and Jack Sheppard. Stanley was brought in, June 27, 1890, by Deputy Marshal, Boynton Tolbert and Deputy Sheriff Powers. Some of Stanley's crimes are thus briefly stated; assisted by two pals, he robbed an old man named Horn, near Eufaula. He and his cousin, Hamp Stanley, shot a young boy, named Jones, who had come bareheaded out of his father's house at their solicitation; they asked him to assist in the robbing one of his father's neighbors; the boy refused and was seriously wounded in consequence. They were captured soon after in December, 1889, at Atoka, and Stanley escaped, having in the meantime been identified by the old man, Horn. Joining in with a negro named George Meyers, he executed a robbery of Judge John Taylor, of Skullyville county, and with Hamp Stanley and two pals robbed

Tom Wood, an old man, near Alma. He also robbed one Hall, near Red Fork, and in April, 1890, he and Meyers, with John Boyd robbed a man named Rigsley, of Dora, Crawford county, Arkansas, and being by that time full-fledged outlaws, they engaged in the disastrous fight at Cache Creek, where Dansby was killed. Meyers and one other of the gang were killed and Boyd was wounded and captured. Stanley was also wounded but managed to hide beside a log, where he lay for a night and a day, too sick to travel; he was Captured soon after by Deputy Marshal Mickle, who conveyed him to Fort Smith, arriving late at night. He placed him in a bed in a hotel near the "Frisco" depot, not knowing what manner of man he was, and the next morning "the bird had flown." He had walked in the direction of Van Buren and then struck into the brush and lost his way, and daylight found him on the highway only eight miles from Fort Smith, but he pushed on and finally arrived at Spadra. Here he committed the indiscretion that landed him fully in the law's clutches. Meyers had left a horse at Lehigh, in care of a friend and had told Stanley of it. Stanley wrote to the man, signing Meyers' name, stating that he had read in the Fort Smith Elevator, to the effect that he had been killed, at Cache Creek; that he was in truth badly wounded but that he was recovering and was out of money, asking him to sell the horse for $50 and send him the money, by express, to Spadra. The letter was sent to Jailer Pape, at Fort Smith, and local officers were communicated with; they failed to find Stanley, as he was assuming the name of Robert Haynes. A bogus express package was then prepared and Stanley was notified (as Meyers) by the agent, through the mails but he did not call for the package for several weeks, and then he was told he must be identified before he could secure the package. While he went after the man he was boarding with, the officers were notified and on his return to the express office he was arrested. He was greatly disappointed when he saw the express package contained nothing but waste paper. Seeing that his career was at an end he readily gave up and confessed his identity. After Boyd and Stanley had been convicted and sentenced, an appeal was taken and their cases reversed. A new trial was granted and they were found guilty of manslaughter and sentenced to imprisonment, at hard labor, for ten years. Stanley was also found guilty of train robbery in three counts and sentenced to fifteen years for each, making for him fifty-five years of confinement.

Gibson Partridge was tried November 15, 1890, for the murder of an old man who ran the pumping station for the Frisco road, near Tulsa, Indian Territory. He was defended by J. Warren Reed, who secured his acquittal; later he pleaded guilty to assault with intent to kill, was sentenced to the penitentiary, at Detroit, Michigan, for five years, and died before the expiration of his term.

THE VERDIGRIS TRAIN ROBBERY

Alexander Lewis was a white man, about 50 years old, formerly a Texan; he had long, sandy whiskers and was of good appearance. The trial was of more than ordinary interest, as there were more than fifty witnesses, including both sides. Alexander was charged with train robbery and murder.

On the night of June 16, 1888, the south bound passenger and express train on the Missouri, Kansas & Texas railroad, was held up at Verdigris (pronounced Ver-di-gree) tank,* two miles south of Gibson Station, by a man who had boarded the "blind baggage" at the station and crawled over the tender to the engineer and stopped the train, at which, three other men, all masked, came from the brush and proceeded through the train, securing only $8.75 and a gold watch, for their trouble.

*Tank is a term used in the west for a small pond created by damning up a stream. This was usually used for watering livestock.—Ed. 2015

A few careless shots were fired at random, to frighten the passengers and one of them struck and killed B. C. Tucker, a stockman, of Rose, Texas, who was on his way home from 'Chicago, where he had been to sell cattle. The express agent was also wounded. The robbery was at once reported at Muscogee and officers started early the next morning and trailed the jobbers to the neighborhood where Lewis lived, fifty-five miles thorn the scene of the robbery. Lewis was suspected but no proof was at hand and he was not arrested. For a long time it was a mooted question as to who were the Verdigris tank train robbers. In December, 1890, J. T. Holleman told his father, in Texas, that he was one of the party who robbed the train and a consultation was held with J. J. Kinney, Chief Detective for the railroad company, and Holleman told a story to the effect that he and one Rogers went to the Indian country at the instance of one Jim Johnson and brought up at the home of Lewis; that Kelp Queen, a notorious desperado and chum of bank robbers, and John Barber, were at the house of Lewis and the five men made an agreement to rob the train, at Verdigris tank; that he and Queen went to Gibson Station, where they were to board the train, while Lewis, Johnson and Rogers ambushed at Verdigris; that Queen boarded the train as agreed, but he (Holleman) weakened and was purposely left; that he then found his way back to the home of Lewis and later was met there by the others, who discussed the details of the robbery, in his presence. He also stated that they planned to go to Seneca, Missouri, and rob a bank, but he and Rogers backed out and went to Texas, where Rogers was afterwards killed. Johnson had been arrested in Texas and sentenced to twenty-five years imprisonment for the part he took with Barber and Queen in the Cisco bank robbery, just before the Verdigris train robbery. Queen had been killed, near Claremore, soon after the Verdigris robbery, by Bud Sanders, then sheriff of Cooweescoowee district, Cherokee Nation. Later on, Barber had been killed by the late Barney Connelley and Deputy G. S. White.

Thus, according to Holleman's story, told as above in open court, all who had been connected with the robbery and killing of Tucker, were dead, but two, Holleman, who was now a government witness and Alexander Lewis, who was quietly engaged at home on his farm. Detective Kinney worked up a lot of evidence, aided by Captain Charlie LeFlore, and the day for trial of the case was set. The number "5," was an important factor in the governments' side of the case; being masked, the identity of all the men was left to the color of their clothing, their height, size and build, and to the color of their horses and to the tracks made by their horses. A spotted horse, alleged to have been ridden by one of the men, was seen by several different persons, as they went to and from the scene of the robbery, there being five men and five horses at every point where witnesses, at the trial, had seen the horses on the trail. These facts and circumstances were urged in corroboration of the testimony given against Lewis by the accomplice witness. Lewis was convicted and his attorneys, Barnes & Reed, took an appeal to the Supreme Court of the United States and secured a reversal and an order for a new trial on the ground of the manner of selecting the jury. It was a novel point but able presentation brought success, and Lewis was again placed on trial for his life. The second trial was very closely contested. The question rested on the identity of Lewis as one of the five robbers. By an ingeniously devised miniature train of cars, made of paste board, and arranged before the jury, Mr. Reed proceeded to demonstrate that his client was not one of the five robbers. He won his point and proved his possession of legal ability, competent to secure acquittals for men charged with high crimes, for which he afterwards became noted. Lewis still resides near Tulsa, in the Creek Nation, and is a respected farmer.

WHISKEY DID IT

Immediately after the acquittal of Lewis, came on the trial of Robert L. Garrett, charged with killing Dolls. Hanshy, at Blue Jacket, in the Cherokee Nation, July 25, 1891. Garrett was an Indian, twenty-five years old, and very intelligent. About July 20, 1891, Garrett and Hanshy went to Southwest City, Missouri, where they purchased some whiskey and returned to Blue Jacket, very drunk, on the night of July 24. The next morning they drank freely and had a good time.

After a while they separated, going to their homes. In the afternoon, Hanshy, while on his way to Blue Jacket, stopped at Garrett's and more whiskey was disposed of. Garrett became highly intoxicated and late in the afternoon he went to a neighbor's house and told that he had killed his companion. An investigation proved his story true. Hanshy was found just outside the door with the fatal gunshot wound in his left side. Garrett at once went to Chetopah, Kansas, where his father lived, and he was soon after arrested. He was defended by Barnes & Reed and W. M. Cravens. Garrett claimed self-defense and his attorneys so skillfully used the argument with the jury that a verdict for acquittal was rendered.

A WICKED OLD MAN

Sheppard Busby was a white man, about forty-five years old. He was the son of "Shep" Busby, who lived on the line between Mississippi and Tennessee and was regarded as the most terrible and dangerous man who ever resided in the former State. His acts of lawlessness were many; he built a four roomed log house, a perfect fort, which he supplied with a complement of fire arms. Many attempts were made to dislodge him but each attempt resulted in failure and he was never seen away from home. At last, he one day went with his family to attend a county fair, a few miles away, in the State of Mississippi, and during his absence the officers visited his home, surrounded his house and awaited his return. Hours after, as he and his family approached the house, Old Man Busby discovered the situation and he at once opened a sharp fire. The officers responded with a fusillade and "Shep Busby" was laid low.

Some years before the crime hereafter narrated, Sheppard Busby (junior) had been a deputy marshal of Judge Parker's-court and was well respected. Being separated from his wife he became enamored of two young Indian women and was living with them, in adultery, in the Cherokee Nation, his son making his home with them. A writ was issued by a United States Commissioner at Fort Smith charging Busby with adultery. The writ was placed in the hands of Deputy Marshal Barney Connelley, a white man, who resided at Vinita, Indian Territory. Connelley was a highly respected citizen and a good officer. Proceeding to Busby's home, August 19, 1891, to arrest him, Connelley met with resistance from Busby, assisted by his son, who hid in the house, Busby opening fire upon the officer, killing him, for which he was tried, convicted December 11, 1891, and was executed April 27, 1892. The son was tried with him and was sentenced to Detroit for ten years on a verdict charging manslaughter. Busby claimed self-defense on the ground that he did not know Connelley was an officer and he thought it was someone come to do him bodily harm. He was a native of Kentucky, born in 1833; he was the oldest man, at the time of his execution, of any of the many victims of the Fort Smith gallows. He served in the Fifty-sixth Illinois Regiment, infantry, under Col. Bob Kirk-ham, and during the last year of the war under Col.

Deal, in the Fiftieth Missouri. After the war he lived for ten or twelve years in Stoddard County, Missouri, then for a few years in Arkansas, going finally to the Indian Territory, where he rounded out his career as a very wicked man. He was a member of the Grand Army of the Republic,* and Hangman Maledon refused to officiate at his execution; the gruesome task was performed by Deputy Marshal G. S. White.

*The GAR was the veteran's organization for former Union soldiers from the Civil War.— Ed. 2015

A BRIDE OF A WEEK MURDERED BY HER FATHER

John Thornton was sixty-five years old, a native of Strasbourg, France; he had come to America at the age of twelve years. He was a jeweler by trade, and at the time of the murder, for which he gave up his life on the scaffold, he lived at South McAlester. He was a profligate, a hard drinker, a dissipated, ungodly man. Twelve years before, he had removed with his family from Rock Island County, Illinois. The crime for which he was called to time in Judge Parker's court was one of the most revolting of all the revolting murder cases which had come before that court. The fact that a father, who should always cherish and protect his own offspring, could wantonly and in cold blood take the life of his own daughter, in the manner here described, seems hard to understand. Human depravity and degradation seemed to have reached its utter limit when such crime was possible. Laura Moyner, Thornton's daughter, had been married six days. She and her husband were happy in a little home at Krebbs, in the Choctaw Nation, with no thought of the horrible tragedy that should soon snuff out the life of one and hang the pall of gloom and sadness over the future of the other. Moyner was an honest, hardworking man, employed by the Osage Coal Company. On the night of the tragedy Thornton visited their home and took supper at the house. After the meal Moyner went to the company store for a keg of powder to use in the mine next day and he asked Thornton to stay until his return. He was gone a half hour and as he again approached his home a ghastly spectacle met his eyes. Lying on the floor, underneath their bed, the brains oozing from a bullet hole under the right eye, was the bride of a week, the spark of life almost gone; assistance was summoned but nothing could be done and the young woman died in a few minutes.

Moyner told the story at the trial in a simple, straightforward manner; several times tears choked his utterances but the jury understood. Other witnesses stated that Thornton went to a drug store and announced that he had killed his daughter. No motive was assigned for the deed unless it was pique. Mrs. Moyner had, the day before, written to a friend in Kansas and mailed the letter; it was found in Thornton's possession, but how he came by it was a mystery that was never solved. He replied, to questions, that he had a machine that made it. In. the letter the girl had stated that she had married "to get away from hell;" indicating that her life at home, before her marriage, had been far from happy. It was believed, however, among their circle of acquaintances that Thornton had been guilty of repeated commission of the crime of incest. The girl had married against her father's will, the reasons for his objections being left to the reader's imagination, and the neighbors reasoned that he had come to the house for the purpose of continuing the awful abuse and that, angered at her refusal he had, in his drunken state, killed her, even after she had crawled beneath her bed for safety.

Thornton's attorneys attempted to prove insanity but Judge Parker, in his charge to the jury, paid particular attention to the theory and cited several eminent authorities who held that a man crazed by drunkenness could not be held unaccountable for his acts. Thornton, when he could not secure spirits, would drink extracts or anything that would intoxicate. He said that when he saw he had killed his daughter he had tried to kill himself; that six times he held his pistol to his temple and pulled the trigger but the weapon missed fire each time; he said that he believed he was prevented from suicide by his Maker, in order that he might have a chance to repent of his sins.

A HORRIBLE SPECTACLE

The sight which greeted the eyes of the spectators as Deputy Marshal White sprung the trap and Thornton's body shot downward and rebounded into space was a most ghastly one, that will never be forgotten by any of those present, while they live, Thornton was of stocky build and he had a small, flabby neck; his muscles and flesh were soft, and this condition his long dissipation had not tended to improve. The weight of the fall almost severed the head from the body, only the tendons of the neck preventing it from falling to the ground. Blood spurted in streams all over the body, saturating the clothing and forming in pools on the ground. A thrill of horror ran through the crowd standing within the enclosure, and strong men turned sick at sight of the hideous wound in the neck. Not only was the spinal column severed but all the flesh was torn away at the neck. It was a sickening finale to a most revolting crime. Thornton had embraced the Catholic faith while in jail and he was given Christian burial. The grave which the assistant sexton had dug to receive his corpse, in the northeast corner of the Catholic cemetery at Fort Smith, is still open. When the undertaker, with the officers, arrived at the cemetery the sexton was informed that Thornton had been promised his body should lie beside that of a friend who had died of measles in the Federal jail; hence, the coffin, with Thornton's blood still oozing therefrom, was placed at one side while another grave was prepared. The ground here is very rocky, with a solid ledge of limestone at a depth of four feet. Thornton's body was, therefore, laid to rest covered by scarcely three feet of earth, about twenty feet from his other still open grave.

ONE YOUNG MAN'S EXPERIENCE

A WARNING TO ALL

John Brown was indicted by the grand jury February 16, 1892, charged with murder in two counts; in the first count, of the murder of Josiah Poorboy on the eighth day of December, 1891, in the Cherokee Nation, near Tahlequah, and the second count charged him with the murder of Thomas Whitehead at the same time and place. Both the victims were Cherokees. Brown was tried on both counts and convicted March 21, and on the thirtieth day of April he was sentenced to be hanged for the Whitehead murder. A bill of exceptions was allowed, an assignment of errors filed and a writ of error taken to the Supreme Court where the verdict was reversed, and at a new trial he was again given the death sentence. An appeal was again taken and at a third trial he was re-sentenced to hang.

Brown was an inoffensive young man, and from the start there was a doubt in the minds of many as to his guilt of the crime charged. His arrest and subsequent imprisonment (secured in lieu of death punishment by hard work on the part of his attorney) was the result of bad company. Had he always sought only that with which a pure-minded man may mingle without a stain he would never have been connected with the killing of Whitehead and Poorboy. These two were deputy marshals. Their presence at the house of Judge Shirley, in front of which they were afterwards slain, was for the purpose of being near the home of one Mrs. Hitchcock. Whitehead applied for and secured permission, four days before the killing, to board a short while at Judge Shirley's for which he was to pay by doing chores. Poorboy came to the Shirley house on the night of the killing to assist Whitehead in arresting one Jim Craig, who had been arrested previously, charged with adultery with Mrs. Hitchcock, and escaped. The officers believed that Craig would return to the home of his illicit love, who kept several girls for immoral purposes. It is supposed that the woman planned the death of her husband, who had sworn to the information causing Craig's arrest. On the afternoon of December 8, Brown, accompanied by Wacoo Hampton, a dissolute character, went to Mrs. Hitchcock's place for the purpose of a "round-up" and there met John Roach who lived in the neighborhood. After dark, at the woman's request, all three went to what was known as Cob Hill, with a message to Jim Craig. On the trip they passed the house where the detectives were staying. They went to Cob Hill, two miles away, but failed to find Craig, and on their return were halted by Whitehead and Poorboy, who evidently mistook one of them for the object of their search. During a fight which ensued, someone, supposedly Hampton, fired the fatal shots which nearly resulted in Brown's execution. Hampton was a Cherokee, eighteen years old, and could not be tried at Fort Smith for want of jurisdiction. Three years previously, he had been tried for murder of a white man and convicted of manslaughter; being under sixteen years old he was sent to the reform school at Washington, D. C., from which he soon escaped and made his way back to the Indian Territory. He was on the scout at the time he met with Brown and became mixed up in the killing of Whitehead and Poorboy. He was killed shortly after while resisting arrest.

Brown's case continued in the courts for five years, during which time he was kept in a cell in murderer's row at the Fort Smith jail. His case was taken the third time, on appeal, to the United States Supreme Court, and finally at his fourth trial, in the last of December, 1896, on a plea of guilty to manslaughter, he was sentenced to one year at Columbus, Ohio. For good behavior he was released on the first of November, 1897, when he returned to Arkansas and secured a position as clerk in a hotel at Clarksville. He fulfilled the expectations of his friends, and, leaving old associations behind, decided in the future to let wine and bad women well alone. His years of confinement gave him plenty of time to study upon the effects of a dissolute life; his near chance of dying for another's crime taught him a lesson, and none better than he realizes the value of temperate habits and a good character.

A YEAR OF FINAL DECREES

The year 1893 was a busy one in Judge Parker's court. Many men were brought in for trial, charged with all manner of crimes, and many were convicted. There were no executions though there were many convictions for capital offenses; since the right of appeal in capital cases had been granted the right once taken advantage of, had let down the bars and new every attorney who could see the least opportunity to pick a flaw in Judge Parker's rulings would, as soon as his client was convicted, make out a writ of errors and away to Washington on appeal, and in this way many convicted felons were ultimately given new trials after the motion before Judge Parker had been overruled, and numbers were given at second or third trials much lighter sentences than at first pronounced, and not a few were finally acquitted or discharged.

Two men were hanged in 1894, however, and thirteen in that year received the final decree that either gave them their liberty or sent them to terms in the various penitentiaries made use of by the government. To some of these latter will this chapter be mainly devoted.

CRIME AND EXECUTION OF LEWIS HOLDER

Lewis Holder was a white man about fifty-two years old. He was first convicted September 19, 1892, of the murder of his partner, George Bickford, in the Sans Bois Mountains Choctaw Nation, December 28, 1891. The two men had gone into the Indian country with a team of horses and wagon, with a camping outfit, all belonging to Bickford (Holder having nothing but an old shotgun), for the purpose of hunting and trapping. Not long after, Holder returned to the Poteau bottoms, near Fort Smith, having in his possession the team belonging to Bickford. When questioned as to how he came to have them he said he had traded a note he held against a man in St. Louis, Missouri, for the property; he added that Bickford had gone to Texas. He was dressed in a suit worn by Bickford when the two men went away together. He explained this by saying he had exchanged a new suit he had purchased for the one in his possession, Bickford desiring the nice new suit to travel in.

Several months passed and all interest in the matter seemed to have subsided, when it was actively renewed by the discovery of Bickford's dead body in a lonely gorge in the mountains about 300 yards from the road, by a traveler, while searching for water. An examination revealed that he had been murdered, having been shot from behind, by a shotgun in the hands of his slayer. The wound was an ugly one, the charge having entered the back of the neck and passed out at the throat, tearing away the larynx and muscles. The discovery was reported to the officers, the body was identified and Holder was finally arrested in the Creek Nation, when he admitted he had killed Bickford but claimed he had done so in self-defense. He said they had quarreled and Bickford had tried to kill him with a sling shot, but he accidently slipped and fell, giving Holder an opportunity to procure his gun and shoot him in the back of the neck. The circumstances surrounding the case, the position of the victim as he lay dead, the stories told by Holder on his return to their home, and all, made a strong chain of circumstantial evidence, and the jury returned a verdict of guilty after being out a few minutes.

AN EXCITING SCENE

Holder's attorneys took a writ of error to the Supreme Court, but after months of weary waiting the decision of the lower court was affirmed, and on September 19, 1894, Holder was once more brought into court for sentence, his face beaming with expectation. All through the summer he had hung on the hope that he would be given a new trial, for though he had taken the life of a brother man, as ruthlessly as he would have spurned a snake, yet life to him was as sweet as to a budding maiden upon whom a sixteenth springtime is just beginning to bloom. The long, weary days, the hot summer months, the anxiety, coupled with the moments of agonizing fear, told upon him, showed in the deep lines of his visage, yet he kept up amazingly well, and his step was as light as a youngster's as he marched into the court room to receive sentence, still hoping that his case was to be called up anew.

He was taken into the crowded court room where were near five hundred men and women who, having heard that Holder was to be sentenced, had flocked as if eager to view the shame and disgrace meted out to a fellow mortal. In a few words, quietly but earnestly spoken. Judge Parker pronounced the sentence, which Holder had fondly hoped he would never hear.

"To be hanged by the neck until dead."

The words died away; not a sound bestirred the court room; all was silent as the grave. To the condemned man it was an awful moment. His face blanched; his frame shook with a tremor that convulsed his whole body. He began to totter; he reeled; a kindly disposed deputy marshal stretched out his hand to save him, but too late; with a scream that reached to the street below, Holder fell forward on his face, senseless. The fall affected the auditors like an electric shock. In an instant all was confusion, as all within reach leaped forward to view the prostrate form, many believing that the man was dead; that he had cheated the gallows at last. A few brisk raps from Judge Parker's gavel restored order, and Holder was carried to the open air where he recovered, but too weak to walk to the van in which he was carried back to prison. From that time until the day set for his execution, Holder was an object of pity. He was a broken down old man from the moment that he heard the words that bade him discard all hope, yet still he hoped; he prayed to the God whose laws he had outraged to save him from the gibbet; he begged the officers who daily passed his cell, to refrain from hanging him; he hoped against hope, and at last came to the belief that the officers would not execute him, declaring that if executed he would return in the spirit and haunt the officers and all connected with the court. Nothing stayed the hand of justice, however, and Holder's fate was the same as had been that of scores of cases before him. As he was placed on the trap he asked that he might make a statement, and walking to the front of the scaffold, he asked all who had a hand in his conviction to step forward. He had previously asked the jury and Judge Parker to attend his execution as he desired to say something to them None of them were present. After a pause, he said that he forgave them all and added that he thought Judge Parker should resign his office and then go down on his knees and ask God to forgive him.

A SOUL-THRILLING MOMENT

Early in December, 1894, about a month after Holder's execution, as Deputy Marshal George Lawson and half a dozen or more fellow deputies were sitting in the office of the jail, just before the yawning hour of midnight, a terrible moan, unearthly and unlike any ever heard by mortal ears before, came from the direction of the scaffold, about 150 yards away, that for a moment froze the blood in their veins and caused each individual hair upon their heads to rise.

"Lewis Holder s ghost" exclaimed one of the deputies in a hoarse whisper. They looked at each other in awe, those men who had faced death many times, and who had never known the meaning of "fear." Lawson was one of the bravest and most desperate men who ever rode the government service. For an instant he was speechless, then, as the hollow, spectral sounds were repeated, he leaped to his feet and exclaimed:

"Boys, if any of you will go with me we will find out what that is; no dead man ever made a sound like that."

His companions responded, and the entire company started for the old gallows, while the hundred or more prisoners confined in the cells, listened with bated breath, all of them having been awakened by the unearthly sounds. Arrived at the scaffold, an old Indian was discovered on his knees before the open trap, looking down through the place where some of his Indian friends had met their deaths several years before, praying for their deliverance. The old fellow had come to Fort Smith, filled up on whiskey and his strange actions were the result.

FAMOUS SMITH

Famous Smith was convicted of the murder of J. J. Gentry near Webbers Falls, in January, 1884. The killing was the result of a difficulty over a horse, in which Gentry was solely to blame. He had borrowed a horse of Smith and had nearly killed the animal by hard riding. He came again at a later period to borrow a horse and Smith refused to loan. Both men met later, while on their way to Webbers Falls, and Gentry began a quarrel, and drawing his pistol fired at Smith, the bullet cutting a hole in the sleeve of his coat. At this Smith drew his pistol and fired at Gentry, killing him. He then rode to Webbers Falls, reported the killing and returned to his home, and from that time until he was arrested, nine years later, he remained at home, quietly attending to his own affairs. At the time of the killing Smith was suffering from hemorrhage of the lungs and weighed only 135 pounds. Gentry was large and strong. Smith was sentenced to hang; he was granted a new trial by the Supreme Court and his case was finally *nollied*.

John Hicks was charged as accessary to the murder of Andrew J. Colevard, who was shot and killed, February 13, 1892, by the notorious Stan Rowe, near Jim Rowe's house, about twelve miles northwest of Tahlequah. The killing of Colevard was in cold blood and there was no excuse. Stan Rowe was killed in December of the same year while resisting arrest. Hicks had been at Rowe's house, where a dance was in progress and whiskey flowed freely, nearly all day, in company with Stan Rowe, Colevard and an Indian named Mixwater. The four men left the house together, starting for their homes.

Colevard insisted on Rowe going home with him, promising to give him a suit of clothes. Rowe and Hicks seemed to think Colevard was trying to entice Rowe into an ambush and after consulting they overhauled him and Rowe accused Colevard of conspiring to turn him over to the officers, covering him with his Winchester. Colevard denied the insinuation and declared he was a friend to both Rowe and Hicks. Three times Rowe brought his Winchester to his shoulder and the third time Hicks pulled off his hat and shouted to Covlevard, "Pull off your hat and die like a man;" and that instant Rowe pulled the trigger and Colevard was killed. Hicks would have been executed on July 12, 1892, but for an appeal to the higher court. He was given a new trial and was again convicted and December 27 1894, was named for him to pay the death penalty. His attorney took a second appeal and on the third trial he was acquitted

Willie Johnson, alias Willie Overton was a negro. He was convicted and sentenced to hang, as accessary to the murder of Sherman Russell, on a Sunday night in July, 1893. The crime was committed near Muscogee. A crowd of negroes, including the victim, were on their way home from evening religious services, held in a country school house, Russel escorting a girl whom Johnson fancied. On the way they were overtaken by Johnson and Sam Woodward (colored). A quarrel ensued and Russel was killed, Woodward, who was claimed to have been the principal criminal, was never captured. Johnson's case was not appealed and on second trial he was given a life sentence.

REDUCED TO FOUR YEARS IMPRISONMENT

John Gourke was a young Italian about 20 years of age, tried and convicted of the murder of a fellow workman at Alderson coal mines, in the Choctaw Nation, with whom he had a difficulty. Dire threats and demonstrations were made by the deceased, after a quarrel that induced Gourke to believe that his adversary intended to inflict some great bodily injury. Acting upon this belief, while in the heat of passion, Gourke went about a hundred yards away, secured a pistol, returned and shot and killed his opponent, who was unarmed at the time. He was sentenced to be hanged, December 27, 1894. He was defended by Thomas H. Barnes and J. Warren Reed, then the law firm of Barnes & Reed. It was urged by his counsel, at the trial, that his crime could be no more than manslaughter; that the killing was in the heat of passion, aroused by serious provocation, and that there was no previously formed design to kill. Judge Parker took a stronger view of the case and instructed the jury in a manner that resulted in a verdict of conviction for murder. The redoubtable Reed and his partner, Mr. Barnes took a writ of error to the Supreme Court of the United States and secured a reversal and a new trial, the Supreme Court, deciding against Judge Parker, and with Gourke's attorneys, that the crime did not constitute murder. Gourke under this decision was permitted to plead guilty to manslaughter on a compromise and accepted a sentence of four years at Columbus, Ohio.

John Graves was charged with having murdered an unknown white man, on the Greenleaf mountain, near Illinois Station, in the Cherokee Nation. The body was found by Robert Williams, about 150 yards from a traveled road, in the latter-part of April, 1891. An attempt had been made to burn the body. It had been thrown into a shallow place caused by a tree being turned over by the wind, then covered with brush and the brush set on fire; none but the small twigs were burned. When the body was found it had been pulled out of its resting place by hogs, the bones partly denuded of their flesh, and the skull, which was separated from the body, lay ten or twelve feet away from where it had first been placed. This was called "the Greenleaf mountain mystery," and it claimed the attention of the court for many days. The evidence was wholly circumstantial and on appeal to the Supreme Court the verdict was reversed, and a new trial granted. His attorney, James B. Rutherford, proceeded to a more complete investigation of the case, obtaining a mass of new evidence for defense and by his masterly handling of the same he won distinction that was recognized by the older members of the bar, and Graves was acquitted.

Frank Collins was a bright mulatto. He was convicted of the murder of Randal Lovely, in the Valley House, at Fort Gibson. The trouble was in a measure invited by Lovely by his action in striking Frank's little brother. In a heat of anger at the blow, Collins slew Lovely. He was sentenced to a place on the old scaffold, November 2, 1894, being named as his execution day. On appeal to the President his sentence was commuted to life imprisonment.

Robert Marshal Hall, through the instrumentation of the right of appeal, was granted a new trial, and was acquitted of the charge of murder and given his freedom, after having been convicted and sentenced to hang. On August 4, 1891, Hall and Jim Yates, a deputy United States marshal, engaged in a game of cards at South McAlester. They quarreled and a fight ensued, in which Yates was killed. Hall was at once arrested and placed in jail at Fort Smith, with final result as stated.

Dennis Davis was a negro; he had the appearance of being only half witted. He was tried for the murder of Solomon Blackwell, also colored. In the summer of 1893, Davis raised a crop of sorghum on land possessed by Blackwell, in the Creek Nation, near Eufaula. By the terms of their compact, Davis was to have half of the crop but was to gather both shares and haul the entire product to a nearby mill. Davis gathered only his own share, leaving Blackwell's standing in the field. This led to a quarrel and threats were exchanged. Davis went away and secured a gun and creeping to where

Blackwell was at work, shot him dead. He did not seem to realize the enormity of his crime for he freely told of what he had done, to several of his acquaintances. On being arraigned before Judge Parker, the court appointed I. D. Oglesby, F. S. Jones, W. B. Cravens and Emanuel Majors to defend him. They made a hard fight for his life, alleging insanity, but the jury returned a verdict of guilty and the negro was sentenced to die. Later he was adjudged insane and placed in an asylum.

Thomas Thompson was a young Creek Indian. He was convicted and sentenced to die for the murder of Charles Hermes, in 1893. Hermes was with his brother and father at work in a corn field, Thompson rode by the field and gave a shout, which was meant as a challenge, a sign of defiance. Then he rode away and armed himself and returned to the vicinity and while Charles Hermes was in the act of turning his horse at the side of the field, Thompson shot him. This case also was reversed by the Supreme Court, and a lighter sentence imposed as the result of a new trial.

Charles Smith killed John Welch and Robert Marshal, at Muscogee, on the morning of September 10, 1894. Smith was a negro, as black as night. He had once before been tried in Judge Parker's court, for killing a man, and sentenced to ten years imprisonment for manslaughter. He was of a particularly vicious nature and while engaged in cutting the harness from some horses, the property of one Newlin, he was discovered by Welch, who was running a booth in the vicinity, and because of the latter remonstrating with him, he became angered and killed him, with a bullet. Robert Marshal was an Indian policeman and in attempting to arrest Smith, he in turn was killed. At the trial, Smith set up the claim that he killed Marshal in self-defense, Marshal having shot at him first. The jury was out only two hours. On reversal by the Supreme Court, Smith was given a new trial and he was sentenced to ten years imprisonment for manslaughter.

The more noted cases of Marshal Tucker, Sam Hickory, Alexander Allen and Henry Starr, which were given final disposition in 1894, will be treated at greater length elsewhere. For the present, let us turn to consider the story of John Pointer, one of the two convicted murderers who were hanged, in 1894,

SPARED THE ROD AND SPOILED THE CHILD

John Pointer seemed to be imbued by nature with a desire to inflict pain upon living creatures. He was born of a highly respectable family in Eureka Springs, Arkansas, and his parents were religiously inclined, but they were lacking in the enforcement of good government. Whatever Johnnie wanted he generally succeeded in obtaining, and if it was in opposition to his parents' wishes he simply overrode them and had his will anyway.

About this time Johnnie committed his first crime. He was less than twelve years old when he attempted to Durn a little boy in the woods; he was roundly reprimanded but that was all. A little later he stabbed, with a pocket knife, a boy by the name of Stites; the boy had several brothers and they were raised in the same neighborhood with Johnnie. The one he stabbed was his own best friend and playmate. For this he was arrested and placed on trial in Carroll county, his home. The attorney who defended him, shrewdly placed him and his gray-haired father on a seat immediately before the jury. The hoary head, the father's tears, the knowledge that his mother lay on a sick bed at home, and the statement that if her boy was punished it would bring her to the grave, had its expected effect and Johnnie was let off with a fifty dollar fine which his father promptly paid, and Johnnie returned home, where he proudly boasted:

"I knew the old man would pay up before he'd let me go to jail."

"The old man" should have flogged him soundly, but he did not. A year later he engaged in a game of baseball on the top of East Mountain, near his home. On that occasion Johnnie received the only real whipping he ever had. A sick boy visited the game and Johnnie picked a quarrel with him and called him a liar. When the boy returned the compliment Johnnie pounced upon him, but fear lent strength to the sick boy and Johnnie was nicely flogged. This so angered him that he went away and, when no one was looking, threw a stone at his chastiser, sending him to the ground, senseless and bleeding. The boy was carried to his home and Johnnie ran off and hid. For this he was never arrested; the friends of the sick boy knew that any fine assessed would be paid by his over-indulgent father, and that the arrest and conviction would only add laurels to Johnnie's imaginary wreath of fame. The Stites boys always intended to catch him and punish him in earnest; Judge Parker's court however, a few years later, saved them the trouble.

In 1891, Johnnie, having become too willful to be endurable at home, was sent to Dallas county, Missouri, where his mother owned a tract of land, to visit relatives, in the hope that a change of scene would have a beneficial effect upon his temper and morals. The attempt was useless. Johnnie had become a bully and a braggart. He must have boys younger than himself to mistreat or he could not be happy. The location was too peaceable to suit him and he soon tired of it and left, a fine riding mare, the property of one of his relatives, going with him. Johnnie rode to Springfield, closely followed by the owner of the stolen horse, and tried to sell it for fifty dollars. So small a price for an animal worth four times that sum, aroused suspicion and Johnnie, failing to make a sale, soon after arrived at Eureka Springs riding a fine brown horse. Placing the animal in a livery stable he went home. He was received with open arms, and after telling several wonderful tales of himself, said to his father that he had purchased a small pony at auction in Springfield, had traded with a man whom he met on the road, for another horse and a saddle, and had finally traded with another man for the fine horse he now had, agreeing to give thirteen dollars "boot" money, and that the man was now in the city, having come with him for the money. The doting father, unsuspecting any wrong (of course he had no reason to imagine his boy could sin), went to the stable, examined the horse, patted Johnnie on the shoulders and told him he was a shrewd trader, and gave him the money to close the bargain. There being no bargain to close Johnnie now had thirteen dollars of papa's money. The next day, while the elder Pointer was at Berryville, the county seat, having ridden Johnnie's recent acquisition, the owner of the mare, with a Missouri officer, arrived in the city; a complaint was filed and Johnnie was arrested on. a warrant charging horse stealing and being a fugitive from Missouri justice. The next day the father returned. He believed Johnnie's story, employed an attorney, secured bail in one thousand dollars, and by the means of shrewd manipulation and a friendly justice, a compromise was effected; before the arrival of the Missouri sheriff with requisition papers Johnnie was spirited away, and six days later, with plenty of money in his pockets, furnished by his father, John (no longer Johnnie) Pointer, walked majestically into a hotel at Brownwood, Texas, and registered at George Gray.

Just what Johnnie did and how he disported himself while on this trip is not revealed, but in a very short time it was whispered about Eureka Springs that John Pointer was "back." The family was in trouble. They knew if he remained at home he was liable to re-arrest for the crime committed in Missouri. What to do with him was the question. At last Johnnie was made to feel, to a slight degree, his danger, in spite of his air of brag and bluff, and scenting another exhilarating trip, at his father's expense, he was finally induced to take a sum of money and, with a good horse and saddle, he was soon once more on his way to Texas, where for a time he disported freely and enjoyed himself, while his money lasted. His funds finally became short and he wrote home for money; he had met with trouble with Texas law and had surrendered his horse and saddle to the Sheriff of Wise County as a temporary bond. About this time, Ed Vandever, a crippled young man, whose parents resided at Eureka Springs, Arkansas, who had, by perseverance and economy, become the owner of a good team and wagon, was preparing to drive from Wise County to his home, accompanied by William Bolding, whose home was also in Eureka Springs. The two young men had driven to Texas on a trading expedition. Pointer, who had known them in Arkansas, asked to accompany them on their trip across the Indian Territory, but as they had no liking for him they tried to avoid him. He followed on foot and after he had overtaken them, his renewed requests were granted by Vandever, who himself paid the necessary expenses entailed by the addition to the party.

This was on December 13, 1891. On Christmas day, following, they stopped in front of the home of W. G. Baird, four miles from Wilburton, in the Choctaw Nation, Pointer talked with Baird, at the gate, asking about a place to purchase hay and was directed properly; as they talked, Baird had a good opportunity to inspect the team and wagon; he saw Bolding, who was standing at the rear of the latter, but did not see Vandever, who was on the other side, driving. After leaving Baird they drove on and a little later went into camp for the night. The next morning the dead bodies of Bolding and Vandever were found in a creek near the camp and Pointer, with the team and wagon and some of the clothing of the murdered men, was missing. Several persons had seen the three young men at their camp, Baird was one of the first to reach the scene of crime, after the alarm was given, and he fully identified the body of Bolding as the man he had seen behind the wagon. On the next day, Monday, Pointer was arrested at South McAlester, while he was attempting to dispose of the team and wagon. He gave his name as Longley. He admitted killing Bolding but said it was in self-defense. He stated that Vandever had spoken roughly to Bolding about his bad treatment of one of the horses and during a quarrel that had ensued Bolding had attacked Vandever with an axe, killing him; that he had interfered in Vandever's behalf and had been himself attacked, and in the struggle had secured the axe (without a cut or scratch on his person) and had been obliged to kill Bolding; that he had then become badly frightened and, scarcely knowing what he was doing, had dragged the bodies to the creek and thrown them in, and on reviewing the trouble he had made for himself by trying to protect Vandever, he had concluded he might as well take possession of the team and other property, An examination of the scene of the killing spoke plainly of a foul murder. Vandever had evidently been sitting near the fire mixing a pan of dough, for bread or biscuits for breakfast, when he had been attacked with an axe and his head split open. A quantity of blood and dough lay on the ground close by the fire. On the body of Bolding were several great, gaping wounds, made with an axe; he had, evidently, attempted to defend himself and had been first knocked into the fire, as his hands were badly burned. During the struggle he had finally been killed, several feet from the camp fire, as the numerous blood stains attested.

Pointer was taken to Fort Smith and locked in jail, December 28, 1891. The bodies of the two unknown victims were buried and descriptions of the three men were published. The fathers of Bolding and Vandever came and identified the bodies. The trousers worn by Pointer were identified as having been taken from Bolding's body and several other articles of clothing he had taken from Vandever. After the killing Pointer had burned Vandever's crutches, the pocket books of the two men and other articles; the irons belonging to the crutches and the rims of the purses were found in the ashes of the camp fire.

Pointer was ably defended, but the chain of circumstantial evidence wound about him was too strong; he had at last fallen into the toils in real earnest and on March 26, 1892, he was convicted of murder. An appeal was at once taken to the Supreme Court, the decision of the lower court was affirmed and he was re-sentenced and finally executed September 20, 1894. His father, mother and sister visited him while in jail; they came to see him on the day before his execution. The mother was very feeble and had to be assisted up the step» leading to the jail. Pointer had kept up a careless demeanor ever since his arrest and his leave taking of his mother and sister was very affecting on their part, exasperatingly calm on his. The father remained until after the execution, that he might take charge of the body and send it home for burial.

THE BRAGGART QUAILS

Pointer was given the privilege of setting the hour of his departure from earth; he named half past three o'clock in the afternoon. When the time came he was beginning to weaken; he asked for a half hour's delay; fifteen minutes were granted. When a few feet outside of the jail building his sight rested on the gallows enclosure and he was visibly affected. He began to talk about some capsules he claimed he had taken just before he had left his cell, asserting that he had swallowed poison that had been given him by a trusty. He kept saying: "If I hadn't taken that poison I would have stood it all right." On the scaffold, he talked for some minutes in a rambling manner, interrupting himself every few sentences to speak of the poison he had taken and how his nerves would have been calm and he would have stood the ordeal all right but for the poison. He grew more pale and at last his knees failed to support him and he was scarcely able to stand. The braggart had become a craven, was showing the white feather at the one time in his life when he needed most to be brave. After his death the physicians discovered that his talk of poison was but affectation, given through shame at his cowardice and to cover his weakness. He had intended to die as he had lived— boastingly—his true nature asserted itself in the hour of death and only by base falsehoods could he seek to hide it.

On the day before his execution he made a statement to Deputy Marshal George Lawson, confessing that his killing of Bolding was not in self-defense as he had asserted, but to the last he maintained he did not kill Vandever. He said that while he was temporarily absent from the camp Bolding had killed his companion with an axe, and as he returned and saw how the poor cripple had been hacked to pieces his first thought had been to knock his murderer down and stamp him to death. "Bolding was standing on the wagon tongue, his back toward me, the axe still in his hand. I rushed at him and secured the axe and struck him a blow with the back of it; he fell and then got partially up and I struck him with the sharp part of the axe and kept on striking him until he was dead."

SAM HICKORY, ALEXANDER ALLEN AND MARSHALL TUCKER

The cause of Sam Downing, alias Sam Hickory, was one similar to many that occurred within this land, where it sometimes seemed that his Satanic Majesty was waging with the Almighty for supremacy, and where conditions existed which often rivaled Dante's Inferno in its horrors. Hickory was captured in "No Man's Land," at the home of an uncle, nearly six months after committing the crime of which he was charged, having scouted during the interval. Joseph Wilson was a young Texan, 25 years old, and was a deputy United States Marshal for the Muscogee district, under Marshal Thomas B. Needles. He was fearless and daring; with a few more years' experience he would become invaluable to the service. On Tuesday, September 22, 1891, Wilson departed from Tahlequah with a United States' warrant, for the arrest of Hickory, charged with conveying whiskey into the Indian Territory, in violation of the law. Hickory was an educated Cherokee, about 20 years old. He spoke both English and Cherokee. He lived with his uncle, "Big Aleck" Stop, ten miles from Tahlequah, on Fourteen Mile creek. Wilson started out in search of the place and after missing his way several times, stopped at the home of John Carey, also a Cherokee, and by him was escorted to within a short distance of Hickory's home. Carey would go no farther, as he feared Hickory and did not care to be mixed up in any trouble with him. As he rode on towards~ the house, Wilson told Carey to wait at a certain point; if Hickory should not be at home he would inquire for Hawkins, the next neighbor, and go on and return to him; if he found Hickory, after arresting him he would fire his pistol in the air to notify Carey of the arrest, that he might come down and meet him on "Brown's Prairie." After waiting half an hour or more Carey heard a pistol shot, then two more almost in unison, then several others at random, followed by the sharp crack of a rifle, Carey was dumbfounded at so many shots, but remembering that the officer had not told him how many times he would fire, he went to the proposed place of meeting and: returned home.

When Wilson left Carey, he proceeded to the home of "Big Aleck," and found Hickory at work in the field with a team of horses. Wilson served his warrant and told Hickory to unharness one of the horses and ride with him to Tahlequah. Sam replied that the team belonged to his uncle, at which Wilson' said: "Well, drive to the house and we will see your uncle about it." Together they went to the house. "Big Aleck" was away from home and Sam went into the house for his saddle, in: response to the marshal's suggestion. As he was about to-enter, Wilson fired in the air as a signal, in accordance with his arrangements with Carey. Hickory, knowing nothing of the pre-arranged signal, took fright, ran in the house for his gun and a moment later appeared with it at the door, Wilson in the meantime having fired another signal. Hickory, supposing that the signal shots were fired at him, at once opened fire on: Wilson, the officer returning with several shots, his bullets-lodging in the side of the house and in the door Hickory's wife took fright and running off, hid among the trees. Wilson made a flank movement to the right and entered the house by a side kitchen door, behind

Hickory, when several shots were exchanged through an inner door, Wilson receiving, one shot full in the breast. The blood gushed forth to the floor, and Wilson ran toward his horse, fell in the yard and died. Hickory, after a short meditation as how best to dispose of his victim's body, loaded it on the wagon, and with some difficulty, hauled it about a mile away and rolled it over a steep bluff into a gulch about thirty feet below, where it was found by a searching party three days later, greatly decomposed. This was substantially the case as claimed by Hickory, who testified on the stand, relying on the law of self-defense, Wilson having fired the first shot, without provocation from him.

The government's theory of the killing was, that Hickory had gone into the house for his saddle, leaving Wilson standing in the yard, and that while inside he conceived the idea of resisting arrest, and seizing his gun, returned to the door, opened fire on Wilson, missing the officer and hitting his horse in the leg. Wilson returned a few shots, striking the side of the house and the door, then fled to the right for safety, into the side room, behind Hickory. Here they exchanged several shots, the officer receiving a shot from the front from which he fell, badly disabled, but lived to the following day, as claimed by the prosecution, and that while here, Tom Shade, a neighbor, learning that the white man was still alive in the house, visited the place and with an axe struck Wilson on the back of the head, killing him.

The horse was found by the searching party, about a quarter of a mile from the house, stripped of saddle and bridle, dead, with its throat cut and with a bullet wound in the knee. Hickory and Shade were tried together on a joint indictment for murder, and were defended by J. Warren Reed and his former law partner, Thomas H. Barnes. Shade was acquitted. Hickory was convicted of murder. Mr. Reed, resolving to save the life of his client if possible, took an appeal to the Supreme Court, secured a reversal and an order granting a new trial. At the second trial, nearly a year later, Hickory was again convicted of murder and again was the death penalty pronounced. Mr. Reed, still bent on saving the life of his client, again appealed to the Supreme Court, a second reversal was secured and a second new trial awarded. At the third hearing of the case the grade of the crime was reduced to manslaughter and Hickory was sentenced to the penitentiary at Columbus, Ohio, for five years, after being confined in the Fort Smith jail for about five years.

ALEXANDER ALLEN

Alexander Allen, a negro boy fifteen years old, was a character such as one may expect to meet in a boy who has never had training, who has been cuffed about (this has no reference to the term "cuffie" often applied to negroes) and had seldom known a friend. He seemed to feel that he was in the way, and that everybody he met had a desire to do him an injury, and being born with an independent disposition his first thought was to oppose or antagonize all with whom he came in contact. Believing everybody his avowed enemy, without a mind development capable of analyzing the intent of any who might attempt to approach him, he resented every speech that seemed like undue familiarity, misconstrued every act of a stranger, imagined that his rights were being imposed upon, and from out the morose disposition thus developed his first thought, where other and better trained boys would have laughed heartily at a joke, was to kill. To say that he did not realize the sin of sinning would be hardly true for he was as apt as any in running from justice, or was it that he fled, not because of a guilty conscience but because he expected to be made the victim of an angered people and punished for the purpose, merely, of revenge? Poor boy! born into the world through no fault of his own, member of a despised race, with a strong self-pride that made him feel more keenly than many colored people do the jibes and thrusts which thoughtless persons often hurl at the negro, it was not unnatural that, imagining every white person his enemy, he should have conceived a hatred for even a white person. Could he have had an early training, have learned that he had the power born within to command respect and to win esteem regardless of his unfortunate color, he might have made a good citizen. He might then have had a very different idea of this world and the people in it than he has now, shut up for life in a penitentiary. Convicted as a criminal when only nineteen years old, how little does he know or will ever know of a life worth living; how different his earthly existence and experience to that of many another boy, born into the world on the same day as he but under more favorable conditions. This is a theme for the true moralist, and the conclusion drawn is, that we who are born under conditions favorable to a high moral status should lose no opportunity to stretch out a hand to elevate those of the human race who are in need of elevation, regardless of condition or parentage, so that all may have a training that will aid in bringing out the best that is in them, even aiding in supplying that which by an error of nature, or rather from a transgression of the laws of nature, has been ignored in building the structure, leaving the individual deficient.

Of the antecedents of this colored boy but little if anything appears to be known. He first shows up at the home of a colored family named Marks, who lived in the Cherokee Nation, four miles south of Coffeyville, Kansas. The Marks family were poor people, and tenants of John Morgan, a fairly well-to-white man. Marks had several children, and the boy, Allen, seems to have fallen in with them without ceremony, and to have secured a temporary home without leave and without opposition. In the same neighborhood lived William Henson and wife with their three sons, of which the eldest was Phillip, aged eighteen years. Another neighbor was named Erne, with two sons named George and Willie. Soon after the arrival of the Allen boy in the neighborhood, about the middle of May, 1891, it appears that Phillip Henson and the Erne boys were in a field on Henson's farm where Phillips was planting watermelon seeds, when one of the Marks boys and Alexander Allen approached. Some more or less disagreeable things were said which Allen construed to be a personal affront, spoken because he was black, and it caused his fire of hatred for the white race to burn more fiercely. Two days later, May 14, 1892, the Erne boys, with Phillip Henson, were passing through a field, not far from the home of Marks, when Allen hailed them from the other side of a fence, drew a pistol and ordered a halt, then went to where

214

they had stopped and, after a few fist blows directed at Phillips' person, deliberately shot at him, the first bullet going high in the air and as Phillip grasped the weapon the other two entered his body causing death within a few minutes. The young murderer ran to the house, procured a valise which contained his few belongings, then harnessed a horse to a cart and rapidly drove to Coffeyville. Two days later he was arrested at Edna, Kansas, by Deputy United Marshal N. M. Clifford and taken to Fort Smith for trial. Here the boy developed all the latent bad that may have been his heritage from generations of a down trodden ancestry. Having committed a crime unpardonable in the eyes of the Fort Smith Court, knowing that his punishment, whatever it was, must be most severe, having nothing to look back to as being a bright and happy spot in his memory, having had, previous to his crime, nothing pleasant or ennobling to look forward to, he could not realize that he, who had nothing to win, had lost aught. He was now more than ever an enemy to all. humanity. He had at least lost his liberty, and in revenge he would grasp every opportunity to cultivate all that was naturally bad within him; he would, if possible, commit other crimes. He was probably the most uncomfortable prisoner the guards ever had to handle. It was necessary to keep him chained a greater part of the time, arid any opportunity that came in his way to perform a mean, contemptible act, he never failed to take advantage of. He was frequently punished, and severely, but as well might one have dealt out punishment to the inanimate prison walls for whatever effect it had, unless to make him worse. A noble fight was made by the attorney for the defense to keep the young savage from the gibbet, but after a long and tedious trial he was sentenced to hang. The case was taken up on appeal and reversed, another trial, sentence, appeal, and another reversal, followed by still another trial, at which Allen was sentenced to serve the balance of his natural life in the Columbus, Ohio, penitentiary. His last sentence to hang was delivered by Judge Parker, October 30, 1895, and the nineteenth day of the following December was set for his execution. Shrewd attorneys saved him from the gallows at last, and he was given a life time to repent of his crime. How many thousands, looking at it from a purely business standpoint, might have been saved to the government if this boy could have been given proper training and instruction in his early childhood!

THE MARSHALL TUCKER CASE

Marshall Tucker was a deputy United States marshal, and he sometimes bought and sold cattle. At the time he committed the crime which placed his life in jeopardy, he was but little past 28 years old. He was generally considered to be honest and upright. He usually had money in plenty and consequently had many friends. He was a native of Sebastian county, Arkansas, but at the time stated his parents lived near Cameron, Indian Territory. He acquired a love for liquor and at times, when off business for a few days, he was apt to shame all good people by his conduct. Gradually he formed bad acquaintances as well as bad habits. On the fifteenth day of October, 1892, he was in South McAlester, and after imbibing freely he started out with some companions similarly conditioned for a tour through what was known as "Chippy Hill," a section near the town devoted to prostitution. When he reached the house he asked admittance, but was denied by one of the inmates, Lulu May, whose voice sounded to him as if she was at another part of the house. For the purpose of frightening her, and making her open the door, he drew his gun and fired through one of the panels. As it chanced she had come forward and when he shot, she was standing directly in range and the bullet struck her, producing instant death. This was the story told by Tucker on the stand. His intent had not been to commit murder nor to injure anyone.

He at once gave himself up and was taken to Fort Smith, for trial. The defense made a strong plea of not guilty. It was urged that as Tucker was intoxicated when he committed the crime, and as the victim of his bullet was only a-common prostitute it was not worthwhile to execute an otherwise good man for a low and degraded woman. But the law regarded a drunken man responsible for his acts, and the life of a degraded woman was of the same value, in a legal sense, as the most upright member of society. It was decided that the crime was murder, and it was no extenuation that the victim chanced to be a human of low degree. Tucker was accordingly convicted and sentenced to hang, and the Supreme Court affirmed the decision. Before the arrival of the day set for the execution, President Cleveland exercised his clemency and the sentence was commuted to life imprisonment.

Tucker's parents were most excellent people. His father served with credit throughout the war, in the Confederate service. During the two years that elapsed between the day of her son's crime and the commutation of the sentence, his mother lived a decade and became an old, disconsolate, heartbroken woman, old before her time. She had trained her boy in the way he should go, but evil associations, with the d(mom drink, had brought ruin to her cherished hopes, and anguish to her heart. Perhaps, too, another mother sat nightly waitings hoping for the footsteps of her once innocent baby girl. Both the slayer and the slain each had a mother, once; each mother had dreamed of the future, when, old and feeble she should be protected and comforted by her own flesh and blood,. "Alas for human hopes!

Tucker's parents are now residents of Fort Smith.

THE MURDER OF ED KING AND OTHER CASES

The case of Berry Foreman, charged with the murder of Ed King, marks with unerring certainty the criminal tendencies of certain of the inhabitants of the Indian Territory. Foreman and King were negroes, each about 25 years old, of the class known In the Indian Territory as "Cherokee freedmen" negroes, whose parents had been slaves of the Indians, before the American civil war.

Berry Foreman was single and was a half-nephew of Mollie King, wife of Ed King, with whose murder they were charged. Foreman lived about four miles from Vian station, on the Arkansas Valley railroad, with his mother, while Ed King and his wife resided one mile and a half from Vian, up in the woodland, among the hills. For a long time Mollie and Ed had not been on congenial terms. It seems that the girl had a sweetheart and Ed did not live with her, although he would sometimes go to the house with her or to visit her. Mollie had two children, partly grown, who kept the house during the day, while their mother worked at a hotel at Vian, returning usually at night. During this time Ed King worked in a livery stable at Vian. He was jealous of his wife, and frequently accused her of being unduly intimate with other men; this incurred her great displeasure and she made dire threats against Ed, declaring repeatedly that she would have him killed.

A few months before the killing, which this tale narrates, she had induced Ed to make a trip with her in the country, passing by a lonely spot where she had arranged with a paramour to lay in ambush; as they passed; he fired upon Ed, inflicting a nearly fatal wound. Two weeks prior to the murder, Ed went to the hotel where his wife was working and there they had a serious quarrel and the woman made violent threats against his life. During the afternoon, preceding the night on which Ed was killed, in the spring of 1894, Mollie met Ed several times and she besought him to go home with her that night. Ed demurred, reminding her how near she had come to causing his death on a former occasion, but at last she wheedled and coddled him into compliance and they started forth on the trip to the hills, after dark. Arriving at the house Mollie performed some errand, then saying to Ed, "We will go on to mother's," a mile further, they proceeded up the mountain. When they had reached a point about half the distance, two men sprang from ambush and began firing upon Ed, shooting six or seven bullets into his body, killing him in Mollie's sight. Then they dragged the body by a mule, a distance of a mile and a half, Mollie walking exultingly by the side of the body. Arrived at a lonely spot in the wilderness they stopped, proceeded to dig a hole and dumping in the body covered it with earth. It was claimed that the two men who-performed this dastardly deed were Aleck Martin and Berry Foreman, who stood indicted with Mollie. The next day Berry ^Foreman and Mollie King were arrested, charged with the murder; they were conveyed to Fort Smith, indicted by the grand jury, and about six months later were put on trial for their lives, were convicted and sentenced to be hanged, Aleck Martin was never captured. A writ of error was taken to the Supreme Court by their attorneys, J. K. Barnes and J. B. Rutherford, of the law firm of Barnes & Rutherford. The judgment was reversed and a new trial was granted. Berry Foreman's mother and his uncles believed that he had been unjustly convicted, and in his especial interest they employed the criminalist J. Warren Reed.

The second trial came on in November, 1897. Mollie was a witness on the stand and testified to facts substantially as here given. It was a tedious case, strongly contested and ably defended, and resulted in the absolute acquittal of Berry Foreman, and Mollie King was convicted of murder, without capital punishment, under the provisions of a law recently enacted, and she was given a life sentence in the penitentiary.

The act of Congress referred to was approved January 15, 1897 (U. S. St. at L, 54th Cong., Sess. I1, vol. 29, chap. 29, p. 487). It provided that "In all cases where the accused is found guilty of murder or robbery under Section 5339, or 5345 R. S." (Whose provisions specified that any person within any place under the exclusive jurisdiction of the United States committing murder or rape should suffer death), "the jury may qualify their verdict by adding thereto: 'without capital punishment,' and whenever the jury shall so qualify, the convicted shall be sentenced to imprisonment at hard labor during life."

A PATRICIDE

John Allison was a young white man, eighteen years old.

He was born in Washington Territory, where his father, William Allison, whom John was charged with murdering, and defendant's mother with his brothers and sisters, had lived since defendant's birth. John was a quiet, peaceful, well behaved boy, well-liked by all who knew him, and was the favorite of his mother. His parents never lived congenially, and the father appeared to conceive a dislike for John because he was his mother's favorite. William Allison was a very boisterous, abusive, cruel man; he frequently whipped his wife and at times beat his children terribly and drove them from home. There were six children, and he pursued this course towards them in Washington Territory until they were nearly all grown, On one occasion, in a terrible fit of anger and fury, the father attacked one of his older sons and one of his sons-in-law with a loaded pistol and tried to kill them; he fired several shots at the son-in-law, some of the bullets cutting his clothing. For this he was arrested, charged with assault with intent to kill, tried, convicted and sent to the penitentiary for one year. For years before his incarceration he had pursued a course of terror in his family, had frequently declared he would kill them all, and he seemed especially to have a spite at John.

Before his conviction Allison's wife had procured a divorce on the grounds of cruel treatment. After he was convicted, in order to escape him, and secure a location where they could live in peace, the family gathered all their effects and removed to the Indian Territory, settling near Claremore, with the exception of one married daughter who settled at Little Rock, Arkansas. As soon as William Allison, the father, was released from the penitentiary, he again declared vengeance against his family, saying he would follow and kill them every one. He followed them, going first to the daughter at Little Rock, where he made all manner of threats against his wife, and more especially against the son, John. Learning from his daughter where the mother and his children were located he continued his pursuit to the Indian Territory and took up his abode with a cousin, residing about a mile from the home of his ex-wife, still breathing his threats of violence, declaring his intention to kill them all, more especially John. Soon after he went to the house of his family, abused the mother shamefully, displaying a pistol, and they were compelled to secure assistance to drive him away from the place. He continued his threats against John and the others. Sometime later, John started toward the house of one of his neighbors, carrying a Winchester for the purpose of going on a deer hunt. Passing by the house of the cousin, with whom his father lived, he saw whom he supposed to be one of his brothers, loading a wagon at the cousin's house. He rode in at the gate and to the barn where two men were at work. Not wanting to go to the house where his father was, for fear of trouble, he waited at the barn, I 50 yards away, until his brother should drive that way with his team. He alighted at the barn, held the bridle rein in hand and stood waiting, with the muzzle of his Winchester resting on his foot. He had been in this position but a few minutes when his father, who had discovered him, left the house and hastily approached directly toward him. Believing his father to be armed, as usual, he watched him closely. When the father had reached a point within four or five steps of the son, as John claimed, he placed his hand behind him, saying, "You've got it, have you?" meaning the gun, and, as John believed, started to draw a weapon; this, at last, turned out to be an error as the old man was unarmed. At that point John raised his gun and fired three times, sending three bullets into his father's body before it fell to the ground.

John was arrested and conveyed to Fort Smith, charged with murder. He engaged Thomas H. Barnes and J. Warren Reed to defend him. John claimed the killing was in self-defense, stating that when he fired he believed his father was drawing a weapon to kill him, as he had so often threatened to do. The case was strongly prosecuted and as ably defended, but the jury did not agree with the theory of the defense and found the defendant guilty of murder. On the ninth day of July, 1895, he was sentenced to be hanged October I following. Numerous exceptions to the rulings of Judge Parker were taken at the trial, and the case was prepared for appeal. Following the sentence of the court a writ of error was taken to the Supreme Court at Washington. The judgment of Judge Parker was reversed and a new trial granted. About a year later, on a compromise with the prosecuting attorney, a plea of guilty of manslaughter was entered in the case and a sentence of seven years and five months imprisonment was accepted by Allison in place of death by the gallows.

HE MURDERED A FOOL

Eli Lucas was a young full-blood Choctaw Indian. His victim was a half-witted negro. The crime was committed in the San Bois country, Choctaw Nation. The negro had wandered into the Indian Territory' from Little Rock, or some point in eastern Arkansas and had stopped for a while at the home of John LeFlore, After a time he became tiresome and he was turned out and made to leave; he went to a base-ball game in the neighborhood and several persons there who knew him, thinking he had strayed, started him back in the direction of the LeFlore home. He was soon followed by Lucas who returned shortly and in reply to questions about a gunshot heard in the direction whence he had been, he said he had shot a squirrel. No more was thought of the affair till, in the course of a month, he told several of his acquaintances of having killed a negro, describing the place. Investigation proved his story true. The body was found, bearing the marks of several bullets. The story told by Lucas was blood curdling in the extreme. He said the negro had no business at LeFlore's, hence he followed him from the ball game and shot him. Several hours later, he returned to see if his victim was dead and the negro was still alive; he told Lucas someone had shot him and asked him for a drink of water. Instead of performing this most simple act of human kindness, instead of giving to the poor unbalanced and suffering negro a drink of water, Lucas drew his pistol and shot again. The poor creature struggled to his feet and started to run but, in his weakened condition, he fell to the ground, and another shot from his inhuman persecutor ended his life.

These stories told boastingly by Lucas to his acquaintances, were repeated in court but, Lucas denied having ever told them and the defense devoted all its energies to breaking down the witnesses who testified to them. It was attempted to prove that no one, to whom the stories were told, believed them; that he told them in a joking manner, often assumed by young fellows who wish to gain the reputation of being "killers." The defense also proved that the firing of guns was of frequent occurrence in the neighborhood, where the negro was killed; that during the day of the ball game, there were numerous shots fired, in the direction of where the dead body was afterwards found and that the killing was as likely to have been done by some other as by Lucas. The jury took little stock in the theory and Lucas was convicted and sentenced to be hanged.

His attorney, James K. Barnes, of the firm of Barnes & Rutherford, appointed by the court to defend, appealed the case and the Supreme Court reversed the decision of Judge Parker's court, on evidence going to show that the negro victim of Lucas, was a citizen of the Choctaw Nation, and thus was, in a legal sense, an Indian, placing his murderer, an Indian, outside of the jurisdiction of Judge Parker's court, and Lucas was. released and returned to the Choctaw Nation.

A CHAPTER ON ROBBERIES

THE HENRY STARR AND JIM DYER CASES

As the reader has observed, robbery formed an important part in the crimes committed by the outlaws, infesting the Indian Territory, and as a slight diversion, a chapter on two of the most noted ones, may prove to be interesting reading.

The Bentonville, Arkansas, bank robbery, in which the People's Bank, of Bentonville, was looted of $11,000 of gold and paper money, occurred Monday afternoon, June 5, 1893 [$289,473.68 in 2015].

It was at first claimed that this piece of business was planned by Jim Dyer but at the trial the claim was disproved. At 2:30 o'clock, on the day named, five horsemen rode into the town (which, shortly after the war, had been made famous by being raided by the James' boys [Jesse and Frank], and the looting of Craig & Son's store) and commenced shooting recklessly, to frighten citizens from the streets. The leader of the outfit was Henry Starr, then known as an Indian Territory desperado. Two of the men were left on the outside to guard against surprise, while the others entered and compelled the bank officers to place their loose money in two sacks; one for the gold and currency and the other bearing $900 in silver. This latter was saved by a courageous young lady, Miss Maggie Wood, employed as business manager in the Sun office. The robbers compelled the assistant cashier to carry the bag containing the silver in the direction of where their horses were stationed, and as they passed the office where Miss Wood was employed, she bravely opened the door, and grabbing the cashier by the shoulders, pulled him headlong into the room and before the others could recover from their surprise, closed the door and bolted it. By this time many citizens had secured pistols and shot-guns and were firing at the robbers from various points of vantage, and they hurriedly left the city, without attempting to recover the silver. They were followed by a sheriff's posse and a desultory fire was kept up for several miles, but the robbers managed to escape. Two of them, Henry Starr and "Kid" Wilson, were captured a few months later, at Colorado Springs, Colorado, and lodged in Fort Smith jail.

THE CAPTURE OF STARR AND WILSON

The capture of Henry Starr and his accomplice, "Kid" Wilson, was the result of the keen sight of William Feuerstine, a resident of Fort Smith, who was in Colorado Springs, Colorado, attending to private business affairs. On Monday, July 3, 1893, Feuerstine saw Starr on the streets, recognized ham and informed the police. A search was instituted and it was learned that late on the Saturday night previous, Starr and his pal, with a woman, had arrived at the Spaulding House and registered as Frank Jackson, John Wilson, Mary Jackson; Joplin, Missouri.

It was at once understood by the officers that they had desperate men to deal with, and if they would capture them without bloodshed they must work carefully; must catch them unarmed, if possible, and singly. A careful watch of their movements was planned. On Tuesday morning the two men went to Oppenheimer's store, made some expensive purchases and told the proprietors they were from the East and desired to see the sights. It was, therefore, arranged that two members of the firm should secure an equipage and the entire party should spend the day at Manitou Springs. The party stopped at the Spaulding House for "Mrs. Jackson," who was in reality Starr's wife, and were shadowed during the day by officers. They returned late at night, Starr and his wife alighting at the hotel, but Wilson rode on to the stable. After going to their room, Starr came down to the office, and on learning that the supper hour was past, went out for a lunch and was followed to the Cafe Royal, where he was arrested a few minutes later as he was regaling ^sumptuously. He submitted to arrest peacefully, and as he was being conducted to jail he enquired:

"Who do you think you have got?"

"Henry Starr," replied one of the officers, to which Starr admitted to his identity. Wilson was shadowed to a house of easy virtue, and half an hour later the officers forced an entrance and took him from one of the rooms without difficulty.

Under the pillow, where rested the pretty head of Mrs. Starr alias Jackson, was found, after the two men had been safely locked in jail, $1,460 in paper money and $500 in gold coin. Mrs. Starr was eighteen years old; she said her maiden name was Jones, her parents being residents of Joplin, Missouri.

The Federal authorities at Fort Smith were notified of the capture of Starr and "the Kid" and Deputy Marshal Wm. Smith was sent to Colorado to bring back the prize rascals. Soon after, Starr was indicted for the murder of Floyd Wilson, a deputy marshal who was seeking his arrest, a year before. He was also jointly indicted with "Kid" Wilson for the Bentonville Bank robbery. Starr was convicted of murder and was sentenced to die. He took a writ of error to the Supreme Court and obtained a new trial. He was tried again a year later and was again convicted of murder, and, taking a second writ of error to the Supreme Court, was awarded a second new trial. Some two years later, in March, 1898, he pleaded guilty to manslaughter and was sentenced to the penitentiary at Columbus, Ohio, for five years. Pending his murder case, he had been convicted of three robberies, for which he was sentenced to ten years in the penitentiary; altogether his sentences were for fifteen years. While in the United States jail, about five years his deportment was most exemplary, and it was plain that he was a changed man and that if again restored to the civil walks of life he would make a good citizen. In view of this manifest reformation of Henry Starr and the fact of his youth, the judge, in passing sentence upon him, said, that if his conduct in future was good in prison where he was going, in a few years he would recommend his full pardon and release.

Kid Wilson, above referred to, was tried and convicted for several robberies, including the Bentonville affair, for which he was sentenced a period of twenty-four years in the penitentiary at Brooklyn, New York.

Henry Starr was a half-breed Cherokee Indian, son of Hopp Starr, who died in 1888, and who was a son of Tom Starr and distantly related to all of the Starr families in the Cherokee Nation, the most of whom were excellent people. Henry was five feet nine and one-half inches in height, had straight black hair and eyes and a good looking, beardless face. At the time of his arrest he was twenty-two years old. His companion in crime, "Kid Wilson," was twenty-five years old, five feet four inches in height, had brown eyes and hair and was smooth faced. The rewards offered for their capture aggregated several thousand dollars, but Wilson was considered the worst outlaw of the two, partly on account of his being older than the other.

Henry Starr was first arrested in June, 1891, by Deputy Marshal Wykoff of the Muscogee Court, on a charge of introducing whiskey into the Indian Territory. For this he paid a fine. He was arrested in February, 1892, on a charge of horse stealing, by Jasper Exendine, and placed in jail February 13, but was released at the commissioner's trial. In August, 1892, he was arrested on a charge of stealing horses and was released on bond furnished by his cousin, Kale Starr, and Chief Harris of the Cherokee Nation;, he failed to appear for trial at the appointed time and his bond was forfeited. His bondsmen offered a reward for his capture and it was while a fugitive from justice that he committed the crime that resulted in his being convicted of murder.

He had, in the meantime, committed several robberies, notably the looting of an express office at Nowata. Detective Dickey, of the express company, went to Fort Smith and obtained a deputy's commission for Floyd Wilson as his posse and the two officers went on a hunt for the youthful bandit. They proceeded to Nowata by rail and just at night arrived at the ranche of Albert Dodge, by whom Starr had been employed before he became an outlaw. It appears that Starr knew of the officers' arrival at his rendezvous but he was personally unknown to them, and while they were in the house, awaiting his coming, he rode by the place several times, peering curiously at the windows. On being apprised of his presence by Dodge, who had seen Starr pass, from where he was engaged about his affairs on the ranche, the officers mounted their horses and scoured the country, continuing the search through a greater portion of the night. On the following day, as the officers, with the family of the rancheman, were at dinner, Starr again rode by the house and Wilson rushed to the stable and mounted a horse already saddled and bridled, on which Mr. Dodge had just returned from a short ride, and started after the outlaw, who, as soon as he discovered Wilson in pursuit, dismounted. The officer followed his example, and the two men stood facing each other not more than thirty yards apart and in plain sight of the house. They parleyed for some time, Wilson apparently trying to induce Starr to surrender, when the officer finally fired over the bandit's head to frighten him. Starr quickly returned the fire and shooting began in good earnest. An empty shell became clogged in Wilson's Winchester, and throwing down the weapon, he tried to defend himself with his revolver. Starr fired two more shots, both taking effect, and at the second

Wilson fell, after which the outlaw calmly walked to the prostrate man and shot him in the breast, holding the muzzle of his pistol so close that his clothing was burned, then rode away to safety. Detective Dickey meanwhile had failed to reach his companion, having mounted a fresh horse, saddled for him by Dodge, and the animal, objecting to a strange rider, had "bucked" badly, preventing the officer's arrival at the place of battle until too late to effect a capture.

This affair placed Starr in the position of a hunted man, where his only chance for freedom or for life was to keep out of the clutches of the officers, and his further commission of crime was but the usual result—a repetition of the old tale, many times told in the Indian Territory. His final capture and conviction was a blessing to humanity and to himself as well.

Of "Kid" Wilson's antecedents nothing was ever learned. Just before his incarceration at Brooklyn he was asked concerning his relatives, but he declined giving any information concerning them. He said:

"My kinfolk have never done anything to place me where I am; they live on the other side of the globe and I prefer to say nothing of them."

THE JIM DYER CASE

The Blackstone train robbery occurred November 13, 1894. The job was done by Nath Reed alias Texas Jack, a white man; Tom Root, Cherokee Indian; Buss Luckey and Bill Smith, negroes. The "hold up" occurred at 9:57 o'clock at night and was attained by throwing the switch and side tracking the north bound passenger train on the Missouri, Kansas & Texas Railroad at what was known as "Blackstone Switch." The railroad company had been carrying armed guards, but owing to the fact that there had been no attempts at robbery for some time, a part of these had been withdrawn. The robbers were disappointed in the booty received, as the $60,000, which confederates had informed them would be shipped on that train by express had been, by some chance, retained until a later train. The usual scene occurred, so familiar to readers of the press of that day. One of the road agents held the engineer and fireman under subjection while two others kept up a careless fire to frighten the other trainmen and passengers. As soon as it was learned that there was no booty obtainable in the express car, Nath Reed went through the train and at the point of a revolver, and with the most fearful oaths, compelled the passengers to "contribute," as he termed it, forcing a young passenger to go with him and hold one side of the sack in which the "contributions" were deposited. Many curious things happened among the passengers when they learned that a train robber was going through the coaches. One young man, who was returning to the East from a trip to the Southwest, was so unnerved that he raised a window and threw out a valuable gold watch, the gift of his mother. His name was engraved on the case and it was afterwards found by section hands and returned to him. Another man became frightened and tried to hide between the backs of two seats; he was discovered by Reed and forced to crawl out and "chip in." A Galveston banker was riding in a seat with a pretty, black eyed young lady, whom he had met that day on the train, for the first time. When word was passed into the car that the bandit was coming that way, he confided to his fair seat-mate that he had five $1,000 bank notes in his possession and a very valuable diamond pin. She said: "Quick, let me take them."

He promptly handed over the money and the diamond and she, making them into a compact roll, deftly lifted her skirts and placed it in her stocking. The banker remarked:

"If you save that roll I'll give you one of the bills."

"Say I'm your wife," she said," and—"have you any other money?"

"Only a silver dollar."

"Then, here, give them this," and quickly reaching into her satchel she drew forth a purse and emptied its contents into her hand—a $5.00 note and a few dollars in silver." Quick," she said, "put it in your pocket."

A moment later Reed came up and pressing his pistol barrel against the banker's temple, yelled out, with a fearful oath, "Shove up!"* The banker drew the joint funds from his pocket and dropped them in the sack, with an air of resignation.

*That is to say, "Hands in the air!"

"How about the young lady there?" asked the robber, in gruff tones.

"My wife," said the banker, in a low tone. "I never trust her to carry money. I wish I had now, for I don't know how we will get our breakfast."

"Oh, well," said the robber, "if it is so bad as all that, take this," and reaching into the sack he gave the banker a dollar. "Enjoy yourselves at my expense," he said.

As he was leaving the train, Deputy Marshal Ledbetter fired and Reed was shot through the hips; his comrades carried him into the woods and cared for him at the home of Dick Reynolds, another desperate character, who was then in jail at Muscogee for stealing hogs, for which crime he was afterwards convicted; from there, a few days later, Reed was conveyed to Seneca, Missouri, and later to the home of his brother in the Boston Mountains, in Arkansas. He was arrested there in March, following the robbery, and lodged in the Fort Smith jail. Smith was never again heard of, and it is supposed he was killed in a drunken brawl.

Tom Root, a terribly dangerous character, was allowed to remain at large, none of the deputies being anxious to engage in a conflict with him, and finally, during the summer of 1895 v the government offered a reward of $250 for his capture. About this time Nath Reed, or Texas Jack, who was hobbling about on crutches in the Fort Smith jail, conceived the idea of clearing himself and securing clemency for one of his companions in crime. He had a violent hatred for Jim Dyer, a well-to-do white man, who had been in constant communication, for a long time, with the marshals, giving them information regarding various crimes committed in the Indian Territory, and the plan which Texas Jack conceived was to turn state's evidence, confess the part he played in the train robbery and swear away Jim Dyer's liberty while securing his own. He also opened up an avenue for his friend, Tom Root, by which with the assistance of Deputy Marshal Smith, a compromise was effected and Root was induced to surrender to Deputy Jim Pettigrew of Muscogee, and on the thirteenth day of August he was brought to Fort Smith, and his testimony assisted materially in the first conviction of Buss Luckey. The terms of Root's surrender included joint testimony with Texas Jack against Jim Dyer, and the story they told was to the effect that Dyer planned the Blackstone robbery, arranged that Texas Jack. Root, Lucky and Smith should do the job, and that all five should share the plunder equally; they also said that it was arranged that all should meet on the night following the robbery, at Vann's ford, on the Verdegris river, and there arrange the division. Upon the strength of their stories the prosecuting attorney promised immunity to Reed and Root and the pledge was faithfully kept. Dyer was arrested and indicted and Judge Parker, believing he had now arrived at the very head center of crime, the leader in all the numerous train robberies which had occurred in that section, placed his bond at $12,000, a sum which he did not believe Dyer could cover, and set the case for trial on the fifth day of the following month. Judge Parker said to me as we were going down the elevator one day, after court had adjourned:

"We have got to the bottom of this business at last. Dyer is the man whose brain has planned these robberies that have so upset business, and I tell you he is worse, a thousand times worse, than those whom he hired to do his dirty work. With him out of the way the others will soon be suppressed."

Judge Parker was mistaken in his estimate of Dyer, as subsequent events will show, and he also misunderstood the energy and ability of Dyer's little black-haired wife, whose eyes snapped fire when she heard the amount of the bond and saw her husband handcuffed and taken back to jail. With the tread of a queen she walked majestically from the court room, took the train for Wagoner, near which was located their home, and returning the next day, proudly produced the required bond, properly filled, and, with stately air, returned home the same day bearing her husband with her. If every wife were like her there would be more good husbands.

Jim Dyer was a native of Fannin county, Texas, born December 19, 1858. He removed to the Choctaw Nation in 1884 and later to the Cherokee Nation, having continued to make the Indian country his home since his first advent there. Several years before the occurrences related in this chapter, he had been tried in the Fort Smith Federal court on a charge of murder and was by the jury acquitted.

The case was commenced on the date mentioned and lasted several days. So certain was Judge Parker of Dyer's guilt, and so cognizant did he become of the ability of his wife and of her untiring efforts in his behalf, that he finally forbade her coming into the court room. It was rather humiliating to the average citizen to see this great government of ours brought to such straits, that to enforce its laws it must stoop to a compromise with criminals, but doubtless the court believed the ends justified the means. The trial proceeded and Dyer was convicted, even though several of the Fort Smith deputies went on the stand and testified to his good character, and to the fact that his house was their stopping place when in the territory in search of law breakers, and that he had rendered them much valuable assistance in apprehending certain noted desperadoes. Dyer was sentenced to fifteen years in the penitentiary and was lodged behind the bars. Here his brave wife showed her true nobility of heart and proved her allegiance. After she had made many attempts in her husband's behalf with as many failures, William M. Mellette, who had formerly been assistant prosecuting attorney under William Id. H. Clayton, took hold of the matter again, and by the exercise of all the power of a masterful nature, after Dyer had lain in prison a year, secured a reversal of Judge Parker by the Supreme Court at Washington, D. C., a new trial was granted, and Dyer was released on bond.

At the former trial Dyer had supposed that his acquaintance with the deputy marshals was sufficient to overcome any adverse testimony that might be presented by men of disrepute like Nath Reed and Root, and he had not attempted to produce a great array of evidence; and besides, Judge Parker had, on his certain belief of Dyer's guilt, obstructed, so far as lay in his power, such evidence as was produced by the defense. Dyer now, with the light of past experience, decided to leave no stone unturned; he also decided to change his counsel, and J. Warren Reed, who had gained a wide reputation by his successes as a criminal attorney, was employed to take charge of his case.

Dyer was released from prison about the time of Judge Parker's death, after the Fort Smith court had fallen from the greatest criminal tribunal in history, to one of comparatively petty dimensions. There still remained on the docket a number of important cases that had not been disposed of before the famous jurist's death; Dyer's case was classed among them—and they were taken up in order by Judge Rogers, who was appointed to succeed Judge Parker, over a court, whose jurisdiction is restricted principally to violations of internal revenue and postal laws, and to civil cases.

After a year and a half, during which new evidence was developed for the defense, on Monday, March 21, 1898, Dyer's case was taken up for rehearing. The trial lasted four days, was hotly contested by the defense; was given to the jury Friday night and the next day, the defendant, with his wife and counsel, were repaid for their energy, by a verdict for acquittal, and Dyer walked forth, a free man.

There were fifty-two witnesses in the case, twenty-four for the government and twenty-eight for defense. The principal witnesses for the government, were the notorious Reed, L. M. Best and the widow of Tom Root. Root had been killed during the previous year and a half, in a quarrel in the Indian Territory, the man who killed him remaining unknown. Nath Reed told the same kind of story as at the former trial, with but little variation. L. M. Best attempted to fill in the gap between. Vann's ford and the robbery. He swore that on the night of the robbery and about the hour the robbery was committed, he saw Dyer at Vann's ford and spoke to him. He also testified that he built the house Dyer occupied at the time of the robbery and made a scuttle-hole, with neat fitting cover and hinges, in the ceiling of one of the rooms; Dyer told him he could use it to "hide the boys." Best was greatly astonished when this scuttle-door was produced. The door was neither neat fitting nor did it have hinges. It was simply an ordinary opening into the garret, such as may be seen in the ceiling of nearly all farm houses. It proved his testimony to be false. Best also made some other wild statements. He gave a date as to the time he saw Dyer at Vann's ford, which was afterwards proven false; he merely saw Dyer at Vann's ford, not upon the night of the robbery, but at a different time, and merely late in the evening, when Dyer had been down to see other persons on business. But it is not necessary to dwell upon Best's testimony. A number of good citizens of Wagoner, showed that his character for truth and veracity was bad, and there his testimony ended. The jury did not consider it as worth anything.

Tom Root's widow attempted to stick to a story which had evidently been coached into her by her husband and her testimony had very little weight. Dick Reynolds' wife, who was also on the stand for the prosecution, said that she went to Dyer's after the robbery, and got from Dyer, for her brother, Tom Root, $15, a portion of the proceeds of the robbery. Testimony on the other side showed that the money she got was loaned to her; that she wanted it to assist her husband, Dick Reynolds, then in jail at Muscogee. The government offered other witnesses to prove its case, but Dyer's twenty-eight witnesses offset their claims. Jim Dyer's testimony showed that late on the day of the robbery he ran a horse race, at Wagoner, at which a number of Wagoner people were present; that he left Wagoner too late to have reached the scene of the robbery; he went home from the race track and stayed there all night. He also showed from the testimony of Col. Sheb. Williams, chief marshal of the Eastern District of Texas, that instead of Dyer assisting outlaws, he was constantly in communication with Col. Williams, giving him information as to the various crimes being committed in the Territory. Nearly one hundred letters were exhibited in court in evidence of what Dyer had written to Williams. These letters showed who were supposed to be committing the crimes, the location of the gangs and a description of the outlaws. Several of Dyer's letters were shown which gave an account of the Blackstone robbery—for which Dyer was on trial—giving Marshal Williams information as to who were the suspected robbers, their probable location, etc. These letters showed that instead of Dyer trying to shield the Blackstone robbers, he was actually endeavoring to effect their arrest

The jury was composed of men of more than ordinary intelligence, and Judge Rogers' charge was clear, explicit and impartial. It was a plain exposition of the law— short and not cumbered with dissertation tending to befog the minds of the jurymen. The jury retired and in a short time returned with a verdict. It was a triumph for honor and justice, over dishonor and outlawry. It was not the first case wherein disreputable men had been made use of by officers of the law, to defame the character of honorable citizens.

I have a case within my own knowledge, occurring about the time of Dyer's acquittal, but in another state, wherein a scheming political trickster, a prosecuting attorney and a sheriff, his willing tool, attempted to secure a pardon for a convicted and self-confessed crook, sent to the penitentiary for safe-breaking, in order that his testimony might be used to convict a man who had lead an honest life for years, in the community where he then resided. The scheme was nipped in the bud, by the refusal of the Governor of the state to grant a pardon.

J. Warren Reed was warmly complimented for his gallant fight in defense of Dyer and for the victory won; he had reason to feel proud. Dyer's truest friend, however, through all his troubles, was his wife. She worked early and late, through thick and thin and against odds, to protect his interests and ward off the blow aimed at his head. To her was due a large share of the credit for her husband's acquittal of the crime with which he was charged. Another true friend, who stayed by him from first to last, was O. D. (Bud) Weldon, of the Fort Smith *Elevator*.

FRANK CARVER AND THOMAS THORNTON

The story of Frank Carver, convicted and sentenced to hang for killing his illicit love, Annie Maledon, an unchaste woman, is one which but illustrates again the fate so apt to befall a man who indulges in the use of intoxicants and the company of bad women. The crime which brought Frank Carver within the pale of the law was committed March 25, 1895, at Muscogee, Indian Territory. There, on the night of the day named, he, through jealousy, slew the girl for whom he had given up honor, wife and his children.

When Carver was yet under nineteen years old he took for a wife a black-eyed Cherokee maiden, and, so far as known, they lived as happily as white men with Indian wives usually do, until he met Annie Maledon, the girl he afterwards killed. He was a gambler; he was reared principally at Muscogee, and when a youth, learned to win money from the Indians who came to Muscogee to draw their quarterly government allowance. He also became addicted to drinking and at the time his crime was committed, at the age of twenty-four years, he had acquired an uncontrollable appetite, to the extent that when he could not procure liquor he would drink bottlefuls of Jamaica ginger, which, being prepared with alcohol, was sufficiently intoxicating to produce drunkenness; but think for a moment the state of paralysis the lining of his stomach must have been in that it could have partaken of such fiery liquid in quantities!

It will be understood that at Muscogee, as well as at any other place in the Indian country, it was an offense against government laws to be in possession of intoxicants, and it naturally followed that when Carver could satisfy his craving in no other way he would go to either Kansas or Texas and return with a supply. For this, he was twice taken before the Fort Smith court but each time he secured an acquittal. It was during one of his trips to Fort Smith that he first met eighteen-year old Annie Maledon, a daughter of George Maledon, the then famous hangman, and she, at that time, had an unsavory reputation for chastity. He at once became infatuated with her, and his unsophisticated Indian wife and the children, the fruits of their union, were for the time forgotten. Carver was an exceptionally fine appearing young man, with regular features and pleasing manner. The girl, Annie Maledon, was beautiful of face and figure, possessed of a wealth of long, heavy black hair and soft, dark brown eyes, and a warm, if illicit, attachment sprang up between them. Carver never returned to his family; he tried to induce his wife to secure a divorce, as he desired to marry his latest flame. The ill-treated wife learned of his illicit attachment and although she had no desire that her faithless husband return to her, yet she refused to obtain the divorce in order to prevent his intended marriage with the girl who had come between them. She might as well have given him legal separation, however, for from the time Carver and Annie Maledon first met, they were together nearly all of the time, appearing as man and wife. It was said of Carter that the first money he ever spent upon the Maledon girl was a portion of $800 which his children drew from the government as their share of an allotment by the United States Government to the Cherokee Indians. From that time, Carver took the girl and cared for her as his wife, regardless of his marital ties, and in May, 1892, they went to Colorado, where he worked on a ranche and made more money than his wages by gambling. They returned to Muscogee in the summer of 1894, Carver, with all the assumption of a characterless man, hiring the girl's board and keeping her within eight blocks of the house where his wife and legitimate children resided with her mother. Open lewdness, however, they were careful to avoid, as they hoped to induce the wronged wife to believe that their attachment was broken and that she would secure a divorce on account of his having deserted her; but they had a place fixed, the home of an old colored woman, where they kept up their unholy meetings to their heart's content.

Meanwhile, Carver's appetite for strong drink was becoming more and more unmanageable. He made several trips away in quest of liquor, and at different times the Maledon woman had, during his absence, taken up her abode at houses where she found conditions very similar to her old time haunts in Fort Smith. One of the men who used to visit her was one Frank Walker and, fickle woman that she was, she encouraged him to an attachment which culminated in her death. Carver, on one of his return trips from a whiskey expedition, learned of the relations existing between his queen and Frank Walker, becoming intensely jealous. He called on her several times at the place where he was boarding her, and on two occasions threatened to kill her. Then he became despondent and drank steadily for two days and rounded off his spree by making away with four bottles of Jamaica ginger, making him crazy drunk, although in this condition he could always stand erect and walk. With his heart fired by jealousy, he continued to drink until, after he was fitted for any crime, he cunningly sent for the girl to meet him on the east side of the railroad track, in Muscogee, near the stock yards, informing her it was the last time she should see him; he was going to Texas, forever. She kept the appointment—going to her death. He at once berated her, and said: "Honey, you're done for to-night; I'm going to kill you before morning." Such women seldom fear a man, and she accompanied him to several disreputable places and at last started for her home accompanied by a mutual acquaintance. Carver several times drew his revolver, shooting in the air. At last the girl saw a gleam in his eye which there was no mistaking, and as he reached for his weapon again she turned to the other man for protection. Carver fired, the bullet striking her spinal column, in the small of the back, inflicting a fatal wound. The mutual acquaintance disarmed Carver (who immediately fled), then tried to raise the girl in his arms; finding her too heavy he started up town for a hack, and becoming frightened, did not return. In the meantime Carver reappeared and found his wounded sweetheart, and raising her in his arms kissed and wept over her, crying, "Oh, Annie, are you dead? Who has done this," then ran away. The girl was found by a crowd where she had sunk to the ground and was conveyed to her boarding place from where she was taken, after eleven weeks, to St. John's Hospital, in Fort Smith and there she died soon after. Carver was arrested on the night of the murder and was conveyed to Fort Smith. On May 29 he was indicted by the Federal grand jury. Carver's brother and other relatives employed J. Warren Reed to conduct the defense, and notwithstanding the case looked hopeless, Mr. Reed fought every inch of the ground and finally saved Carver's life.

The case came on for trial June 26, 1895, and lasted four days. At the trial the government introduced Annie Maledon's written dying statement, made the day after the shooting, which was to the effect that Carver had shot her in a murderous way. To the introduction and competency of this statement Mr. Reed saved four separate exceptions which were embodied in the record, and are too long to be here given. Numerous other exceptions were taken by the attorney during the progress of the trial, and it could be clearly seen that he was preparing a case for the Supreme Court. The case was hard fought and resulted in the conviction of Carver, and on July 9, he was taken before Judge Parker for sentence, and the first day of October following was named as his last of life.

Mr. Reed took a writ of error to the Supreme Court, and about half a year later Judge Parker was reversed and a new trial granted to Carver. Within about a year the case came up again for a second trial. The previous rulings of the court had narrowed the evidence until but little additional testimony could be offered. However, the attorney made a very strong defense; the jury were less willing to convict and were out two days deliberating upon a verdict. They finally convicted Carver again of murder in the first degree; at this trial, however, Mr. Reed sprung upon the court a new point, on which it was found later but little authority could be found in the books; but Mr. Reed urged his point, saved full exceptions in the record and again took a writ of error to the Supreme Court at Washington, reversed the judgment of Judge Parker and obtained a second new trial.

After a year's delay the case came on a third time to be tried. The last decision of the Supreme Court had enabled Mr. Reed to offer an additional class of testimony, and about a dozen additional witnesses were used. This time the defense made a stronger fight than ever and obtained a verdict of life imprisonment in place of the hangman's noose, and Carver exulted. The verdict was a. high compliment to the tireless labors and energy of his attorney.

A BROTHER-IN-LAW KILLED

Of all the unfortunate killings that ever occurred in the Indian. Territory, one of the saddest was that of the murder of his brother-in-law, John Ortner, by Tom Thornton, a well-to-do Cherokee Indian, at Bartlesville in the Cherokee Nation, in the summer of 1894. Thornton and his wife had been having trouble and were separated, Thornton being in charge of a store on Double Creek, ten miles from Bartlesville, while his wife, a German woman, ran a boarding restaurant at Bartlesville. Her brother lived with her in the absence of Thornton, and between, the two men existed a feud. Thornton had a young son to whom he was very much attached; it lived with the mother, and Thornton would occasionally call at the restaurant to see the child. On the day of the killing Thornton had driven to Bartlesville accompanied by a man named Morgan. He stopped in front of the restaurant kept by his wife and entered. While in the restaurant engaged 'in an unpleasant interview with his wife, the brother-in-law, Ortner, armed himself with a pistol, and going out of a rear door passed between the buildings and crossing the street took a seat upon the porch of a store building occupied by Johnson & Keener, and there waited until Thornton appeared a few minutes later. As he started to enter his buggy he was attracted by a scream from his wife, who had followed him, and looking across the street discovered the brother-in-law.

The prosecution and the defense had different theories of the killing. The latter held that the brother-in-law had gone across the street by pre-arrangement and that the wife gave the scream as a signal, at which he fired at Thornton, and that the latter shot in self-defense, killing his antagonist instantly. The government's theory was that the brother-in-law had sought to evade Thornton and that the scream by the woman was caused by her discovery that Thornton had seen her brother and that Thornton took first aim, killing the other in a murderous way.

Thornton was arrested the next day, conveyed to Fort Smith and placed on trial. He first employed Barnes & Mellette to defend his case. He was convicted and sentenced to hang. A writ of error was taken to the Supreme Court. The lower court was reversed and a new trial granted. Meanwhile Thornton had become convinced of the superior ability of the criminal lawyer, J. Warren Reed, and he engaged him to assist at the new trial, which came on in the early part of 1897, and resulted in the grade of his crime being reduced from murder to manslaughter, and he was sentenced to eight years in the penitentiary at Columbus, Ohio.

A FIENDISH OUTLAW'S LIFE RECORD

CRIMES AND EXECUTION OF CHEROKEE BILL

The most fiendish murderer of all those appearing in the annals of the Fort Smith court, considering his age and the time of his operations, was Crawford Goldsby, alias Cherokee Bill, executed for the deliberate killing of Earnest Melton, while robbing the store of Schufelt & Son, at Lenapah, ninety miles from Fort Gibson, in the Cherokee Nation, on the eighth day of November, 1894. But for the fact that courts can go no farther than to destroy life, and that one execution must serve to mete justice to the multiplex [sic, multiple] murderer, the same as to those who have only one such crime to answer for, Goldsby might have met the terrible fate of a murderer seven or more times, once, for each, of the cold blooded crimes he was said to be guilty of.

Among the awful crimes he was charged with having committed during his short but tumultuous career, was the killing of a railroad agent, named Richards, at Nowata, for the purpose of securing a few dollars; he also killed his brother-in-law, George Brown, and in fiendish glee, filled his body full of bullet holes, for no other cause than that Brown's father, the owner of a hog ranch, had given Brown's wife, Bill's sister, a few more hogs than he had given him. Many other crimes were charged to Goldsby. The cases, other than murder charges, in which he was indicted, were: The robbery of Scales' store, at Wetumpka, Creek Nation; the robbery of a train at Red Fork, Creek Nation, July 18, 1894; the robbery at Parkinson's store, at Okmulgee, Creek Nation, September 14, 1894; the robbery of an express office, at Choteau, Cherokee Nation, October 9, 1894; the robbery of a train at Coretta, October 20, 1894; the robbery of A. E. Donaldson, in the Cherokee Nation, October 22. 1894; the robbery of Schufelt's store and post-office, at Lenapah, November 8, 1894. Many other crimes, of various degrees, were charged to him but investigation was useless, in the face of indictments on more serious charges, and finally, after having been sentenced to hang for the murder of Earnest Melton, as if to wind up his criminal career with a grand finale that should cause even the imps of hell to shudder, he deliberately shot down Lawrence Keating, one of the guards at the Federal jail, who had always treated him kindly, while in jail. This, the last of his crimes, was committed while he was awaiting the action of the Supreme Court upon the verdict condemning him to death. His turbulent course was of less than two years duration but in that time he made a record that was most unenviable.

Crawford Goldsby was born at Fort Concho, Texas, February 8, 1876, his father being a soldier in the Tenth Cavalry, United States regular army. He was George Goldsby, now a well-to-do and respected farmer, at Cleveland, Oklahoma, where he is known by the name of Bill Scott. He is of Mexican extraction, mixed with white and Sioux Indian. The maiden name of Crawford Goldsby's mother was Ellen Beck; she was half negro, one-fourth Cherokee Indian and one-fourth white. When he was quite young, Crawford Goldsby's parents separated and until he was seven years old, he lived at Fort Gibson, with his nurse, an old colored aunty, named Amandy Foster; both she and the mother witnessed his execution. At the age named, the boy was sent to school at Cherokee, Kansas, for three years, and was then sent to the Catholic Indian school, at Carlisle, Pennsylvania. Up to that time he had not been considered a bad boy, but he had always been counseled by his mother: "Stand up for your rights; don't let anybody impose on you," and having been true to the teachings, his prowess, as a youth, was considerable. When he returned from school, at 12 years old. he was then at just the right age, when, with the education he had received, he might, with proper discipline, have been made a fairly useful citizen, to the extent, at least, that his peculiarly constructed mentality would permit, but he found himself alone; his mother had remarried, to William Lynch, of Fort Gibson, and as usual, with second marriages, there seemed to be no room for the issue of the first. The boy, having no guidance, fell in with first one and then another, learning new evils at every stage, among them being the taste for intoxicants, and at the age of 18, having become a lusty, burly fellow, who had never been curbed, he came to the conclusion that none could curb him, and about this time he had his first serious trouble; it was with Jake Lewis, a negro of about 35 years (now a resident of Braggs). They met at a dance, in the portion of Fort Gibson, known as "oldtown," and as the result of a quarrel, Goldsby, with true grit, called his antagonist out of the house, to settle their difficulty, by a fistic encounter. The lad was much the heavier but his youth was against him, and he received a brutal whipping. It is safe to say that he never again trusted himself to his fists. Smarting under the blows, the boy determined to have revenge and one morning, two days later, as Jake went to the barn of his employer (C. L. Bowden, of "oldtown") he was met at the door by Goldsby, who flourished a six-shooter and threatened to kill, following the threat with a shot into Lewis' body. Lewis started to run and Goldsby shot again; the victim fell, and leaving him for dead the boy mounted his horse and fled. The Cherokee authorities tried to arrest him, but Goldsby, now a scout, left the Cherokee Nation and went into the Creek and Seminole Nations, where he became acquainted with Jim and Bill Cook, who afterwards became noted outlaws. This was in the early spring of 1894.

During the first week in June, following, Treasurer E. E. Starr, of the Cherokee Nation, commenced, at Tahlequah, the task of distributing among the Cherokee Indian citizens of the Tahlequah and Going Snake districts their individual portions of a large sum of money, $6,640,000 [$184 billion in 2015], that was appropriated by the United States government, as payment for what was known as the Cherokee "Strip." Goldsby and the Cooks started for Tahlequah, for the purpose of obtaining their shares of the money, $265.70, each, but as they did not care to be seen in Tahlequah, Cherokee Bill on account of his trouble with Jake Lewis and Jim Cook on account of his larceny charge, they stopped at what was known as the "Half-way Home," on Fourteen Mile Creek, near the former home of the Cook's, fourteen miles from Tahlequah, a place where travelers between Fort Gibson and Tahlequah, were wont to stop for meals, kept by Effie Crittenden, who had Bob Hardin, a brother-in-law of the Cooks, employed as a cook, in her establishment. The three boys gave the Crittenden, woman an order and she proceeded to Tahlequah and drew their money. Effie was the wife of Dick Crittenden, of Cherokee extraction; they had separated and were on unfriendly terms. The fight that occurred at her house on the evening of July 18, between Sheriff Ellis Rattling Gourd and a posse of seven men on one side and Goldsby and the Cooks on the other, is alleged by some, to have been planned by the ex-husband., in the hopes that Effie would be killed.

The payment at Tahlequah closed on Saturday, July 16, and on the following Wednesday, Treasurer Starr commenced' paying at Vinita. Goldsby and the Cooks, through the medium of Effie Crittenden, drew their pay on the last day of the treasurer's stay at Tahlequah, and supposing that their presence at the house was unknown to the officers, they continued for a couple of days, resting from their trip, intending on Monday night, July 18, after dark, to quietly leave the country. Just at night, as Goldsby sat outside the door, under a tree, they were all apprised of the approach of the officers by the noisy demonstrations of some of them who were under the influence of drink. The sheriff had a Cherokee warrant for Jim Cook, on the larceny charge. His posse were, Sequoyah Houston, Dick Crittenden, and his brother Zeke, Bill Nickel, Isaac Greece, Hicks and Bracket. Goldsby and the Cooks hastily grasped their Winchesters and as the posse opened fire, they were met by rattling shots from the others. A hot fight ensued, during which Sequoyah Houston was killed and Jim Cook was wounded seven times, Dick Crittenden shooting his gun from his hand as he was about to fire from a corner of the house. After Houston fell, the sheriff and four of his posse fled, leaving the Crittendens to face the danger, and the brothers, knowing that to turn their backs meant death, held their antagonists at bay, behind the house, until they escaped in the dark.

It was here that Crawford Goldsby is said to have gained the alias which clung to him so tenaciously that, before his death, even his mother came to use the term in speaking of him. On the day following this fight with the sheriff's posse, Lou Cook was asked if Crawford Goldsby had been there. She replied, "No, it was Cherokee Bill."

After Jim Cook fell, he was taken away by his brother and Goldsby and at Fort Gibson they pressed a doctor into service and the outlaw's wounds were dressed; but while the operation was in progress they were so closely pressed by officers that Bill Cook and Gold-by were forced to flee and Jim Cook was captured. He was tried in the Cherokee courts and sentenced to seven years in the penitentiary at Tahlequah. He escaped and was captured several times, and at last the Cherokee authorities abandoned the chase, sometime after the final incarceration of his brother, Bill Cook. He had been a trusty, and before he escaped the last time he was a familiar figure on the streets of Tahlequah. For the killing of Sequoyah Houston, Bob Hardin was arrested and tried at Fort Smith; it was proven that he had taken no part in the battle but had tried to get away before the shooting began, and he was acquitted.

Soon after the fight at Fourteen Mile Creek, the famous Cook Gang was organized, composed of—besides Bill Cook and Cherokee Bill—Henry Munson, Curtis Dason, "Chicken," "Skeeter," "Long" Gordon, and later, Sam McWilliams alias "Verdigris Kid," Jim French and others, although the friends of Skeeter always claimed he was only led into a few of their raids after having been made intoxicated. The title, "Skeeter," was given him on the occasion of a horse race; he was of slender build and the rider against whom he was pitted said, scornfully, that he "had not agreed to ride against a mosquito." Others became allied to this precious gang of outlaws during the summer; some of them were afterwards killed, during certain desperate fights with deputy marshals, and others were captured and were given penitentiary sentences.

The crime which finally led to Cherokee's incarceration, and for which he at last died on the gallows, was committed November 8, 1894. On that date, Lenapah, a little town on the Kansas & Arkansas Valley Railroad (now the Missouri Pacific), twenty-four miles south of Coffeyville, Kansas, and twenty-six miles from Tulsa, Indian Territory, was the scene of the dastardly act which cost Cherokee Bill his life. It is a historical place in the annals of the Indian country, as it was the scene of one of the first "hold ups" committed by Henry Starr; it was near here, too, that Starr killed Floyd Wilson. Clyde Barbour and Dooley Benge started out as outlaws from this vicinity, but their career was soon after nipped. At that time the principal store in Lenapah was operated by Schufelt & Son. John Schufelt, the junior member of the firm, was also postmaster.* Just before noon, on the day noted, two men rode rapidly into Lenapah, from the south, but attracted little attention, as their appearance differed scarcely from the hundreds of cowboys who came there to trade. The pair halted, in front of the Schutelt store and dismounted upon a large platform scale. Then it was seen that they were strangers, a large man and one of smaller size. Those men, it is claimed, were Cherokee Bill and either Jim French or "Verdigris Kid.' As soon as they dismounted they brought their Winchesters to bear upon the men in the store and, with terrible oaths, commanded, "Hands up," a request that nearly always meets with speedy acquiescence within the borders of the Indian country, when emphasized with a flourish of loaded weapons. Then Bill entered the store, while the other remained outside on guard and fired an occasional volley up and down the street to warn citizens to keep a safe distance. Cherokee Bill's first act, after entering the store, was to march John Schufelt back to the safe, which he commanded him to open. Hastily securing all the cash contents, Bill made a careful selection of goods, then marched Schufelt to the front of the store and was about to depart when his companion spoke to him. Bill then turned back and asked for cartridges. He was told they were in the back, part of the store, and he ordered John Schufelt to go back and get them, then changed his mind and started back himself.

ERNEST MELTON MURDERED

Parallel with the store, but separated by a vacant lot, was a small restaurant. A glass door on the side of the store was opposite a window in the restaurant. Several paper-hangers were in the restaurant at work. When they heard the shots fired by the outlaws, all rushed to the windows to see what the noise was about; one of them, Ernest Melton, went to the side window overlooking the store. As Cherokee Bill passed the glass door mentioned, on his way after cartridges, he chanced to look across and saw Melton. Angered at being thus watched, he swore a great oath and brought his rifle to his shoulder; its sharp crack rang out and Melton fell dead, his brain pierced with a bullet from the rifle of one of the most desperate and bloodthirsty outlaws the Indian Territory ever produced. He fired several other shots but no one else was injured. After the crime the outlaws rode rapidly out of town in the direction from which they had come. During the next two months the section of country about Lenapah and south into the Creek Nation was scoured by deputy United States marshals in search of the one desperado who, in spite of his youth, was more generally feared than any other in the Indian country. He could shoot faster than two ordinary men and few marshals had the bravery to attempt a capture, but when a reward of $1,300 was offered for him "dead or alive," soon after the Lenapah murder, it put the marshals upon their mettle. Among these were Deputies VV. C. Smith, now a druggist at Fayetteville, Arkansas, and George Lawson, of Fort Smith. They stopped at the house of Charles Patton, at Wealaka, for several weeks, reconnoitering the while, and they sent Patton out into the hills to look for the man whom, though they feared, yet were anxious to capture. Patton found Bill and the "Verdigris Kid" skulking about the hills and he stayed with them from 3 o'clock in the afternoon until 9 o'clock at night. Had they imagined Patton to be a spy, Bill would doubtless have added another to his long list of victims. During this visit Bill, told Patton that he had secured $164 "in a little hold up at Lenapah and had to shoot a fellow." Before he left them the "Kid" gave him a locket which Bill took from John Schufelt on the day of the murder, telling him to be careful or it might get him into trouble. Patton met Smith and Lawson at Sapulpa that night and turned over the locket and the knowledge he had gained. He was a witness against Cherokee Bill at the trial and his testimony, together with the locket, which was admitted in evidence, was the most interesting of any produced by the government. About this time Goldsby encountered Deputy United States Marshal John McGill and posse. Numerous shots were exchanged and Cherokee's horse was shot beneath him but he escaped, leaving his hat as a trophy to the officers.

ROMANCE AND STRATEGY COMBINED

Deputy Marshal Smith was the first to conceive of coupling romance with strategy as a means of capture. He learned that Bill was fond of visiting at the home of Isaac Rogers, a mixture of Cherokee Indian, negro and white, who lived five miles east of Nowata, to call on Maggie Glass (negro and Cherokee), a relative of Rogers, with whom the bandit was desperately in love, though he had begun to suspect Rogers, and during such visits he always kept his Winchester ready for an emergency. Soon after the Lenapah tragedy he had attended a dance at Rogers' house, and during the night he had told Ben Vann, a negro, that he did not mean to shoot the man at Lenapah, but that he shot to scare him. This, too, was considered important evidence at the trial.

Rogers had been a deputy under United States Marshal Crump, and the latter learned of his intimate acquaintance with the outlaw, as well as the latter's infatuation for the girl, Maggie Glass, from Deputy Marshal Smith, and he arranged with his ex-deputy to invite the girl, who lived near Rogers' place, to visit his home and also to invite Bill to come and visit the girl. Maggie readily consented to the arrangement, and on Tuesday afternoon, January 29, 1895, Rogers saw Bill ride towards the house of a man named Jackson, and he sent his boy to tell Bill he wanted to see him. Shortly after dark the outlaw came to Rogers' house, dismounted and entered, and from that moment until 9 o'clock Wednesday morning, not one moment elapsed that the outlaw was not on his guard, prepared to-use his Winchester. The girl, too, was suspicious of Rogers, and she warned Bill to leave, but Bill refused to run away, telling the girl he would show Rogers how long it would take him to commit murder, his plan being to let Rogers make the first break, then shoot him in his tracks. Rogers in turn was wiley; he knew the kind of a man with whom he had to deal, and while acting the part of the generous host, he watched for an opportunity to strike a deadly blow that should give him part of the promised reward. He treated the outlaw with the greatest kindness and managed to gain his confidence somewhat, and urged him to stay all night. He suggested that the outlaw lay aside his Winchester, but he replied:

"That is something I never do."

He then tempted him with whiskey, doctored with morphine, but Bill refused to drink. Supper time came, and after the rest had seated Cherokee took his place with his back to the wall and his Winchester across his knees. After supper, cards were proposed and Bill played casino with Clint Scales, a neighbor, who was acting in concert with Rogers to effect Cherokee's capture. While the game was in progress Rogers watched for an opportunity to overpower him, but Cherokee was observant of every movement. The weapons of the would-be captors were necessarily kept from sight, as Rogers knew the first effort to raise a gun would be a signal for a fight, and he did not desire to give his guest any excuse for a fight. The night lengthened, and it may well be imagined that Bill himself was awaiting the climax with some interest, intending then to punish his pretended friend for intended treachery, and Rogers, in turn, watched for opportunities that failed to appear. The card playing continued, and they talked until 4 o'clock in the morning, in the nervous but distrait manner of men who would appear calm while secretly striving to conceal the turbulence in their breasts; it was an outward and unnatural calm preceding a storm. At the hour named they retired, the outlaw and his treacherous host sleeping in the same bed. Rogers laid awake for some time, hoping to catch Cherokee asleep, but whenever he would move the other would instantly rise in bed, ready to use his Winchester. At breakfast time it began to look as if the game would surely escape. The rest is best told in Rogers' own language, as given to Hon. Frank Weaver, then court reporter for the weekly *Elevator*.

THE BANDIT STRUCK DOWN

239

"I had been instructed by Col. Crump to get him alive, if possible, and I didn't want to kill him but I made up my mind to kill him if I couldn't get him in any other way Scales and I had our guns hidden where we could get them in a hurry but we didn't want to give them any show to fight. After breakfast, we talked along for some time and he began to talk of leaving. He and Scales and I sat in front of the open fireplace. 'I knowed that we had to make a break on him pretty soon and I was afraid the girl would take a hand in it when the trouble began, so I gave her a dollar to buy some chickens at a neighbor's, so as to get her out of the way. I also sent my boys away as I had not told them of my plans. Bill finally took a notion that he wanted to smoke and he took some paper and tobacco from his pocket and rolled a cigarette. He had no match, so he stooped over towards the fireplace, to light it, and turned his head away from me for an instant. That was my chance and I took it. There was a fire stick lying on the floor near me and I grabbed it up and struck him across the back of the head. I must have hit him hard enough to kill an ordinary man but it only knocked him down. Scales and I then jumped on him but he let one yell and got on his feet. My wife grabbed Bill's Winchester and we three tussled on the floor, full twenty minutes. I thought once I would have to kill him, his great strength, with his 180 pounds weight, being almost too much for me and Scales, but finally we got a pair of handcuffs onto him. He then plead and begged me to kill him or release him. He promised me money and horses, all I wanted. Then he cursed. We put him in a wagon and Scales rode with him and I went on horseback, and started for Nowata. In accordance with the prearrangements, Deputy Marshals Smith and George Lawson, had, on January 29, gone to Nowata, to await The coming of Rogers and Scales, with their prisoner.

On the way Cherokee broke his handcuffs and grabbed at Scales' gun and Scales had to fall out of the wagon to keep from losing his Winchester, while I kept Cherokee covered with my shot gun. At Nowata, we turned him over to Bill Smith and George Lawson."

The reader might wonder that a desperate man like Cherokee Bill would consent to be driven to a meeting with the officers, unshackled, but a desperado of the Indian Territory type is brave only, when, by the aid of his arms, he is master of his opponent; a hand to hand conflict they know nothing of and unlike many desperate men raised in a more northern climate, would never think of trusting their lives to their fists. Down in the Indian Territory men only draw their guns when they intend to shoot, and a citizen of that country, when a gun is drawn upon him, realizes on the instant that the weapon is in dangerous hands and though he might be heavily armed, himself, he knows better than to make a movement after a weapon as long as his opponent has him covered. This fully accounts for the fact that the bandit, Cherokee Bill, remained riveted to his seat; he knew that his every act was being closely watched by Ike Rogers, who rode silently behind him, with a loaded, double barrel shot gun.

While Deputy Marshals Smith and Lawson were on the way to Fort Smith, with the prisoner, they stopped at Wagoner, to be photographed. The illustration here given is a copy from the photograph taken that day. It shows Ike Rogers, Clint Scales, Deputy Marshal Smith and Dick and Zeke Crittenden, with Cherokee Bill, his feet in chains, as the center piece. When told that his photograph was to be taken he refused to allow Rogers to stand by him but threw his right arm about Dick Crittenden, and said:

"Here's a fellow who once stood up and fought like a man, I will have my picture taken with him;" at the same time reaching for Crittenden's revolver; had he obtained it, the officers would not have lived to take him to Fort Smith, nor Rogers to receive his share of the cash reward. Cherokee afterwards said, that if he had secured that gun some of the men in the crowd, "would have worn away wooden overcoats."

At the trial before Judge Parker, Goldsby attempted to establish an alibi. He introduced several witnesses to prove that on the morning of November 6, he was in Fort Gibson, nearly ninety miles from Lenapah; that from there he went to near Claremore, stayed all night at the home of a Mrs. Cochrane, and that from thence he went south into the Creek Nation, sixty miles from the scene of the robbery, staying there all night with a friend and consequently on the next morning, when Schufelt's store was robbed and Earnest Melton received his death wound, he was sixty miles from Lenapah. One of the important points brought out in the trial, was the rapidity with which bandits travel from place to place. A few days previous, it was testified in court that soon after the Red Fork robbery, the Cook gang rode sixty miles in a single night, and this had a tendency to weaken Cherokee Bill's alibi. Goldsby did not go on the stand, but "Bud" Vann, a Fort Gibbon colored boy, who was at Lenapah at the time of the murder, testified that he witnessed the robbery and that Cherokee Bill was not one of the robbers, but that one of them was Jim French, and he did not know the other. Several witnesses from Lenapah, testified that within a few hours after the crime, Vann had stated to a large crowd, assembled to discuss the affair, that one of the robbers was Cherokee Bill and the other, he thought, was Jim French, but he was not sure. Three other witnesses told the story of the robbery and killing and identified Goldsby as the man who shot Melton. Deputy Bill Smith testified that while bringing Goldsby to Fort Smith on the train, and discussing the various crimes committed by him, including the one at Lenapah, Goldsby said:

"I don't see how they can prove the killing on me, for there were others shooting besides me."

J. Warren Reed had been employed to conduct the defense, but the conditions were against him and his client was convicted of murder. Goldsby's finances were limited and Mr. Reed's chances for collecting his fees were uncertain, yet this hard-working attorney threw his whole soul into the defense of the poor Indian boy with the same zeal that he would have exercised had his client been a Rothschild or an Astor, was untiring in his efforts to save him from the gallows, and when, a few weeks after the trial, Mr. Reed took a writ of error to the Supreme Court, he paid the expenses from his private funds. Realizing from the first that he had a desperate case, he worked every inch of ground, contesting step by step, and never for an instant wavered an iota. His efforts, while not successful, were worthy of commendation, and his constant and faithful devotion and strenuous endeavors to win in a case that from the outset was worse than helpless, was worthy of appreciation and emulation.

Judge Parker, restricted Goldsby in his witnesses at the trial. Months after his conviction, the affidavits of several eye witnesses of the killing of Melton, whose testimony was denied by the judge, were used on an application for pardon. The affidavits showed substantially that all these witnesses knew Cherokee Bill; that they saw the men who committed the robbery and killed Melton, and that Cherokee Bill was not one of the men.

Arguments in the case were commenced at noon, February 26, 1895, and lasted until 10 o'clock at night. Judge Parker instructed the jury next morning, occupying only fifteen minutes in his charge. The jury returned a verdict within a few minutes after retiring. Goldsby simply smiled when the verdict, "guilty," was read, but his mother and sister, who attended the trial, wept loudly.

"What's the matter with you? I'm not a dead man yet, by a long ways," he harshly ejaculated. Over at the Federal jail that afternoon, Cherokee Bill was engaged in a game of poker with Bill Cook and several kindred spirits, as if nothing had happened.

Immediately after the conviction, his attorney, Mr. Reed, made application for new trial, but the motion was overruled, and on the thirteenth day of April Cherokee was taken to the court for sentence, June 25 being set for the day of his execution. An appeal to the Supreme Court resulted in the finding of the lower court being affirmed and he was re-sentenced, and March 17, 1896, named as the day which should end his earthly career. Just a few days before the latter date, Mr. Reed, tireless in his efforts to save Bill's neck, applied to President Cleveland for a pardon, the petition being based upon the sworn affidavits of the seven persons noted, that it could not have been Bill who fired the fatal shot that killed Melton. The petition was ineffectual, but it proved the relentless and tenacious spirit of the persistent attorney to save the neck of his client from the deadly noose.

CHEROKEE'S LOVE FOR GUN

J. E. Kelly, the founder of Kellyville, in the Creek Nation, who is postmaster and merchant there, and who has spent a greater portion of his early life on the frontier and was a cowboy in the 70's, in Wyoming and Nebraska, knew the Cooks and Cherokee Bill intimately, long before they became outlaws. He visited Cherokee Bill in the jail at Fort Smith, after his incarceration, and he thus aptly describes an incident showing the great love borne by the outlaw for a gun:

"Cherokee Bill was game as a hornet, and a true friend but a bitter enemy. He was quick and active and always wide-awake. He was not shamming, he was an outlaw in good earnest. I saw him at Fort Smith shortly after his arrest.

George Lawson, who figured in his arrest, asked me up to the jail to see him. He brought Bill out to have his photograph taken. Bill was 'hot' and was crying with madness when he appeared. Lawson said: 'Bill, quit your crying; here is Kelly who has come to see you; why don't you ask him about some of your old friends?' Bill, who up to this time had not raised his eyes, looked up quickly, and as he saw me he smiled through his tears and grabbing my hand exclaimed: 'Hello, old friend! I never thought you would see me down here. I thought you might see me all shot to, but I never thought you would see me here.' He was handed a beautiful Winchester, the property of Post-office Inspector Houk, and was asked to pose for his picture. The gun was empty. Bill's eyes snapped with the old time fire; he took a position as if he had been surprised; he brought the gun into position and every nerve seemed on the alert. Oh! how he would have loved to be out in the jail yard with the gun full of cartridges. After the photographer had finished, Bill fondled the gun and asked several questions about it; he seemed loth to give it up, and before returning it he worked the lever and the trigger until it clicked like a sewing machine. It was the wonder of all the deputy marshals, how he could shoot so fast. Bill said he knew his rapid firing was not always accurate, and he might not always hit the target, but he would shoot so—fast that he would 'rattle' his antagonist 'so he could not hit me.'"

When June 25, 1895, arrived, the day first named as Cherokee's execution day, his appeal was still in the hands of the Supreme Court, and Judge Parker issued a stay of execution to give the Supreme Court time to act. It is, indeed, a pity that the execution could not have been carried out according to schedule and thereby have prevented another crime by the desperate fiend, the killing of a brave officer, who had a wife and four children dependent upon him. This last murder was, if anything, even more blood-thirsty than any of the others he was connected with.

THE MURDER OF LARRY KEATING

For several weeks Goldsby had manifested a spirit of unrest. His unruly and obstreperous conduct had affected the other prisoners, and many who had a knowledge of the jail and surroundings, had predicted that something terrible would occur. The lower floors of the jail was filled with murderers, there being fifty-nine then under sentence of death, awaiting a hearing by the Supreme Court, and as if to make matters worse, the number of guards had been cut down by the government for the purpose of saving expenses. On the tenth of July a revolver of 45-caliber, nicely loaded, was found in Cherokee Bill's cell, and on the next floor above nine additional cartridges were found. Vann, a trusty [sic, trustee], was suspected of complicity in the affair, but it was never known just where the weapon came from. Again was it whispered about the city that Cherokee Bill would yet kill somebody in the jail, but no precautions were taken, and foolishly enough, the noted murderer was allowed the freedom of the jail during the day, unmanacled, the same as were other prisoners, although the press gave warning of the danger. The finding of the loaded pistol in Cherokee's cell did not lessen his endeavor to plan some means of escape. Ben Howell, a straggler from Bill Doolan's gang, was at that time serving a ninety-days' sentence for stealing groceries at Ingalls, Indian Territory. In Oklahoma he bore the reputation of being a confederate of the Doolan and Dalton gang, but too cowardly to join in their raids. He was given the privilege of the jail and yard, and early in July he made his escape. After the killing of Keating, Cherokee Bill stated that Howell smuggled two pistols to him on the twenty-seventh day of June. One of them he hid in a bucket and it was found as stated, July 10. The other he hid in a hole in the wall of his cell made by removing a brick; the white-washed end of the brick, after the other half had been broken off, was replaced, and the trick was not discovered, and Bill watched his opportunity to make use of the weapon there in hiding.

The opportunity was presented Friday evening, July 26. The climax was reached when, at just before 7 o'clock on the evening of the day named, Cherokee Bill shot and killed Lawrance Keating, one of the night guards, one of the oldest officers of the court, as well as one of the best citizens of Fort Smith, and who had served as guard at the Federal jail for nine years. The tragedy occurred when the prisoners were being locked in their cells for the night. It was the custom for the day guards to go off duty at 6 o'clock, when they were relieved by the night guard, and 6:1 5 was the time for locking the cells on each of the three floors. Owing to long days and hot weather, the prisoners, at this time, were allowed to remain in the corridors until near 7 o'clock. On the occasion mentioned, Turnkeys Eoff (pronounced Ofe) and "Uncle" Bill McConnell were on duty and Guard Will Lawson and Night Guards Lawrance Keating and Tom Parker had just come on duty. Turnkeys McConnell and Eoff guarded the lower tier of cells, known as Murderer's Row, in the day, and it was one of the duties of Turnkey Eoff, after "ringing in" the prisoners on the east and west sides of the lower floor, to go inside the "bull ring," or corridor, and lock each cell door, having first pulled a lever connecting with a long bar which was intended to fasten the closed cell doors at the top. Before pulling this lever, it was customary for a guard to walk along the outside corridor and see that each prisoner had closed the door of his cell, in order that the "brake" should work properly. The "brake" on either corridor could be opened, however, by a broomstick or similar instrument in the hands of a prisoner in a cell at the north end of the tier, and on this particular occasion, in compliance with a concerted movement on the part of several prisoners in the west corridor, the "brake" was thrown open by someone of the prisoners while Eoff and Keating were attending to locking the cells on the other side, thus releasing the doors of all the cells on the side where Cherokee Bill was confined.* After laying off all his weapons, Eoff went inside the corridor, on the east side, and was locked in, being provided with a key to let himself out at the north end of the west corridor. His weapons were left outside lest, in the case of an unruly prisoner, they should be taken from him—leaving him at the prisoners' mercy. Meanwhile, Cherokee Bill, with his cell door, like the others, free to be pushed open from the inside the cell, calmly waited, with drawn pistol, the coming of the officers. The doors on the east side were first locked, Guard Keating meanwhile, according to custom, keeping pace with Eoff, on the outside, and the latter passed around the south end and began locking those on the west side.

Cherokee's cell was "No. 20 and was the third from the south end. Adjoining his cell on the south, was the one occupied by Dennis Davis, the half-witted negro convicted of murdering Solomon Blackwell, previously noted. A wad of paper had been crowded into the keyhole and when the key was placed in the lock it became fastened and Eoff was thus delayed. Turning slightly, he remarked to Keating: "There's something wrong here;" and Keating walked closer.

This is contrary to the general understanding of the case, it being popularly supposed that Bill left his door slightly ajar when the "brake" was thrown to close, thus leaving his cell the only one not fastened. The statement above is on the authority of a prisoner then awaiting trial on a capital charge and who. more than two years afterwards, was acquitted.—note in original

THE DREADFUL FIGHT BEGINS

At that instant the door of Cherokee Bill's cell was pushed suddenly open and Bill leaped out across the short space, shoved the muzzle of a revolver through the bars at Keating and shouted:

"Throw up,* and give me that pistol!"

i.e. "Put your hands in the air."

Had the officer complied, Cherokee would have held him and Eoff under subjection while he unlocked the door leading out of the corridor and after releasing the other prisoners all hands would have made a break for liberty, and had he been successful in passing through the gordian of officers on the outside, alive, he intended, after he was safely away, to send a letter back to the chief marshal thanking him for his kindness in the past and telling him he did not need his hospitality longer. Instead of complying with Cherokee's order, Keating made a movement for his weapon and immediately a shot was fired, followed closely by a second, and Keating staggered backward, mortally wounded. Eoff was standing within five feet of Cherokee, but unarmed as he was, he was in no shape to make a. fight, and he turned and ran around the south end and up along the east side, leaving the keys still in the lock of Davis' cell, door. Twice during this run he was fired upon by the bloodthirsty criminal, and when he reached the door at the north end of the east corridor he was still in danger and but for the timely arrival, at this moment, of Brass Parker, McConnell and Will. and George Lawson he might have been killed. They had been in the yard and in the jailer's office and had rushed below when they heard Cherokee's shots ring out. As they entered they saw Keating, pistol in hand, staggering around the southeast corner—having walked the length of the south corridor—showing, that wounded to death though he was, he was making a last effort to reach a point where he could defend Eoff from attack. The effort, however, was his last and, sinking to the floor, he shouted, "I'm killed;" gasped a few times and was dead.

Meanwhile, George Pearce, who was under sentence to hang; and who was a plotter in the devilish scheme, armed with a club, the leg of a broken table, had rushed out after Bill's second shot, and advanced rapidly upon Eoff, thinking he had the keys, when, in fact, they were fast in the lock of Davis' cell. This, perhaps, saved Eoff's life, as Bill could not shoot squarely at him without endangering Pearce. A shot from George Lawson drove Pearce back around the south end. Guard McConnell, who saw Keating fall, stopped an instant to ask, "Are you hurt, Larry?" but Keating was already unconscious and unable to reply. McConnel grabbed up the pistol that had dropped from his hand and fired point-blank at Cherokee Bill, who returned the fire twice, and then made another rush back around the south end and exchanged several shots with those who were guarding the jail. Every time he fired a shot he would gobble like a turkey. After he had emptied his pistol he ran into his cell and reloaded and again opened fire. By this time Deputy

Marshal Heck Bruner and several others, attracted by the many shots, had hurried upon the scene, armed themselves and joined in the chorus. Bruner fired once with a shot-gun, but by this time Cherokee had retired into the cell and was firing at random from the cell door, never putting his head out. The smoke was dense and the guards could only fire at the puffs of smoke as they came from the weapon of the enraged man. In this way the firing continued until Bill-saw that further fighting was useless. He did not signify any intention of giving up, however, and Henry Starr, who occupied the north end cell on the west side, volunteered to go and get Bill's pistol if the guards would promise not to fire upon him. He was given permission, and walking to the cell he induced Bill to give up his weapon, then handed it out to the officers.

Jim Shannon and another man were fired upon by Cherokee as they were carrying Keating's remains outside. The bandit fired at every form he could see, and it was not his fault that a dozen men were not killed.

It was always claimed by the officers that just after the first shot (instead of before any shooting had commenced, as stated in the foot-note), the lever heretofore mentioned, which fastened the cell doors at the top, was thrown, thus liberating all the cells which had not been locked with a key. Who was responsible for this act was never settled further than that it was by someone near the north end. Henry Starr was suspected of the deed, but none saw him in the act. It was this act, whenever done, that allowed Pearce to leave his cell and start around the corner on the rampage, and if the rest of the prisoners on that side (excepting the inmate of cell No. 24, whose door was locked) had not been too badly frightened, they might have come out into the corridor.

THE PEOPLE EXCITED

The greatest excitement prevailed from the time of the first shot which killed Keating, until late into the night Crowds gathered in an incredibly short space. They heard the cannonade going on within the jail and some were frantic. Not less than 100 shots were fired, Winchesters, shot guns and revolvers being brought into play. To the person entering the jail after the firing ceased, excitement and confusion was

246

apparent at every hand. Fire arms were at every step and the place was redolent with the smoke of gun powder. The prisoners were for the most part badly frightened and huddled in the corners of their cells. On the west side in the outside corridor, were twenty or more men, all armed to the teeth. Standing in the inside corridor, was the vile murderer himself, Cherokee Bill. Captain Berry, the jailer, was vainly endeavoring to induce him to tell who furnished him the weapon. A steady refusal was the only response. Among the armed men were several who had known the murdered guard for many years, and at one time, as the result of a short but earnest consultation, it was decided to kill the outlaw then and there. It looked as if justice, swift and certain, was about to be meted out to him. The spirit of vengeance boiled in many breasts, but reason finally triumphed and Cherokee's life was saved to the mercies of the old gibbet.

Outside, the crowd continued to increase until it assumed alarming proportions. The cry "Lynch him" "Hang him" was frequently heard. The guilty wretch, himself, heard the shouts; he saw the temperament of the men; he feared he was about to be brought out to a terrible death; with the cringing cowardice of a bully disarmed, he pleaded for mercy, for the protection of the law he had so many times and so lately outraged.

"Larry Keating was a good man," he pleaded, to the crowd, "I didn't want to kill him, indeed I didn't, but I wanted my liberty. Damn a man who won't fight for his liberty!" And to Marshal Crump, who arrived just then, from his home in the suburbs, he said; "Colonel I'm sorry this happened, but I couldn't help it. If I hadn't shot him he would have shot me. If I could have captured the jail as I expected and planned, no one would have been killed."

As a precaution he was taken out and searched and his cell, was given a thorough overhauling [searched], after which he was shackled and locked in and the jail cleared of sight seers.

The act of Lawrence Keating, in refusing to give up his pistol to the outlaw, thereby drawing his fire and arousing the other guards was one which was far more reaching in its effects, than he could have known, during the short time he lived thereafter. Had he complied with Cherokee Bill's order, as might have been done by a less fearless man, who knew as Keating did the danger of disobeying such an order, given by an armed desperado, the result must have been most dire for the people of Fort Smith. The time chosen by Bill and his confederates for the delivery was most opportune, Keating and Eoff were the only guards in the jail; had Keating thrown up his hands as commanded, Cherokee Bill would have reached through the bars and secured his pistol, then would have covered both Keating and Eoff, commanding silence, while George Pearce would have come out and taking the keys, would have released all the desperate characters on that floor and leaving Keating and Eoff bound and gagged, Cherokee, with that peculiar much meaning smile, which is so well shown in his photographs, would have led the entire gang up one flight of stairs into the jailer's office, where was an arsenal sufficient to equip the entire lot. To have overpowered the few remaining guards would have been the work of but a moment and the next move would have released all of the rest of the 250 prisoners in the famous jail, and the scenes of rapine and murder, of monstrous and petty crimes that might have been committed in Fort Smith before the dawn of another day, are too horrible to contemplate. Thousands of dollars' worth of property might have been destroyed in spite of its handful of police, and that night's work in Fort Smith would doubtless have been the most villainous, the most terrible and heartrending of any in the history of any city of America. Well may it be said of Larry Keating, that he gave up his life, not only for his friends but for the honor of his country.

After all had become quiet in the jail, Bill began to cry and continued to sob the entire night through, from disappointment, at the failure of his plan. From anger at being shackled and denied the run of the corridor, he finally became sullen and morose and for several days almost entirely refused food. He was like a lion in captivity; having failed in his efforts to escape to his native forest and plain, he had all at once discovered how much really greater was the law he had become subject to, than himself, and the knowledge was enough to throw him into the most sullen mood.

The night following the murder of Keating was an exciting one on the public streets of Fort Smith, and for several days but little else was talked about in public places. The streets were thronged with people until long past midnight following the murder and there was much talk of lynching, but District Attorney James F. Read and a number of prominent Irish-Americans mingled quietly with the crowd, arguing against mob violence, and the night passed off without incident. As an illustration of the deep feeling of the people over the killing of Keating, and their hatred of his murderer, the following editorial expression, which appeared in a current issue of one of the Fort Smith newspapers will suffice:

"The murder of Larry Keating, on Friday last, in the United States Jail, has been the theme of conversation on the streets nearly all the week, and the general expression is that the people should have taken Cherokee Bill from the jail and hanged him to a limb, for that is the fate that such hyenas deserve. Lynch law is to be deplored in any community, but there are cases where the people are justified in taking the law into their own hands, and this was one of them. The government, in this instance, demonstrated its inability to properly take care of such men as Cherokee Bill, and the people should have taken the job off the hands of Marshal Crump and put the monster out of the way forever. It has been common talk on the streets and about the court house, for several weeks past, that Cherokee Bill would kill somebody about the jail. Pistols and ammunition found their way into his cell without hindrance; one was found and taken out, and it was hinted that there were more in there, yet the desperado was allowed the freedom of the jail unmanacled the same as ordinary prisoners, and when it culminated last Friday, in the death of* poor Larry Keating, it was no surprise to many in this city, as such a tragedy was anticipated. Now that the devilment has been done Cherokee-Bill has been securely locked in his cell, where he should have been from the day he was brought in. He is one of that class who have to be dealt harshly with, and do not deserve the same treatment accorded to other prisoners. His crimes were too numerous and atrocious. He should have been hanged according to the sentence of the law, as an appeal in his case was hopeless, and was only to delay justice, yet it has given the monster a chance to murder another man, and deprive a mother and her children of a protector,"

After speaking of some pf the more heinous crimes committed by Cherokee Bill, the article continued:

"To cap the climax, he wantonly murders Larry Keating, who had never done him an injury, and who had always treated him kindly. The cutting down of the number of guards at the jail, we understand, was done at the instance of Jailer Baxter, before he was retired, and while we think it should not have been done, yet it made it all the more necessary to keep such men as Cherokee Bill securely locked up or in irons all the time."

JUDGE PARKER'S ST. LOUIS INTERVIEW ON CHEROKEE BILL AND CRIMES IN THE INDIAN TERRITORY

At the time of the Keating murder, Judge Parker was away on a vacation, having visited Little Rock, Arkansas, and St. Louis, Missouri. On Thursday following the crime the Judge left St. Louis returning to Fort Smith for the purpose of re-convening court and calling the grand jury together, that they might return an indictment against Cherokee Bill for the murder of Keating. In an interview with the St. Louis Globe Democrat, published July 30, Judge Parker was quoted as saying:

"What is the cause of such deeds, do you ask? Why, the cause lies in the fact that our jail is filled with murderers, and there is not a sufficient guard to take care of them. There are now fifty or sixty murderers in the Fort Smith jail. They have been tried by an impartial jury; they have been convicted and have been sentenced to death. But they are resting in the jail, awaiting a hearing before the Supreme Court of the United States. While crime, in a general way, has decrease^ very much in the last twenty years, I have no hesitation in saying that murders are largely on the increase. This has been noticeable, chiefly in the last two years. I attribute the increase to the reversals of the Supreme Court. These reversals have contributed to the number of murders in the Indian Territory. First of all, the convicted murderer has a long breathing spell, before his case comes before the Supreme Court; then, when it 'does come before that body, the conviction may be quashed, and wherever it is quashed it is always upon the flimsiest technicalities. The Supreme Court never touches the merits of the case. As far as I can see, the court must be opposed to capital punishment, and, therefore, tries to reason the effect of the law away. That is the sum total of it. Next, the guard at the Fort Smith jail ought to be doubled. In speaking as I do of the Supreme Court, I am mindful, of course, of the wise and merciful provision of the law, which declares it is better that ninety-nine guilty ones should escape than that one innocent man should suffer. Nor am I devoid of human sympathy, because I have endeavored to carry out the law justly and fearlessly. But sympathy should not be reserved wholly for the criminal. I believe in standing on the side of the innocent. Take that man Keating. He was a quiet, peaceable, law-abiding citizen. Is there no sympathy for him and for the wife and children who have been deprived of his protection and support? Wasn't his life worth more to the community and to society at large than the lives of one hundred murderers? If one man can shoot another in self-defense, cannot the third, representing society, extend its protection in a similar manner, though, of course, in a strictly legal and judicious manner? Now, as to the condition of the Indian Territory in the matter of murders; these are confined, to a great extent at least, to what I call the criminal intruders—men who have committed crimes in the States and come to the Indian Territory for purpose of refuge. Take the resident population, and it is as orderly and as quiet as any to be found anywhere. During the twenty years I have been engaged in administering the law there, the contest has been one between civilization and savagery, the savagery being represented by the intruding criminal class of which I have spoken. I have never found a time when the Indians—the Cherokees, the Osages, all of them—have not been ready to stand by the courts in the carrying out of the law. The United States government in its treaties, from the days of Andrew Jackson down to the present time, stipulated that this criminal element should be kept out of the country, but the treaties have only been made to be broken. The same treaty was made when the last strip was purchased. But this is the old story over again. Thus this class keeps on increasing; its members marry, and the criminal population keeps ever growing larger. A criminal example is set to the young Indians and so crime spreads, but were it not for this intruding criminal class the Indian Territory would be fit for statehood to-day. During the twenty years I have been sitting on the bench I have only known of three cases of mob violence. Prisoners have been brought to the court from a distance of 300 to 700 miles. The reason is that the people have confidence in the court and in the laws, and in this there is a great object lesson. I used an editorial from the Globe-Democrat the other day in charging the grand jury. The editorial commented on the laxity of the courts in carrying out the laws, and it hit the nail on the head. At the present time there seems to be a criminal wave sweeping over the country, the like of which I have not seen before. It is due to the laxity of the courts.

I have this much satisfaction, after my twenty years of labor; the court at Fort Smith, Arkansas, stands as a monument to the strong arm of the laws of the United States, and has resulted in bringing to the Indian Territory, civilization and protection."

INDICTMENT, TRIAL, CONVICTION AND EXECUTION

Judge Parker returned to Fort Smith, Saturday afternoon, August 3. I met him as he stepped from the train and questioned him with reference to the action that would be taken with Cherokee Bill, for the murder of Keating There had been grave doubts expressed by some of the attorneys, as to whether Bill could be tried for his latest crime, in view of the fact that he then had one case pending in the Supreme Court.

Judge Parker set all doubt at rest. He said there was no question but what the trial could proceed, and that the grand jury could take up the case at once and report their findings.

"He is under no sentence at present," said the Judge: "His case stands the same as if he had never been sentenced, and there is nothing to prevent his trial on any other charge."

The United States Court began its work of the August term, at 9 o'clock, Monday morning, August 5. Judge Parker had had but little rest since closing the criminal docket three weeks before. Immediately after the close of business for the May term, he had gone to Springfield, Missouri, where he disposed of a number of important cases. From there he went to Little Rock, Arkansas, presided for two days, and then went on to St. Louis for a short visit with his son, Charles Parker, who was a practicing attorney, in the civil courts. After returning to Fort Smith, he immediately went to work, disposing of some business which yet remained on hand and the next Monday he opened the August term. It was the first time in three years that the court had opened in August for jury trials. The docket was extraordinarily heavy. It showed 193 criminal prosecutions pending, divided as follows:

Murder, 24; manslaughter, 2; assault to kill, 22; larceny, 14; introducing liquor into the Indian Territory, 9: violating revenue laws, 3; selling liquor to Indians, 1; obstructing railways, 1; bribery, 1; robbery, 2; arson, 3; violating postal laws, 5; fraudulently obtaining letter from post-office, 1; embezzling, 1; presenting false claims, 1; perjury, 3; forgery, 2; and ninety-nine cases of less degree.

This did not comprise the large number of new cases to come up. There were a large number of cases which had not yet been presented to the grand jury, and from these nearly 200 indictments were afterwards returned, twenty being for murder. When court opened, Monday morning, the room was well filled with spectators, as had come to be the custom at the first day of court, ever since the opening of the new court house; there were many who were there through curiosity; others who were mere idlers, found the court room an interesting loafing place, and others still, by no means a minority, were there to listen to the opening words of the court and his instructions to the grand jury. His remarks on this occasion, were particularly, instructive and forceful; his charge was said to be the masterpiece of his life. He spoke "off hand," as usual, without even notes to guide him. This charge, with only the less important portions eliminated, is given in another part of this work. When the grand jury was brought before him for instructions, he questioned them carefully upon a number of points; particularly in regard to their scruples against or in favor of capital punishment. Only one juror expressed himself as opposed to it and he had previously given an excuse, which Judge Parker considered valid; he was excused. Eli J. Black, was appointed foreman of the jury. The petit jury was next empaneled, after which he delivered the memorable charge, and the grand jury returned to their deliberations. Judge Parker then turned to the petit jury, of which I was a member, and delivered a brief charge of about fifteen minutes duration. As in the case of the grand jury, he looked carefully into the qualifications of each and sought out their opinions regarding capital punishment. In the charge he said, among other things:

"We want jurors who will do their duty honestly; who, when the proof shows guilt, will convict, and will acquit when the proof shows the accused to be innocent. When a man has done his whole duty he has climbed to the highest summit of good citizenship."

Shortly after Judge Parker had completed his charge to the petit jury, the grand jury returned with an indictment charging Crawford Goldsby, alias Cherokee Bill, with the murder of Lawrence Keating. It was probably the quickest indictment ever returned in this country by a grand jury. They had been from the court room less than forty minutes; the grand jury returned to their room and court was adjourned for dinner.

At 1 o'clock Crawford Goldsby was brought into court to answer the charge against him. After his shackles had been removed he threw back his head and with a quick jerk took in every detail of the court room, apparently, at a glance, evidently looking for possible chances of escape. His range included Court Bailiff Arch Stocton, who stood close behind him armed with a heavy billy [club], alert and ready to smash him to the floor if he should make any such attempt; at sight of him a look of resignation overspread his features and he doggedly awaited results. There were some in the crowd who expected to see him make a break for liberty and their faces blanched in anticipation of the possible scenes that should occur. When the arraignment, charging him with the death of Keating, was read he pleaded not guilty. He displayed no sign of emotion, though his voice was more husky than usual. Judge Parker turned to J. Warren Reed, counsel for the defense, and asked:

"Are you ready for trial?"

"Your honor, I know nothing more of the facts in the case than I have learned through the press. My client has been locked in his cell and I have had no opportunity to consult with him. I would like to have until Monday morning to announce," answered Mr. Reed.

Judge Parker: "I think this case should be disposed of at once. All the circumstances call for speedy action. I will set it for 10 o'clock Thursday morning, and I want it distinctly understood the case will go on trial then."

A slight digression just here for the purpose of showing the vast amount of work that was often turned off in a single day may not lack interest. After Cherokee Bill had been taken from the court-room, after the scenes above narrated, the court took up a lot of petty cases, one after the other, and before the day was done eleven separate convictions had been secured and eleven criminals sentenced, as follows: John Etter, introducing and selling liquor in the Indian Territory, thirty-two days in jail and a fine of $100; Leslie Davis, larceny, three years at Leavenworth, Kansas; Cain Tobin, violating internal revenue laws, ninety days in jail and $100 fine; Rufus Hollenbough,

252

violating internal revenue laws, ninety days in jail and $100 fine; William Jones, retail liquor dealer, eighteen months in the penitentiary and $100 fine; Allen Whitefield, violating internal revenue laws, sixty days in jail and $100 fine; Alph Shotwell, retail liquor dealer, thirty days in jail and $100 fine; Riley Snowden, larceny, three months in jail; Walter Kennedy, larceny, sixty days in jail; Charles Foush, larceny, three years at Leavenworth, Kansas.

During that week there were twenty-five jail arrivals charged as follows:

Murder, 2; robbery, 2; assault, 5; larceny, 4; perjury, 1; introducing, 2; introducing and selling, 2; selling, 1; larceny and introducing, 4; violating internal revenue laws, 2. Berry Foremen and Mollie King were brought in that day, charged with killing Mollie's husband, Ed King, near Vian, Indian Territory. Will Benton was brought in charged with shooting Engineer Gibson, near Cherokee, the week previous; Benton was a negro. Tom Root, a negro, accused of being a train robber and all-around crook, was brought in from the Verdigris bottoms, in the Cherokee Nation. He was under indictment for the Blackstone train robbery, and was thought to have had a hand in a holdup at Coretta, and was also charged with being implicated in the murder of Deputy Newton LeFlore, in the Creek Nation, one year before. Ben Howell, the trusty, who has been previously mentioned as having escaped from the jail in the early summer, and who was said by Cherokee Bill to have furnished him the pistol, with which he killed Keating, was brought in that day. He denied Bill's statement and said that the relations between himself and Bill were never pleasant. On the previous day, Sunday, Louis Girard was brought from Louisville, Kentucky, charged with the robbery of the Eureka Springs,' Arkansas, post-office. When brought in, he was stylishly dressed, wore a fine diamond scarf pin and had $165; three days later he was visited by his wife, a beautiful, modest appearing woman, who was reared near Berryville, Arkansas. Girard had several aliases, but when arraigned, the day of his wife's visit, he pleaded not guilty, under the name of Louis Girard. Tuesday morning, Lock Langley and Bill Camming were brought to the jail, on a charge of killing a man named Seay. They denied that Seay was dead, and he was afterwards found alive, in North Arkansas. On Wednesday; Chief Marshal Crump received a telegram from Deputy Marshal George Lawson, announcing the arrest, in St. Louis, of Ed Alberty, charged with killing a man named Duncan, at Fort Gibson, in 1880. On that same Monday on which Cherokee Bill was indicted, eight prisoners were discharged on bond and twenty-three were discharged from custody, having been acquitted or having served out jail sentences. And the reader will ask, "Was not this a blue Monday.' Was it not an exceptionable day, and an exceptionable week, even for the Fort Smith court?" And I assure you that it was not exceptional; on the contrary, there were many days, during the ten years that I served occasionally on the panel, as petit juror, from Bentonville and Rogers, Arkansas, when the business transacted, even exceeded that of the day mentioned; otherwise, how could the many thousands of criminals, who stood before the Fort Smith bar, from the time of opening of the court in 1871, until its practiced abandonment in September, 1896, have been arraigned arid their cases disposed of,

At 2 o'clock, Thursday afternoon, Cherokee Bill was placed on trial for the murder of Lawrence Keating. Not since the famous Kettenring trial had the court been so crowded with visitors. The case had been set for 10 o'clock in the forenoon, and when court convened at the morning hour much of the available space had been taken up, everyone being in expectancy. The notoriety given the prospective defendant by reason of his numerous crimes and the dare-devil recklessness which characterized them made each one anxious to get a glimpse of him. There was disappointment in store for them however, as when after a couple of hours had been spent in the transaction of other business and Cherokee Bill had been brought over it was found that his attorney was not present. He was engaged in a trial in the commissioner's court and the prisoner was taken back to jail.

The afternoon session, though, found even a larger number present, as those who had been on hand earlier in the day had spread the news and there was scarcely enough room for the jurors, many of us being compelled to stand. "Beauties row" was crowded as usual and I gave up my seat to a handsome brunette, and stood behind her for nearly an hour until I was called to the box. Before the arrival of Cherokee about a dozen other prisoners were brought over for arraignment, this taking up perhaps a half hour. Everyone waited patiently, however, and were finally rewarded, the clanking of chains announcing the approach of the desperado. Handcuffs were about his wrists and shackles around his ankles as he walked to his seat. Little time was then lost. The case was called, and the government, through its representative, J. B. McDonough, the assistant district attorney, announced readiness for trial. When J. Warren Reed was asked if he was ready, he took from his pocket two documents and handed them to the court. One proved to be a motion for continuance on the ground that in view of the public sentiment in Fort Smith, the excitement attendant upon the killing and the prejudices of the people against the defendant he could not get a fair and impartial trial at this time. The other was a demurrer alleging that the court did not have jurisdiction to try the case in view of the fact that the killing occurred in jail. It was one of this astute attorney's attempts to drive a wedge, that might, by some "hook or crook," succeed in giving his client more time, thus putting off the almost certain day of execution to as late a date as possible.

Scarcely a moment was taken up with a consideration of these legal documents, however, Judge Parker holding as a legal proposition that there could be no question as to the jurisdiction of the court in the matter and as a common sense proposition, that the documents were merely intended for effect in another tribunal. He became highly indignant, as he proceeded, at the idea that a fair and impartial trial could not be given in his court, and he took occasion to state that many of the allegations set out in the demurrer were wholly false and without foundation. Both were accordingly overruled and the panel of jurors was ordered called. This consumed nearly an hour as each of us, in turn, were questioned as to our qualifications, unusual precaution being taken in passing upon it. Of the twelve finally chosen none of us lived nearer than forty miles from Fort Smith. The defense was entitled to twenty peremptory challenges and every one of these were exhausted.

Judge Parker questioned each of us regarding our ability to give Cherokee Bill a fair and impartial trial, all of us having read of the killing. Each of us answered, though we had read of the sad case and heard it spoken of repeatedly, we were not prejudiced and could render a verdict in accordance with the law and the evidence. "Then," said Judge Parker, "you are qualified jurors."

As for the Fort Smithians on the panel they disqualified themselves promptly by declaring that they had formed and expressed an opinion and stepped aside. At least six of the twelve jurors empaneled were found to live further than 100 miles from the city. There was much curiosity to know what kind of defense was to be made. It was very plain from the time the demurrer and motion for continuance were filed that Mr. Reed had gone into the trial prepared to fight to the last and that seemingly he was not overawed by the desperate case he had before him, and though there was not the slightest feeling of sympathy among the audience for the defendant, one could not help but admire the faithfulness to his client shown by the brilliant attorney.

The opening speech by Mr. McDonough was free from argument, contenting himself with a brief and concise statement of the killing and the circumstances surrounding it. For the defense Mr. Reed said he was willing to await the evidence and judge from it what the nature of the offense might be if any had been committed. It was not his province nor that of the attorney for the government to dictate to the jury how they should characterize the crime if one was proven. He thought there was too much prejudice and ill feeling against his client and hoped that only the law and the testimony would be permitted to have a place in our deliberations.

Mr. Eoff was then called and taking the stand he related the story of that fateful July afternoon. He was the one who had such a thrilling experience, he being the one who was on the inside locking the cells when the break was made and was the only eye witness to the bloody tragedy. He was shot at twice, he testified, before reaching partial shelter in the recess of what was known as John Brown's cell and was in more danger of his life than any of the others who came to his assistance and who engaged the outlaw in battle. His statement was in accordance with the story as given in previous pages and it is unnecessary to repeat it here. Arch Stockton followed Mr. Eoff and related his experiences. He arrived in time to be of some assistance to the others and was one of the two to make the search of Bill's cell after the battle was over. Jailer Berry detailed what he knew with reference to the affair, the damaging feature of his testimony being the narration of conversations he had had with Cherokee Bill relative to the killing, in which the latter stated that he had killed Larry because he refused to put up his hands. Will Lawson's testimony was merely corroborative of the others the testimony of any one of the witnesses being sufficient to convict the defendant. Col. Ben. T. DuVal was here introduced as a witness to prove that the jail was on government ground. He went back as far as 1840 in his history of Fort Smith. It was a few minutes after 6 o'clock when court adjourned and it was five minutes before the crowd could make their way out. At the bottom of the stairs and on the sidewalk groups of men and women formed and only dispersed when the prison van had driven off to the jail.

We were taken in charge by Bailiff, D. S. Patrick, and conducted to Arch Stockton's boarding house, inside the old government barracks near the jail, operated by the government as a boarding place for jurors when under care of the bailiff. We were not allowed to converse with anyone except to each other and were not allowed to separate until we retired to sleep. I afterwards learned that nearly all night long on the streets of Fort Smith, in hotel lobbies and all public places, crowds congregated and discussed this, one of the most noteworthy murder trials in history; the next morning, as we were marched to the court house just before nine o'clock, knots of men were gathered here and there and all seemed to be discussing the all-important subject. I could hear men say in a respectful undertone, "There's Cherokee's jury; they look as if they were the kind to convict," and many remarks of a similar nature, indicating the intensity of feeling held by the people who had known Keating in life. One of the Fort Smith papers that morning contained the following editorial, under the caption, "'Law's Delay:"

"Fort Smithians were treated yesterday to a beautiful exemplification of the law's delay that one hears so much of. It may be that we have had some striking examples before but still it came home with peculiar force to all who were in the United States court yesterday and to the rest of us who heard of the transactions there.

"Some days since Cherokee Bill, a noted desperado, shot and killed a faithful guard at the United States jail. There could be no possible doubt of equivocation about the murder. It was plainly seen and confessed and coolly discussed. There is no possible way to deny the killing that a lay mind can see. But a legal mind can see further and the spectators were treated to an exhibition of the seeing. It was exceedingly annoying to those who hoped to see justice speedily executed and they were treated to a bitter disappointment in the frequent and fertile suggestions put forth by the bright lawyer for the defense. True, the mock barriers may avail naught, the chances are very largely that they will avail nothing, but yet the defense is possibly sufficiently comprehensive to insure a delay of justice by the defendant carrying an appeal to the Supreme Court. This is the right accorded by the law to every man and it ought not to be grudgingly denied any murderer, no matter how red-handed he may be. This is the way at least fora lawyer to view the case. But the civilian frets at the manner justice drags along her leaden feet. When the law is plainly broken, punishment swift and meet should follow.

"France tries her men-immediately. We ought to do the same. Judge Parker has been duly and commendably expeditious. If the Supreme Court has to review the case it should take it up as rapidly as Judge Parker. That would be both justice and common sense. If such were the course adopted there would be less socialistic and other discontent at the laws snail pace. As for the quibbles, one can admire the ingenuity that finds them and recognize the fact that the untrained mind loves not niceties and is unable to grasp subtleties."

Court opened promptly at nine o'clock, with Jailer Berry's wife on the stand for the defense, the government having rested the night previous. Mrs. Berry had visited the outlaw at his cell and asked him why he committed the horrible crime, but he had maintained a stubborn silence throughout, refusing to talk to her. Mr. Reed expected to prove by her that Cherokee killed Keating while laboring under an aberration of mind the result of long imprisonment. Mrs. Berry had been a frequent visitor to the jail, had acted as guide to hundreds of women who desired to go through the corridors; she was a very sympathetic woman, and having taken a great interest in the criminals confined there, was believed to have a knowledge of prisoners of that class. She told of escorting a party of women through the jail a few days previous to the killing of Keating; as usual, they had a curiosity to see Cherokee Bill. Always, before, he had acted kindly and come up to the side of the cell and spoken to her, but this time he had held a blanket up so as to prevent her or any member of the party seeing him, and when she spoke to him he refused to reply. Mr. Reed attempted to draw from this that Bill was temporarily insane, but when the witness was asked by the prosecution: "Mrs. Berry, you do not intend to lead this jury to believe that Cherokee Bill was insane?"

"Oh, no!" she replied with emphasis, "I never thought him insane. He might have been thinking then of a plan to kill one of the guards and escape and, perhaps, had a guilty feeling. He appeared morose and stubborn."

Several of the prisoners, who occupied cells near Cherokee Bill's, were sworn, but none of them had seen any signs of insanity on Bill's part. The most interesting testimony, however, was given by Ben Duff, who was confined in the jail for murder. His testimony showed that a conspiracy had been formed among some of the prisoners in the lower cells, and in proof a letter was submitted which had been taken from one of the trusties several days before the death of Keating. The letter, among other matters, contained the following sentence: "We are doing away with them every day and are going to kill a guard next week." Duff said that Cherokee Bill had written the letter, and that it had been given to Will Rail to give to Kirk Barnes, a man on the outside. By some means, he did not know how, it had fallen into the hands of the officers. Duff's testimony disconcerted Cherokee Bill. It was the only incident of the trial that caused him to show the least degree of nervousness.

After the defense had rested, at the request of one of the jurymen, who was a stranger in the court, I asked Judge Parker to have Mr. Eoff brought to the stand again, that the juror might ask a few questions, in order to become better acquainted with the position of the cells and the relative position of Bill to the others when the fatal shot was fired. I asked the questions which the stranger desired answered in order to procure the necessary information. Mr. Eoff said as he was leaving the box:

"That fellow understands the inside of that jail as well as I do."

Mr. Eoff was the last witness and at 2:30 o'clock p. m. Judge Parker announced to the attorneys that he would allow two and one-half hours for each side to present the case to the jury. Mr. McDonough opened the argument and spoke for an hour, setting forth the loyalty of Keating and his associates, as well as the desperate characters of the men with whom they had to deal. At 3:30 o'clock Mr. Reed began his argument for defense, and for two hours and thirty minutes he pleaded most eloquently for the life of his client. He based his claim for acquittal on the plea that it was not, in fact, a shot fired by Cherokee Bill which killed Keating but a stray shot from one of the guards; that while Bill shot at him and tried to hit him he had missed him and the bullets lodged in the wall beyond, and if eloquence could have convinced us jurymen that Cherokee Bill was innocent of this murder, as charged, we must surely have rendered a verdict of acquittal. While he was in the midst of a flight of oratory that seemed to be of sufficient subtleness and power to move a nation of beings— unmindful of time—Judge Parker suddenly cast his eye over his right shoulder to where the hour hand of the court clock pointed to six and raising his gavel brought it down with a bang. Mr. Reed continued to talk, not heeding the interruption, and again Judge Parker's gavel rang out.

"Time's up," he said, sharply.

"Just a few minutes more, your honor, please," said the attorney.

"Mr. Reed, the time is up; we will adjourn court," said the judge, sternly, and, with one last appealing look at the jury box, the Trojan submitted and without another word picked up his silk hat and the court adjourned.

As soon as the room was cleared we were once more conducted to the boarding house. In the lobbies of the building and in the yard outside crowds were congregated to discuss the plea of Mr. Reed. Many were the expressions we heard as we passed, in wonder that any man could stand before a jury and plead for so evident a criminal, for a blood-thirsty wretch so steeped in the darkest measure of crime as was Cherokee Bill. All, however, complimented the attorney for his powerful and magnificent endeavors for his client and his dogged determination which caused him to hold on as long as there was a single straw in sight.

"Why," said one, more loud spoken than the others, "he was just a butting his head ag'in' a stone wall all afternoon, but it didn't phase him a bit. Reed is the most powerful lawyer I ever saw; he'd a been talkin' yet to-morrow morning if the old judge would a' let him."

"Yes," said another, "when Reed has got a job to do he goes about it in full earnest; nothing dead about him." And so it was until we finally passed through the crowded streets to the quiet of the boarding house.

"BUCK" MCDONOUGH'S SPEECH

The next morning we were escorted again to the court house, and at 9 o'clock Assistant Prosecuting Attorney J.B. McDonough again took the floor for the government. He had an hour and a half in which to close and he filled the time to advantage. He spoke of the evidence produced and of the further fact that Cherokee Bill was a ferocious villain, as unprincipled as he was terrible. He spoke of the blood-thirsty gang to which Cherokee Bill belonged and with whom he trained; of the reign of terror they had inaugurated in the Indian Territory; of the bloody crimes they had participated in; and under the very eaves of this court! Cherokee Bill belonged to a gang of worse than ruffians, such as had been known nowhere except on this border land where in the fastness of its mountains, its broad prairies and the dark recesses of its forests, unobserved by the eye of civilization, yet almost at our very thresholds, they committed crimes of the blackest hue until the blood of their brother men poured forth to enrich the plains of the Indian country, given by the government to the Indians, with a guarantee of protection they have never received. He belonged to a gang at the sound of whose name brave men trembled; to a gang of fiends of which he was the most fiendish. He gloried in crime, and boasted within himself of the numbers who had bit the dust at his command, or at the crack of his trusted rifle.

"While this band of outlaws stalked the land business became paralyzed and was at a standstill. Merchants with their little stocks of merchandise grew timid, and though living miles from the scenes of their crimes, fled from the country through fear of their lives and those of their wives and children. Schools or any form of education were impossible, as none would risk the chances of being slain and their bodies left festering on the plains, a feast for the wolves and buzzards. Even physicians feared to visit their patients, such was the terror which this band inaugurated, and the cases of sickness, from the lack of proper medical treatment, increased many times; the tide in the affairs of men turned backward and the advance of civilization was retarded to an extent incalculable. The bad repute given a most fertile country kept settlers away, and the time when, the wilderness should be made to blossom as the rose was retarded and the fertile plains were left to the howling coyote and the banditti. The announcement that the band was near, the distant cloud of dust away on the horizon, warning the few squatters that the scouts were coming, was sufficient to cause them and their families to flee in terror.

"To effect his capture and prevent a further gorging of his appetite for a brother's blood, brave men risked their lives, and it was only by the keenest strategy that his capture was effected

Even after he had been placed within the prison walls, with the majesty of the law frowning upon him, his ferocity prevented docility, and his only thought was to break away that he might return to the scenes of bloodshed from which an outraged law had estranged him. In order to make his escape he would have trampled underfoot the will of the people, and releasing hundreds of his ilk, would have slipped away to his mountains and his forest haunts, there to gather about him a larger and more blood-thirsty band; there to defy all power under heaven while he indulged his passion for crime: there to burn and pillage, and. destroy the lives of whoever stood for a moment in the way of his campaign of destruction.

"Life, honor, property, all were unsafe, so long as this red-handed fiend stalked abroad, unmindful of another's rights or another's life. His love of crime was his controlling passion, and even the mighty power of the law seemed almost unable to keep it in check. Failing to work out his plan for escape, he deliberately, without a moment's hesitation, let out the lifeblood of a fellow being, one who was beloved by all, and who had been the best friend he had known in his incarceration; then, nerved by the very scent of the fresh blood he had spilled, he would add other terrors to the occasion by shooting even those who had come to carry away the poor quivering, dead body of the friend he had ruthlessly slain. With the hideous mien of a double-dyed monster he stood at bay and fired shot after shot at the brave officers who gathered to prevent him from adding other and heavier burdens upon his soul that was already foul with crime.

"And now he comes here, with his hands steeped inhuman gore, with a long list of misdeeds that should cause even the imps of hell to shudder, with a plea that is untenable-, asks mercy at your hands; mercy! for a series of crimes that knows no equal among men of the Nineteenth century; with his heart reeking with infamy, he pleads for mercy, this most ferocious of monsters, whose record is more atrocious than all the criminals who have hitherto stood before this bar; a creature whose very existence is a disgrace upon nature, a grievous burden to the atmosphere from which he draws his breath.

"And here is a strange fact, that the women of our city, ladies, our fair mothers and sisters, should flock to this court room to satisfy their curiosity, that they may but look upon this [man].

"It is the most incomprehensible of all that the fair and gentle creatures of our land should desire to attend scenes like this, where they may revel in the ghastly mire that is here revealed. Why are they here? We do not ask them to come. Is it that they may drink to the dregs the cup of infamy here exposed in order that they may instill the minds of the children yet unborn; that we may keep on rearing up criminals, generation after generation, until we have a race of them, with none to stay their hands?

"Is the craving of the feminine heart for the essence of sin so strong, are the beautiful creatures of God's handiwork, whom men adore, whom we love to call by the hallowed name of 'wife' and 'mother,' who were last at the cross and first at the tomb?

"Has she become so low, her appetite so depraved, that she cannot exist in comfort without coming here to gorge her mentality with a consideration of crime in all its shades and all its horrid bearings? And is this the result of an era of criminal procedure within this borderland of which history, neither modern nor ancient, knows its equal? Then away with its perpetrators; away with this, one of the most fiendish of the entire monstrous lot! Life is to him but a hollow mockery; why should he plead for life, he who has destroyed it so recklessly and without even the slightest provocation? Away with creatures of his ilk, not fit to exist upon this fair land while there is the remotest possibility of his contaminating influence being exerted upon those who have not yet descended lo the depths of depravity in which he loves to wallow. May the Good Giver of All forbid that ever another such a creature should be given the breath of life; might he have been strangled at his birth rather than that he should ever have arrived at the age we call manhood, which title he has desecrated, until all nature points the finger of scorn towards those who are responsible for his having been born."

Mr. McDonough had grown intense in his masterful eloquence. His blue eyes, mild, ordinarily, flashed and seemed to become as black as night. With his head thrown back and his breast forward he "heaved" away, his deep voice reaching to the far corners of the court yard where were massed many who were unable to secure entrance to the court room. Small of stature, though perfect in build, he looked the very "Apollo" as he pounded blow after blow upon crime and its perpetrators. At last he paused; he seemed to have reached the limit of his endurance, yet showed no sign of fatigue. As he turned again to the jury, a look of sympathy came from his eyes and he spoke of poor Larry Keating and his untimely death; of his kind heart and those whom he loved; of his wife and fatherless children; then said:

"I have no fears of the jury; I know full well you will avenge, as the law gives you the right to do, this, one of the foulest of murders, a crime for which there was not the least excuse. It was a terrible crime. All murders are terrible; but when we consider this one, in all its horrible bearings, it seems to be far more terrible than the ordinary. We who have occasion so often to listen to the wrongs perpetrated by a class of beings who make the world worse by their having lived in it, are apt to become hardened to even the acts of the worst criminals, but there was something about this act that is so heartrending in its incipiency that it causes us to shudder at the thought of it. We all loved Larry Keating, who knew him. He loved his family, idolized his children; few men were ever blessed with his splendid temperament. He had always a kind word for those he met, always a smile and a hearty handshake for his friends. We cannot allow his murder to go unavenged. Avenge is a hard word, but it is most mild when applied to this case. I know you men will do your duty. I feel it. I can read it in your faces. You are honest men; you are sworn to decide in accordance with the law and the evidence. The law is plain and so is the evidence. There is nothing complex about this case, no technicalities to be cleared away; all is as plain as the noonday sun. There is not a particle of doubt in the minds of any of you that the crime was committed; not a

261

particle of doubt as to who committed it. You will do your duty, I have no fear of that, and may God bless you for it."

Gradually, as he spoke, his voice took on a milder tone and as he delivered the last word it sank almost to a whisper, and turning, he left the court room.

He had made a telling address but it is more than probable that it had not affected the opinions of any member of the jury. The evidence had been so plain, and even the testimony of the witnesses put on by the defense had only tended to strengthen the prosecution. A subdued ripple of admiration passed over the crowd as he closed and then all turned to Judge Parker, it being supposed that he would deliver a lengthy charge. They were disappointed in this, for Judge Parker in all his experience had never had before him a case where facts were so self-evident, as in this. He had been annoyed by the intense persistence of Mr. Reed but he had confidence in the jury to believe they would not be led away by unwarranted assumptions; his charge was very brief, lasting only thirteen minutes, and then we were escorted to the room reserved for the jury. Once there, I was chosen foreman, by unanimous vote; but a few minutes were engaged in discussing the case, and when the poll was taken it was found that all twelve had voted to convict. We were conducted back to the court-room and it was then discovered and remarked upon by the superstitious, that we had been just thirteen minutes, in arriving at a verdict.

There is much comfort here for those who believe that the number 13 is an unlucky one, for the number occurs many times in connection with Cherokee Bill, and his conviction and sentence. First, Cherokee was believed by some to have killed thirteen persons during his career; the offer of $1300 reward affected his capture for killing Earnest Melton; his first sentence to die was pronounced on April 13; he killed Keating on the 26th day of July, or twice thirteen; Bill was said to have fired thirteen shots, during the fight with the guards; Judge Parker occupied thirteen minutes in charging the jury in the Keating case: the foreman of the jury, myself, boarded, during the term of court, that convicted Bill, at a house numbered 313; the actual hours occupied in the trial, numbered thirteen; the jury were thirteen minutes in arriving at a verdict; the jurymen and deputy, who ate and slept together during the trial made a company of thirteen; there were thirteen witnesses for prosecution and there were many who believed execution should have followed within thirteen minutes after conviction, a total of thirteen 13's.

Judge Parker paid us a high compliment for the speedy verdict. He said: "You have done your duty." Turning to Arch Stockton, he asked, "Have you prepared dinner for these men?" Receiving an affirmative answer, he continued, "Then take them over and give them a good dinner; they deserve it." As we passed out of the court-room I stepped over to a nearby telegraph office and sent a dispatch to my home paper, the *Rogers Democrat*. It read:

"Cherokee Bill convicted of murder."

The editor of the Democrat was my friend. His usual press time was 2 o'clock p. m. This gave him plenty of time to tell the story in print and the Rogers, Arkansas, Democrat, was the first paper to publish the announcement of the verdict. The Fort Smith papers came out at 5 o'clock and contained long articles regarding the last hours of the trial, and telling of the verdict.

Sentence was passed upon the outlaw Monday, following. Promptly at nine o'clock court convened. The room was packed to suffocation. Cherokee Bill was not on hand, but he arrived a few moments afterwards and took his seat near the end of the long table at which prisoners were generally seated. Nearby stood heavily armed guards. He looked quietly about, as though sizing up the crowd of people who had gathered to listen to his doom. He was shackled and handcuffed, and so remained until ordered to stand up. Mr. Reed, his attorney, moved for a new trial and a stay of sentence. In his motion he alleged that the jury had been influenced against the prisoner by reason of remarks made by the court at the time the grand and petit juries were empaneled. He also claimed that certain evidence had been admitted at the trial which should have been excluded, while other evidence, which might have benefitted the prisoner, was excluded; that certain jurors were not free from prejudice when they passed upon the case, and that one of the witnesses had shown a disposition to lead a crowd in the lynching "bee" which was proposed on the night of Keating's murder. When asked if he wished to submit an argument in support of these allegations, Mr. Reed said that he did not. The court sententiously joined, "I should think not." Mr. McDonough had nothing to say concerning the matter, so the court passed upon them, saying: "Both the motion for a new trial and for a stay of sentence are overruled without comment." There was some vinegar in the court's voice as he made his ruling.

Cherokee Bill then stood up and the court passed sentence, and September 10, just a month from the date of his conviction, was named as the day for his execution. It did not affect him much. He stood carelessly by the table, rocking to and fro, shifting his weight from one foot to another, and gazing most of the time out of a side window of the court room.

After the sentence, Cherokee Bill was placed in solitary confinement. He did not seem to mind it, but he complained bitterly at his inability to obtain his mail, as under the rules felons were not allowed to either receive or send mail when in solitary confinement, and letters addressed to Cherokee Bill were, of course, opened by Jailor Berry and carefully read.

One of his most persistent correspondents was a young mulatto girl, who lived in Indianapolis, Indiana', who claimed to be a relative She had corresponded with Bill for some months and had sent him her photograph. She wrote frequently after he was sentenced and at last her letters showed that she was greatly worried at receiving no replies, fearing she had written something to incur the desperado's displeasure. She finally wrote him a sad and last farewell, expressing the deepest sympathy and begging him, if he ever came free, to be sure and visit her. It was, doubtless, a blessing to the girl that Bill never "came free."

Very soon after the sentence the case was appealed to the Supreme Court, and when September 10 arrived no answer had been returned. Judge Parker, therefore, issued a stay of execution to await the action of the higher court. The fact that the case had been appealed, however, seemed to have been generally overlooked, for on Tuesday, September 10, from 500 to 600 people came into the city, mainly from the Indian Territory, to witness the execution. Some of them came a distance of seventy-five miles, and one man was known to have walked a distance of twenty miles. An amusing scene occurred in the jail yard that day. The greater portion of the people who came to witness the execution of the noted bandit went to the jail yard and remained there during the greater part of the day, in spite of the assurances of Jailer Berry that the execution would not take place. A scheme was finally fixed up to scatter the crowd, and a pet bear belonging to the jailer was turned loose; for a while there was a lively scrimmage; the bear tore through the crowd knocking men down and rolling them over, frightening some of them terribly. The fun was of short duration, however, for someone in the crowd, more venturesome than the others, grabbed Bruin's chain and fastened the animal to a tree. A couple of hours later, the guards shackled a trusty, dressed him in a long, black coat and broad-brimmed hat and led him to the gallows yard, between two guards, preceded by a third. Seeing this, the crowd rushed towards the gallows, and finding the door shut many of them climbed the walls.

When they finally became convinced that it was not Cherokee Bill and that the noted desperado would not be hanged that day, they, sorrowfully, left for their homes. They had made their long trip to satisfy their appetite for a gruesome sight and were sadly disappointed.

A few months later a decision was handed down from the Court of Appeals affirming the decision of Judge Parker's court, convicting Cherokee Bill of the murder of Ernest Melton, and a third time was he brought out and sentenced to hang, on the seventeenth day of March, 1896. Again, as previously stated, did "Reed, the Trojan," attempt to save the life of his client, by appealing for a pardon just a few days before the time set for his execution, but all to no avail, and on March 14 the last hope of Bill's noble defender was dashed to the ground by the following dispatch:

Washington, D. C., March 14.—Read, United States Attorney

The President has denied the application for pardon of Crawford Goldsby, alias Cherokee Bill, sentenced to be hanged Tuesday, March 17. The judgment of the court must be carried out, acknowledge receipt by telegraph.

Harmon, Att'y General."

The next day the condemned man was informed that the last chance was gone and fully realizing the terrible ordeal through which he must pass, he began making some effort of preparation for the fate, so soon to be his. The day was eventful, in that it worked a change in his cell quarters. His new cell was the one occupied by Alexander Allen for so long a time. His games of poker were ended. No prisoner was allowed to come in front of his door nor converse with him. A guard was appointed to sit in front of his cell constantly. He was allowed a deck of cards with which to play "solitaire." He appeared to be in a fairly happy state of mind and conversed freely upon the subject of his execution, saying that the worst feature of it, to him, was the way his mother would take it. He seemed to take great pleasure in paying high tribute to Mr. Reed, his attorney, who, he said, had worked with the same zeal as if he had been certain of a heavy fee for his efforts; to the last he maintained his innocence of the majority of the crimes charged to him, and even refused to admit that he killed Lawrence Keating. Saying: "I don't know whether I killed him or not. I don't know whether my shots struck him. He may have been shot by the guard." On the day previous to that upon which he was to expiate his crime, his mother arrived in the city and for the first time she was allowed to converse with him in his cell. She was with him for several hours and during the afternoon he made his will, drawn up by his attorney, giving his claim in the Cherokee Nation to his mother. Just before the close of the interview, the old negro Aunty, who nursed him in infancy, arrived at the jail and had a few words with him. His brother, Clarence Goldsby, also visited the jail yard and viewed the scaffold and rope and the gruesome preparations. On that day the rope was tested by the heavy wooden dummy; it worked satisfactorily. The dry grass that had stood all winter in the gallows inclosure, was burned. The black cap used in the last execution had been cut into pieces to form relics for the members of a traveling troupe and another was made.

During the time, after the return of the indictment charging Cherokee Bill with the murder of Lawrence Keating and the reception of the announcement of the refusal to honor the petition for pardon, true bills of indictment had been returned, by the grand jury, charging Edward and John Shelley, brothers, Lu Shelley, wife of one of the brothers, Sherman Vann, the trusty heretofore noted, and Henry Starr, with the crime of murder, as accessory to the killing of Keating. Cherokee was appealed to for the truthful statement regarding the guilt or innocence of these five fellow prisoners and on the day preceding his execution, he swore to an affidavit, which is here copied from the original, and which has never before been published. It contains an interesting statement concerning the manner in which the two pistols found their way into his cell, which will be a surprise to many, into whose hands this book will fall:

CHEROKEE BILL'S AFFIDAVIT—A MYSTERY HALF SOLVED

This day, personally appeared before me the undersigned authority, Crawford Goldsby, to me personally known to be the person represented and who being by me first duly sworn, as the law directs, deposes and says:

That he is fully advised and knows and understands the certainty of his impending dissolution by being hanged on to-morrow, the 17th day of March, 1896; that in view of his said impending dissolution and death, he desires to make a sworn statement as to the charge

265

of conspiracy and agreement among prisoners in this jail, to bring about a jail delivery from the United States jail at Fort Smith, Arkansas, just before the killing of Larry Keating, on the 26th of July, 1895, who was a guard at said jail.

Affiant, Crawford Goldsby, says that neither Edward Shelley, nor John Shelley, nor the woman Lu Shelley, nor Sherman Vann, nor Henry Starr had anything whatever to do with putting the pistols or pistol used by affiant, Crawford Goldsby, at the time said Keating was killed, into said jail.

Affiant, Crawford Goldsby, further says that neither of said Shelley brothers nor the woman Lu Shelley nor Sherman Vann nor Henry Starr knew, so far as affiant knows or can state, that said pistols were coming into said jail.

Affiant, Crawford Goldsby, further says that both of said pistols which were put into said jail, came from the outside of said jail and were put in on a pole, through the open window and came directly to affiant in his cell, on the west side of said jail and were not handled by either of said Shelley brothers nor the woman Lu Shelley nor Sherman Vann nor Henry Starr.

Affiant further says that the pistols which were put in the jail to him for the purposes of said jail delivery, one of which pistols was used by him at the time said Keating was killed, were put into said jail as before stated, about 11 o'clock at night, about ten days, perhaps, before said killing and put in about one hour apart on a pole, as before stated, and both were taken off the pole by affiant and concealed, and no one had said pistols, until, for fear of detection, one of said pistols was put in a bucket and the other pistol kept by affiant in his cell, until the time of said killing, sewed up in his bed. Affiant knew that said pistols were to be put into said jail to him by a note that he found in his cell, directing him where and when to look for the coming of said pistols.

Affiant, Crawford Goldsby, further says that there was no plan nor agreement among said Shelley brothers nor said woman, Lu Shelley, Sherman Vann nor Henry Starr nor either of them with this affiant to break jail before nor at the time of the killing of said Keating; but that all the agreement and plans for said jail delivery were made with other persons, and not the five persons hereinbefore named.

Crawford Goldsby.

Subscribed and sworn to before me the undersigned, at the United States jail, by Crawford Goldsby, this 16th day of March, 1896.

Stephen Wheeler, Clerk,

By j. d. berry, d. c.

It had also come to Cherokee's ears that his mother, Ellen Lynch, and his sister, Georgia Brown, were believed by some to have provided the pistols, and in some manner to have smuggled them into his cell, and he made an affidavit similar to the above, and at the same time in which he swore positively that neither his mother nor sister had anything to do with the pistols being placed in his cell, nor knew anything whatever of the plan and agreement for the said jail delivery so far as affiant knew, and that they were entirely innocent of anything connected with the pistols coming into the jail, so far as affiant had any knowledge. To his attorney he said that he did not know by whom the pistols were placed within his reach, and that his knowledge of their coming was by means of written information dropped into his cell by a trusty. The findings of the grand jury against the five prisoners named in the above indictment were quashed, without the prisoners ever being brought for arraignment.

HIS LAST DAY

The final chapter in the life of Crawford Goldsby, alias Cherokee Bill, the most noted of all the Indian Territory desperadoes, was closed at 2 130 o'clock on the afternoon of March 17, 1896. At that moment, Jail Guard Eoff, whom Cherokee Bill tried to kill in July previous, threw the fateful lever and sprung the trap that launched the murderer into eternity. The hour for the execution had been announced for II 130, but before 9 o'clock the people began to wend their way from all parts of the city to the jail yard. One hundred tickets had been issued, and every person so supplied was on hand early. The thousands who were without passes swarmed outside the gates, and all space on top of the walls was taken up. Many of them succeeded in slipping from this point of vantage to the yard below, and mingled with the others until the yard was fairly alive with humanity, and the coarse laughter and ribald jests contrasted queerly with the solemn scenes about to be enacted. In the jail several representatives of the press were assembled, all taking notes of events. Behind Bill's door hung a blanket, shutting from view those on the inside. They were, the felon, his mother, the old colored auntie and a Catholic priest. That the other prisoners felt the solemnity of the occasion, was apparent. They refrained from the usual daylight disturbances, and many of them crowded to the east side in order that they might watch whatever was to be seen. One game of cards was in progress. Three of the players were: the Pearce brothers and Charley Smith, the two former under sentence to hang. While the time was dragging slowly, the announcement came that the hour of execution had been postponed till 2 o'clock in order to allow Bill to speak a last word with his sister, Mrs. Georgia Brown, who was expected to arrive by an afternoon train. On learning of this the crowd gradually dispersed, and when, about 1 o'clock, they re-assembled, Chief Marshal

Crump had issued an order restraining every one from entering the yard before 1:30 o'clock. It was a struggling mass of humanity that gathered at the big gate, on and around the steps and walls, and when the time came to admit those who were provided with tickets, a crush and jam ensued that reminded one of a lot of wild animals rushing ravenously to a gluttonous feed. Order, in a measure, was finally restored by the guards, and all awaited the moment when the door of the jail should open for the coming of the doomed. Outside the jail yard the crowd increased. They continued to come until they were numbered by thousands. For blocks about the enclosure the scene was one of indescribable excitement, though the crowd was not disorderly. The roofs of the nearest buildings were covered with people who eagerly peered and watched every move made about the jail. Occasionally a form would slide over the wall and endeavor to become lost in the crowd within the yard. Some succeeded, but, usually, the eagle eye of the guard singled them out and escorted them back to the entrance and unceremoniously ejected them. A rickety old shed on the outer east wall collapsed under its unusual burden, and the crowd massed thereon made a lively scrimmage before they were extricated. Those inside the yard, who were eager to drink in all the horrible details, passed the time while waiting for the prisoner to arrive, by visiting the gallows and closely examining the huge instrument of death to the minutest degree. Inside the jail was a repetition of the scenes of the morning. Bill's mother and the old nurse were taking their leave, and the former was admonishing her wayward son to show his nerve and never break down. The women did not expect to see him again, but after they were in the open air Col. Crump suggested that they walk with Bill to the gallows. Just before 2 o'clock Bill said:

"Well, I am ready to go now, most any time," and the jail was cleared. Outside, the crowd had swollen and there was a dense jam about the side entrance to the jail. A pathway was cleared, and at 2 o'clock the huge door swung open and the march to the gallows was taken up, the condemned man walking between Guards Eoff and George Lawson. Bill was pale as death but he stood erect. As he gained the outside, walking slowly on account of his shackles, he said: "Hell, look at the people; something must be going to happen!" Then looking up at the sky, he said: "This is about as good a day to die as any." At the south end of the jail he looked about and remarked:" It looks like a regiment of soldiers," and continued to eye the crowd, curiously. At the door of the gallows enclosure there was a jam. Everybody crowded up eagerly, and, there was a delay of a few moments; then, as the death party went through, a disgraceful scene ensued. The mob behind, fought and cursed. The crowd had followed close upon the heels of the condemned man and now those who were without tickets were striving to gain an advantage over those who had' them. By the time the tangle had been straightened out, Bill and his guards had mounted the scaffold and were followed by two women, several representatives of the press, physicians and deputies, and Chief Marshal Crump. Bill walked with a firm step and took up his position near the back of the gallows, waiting for the end. Turning, he saw his mother; he said to her: "Mother, you ought not to have come up here." Her answer was:" I can go wherever you go."

One of the deputies asked him if he wanted to say anything. "No," he replied;" I came here to die, not to make a speech."

The marshal then read the warrant, during which Bill gazed about but showed no emotion. The marshal asked him:

"Have you anything to say?"

"No," in a low tone; "except that—I wish the priest would pray."

Hardened wretch though he was, he feared to go into the great beyond, with all his heartless crimes hanging over him, without any assistance, ever so slight, to guide him over the dark river. The priest complied with a few brief sentences. Bill listened attentively, then walked over and stood upon the trap. Deputies George and Will Lawson adjusted the ropes, binding his arms and legs, Bill meanwhile bidding his acquaintances good bye. Then he suddenly discovered a score or more of young men in the act of taking "snap shots" with "Kodaks," and he called the attention of the guards, asking that none of them be allowed to take photographs of the scene.

"Don't take any pictures here," said Marshal Crump, peremptorily, and the Kodaks were put away—all but one. That one was held by a persistent youth and the plate he secured was finished by John Gannaway, of Fort Smith, and was used in making the engraving, here given, illustrating Cherokee Bill's execution.

Again Bill hailed his friends good bye, and said to Marshal Crump:

"The quicker it is over the better."

The black cap was adjusted by the Lawsons. "Stand over a little more, Bill," said Guard Eoff, who stood ready to spring the trap, and Cherokee Bill obediently moved his feet until he stood directly over the center of the trap.

The rope was placed around his neck and drawn taut. The deputies stepped back, excepting Will Lawson, who remained directly in front to assist in steadying the condemned man in case it became necessary. The black-capped figure stood erect and motionless as a statue, for a moment; the bolt was withdrawn, and Guard Eoff, who stood with his hand upon the lever, shouted: "Ready!" then sprung the trap, and at 2:13 the body of Cherokee Bill shot through the opening, dropping eight feet, and that was the end.

In ten minutes the doctors pronounced life extinct; he had died without a struggle.

At 2:30 the body was cut down and placed in a neat but plain coffin, provided by his mother. The remains were next conveyed to undertaking rooms and boxed for shipment to Fort Gibson that afternoon at 3:20 o'clock.

The morbid curiosity that had caused thousands to gather about the jail yard, before and during the execution, still prompted, and crowds followed the corpse to the undertaker's, hung about listlessly, and followed again to the depot, apparently anxious to peep at the coffin as the next most gratifying occupation to seeing the body. Not until the train moved away from the platform and from their sight was the full measure Of their curiosity satisfied.

Thus ended the career of a youth, who was a man terrible among men, one of the most noted criminals in history. He died believing in the transmigration of the soul; that he would sometime return in the shape of a horse, a dog or a wild beast, to further annoy the human race.

A MASTERFUL SENTENCE

The sentence of Cherokee Bill for the Keating murder, though unusually brief, was said by some of the members of the Fort Smith bar to be Judge Parker's masterpiece, in its line; it is here given:

The court said: "Cherokee Bill, stand up. Crawford Goldsby, alias Cherokee Bill, you have been convicted of the murder of Lawrence Keating. Under the law it becomes the duty of the court to pass upon you the sentence of the law, that sentence which the law says shall follow a conviction of the crime of murder. Have you anything to say why that sentence shall not now be passed?"

The prisoner: "No, sir."

The court: "The crime you have committed is but another evidence, if any were needed, of your wicked, lawless, bloody and murderous disposition. It is another evidence of your total disregard of human life; another evidence that you revel in the destruction of human life. The many murders you have committed, and their reckless and wanton character, show you to be a human monster from whom innocent people can expect no safety. The killing of Lawrence Keating shows three wicked and unprovoked murders that we know you have committed. If reports speak the truth, two or three more 'innocent human beings have been robbed of their lives by you. The evidence in this case shows that you most wantonly and wickedly stole the life of a brave and true man; that he died by your murderous hand—a martyr at the post of duty, while bravely guarding you and the desperate criminals in the jail with you. You wickedly slew him in your mad attempt to escape that you might evade the punishment justly due for your many other murders and robberies. It was, no doubt, a concerted movement between you and many of the other murderers in the jail to effect an escape. You were lawfully confined in the United States jail for murder and robbery. The evidence shows that by some wicked agency—it is difficult to tell what that agency is—you had weeks before obtained a revolving pistol and many cartridges; that you concealed the same in your mattress, awaiting an opportunity to do the deadly act you did do. The time came, to Lawrence Keating the fatal hour struck, and you, without remorse, in cold blood, in the most devilish and wicked way, shot down poor Lawrence Keating, one of the guards at the prison, while he was faithfully discharging the duty in the station he filled, to peace, to order, to the security of human life, to the supremacy of the law, and to his country'. He died like a brave soldier. He gave up his life rather than fail to perform his duty. You ordered him to throw up his hands, co surrender to you—a murderer and a bandit! The brave and honest man was no doubt startled. He was shocked; but he never quailed. And because he did not surrender to you, that you might escape yourself, and lead the host of other criminals to escape judgment, you, with your murderous hand, directed by a mind saturated with crime, while he was gallantly and bravely upholding the laws of his country, shot him to death. He was a minister of peace; you were and are a minister of wickedness, of disorder, of crime, of murder. Lawrence Keating was in the discharge of a great duty when you killed him. Your fatal bullet destroyed the life of a gallant and brave man, who died like a true citizen and faithful officer. He died as gallantly and bravely as if he had given up his life for the flag upon the battle field. His family deserves as well of his country, and of every lover of peace and order, as though he had so died. He died at the hand of an assassin, at the hand of the wicked man of crime.

"You have taken the life of a good man, who never harmed you—of a faithful citizen, of a kind father, and a true husband. Your wicked act has taken from a home its head, from a family its support. You have made a weeping widow; your murderous bullet has made four little sorrowing and helpless orphans. But you are the man of crime, and you heed not the wails and shrieks of a sorrowing and mourning wife no more than you do the cries for a dead father of the poor orphans. Surely' this is a case where all who are not criminals or sympathizers with crime should approve the swift and certain justice that has overtaken you.

"All that you have done has been done by you in the interest of crime, in furtherance of a wicked criminal purpose. The jury in your case have properly convicted you; they are to be commended for it, and for the promptness with which they did it. You have had a fair trial, notwithstanding the howls and shrieks to the contrary. There is no doubt of your guilt of a most wicked, foul and unprovoked murder, shocking to every good man and woman in the land. Your case is one where justice should not walk with leaden feet. It should be swift. It should be certain. As far as this court is concerned it shall be, for public justice demands it, and personal security demands it. If Lawrence Keating had thrown up his hands and surrendered to you, he might have lived, but there is no telling how many other innocent and brave human lives would have been taken. He died for others, and a greater death than this no man can die. I once before sentenced you to death for a horrible and wicked murder committed by you while you were engaged in the crime of robbery. I then appealed to your conscience by reminding you of your duty to your God and your own soul. The appeal reached not your conscience, for you answered it by committing another most foul and dastardly murder. I shall therefore say nothing to you on that line here and now.

"You will listen to the sentence of the law, which is, that you, Crawford Goldsby, alias Cherokee Bill, for the crime of murder committed by you, by your willfully and with malice aforethought taking the life of Lawrence Keating in the United States jail in Fort Smith, and within the jurisdiction of this court, of which crime you stand convicted by the verdict of the jury in your case, be deemed, taken and adjudged guilty of murder; and that you be therefor for the said crime against the laws of the United States be hanged by the neck until you are dead; and that the marshal of the western district of Arkansas, by himself or deputy or deputies, cause execution to be done in the premises upon you on Tuesday, September tenth, 1895 between the hours of 9 o'clock in the forenoon and 5 o'clock in the afternoon of the same day. And that you now be taken to the jail from whence you came, to be there closely and securely kept until the day of execution, and from thence on the day of execution, there to be hanged by the neck until you are dead.

"May God whose laws you have broken and before whose tribunal you must then appear, have mercy on your soul."

RETRIBUTION OVERTAKES THE BETRAYER

Valuable as was the act of Ike Rogers, to society, and the officers of the government in betraying to the latter the noted bandit, Cherokee Bill, and precipitating him into the clutches of the law, yet was the deed a dastardly one, prompted merely by the hope of reward and not with a view of relieving the Indian Territory of a dangerous criminal, and not a few will read this chapter with a degree of satisfaction, learning of the retribution that followed the footsteps of the foul betrayer, meting out to him a similar but baser punishment to that which his victim suffered at the hands of the law.

Crawford Goldsby, alias Cherokee Bill, had been a friend to Ike Rogers, in the days when his name was a terror to the people of a considerable portion of the Indian Territory and the man who bore it was making a national reputation, as a desperado of the worst class. It was Cherokee Bill to whom, much of the time, Ike Rogers looked for sustenance for his family. At the latter's house Bill often made his home, when he chose to. rest quietly for a few days or weeks and after a raid or a hold-up, he was wont to retire to the home of his false friend, to remain in hiding until such time as he could once more go forth in comparative safety. Rogers was not a "munificent provider," and had it not been for the supplies often brought to them by the reckless Cherokee Bill, when returning from his raids, they would often have suffered for the bare necessaries. More than that, it is claimed, that it was not infrequently that Rogers looked out for opportunities and planned burglaries of the country stores or other places containing the articles most needed by his family, and after divulging his plans to Bill, sat down to await his return, well laden with the fruits of his crime, in the shape of food, clothing or money. Here it was that Cherokee Bill was lured to his doom, soon after the killing of Earnest Melton and by the very man who had fed upon the proceeds of his felonies, Ike Rogers, for the mere purpose of obtaining a portion of the gold, offered by the government, for Cherokee's capture.

Retribution could not come more justly than at the hands of a brother, and to Clarence Goldsby, a full brother of Cherokee Bill, fell the lot of meting punishment to the betrayer. Clarence was several years younger than his outlaw brother, and he had always been a quiet, inoffensive and well-mannered youth, not given to unlawful acts, and he bore the respect and confidence of all good citizens of Fort Gibson, his home. A certain animosity naturally grew into his heart against Ike Rogers, on account of the latter's betrayal of his brother, but never did it show forth in any overt act; the difficulties which finally resulted in Ike Rogers' tragic death began at the little town of Hayden, in the Cherokee Nation, in the winter of 1897, nearly a year after Cherokee's execution. At Hayden, for a month or more, were located the men having in charge the payment, to the negro citizens, of the Cherokee Nation, of their individual shares in the money received by the United States government, from the sale of the Cherokee Strip. Clarence Goldsby was entitled to a portion Of this money, on account of his being the son of a negress citizen, and was one of the thousands who repaired to

Hayden to receive his money. There he met Ike Rogers, who was present for the same purpose as himself. Rogers attempted to quarrel with Clarence, doubtless from a sense of guilt, at the wrong he had done him, through betraying his brother, and for several days he continued to abuse him, addressing him by all manner of vile names and epithets and even threatening his life. At last, friends of Mrs. Lynch and who had stood by Cherokee Bill until the last, fearing that Clarence would turn upon his tormentor and feeling that with the state of public sentiment against Cherokee Bill at Fort Smith and elsewhere, such an act would get him into serious difficulty and heap more sorrow upon the head of hi& mother, induced Clarence to return to his home and await a future opportunity for drawing his money. It is asserted, however, that had he killed Rogers, at that time, he would have been supported by the best citizens of the Cherokee Nation.

A few months later, early in August, the paymaster and his deputies established at Fort Gibson, for a month or more, and, as it happened, Clarence Goldsby was employed as one of the numerous guards, which the presence of so much money and the conditions then existing made necessary; he was therefore authorized to carry weapons. While thus employed as a guard, Rogers sent him notice that he was coming to Fort Gibson to kill him. One day, a short time later, as a passenger train entered the town and stopped at the depot, Clarence Goldsby was on the platform. Rogers was on the train and someone who had heard him say, boastingly, that he was going to Fort Gibson for the purpose of killing Cherokee Bill's brother, hastened from the train and informed Clarence of the threat, placing him on his guard. A moment later, Rogers stepped from the train and Clarence, raising his pistol, took deliberate aim and sent a bullet flying into his anatomy, breaking his neck and killing him instantly. The next instant, with his pistol still smoking, Clarence made a dive beneath the coach, near where he stood, and coming out on the other side, he ran away towards the forest covered hills, followed by several deputy United States marshals, firing as they ran but failing to bring him down. One of these deputies was Bill Smith, who had taken advantage of Ike Rogers duplicity, and aided thereby had affected Cherokee Bill's capture. Smith mounted his horse and followed to a point where he considered it prudent to dismount and run across a field to head off the fleeing man, and the latter, with exceptionally keen cunning, discovered the situation and ran back, mounted the officer's horse and rode away, much to the officer's discomfiture and chagrin.

During the following month Clarence returned, under cover of darkness, two or three times, td his mother's house, when, acting on the advice of friends of the family, he left the country, his whereabouts still remaining unknown.

After the first dash by the officers, there was never a concerted effort made for his capture, and it is likely, that with public sentiment, strongly in his favor, he might have openly returned to the scene of the killing as soon as quiet was restored and cool judgment prevailed, with perfect impunity.

THE BUSS LUCKEY CASE

RAPE OF THE CHILD WIFE

Saturday morning, September 7, 1895, Judge Parker pronounced the sentence of death upon Buss Luckey, a big mulatto, for the murder of Deputy Marshal Newton LaForce.

His was the first murder trial after that of Cherokee Bill for killing Lawrence Keating. The case was called up Wednesday, August 21. He was charged with killing Deputy LaForce in the Broken Arrow Settlement, in the Creek Nation, fifteen miles from Tulsa, on the fifth day of the previous December. LaForce, with Deputy Birchfield and six other men, the most of whom were deputy marshals, were sent out to bring in Luckey and Tom Root. They were wanted at Fort Smith for participating in the Blackstone and Correta train robberies. The morning was heavy with fog, and very early six of the party surrounded the house where Luckey and Root were supposed to be, and LaForce and Birchfield proceeded about 200 yards to several hay stacks, where they were thought to be lying, in the event they were not at the house. Dogs at the house discovered the officers and set up a loud barking, which awoke Luckey and Root and Root's wife, all of whom were, in fact, sleeping at the hay stack. By this time the two officers who had started in the direction of the stacks had separated about 100 yards, leaving the stacks between them.

The dense fog prevented objects being clearly visible more than a few yards distant. As Lucky and Root rose from their beds in the hay they caught a glimpse of the officers through the fog and opened fire; the officers commanded a surrender, returned the shots and a running fight ensued. The officers at the house, hearing the shots, ran towards the stacks, firing as they ran at objects barely discernible. Root and Luckey escaped, and as the battle ceased LaForce was found lying, shot, the bull having entered his back and gone through his body. He died the next day. Root was lodged in jail during Cherokee's Bill's last trial, as previously stated, and Luckey was brought in from Muscogee some months later.

He employed J. Warren Reed to defend him. He was soon indicted, charged with the murder of LaForce. In the meantime, Root had turned state's evidence against Luckey. His trial came on; Luckey had no witnesses in his behalf, while on the part of the government were eight deputy marshals and Root arrayed against him. It was a very interesting and hard fought case, but Luckey was convicted and sentenced to be hanged. When Luckey was brought out for sentence he exhibited very little interest in the remarks of the court, made prior to naming the date for his execution, and when asked whether he had anything to say answered:

"I have nothing to say, only I never did it."

Judge Parker replied: "Twelve true and tried men of your country have said that you did, and it becomes my duty to pass sentence."

"You have been convicted of the murder of Newton LaForce, a United States deputy marshal of the court, in the Indian country. He is one of more than three score of marshals, who, in the last twenty years, have given up their lives in the Indian country while in the discharge of duty to their country, these brave men representing the government and the law in a bloody struggle with outlaws and banditti. They represented peace and order. The banditti represented lawlessness, bloodshed and crime. The killing of Marshal La Force was but one act in the great war of civilization against savagism which has been waged against the men of crime by this court and its officers for twenty years. The history of this court in its efforts to overcome bloody violence and murder is unequalled in the history of jurisprudence of this country.

"You, by the evidence, are a man of blood. You belong to the banditti, to the bands of men who robbed and plundered peaceable citizens, express cars and passengers on railroad trains. The officers were seeking your arrest for robbery, and the crime of obstructing a railroad train. You evaded the officers who were lawfully and properly seeking your arrest. There seems to be a great misconception in the minds of lawless men, as well as many others, in regard to the rights of officers. The idea prevails that they, while in the interest of the law and of peace and order are entitled to no protection. The truth is, while in the right, in the performance of the responsible duties that devolve upon them in this jurisdiction, they are entitled to all protection. The officers in your case were clearly in the right. You did not permit them to make their mission known before you fired on them and killed Marshal La Force. Your act can be nothing but murder. It was clearly proven. The action of the jury in finding you guilty is entirely justified by the law. Your conviction but emphasizes a life of crime. You are now about to be sentenced to death for this wicked murder. This is the punishment the law says shall follow the conviction of this crime, and the court when it pronounces sentence but voices the law of the land.

"My advice to you is to make an honest effort to obtain forgiveness of your God for this terrible crime, as well as for the other crimes you have committed. The highest duty you owe is to your God. The duty to him demands that you implore him for that mercy you now so much need. Your past life has been such that you specially need the assistance of your Maker to enable you to get away from the condition in which your crimes and wickedness have placed you. For your own sake I request that you honestly and sincerely seek the assistance of your God."

The sentence in Luckey's case however, was never carried out. The irrepressible J. Warren Reed took a writ of error to the Supreme Court at Washington and reversed Judge Parker's decision, securing a new trial, which came on about two years later. Meanwhile, Mr. Reed lost no time in securing additional evidence and more fully developing his client's case. At the new trial he produced a large map, some three feet square, which he used before the jury, indicating the position of the haystacks, the field, the fences, house and all the premises about where the killing of LaForce took place, and the course which the marshals ran when firing in the direction of the haystacks, through the fog. By shrewd management, and application of the facts in the case to this map, Mr. Reed made the point and contended before the jury, that notwithstanding, Luckey and Root were firing at the marshals as they fled from the stack, and that a fight ensued, yet in fact, neither Luckey nor Root had shot Fa Force, or he would have been struck from the front; that La Force being shot in the back must have been shot unintentionally by one of his companions as they came from the house firing towards the stacks; it was a most ingenious defense, and it was so logically presented that Luckey was acquitted. He was subsequently convicted of participation in the Blackstone train robbery, in which case he could make no defense, and was sentenced to the penitentiary at Columbus, Ohio, for fifteen years.

RAPE OF THE CHILD WIFE

The Federal criminal court for the Western District of Arkansas, was given to examining into a greater variety of crimes than any court in history and before its bar were arraigned, from time to time, men from every state and territory. Next to murder, if not fully equal to it, the vilest and most vicious crime committed within the jurisdiction of this court was that of rape. While it is true that life was not safe, was not held sacred by the base wretches who constituted the roving class, whom Judge Parker styled "Criminal intruders," neither was a woman's honor; that which is, among honorable men, a strong armor of defense. Womanly modesty, was to them as nothing, and when urged by an unholy passion, they would invade the sanctity of a home, no matter how humble, and would violate a woman's virtue as ruthlessly as they were wont to tread underfoot the wild grasses of the prairies.

A sad and the same time most heinous and disgusting case on which I chanced to sit as juryman, was that of Ed Wilkey alias one Davis, who committed rape upon one Mrs. Lillian Arnett, a child-wife and mother of a babe only a month old. James Arnett and his wife were of the untutored and unsophisticated country folk, born and raised in Catoosa county, Georgia. On Christmas day, 1893, less than five months after the bride's fifteenth birthday, they were united in marriage, and a week later, in company with Mrs. Arnett's parents, removed to Pawpaw, in the Cherokee Nation, only a few miles from Fort Smith. On the twenty-fifth of May, 1895, the child-wife became a mother; a babe was born to brighten the little home and be company for its mother while the husband and father was away at work, earning a subsistence for the family. One day a month later, while she was yet in a weakened condition, the defendant, Wilkey, stopped in the road in front of the humble abode, and shouted for water. Mrs. Arnett started to comply with the request, intending to carry to him a cupful of water in order to keep him from entering, as she did not like his appearance, and, besides, her husband was a mile or more away at work for a neighbor, and she was therefore timid of strangers. While she was preparing to carry the water to the road, Wilkey climbed through the fence and approached the house, meeting Mrs. Arnett at the door. After quenching his thirst, Wilkey engaged the woman in conversation and learned that she was alone; it was now between eight and nine o'clock in the morning, and he discovered that the husband was not likely to return before noon, or after. Again he asked for a drink of water, and as she turned a second time to put away the cup he had drained, her baby, lying on one of the two beds the one room contained, awoke and commenced to cry; as she turned towards the little one, Wilkey entered silently, and catching her unawares, threw her upon the other bed and quickly accomplished his vicious purpose, after which he coolly and with unconcern, remarked:

"There, I haven't hurt you a bit' then picked up his coat and walked away. As Wilkey left the house Mrs. Arnett, who had grabbed up her babe, rushed frantically out of a back door and ran with all possible speed to the house of her nearest neighbor, about 400 yards distant, reaching there in such a frightened and exhausted condition that she was unable to utter a word for several minutes. When she could tell her story, the neighbor woman dispatched a little girl, the only available messenger, in quest of the young husband of the wronged woman. He came hastily, and organizing a small posse, at once set out in search of the rapist, aided by such description as Mrs. Arnett was able to give. The principal clue was the condition of his shoes, one of them being worn so badly that a toe protruded, making a track in the dust that was easily followed, and thus resulted in his capture. The husband was armed with a double barrel shotgun when he came up with the desperado, but he made no attempt to take the villain's life, each member of the party feeling sure that the Fort Smith court would mete justice. They arrested him within a mile of the bridge crossing the Arkansas river, and marched him to the Federal jail and swore to, a complaint.

Three months after the commission of the offense Wilkey was indicted by the grand jury and brought out to be arraigned and it was found that he was penniless and unable to employ counsel. It therefore became the duty of the court to appoint an attorney to defend him, and J. P. Mullen and J. Warren Reed were chosen to take charge of his case.

The trial came on; Wilkey had no witnesses in his behalf and it was left only for his attorneys to take advantage of whatever failures there were on the part of the government to make a case and of the technicalities of the law. Wilkey did not go on the stand as a witness in his own behalf. The government testimony was that of the woman charged to be raped, together with the testimony of the men who followed his tracks, plainly identified by the hole in the side of his shoe where his toe pressed upon the ground. The testimony seemed to be conclusive that he was the man, and the jury returned a verdict of guilty, September 25. On the ninth day of the following October he was brought out for sentence, and December nineteenth of the same year named as his execution day.

Mr. Reed took a writ of error to the Supreme Court, and while it was pending there he secured a commutation of imprisonment in place of the death sentence.

YOUR SIN WILL FIND YOU OUT

The case of Ed Alberty, alias Charles Burns, a negro, charged with killing Philip Duncan, in the Cherokee Nation, was an apt illustration of the inexorable tenacity, of the once famous Federal court at Fort Smith, and of the almost impossibility of a criminal escaping its talons, once they were outstretched for his capture. Alberty was born—just across the river from Fort Smith—a slave to a Cherokee Indian. His father's name was Burns, but the child, in line with a custom that prevailed, adopted the name of his master, retaining it even after emancipation had been declared. He subsequently married and settled at Fort Gibson, and at the time of the killing, for which he was convicted fifteen years later and sentenced to hang, he had become the father of three children, one a babe in arms. For a year he had not been living with his wife, directly; there had been disagreements between them, and his wife was working as a domestic in the family of a retired merchant, named Lipe. She had the babe with her. Alberty was at the same time in the employ of Lipe, as gardener and man of all work, but with his two older children he lived some distance away, at the home of Thomas Graves. He was twenty-seven years old, and was generally considered quiet and unoffensive. Duncan, the victim, was also born in slavery and was the illegitimate son of a Choctaw Indian and a negress, his slave. He removed to the Cherokee Nation when he was seventeen years old, and at the time of his death was twenty-five, and had been living with a cousin of Alberty as his common law wife. Duncan was a cross between the Indian and negro and was what was known in that locality as "a bad nigger." Several times he had threatened Alberty's life, for some fancied wrong, had at one time driven him and others from a barber shop at the point of a weapon and at another time had fired a bullet through a door of a house where Alberty was sleeping.

It is possible Duncan's persecution arose from a sense of guilt, for it was generally believed, in their circle of acquaintances, that illicit relations existed between him and Alberty's wife. This came to the ears of Alberty but, with the usual confidence of a husband, he refused to believe the tale. On the night of May 15, 1880, Alberty accompanied his wife to church and returned with her as far as the gate leading to Mr. Lipe's house, then went to his employer's horse pasture to make sure that the team, which he was to use early the next morning, was safe. Evidence was produced at the trial to prove that Duncan, who was also at church, was heard to make threats against Alberty's life after church was dismissed and that he said he was going that night to see" Mandy," Mrs. Alberty, and was advised to stay away.

When Alberty returned from the horse pasture, at the rear of the house, he happened to glance up at the window of the room occupied by his wife and saw it raise and then discovered the form of his wife standing by the opening. She could not see him for the semi-darkness and he, wondering why she had raised, the window and thinking sadly of the stories he had heard but never believed concerning her alleged unfaithfulness, walked along to the house and suddenly discovered Duncan standing at the foot of a ladder whose upper end rested against the roof of a porch overlooked by the open window above. Duncan was nonplussed, as he supposed Alberty had gone to his boarding place; but angered at the trap he had been caught in, he made a lunge at Alberty, who drew a pistol he was carrying for fear of Duncan, and who, while holding him at a distance, allowed himself to be backed by the end of the house and around to the front, where he aroused the family and sent for his wife. She came down and met her husband, who at once engaged in a scuffle with her, and crying, "Don't let him kill me," she at last broke from him and ran up the stairway. Then, angered and despondent at the perfidy of his wife and with a wholesome fear of Duncan, seeing the latter approach him again, with knife drawn for a blow, he fired and Duncan fell, mortally wounded. He died the next day.

Alberty at once fled. He went direct to Fort Scott, Kansas, where a sister resided, and after two days proceeded to Kansas City, Missouri, and secured a place as porter in the St. James Hotel. After six months, he took a similar place at the Pacific Hotel and continued there two years. Later, he worked at odd jobs around one of the large slaughter houses, for a while, and then went to Fort Leavenworth, Kansas, where he made a living as lackey for the military officers, staying there a year. At last, he went to St Louis, took up the name his father gave him, married and settled down to work, and when the new union depot was built, secured a position as porter at $45 a month, It is said that he was a faithful employe and good citizen. His wife died in 1893 and he continued to make St. Louis his home, and had succeeded in forgetting the one sad event of his life. On the day that Judge Parker passed through the union depot, enroute to Fort Smith, for the purpose of calling the grand jury together to indict Cherokee Bill for the murder of Lawrence Keating, he met Alberty and employed him to perform some slight errand; they conversed* neither of them aware of the other's identity until later, when Alberty was brought to trial at Fort Smith.

There was quite a romance connected with the man's going no farther away than St. Louis. There, near the Union Depot where any number of people from Fort Smith and the Indian Territory were passing almost daily, he lived for years under a changed name and as far as his real self was concerned, unknown and unnoticed. Think of a murder charge hanging over his head and he yet remaining in confidence at his pest! But it all ended one day when a returned prisoner from the penitentiary at Brooklyn recognized him, and on the following Sunday, August 4, 1895, Deputy Marshal George Lawson, with Henry Starr, the famous bandit, stepped from an incoming "Frisco" train. Starr, who had known the negro in the days before he had commenced to be a law breaker, identified Alberty and Lawson and Starr proceeded to the Four Courts and after a talk with Chief of Police Harrigan, the latter sent an officer to bring Alberty in. Again Starr identified the negro, and with the usual style so long employed by the St. Louis police force, he was placed in the "holdover," and held four days, then turned loose. Lawson at once wired his chief, at Fort Smith* announcement of the capture and on receipt of a warrant, the following Sunday, Alberty, who had not attempted to escape, was again arrested and returned to Fort Smith.

Many changes had gone on during his absence; when he first arrived at the jail he strongly denied his identity, but even in the jail there were old friends who recognized him, to his intense disgust. He had to own up finally, but it was with much reluctance. Three days after his arrival there called at the jail to see him a hearty looking young negro woman. Ed looked at her and of course did not have the lea-t idea who she might be. At last she introduced herself. I am your daughter. "Indeed," thought Ed. When he left home she was a small child, yet now she was a grown young woman and was married. It was an Ethiopian Enoch Arden tale. Ed began to inquire about the girl's mother, his wife. Here the story of Enoch Arden comes in once again. The wife mourned him awhile, and there came a Phillip on the fit Id, and she, thinking Ed would never come, married the dusky Phillip.

"Well, well," said Alberty, "Here I am after so many years to find my child grown out of my recollection and married; my wife is now another man's wife and the only thing remaining the same, through changes of friends and enemies, is that *old charge of murder*." On the twenty-sixth day of August, he was arraigned on the old indictment; he pleaded not guilty as charged, his case was continued to the November term of court and set down for trial, November 12. His attorneys were Barnes & Mellette. The trial commenced on the thirteenth, lasted two days, the jury returning a verdict of guilty of murder. A motion for a new trial was filed and overruled, and on the fourth day of December, Alberty was taken before the court for final sentence, the twenty-ninth day of January, 1896, being named as the day he should tread the fatal plank. A writ of error in his case was taken to the Supreme Court of the United States and a new trial was granted, which did not take place until more than a year later. In the meantime Alberty grew restless; fearing that he might be again convicted of murder he concluded to employ an additional attorney. Having lain in jail so long he had gained a thorough knowledge of all the attorneys practicing before the Fort Smith court, and as a choice he selected J. Warren Reed, (who was just then fresh from several victories gained by hard fought battles) who should be his Moses and carry him through to the promised land of liberty.

Mr. Reed investigated the case thoroughly; went to Fort Gibson to the scene of the killing, examined the premises and made a plat of the house and yard. He developed other facts and evidence in his behalf, and returned to Fort Smith, and with Alberty's former attorneys, proceeded to a trial which lasted several days. It was a close case, ably defended, and resulted in a victory for the defense, and the acquittal of Alberty. A short time later he returned to St. Louis for permanent residence.

WEBBER ISAACS AND THE PEARCE BROTHERS

Webber Isaacs, a Cherokee Indian, was executed April 30, 1896, for the murder of Mike P. Cushing, a white man.

He was indicted on four counts, two charging him with the murder of Cushing and two naming the victim as an unknown white man. He was convicted February 11, 1895, and sentenced April 15 to be hanged on June 25, following. No witnesses testified to having seen the murder committed, but the uncontroverted evidence of several witnesses showed that a peddler, about sixty years old, with gray whiskers, riding a gray pony, was seen going in the direction of Isaacs' house, and that several days thereafter, within a mile of the house and some distance from the highway, the dead body of a gray horse, like the one the peddler rode, was found, its appearance indicating that it had died from gunshot wounds; near the horse were the remains of a man, the clothing and flesh from which had been almost entirely consumed by fire. A trail on the ground indicated that the body had been dragged from where the horse lay to where it was found, by means of the bridle rein, which had been cut from the horse and tied about the victim's feet. Several witnesses swore that the burned body was that of the gray whiskered peddlar. Under the chin, unconsumed by fire, was a tuft of gray whiskers, and near the body were found bills and letters bearing the signature of Mike P. Cushing. The head was mashed to a jelly and under the arms were large holes, presumably made by a shotgun. There were two theories about the burning: one was that the wadding of the gun ignited the victim's clothing causing the fire by which the body was so terribly burned, the other that it was saturated with coal oil and set on fire to remove chances of identification.

Soon after the body was found, Webber Isaacs was seen to be in possession of an unusual amount of money. Isaacs admitted on the stand that the peddler was at his house on the day that the peddler above referred to was last seen alive, but claimed that he rode away with one Jack Chewey, who told him the next day that he had killed the peddler. He had never, he said, asked Chewey any questions about the killing nor told any one of Chewey's confession. Five reliable witnesses testified that Isaacs told them he and Chewey had killed a white peddler at a time corresponding to that of the unknown peddler's disappearance, and the jury, regarding Isaccs' defense untenable, found him guilty of the murder of Cushing. June 25, 1895, was set for Isaacs' execution, and he would have been a companion on the gallows of Cherokee Bill had it not been for a stay of execution in both cases to await the action of the court of appeals. But the avenging of the death of the poor old peddler, who was mercilessly slain and left as carrion on the plains, was not to be delayed for long. The evidence was so plain that the higher court refused to interfere; the decision of Judge Parker's court was quickly affirmed; Isaacs was therefore re-sentenced and was executed on the last day of April, 1896.

TWO BROTHERS HANGED

John and George Pearce were executed April 30, 1896, at the same moment that Webber Isaacs met his fate, for killing William Vandever, with whom they had played as brothers, in their childhood days.

The young men were reared in Texas county, Missouri, and were from respectable families. On the twenty-first day of November, 1894, they left their homes for the purpose of seeking employment in the Indian Territory. John Pearce, the elder brother, twenty-nine years old, owned a span of mules and a wagon; his brother, George, ten years younger, had nothing except the clothing he wore, and William Vandever had a mare and a colt. Together the two, with the property named, set out on that November morning bound for the Indian country. At Spring River, eight miles within the Cherokee Nation, they stopped at a lumber mill and worked for a few weeks, then drove to within a few miles of Coffeyville, Kansas, and from there the two brothers, leading Vandever's mare and colt hitched to their wagon, veered off and drove in the direction of Tahlequah. Two weeks later they were overhauled by deputy marshals while camped by the roadside near Tahlequah, as they were preparing to retire for the night, and were taken to Wagoner and subsequently to Fort Smith for trial. On the stand both testified that Vandever, who was never seen again alive, left them in an excited state of mind while they were at the point nearest to Coffeyville and said he was going to Texas by rail and, possibly, to California. They explained his hurried departure by a statement to the effect that he had, for fun, shot a dog belonging to a mover, as he was camped alongside the road, and that the owner of the dog became very angry and threatened to have him arrested. They said he gave them ten dollars to care for his mare and colt and return them to his family in Missouri. A pair of boots and a suit belonging to Vandever were found in their possession, but they declared they found the boots on the prairie, that they were never Vandever's property, and that the suit was given to them by the fleeing man, who was so frightened over the mere threat of arrest for killing a dog that he desired to be free of all luggage. After being arrested, they were taken back over the route they had come and shown the dead body of a man, identified as that of Vandever. They both denied the identity and said the corpse was that of a man they had never seen. At the trial they spoke of a stranger, named Voschel, who they claimed was at their camping place two weeks before the arrest, on the very night that Vandever was claimed to have started for Coffeyville, intending to catch a train for Texas, and the defense attempted to show that this man Voschel was the murderer of

Vandever, who was, as claimed by the prisoners, not dead. It was proven that the Pearce brothers left their camp very early in the morning, without waiting to cook breakfast.

They were arrested January 15, 1895, by Deputies Charles Lamb, Bob Clark and Ed Reed. They were convicted March I and sentenced to die. A long delay was occasioned by their attorney, J. C. Rogers, taking an appeal to the Supreme Court, and for over a year they were inmates of the Federal jail, awaiting their fate, which finally overtook them, as stated, April 30, 1896.

There were many of us who believed that John Pearce need not have suffered the full penalty had he testified to all that he knew concerning the killing, as many incidents of the trial seemed to indicate that the killing was done by the younger brother to secure the mare and colt and that the elder swore falsely to save him.

THE FAMOUS GRAND JURY CHARGE

On the fifth day of August, 1895, Judge Parker delivered what was considered by the Fort Smith bar and by himself, the most notable grand jury charge ever delivered by him, the masterpiece of his life in this class of charges. It is here given in full and will be found replete with law points and of value to every attorney in the land. It was this grand jury which had to examine the case of Crawford Goldsby, charged with killing one of the jail guards, and there were numerous other cases, a large variety of crimes to investigate, making the task imposed upon this particular grand jury the hardest in the history of the court. Judge Parker said:

"Gentlemen of the Grand Jury, before proceeding with your deliberations, I desire to address to you a few remarks by way of a reminder of what your duties are under the law. That reminder has already been given to you in the shape of your oath, which is an epitome of the great duties that devolve upon you as the accusing power of the government, in this district, for this term of court, but it is sometimes considered to be more impressive, and we are more apt to understand our duties, when we can converse for a brief time about them, and when we understand them properly we are apt to perform them better than we would if we did not fully comprehend the great responsibilities resting upon us.

"I never open a term of court that I am not impressed again and again with the greatness of this government of ours. Its greatness consists in the fact that all of its power is in the hands of those who are to be benefitted or injured by the execution or the neglect to execute that great power—in the hands of the people themselves. There is not a step taken in the execution of these laws enacted by this government that is not taken by the people. In the first place, the laws are made by their agents. They are made for their protection, to secure their rights, and when they do not bring to them that protection, and do not secure to them these rights, they are bad laws, they are vicious laws. Every good citizen comprehends this fact. No good citizen should ever let his partisan opinions or his political views, no matter what party he belongs to, run so high as to forget the great truth of the principle as to what his duty may be as to the government of his country, and its laws. Now, what I have said is based upon the fact that laws are worthless to protect the rights of the people unless they are executed. Society cannot live without the execution of the law. It cannot live, it cannot exist, it degenerates into anarchy, into riot, into bloodshed, and into that condition which brings about destruction of all order, and of all peace, unless these rules of government called the law are executed promptly and vigorously; the protection of every right that belongs to the citizen. The laws of the United States cannot be executed in this district until you as a grand jury first act in the premises. You occupy such a position as that the government through its officer comes to you and says: 'I present this man, or that, or the other, and charge him with a crime.' The government is the charging power. The government brings the case before you. Before any action can be taken to ascertain finally the guilt or innocence of a man you must first accuse him in a lawful way by an indictment. That is to say, you must pass upon his case, and see it by the light of the evidence that the government offers to you, because the government says to you, 'I charge this man with crime, and here is the evidence supporting that charge.' That evidence is presented to you through the district attorney, or someone of his assistants, and you pass upon the question primarily as to whether he shall be called upon in a court of justice to have the question determined as to whether he is guilty or innocent.

"We have but to cite this fact to show the great responsibilities that rest upon you, to show you the importance of the position you assume or that is cast upon you, when you are chosen from the body of the people and brought into this court, placed under the sanction of an oath to perform this great duty, to perform it thoroughly, to perform it well, to perform it so that the rights of the citizen which are protected by these laws are really made secure by the proper enforcement of them. That is why you are brought here. It is a principle of law, arising under the Constitution of the United States, that if man is the accused of a capital, or otherwise infamous offense, he cannot be tried for it, no matter how guiltily he may be, no matter how injurious to the community it may be not to try him, unless he is first indicted by a grand jury. That is a matter that is enacted by the law as a safeguard to the liberty of the citizen who may be improperly accused, who might be wrongfully accused, who might be accused in an *exparte* way, but the presumption is that if the grand jury investigates his case, and they find facts showing, first, that a crime has been committed, and secondly, that the man accused committed it, then there exists a condition of things that demands the intervention of a petit jury to pass upon that case, and he is accordingly indicted. The grand jury system, in my judgment, is one of the guarantees thrown around the liberty of the citizen, in this country. At the same time it is a method by which it is made easier to determine the guilt or innocence of the party accused when he is put upon trial in a court before a petit jury, because the evidence is sifted out, the facts in some degree are ascertained, and it becomes easier to find out whether he is guilty or innocent than if an indictment was not had, but he was simply tried upon information. When there is an investigation of that kind, the facts are better developed than they would necessarily be if there was no investigation.

"The duties of this grand jury are much more onerous than those of a Federal grand jury usually are. Most Federal courts only deal with cases directly affecting their government, but here we have nearly all the Indian Territory attached to this jurisdiction, and the laws of the United States are extended over it, to protect that country which for years has been cursed with criminal refugees. They committed some crime back at their homes and fled from justice, taking refuge in the land of the Indians, where, by their acts and their influence over the young men, they have made a hot-bed of crime. The government, in its treaties with the Indians, obligated itself to keep all these characters out, to remove them as fast as they moved in, but that promise has never been kept except insofar as the court having jurisdiction over that country has brought these criminals out to punish them. For years this court stood alone in the work but of late years the jurisdiction has been divided, and now other courts are exercising the same wholesome influence.

"Taken as a whole, the juries have done their duties fairly, honestly and impartially, though some grave mistakes have been made and the cause of justice scandalized. By finding a verdict of guilty where guilt exists, you are doing your duty, and also are teaching one of the greatest object lessons. Judging from the vast volume of crime, which has almost submerged us in a sea of blood, we have gone astray, and are almost at the mercy of the man of crime. The greatest question of the hour is, can we properly inforce the law? Crime is gaining strength, especially those crimes affecting human life. This is not caused entirely by the failure of the people to enforce the laws. There are other causes and sources. One of our leading newspapers in commenting upon the trial of Dr. Buchanan, printed an editorial under the head of 'The Laxity of the Law.' The article went on to say that technical pleas of cunning lawyers often defeat justice; that the appellate courts consider alleged flaws and encourage a system of practice of the law entirely in favor of the criminal and against the cause of right; that they never look to the merits of the case, but seem to be co-operating with the unscrupulous attorneys whose object is to circumvent the law. This is as true as the words of Holy Writ. However honest and fair the trial court may be, it is impossible to bring assassins to merited punishment when appellate courts allow the cases to linger along, and give these murderers an opportunity to take other innocent life in cold blood.

"Now, you will understand that you organize as an accusing body. You are organized now as such body, with a foreman to preside over your deliberations—with a foreman as your presiding officer, and who presides over you during these deliberations as he would over any other deliberative body. He puts all questions to a vote that come before you, he determines whether the proposition accusing the man of crime has received the requisite number of votes to authorize the findings of a true bill against a party. He may determine this by counting the votes. He may determine it by calling the roll when there is any question of doubt about it. He has the power, under the law, to swear witnesses, to administer an oath to a witness that is as binding upon the witness as though it was administered by the judge of this court, or by the clerk of the court. He leads in the examination of the witnesses, though any gentleman on the jury has a right to ask a witness questions, with his consent. You will bear in mind that the law prescribes the number of votes that shall be cast in favor of indicting a man before you are authorized to return a true bill against him. The law says that at least twelve of your number shall concur in voting the man guilty of the crime charged before an indictment can be returned. You will understand that it takes sixteen of your number to constitute a working quorum. You cannot transact any business unless there are sixteen members of the grand jury present. Now, in this connection, I remark that it is highly important that the whole body should be promptly present at every meeting after recess or adjournment, because you are all interested, of course, in the investigation of these cases. You all want to understand them, and you all want to perform your duties, and prompt attendance is the way to accomplish that, and if this rule is observed strictly it becomes a fact that you are all present, and there could never be any question raised about the quorum.

"You will bear in mind that there is a veil of secrecy thrown around your proceedings. There was a much greater necessity for that in the beginning of the grand jury system than there is now, though at times now the rule is necessary in order to secure the independence of the grand jury in their action. The language of your oath is that you are to pass upon these cases without fear, favor or affection; you are not to be controlled by any outside influence; you are not to be controlled by any outside opinion; in fact, you have no right to talk to anybody outside the grand jury room about cases, unless it may be the judge of the court or the district attorney, or someone of the assistants of the district attorney. The matter of passing upon the guilt or innocence of a man is to be determined by you just as it is to be determined by the petit jury, by the law bearing upon the question of which you will be advised by the district attorney or someone of his assistants, and by the evidence that is offered upon that case, and by these, and these alone, are you to be governed. Therefore, you are not to make known what proceedings are transpiring in the grand jury room to anybody on the outside; you are not to inform anyone what you are doing there, whether you have indicted anybody for a crime, or whether anybody has been charged, before you, with a crime. Nor are you permitted to make known how any member of your body votes upon a proposition, or what opinions he expresses upon questions that may be pending before you. Nor are you permitted to make known the testimony of any witness before you, unless you are called upon in a court of justice to make known that evidence and the character of it. You may be called upon, for instance, in a case of perjury, where a party is accused of perjury before you, or in a case where it becomes necessary to impeach the testimony of a witness by proving contradictory statements made before you different from those made in court, and in such cases you may be called upon legally as a witness to disclose the testimony of the witness, but outside of this exception you are to keep that matter a profound secret so that witnesses may act independently. It sometimes is the case—very often is the case—that witnesses are afraid to go before the grand jury and tell the truth if that evidence is to go out before the party is arrested, or the party or his friends might be informed of it, and the witness might, perhaps, be assassinated, or interfered with, or run out of the country. You see there is wisdom in all these rules. Now, of course, this rule I have given you, requiring you to keep these matters a profound secret, is a rule, when properly observed, which secures the administration of justice in the proper way. At the same time it may be taken advantage of unduly—not apt to be, here, because we have safeguards against that, but still you are to see to it that men do not come into the grand jury room and take advantage of this rule of secrecy by falsely accusing other men of crime. We have rules, I say, that prevent that as far as possible. For instance, a party who desires to make complaint, if the case has not been examined by a commissioner, and he has not already given his evidence, is required to go to the district attorney and make his complaint to him, and then the district attorney passes his judgment upon the question as to whether the man is telling the truth or not. If, in the judgment of the district attorney, the man is telling the truth, he is sent to the grand jury. If he is not, if it is a fictitious charge, if it is something that is invented for the purpose of venting spleen or malice or hatred or ill-will against an innocent citizen, the district attorney is apt to detect that, and, consequently, you are not liable to be imposed upon. You are not troubled much by false witnesses, who seek the privacy of your chamber, and who become false accusers. Sometimes men go there who may be mistaken as to whether an act is a crime or not. They may be mistaken as to the identity of the man committing that crime, and they may be mistaken honestly, but it does not often happen. It sometimes occurs, though, that witnesses appear before the grand jury for the purpose of committing downright and deliberate perjury. The perjury is more apt to be committed where the motive is greater. The motive upon the pert of the government does not exist to have a man falsely convicted. There is nobody who represents the government who wants a man falsely accused or falsely convicted. It generally occurs that the perjury is upon the other side, where the motive is strongest, where a man is in danger of conviction, where he is likely to pay the forfeit with his life or lose his liberty. The inducement is greater there to invoke this terrible agency of crime, called perjury, which is so often resorted to in this age, than it is upon the part of the government, whose duty it is to see to it that the innocent are protected as well as the guilty punished. No-one connected with the court, or with the government, has any interest in that direction, much less have they any desire of that kind; but. they have a desire to uncover perjury, to uncover falsehood, and bring to justice false accusers or false witnesses, whenever they can be found, whether they are upon the side of the government or against it.

"Now, there is another remark I desire to address to you in regard to the character of evidence you are required to act upon in the grand jury room. You cannot indict a man upon affidavits, or upon *exparte* statements that come to you second hand. The general rule is that the witness whose testimony is relied upon must be produced before you. He is to be sworn by the foreman, and you proceed then to examine him. You judge of his credibility, and you use exactly the same means that a petit jury may use for that purpose. You look at the very way he gives his evidence, the very consistency, and reasonableness and probability of the story as he gives it, his very manner of testifying. All of these things are passed upon by you. That is the benefit of having the living witness before you. You can see the manner of evidence he is giving sometimes from the way he gives it. There are exceptions, however, to this rule from necessity, and in the interest of public justice. If a witness has once appeared before a man accused of crime in an examining court, for example, and has there given his evidence, and he subsequently dies, that evidence from necessity, and in order that justice may not be defeated, may be relied upon by you, and it may be produced before you properly, more properly by the officer who heard the evidence. He can go before you, or anybody else who heard it, may go before you and reproduce it, and tell you what that evidence was, and you may act upon it just the same as though that witness had stood before you and given that testimony; or, if may be shown from the notes of the officer who takes it down, the Commissioner. That is one exception to the rule. The other is, where a witness is permanently sick, and he has given his evidence before an examining court, and his sickness is of that permanent nature that it is hardly probable or reasonable to believe that he will ever recover; his testimony then, I say, maybe reproduced in the way I have indicated the same as though he were dead. In that sort of case, before evidence can be used, it ought to be shown that the sickness of the witness is not merely temporary, but is of that permanent and serious character as to disable the party for all time so he would not be able to come, and that in all reason and probability he would die before he could be produced before you. Another exception to the rule is where a witness is improperly used by a party accused of crime, or somebody in his interest, where he is induced to leave the district by corrupt means used upon him in the shape of bribery, or by threats or violence, or intimidation, he is induced to absent himself from the district, or to so hide himself away as that the officer cannot serve a subpoena upon him. In a case of that kind, if he has once given his evidence before the commissioner, that testimony may be reproduced before you, and you may act upon it just the same as though the witness were dead. Now, these are exceptions to the rule, but with these exceptions you are required to have the presence of the witness before you, and you are to so examine them as to satisfy yourself, first, of their telling the truth, an then, of course, you are to pass upon the proving power of the story given by them as witnesses to see whether the testimony of any one witness alone, or in conjunction with other testimony, is sufficient to lead you to the belief, first, that a crime has been committed, and, secondly, that the party or parties accused, is the one, or are the ones, who committed it. If the two propositions are then established, your duty calls upon you to say so by presenting your conclusion from that evidence in the character of the charge drawn up by the district attorney's office, and presented' by you in the shape of an indictment, signed by Mr. Brooks, as your foreman, and returned into court by you as a body-headed by your foreman. That completes your duty as to that case. That case is then in a condition where the court can dispose of it in the way prescribed by law.

"Now, it is your duty to pass upon all violations of the-laws of the United States where those violations are alleged to have occurred in this district. These violations may be classified. There are violations of laws which affect the operations of the Treasury Department of the United States, for instance. If a party counterfeits the money of the United States, or such counterfeit is found in the possession of a party with guilty knowledge and for fraudulent purpose, that becomes a crime against the operation of the government. This is a matter that you are to look to carefully, because the circulating money of' the country which passes into the pockets of the people, and-which they receive in exchange for the products of their toil, is required by the law to be kept entirely pure. You cannot keep it pure unless this law against counterfeiting, or passing counterfeit money, and having it in possession for fraudulent purposes, is rigidly enforced. There are always enough bad men who are disposed to violate the law if they can make gain of it, if they can benefit themselves by it, and the only thing that restrains them is the fear of punishment; it is the fear of capture, the certainty of conviction, and the certainty of punishment following that conviction that restrains them. The treasury department is, therefore, one of the departments of the government that must be protected by you, and by the petit jury, in all cases where you and it are called upon to enforce the law.

"Then there is the postal department, one of the great agencies of the government, which is of the highest character because of its great importance to the people of the United States' everywhere, so important and so much of a necessity, that we would rather do without one of our meals than to miss our mail one time. We become so anxious about it and so used to it, that it is one of those agencies we depend upon to such an extent that we cannot do without it. And if you wanted to produce a revolution in this country, if you wanted to upset things generally, I think you could do it quicker by suspending the mails of the United States for six months or a year than by any other means. This agency is a matter of great benefit to the people. They enabled by it to transmit valuables and letters to one another; to transmit letters containing matters that are private between relatives and friends; to transmit packages and things of that character. And they now transmit them as a rule by depositing them in the office with the belief in their minds that they will as certainly arrive at their destination as that they deposit them. Somebody has said, somewhere, that the postal laws of the government, from the way they are executed, make this mail matter just as secure as though each letter was surrounded by a battalion of cavalry to convey it to its destination. And that is true. You take that great system and consider the millions and hundreds of millions in money that is transmitted through it by the people of the United States from one to another, and the millions of letters, and the thousands and hundreds of thousands of papers and magazines that pass throughout the country by the means of this great agency, and all with entire safety, and there is the greatest lesson in it in favor of the administration and enforcement of the law that can be taught anywhere. It is an object lesson that teaches us what the security of the law means; it teaches us how secure all the rights of men can be made if we look to the proper enforcement of the law. What do I mean by that? This branch of the government is better protected by the agency of the postal department, intended to discover, arrest and bring to justice all violators of this law than any other department in it. It is a fact that may be asserted with truth with reference to this department that a robber or an embezzler, or a man who would open a letter wrongfully, or a man who would commit the larceny of a letter or of its contents, has not any possibility of escape, as a rule. Its agents follow him to the uttermost ends of the earth; they arrest him and he is brought to justice before the juries of the country through the means of this great agency of the government. The consequence is that it has this security. How much better would the condition of the country be in, how much happier would the people be, if we could only assert this fact with reference to that which is the most sacred thing possessed by any citizen—his life? If the same measure of security, if the same degree of protection, if the same enforcement of the law to protect human life, existed in this country as it does with reference to this department of the government, this tide of bloodshed that is now deluging this land, would, in a measure, disappear and human life would have at least the highest possible degree of security thrown around it that could be thrown around it by the power of the law. I say there is an object lesson to be found in the way that the law is enforced as affecting the postal department of the government.

I ask you to continue to teach that object lesson in this jurisdiction by indicting every man who violates the postal laws in any way. There is another branch of the postal department I desire to call your attention to especially. While it is important to protect the property of the citizen, his money in the letter, or his secret in the letter transmitted to his friend, or the transmission of these confidential family matters that exist, and with which the public have no business, it is equally as important to protect the morals of the young of this country against the vicious and vile acts of men who would use the mails as a conduit for corruption, for villainy and vice and crime of that character. The law therefore says that the mails cannot be used for the transmission of anything that vitiates the morals, or has that tendency. And this is one of the best laws ever enacted by the congress of the United States in the interest of good morals. All those who violate this law in the interest of licentiousness, vice and crime are guilty, and should be punished. He who makes a threat in an open manner upon a postal card so that it would have a deleterious influence upon the party to whom it is sent, is subject to punishment. The mails paid for by the people are not to be used as a conduit for crime, for the perpetration of crimes, or for the production of bad morals, vice and licentiousness. And I ask you especially if any cases of that kind are discovered by you to indict the parties who may be guilty of having used the mails in this unlawful way.

"There is another department of the government, of which I remind you especially, and it is connected with, and grows out of, this department I have called your attention to already, the treasury department. This treasury has to be supplied with funds, with money, and it is necessary that the agencies used to do that should be protected by the courts and juries of the country. There is one system of collecting revenue, growing out of a direct tax on products produced in the country, known as liquors, such as whiskey, brandy, distilled or fermented liquors, etc., and the law is of that character that unless a man complies with these provisions he is guilty of a crime. If he runs an illicit distillery without complying with the many regulations prescribed by the statutes, he is guilty of crime; he is running what is called a "moonshine" or illicit distillery, and he is subject to punishment. If he carries on the business of a wholesale liquor dealer, without having first paid the tax required by the law, he is guilty of crime. If he sells malt or fermented liquors, without having paid the tax, he is guilty of crime. Or if he carries on a retail liquor business, without having first paid the tax, he is guilty of crime. It is highly important that this law should be enforced, for the reason if it is not enforced the government will get but little revenue from that source, and if the government is to recognize this traffic at all, the law should be so administered as to fall equally upon all, and that the man who honestly pays the tax and complies with all the requirements of the law should not be put to a disadvantage, compared with the man who disregards the law and pays no tax. If you do not enforce it, even against the smallest violators, the consequence is that, in a small way, it is evaded, and the traffic is wholly carried on in that way, For instance, you take the business of carrying on a retail liquor dealer's traffic: the law says that if a man sells or offers for sale any foreign or domestic spirits in quantities less than five wine gallons at one time, he is carrying on the business of a retail liquor dealer. He is required by the law to pay twenty-five dollars tax per year, and if he does not pay that tax, the act of entering the business becomes a crime. The law is very comprehensive. It says: 'whoever sells or offers for sale this liquor in any quantity.' A man can go out here with a pint cup and he can sell, or offer to sell, a drink of whiskey, and if he does he is carrying on the business of a retail liquor dealer. It looks like a trivial thing upon the face of it, but when we look at the consequences arising from it if the law is not enforced, it becomes a serious matter. If the business could be carried on in that way, without paying any tax, of course that is the way it would be carried on. Nobody would put himself in a position where he could be caught up readily by the officers, but he would peddle it around and sell it to single individuals in small quantities. The law is made comprehensive for the purpose of saying to all men: 'if you sell it or offer it for sale in any quantity less than five wine gallons, you must pay the tax. If you sell it in quantities more than that, you are a wholesale dealer, and you must pay the tax.'

"Now, these are the principal departments of the government that may be affected by these violations of the law, that may come before you, and I ask you to see to it that every department of the government, that is effected by these violations of the law, is sustained. You are emphatically and truly upon the side of the government when you come into a court of justice, not to use that government for the purpose of wrongdoing, but to see that these laws are sustained, and the same thing is true with reference to the petit jury—to see to it that no guilty man escapes and that no innocent man is wrongfully accused or punished.

A UNIQUE JURISDICTION

"Now, there are other matters that will come before you because of the peculiar jurisdiction of this court. What I have heretofore stated has been stated with reference, more especially, to the established jurisdiction of Federal courts, but in this jurisdiction up to this time, and as it will remain for some time in the future, there is an increased jurisdiction belonging to this tribunal; and this being so, there is cast upon you additional responsibilities. For instance, there comes before you for investigation cases growing out of the taking of human life, or of attempts upon hum in life in the shape of assaults with intent to kill, and cases growing out of acts affecting the property rights of citizens. And there are cases to be brought before you which grow out of violations of what is called the intercourse law—the law that regulates the intercourse between the people of the United States and the Indian tribes or nations that are rightfully in the Indian country. This does not exist as a part of the jurisdiction of the United States courts generally. Now, in coming to that part of the jurisdiction belonging to us because of this traffic that is carried on in liquor in the Indian country, we approach a subject that is of the gravest importance to the welfare and peace of that country; and while it is impossible to make that country a prohibitory one, we can: largely suppress, if we do our duty this traffic in liquors there, or the taking of them into that country. Of late years there has been much legislation upon that subject. The law as it existed originally is found in that section of the statute which has stood as the law of that country for a great many years. That section is 2139 of the Revised Statutes of the United States, which provided:

"No ardent spirits shall be introduced under any pretense into the Indian country. Every person, who sells, exchanges, gives, barters, or disposes of any spirituous liquors or wine to any Indian under the charge of any Indian superintendent or agent, or introduces or attempts to introduce any spirituous liquor or wine into the Indian country, shall be punishable by imprisonment for not more than two years, and a fine of not more than $300.

"That is the law as it has stood ever since Indian reservations were set apart by the laws of the United States. That act was repealed by the act of July 23, 1892, upon the subject of the introduction of liquors of an intoxicating nature. The very gravamen* of these-statutes is that liquor is prohibited, and liquor of any kind that will intoxicate, or that is spirituous in its nature, is not to be introduced. By the act of July 23, 1892, it was provided:

"Every person who sells, exchanges, gives, barters, or disposes of any ardent spirits, ale, beer, wine, or intoxicating liquors of any kind to any Indian under charge of any Indian superintendent or agent, or introduces or attempts to introduce any ardent spirits, ale, beer, wine, or intoxicating liquor of any kind into the Indian country, shall be punished by imprisonment for not more than two years, and by a fine of not more than $300 for each offense.

"That stood as the law repealing the old statute until the last legislation upon the subject, which was upon the first of March, 1895, by an act entitled 'an act to provide for the appointment of additional judges of the United States court in the Indian Territory,' and for other purposes. I note these different stages of legislation upon this subject because I am coming to the proposition as to whether or not this court has jurisdiction of violations of this law at this time. Section 8 of the act of March 1, 1895, provides:

'That any person, whether an Indian or otherwise, who shall, in said Territory, manufacture, sell, give away, or in any manner or by any means, furnish to anyone, either for himself or for another, any vinous, malt or fermented liquors, or any other intoxicating drinks of any kind whatsoever, whether medicated or not, or who shall

293

carry, or in any manner have carried, into said Territory, any liquors or drinks, or who shall be interested in such manufacture, sale, giving away, furnishing to anyone or carrying into said Territory, any of such liquors or drinks, shall, upon conviction thereof, be punished by fine not exceeding five hundred dollars and by imprisonment for not less than one month nor more than five years.'

"This section of the act of March 1, 1895, as this court construes it, as far as such law has reference to acts done in the Indian country, works a repeal of the law passed upon the twenty-third of July, 1892. It takes up the whole subject. It legislates fully upon it. It changes the penalty. It embraces, as I have said, the whole subject embraced in the other statutes, and more, too. It is more comprehensive, because it makes it an offense to manufacture in the Territory, or to sell, or to give it away to anyone, or in any manner or by any means furnish to anyone, whether he be an Indian or not, either for himself or for another, any vinous, malt or fermented liquors, or any other intoxicating drinks of any kind whatsoever, whether medicated or not, and it prohibits the carrying in, or in any manner having carried into said Territory, any such liquors or drinks. It prohibits parties from being interested in such manufacture and sale or giving away or carrying into the Territory. As I say, it embraces the whole subject embraced in the other statutes, comprehends even more, and it changes the penalty. It is, therefore, new legislation, inconsistent with the other statutes, and they both cannot stand together. That being true, by the rules of law declaring that when one statute repeals an older one, as asserted by the following authorities, the statute of March 1, 1895, manifestly being intended as a substitute for the act of July 23, 1892, repeals the same. In King vs. Cornell, 106 United States, 396, the Supreme Court said:

'While repeals by implication are not favored, it is well settled that where two acts are not in all respects repugnant, if the later act covers the whole subject of the earlier, and embraces new provisions which plainly shows it was intended as a substitute for the first, it will operate as a repeal. United States vs. Tynen, 11 Wall., 88; Redrock vs. Henry, 106 U. S., 596; Wood vs. United States, 16 Peters, 342, and Murdock vs. City of Memphis, 12 Wall, 590, fully sustain the principle asserted in King vs. Cornell.'

"Under the subsequent provisions of the statute defining the jurisdiction of the courts in the Indian Territory, which say that the United States courts in the Indian Territory shall have exclusive original jurisdiction of all offenses committed in said Territory, of which the United States court in the Indian Territory now has jurisdiction, if they had jurisdiction of this offense, as prescribed by this statute, they would have, under this legislation, exclusive jurisdiction of it, and this court would have nothing to do with it; but they could not have had jurisdiction of this offense as created by this statute—*it being a new offense and punished in a different way*—they could not have had jurisdiction of this offense at the time the act passed, when there was no act in existence providing for the offense as it is prescribed here, and the manner of committing it, and the punishment as prescribed by this statute. Therefore, they did not have jurisdiction of this offense as prescribed by Section 8, and consequently they do not have jurisdiction now, but this court has jurisdiction of it, and will continue to have jurisdiction under the provisions of this statute until the first day of September, 1896. Therefore, I say to you, that as to all offenses committed, which are prescribed as offenses by that section, growing out of the manufacture in the Territory, or of the selling, the giving away, or in any manner or by any means furnishing to anyone, either for himself or another, any vinous, malt or fermented liquors, or any other intoxicating drinks of any kind whatsoever, whether medicated or not, or who shall carry or have carried into such Territory any such liquors or drinks, if any of these things are proven before you, your duty is to indict the party. There has never been a Congress yet, except one, where there was an exception made, and that was by a legislative trick, where any of the provisions in any of these laws that I have read were not regarded of the highest importance. They were enacted, in the first place, upon the petition of Indian settlers of that country who looked upon the traffic in intoxicating liquors as a method adopted by vicious, vile and evil-disposed white men to destroy their people and take advantage of their condition and their tribal weakness.

And this destruction has been brought about in many instances until whole nations have been wiped from the face of the earth by means of liquor carried to them by white men, who were desirous of using them in that way in order that they might get some advantage of them. It is your duty, and I know you will perform it, to see to it, as the people of this goodly state have seen to it for over fifty years, that this provision of the law is enforced.

"You will understand that upon the organization of this Indian country, the power to uphold the laws of the United States over that country was put into the hands of the good people of the State of Arkansas, and it has remained there for fifty years and over—ever since 1834. The law at first provided that the court of the United States for the Territory of Arkansas, sitting at Little Rock, was to enforce the laws of the United States over the Indian country. Subsequently, after the territory had been admitted to statehood, when there was a division of the State into two districts and a court was established at Van Buren, the same law prevailed, and the same people of this State were the jurors in whose hands was placed by that law the power to protect these people of that nation, to use all the power that belonged to them to protect them in all the rights which they possessed.

JUDGE PARKER, THE CHAMPION OF HIS COURT

"Again, in 1871, when the court was removed from Van Buren to this place, the same power of protecting them remained in the hands of the people of Arkansas. And I want to say that for twenty years, just about now, since the opening of the first court here, as a rule these people have performed that duty faithfully and well. Why a distrust has been entertained of them, or why the jurisdiction was changed, I am not prepared to say, nor is it material that anything should be said upon the subject. All I have to say upon that subject is that the jurisdiction yet remains, it still is in your hands, and as long as it does remain I ask you to vindicate the character established by the people of this State for enforcing the law in that country. Much has been said in that regard. Much has been falsely asserted in regard to it. I can say, in vindication of these jurors and of these people, that the law has been at least as well enforced by them as effecting that country and the rights of its people, as it is enforced in any State of the Union, anywhere I can say more than that. I can say even more than that. I can say that there has not been a band of robbers or highwaymen or assassins in the Indian country that has not been, by the officers of this court and by the juries passing upon their cases and finding them guilty, if they were guilty, more promptly broken up, destroyed and wiped out, than has been the case in the Indian country for twenty years past. This is the truth. More cases of criminals committing high crimes have been tried, a higher percentage of arrests have been made, more convictions have been obtained, although justice has often failed from corrupt influences, as it does everywhere, from improper influences exerted, not always felt, known and understood by the jury when the mistake is made; but, I say, notwithstanding this there has, altogether, been a greater percentage of convictions, more men brought to justice, the law better vindicated, better upheld, and better sustained, and the rights of the people better protected by the people who come to this court as jurors than in any court in the country, I care not whether it is in the old States or in the new States, and when the history of this court comes to be written; when the passions of the hour, prompted by cupidity, avarice and self-interest, and desire for gain shall have all disappeared, those who have been connected with it in upholding the majesty, power and dignity of the law of the United States shall not suffer from that true history. I ask you to keep it up. I ask you to vindicate it still, because when you are doing that you are seeking to protect the people under the protecting agency of the law of the United States, and, as I have already said to you, the only way to protect men in their rights is for the juries of the land to come into the courts with a desire to fearlessly enforce the law, no matter whom it affects. The truth about it is that we are in a peculiar condition in this nation today—in such a condition that, in my judgment, the greatest problem that has ever presented itself to the minds of the people is confronting us now, and that is, whether crime shall be triumphant; whether the man of blood, the man of crime, the man of vicious disposition, the man who destroys human life, who tramples upon the rights of others, shall be the ruler, or the law of the land shall exert its peaceful sway, and by its protecting power, all men made secure under their own vine and their own fig tree, and under their own roof-tree. It is a great problem. It is one that is exciting the interest of all good men in the land. You find it in the law journals of the country; you find it in the lectures of judges; you find it as delivered by professors in colleges who are discovering this terrible condition where this wave of blood is about to deluge us and overpower us. Now, what is the reason for that? The reason for it in our jurisdiction is, because we have had to contend with almost the whole earth—the criminals, at least, of all the country. It has been the custom for all these years that when a man committed a crime in an older state, or in any state, and he could get away from the officers, he would run to the Indian country. He became a refugee criminal. And while there are many good men, hundreds and thousands of good white men in that country who are properly there, who are there by invitation; there are hundreds and thousands of others who are stained with crime, whose tendencies are corrupted by the crimes that they have committed elsewhere, and it is with this corrupt element assembled from all the States of this Union that this court, and the juries of this court, have-had to contend with. That is why the volume has been great. That is why it has been said: 'You convict so many men there; you must be cruel, you must be harsh, you must be tyrannical.' In fact, that reputation of this court has gone abroad, it has reached the whole land, and it started right here. Often, lawyers who would lose cases, whose client's neck was placed in the halter by the evidence and the law of the case, to vindicate themselves with their clients, would go off and damn the court, and talk about its cruelty, and its inhumanity and wickedness in that direction. There is where it started from; there is the origin of it. Many have acted outrageously in that particular, disgracefully, unprofessionally, and in every other way that ought to be reprimanded. That is the truth about it. There is where it started. But let the record of the court speak for itself and it will vindicate itself. The juries in this court, under the guidance of the court, as a rule have endeavored to uphold the law, to vindicate it. Now, then it is not only your duty to continue to do this for the sake of giving protection to these people under that law, but you, as well as the petit jury, are, for the time being, educators. You are to teach the people, everywhere, a wholesome lesson, and that is that they must rely, upon the law and upon its enforcement, for their protection, and not upon mob violence, not upon that spirit that causes people to degenerate into a mob and become criminals themselves in an effort to seek protection. There is a prevalence of this crime everywhere, that men, instead of arresting criminals, and bringing them before juries of the country, take them out and put them to death without judge or jury, and without investigating their cases, and not being competent to properly investigate them. Every day they do that. Sometimes you will find that good men are involved in things of that kind. It is because they have lost confidence in courts and juries. You say to a community that as sure as a crime is committed, so sure will the party who has committed it be brought to merited justice, as the law prescribed that punishment, and you won't find any mobs in that community. There are no mobs in the counties of this state which are in this jurisdiction. Have you noticed that? Why is that? It may not be that this court is entitled to the credit of it, but it is a fact that three or four times a year sixty or seventy-five men come up here, assist in the enforcement of the law, and they go home as educators among their people, and who are in favor of depending upon the law for the protection of every right, and the consequence is that mob violence does not exist in these counties. Everything is peaceable. It is quiet. A man commits a crime and the people seek to arrest him, as they have a right to do, and they bring him into the courts that he may be punished. And it is a rare exception that mob violence exists in the Indian country. There are cases of it (we have tried in this court three cases of mob violence since I have been here), but there is not the amount of it that you would naturally expect from the criminal condition of that country. And it is because the people have a belief that we will at least endeavor to enforce the law. Now, when we are teaching the lesson to all people that we must rely upon the law of this country to secure peace and good order and the consequent happiness and prosperity of the people, we are teaching the greatest lesson that can be taught; and we do that every day and every hour when we are in the courts of the country seeking to honestly, impartially and dispassionately uphold and enforce the law. It may not be inappropriate to give you the opinions of eminent jurists, of eminent men, showing our condition at this time in this country, and outlining to us what the duties of every good citizen are when they go into the courts of the country, and even when they are outside of the courts. Now, reading from the lecture of Judge Elliot Anthony, President of the Illinois State Bar Association, at its eighteenth annual meeting, held January 24, 1895, at Springfield, Ill., in which he said, in relation to criminal law:

"'There is no subject at the present time before the American people of such transcendent importance as that of the administration of the criminal law.'

"Much criticism has been indulged in regarding our jury system. The jury of the vicinage is, today, the most complete humbug. It was all right when it was originated 500 years ago, but the jury system has been reversed since. Then the jury tried the case on their own knowledge of it; now that knowledge of it would disqualify you. The majority of criminals do not want a trial by a jury of the vicinage. They committed crimes at their former homes, and fled because they did not have a good opinion of that law system. All they are entitled to is a fair tri d by an impartial jury, and that I am sure they will get here.

The truth about it is, for some reason or another (and the reason to my mind is manifest) that the administration of the law affecting the civil rights of the citizen, his property rights growing out of the controversies between man and man, has become to be regarded of much more importance than the enforcement of the law which protects the life of the citizen. Did you ever notice that? The criminal law and its administration has rather fallen into disgrace. That is especially true of the large cities of the country. Now, is it not more important to protect a man's life than it is his property? A man may lose every cent he has on earth, and he can earn more; if he cannot, he can depend upon his neighbor, or upon charity. He has still his life. But if his life is destroyed, if the assassin fires into his house and takes his life, robs his family and himself of that which belongs to him, is not that a greater deprivation than to deprive him of his horse, or his cow, or even of all the property which he possesses? Yet I say it is true that the administration of the criminal law has to some extent fallen into disgrace. I apprehend it is because of the corrupt methods resorted to to defeat its administration, and for this reason the people have become so that they look upon it with a kind of contempt. This eminent jurist, continuing, says:

"'It is as a general rule the least studied and the least understood by our judges of any other branch of the law. Many, up to the time of their accession to the bench, never tried a criminal case in a court of record, and consequently they have no appreciation whatever of the fine points of the law, or what is required by the Supreme Court to sustain a verdict in a case wherein it has once been obtained, and what is worse, they do not study to master the subject. Our methods of criminal procedure are vicious, and our criminal practice still worse. The rights of the defendant are regarded as supreme, while those of the public are almost entirely disregarded and ignored. Those who are charged with a criminal offense in Illinois are privileged characters and dominate the state. They can, under our practice, generally choose their own judges to try them, can fix the time and the season, can select just about such a jury as they see fit, and can then prolong the trial long enough to wear out the patience of the jury and drive the judge to madness.

Everything is, as a general thing, ruled against the state, and If they cannot win in the court below, they can in the Supreme Court.

"The history of crime is interwoven to a greater or less extent with every government, and will always be the most momentous question with which the human race has to deal. It is the great problem of civilization. He who has not thought upon it, has thought little about humanity, and he who has not paid some attention to the criminal law of his country has not received a liberal education. It ought to be administered with intelligence and enlightenment, but it is not. The great effort seems to be to involve every investigation of crime in a network of subtleties, artificial distinctions, and downright quibbles, shut out all incriminating evidence possible, then decide every case on some technicality. There is dissatisfaction everywhere throughout the country in regard to the methods adopted and the course pursued by our courts in dealing with the violators of the law, and it is but little wonder that the people in some of the oldest portion of the Republic have at times become exasperated at the trifling and juggling which are allowed, and have wreaked summary vengeance on thugs and assassins, to the disgrace of civilization and the age in which we live. Public rights seem to be held in much lower estimation than private rights, and as between the living and the dead there is no equality whatever.'

"'In 1889, David Dudley Field said, in addressing the American Bar Association, of which he was at that time the president:

"'We are a boastful people: we make no end of saying what great things we have done and are doing; and yet behind these brilliant shows, there stands a spectre Of halting justice, such as is to be seen in no other part of Christendom. So far as I am aware, there is no other country calling itself civilized, where it is so difficult to convict and punish a criminal and where it takes so many years to get a final decision between man and man. Truly may we say, that justice passes through the land on leaden sandals. The judges of the Supreme Court have it in their power to establish by their decisions, such a body of criminal law as they see fit. They are hampered very little by statutes and none whatever in regard to the determination of the guilt or innocence of the accused. To build up and establish an arbitrary system of rules and regulations is not the true object and aim of an enlightened judiciary. What society demands and common sense demands, is this: If a man is charged with a crime, then the question should be, is he innocent or guilty; not did the judge err when he told the jury that they must be "satisfied" of the guilt of the accused, instead of "believe" him guilty, after a full consideration of all the evidence.'"

"These are the expressive sentiments of men who are observing men, who are good men, who are skilled in the laws of the country, who are devoted to the true interests of the people everywhere in this land. You cannot pick up the proceedings of a bar meeting, a meeting of lawyers, nor can you scarcely find a lecture delivered on that line in any institution of learning in the country, that does not treat on this subject just as these eminent jurists have spoken of it. It is the solemn truth, and it should be the duty of every good citizen to see to it, in court and out of it, that no stone is left unturned to undo this condition where the man of crime is in power, where he is practically the ruler, where, if he has things in the shape of money or social power and standing, he breaks through the meshes of the law and makes his trial a mockery, a sham, a delusion, as is manifested in every court in this land, time after time. Juries are deceived; they are humbugged; they are imposed upon by the tricks and artifices resorted to for the purpose of circumventing justice, to cheat the law of its rights and its just demands. I ask you to see to it that nothing of that kind will occur as far as you are concerned, that no effort can be brought forth strong enough or powerful enough to cause you to swerve from the line of duty which is marked out for you by the law, and that is indicated for you by the oath you have taken. See to it that every apparently guilty man accused of crime is properly and promptly indicted so that he may be put upon his trial, and it may be finally ascertained whether he is guilty or innocent. It is the duty of all of us, as citizens and as officers, to see to it that these great principles of the law, enacted for the preservation of the rights of each and every citizen, whether it be the right to life, to liberty or property, shall in every case be enforced, and in every case be vindicated. That no distinction shall be made; or, if any distinction is made, make it against the intelligent and powerful and those who ought to know better, rather than against a man who has less reason and who is ignorant and who may have become criminal from environment, from his surroundings, as is often the case. If any distinction shall be made in the way of punishment, in my judgment, it should be made in favor of a man of that kind, and not in favor of the man with power behind him, who breaks through all of these statutes that have been enacted. And you are to especially see to it ii he is a violator of the law that he shall suffer punishment. It is abhorrent, it is disgusting in the extreme, to see this manifestation exhibited all over the land, which has gone so far that there is a sickly sentimentality today in favor of crime. The man who is a criminal is apparently a little better than you who are honest and upright and who have not stained your hands with the blood of a fellow man, or committed some other high crime. There is that sickly sentimentality in favor of crime upon the part of large numbers of the people of this land. When you come into this court as jurymen, if you ever had a lingering fragment of such a sentiment, leave it outside the door, because you are here panoplied with the power of your country to uphold the laws of this land, to assist in seeing to it that justice is done in every instance, no matter who may be charged, no matter who the criminal may be, no matter who the innocent person may be. If a man is innocent, protect him in his innocence; if he is guilty, see to it that you assist in bringing him to merited punishment.

"I want you to return indictments in every case wherein it is probable that a murder has been committed, and first, I want you to take up the case of one Crawford Goldsby alias Cherokee Bill, who has been regularly convicted in this court of a foul murder, but upon which the sentence was set aside by his appeal to the Supreme Court, which is now pending. He is accused of, while lawfully committed to jail, having secured a pistol and killed Larry Keating, one of the guards, as the result of a conspiracy on the part of the prisoners to escape from custody. I want you to especially given that case your attention, and if you think an indictment should be returned, do so speedily, that he may be put on trial to answer for his crime. There are a large number of murderers confined in the jail, and in the interests of good government and humanity, you should act promptly. Something must be done to hold these characters in check.

"It is not the severity of punishment but the certainty of it that checks crime nowadays. The criminal always figures on the chance of escape, and if you take that away entirely he stops being criminal. The old adage of the law, 'certainty of punishment brings security,' is as true to-day as it ever was.

"You will have someone from the district attorney's office, either himself or one or the other of his assistants, Mr. McDonough, or Mr. Smith, who will wait upon you, to give you advice upon questions of law, because you have a right to have information upon these matters to aid you in correctly and properly performing your duties. The district attorney, or one of his assistants, has a right to assist you in the examination of witnesses. Of course, he knows more about these cases than you can possibly know. He has become conversant with them and in that way he can render you very material aid. I desire to say to you in this connection that when you come to vote upon a proposition no one is permitted to be with you when you vote except a member of your body. The district attorney, or whichever one of his assistants may be waiting upon you at the time, will retire at that time. Nobody will be present with you. At all other times the representative of the district attorney's office has a right to be present with you to assist you in the manner I have indicated. There will be a bailiff at your door for the purpose of calling witnesses, and make you as comfortable as is possible in the room we furnish you.

"Now, of course, it is your duty to proceed as fast as you can with the business before you, yet at the same time not to proceed so rapidly with it that you would overlook it, or that you would hastily indict a man without fully understanding the case, or that you would hastily ignore the charge against a man without understanding the case. See that you get all the facts in every case. If the witnesses are not all here, examine those who are here, and lay the case over until the others can be produced. You are, of course, to take up the cases first where parties desire to plead guilty before you. It is a rule of law that if a man is brought before you and is informed of the nature of the charge, and you are satisfied he understands its nature, and the consequence of pleading guilty, and the party says, when interrogated by the foreman or any other member of your body, or the representative of the district attorney's office, that he desires to plead guilty to the charge, that you can indict him upon that plea alone. You have a right under the law to do that. I would suggest that you take up these cases first, if there are any. I do not know whether there are any or not. If there are, they will be brought before you, and you will proceed with them as rapidly as you can that they may appear before the court and receive their sentences, whatever they may be. I might outline the order in which you may conduct your business, but of course I do not undertake to make it absolutely binding upon you, it being only directory, because you have necessarily to change it owing to the varying circumstances that will transpire in the course of your deliberations, but dispose first of cases where the parties are in jail—that is, if you can do so, if the witnesses are here. Next, dispose of cases where parties are upon bond. Next, where parties are not in arrest. Now, vary this order of business according to the circumstances. That is to say, if witnesses are here in cases where parties are upon bond, and are not here in cases where parties are in jail, take up the cases first where parties are on bond. If there is a case where it is urgent to get an indictment where the party has not been in arrest, proceed with his case first that he may be arrested upon your indictment returned in his case, if you return one. In other words, vary the order of business according to the circumstances, so you will be enabled to discharge the business before you as rapidly as possible.

"You have a right to fix your own hours of meeting and adjournment. The court usually fixes its hour of meeting in the morning at half past eight o'clock, a recess of an hour and a half at noon, and adjourns at 6 o'clock in the evening, You may conform to that time, or fix other hours, just as you see fit. I say to you, make use of all the time you can in justice to your health to dispose of the business before you as promptly as possible.

"In conclusion I say to you that for the time being I put the laws of the United States applicable to this jurisdiction in your hands, and I ask you to sustain them upon your part by a fair, just, impartial and deliberate investigation in every case that comes before you. If guilt is established, you cannot help it; you must proceed to return your indictment. If guilt is not established, the man who has been charged is vindicated, and you ignore the bill, and so return it into court. When you proceed in this way, as you have taken your oath to proceed, and as I know you will do, you have performed your duty as good citizens and good jurors and in such a way as to become an educating influence in the country, and at the same time to give fully the benefit of the law of the land to those who are entitled to its power as a protecting agency.

"Gentlemen, you will retire to your room and proceed with your deliberations."

THE INFAMOUS BUCK GANG

I have spoken in previous chapters of the fact that rape was one of the prevailing crimes committed in the Indian Territory by the lawless bands of marauders, by which it was infested, and have given accounts of a few of the crimes of that nature which came under the jurisdiction of the Fort Smith Court.

Of all the rapists tried however, the Buck gang, composed of Rufus Buck, a Uche Indian; Lewis Davis, Creek Indian; Luckey Davis, Creek negro; Sam Sampson and Maomi July, Creek Indians, were the most desperate, and for the short time the gang operated, they committed more heinous and terrifying acts than any of the numerous gangs of desperate characters which infested the Indian Territory, cursing it by their presence. It is generally conceded that outlaw Creek Indians and Creek "niggers," are the worst of the natives of the Territory, and this was doubtless the most desperate band of outlaws ever in America. Their only object was to commit crime because it was crime.

It was not until late in July, 1895, that the members of this gang organized into a band, although all of them had been lawless and law-breakers for months, some of them for years. Buck had already been before the Fort Smith court on a charge of introducing whiskey into the Indian Territory and was given a ninety-day sentence. During his confinement he was an exemplary prisoner and was made a trusty.

The Buck gang sprung up suddenly near Okmulgee, Cherokee Nation, flourished thirteen days, and were taken in, but during that thirteen days they made a criminal record that faded the Dalton gang, the Starr gang or the Cook gang, considering the length of time they operated. In fact it is known that they boasted that they would make a record that would cause the above-mentioned gangs to fade into insignificance.

They started out as a band on Sunday, July 28, by killing a negro deputy marshal at Okmulgee. Rufus Buck himself was said to have done this job, and it was the first act in a carefully laid plan to first get the officer, who was watching them, out of the way and then start out on a campaign, to murder, burn and pillage. After this the band started out raiding through the country, terrorizing every section they visited. Four of them met Mrs. Wilson, who was moving from one farm to another with two wagons. Her fourteen-year-old son and a young man who was with her were made to drive on with one wagon, while they kept the woman and the other wagon. They made her get out, and each one of them brutally assaulted her, after which she was allowed to go her way, nearly dead from fright and abuse.

A day or two later they went to the house of Mr. Hassan, between Duck and Snake Creeks, and after forcing the wife to prepare dinner for them and partaking of it, all five of the scoundrels assaulted her, holding her husband at bay with Winchesters. They then amused themselves by making Hassan and another man who was present fight each other and dance, shooting around their feet to make them move lively. They met a man named Shafey on Berryhill Creek, eight miles from Okmulgee, robbed him of his horse, saddle and bridle, $50 in money and a gold watch. They then discussed the advisability of killing him, and took a vote on it. Three of them voted to let him go, and he was allowed to go on foot. Afterwards they robbed a stock man named Callahan, even taking his boots, and then shot at him, one ball grazing his ear. At the same time they shot a negro boy who was with Callahan; he afterwards died of his wounds.

They visited the home of Gus Chambers on Duck Creek, ten miles from Sapulpa, to steal some horses, at night. Chambers made a fight and they filled his house with lead, but harmed no one. They secured one horse. They robbed Nor-berg's store, near McDermott, and also Orcutt's store, in the same locality. The next day after the Norberg robbery, Saturday, August 10, Capt. Edmund Harry, of the Creek Light Horse, with Light Horsemen Tom Grayson, George Brown and Skansey, accompanied by Deputy United States Marshals Sam Haynes and N. B. Irwin and over one hundred citizens of the Creek Nation, ran on to the outlaws while they were dividing their plunder, just outside of the village, and after a fight in which hundreds of shots were fired, all the outlaws surrendered except Lewis Davis, who escaped during the fight but was captured later. Deputy Marshals Ledbetter, Tolbert, Jones and Wilson were hot on the trail of the outlaws, and they arrived at the scene of the fight a few minutes after the surrender.

A BATTLE WITH OUTLAWS

The fight commenced soon after noon and lasted until nearly dark. The officers had surprised the bandits, as noted above, while they were dividing their plunder. The day was one of torrid heat, and the swarthy outlaws, each wearing the inevitable wide-brimmed, white or black felt hat, jeans trousers and high heeled, high topped boots, fitted with clanking spurs, their vests flung open, their necks encircled with fancy colored bandanas and their waists with heavily loaded cartridge belts, sat tailor fashion, in the shade of a clump trees, about a big pile of merchandise, the proceeds of their depredations, consisting of cigars, tobacco, clothing, ammunition, and whatever fancy had impelled them to carry from the stores they had looted. Their horses stood close by, too busily occupied in switching flies from their sides to pay any attention to the half dried prairie grass; each horse stood obediently behind his rider, each still bridled and saddled, ready for instant mount. So interested were the bandits in the division of their spoils, so sure that they were incapable of capture, and little thinking that an outraged people were hard upon their trail, that they neglected to place a sentry. This they might easily have done, for from just where they sat the ground began an upward slope and terminated abruptly in a high knob, about 200 feet high, and whose top was of about one-fourth of an acre in extent. A sentry posted here could have viewed the country for miles around and could have warned his fellows in crime of the approach of an enemy long before they reached "shooting distance," and have come rome [sic] rolling down to the place of rendezvous and the entire gang could have grabbed up their plunder, mounted and rode away at break-neck speed and the next heard of them would have been the report of a terrible crime of some nature, committed by them many miles away. But they felt too secure for caution, and while they were enjoying the occasion, their eyes gloating over the proceeds of their crimes, the officers noted above, re-enforced by the outraged Creeks, crept up carefully from the other side of the knob, slipped around to one side, and the first the bandits knew of their danger was the loud report of a score of rifles fired into their midst. Strange to say, none of the five were wounded, but the onslaught was so sudden, so unexpected, that they had not time to mount, and, with a muffled oath, each man grabbed his rifle and with the agility of panthers they rushed to the top of the knob, from where, a moment later, they commenced firing volleys at the pursuers below. The scene was an inspiring one. The bandits would fire rapidly from their vantage ground until their magazines were exhausted, then retire to the center of the little plateau to reload, then creep to the edge, keeping their bodies from exposure, and fire again and again. Brave and desperate men by degrees ascended the slope, closer and closer, and it can be naught but a miracle that scores were not shot to death. The pursuers kept up a rattling fire for hours, and not one of them were wounded.

HOW THE NEWS WAS RECEIVED AT FORT SMITH

A little after one o'clock, just as court had convened, there came a dispatch to Fort Smith which said that a big posse had rounded up the Buck gang. Everybody in Fort Smith had heard of the Buck gang, the report of whose dare-devilishness had spread over the entire country. Coming so soon after the Keating murder, their acts had filled the people of the city and country with horror, and women and children feared to step out of doors after dark. The news of the "round up" spread like wild fire; "The Buck gang" was upon every body's lips. The news reached the court house. There were in the yard and corridors over 400 persons who had been summoned before the court as witnesses. The court room was crowded, to listen idly to the numerous petty cases that were invariably called up after the disposal of a noted murder trial. Inside the court room word was passed from lip to lip, to the effect that officers had corralled the "Buck gang;" almost instantly all was in a bustle. A bailiff whispered the news to Judge Parker; he nodded, pleasantly, called for order in the court and proceeded with the regular business. Soon another dispatch came; it read:

"Deputy marshals and Indians are engaged in a hand to hand conflict with the Buck gang."

Like a flash the contents of this second dispatch found its way to every nook and cranny in the city. In the court room the bustle increased; attorneys for once forgot to ask questions, and witnesses to answer them, and again and again Judge Parker called for the bailiffs to preserve order. His tone was kindly, however, and he seemed to join in with the crowd in secret exultation at the fact that the murderous and unholy gang had been tracked to their lair. All through the afternoon this eager uneasiness continued and Judge Parker's voice would sing out ever and anon.

"The United States against—; Mr. McDonough are you ready in this case?"

"Yes, your honor."

"Bring in the prisoner; swear the witnesses; order in the court!" And when court finally adjourned every one hurried to the streets to learn of any possible later news of the fight, and gathered in little knots to discuss the probable outcome.

Just after dark there came a dispatch which told of the surrender and then the high tension under which the people had been held for a half a day was loosened and normal conditions were restored, though many continued about the telegraph and newspaper offices all night, to learn of any possible later developments.

As soon as he heard of the "round up," United States Marshal S. M. Rutherford, of the Northern District, Indian Territory, hurried to the scene, from Muscogee, reaching there while the fusillade was in progress. All this time the assaulting party had been lying at full length on the ground, hugging the grass roots, and firing upwards at an angle of probably thirty degrees. The constant "pumping of lead" with the accompanying flashes, gave the appearance of a constant blaze of fire and the smoke at times hung over the knob until the belligerents were hidden from each other. At last, an old Indian, whose misfortune it is that his name was not preserved to history, rose bravely to his feet and said:

"Let us stand up and fight like men; I've had enough of this,", at the same time pushing a dynamite cartridge into his rifle.

This act was even more brave than the other. There was probably not another man in the posse who would have dared fire a dynamite cartridge from a rifle intended to stand only the force exerted by exploded gunpowder. Quickly he raised his gun and fired. The terrible explosive struck a tree behind which Buck was standing. A piece of the shell cut his belt and as it dropped to the ground, he threw away his rifle and ran. This demoralized the gang and all ran pell mell down the opposite side of the knob, and into the arms of a fresh posse and were captured, with the exception of Lewis Davis, who, twice wounded, had escaped while the fight was in progress. He was captured a few days later.

A LYNCHING NARROWLY AVERTED

The worn out but desperate men were at once shackled, hands and feet, and chained together and taken to the village where it was intended to keep them under heavy guard all night. A vast crowd of citizens and settlers gathered about. The noise created by the guns fired during the battle had reverberated through the valleys and had caused an outpouring, as the glad news sped over the country, of hundreds of people who a few days before would rather have met old Satan himself, than the gang that had so terrified them; but now that they were safely manacled, all were eager to get a peep at the vicious wretches who were at last overcome but not subdued. During the early evening, muffled threats were heard. Citizens of the Creek Nation, born to lead, were working quietly in the crowd, and it was not long until lynching was openly talked of. Marshal Rutherford addressed them, coolly, dispassionately, and assured them that the bandits, if left to him, and his deputies, should be landed in the Fort Smith jail and that swift justice should be meted out. The manner of his address pacified them for a while, but there were those of the Creeks, whose fingers itched to mete out to the outlaws the ignoble death of strangulation at the rope's end. The Creeks had been repeatedly accused of looseness in upholding the laws and of failure to assist in its prosecution; they smarted under the accusation and here was an opportunity to work summary punishment, which they could not bear to let pass by; after the marshal's address the mob scattered aimlessly for a half hour, then gradually gathered again at a distance and finally posted sentries to prevent the officers and their desperate prisoners escaping. The marshals watched the proceedings carefully, and their experience taught them that they must act quickly and wisely, if they would convey the outlaws to the Federal jail. It was now dark; the sky was cloudy and except for a fitful bonfire here and there, or when an occasional sheen of light was given from the moon as the clouds parted for an instant, nothing could be seen at a distance of twenty yards. There was an ominous silence, broken only now and then by muffled voices from the vicinity of the bonfires; the officers became uneasy for the safety of their prisoners, who had heard the threats, and were now begging with all the earnestness of innocent men, that their lives might be spared. By degrees the mob grew more noisy, and now and then a threat and a curse could be heard. The officers consulted earnestly, while the prisoners quaked with fear. In the darkness they believed they could easily steal through the crowd and away to safety, but for the clanking of the heavy chains that bound the bandits together, the noise of which would be certain to betray them. Finally the prisoners were told that the mob were bent on wreaking out vengeance and that if they remained there the entire four would be lynched; that if they would pick up their chains and carry them without a sound, the officers would try and steal through the line and away from the mob, and conduct them safely to Fort Smith. The bandits eagerly agreed, and here I have to record one of the strangest facts known. Those vile wretches who had so little regard for the lives of others, but valued their own so highly, picked up the chains and carried them for a full half mile, without a sound from the chains. From that point the prisoners were conducted fifty miles to Muscogee, where they hastily boarded a convenient train and were safely carried to Fort Smith.

THE ARRIVAL AT FORT SMITH

From near the Missouri Pacific Railroad depot, near the Arkansas river bank, a half mile from the center of the city, Garrison avenue runs southeasterly, and three blocks away from the depot was a gate which opened into the old government barracks enclosure, from where a path leads diagonally in a southerly direction to the Federal jail. As the train bearing the officers with members of the Buck gang, heavily ironed, reached the depot on that memorable Sunday morning, it was met by a crowd of several hundred men who had assembled to take advantage of the first opportunity to gaze upon the fiends in human form of whom so much had recently been said, and who had created such an unenviable reputation within less than two weeks. As the prisoners came off the train, with officers in front and behind, the chains clanking at every step, I could not help saying to myself:

"If, by some manner of means those men could be unshackled and all provided with Winchesters, what a scattering there would be!"

As for the bandits themselves, they appeared wholly unconcerned, though their covert glances took in every face and every detail, and no doubt they longed for the opportunity to make the scattering I have suggested. There was no time lost; the marshals headed for the sidewalk, the crowd separated and with officers leading the way and others bringing up the rear, the strange procession marched slowly and silently up the Avenue, while the morning church bells tolled a requiem to the dead victims of this blood-thirsty gang, the only sound except the clank, clank of the chains as they struck upon the sidewalk. Profoundly impressive it was, but the impressiveness was lost upon the bandits, whose only thoughts were that they might escape. The crowd closed in and followed at the officers' heels, continuing until the jail was reached and the creak of the hinges told that another band of outlaws had been brought to know the majesty of the law. Here the crowd was augmented by others who had learned of the arrival, and was quickly swelled to hundreds. Gradually they dispersed, their curiosity temporarily satisfied. The prisoners could no longer be seen, and every man in that vast crowd knew that, once behind the gates of the Federal jail there was no escape, and all felt easier, and Fort Smith breathed freer, knowing that at least one gang of murderers had been placed where they could no longer gloat over human blood.

During the week a flood of evidence concerning the rape of Mrs. Hassan, considered the most shocking of all the dastardly crimes committed by the Buck gang, was laid before the grand jury, and an indictment was returned. It appears upon the court records in the following language:

INDICTMENT.

United States of America, Western District of Arkansas.

In the Circuit Court, May term, A. D., 1895.

United States

VS.

Rufus Buck and Lewis Davis and Luckey Davis and Sam Sampson and Maoma July.

Rape.

The grand jurors of the United States of America, duly selected, empaneled, sworn and charged to inquire into and for the body of the Western District of Arkansas aforesaid, upon their oath present:

309

That Rufus Buck and Lewis Davis and Luckey Davis and Sam Sampson and Maoma July, on the 6th day of August, A. D. 1895, at the Creek Nation, in the Indian country, within the Western District of Arkansas aforesaid, in and upon Rosetta Hassan, a white woman, and not an Indian, feloniously, forcibly and violently an assault did make, and her, the said Rosetta Hassan, then and there, and against her will, forcibly, violently and feloniously, did ravish and carnally know, contrary to the form of the statute in such case made and provided, and the peace and dignity of the United States of America.

E. J. Black, Foreman of Grand Jury.

Jas. F. Read,

U. S. District Attorney, Western District of Ark.

At 8:30 o'clock on the morning of Tuesday, August 20, the prisoners were taken into open court and arraigned; they entered pleas of not guilty and September 23 was set for a hearing of the case, time being allowed for the assembling of witnesses.

On the day of the trial court opened at 8:30. Within a short time the court room was packed with an eager crowd, of all kinds and classes, and the whole motley throng, unmindful of the suffocating heat, sat through the trial, eagerly drinking in the loathsome details of the horrible crime; some out of pure depravity and for the mere sake of feeding upon a recital of an awful wickedness, others drawn thither by an inborn craving, as the buzzard or the vulture is attracted to the polluted carrion whose odor ascends to the heavens; others that they might gain a knowledge of the minutest details of the frightful crime and so work themselves to a pitch where they could more fully enjoy the punishment, even if inadequate, so certain to be dealt them.

Henry Hassan, the husband of the injured woman, was the first witness examined. He described how, on Monday, the fifth day of August, as he lay sleeping beneath an arbor, his wife sitting nearby preparing fruit for the family larder, the gang rode through the front gate. Awakening, he greeted them pleasantly and asked them if they were hunting. Buck replied in the affirmative and called for water. Sending his wife's little brother for a pail of fresh water he started to meet them and then discovering that one of the number was Lewis Davis, with whom he had previously had some slight difficulty, he knew he was at the mercy of the terrible band of whose recent depredations he had heard. He hesitated a moment, then started for a corner of the house, hoping to reach cover, then enter a door, inside of which hung his Winchester. He gained, the corner safely, then ran towards the door and as he started to enter was stopped by Maoma July, who had entered from an opposite door and securing the coveted rifle now brushed his face with its muzzle, while Sampson at the same time covered him with a six-shooter. Hassan backed away, and the others coming up, Buck, with an air of bravado, said: "I'm Cherokee Bill's brother; we want your money." With vile curses they commanded Hassan to sit in a place designated, then ordered his wife and her mother to prepare dinner. The women hastened to cook a

310

meal, and meanwhile Lewis Davis stayed with Hassan to keep him under control by threats of death, boastfully declaring himself to be Tom Root. While the meat was being made ready the rest of the gang searched the house and appropriated $5.95 cash, a suit of clothing, some baby's dresses, together with various articles of feminine apparel, handkerchiefs and whatever struck their fancy. After having appeased their appetites, they came out and stood guard over Hassan while the negro went in to dinner, after which the assault on Mrs. Hassan was made.

Having satisfied their lusts, they mounted their horses and ordered Hassan to go with them; just then a young man came, unsuspectingly, to the house from a little distance and they held him up, and marched both him and Hassan two miles away and, after dire threats of death, amused themselves by making the men dance while they fired random bullets at their bare feet. Their next amusement was to compel the men to jump into a pool of water, then forced them to wrestle and fight, then commanded Hassan to kill the other. Finally, when their ideas of fun were exhausted, they ordered the men to go-home, warning them: "If you ever appear against us our friends will kill you." Hassan hurried to his home as soon as released, but found his wife was missing. She had been so. wrought up over the ordeal through which she had passed, believing it the only means of saving her husband's life, the continued absence of the latter had caused her to believe her sacrifice had been useless, and that he had already fallen a victim to their love of crime, and finally, overcome with fear, she had fled to a nearby cornfield and hid. After a continued search, her husband found her, in a paroxysm of fear, nearly dead from, apprehension. Hassan's story, as related on the witness stand, was straightforward, and was given with but little interruption on the part of the prosecuting attorney and none whatever by the attorneys for defense. Through it all the members of the gang sat unmoved, pretending an inability to understand English. If the testimony of the husband was listened to by the vast assemblage with thrilling interest, then there is no adjective capable of describing the interest shown during the time that the injured wife and mother was giving a recital of her wrongs.

MRS. HASSAN'S STORY

The murmur of indignation that ran through the crowd when Hassan stopped speaking and retired, ceased as Mrs. Hassan was escorted into the court room and took her position on the stand, and but for the bustle occasioned by the shifting and craning of necks by the members of the crowd to secure a view of the witness, all was silent. Mrs. Hassan was a well-proportioned woman, of beautiful features, and a look that betokened a kindly disposition. She appeared to be about 30 years of age. She was very nicely dressed, but wore nothing that could be considered gaudy. Her appearance was most modest and it was evidently with a great effort that she was able to sit there, cynosure of so many curious pairs of eyes. She still showed the effects of her frightful experience. She spoke slowly and in ow but tremulous tones showing the strong nervous tension under which she was still laboring; at times her breath came quick, her bosom heaved, the hot blood surged to her temples and with her head bowed low she would give way to heartrending sobs, as the questions propounded by the prosecution or the court brought back with awful vividness the horrible scene through which she passed but a few weeks before. She related, much as her husband had done, the coming of the gang to her home, to ask for water, of her fears for the life of her husband, of the hastily prepared meal which she hoped might be the means of saving him. Urged to tell what occurred after they had eaten, she described between sobs, how Luckey Davis, the negro, had told her: "you have to go with me," and how she pleaded with him not to take her away from her babies; how he had replied, "We will throw the G—d— brats in the creek;" how he had commanded her to mount his horse and ride away with him, only desisting when she declared she could not ride; how he then ordered her to go with him a little way, and she hesitated and had finally obeyed, believing if she refused they would kill her and the rest of her family, and marched on, while the colored brute held the muzzle of his Winchester close to her head. She told how they continued until they reached the back side of the barn, out of sight of the house and 200 feet away, and of Davis then laying down his rifle and drawing a pistol from his belt—then paused.

Judge Parker said kindly, "Just go on and tell everything that occurred there. The law makes it necessary to tell it. It is a very delicate matter, of course, but you will have to tell about it."

"Did he tell you what to do?" asked Mr. McDonough.

"Yes sir," in a tone barely audible.

"What did he say?"

"He told me to lie down;" and the witness broke down completely, while her frame shook with convulsions and she sobbed like a child, yet as a child could not. The effect upon the audience was magnetic. They had listened with sympathetic eagerness, forgetful of their own existence even, and the result, when the climax was reached is indescribable; during the several minutes that elapsed before the witness could regain her composure there was the most profound silence, broken only by her sobs; the conditions, the awfulness of the crime committed, the story so clearly told and the woman in tears, had a reflex action upon the auditors, and a wave of sympathy swept through the room, and left scarcely a dry eye. Not one of the jurors, accustomed though they were to recitals of brutality, somewhat hardened no doubt, but who shed tears, sympathetic, manly, noble tears, of which they were not ashamed, neither had reason to be. It was a supreme moment, such as I never expect to experience again. The few women in the crowd gave way to a mighty surge of grief, and even Judge Parker, notwithstanding that he had been inured by many long years of experience with brutal crimes, removed his spectacles and while a suspicious moisture twinkled upon his lashes, drew a handkerchief from his pocket, wiped the lenses, then spoke a few words of gentle encouragement to the witness.

Let us draw a charitable veil before the remainder of her testimony, her unwilling description of what followed, and was repeated, one, two, three, four times, each one of the brutal ruffians taking their turn at the revolting crime while at all times, three of the gang remained on guard over the husband, ready to send a bullet crashing through his brain, if he attempted a remonstrance or made an outcry. Gently the court drew from her that it was only for the sake of her husband and children, and through fear that they would kill her loved ones that she submitted to the indignities, and as she proceeded, the terrible iniquity of the deed came upon him with such power that Judge Parker became livid with rage; it were well for the prisoners that the law prevented him dealing out punishment then and there.

Without cross-examination Mrs. Hassan was allowed to step down from the witness stand and retire; the attorneys standing aside and bowing reverently as she passed out, bearing the sympathy of every one in the court room. At the conclusion, Assistant District Attorney McDonough rose, and in a subdued tone, said to the jury:

"Gentlemen: You heard the evidence. It was so plain it is unnecessary to argue the case. The court will give all necessary instruction, and we will expect a verdict of guilty at your hands."

Wm. M. Cravens, one of the five attorneys appointed for the defense, arose and said, simply, "May it please the court and you gentlemen of the jury, you have heard the evidence. I have nothing to say," then resumed his seat. It was probably the shortest plea for defense ever recorded.

Judge Parker then delivered a short but impressive charge and the jury retired. It required no effort on the part of any member of that jury to arrive at a verdict of guilty. They did not even take time to ballot. One of their number was chosen foreman, his signature was affixed, and the jury at once returned to the court room, where in silence, the verdict was awaited. It read: "We, the jury, find the defendants, Rufus Buck, Lewis Davis, Luckey Davis, Sam Sampson and Maoma July guilty of rape, as charged in the within indictment.

(Signed) JOHN N. FERGUSON, Foreman.

A most remarkable fact is here to be related. Immediately after the finding of the indictment for the rape of Mrs. Hassan, the grand jury had returned a true bill charging the Buck gang with murder, the victim named being the negro marshal, the killing of whom was the first crime committed by them as they started out on their short and terrible career. As soon as the verdict convicting them of rape was read, Judge Parker excused the jury and at once another panel was drawn, a new jury was selected, and, without being allowed to leave their seats, the prisoners were placed on trial for murder. The case continued until the next day, resulting in a verdict of guilty.

THE SENTENCE

Two days later, Wednesday, September 25, a large crowd gathered in the court room to listen to the sentence of death pronounced upon the members of the famous gang. The occasion was remarkable, in that it was the first time, and proved to be the last, that sentence was pronounced upon so many as five convicted rapists at once. The crowd, as usual, was variegated, such a one as could be seen almost nowhere else on earth, composed of all possible classes and conditions, from the very apex of society to the very lowest; from the highly cultured and refined, by stages, down to the most degraded specimens of the human race. A petty case, assault with intent to kill, occupied the attention of the court all of the first half of the day, and when court opened at 1 o'clock it took but a few moments to fill the court room to suffocation. This time they were not disappointed. The men were brought in and sentence was pronounced, Judge Parker speaking as follows:

"Rufus Buck, Lewis Davis, Luckey Davis', Sam Sampson Maoma July, stand up.

"You have been convicted by a verdict of the jury, justly rendered, of the terrible crime of rape. It now becomes the duty of the court to pass sentence upon you, which the law says shall follow a conviction of such crime. Have you anything to say why the sentence of the law should not now be passed in your cases r"

Lucky Davis said, "Yes, sah."

Judge Parker asked "What is it?"

"I want my case to go to the Supreme Cote."

Judge Parker replied: "I don't blame you a bit," then continued:

"I want to say in this case that the jury, under the law and the evidence, could come to no other conclusion than that which they arrived at. Their verdict is an entirely just one, and one that must be approved by all lovers of virtue. The offense c f which you have been convicted is one which shocks all men who are not brutal. It is known to the law as a crime offensive to decency, and as a brutal attack upon the honor and chastity of the weaker sex. It is a violation of the quick sense of honor and the pride of virtue which nature, to render the sex amiable, has implanted in the female heart, and it has-been by the law-makers of the United States deemed equal in enormity and wickedness to murder, because the punishment fixed by the same is that which follows the commission of the crime of murder.

"Your crime has been proven beyond question, and the evidence, showing the manner of its commission, exhibits it as of the most repulsive and abhorrent character. The proof shows that each of you first took part in the robbery of the house of Henry Hassan, and afterwards that each of you, in the most revolting and brutal manner, in turn, outraged his wife, Mrs. Rosetta Hassan. Some of you held the family at bay. Some of you overcame all resistance by armed violence while each of you in turn committed this terrible crime against decency and virtue, and you all exhibited the most horrid and brutal depravity. The acts so aroused the indignation of your own people, the Creek Indians, that they were almost persuaded to take you from the officers and execute upon you summary vengeance. It was only through respect for the law, and the belief that it would be enforced in this court, that induced them to permit the officers to bring you here.

"The enormity and great wickedness of your crime leaves no ground for the extension of sympathy to you. You can expect no more sympathy than lovers of virtue and haters of vice can extend to men guilty of one of the most brutal, wicked, repulsive and dastardly crimes known in the annals of crime. Your duty now is to make an honest effort to receive from a just God that mercy and forgiveness you so much need. We are taught that His mercy will wipe out even this horrible crime; but He is just, and His justice decrees punishment unless you are able to make atonement for the revolting crime against His law and against human law that you have committed. This horrible crime now rests upon your souls. Remove it if you can so the good God of all will extend to you His forgiveness and His mercy.

"Listen now to the sentence of the law which is, that you, Rufus Buck, for the crime of rape, committed by you upon Rosetta Hassan, in the Indian country, and within the jurisdiction of this court, of which crime you stand convicted by the verdict of the jury in your case, be deemed, taken and adjudged guilty of rape; and that you be therefor, for the said crime against the laws of the United States, hanged by the neck until you are dead; that the marshal of the Western District of Arkansas, by himself or deputy, or deputies, cause execution to be done in the premises upon you on Thursday, the thirty-first day of October, 1895, between the hours of 9 o'clock in the forenoon and 5 o'clock in the afternoon of the said day; and that you now be taken to the jail from whence you came, to be there closely and securely kept, until the day of execution, and from thence on the day of execution as aforesaid, you are to be taken to the place of execution, there to be hanged by the neck until you are dead.

"May God, whose laws you have broken, and before whose tribunal you must then appear, have mercy on your soul."

The sentence was then pronounced upon each of the remaining four, being interpreted to Maomi July, by a Creek squaw. The men upon whom the sentence of death was thus pronounced, exhibited no sign; they seemed to care nothing for it.

A stay of execution was afterwards issued to await the action of the Supreme Court, to which an appeal was taken because of the claim put forth by Buck, that if given an opportunity, he could prove an alibi; but the higher court affirmed the decision of the lower, and the members of the gang were resentenced and were finally hanged, July 1, 1896.

CASHARAGO, ALIAS GEORGE WILSON

I have given, in one of the early chapters of this book, an account of the first execution performed at Fort Smith, on a gallows built expressly for the purpose of taking the life of John Childers, as a punishment for his having killed a white peddler that he might secure possession of a horse he coveted. This execution occurred August 15, 1873, and for almost twenty-three years thereafter the cumbersome death machine continued to deal out justice, until just before the-time named by Congress for the cutting down of the powers of the famous court. The very last man to be executed on the old scaffold was James Casharago, alias George Wilson, twenty-six years old, convicted of the cold-blooded murder of Zacharia W. Thatch, a highly respected citizen of Washington County, Arkansas, near Keokuk Falls, in the Creek Nation, about May 13, *895. His execution occurred July 30, 1896.

Casharago's murder of Thatch was not his first advent into the realms of crime; at the time he committed the most heinous act of his life, he had been for years under the ban; he was already a hardened criminal, but his illegal acts had previously been limited to larcenies and kindred crimes, less than those punishable as capital offenses, and by which he could obtain a living without work. He was a native of Arkansas, born in Faulkner County, in January, 1870, of an Italian father and an American mother; they were poor but honorable people, engaged in farming. The elder Casharago was killed while the son was a mere boy by falling from a stable loft, breaking his neck, after which his widow married a man by the name of Jones, a respected citizen of Faulkner County.

Jimmie Casharago's rearing was like that of the majority of country boys; he was given a limited education and as a child was pleasant and companionable, agreeable of address and manners and of temperate habits; but "Jimmie would steal." While still in his tender years he developed a tendency to taking other people's property, by numerous petty thefts, and on convenient occasions he stole money from cash drawers, but was not prosecuted because he was too young to be subjected to the State laws. The fact that his mother would make restitution, so far as lay in her power, seemed only to accentuate his love of crime and he grew from bad to worse.

When he was eighteen years old his grandfather died leaving to him a considerable property, and proceedings were instituted in the court of chancery to enable him to gain the benefit, during his minority, of his interest in his grandfather's estate. A few months later, April 29, 1888, he married Miss Mary A. Salter, seventeen years old, the pretty daughter of a prominent Faulkner County farmer. For a year and two months they lived together, Jimmie meanwhile spending his money freely and going, by degrees, deeper into crime, and in the latter part of June, 1889, he was forced to leave his home and wife on account of some shady transactions, embracing forgeries on prominent men of the county and obtaining money by false pretenses. His plan of operations was to draw notes purporting to have been given him by men, real or imaginary, whose names he signed as having purchased from him certain real estate, the notes being due in from two to three years; the amounts of these notes aggregated $10,000 and were sold or traded in various ways. In one instance he traded several of these notes for small stocks of goods with which he intended to start a mercantile business, and when finally brought to account he said he could see no other way to make a living; that he intended to sell the goods at a profit and then redeem and cancel the notes before they became due. The sudden discovery of his schemes caused him to leave the vicinity before he had begun to realize upon them; he was followed and was arrested by L. B. Dawson, sheriff of Faulkner County, and lodged in jail at Conway but he soon broke out and fled to the mountains of northern Arkansas.

Officers pursued and routed him from his hiding place, but he eluded arrest and went to the eastern part of the State, obtained employment with a country merchant, remaining quiet and law-abiding for a season, when, yielding again to his itching palm, he rifled his employer's trunk of money, a pistol and other valuables and escaped to other climes.

Nothing more was heard of him, in official circles, until about the first of the year, 1890, when he was arrested in Obion County, Tennessee, for breaking into a business house and stealing money and merchandise. He was tried and convicted of burglary and larceny, on February 20, 1890, and was sentenced to a term of three years in the State penitentiary at Nashville. He was a model prisoner and after serving his term and being released he gravitated to his old home, on the scout.

His love of crime was not dead, however, and his next move in the direction of the terrible fate awaiting him was the most peculiar and foolhardy, not to say ingenious, of all his crooked transactions. His friends welcomed his reappearance and helped to shelter him for a few months, and when he asked his step-sister for the loan of a mule he was not refused; he borrowed the animal with a purpose, or if not, his purpose formed as he rode away, shaping in his mind his next plan for making money without work. He proceeded to Conway County, Arkansas, next adjoining Faulkner County, and succeeded in mortgaging the mule for enough money to buy another. He then mortgaged both mules and bought a wagon; then mortgaged mules and wagon and bought a load of merchandise, and after loading the latter on his ill-gotten wagon, drove away to the mountains and began peddling, having performed one of the most unique acts of swindling on record. He was pursued, captured and returned to the Conway County jail at Morrillton. He escaped before the day set for his trial and went to the home of an uncle in Faulkner County. His relative had heard of his latest fraction of the laws, but he disliked to turn his own sister's son over to the officers, besides. the young man pleaded for assistance, asserted that he had committed his last of crime and promised to do right and go at honest labor, if given an opportunity, at some place among strangers where his being unknown would give him immunity from arrest. His uncle's heart filled with pity and finally he gave him a letter of introduction to. an old friend, Zacharia VV. Thatch, a farmer, in Washington County,

317

in the western part of the State, knowing that on his request, his friend would at least give the boy a home for a while and an opportunity to earn an honest living.

Meanwhile, a period of nearly a year had elapsed since his release from the Tennessee penitentiary and young Casharago arrived at the home of his new friend, as a fugitive from justice, late in autumn, 1894. The farmer perused his letter and readily gave him shelter and a home. There was little work required on the farm during the winter months and Casharago managed to endure the conditions surrounding him with a fair degree of contentment.

In the following April, Thatch, being in poor health and wishing to inspect the land in the new country recently opened to settlement, decided to take a trip west into Oklahoma, and desiring company he took the young man with him, having become somewhat attached to him by reason of his agreeable manners. They started with a two horse wagon and a camping outfit and several horses for trading purposes, among the litter being a stallion upon which was pi-iced considerable value. They proceeded by easy stages and about May 13, they reached Buck Creek, a few miles from Keokuk Falls, near the line between the Creek Nation and Oklahoma.

The two men were seen together several times in this vicinity and on the night of the murder they camped at the place where the dead body of Thatch was afterwards found. On that night two shots were heard at or near the camp, and on the following day, Casharago broke camp and drove away. He passed the house of a farmer named King, with whom he conversed, giving his name as George Wilson and claiming the horses and other property as his own. After proceeding a short distance he again went into camp.

On the morning of May 26, a man named Lee discovered the dead and decomposed body of Thatch floating in the creek near the late camp. It was partly covered with rocks and logs and examination showed that the head had been crushed by a blow from an axe and two fingers of one hand had been shot away. It was also discovered that the murderer had tied rocks to the body as a means of holding it beneath the surface of the water, and investigation of the ground about the camp disclosed that a fire had been built over the spot where Thatch's blood was spilled, in a frantic endeavor to destroy the tell-tale stains. Owing to the nature of the soil and on account of dry weather, the ground was traversed by large cracks or seams and into one of these the blood had run; at the trial of Casharago, for the murder of Thatch, chunks of earth, saturated with the blood of his victim, taken from below the surface were exhibited as evidence. Alluding to these circumstances, when pronouncing sentence on the murderer, Judge Parker said, in tones that will never be forgotten by us who heard them:

"Even nature revolted against your crime; the ground cracked open and drinking up the blood held it in a fast embrace until the time that it should appear against you; the water, too, threw up its dead and bore upon its placid bosom the foul evidence of your crime."

At the time the body was found Wilson was still camping in the vicinity, not far away. He was arrested, and on viewing the body he identified it as that of Thatch, his uncle. Investigation of Wilson's effects discovered blood on the bed clothes and other garments and also on an axe. Wilson's explanation of the blood stains was that he and his uncle had killed and dressed a prairie chicken and had performed an operation on a horse. At the trial, before Judge Parker, Wilson testified that the body was not that of Thatch; that Thatch had left to go to the Kickapoo opening; that it was true that part of the stock found in his possession belonged to Thatch, but that the latter was not dead but had been seen soon after he went away, at El Reno, Oklahoma. He made as vigorous defense as possible under the circumstances, but he was convicted and sentenced to hang. His attorney, C. J. Frederick, appointed by Judge Parker, appealed to the Supreme Court, and the verdict of the lower court was affirmed.

S. C. McMillin, one of his cousins, visited the city a few days before the execution, and, under his directions, the body was placed in a coffin and conveyed to Conway for burial.

Just before he was executed he admitted being guilty of a number of crimes, but to the last moment he denied having killed Thatch. Among the crimes he confessed to having been implicated in were the Bentonville bank robbery and the train robbery at Pryor Creek; he added:

"Frank Chaney is now serving a ten year penitentiary sentence for participating in that crime, of which I am guilty."

When Casharago was first arrested he was only known by the name he gave the officers and he was indicted under the name of George Wilson. Gradually his real name leaked out and by the agency of the press it became known about his former home that a man named George Wilson, said to be also James Casharago, was under indictment at Fort Smith for a murder committed in the Indian Territory. Many doubted the truth of the rumor, though some of his former acquaintances who saw him in the Federal jail vouched for the story. The majority were still not satisfied, however, and a vast crowd of people who had known Jimmie Casharago gathered at the depot to view the remains and make sure that the boy they had known and the murderer, George Wilson, were the same.

Appended is Judge Parker's charge to the jury that convicted Casharago, delivered Wednesday afternoon, December 18, 1895. It was considered the masterpiece among all his numerous charges to petit juries.

JUDGE PARKER'S BEST PETIT JURY CHARGE

"Gentlemen, a moment's reflection satisfies us that in every trial of this character, there is involved one of the gravest propositions upon which depends the social happiness of men, women and children living in a state of civilized society and under a civilized government. That proposition is whether the law of the land, that rule of action which prescribes the conduct of men, when in the hands of the intelligent jurymen of the country, affords a sufficient safeguard for all the rights of the governed, and especially that highest of rights known as belonging to man—the right to life. I say, in every trial of this kind, there is involved that proposition which determines the weal or the woe of the people of this land; that proposition upon which depends the enforcement of the law of the land, the mission of which is the peace and social order and security of all innocent and law-abiding people of the nation. This being a proposition of this magnitude it can be seen at a glance that the responsibility placed upon you by the law as a part of the good people of this land, is the greatest responsibility which you are ever called upon to assume as citizens. Nothing, I say, can ever be done by you, if you perform your duties properly, which, will so subserve the true interests of the people of this land. Because of the magnitude of this responsibility, because of the greatness of the issue, you are entitled to the sympathy and honest support of all good men in the faithful discharge of your duty according as you may see the right as God gives you to see it. But notwithstanding you are entitled to this sympathy, when you consider the attributes which you possess, the duty is lightened. When we but reflect for a moment that you are ^possessed with memories, with judgment, with reason, with the power of observation, with the knowledge of right and wrong, with a high sense of justice, a strong desire to see the right prevail, an inherent love of equal and exact justice to all under all circumstances, a reverence for the truth, and high regard for the law of the land—when you have all of these things as attributes of your nature, and as a part of the qualifications which enable you to perform rightfully, honestly and well this high duty cast upon you by the laws of your land; I say the consideration of sympathy is lessened, because when you can apply, in the discharge of this great duty, these great attributes of your nature, the duty is easier of solution, easier of performance, than it would be if you did not possess them. Besides these attributes you have all nature to aid you in your search for the truth in this case. It has been truthfully said, it has been well said, that Providence always throws a protecting shield around the innocent, and it may be as truthfully said as a corollary to that proposition, that Providence always points to the guilty as unerringly as it protects the innocent. There may be exceptions, but nature, when properly studied by her subjects, never lies to them. They may sometimes misinterpret her on abstract questions, it may take long to understand her rightly, but when once properly understood the Almighty never lies, and nature is but his revealed will. When he has forged a chain of circumstances around an individual, he has done it for the wisest of purposes—to protect human life, to teach those who think they have a safeguard in the secrecy which is to accompany the commission of a crime that detection is all around them, and justice is certain to overtake them. For centuries, yes, for ages, if geology be true, the lightnings had played in the heavens and men were awed and terrified from their sight. Morse came with the capacity to read their laws, and he chained them, and taught them to carry our messages of affection, our messages of fortune and misfortune, to friends thousands of miles away. When nature is correctly read she never deceives. For centuries the blood had gone to the heart and returned again to the extremities. For centuries physicians had

320

dissected the human frame and had failed to discover the great law of life, that the lungs received the oxygen from the air we breathe and transmit it to the blood; that the blood thus provided with new life was sent out to feed the most remote organ, it may be said by a mechanism more delicate than human genius has ever been able to construct. Harvey came, read nature's law aright, made the discovery, and it was no longer a mystery. And so it is with nature everywhere. We look out of that window and see the leaves falling from the trees. The unthinking say the frost has come and killed the leaf, and so it falls. Pick it up, and examine it. At the end of the stem you find a little cavity which covered a bud that had been gradually growing and growing and crowding the little leaf off until it fell, and next spring that little bud, which will remain torpid through the cold winter, will expand with the increased heat and grow into a green leaf. These are nature's laws which always tell the truth. These are nature's laws which are a part of the great system of nature, designed by its God. Nature's laws to govern the workings of nature in their innocence, and that they may serve the purposes of man. Nature has a set of laws which apply to the criminal acts of men as well as to their innocent acts. And let us read what one of the greatest American thinkers says upon that subject:

'The league between virtue and nature engages all things to assume a hostile front to vice. The beautiful laws and substances of the world prosecute and whip the criminal. He finds that things are arranged for truth and benefit, and that there is no den in the wide would to hide a rogue. Commit a crime, and the world is made of glass. Commit a crime, and it seems as if a coat of snow fell on the ground such as revealed in the woods the track of every partridge and fox and squirrel and mole. You cannot recall the spoken word. You cannot wipe out the foot track. You cannot draw up the ladder so as to leave no inlet or clew. Some damning circumstance always transpires. The laws and substances of nature, water, snow, wind, gravitation, become penalties to the thief.'

"So I say it is true that you have nature in her honesty, in her great purpose to subserve men, and especially to protect innocent life, to aid you in the solution of this problem, if you will but read her aright, and you can apply to her, and to her laws, these great attributes which belong to you, and which I have named, and when that application is properly made the solution of the problem of ascertaining the truth or falsity of the charge preferred against this defendant becomes, in my judgment, comparatively easy, one which is easy to solve one way or the other. You will find that by nature's law these things which are invariably left around human action, human conduct, called circumstances, if read aright by the true law of nature, will either always point towards innocence, and therefore it is truthfully said in the language of the book I read from that 'nature reveals innocence,' or if guilt exists they will invariably point, if read aright, towards guilt. And therefore, while nature, with all her mighty power protects innocence, she at the same time, in the interest of man, in the interest of the enforcement of the law, in the interest of the upholding of the dignity and power and supremacy of government that it may be reverenced by men and its laws obeyed by them, is equally all powerful in uncovering guilt. Then it is that we are to solve these problems by these tracks which nature has left around the occurrence, and which nature permits us to read. And I say to you, in this connection, that it is but these natural things which make up what we call in the law that volume of testimony so often resorted to in the courts, called circumstantial evidence. When true, when forming a connected chain, when properly produced to the jury, it is as all-powerful in its proving power as though a human agent in the shape of a living being had applied to the transaction at the time of its occurrence someone of his five senses in order that he might come here as a positive eye-witness before you and tell you of the occurrence. You see and understand that in this case, as in a large proportion of cases where human life has been taken, there is no human eye which witnessed the destruction of that life, except the eye of the author of the crime. The eye of the man who has been murdered, if murder exists, is closed in death. His tongue is silent. No one of his five senses can be used to reproduce the occurrence before you. It is true that he can be brought here with all of his gaping wounds, from which there was streaming his heart's blood, with his mangled clothing, with the bloody garments which were found near him—they can all be produced before you as inanimate circumstances upon which no influence can be exerted to induce them to tell that which is false. They are motiveless, they are inanimate, and therefore no motive can cause them to be influenced, and yet, though they be inanimate, in the language of the great poet, Shakespeare, they are made upon occasions like this to speak with wondrous power to enable you to see the truth of this case.

THE NATURE OF THE CHARGE

"Now, gentlemen, it is necessary that we should proceed in detail to see what this crime as charged is, then see whether or not it exists as charged, then whether or not this defendant is the author of that crime. These are the several general propositions which make up the one asserted here by the government in this indictment. It is stated in the first count of this indictment that this defendant took the life of the man who is alleged to have been murdered, named Zacharia W. Thatch, and that he did it willfully and with malice aforethought; that he did it with a blunt instrument, a more particular description of such blunt instrument being to the grand jurors unknown; that he used that blunt instrument in such a way as to willfully and with malice aforethought destroy the life of Zacharia W. Thatch. That is the charge in the first count of the indictment. The charge in the second count of the indictment pertains to the killing of the same man, of the same name, by the same party, the defendant, George W. Wilson. It is alleged in that count of the indictment that the means used by the defendant in taking the life of Zacharia W. Thatch were unknown to the grand jury, but that he used these unknown means in such a way as to willfully and with malice aforethought destroy his life. Now, if you believe this charge to be true, as I have named it to you, then you are to designate the count in the indictment which is appropriate as the one upon which you will find your verdict. If you find, from the circumstances of this case, that it was a blunt instrument used, and its nature was unknown to the grand jury, judging from the character of the evidence here, then your appropriate finding would be upon the first count of the indictment. If you are unable, as was the grand jury, in your judgment, from the testimony here, to find beyond a reasonable doubt the nature of the instrument used, then the appropriate finding would be upon the second count of the indictment, where the instrument is alleged to have been unknown to them.

"We now proceed, I say, in detail, to ascertain what propositions are necessary to be found. First, we are required to find that Zacharia W. Thatch is dead. That is the very initial point in this case. It is the point from which we start, because, if it should turn out in an investigation that a man was not dead, that stops the inquiry. We need not go any further. And by proceeding in this way there might be cases where the work could be shortened. I take up these propositions in detail because it makes it easier for you. If I were to tell you in a general way, by so many sentences, that certain things must be found, and stop there, you might overlook them when you came to make the application of the law. So we must enter into this charge in detail in order that you may the better recall the testimony bearing upon each proposition as we go along and have it fixed in your mind as to whether or not that proposition is established and established to the extent required by the law.

AS TO THE IDENTITY OF THE DECEASED

"In ascertaining the proposition that he is dead, that inquiry necessarily involves the identity of the body found, with the dead body of Zacharia W. Thatch. Then it becomes, right at this point, a question of identity, because the government does not produce the body; the government claims that was the body of Mr. Thatch, and it is to the identity of that body that we are to confine our investigation here. Now we are to proceed to ascertain how this identity may be established, and in doing that we cannot do better than to read from the charge of the court here, delivered to the jury which tried the case of the United States versus Graves, a man tried in this court some time ago, and you will ascertain from the principles of law laid down in that charge exactly how you may ascertain that this was the body of Mr. Thatch; but you will bear in mind all the time that all these propositions I will enumerate to you in detail—the fact of the death of Thatch, involving his identity; the fact that he died by violence of the kind described in the indictment; the fact that violence was criminal, and the concluding fact that the defendant was the author of that violence, may all be established by these things called circumstances, which are a part of nature.

"This is a case like hundreds of others which occur in the administration of justice in this country where you may not be able to look upon the face of a dead man, or look into it and see that it is the face of a certain man, because the face may have been destroyed. The decaying finger of time may have touched it. It may no longer exist, and the question then becomes pertinent right here: how we are to establish the identity in this case of Thatch, how we are to ascertain that proposition. You see a man alive, with whom you are acquainted—your friend, a man you have met often;

you can look into his face and from the nature of that face, its form or appearance, and its very cast, its features, its lineaments, made up of a number of things combined, you can swear, from an observation of these, to the identity of the person, from that face and from this combination of things which produces a certain appearance, and this combination, as it is illuminated by the light which comes through the windows of the soul, his expression and intelligence which exists in the human mind and which beams out over the face, you are able to know it. You can look into the face of a friend or an acquaintance and name him as a man whom you know. When a man is dead this illuminating power which is connected with the human mind, and which comes from the mind, disappears, and, necessarily, the human face, while it is preserved, until it is destroyed, only presents the general outline which it had when the person was alive. There was something about it in life which is gone forever, it is destroyed, and you will have a little more difficulty in recognizing the face of a man. although he may be an acquaintance, yet, as a general rule, you can recognize him by his face. But suppose his face is gone, the body is partially, or it may be entirely, destroyed; what then are you to do? When a man has been murdered the rights of society and the rights of its members have been thus wickedly trampled upon by a brutal assassination; are you to make no effort to discover the crime and punish the criminal because the identity of the remains of the person, by the means I have named, cannot be ascertained? Not at all. You can go to the means extraneous to the body of the person. You can, in other words, fall back upon that evidence which is so often and so generally and usually relied upon, called 'circumstantial evidence,' to ascertain that fact. Now, the fact to be proven under this proposition is the identity of Zacharia W. Thatch, the man alleged by the government to have been murdered. That is a proposition which, if a man would come before you and say he had looked at the dead body, he saw it, and from its face, its form, its appearance he knew it, then you could take the statements of a witness of that character as the positive statements of an eyewitness to that fact. As I have already told you, in regard to a live person j we can recognize it from a combination of things, such as the character of the nose, the appearance of the eyes, the shape of the mouth, and the general appearance and outline of the face of the party, and all these things which are illuminated by that light which comes from the soul, from the mind. When there is no opportunity of that kind, identity may be made in that way by a person having looked at and observed the man, and being able to tell what he observed at that time and to tell it to a jury. Now, in the absence of both of these opportunities, the man being dead, and thus one of the means of recognition gone, or if the face is so far decayed as that persons cannot look into that face, the inquiry naturally arises whether there are other means of identification. Mr. Burrill, an eminent writer upon the subject of circumstantial evidence, says:

"'Where the body is found, shortly after the commission of the crime, and the face has not been disfigured by the violence employed, or by accident, or in the natural course of decay, the identification is made in the form of direct and positive proof of

324

the fact by those to whom the deceased is known. But where the features have been destroyed the body may be identified by circumstances, as by the dress, articles found on the person, and by natural marks upon the person. In Colt's case, where a considerable portion of the face had been beaten in by blows—Colt was the brother of the inventor of Colt's pistols, and he murdered a man in the city of New York, mutilated him by cutting him up, put him in a barrel, started to ship him to Charleston, or New Orleans, or some other place, and was discovered—and the progress of decay had otherwise rendered direct recognition impossible, the body was identified in this way. In McCann's case, where the face of the deceased had been eaten away by the hogs, identification was effected in r. similar manner. Even where nothing but the skeleton has been found, it may sometimes be identified by peculiar marks, and by objects discovered near it. In the case of Rex versus Clews, the body of a man, after the lapse of 23 years, was identified by his widow from some peculiarity about his teeth, and by a carpenter's rule and a pair of shoes found with the remains, and also identified. But in examining skeletons, great attention should be paid to their anatomical characteristics, upon which the important fact of the age and sex of the person depends, as these may be decisive of the whole case in favor of the accused. Where the body has been purposely mutilated, and especially where it has been dismembered, with a view to its destruction, by fire or otherwise, its identification becomes a matter of greater difficulty, the head being usually destroyed first, for the very purpose of preventing recognition, but it occasionally' happens that even the agency of fire, which is generally selected as the readiest and most effectual means of destruction, proves inadequate to the purpose contemplated.'

"Sometimes it may happen that it will not even dry up and destroy his blood.

"In Webster's case, the head of the deceased had been placed in a furnace, and exposed to a strong heat for a considerable time, but some blocks of mineral teeth resisted the action of the fire so effectively that they were identified by a dentist as part of a set of artificial teeth which had been made for the deceased, and which the latter wore at the time of his disappearance. Some other portions of the body, which had not been subjected to the action of the fire, were also identified by peculiar appearances. A case is mentioned by Mr. Wills, in which the remains of a female, consisting merely of the trunk of the body, from which the other parts had been cut, were identified by a curious train of circumstantial evidence, embracing several facts of conduct on the part of the prisoner.'

"Mr. Wills, on circumstantial evidence, further says:

"'It is not necessary that the remains should be identified by direct and positive evidence, where such proof is impracticable, and especially if it has been rendered so by the action of the person accused. A man was convicted of the murder of a creditor, who had called for the payment of a debt, and whose body he cut in pieces, and attempted to dispose of by burning. The effluvium and other circumstances alarmed the neighbors, and a portion of the body remained unconsumed, sufficient to prove that is was that of a male adult, and various articles which had belonged to the deceased were found on the person of the prisoner, who was apprehended putting off from Black Rock, at Liverpool, after having ineffectually attempted to elude justice by drowning himself. The identification of human remains has been facilitated by the preservation of the head and other parts in spirits; by the anti-putrescent action of the substances used to destroy life; by the similarity of the undigested remains of food found in the stomach with the food which it has been known that the victim has eaten; by means of clothing or other articles of the deceased traced to the possession of the prisoner, and unexplained by any evidence, that he became innocently possessed of them; by means of artificial teeth and by means of other mechanical coincidences.'

"Mr. Wills further says upon the subject of identification:

"'Identification is often satisfactorily inferred from the correspondence of fragments of garments, or of written or printed papers, or of other articles belonging to or found in the possession of persons charged with crime, with other portions or fragments discovered at or near the scene of crime, or otherwise relating to the *corpus delicti*, or by means of wounds or marks inflicted upon the person of the offender.'

"I think that is sufficient upon that proposition. You are told by these cases I have referred to (and they are simply the declarations of the law which are recognized everywhere as being the law) that the identity of the remains may be proven purely by circumstances, may be proven by circumstances extraneous to the body—that is, that there are garments found which belonged to him, f:und upon him, or identified as his, and garments found near where the body was found, or garments or property of his, proven to be his, found in the possession of a defendant and not satisfactorily accounted for upon the theory that his possession is an innocent one. All these meanings, then, in this case may be used for the purpose of enabling you to come to the conclusion as to whether the body of the man found in Rock Creek, at the place described by the witnesses, was the body of Zacharia W. Thatch. If so, if these circumstances all combined, whether connected immediately with the body or extraneous of it, in your judgment, as honest, as intelligent and as just men, are sufficient to establish this proposition beyond a reasonable doubt, then you have proven the fact that Zacharia W. Thatch is dead, because that body was dead; there can be no controversy over that proposition. If that was his body, then he is dead. That is the first proposition to be established.

AS TO HOW DEATH WAS PRODUCED

"The next proposition to be established is, did he die by violence, either of the kind named in the first count of the indictment, or by violence exercised in such a way as that the means by which it was exercised—that is, the weapon with which death was produced—was unknown to the grand jury, and is not known to you, beyond a reasonable doubt. That is the second proposition to be established. Now, how are you to get at that? By the same method by which you may find the other one. You are to see in what condition that body was; whether or not it presented any evidence of violence. You go to the evidence and see what the condition of the skull was; whether the testimony shows to you that it was crushed or that it was broken. If so, that is a fact which would ordinarily satisfy reasonable men that that act was one which might produce the death of Thatch, that it might cause his death, and you would be justified, in the opinion of the court, in so finding. But, of course, as to what the evidence is, and as to its weight, you are to finally determine, and any suggestions which may be made by the court upon the weight of testimony are made to you with the distinct reservation to you that you are the ultimate arbiters, not only as to what the testimony is, but as to what its proving power amounts to. While the Federal courts, under the practice prevailing in them, may take up the testimony of each witness, even, and detail it to the jury, tell them, in the judgment of the court what it proves, I do not do that but if I were to do it, it is always done by leaving to you the ultimate right of passing upon that very proposition and solving it for yourselves. Then, upon this point, you look to the testimony and see from it whether or not the second requisite: of this charge is established beyond a reasonable doubt.

MURDER DEFINED—(a) 'WILLFULLY.'

"The third proposition is, was he killed willfully, and with malice aforethought. These are the attributes of murder. In addition to the physical fact that he is dead, he must be killed in a certain way so that we are able to say, under the law, that he was murdered, that his life was taken in that wicked and wanton way defined by the laws of the United States to be murder. These attributes—that is, that it was done willfully and done with malice aforethought—are the things which go to characterize an act so that it may be named as murder. They have a legal meaning attached to them. Each expression has a legal meaning attached to it. For that reason we must stop here long enough to get that meaning, to ascertain what it is. We will inquire first, whether that killing was done willfully; we will see what is meant by that. We will then go to the method that may be adopted by you in finding that proposition. What is meant by 'willful' as used in this connection? The law says it means intentional, and not accidental. That is a definition of willful which is remarkable for its brevity, and also for its power. It is the most powerful definition which could be given when we get in mind the strong contrast existing between a death produced by an accident and one where there has operated to produce the act which results in death the agency called the human mind. In the law a thing which is called an 'accident' is something which transpires after a man has used the care exacted of him by the law to prevent its occurrence. When he does that, although human life may be destroyed, it is called an accident; it is called misadventure; it is not a crime. Whenever he uses that care which the law says he ought to use under the circumstances, considering the character of the weapon handled or being used, and the dangerous consequences which may be produced by it, you have a condition which is not willful, a condition which is outside of the domain of willfulness, and it is called a case of misadventure. Now, the opposite of that is this expression which enters into the crime of murder, known as an intentional act. It means this: If the evidence in a case shows that the act which produced death was intentionally done, because of the intimate connection between an act which will produce death known as a deadly or dangerous act and death, the law says you are authorized to find not only that the act was done intentionally but that the death was intentional, because of that connection between cause and effect, between action and result, between the deadly act and the death. Then in this case, if, from the circumstances of it, from the character of the wounds, from the fact that the skull was crushed, from the concealment of the remains, from the effort to cover up all traces of the fact of the killing, and of the manner of the killing, and from all these facts and circumstances combined which have gone to you as evidence it this case, you are able to conclude as rational men, as just men and as men loving truth, beyond a reasonable doubt that that killing was done willfully, then you may take that proposition as established, you may take it as proven in the case. You can only know it, when a murder is alleged to have been done, in secret as this is alleged to have been done, by the means of these circumstances, by these means which nature by her great law presents to you as proven facts either to show the truth or falsity of the proposition alleged. You can only know it that way, as you can only know all the elements which enter into any and every secret crime committed as this was committed, if it was committed, in the hour of night, when no human eye except the eye of the author of the crime beheld it. You can only know it by the light of these things left around it, and which can be seen through nature and by nature's laws to enable you to fathom this mystery, to know the truth of this case. Then, look at the evidence. You must understand the meaning of this expression, not only because it is necessary for you to understand it as an element which enters into the crime of murder, but because if you find this to be a case where the killing was done without provocation, and therefore outside of a state of case where the law of self-defense would be applicable, or a killing in the absence of mitigating facts and therefore outside of a state of case where the law of manslaughter would be applicable, and you have a set of facts and circumstances which show that it was done willfully, done wrongfully, done illegally, you have that which establishes the other element of the crime known as 'malice aforethought,' which is the distinguishing characteristic of the crime of murder, that which stamps it as murder and gives it a character different from any other homicide, or from any other crime which results in death.

(b) 'MALICE AFORETHOUGHT.'

"Let us now see how 'malice aforethought' is defined. The law says that this characteristic of murder means the doing of a wrongful and illegal act in a way which is not justified or mitigated, and which act results in the taking of a human life causelessly and wickedly in such a way as to show premeditation, to show that, it was thought of beforehand, to show that it was planned by its perpetrator, by its author, and that it was executed by him in pursuance of a previous purpose to take that human life. We cannot entertain a purpose to wrongfully destroy human life. We can entertain a purpose to defend ourselves and be justified in entertaining it, and we can deliberate upon it, we can premeditate upon it, but if it be a case of killing where there is nothing of that kind in it, and the killing is shown to have been wrongfully and illegally done, and the facts and circumstances show, under such a state of case, premeditation and deliberation, these are evidences of malice aforethought, because they show the existence of a state of case where human life has been destroyed in such a way as to show that it was wrongfully and illegally destroyed, without just cause, or in the absence of mitigating facts. Mr. Wharton, of his work upon Homicide, says:

"'Malice is implied from any deliberate, cruel act committed by one person against another, however sudden, as where a man kills another suddenly without any, or without considerable, provocation, and with a deadly weapon, it being a maxim based on ordinary experience that no person unless under the influence of malice would be guilty of such an act upon slight or upon no apparent cause.'

"Again, upon this subject:

"'Where there is a deliberate intent to kill, unless it be in the discharge of a duty imposed by the public authorities, or in self-defense or in necessity, the offense must be murder at common law, as evidenced by the execution of the deliberate intent, wrongfully and improperly.'

"Further, upon the definition of malice aforethought—and I want you to observe in this connection that there is a proposition referred to which will be a little more elaborately given after awhile, and which has reference to the fact that you are not required in the investigation of these cases, before you can come to a conclusion of guilt, to find the existence of a motive for the crime, or the adequacy of that motive, for if you were to stop, to hesitate and to fail to enforce the law and thus stop the wheels of justice until you could find an adequate motive for a deliberate and wicked and unprovoked killing, you never would, in the judgment of honest men and of men with pure hearts and proper minds, find a motive which was adequate, because all this world, with its riches, if it be a case where lucre was the cause, was the motive, is not a motive sufficient in the judgment of a good man to destroy an innocent human life, and therefore we never do find motives which are adequate, and if we are to wait until we do that is the end of all enforcement of the law, that is the end of all the protecting power arising from the enforcement of the law; but we are not required to do that, as you will learn further on. I read to you now from the case of Lander vs. The State, upon the subject of malice aforethought:

"'When the law makes use of the term 'malice aforethought' as descriptive of the crime of murder, it is not to be understood merely in the sense of a principle of malevolence to particulars, but as meaning that the fact has been attended with such circumstances as are the ordinary symptoms of a wicked and malignant spirit.'

"It is not necessary to show that a man had special spite or hatred or ill will against the man whom he may have killed, because it very often happens that men kill when there is nothing of this kind existing. But there is another motive which prompts them. There is always a motive to cause the hand of the murderer to strike its victim. There always does exist a motive for that, but sometimes we lose it because of its inadequacy in our judgment—we overlook it sometimes. It is not necessary that that should be proven. It is not necessary that it should be shown that there was any special spite or hatred or ill will, against the party slain. That sometimes exists as a motive, as a cause, and sometimes it does not; sometimes there are other reasons for the killing. A man may kill for revenge, he may kill from jealously, he may kill from a great many things from, which spring special spite, or a grudge, or a state of ill will which he desires to satisfy, but there are many other reasons, for a killing which are equally as wicked, and even perhaps more so, because it often happens when a man kills from ill will that he has considerable provocation. He goes too far, he exceeds his authority and takes human life. But still, when we look at the uniformity and the wickedness of the mind of men there are many things which are highly provocative in the law which are not justifiable, nor can they be mitigated, and that is. a case where the man who takes human life is entitled to the greatest sympathy, if he is otherwise a good man. It often happens that this is true. But when we come to a case where a man kills for gain, for lucre, to get that which does not belong to him, we must all agree in the truthfulness of the proposition that that is a motive of the basest character, that that is a motive of the most degrading nature, showing a heart void of social duty and a mind fatally bait upon mischief. Further, upon this line:

"'Malice, in its legal sense, denotes a wrongful act done intentionally, without just cause or excuse. The legal import of the term, it has been said, differs from its acceptation in common conversation. It is not, as in ordinary speech, only an expression of hatred or ill will to an individual, but means any wicked or mischievous intent of the mind. Thus, in the crime of murder, which is always stated in the indictment to be committed with malice aforethought, it is neither necessary in support of such indictment to show that the person had any enmity to the deceased, nor would proof of the absence of ill will furnish the accused with any defense when it is proved that the act of killing was intentional and done without justifiable cause. Malice in law is a mere inference of law which results simply from a willful transgression of the law. It imports simply the perverse disposition of one who does an act which is unlawful without sufficient legal excuse therefor. And the precise and particular intention with which he did the act, whether he was moved by anger, hatred or a desire for gain, is immaterial, He acts maliciously in willfully transgressing the law.'

Now, the other expression which denotes the meaning of malice aforethought is: The killing of a human being done in such a way as to show that he who did it had a heart void of social duty and a mind fatally bent upon mischief. That implies that the man who thus kills has forgotten the great obligation which we all owe to each other not to destroy innocent human life but to protect it. And when we do destroy it without just cause, when we do destroy it for gain, in order that we may get property, or from a spirit of vengeance, or from any other motive which stamps the killing as a crime of a high degree, and which is of a character that may be taken into account by those who pass in judgment upon the case as evidence of a malignant spirit, as evidence of a heart which is void of this duty, when the circumstances, from their wickedness, from their unprovoked character, from the fact that there is nothing shown to mitigate the act or to justify it, are in existence as evinced by the testimony, the very fact that such an act is proven shows that he who did it had a heart fatally bent upon-mischief. There are degrees of crime by the law of morals, and there are degrees of crime by the laws of the land. If a crime which results in the taking of a human life is committed by lying in wait, by watching an opportunity in the darkness of the night, by taking action when the party is off his guard, such a crime is known to the law of the land as assassination, as the highest crime which can be committed which destroys human life, because it is done by taking advantage of the unsuspecting victim; the party who commits it awaits his opportunity, he takes advantage of the helpless condition of the innocent and murdered man; and it is known, I say, as assassination; it is known as a killing by lying in wait, and it is denounced by the legislatures in every State and in every civilized country as a killing which alone is murder—a killing by lying in wait, a killing by assassination.

THE LAW AS TO MOTIVE FOR A CRIME

"I told you a while ago that to enable you to find the existence of malice aforethought, or that the act was done willfully, you need not stop to hunt for motive. If the motive exists, if it is proven, it becomes evidentiary in the case and you may use it. You may use it not only to enable you to characterize the killing, to show what manner of killing it was, but you have the right to use it also to bring that killing home to a particular individual charged with it, because if you can trace the connection between the motive existing in the breast or mind of a particular party as the cause which produces the deadly act, you have a fact which brings the crime home to the party who possessed that motive, and, I say, if it is manifested in a case, you are not required to look after it, you are not required to pass upon its adequacy, you may still use it as evidence in the case for the purposes I have named. Now, Mr. Wharton, that eminent author upon the subject of criminal law, in his work upon Homicide, Sec. 670, A, says:

"'It is sometimes urged, is it likely that one man should kill another for so small an article? Are we not to infer when there is a homicide which is followed by the stealing of a mere trifle that the homicide was the result of sudden passion rather than lucre causa? Or for some prejudice or spite is it likely that one man would assassinate another, and thus expose himself to the gallows? No doubt, when a tender mother kills her child or a friend kills a friend, and nothing more than the fact of killing is proved, we may be led to infer misadventure or insanity from the motivelessness of the act. But we have no right to make such an inference because the motive is disproportionate. We are all of us apt to act upon very inadequate motives, and the history of crime shows that murders are generally committed from motives comparatively trivial. A man unaccustomed to control his passions, and unregulated by religious or moral sense, exaggerates an affront or nourishes a suspicion until he determines that only the blood of the supposed offender can relieve the pang. Crime is rarely logical. Under a government where the laws are executed with ordinary certainty, all crime is a blunder, as well as a wrong. If we should hold that no crime is to be punished except such as is National, then there would be no crime to be punished, for no crime can be found that is rational. The motive is never correlative to the crime, never accurately proportioned to it. Nor does this apply solely to the very poor. Very rich men have been known to defraud others even of trifles, to forge wills, to kidnap and kill, so that an inheritance might be theirs. When a powerful passion seeks gratification it is no extenuation that the act is illogical, for when passion is once allowed to operate reason loosens its restraints.'

"There is the germ from which springs this bloody crime which results in the death of innocent human beings—unbridled passion—a desire for gain—a mind which has never been regulated by that high moral sense which governs honest men, a mind which is not prompted by that spirit of amity and good-fellowship which causes a good man to love another as his brother. That is all out of the mind. He may be shrewd, he may be quick-witted, in some respects, he may be sagacious, but when he becomes a criminal by assassination, by killing another in an unprovoked way, in the darkness of night, he does it because he is entirely void of moral nature; he has not that principle of right imbedded in his mind which teaches him the difference between right and wrong, and that is the secret of the commission of a crime committed in that way. A little further upon the subject of 'motive,' reading from the charge of Judge Landon in the Billings' trial, a noted case in the State of New York, where he said:

"'I speak first of motive. No man commits a crime without some motive leading him to commit it. That motive may seem to be strong or weak. You are not to inquire whether the motive is one that would ordinarily lead to the commission of the crime charged. It is difficult for the mind that is fortified by the consciousness of its own rectitude to conceive of an adequate motive for any crime. No motive will lead an entirely just man to the commission of any crime. You could not be moved to take the life of your fellow-man except in the just defense of your own lives and rights, or the just defense of the lives and rights of those whom it is your duty to defend. But just defense is no crime. You may, however, properly inquire what motives usually lead men to the commission of crimes, and you will find where mens' consciences and morals are depraved they are often led into the gravest of crimes by the simplest of motives. A small sum of money, a word spoken in anger or insult, wrongs real or imaginary, revenge, jealousy, hatred, envy and malice often lead to the crime of murder.'

"We find that any one of these may become the mainspring of high crimes of this nature.

FURTHER AS TO 'MALICE AFORETHOUGHT.'

"A word or two further as to how you may find this distinguishing trait of murder known as 'malice aforethought.' I have already told you that you may find it, as well as other propositions in the case, from the circumstances surrounding that case.

I will add to that by saying that you must find it in that way if you are to find it at all, because it is a condition of the mind, just like 'willfully.' You cannot know a mental condition except by the light of circumstances. No human power has ever devised any scheme by which we can apply to the working of the human mind directly or immediately any one of the five senses. You cannot touch it, you cannot taste it, you cannot feel it, you cannot hear it, you cannot smell it; therefore, there is no direct method of understanding the movements of the mind, but we are to bear in mind all the time that by law and by logic it is a legitimate method to reason from effect to cause, or from cause to effect, and when you have an effect produced, when you have a dead body presenting marks of deadly violence, you are to gather up all the circumstances connected with that death, if you find that to be the condition as an effect, and to reason back to the cause of it. If it is an act which evidences that it was done deliberately, done because the mind dictated it should be done, and not done accidentally, then we have that which shows the existence of premeditation, of thought of beforehand, and consequently that which shows malice aforethought. We may take into consideration all the facts showing the time of the killing, the manner of the killing, the concealment of the fact of death, or the attempt to conceal it by placing the body under water and putting logs upon it, the attempt to obliterate evidences of the death—all these things are pertinent facts, pertinent circumstances surrounding the transaction to show, first, that a killing occurred, and to show it was a crime, and to show that it had connected with it this attribute of murder known as 'malice aforethought.' We may resort to all these circumstances for that purpose as means which we must use if we are to get at the proposition as to whether the killing was one which was murder or not, because, as I have already told you, you cannot know it in any other way.

AS TO THE EVIDENCE

"There are but few more things to be said by the court in this case. You are to bear in mind that there are just two general propositions entering into your verdict, the truth of the case and the principle of the law applicable to that truth. I have given to you the language of the law defining this crime of murder charged in this indictment. Then the question becomes pertinent upon my part to ask you whether or not, in your judgment, the proposition asserted in this indictment has been so proven, as under the principles of the law which I will give you in a moment, the crime of murder has been established. If that is the truth of the case, then the principle of the law applicable to that truth is that which defines the crime which tells you what is murder. In that way you get at a rational result; in that way you arrive at what is called your true speech, your very dictum—your verdict. That is the way you arrive at it by finding the truth and applying the law applicable to that truth, and these are the two general propositions which enter into your verdict. Every proclamation which you make here

333

in the shape of a verdict has involved in it and interwoven with it, I say, the law of the case which is applicable to the truth of it as you find it by your judgment and by your consciences.

"Now we come to the point where I am to remind you, as I have already, but I remind you again, that your certain duty is to find out what the truth of the case is as ascertained by you from the evidence which has been offered before you. As we so often remark, it is impossible to reproduce actually and really this occurrence, or to reproduce it as it would be reproduced upon a stage. It is a drama which cannot be presented to a jury in that way. The bloody drama can only be seen by the light of the testimony which illuminates it, which lights it up, so you are able, as honest, conscientious, and intelligent men, of judgment and reason and memory, having a desire to arrive at the truth, to see it by the light of these circumstances which are brought here as witnesses and offered before you in this case. Then let us go over again the general propositions necessary to be found. First, you are to find whether the man alleged to have been killed is dead, and in passing upon that you are to take into consideration all of these circumstances surrounding it, and whether he was killed in such a way as to make the crime the crime of murder. Then when we come to the proposition as to the guilt or innocence of the defendant you are to ascertain whether by the light of this testimony he had the means at hand to produce this deadly result, and, secondly, whether he had the opportunity to produce it. Then what are the circumstances in the case pointing to the guilt or innocence of the defendant. All these facts and circumstances you have a right to take into consideration; you have a right to have them all pass in review again and again, if necessary, when you come to consider the case in your jury room, in order that you may the better see whether guilt or innocence exists here. Every item of testimony is to be considered, not by itself alone, because some of it may be very insignificant when considered alone, but when considered in conjunction with other facts, when considered as a link going to make up the chain of evidence, it may have great proving power, it may have great weight as a fact in the case. Then it is your duty to see what presumptions you can legitimately draw from the facts and circumstances in this case. The law says that if a mm has been killed, and killed in such a way as to show it was done murderously under the law I have given you defining the crime of murder, then you are to look to see whether the party accused of the killing was found in possession of any of the property of the man killed. If so, that is the foundation for a presumption; it is not conclusive in the beginning, but it is a presumption which you are to look at just as you would look at it as reasonable men outside of the jury box. The party so found in possession of such property, recently after the crime, is required to account for it, to show that as far as he was concerned that possession was innocent, and was honest. If it is accounted for in that way, then it-ceases to be the foundation for a presumption. If it is not accounted for in that satisfactory, straightforward and truthful way that would stamp it as an honest accounting, then it is the foundation for a presumption of guilt against the defendant in this case, just upon the same principle as if a certain man is charged with robbery or larceny, and is found in the possession of the property stolen or robbed, recently after the crime, he is called upon to explain that possession. If his explanation of it is truthful, if it is consistent, if it is apparently honest, if it is not contradictory, if it is the same at all times, if it has the indicia of truth connected with it, that may cause to pass out of the case the consideration of the presumption arising from the possession of the property, but if it is not explained in that way it becomes the foundation of a presumption against the party who is thus found in possession of that property. Now, that is not the only foundation for a presumption, but you take into consideration the very appearance of this property, whether there were blood stains upon it indicating that there was blood of some kind there, and if so, whether that fact has been satisfactorily explained by the defendant in this case. If not, whether in your judgment there is that in these numerous blood stains upon these clothes, bed-clothing and found upon the straw in that bed, whether or not that fact, if it has not been satisfactorily explained, is a fact upon which you may base a presumption that there was an act of deadly violence perpetrated while the party was upon these bed-clothes, or while he was connected with them in such a way as that the blood was the blood of the murdered man, or the missing man. Now, another foundation of a presumption is the fact of his false statements. You understand that nature, in her bountiful provision, has given to man a set of rules by which he may know the truth above all other things that rule, which underlies all nature, and which comes from the same source that this state of nature comes, which has its abiding place in the very breast of God himself, because God is truth—the truth. The truth is the same yesterday, today, tomorrow and forever. If a man makes a statement to you today about a transaction which is one thing, and details to you another one tomorrow which is something else, and another again which is something else, you necessarily call upon him to explain why he has made these contradictory statements, because you know they are not the attributes of truth, you know they do not belong to the truth, because the highest attribute which it possesses is its harmony, its consistency, and it possesses these attributes at all times, whether it is spoken in the stillest and smallest voice with which it can be uttered, or whether it is heard in the thunders of the clouds, or in the roar of the waters of the ocean, or in the voice of the mighty earthquake, it is still the voice of truth and the voice of nature, and it speaks the same at all times, and it has always attending it that which stamps it as true. Therefore, if statements in this case before you which are false were made by the defendant, or upon his side of the case, if they were made by his instigation, and knowingly instigated by him, you have a right to take into consideration the falsehoods of the defendant, to see whether they are falsehoods. Then you are to look at them to see whether he satisfactorily explains to you the making of those false statements, and if he does not they are the foundation of a presumption against him for the reasons I have given you, because they are not in harmony with nature, they are not in harmony with truth, they do not speak the voice of truth, they speak the voice of falsehood, they speak the voice of fraud, they speak the voice of crime, they are not in harmony with that great law which in all of its parts is consistent and harmonious. Then look to these statements and view them, not alone, but in connection with the other circumstances in the case, all the other circumstances which have gone before you as evidence, to see whether or not the conduct which is urged by the government as accusatory, as inculpatory, has been satisfactorily explained by the defendant upon the theory of his innocence. If so, then that conduct passes away as proving facts in the case; it is no longer the foundation as proving facts; but if these explanations are not satisfactory, if they are not in harmony with the truth, the presumption must remain in the case and you have a right to draw that inference from these circumstances I have named.

"In passing upon the credibility of the evidence you consider the relation the witnesses bear to the case, their interest in it—not because they exhibit zeal in hunting up the evidence as to whether a crime had been committed or not, for that is commendable, that is the duty of every citizen, and if all of us performed it in all circumstances as we ought to, crime would virtually disappear in the country; and when witnesses exhibit zeal, when they exhibit energy, when they exhibit enterprise in gathering up all the circumstances and minutiae which surrounds a case, they are entitled to the commendation of all. That does not show an interest which would create any undue bias in the judgment of the law against any man who might testify. If a man is related to the case, however, so as to be affected by the result of it directly or immediately, that is a condition which you are to necessarily look at, because we are all largely creatures of self-interest. If that self-interest is great, if it involves the result which may deprive us of life, it is the greatest which can ever confront us. If that is the condition, in passing upon the testimony of such a witness we are to view that evidence in the light of that condition, not that we are to necessarily exclude the testimony because of that condition, but we are to apply this self-evident principle which is applicable to all of us, that when we are so situated we are more apt to testify so as to benefit ourselves than to testify against ourselves, or even to keep along the strict line of truth. We are more apt to wander from that line when there is that condition confronting us than if we are entirely disinterested. Such testimony is to be looked at in the face of that condition, and above all things in the face of the other facts and circumstances. The defendant goes upon the witness stand in this case, and you are to view his evidence in the light of his relation to the cast in the way I have named, and in addition thereto you are to look at all the other facts and circumstances in the case as bearing upon his evidence to see whether it contradicts what he says, and therefore weakens it; whether it is so as to be contradictory and inconsistent from statements made by him at other times; whether it is shown to lack these elements of truthfulness known as rationality, consistency, naturalness; whether these things are all absent from it, and whether, in your judgment, it seems to be consistent and probable in itself when you come to look at the story and listen to it and weigh it by your judgment. If has these attributes they are evidences of its being true; if it hasn't them, but has the opposite, this opposite condition made up of these circumstances is an evidence of its being false.

"The law says it is your duty in the investigation of these cases to gather up all the accusatory facts, see what their combined proving power is, and if it is equal to the testimony of one positive, credible, uncontradicted eye witness, then you proceed further in the case to see whether that condition is destroyed or broken down or eliminated from the case by the testimony which is exonerating in its nature, which goes to show innocence. If it is not, then the condition remains as one that sufficiently proves the case. That does not mean that you have to have a witness of that kind before you can convict a mm, that you have to have a man who stood by and saw this act of deadly violence committed. That is impossible in a majority of cases. But it means that the facts and circumstances left around that occurrence, under nature's laws, are equal in proving power to what would be the testimony of one such witness. When there is that amount of evidence in the case the law says the case is established beyond reasonable doubt, and when it is proven in that way guilt is established, and conviction of that guilt is a matter of solemn and imperative duty under your consciences and your oaths.

"PROOF BEYOND REASONABLE DOUBT."

"Now, what is meant by that proposition? When we have given that to you we are done; we have submitted the case to you, we have passed it to your judgments, we have placed it in your hands that you may deliberate upon it, that you may discharge this great and solemn duty which I told you in the beginning, rests upon you as the highest duty, the greatest responsibility ever cast upon any citizen of this proud government. I say, it is to be proven beyond a reasonable doubt. Not absolutely demonstrated, because the law recognizes that you cannot demonstrate a proposition growing out of human conduct. It is impossible to do that. The law does not exact of you, in the performance of this great duty, impossibilities. It does not command you with one voice to uphold the dignity and power and supremacy of this mighty protecting agency called the law of the land, and at the same, time make it impossible for you to do so. It permits you to do it in a possible and reasonable way. Now, to what degree of certainty, then, must the several propositions making up this crime be established? First, the proposition of law, which is an axiom, supposes that all men, when they enter upon the trial of a case are clothed with the presumption of innocence, which presumption surrounds all of us, just as does the presumption of sanity. The law, from public policy, for the encouragement of the good and the discouragement of vice, holds out to all mankind that men are innocent. It does not always hold that out, because if it did there would be no crimes existing, no matter what the conduct of men might be, but it declares when a man is charged with a crime that he is panoplied by this presumption of innocence, and it further declares that that presumption remains with him until the proof in the case drives it out of the case. The proof in the case does destroy it, does drive it out, when it carries the propositions making up the crime to a point where you are able to say, as reasonable men, that you have an abiding conviction to a moral certainty of the truth of the charge, or so it is established that there is no longer confronting the conclusion a

337

doubt for which a good reason can be given. In other words, if all doubts are driven out of the case for which good reasons can be given, no other doubts are to be paid any attention to, we are not to consider them for a moment, because they exist as confronting every human proposition. Men doubt the existence of the Deity. They sometimes are so skeptical that they doubt their own existence. There are so many doubting Thomases in the world that they will not even believe a proposition when it is proven absolutely. Well, of course, that is not the deliberate mind, that is not the reasonable mind. The reasonable mind is the one which takes into consideration deliberately and dispassionately and coolly all the proving facts and all the disproving facts, and whenever that mind is brought to a condition that its possessor is able to say he is satisfied with the truth of the charge, that it is proven to that degree of certainty that he willingly and readily believes it, and will take whatever action upon that belief that duty calls upon him to take, it is then established as such propositions ate usually required to be established by reasonable men, and that is the test, that is the source of the rule. I will read to you, briefly, the opinion of the Supreme Court upon this proposition, commenting upon the charge of the court in the case of Haupt vs. Utah, where a man was upon trial for murder, and where the court below gave this charge to the jury:

"'The court charges you that the law presumes the defendant innocent until proven guilty beyond a reasonable doubt; that if you can reconcile the evidence before you upon any reasonable hypothesis consistent with the defendant's innocence you should do so, and in that case find him not guilty. You are further instructed that you cannot find the defendant guilty unless from all the evidence you believe him guilty beyond a reasonable doubt. The court further charges you that a reasonable doubt is a doubt based on reason, and which is reasonable in view of all the evidence, and if from an impartial consideration of all the evidence you can candidly say you are not satisfied of the defendant's guilt, you have a reasonable doubt. But if after such impartial comparison and consideration of all the evidence you can truthfully say that you have an abiding conviction of the defendant's guilt, such as you would be willing to act upon in the more weighty and important matters relating to your own affairs, you have no reasonable doubt. It is difficult to conceive what amount of conviction would leave the mind of a juror free from a reasonable doubt if it be not one which is so settled and fixed as to control his action in the more weighty and important matters relating to his own affairs. Out of the domain of the exact sciences and actual observation there is no absolute certainty. The guilt of the accused in a majority of criminal cases must necessarily be deducted from a variety of circumstances leading to proof of the fact Persons of speculative minds may in almost every such case suggest possibilities of the truth being different from that established by the most convincing proof. The jurors are not to be led away by speculative notions as to such possibilities. In the case of the Commonwealth vs. Webster, the Supreme Judicial Court of Massachusetts said in its charge, that it was not sufficient to establish a probability, though a strong one, arising from the doctrine of chances, that the fact charged against the prisoner was more likely to be true than the contrary, and said:

"'The evidence must establish the truth of the fact to a reasonable and moral certainty, a certainty that convinces and directs the understanding and satisfies the reason and judgment of those who are bound to act conscientiously upon it. This we take to be proof beyond a reasonable doubt. It is simple, and as a rule to guide the jury is as intelligible to them generally as any that could be given with reference to the conviction they should have of the defendant's guilt to justify a verdict against him. In many cases, especially where the case is at all complicated, some explanation or illustration of the rule may aid in its full and just comprehension. As a matter of fact, it has been the general practice in this country of courts holding criminal trials to give such explanation or illustration. The rule may be, and often is, rendered obscure by attempts at definition which serve to create doubts instead of removing them, but an illustration like the one given in this case by reference to the conviction upon which the jurors would act in the weighty and important concerns of life, would be likely to aid them to a right conclusion when an attempted definition might fail. If the evidence produced be of such a convincing character that they would unhesitatingly be governed by it in such weighty and important matters they may be said to have no reasonable doubt respecting the guilt or innocence of the accused, notwithstanding the uncertainty that attends all human evidence.'

"'The instruction in the case before us is as just a guide to practical men as can well be given, and if it were open to criticism it could not have misled the jury when considered in connection with the further charge, that if they could reconcile the evidence with any reasonable hypothesis consistent with the defendant's innocence they should do so, and in that case find him not guilty. The evidence must satisfy the judgment of the jurors as to the guilt of the defendant so as to exclude any other reasonable conclusion. The instruction is not materially different from that given by Lord Tenterden as repeated and adopted by Chief Baron Pollock in the case of Rex vs. Muller.

"'I have heard,' said the Chief Baron, addressing the jury, 'the late Lord Tenterden frequently lay down a rule which I will pronounce to you in his own language:

"'It is not necessary that you should have a certainty which does not belong to any human transaction whatever. It is only necessary that you should have that certainty with which you would transact your own most important concerns in life. No doubt the question before you to-day, involving, as it does, the life of the prisoner at the bar, must be admitted to be of the highest importance, but you are only required to have that degree of certainty with which you decide upon and conclude your own most important transactions in life. To require more would be really to prevent the repression of crime, which is the object of criminal courts to effect.'

"Gentlemen, that is the definition of the degree of certainty you are to arrive at in this case before you find the defendant guilty. When you have arrived at it, as sensible men, as just men, I say to you, under the law it is your duty to find the defendant guilty, and to specify in your verdict under which count you find him guilty. If you do not arrive at that conclusion to that degree of certainty, it is equally your duty to pronounce him not guilty. I say to you, in conclusion, as I said to you in the beginning, that the very power and majesty of this government and this law is in your hands in every case as a part of the people of this land. You represent them, and you represent the whole of them, to see to it that the maxim, (while it is not there in burning letters, it has been pronounced as existing in this court, and as engraven over its doors) that I no guilty man shall escape and no innocent man shall be punished', shall be verified in this case, as it should be in every case. You will find forms upon the back of the indictment. I submit the case to you. I ask you to pronounce your solemn, your just, and your impartial judgment, as good men and good citizens and good jurors, upon this case.

"You will retire to make up your verdict."

Perhaps the most dreaded of the many desperadoes who infested that land of outlaws, but who did not live to meet his fate on the gallows, was Ned Christie, the noted Cherokee outlaw, charged with all manner of crimes, from murder to whiskey peddling. He was once a cultivated, civilized Indian. His career of crime began in 1885, at which time he killed a very popular United States Deputy Marshal, Dan Maples, of Bentonville, Arkansas. This crime was committed near Tahlequah, Indian Territory, and just why he killed Maples was never known. Maples was a splendid citizen, and his murder nearly drove the citizens of Bentonville wild.

Christie was a full-blood Cherokee, but was an unusually handsome man up to the date when he got shot in the face during a fight, in 1889, with deputy marshals commanded by Heck Thomas, who was trying to arrest him, but failed. In this fight Deputy Marshal Isabell was wounded in the shoulder and arm, making him a cripple for life.

Christie had served with honor and distinction in both houses of the Cherokee legislature, and spoke the English language fluently, but after he launched out in a life of crime he dropped this and was never induced to speak a word except in his mother tongue. He was a gunsmith by trade and an expert in the use of firearms. After the killing of Maples he gathered about him a few trusted native friends, who stayed with him with a valor worthy a better cause. He was soon charged with horse stealing, robbing stores and whiskey peddling, together with the crime of murder hanging over Him, which put numbers of United States officers on his track, and many fights took place between them and Christie and his band, which, up to the second and third day of November, 1892, always resulted in favor of Christie. Deputy Marshals Barney Connelly and Heck Bruner, with organized posses, gave him several lively chases. Heck Thomas and Isabell tried their hands with no better success. William Bouden and Milo Creekmore made two efforts at his capture and were routed. David Rusk and Charlie Copeland, together with a large number of friendly Indians, also gave him battle, and during these fights Isabell, Creekmore, Bouden, Fields and several others were badly wounded,

The full history of Christie's crimes will never be recorded. About the latter part of October, 1892, Marshal Jacob Voes and the officers under him decided to make one more effort to effect his capture, and the preliminaries were turned over to Paden Tolbert, United States deputy marshal, of Clarksville, Arkansas, Heck Bruner and Capt. G. S. White. Tolbert and Bruner went to Coffeyville, Kansas, and secured a three-pounder cannon, while Capt. White, of West Fork, Arkansas, sent an invitation to Wm. Ellis, of Hartshorne, Indian Territory, David Rusk, of Oats, Indian Territory, Ennis Mills, of Middle Fork, Arkansas, Ab Allen and Wess Bauman, of Johnson county, Arkansas, Marry Clayland, of Fort Smith, E. B. Ratteree, of Poteau, Indian Territory, and Chas. Copeland of Siloam Springs, Arkansas, to join the fight. They started from Fort Smith by rail to West Fork, Arkansas, thence overland on horses and wagons, to near Tahlequah, Indian Territory. They were joined also by Thomas Johnson and Policeman Birkett. of Fayetteville, Arkansas. They soon found Christie and his friends, lodged in a first-class log fort built for the purpose. The first gun was fired at daylight by Arch Wolf, a member of Christie's band. Fortunately, only two of his men were in the fort with him. The fight lasted all that day, November 2, 1892, and till near daylight the next morning. Over 2000 shots were fired by the attacking crowd. Many shots were fired from the fort and about thirty shots were fired from the cannon. It was the first time in history that a cannon was used by an attacking party against a single individual.

Several of the officers had holes shot through their clothes and there were many hair-breadth escapes. The fort seemed impregnable, and several times the marshals were undetermined what course next to pursue. At last Bill Smith and Charlie Copeland stole a march on the outlaw and secured a position within twenty two yards of the fort and built a little fort of their own, which was enlarged by standing rails up against a wagon near the fort. They were reinforced by William Ellis, Paden Tolbert and G. S. White, and the decision was reached to dynamite Christie's stronghold. Six six-inch sticks of dynamite were prepared, and Copeland was to place the bombs. At the word Tolbert and Smith stepped out on the right and Ellis and White to the left, and the Winchesters began their work. Under this fire Copeland placed the dynamite and returned, when they all took shelter behind their scanty breastworks. Only a moment, and a terrific explosion was heard, after which the five marshals charged the fort, several shots being fired on them before they could locate them. Having discovered that they were coming from under the floor they returned the fire. Christie crawled out on the opposite side, where he encountered several guards, who mistook him for one of the marshals till he had fired on them; so close was he that the powder burned their faces. They quickly rallied, returned the shots and ended Christie's earthly career. Between the firing on the two sides Wolf made his escape unobserved. The house took fire, and Charlie Hare; a boy, came out and surrendered, having remained till he was badly burned.

Every man in the attacking party obeyed orders to the letter, and, strange as it may seem, not one of the officers were hurt. Christie was about forty-five years old at his death. His burial was a signal for great rejoicing by the citizens of a good portion of the Territory, where the speaking of his name had been sufficient to strike terror to the stoutest hearts. The body was removed to Fort Smith for the purpose of identification and for the rewards that had been offered by the government through the Chief Marshal and by private individuals.

A noted French magistrate is said to have traced all crimes committed in his jurisdiction to women. Whenever he was informed of an especially desperate breach of the law he would call his chief officers about him and after inquiring into all the particulars, so far as known, would ask:

"Who is the woman in the case? Find the woman in the case and bring her to me; the rest will be easily accomplished." It is claimed that by working on this hypothesis alone, he was enabled to ferret out nearly every detail of all the desperate crimes committed in Paris during his reign. His plan of action was based upon the theory that the acts of men, be they good or bad, are nearly always, whether consciously or otherwise, the result, direct or indirect, of feminine influence, the outgrowth of a center of attraction by which their impulses are governed. Whether or not the hypothesis be worthy of reliance, certain it is that no important act in history is without its noted women, and one might write volumes on events drawn from the world's archives dealing exclusively with members of the gentler sex and showing the very important roles they have played in history ever since the dawn of creation.

In peace or in war, in solitude or in the most important public events, we have woman always with us, and though she was second to man at the creation, she has necessarily taken a place foremost in our hearts; is first at the cradle and last at the death bed; and wherever she appears, whether as a ministering or an avenging angel, her influence upon mankind is most potent. History teems with the records of the acts of good women in times of war, of great public distress, but its pages are less minute, rightly, no doubt, regarding the deeds of women no less brave, whose influences were, unfortunately, turned in the wrong direction.

Of all the noted women ever mentioned by word or pen none in history have been more brilliantly daring nor more effective in their chosen roles than the dashing Belle Starr, champion and leader of robbers; herself a sure shot and a murderess, who never forgot an injury nor forgave a foe; who was a terror alike to those she hated and to false friends, and about whom more has been said and written (much of the former being false) than any member of her sex in America. During her career she is supposed to have directed, from the background, many of the most daring acts of the Spaniard and numerous other desperate gangs, and while the records do not point definitely to one murder that she committed, yet it is believed that not a few men were laid low by bullets fired by her, though she is known to have said that she never killed a man unless compelled to, adding, "Wouldn't you kill rather than to be killed?"

Her ideas of outlawry seemed to have been more for the wild pleasure of the chase than for any desire to take human life, and it is claimed that it was only when angered beyond control by some act of betrayal or when driven to a corner, that she committed the crime of murder. Love of money, horses and books was with her a ruling passion, and she would go to almost any ends to procure the former; it was on that account that she confined the greater part of her efforts, while on the scout, to directing raids that should result in available plunder. Her mature life was a strange mixture of the sentimental, the terrible and the grotesque; her childhood was as sweet and innocent as the new blown flower; her end was tragic. Her life's history is given in this work, not with an idea of posing her as a heroine, not with the hope that a moral may be drawn (though that is indeed possible), but simply because a book that aims to give a history of the Fort Smith Criminal Court and its environments would be strangely lacking in a principal feature if Belle Starr's history were to be eliminated.

Belle Starr, or, as she was known in girlhood, Myra Belle Shirley, was born in Carthage, Missouri. February 3, 1846; she died on her forty-third birthday, February 3, 1889. She was the only daughter of Judge John and Eliza Shirley, wealthy people of Southern antecedents, who for twenty-five years conducted the best hotel in that pretty little Southwest Missouri city. The judge owned, as well, large landed estates and was the possessor of many slaves. He and his family, naturally, took up with the Confederate cause in 1861, and with the closing of the war the judge and his wife found it more to their liking to go south and reside among those of a similar temperament, owing to their strong antipathy, openly expressed, to Northern institutions and innovations. They left valuable property uncared for and settling at Sceyene, Texas, ten miles east of Dallas, again amassed large landed possessions.

Belle had a twin-brother, Ed, known as Captain Shirley, to whom she was devoted. He, too, was wild and daring, and in the rough and ready times which preceded secession he joined the Missouri Bushwhackers and became a captain of guerrillas under the intrepid Quantrill. Belle Shirley was just past fifteen years old when the first gun fired upon Fort Sumter warned the people living north of Mason and Dixon's line that the desire of the South to secede was no longer a theory, and it was only natural, considering her surroundings, with parents in full sympathy with the Southern cause, and with a brother whom she idolized in the active service, that her hot Southern blood should be fired to deeds of valor, and that she should early come to regard the supporters of the Stars and Stripes as her enemies. She was brilliant as a child, tractable and apt to learn and as the means of education had not been stinted in her case, she was already, at fourteen years old, the possessor of a liberal education, and withal was an excellent musician. Early in the conflict Belle, a competent horsewoman and always fond of out of door exercise, had rendered valuable assistance to the force with which her brother trained, in the way of carrying messages, and at times acting as a spy, and her dark hair and smiling, rosy cheeks became a synonym, among the guerrillas, for all that was beautiful.

BELLE'S FAMOUS THIRTY-FIVE MILE RIDE

On her sixteenth birthday, February 3, 1862, as Belle, returning from a scout, was riding through the village of Newtonia, in the eastern part of Newton County, Missouri, thirty-five miles, as the crow flies, from her home town, Carthage, she was intercepted by a Major Enos who, with a troop of cavalry, was stationed in the village and who had his headquarters at the home of Judge M. H. Ritchery.

It is a quaint old place; the house, a long structure of red brick, with broad verandas and an L, located at some little distance back from the highway, the centerpiece of beautiful grounds, dotted here and there with fine old shade trees. The house is still standing, and is the home of Professor and Mrs. S. C. Graves, the latter being a daughter of Judge Ritchery. The place is a romantic one; scattered here and there are seven solid shot that were dropped on the grounds during the cannonading incident to several lively skirmishes about the time the battle of Pea Ridge, in Arkansas, was fought. The cornice of the house, in several places, still shows where portions of the architecture were carried away by shells; it was the desire of Judge Ritchery that the marks of battle be allowed to remain as they were, and that the cannon balls be not disturbed, and those who came after him have respected his wishes. Across the road from the grounds still stands a large, but considerably dilapidated, stone building, first built for a mill and afterwards successively used for a hospital, first by the Confederate and then by the Federal troops.

On the day of Belle Shirley's capture, as noted above, Major Enos had sent a detachment of cavalry to Carthage for the purpose of capturing her brother, Captain Shirley, who was known to be on a visit to his home, Belle, or Myra, as she was then called, had ridden into that section of the country for the purpose of obtaining information that might be of value to her people, and having discovered that men had been sent to capture her brother, was on the point of hastening to warn him, when she was arrested and detained. She had been in the habit of riding recklessly where she pleased, and as scarce any Union soldier would think of molesting a woman, especially when the woman chanced to be a beautiful and buxom girl, her plans had not, hitherto, been disarranged. It happened that Major Enos, who had resided in Carthage, was acquainted with both her and her brother, as children, and this was why he had ordered her arrest; he rightly surmising that she was about to go to her brother's assistance. The girl was taken to the chamber of the Ritchery home and guarded by the major himself, who laughed at her annoyance. This served to anger her and she gave expression to her rage in loud and deep curses. Then she would sit at the piano and rattle off some wild selection in full keeping with her fury; the next instant she would spring to her feet, stamp the floor and berate the major and his acts with all the ability and profanity of an experienced trooper, while the tears of mortification rolled down her cheeks, her terrible passion only increased by the laughter and taunts of her captor. At last, believing his men to have had plenty of time to reach Carthage ahead of her, Major Enos said:

"Well, Myra, you can go now. My men will have your brother under arrest before you can reach him."

With eagerness, trembling in every lineament, she sprang to the door, rushed down the stairway and out to a clump of cherry bushes, where she cut several long sprouts for use as riding whips. The judge's daughter, now Mrs. Graves., accompanied her.

"I'll beat them yet," said the girl, as with tearful eyes she swallowed a great lump in her throat. Her horse stood just where her captors had left it; vaulting into the saddle, she sped away, plying the cherry sprouts with vigor. A short distance from the house she deserted the traveled road and, leaping fences and ditches without ceremony, struck a bee line in the direction of Carthage. She was a beautiful sight as she rode away through the fields; her lithe figure clad in a closely fitting jacket, erect as an arrow, her hair unconfined by her broad-brimmed, feather-decked sombrero, but falling free and flung to the breeze, and her right hand plying the whip at almost every leap of her fiery steed. The Major seized a field glass and ascending to the chamber watched her course across the great stretch of level country.

"Well, I'll be d—," he ejaculated, admiringly, "she's a born guerrilla. If she doesn't reach Carthage ahead of my troopers, I'm a fool."

The Major was right; when his detachment of cavalry galloped leisurely into Carthage that evening they were greeted by a slip of a girl mounted on a freshly groomed horse. She dropped a courtesy and asked:

"Looking for Capt. Shirley? He is isn't here—left half an hour ago—had business up Spring River. 'Spect he's in Lawrence county by this time."

The famous ride by his little sister availed Capt. Shirley but little after all, except that it gave him an opportunity to give up his life in battle; he was killed a few days later while at the head of a band of guerrillas during an engagement in the brush with Federal cavalry.

Her brother's death enlivened all the animosity of which her untrammeled nature was capable, and to her dying day there was nothing so hated by her as a "Yankee." She still continued her rides as a scout as occasion encouraged until the close of the war, and during the three years after her brother's death was frequently with Cole Younger and the James boys, whose acts of recklessness and daring in after years astonished the world. In 1866, soon after her twentieth birthday, she became the wife of James Reed. They had first met in her home city in their childhood. Reed was the son of a wealthy farmer residing four miles from Rich Hill, Missouri. As a boy he was of a quiet, even religious turn; he attended church regularly, and his mother used to say of him that he was the most helpful and kindly disposed of any of her several sons. It may be surmised, with reason, that he was a reader of cheap novels, or it may have been that the thrilling events connected with the civil war stirred the blood of some adventurous ancestor, flowing in his veins; at any rate it appears that Jim Reed, too, was a close friend of the James boys, that he was more than once their companion during their raids, and it was doubtless while riding with them that Jim Reed the man came to admire and love, in the brilliant horsewoman of twenty years, the sweet and attractive girl he had seen in childhood.

The marriage of this pair smacked of adventure and was as romantic as their natures. It came about as follows: About the close of the war Judge Shirley had removed with his family to Texas, where the social atmosphere was more to his liking and as his home in Missouri had been a rendezvous for Quantrill and his guerrillas, the companions of his only son, he was visited at his new home in the Lone Star State, after the close of the civil war, by Quantrill and a score or more of his men. Jim Reed had served in the Confederate army, of his own volition, without regular enlistment. Members still living of Company B, of Sidney G. Jackson's famous Sixteenth Regiment of Cavalry, tell of Jim Reed's joining their command in 1864, in Texas and continuing until the close of the war, making a good soldier. He, too, was with his old comrades when in 1866, the remnant of the guerrilla band visited their old sympathizer and friend, Judge Shirley. It was a pleasant reunion and Belle assisted her father in supplying their guests with every luxury. When they departed they were accompanied by Belle. Jim Reed had failed to gain the consent of Judge Shirley to the request for his daughter's hand, but he had the girl's consent and the pair were married on horseback, in the presence of twenty of his companions. The horse upon which the girl sat was of high mettle and was held, while the ceremony was performed by John Fisher, afterwards a noted outlaw.

Soon after this Reed found it necessary to leave the country for a season, and Judge Shirley sent his daughter to school, in Parker county, Texas, for about six months, when the young husband again stole his bride and bore her away to his father's home in Missouri, and Belle Shirley once more breathed her native air.

By some means Judge Shirley managed to treat his energetic son-in-low as he had been treated; he succeeded in stealing his daughter away from her husband, within a few weeks, and sent her to live with a brother among the mountains of the far west. Young Reed had a sister who was very sedate, had scarce been away from her birth place and was thoroughly unacquainted with the ways of the world; she was not one such as would ordinarily be selected for purposes as a confidential spy in a love affair, but she was the only one at his command and in his desperation Reed grasped at straws; he induced his unsophisticated sister to go to the home of his unwilling father-in-law, in Texas, to investigate matters and ascertain what had become of his bride of less than a year. No sooner had she returned bearing the information he desired, than he at once started away on his long trip full of hope and determination to have his wife or die. That he was successful was only what might have been expected of a plucky American youth and taking her "up behind," he hurriedly left the uncle's ranch, only to be followed by uncle and cousins and he was finally brought to bay, after a chase of several miles, and after numerous shots had been fired, without injury to himself or the others, he continued to where a fresh horse could be secured for Belle and in due course of time the husband and wife were once more enjoying their honeymoon at home.

In September, 1869, Belle became the mother of a beautiful baby girl. Belle idolized her and named her "Pearl," though the baby's grandparents and uncles always insisted on calling her "Rosie." A year after Pearl's birth her father became a fugitive. He had taken the law into his hands and killed the slayer of his brother. It was the outcome of the attempt of three brothers named Shannon, to murder a man named Fisher, at a point in the Indian Territory only a few miles from Fort Smith, Arkansas. By chance, a brother of Jim Reed, named Scott Reed, passed where the brothers were in ambush, and was mistaken by them for Fisher and killed. When Jim heard of it, the lines of his face contracted and taking Belle and her baby down by a large oak tree, that grew on the bank of a creek coursing through his father's farm said to her:

"Be here with our baby, twenty-one days from today, at 1 o'clock and I will meet you;" then kissing her and the baby, he disappeared.

JIM HEED BECOMES A FUGITIVE

Belle counted the days, and an hour before the appointed time was at the bank of the creek, wondering whether her husband were dead or alive; the time drew on, minutes seemed hours, and just as the hands of her watch announced the hour she heard a smothered laugh and the next moment, her husband reached over her shoulder and taking the baby from her arms tossed it in the air, then kissed the baby and her. He was accompanied by a young man whom Belle had never seen.

"Humph," said the stranger, "Is that the child I've heard you raving over for the past ten days? Why that is the blamedest, ugliest looking baby! ever seen."

The young husband had avenged his brother's death but in doing so he had committed the fatal act of his life, the act that should eventually be the means of making him bite the dust. Not daring to remain in Missouri he at once left, taking wife and child with him and in the course of time landed in Los Angeles, California. Here he remained two years and here in 1871 was born to them a boy, whom they named "Eddie," and who was eighteen months younger than baby Pearl. It soon became known to the government authorities that Reed was a murderer and a large reward was placed upon his head. When Pearl was three years old her father decided it unsafe to continue longer at their home on the Pacific coast, and leaving his family he "took to the scout." Going to Texas he purchased a beautiful home, nine miles from Dallas, not far from the ranch of Judge Shirely, who, since the birth of the children had become somewhat reconciled to the marriage of his daughter, and sent word for Belle to come. She in some way discovered that she was watched by officers with a view to following her and thus apprehending the husband and securing the reward. Officers in various parts of the country were notified to look out for "a woman with a little girl and a baby." Belle dressed Pearl as a boy and thus eluded the sleuths. At one place where it was necessary for them to stop at a hotel for a night the proprietor was greatly attached to Pearl, whose golden hair hung in beautiful curls, and calling her to him, said:

"Oh, what a pretty little curly headed boy!"

Pearl replied: "No thir! I ain't a boy; I'm my papa's little turly headed girl," whereupon Belle, controlling her emotions, explained that on account of the little boy's pretty curly hair her husband called him his little curly headed girl.

The innocent, happy life they had enjoyed at Rich Hill 'was never again to be experienced. Belle reached her new home in safety, but though it was supplied with everything needful, yet the lover for whom she had left her home was only able to be with her at times and for only brief periods. The greed of gold, since the reward was offered, made him fear every man his enemy, and when he came home at all it was by stealth. A good portion of his time was spent in the Indian Territory and it chanced that he chose as a rendezvous the home of Tom Starr, a noted Cherokee Indian, living some eighty miles west of Fort Smith, with a half-breed wife.

Tom Starr was a son of Ellis Starr, a "Southern Cherokee." He had gained the reputation of being the "worst Indian" the Cherokee government had ever had to deal with. He had joined the Confederate forces as a scout during the civil war, after suffering the loss of near relatives by assassination, at the hands of the Ross party, and had committed many depredations against them, and at the declaration of peace he continued on the rampage, becoming a foe so deadly that in 1866 the Cherokee government made a special treaty with him, guaranteeing immunity from punishment for his former crimes in order to induce him to settle and cease to roam the plains. At Tom Starr's home Reed found the seclusion necessary to the safety of a man on whom a price is set, and here for weeks at a time he would stay, sending word to Belle, who would leave her children with "Grandma Shirley" and go to him fora visit. Belle kept a stable of several fine horses at Dallas, and was ready at any time to mount and away to meet her bandit husband at the home of the noted Cherokee. Tom Starr had a son, Sam Starr, who was several years Belle's junior. During Belle's visits to Jim they often attended dances together, often riding twenty to thirty miles for the purpose, and it was not unusual that Sam Starr rode behind, on Belle's horse, the three attending the homely fetes together.

It could scarcely be expected that a man existing under the conditions surrounding Reed would lead a life in strict conformity to law and gospel, and it is little to be wondered at that during the four years after he returned from California that he was on the scout he is said to have committed deeds that would have gained for him severe punishment had he been apprehended.

THE WATT GRAYSON ROBBERY

On the night of November 19, 1873, Watt Grayson, a prominent citizen of the Creek Nation, was robbed of $30,000 in gold coin. It was money which the Indian had secured by a system of official thievery from the tribal funds, and the fact of his being in possession of so much money he endeavored to keep secret even from the members of his own tribe, as it would have been proof of his malfeasance. At the first announcement of the robbery Grayson placed his loss at $3,700, for reasons the reader will understand. He had kept the money hidden away in the mountains during the civil war, but afterwards he removed it to his home, burying the sacks containing the coins under his house.

On the night in question his house was visited by three white men who had been in the neighborhood for several days. Grayson's immense wealth was known to the robbers, but they did not know its hiding place. They tried the virtue of a rope, placed about the Indian's neck, by which they stretched him off the ground seven times without obtaining from him the information they desired; they next threw the noose over the head of his wife and she was "elevated" three times, when the Indian gave up and disclosed the location of his gold. He could withstand much himself, but the torture to his wife was too painful and he let go his hold on his ill-gotten lucre, and with it the robbers left. The money was never restored, but one of the robbers, named Wilder, was arrested and was given a penitentiary sentence. Attorneys at the Fort Smith Court and some of the former jail guards still remember the eloquence with which Wilder described his sensations as he handled the glittering coins and dabbled his fingers in the pile "like wheat" His partners in crime escaped, but it was generally understood that Jim Reed was one of the three, and in early June, 1875, Dan Evans, one of the famous sextette, executed on the twenty-sixth of that month, made the assertion that he was one of Jim Reed's pals in the job for which only Wilder suffered the penalty. He claimed that Reed first made several trips to the home of Grayson, but he lacked nerve to attempt the robbery alone.

SLAIN BY HIS SCOUTING MATE

In the summer of 1875, Jim Reed made his last trip home to wife and children. As usual, he came by stealth and was met by Belle in a strip of timber and conducted to their home after night fall. On leaving again, after a few happy but nervous days, he was accompanied by one John Morris who, attracted by the offered reward, sought to encompass Reed's death, and, strangely enough, the man who had come to doubt all men, placed confidence in the very one fated to destroy his life. Morris, who had never committed a serious offense, professed to be on the scout and as companions in tribulation they rode away. Belle never saw her husband again in life. A few days later they rode up to a farm house near McKinney, the county seat of Collin county, Texas, about the noon hour, and stopped for dinner. Morris suggested that they leave their guns on their saddles as, if they went into the house armed, it might create suspicion. As do all fugitives, sooner or later, Reed trusted once too often. He laid aside his arms. It was his last, his fatal mistake. During the meal, Morris, making some excuse, left the table. Going to his horse he procured his Winchester and returned to the house. Reed sat at the opposite side of the table facing the open door, and as his betrayer stepped into sight, he, scenting the danger, cried, "traitor," and teaching out both hands grabbed the far edges of the table and raised it between himself and the assassin, while dishes and contents went to the floor in a smash, echoing the three shots which rang out in rapid succession, piercing the table top and releasing Reed's life blood. Even then, had it not been for the farmer he would doubtless have killed his murderer with a small pistol he had in his pocket, but Morris shouted:

"Kill him; he's a murderer! He's a murderer! There's a reward for him dead or alive!" and the farmer rushed for-, ward and preventing the use of the pistol, assisted in finishing the work Morris had begun.

Later, the farmer started to write a letter, addressed to the murdered man's bachelor brother, F. M. Reed, then and now a resident of Metz, Vernon County, Missouri, telling the story of the killing. He described the affair more minutely than is here given and when he came to speak of his own connection with the crime his reason suddenly deserted him; he was conveyed to an asylum a raving maniac. The letter was afterwards sent to the bachelor brother by a neighbor, who completed the story, and it is still in his possession.

A NERVY ACT

An event in connection with this cold-blooded murder exhibits the steady nerve and the powerful command which Belle had over herself. It was necessary for the assassin, in order to secure the reward offered for Reed "dead or alive," to furnish proof of his death, and as the murdered man was a stranger in that portion of the country where he was killed there were none to identify the body. The weather was sultry, making an early burial imperative, and word was sent to Belle-informing her of her husband's death, the supposition being that she would weep, as would ordinary wives, over the remains, thus establishing their unquestioned identity. But Belle was far from "ordinary." When she received word to come and take charge of her husband's dead body her eyes took on a hard look and she said, "They've killed him for the reward but they will never get it," and rode to the house where the body lay. As she entered the room where a number of men, Morris among them, were gathered about the corpse, one of their number removed the covering, exposing the features, while the others silently fell back expecting to witness a heartrending scene of weeping. They also expected to make oath to what they saw, and thus assist the murderer to obtain the reward. Belle walked to the body, gave a glance at the face of her loved one and without the least sign of emotion, but with a scornful curve of the lips, quietly remarked:

"I am very sorry, gentlemen, that you have made such a mistake and killed the wrong man; very sorry, indeed. John Morris, you will have to kill Jim Reed if you desire to secure the reward offered for Jim Reed's body."

Since Morris had but a few days previous visited the man who now lay before them dead, at his own home, and Belle's, this was a turn in affairs on which he had not counted. Belle rode calmly away, suffering the anguish she would not indicate, and her husband's body was buried in the potters' field.

BELLE AS A WIDOW

For a year, thereafter, Belle led a more or less quiet life, taking occasional long rides about the country on one of her thoroughbreds. She left her farm property in the care of a renter and with "Baby Pearl" removed to Dallas. "Grandma" Shirley had cared for the younger child since their return from California. In Dallas, Belle made many friends among the men, and her stable was the envy of all. A letter still in existence, written on stationery of Sheriff James E. Barkley, of Dallas, the envelope bearing date of August 10, 1876, and addressed to the aforementioned "F. M. Reed, Metz P. O., Vernon County, Missouri," may interest the reader, as it reveals certain traits of her character better than can be otherwise described. The letter follows:

Dear Mother and Brothers and Sisters:—I write you after so long a time to let you know that I am still living. Time has made many changes, and some very sad ones indeed. My poor old father has left this world of care and trouble. He died two months ago today. It seems as if I have more trouble than any person. "Shug" got into trouble here and had to leave; poor Ma is left alone with the exception of little Eddie. She is going to move away from here in a few days and then I'll be left alone. Eddie will go with her, and I don't know that I shall ever see him again. He is a fine, manly looking boy as you ever seen and is said to resemble Jimmie very much; he is very quick motioned, and I don't think there is a more intelligent boy living. I am going to have his picture taken before he leaves and I will send you one; would like for you to see and know him. I know you would love him for the sake of the dear one that's gone. Eddie has been very sick and looks pale and wan, but I think my boy will soon mend up. Rosie is here in Dallas going to school; she has the reputation of being the prettiest little girl in Dallas. She is learning very fast. She has been playing on the stage here in the Dallas, theatre and gained a world-wide reputation for her prize performance. My people were very much opposed to it but I wanted her to be able to make a living of her own without depending on any one. She is constantly talking of you all, and wanting to visit you, which I intend she shall sometime.

Jno. L. Morris is still in McKinney, at large. It seems as if justice will never be meted out to him. Pete Fisher is in. Colin City, where he has always lived. Solly hasn't the pluck and love for Jim I thought he had. I have Jimmie's horse (Rondo) yet; I was offered $200 for him the other day. If Sol had come to Texas, freely would I have given the horse to him. if he had sought revenge.

I think Brocks are in Montague county. I will realize nothing from my farm this year. Brock rented it out in little pieces to first one and another, and none of them tended it well, so I made nothing. I am going to sell it this fall if I can.

I am far from well. I am so nervous this evening from the headache that I can scarcely write.

(No signature.),

Copied from the original October 4, 1898, at Fort Smith, Arkansas. most peculiar trait of this peculiar woman was that she made it a rule never to sign her name to a letter, and she never recorded thereon the date on which they were written, neither the address.)

The person spoken of as "Shug," was a young brother of Belle's, thus nicknamed. As will be observed, she was then training Pearl for the stage, and it is a fact that the little girl gained much local renown as a dancer, but in the autumn of 1876, soon after this letter was written, she was overcome during a performance, by a sudden rush of blood to the brain and for a time death was feared. On her physician's advice, Belle thereafter kept Pearl away from the theater. The "Pete Fisher," named in the letter was the man whose death was intended by the Shannon brothers, who killed Scott Reed by mistake. "Solly," was a younger brother of Jim Reed, living at home in Missouri. The drift of Belle's mind and the desire that her husband's death be avenged is very clearly shown, but "Solly" was wise in his generation, and appreciated a safer course. Belle's mother, Mrs. Shirley, removed from her home after the death of Judge Shirley, as predicted in the letter, but instead of her taking "Eddie," the boy was left with Belle who soon after made a visit to Rich Hill, taking the child with her and he remained with his grandmother Reed until he was past twelve years old. Belle returned, shortly, to Dallas, and taking her daughter with her made a trip to Conway, Arkansas, where, for two months she visited with an old school friend and at the end of that time she returned to Texas, leaving Pearl behind; she remained for two years, after which Belle again placed her in school in Dallas.

After returning from the visit to her friend in Conway, Belle began to exhibit her former roving disposition once more and about a year later, she met with her first serious difficulty. She was out on a reckless ride with another girl as wild as herself, Emma Jones by name, between whom and Belle a strong intimacy had sprung up. The day was windy, and their route lay through a small prairie village. In a spirit of bravado, the Jones girl attempted to build a fire at a back corner of a small building occupied by a merchant, with a stock of goods. The wind blew out the matches and prevented her attempts. Belle came upon her and said, "You can't build a fire; let me." Belle did and the store was consumed.

Her companion told of the act and Belle never again placed confidence in a woman. Belle was arrested and tried at Dallas. While the trial was in progress, a wealthy Texas stockman, named Patterson, entered the court room. He had known Judge Shirely and had heard of Belle's nervy action at her husband's bier. He fell in love with her at first sight. He secured her release and gave her a large sum of money; whether he expected to make her his wife cannot be stated authoritatively. Belle went to Conway where Pearl was still living, and after giving her old friend a sum that seemed to her a fortune, took Pearl out to a stretch of timber land, and seated on the bank of a little stream, counted out' the large roll of paper money remaining from the wealthy Patterson's gift. Kissing her child she said:

"Baby, here is $—," stating the amount; "enough so you and I will never want again, mamma will go up into the Territory and fix up a nice home and have lots of music

353

and nice horses and then come and get her baby and we will always be happy." But if Belle loved money, she loved to spend it also, loved the prestige its spending gave her, and none of the stockman's gift was ever used in fixing up the nice home as mamma intended.

About a year later, Belle, who had spent the most of the intervening time in Texas and the Indian Territory, the while keeping up her magnificent stud at Dallas, was arrested in Texas on a charge of horse stealing. She was committed to jail at Dallas, where she soon succeeded in winning the heart of a deputy sheriff, who guarded the jail, and induced him to break her bonds and elope with her. The officer returned to the bosom of his family a month later without his prisoner, of course, his infatuation, from some cause, having cooled.

Gradually Belle gathered about her a set of male admirers-as reckless as herself, to each of whom she was at one time or another especially gracious and who was for the time counted as her lover. Among these are named Jack Spaniard, Jim French, and "Blue Duck." Naturally, such men and those whom they influenced stood ready to obey the wishes of the woman-they admired yet feared, who could out ride, out jump and out shoot them all, who could draw her pistol from its convenient holster at her side in a twinkling and who never missed a mark, and she finally gained the title of "Prairie Queen" and "Queen of Desperadoes," though there is no doubt that, like the majority of bandits, she was charged with more unlawful acts which she never performed or planned than would number all deeds of outlawry she ever committed.

Many amusing stories are told of Belle's recklessness, enough to fill a book; let a few suffice. One of her lovers named above, a white man, who operated under the alias, "Blue Duck," was a leading figure in a highly sensational act performed by his mistress in 1877. They were scouting in "No Man's Land," a long and narrow strip of the Indian Territory lying between Kansas and Texas and reaching to the Colorado line, and "Blue Duck" borrowed $2,000 from Belle, went to Port Dodge, Kansas, and lost the entire amount in a gambling house. Fort Dodge was then the extreme western terminus of the Santa Fe railroad and was the shipping point for cattle driven from the vast plains lying south and southwest. Money was therefore plentiful and gamblers were seen at every turn. The day after losing his mistress' money "Blue Duck" returned to her and in answer to her question, "'Blue Duck, what did you do with that money?" confessed that he had lost it at the tables. Belle swore a string of oaths, declared she could, never allow such work as that, then mounted and headed for Fort Dodge.

Entering the saloon, in an upper apartment of which was the gambling hell, she strode up the stairway, covered the players with her pistol, grabbed up the entire stakes, amounting to $7,000, and backed away, saying:

"Gentlemen, there is a little change your due; I haven't time to give it to you now; if you want it come down into the Territory." There is no record to show that they ever called for the "change."

In January, 1886, "Blue Duck" was convicted of murder at Fort Smith and was sentenced to mount the ghastly old scaffold on the twenty-third day of the following July. Belle remembered him in his tribulations and spent many hundred dollars to save his rascally neck. The attempt succeeded, his sentence being finally commuted to life imprisonment and after a year he was pardoned. c Belle was facetious and had times when she remembered her early training and demanded from the rough and uncouth dwellers of the plains the full courtesy due a lady in civilization. On one of these occasions, as she was riding on the Skullyville Prairie, Indian Territory, her hat was blown off by the wind. She saw William Kayser riding at a short distance and hailing him she told him to get down and pick up her hat. Kayser refused. Instantly grasping her pistol she "drew a bead" and with telling oaths commanded:

"Get down and pick up my hat!" Adding, after he had hastened to obey: "The next time a lady asks you to get down and pick up her hat, do as she tells you."

An interesting story of one of her alleged escapades, for whose absolute truth, however, I cannot vouch, tends to show the wonderful ability of this cultured Amazon and is indicative of her strong magnetism. Whether true or false, the story is too good to lose. It is as follows:

A SMOOTH PIECE OF WORK

"Being short of money, she decided to make a change from her usual manner of replenishing her purse and at the same time perform the lady act. Decking herself out in raiment suitable for appearance in a civilized community, she proceeded to one of the stirring Texas cities and had no difficulty in ingratiating herself with the best 'society.' She adopted her silver-toned voice, put on graceful airs, attended church and Sunday school, and was soon a recognized leader of fashion. Among her many admirers, she seemed to be especially gracious to a middle aged bachelor, who was cashier of one of the leading banks. She kept up her saintly demeanor for several weeks until the banker was in love with the brilliant enchantress and was on the point of proposing. This was Belle's opportunity. She entered the bank one day while the cashier was alone, the others being at dinner, and after a pleasant chat he invited her behind the railing. Once there, she became very solicitous of his health and standing close to the stool upon which he was sitting told him he must take more out-of-door exercise, as it broke her heart to see him looking so pale and wan. She murmured away in sweetest tones, pulling at his heart-strings at every breath; suddenly she slipped an ugly looking, 45 calibre pistol from the folds of her skirt and, pressing the glittering steel beneath his chin, said in a low but determined voice, 'Don't make a sound,' at the same time lifting a flap of her basque, displaying a sack made for carrying the funds of this especial bank.

"'What does all this mean?' he stammered.

"'Sh, not a word; put the money right in there, and be quick about it.'

"The thoroughly surprised and frightened banker slipped down from his stool and going to the safe procured $30,000 in paper money and placed it in the sack, the mouth of which she obligingly held open. Then she continued:

"'Now, dear, don't make any outcry; your life depends upon it; good bye sweetheart; come and see me when you come up into the Territory; and backing out of the building she proceeded quietly to a nearby livery stable where she had left her horse, vaulted into the saddle without first placing her foot in the stirrup, a feat that surprised the stable hands, and was away like the wind. And that was one time when that bank at closing time found itself $30,000 short on the credit side of the ledger."

THE NOOK IN THE MOUNTAINS

About this time she spent two years in Nebraska, and in 1880 Belle became the wife of Sam Starr and she at once decided to take advantage of her opportunities and secure a claim to which she was then entitled as a citizen of the Cherokee Nation. Not caring, even for baby Pearl's sake, to make a home too near civilization she went into the wild country on the Canadian river, in the southwest part of the Cherokee Nation, and located a fine claim of near a thousand acres of forest and bottom land, causing a log house to be built, in a picturesque and charming spot nestling between two mountain peaks overlooking the bottoms, a mile and half back from the river, eight miles above Briartown on the same side of the river, sixteen miles below Eufaula, Creek Nation, and ten miles from Whitefield, down the river in Sans Bois county in the Chickasaw Nation, at one time designated as Oklahoma Post-office. A circle in the river partly encircled Belle's claim and she named her possessions "Younger's Bend." No wagon roads led to this cosy home in the wilderness and none were needed. Bridle paths here and there alone marked the routes taken by Belle and her companions as they rode to and from what was to many of the latter, at times, a hiding place from the officers. The home to which Belle took Pearl, then a modest girl of eleven years, was not a palace, nor was it furnished in regal style; it was superior however, to any of its class in that part of the country; its puncheon floor was laid as straight as the axemen could lay it, and the interior walls were covered with bright hued calico, which was renewed as often as was necessary to prevent its showing too plainly the stains of age. Buffalo horns and the antlers of prairie deer occupied prominent places above the rough but tasty mantle and at other places, and at times sprigs of cedar with clusters of mistletoe festooned the walls, while photographs or life sized portraits of her friends occupied commanding positions here and there tastefully arranged by herself or by "Baby Pearl." Very little of modern fragile bric-a-brac was to be seen, but nature's curios that would be readily granted a place in the millionaire's drawing room, were posed so as to best set off their rough beauty, and altogether the place bore the aspect of a home, such as is seldom found on the frontier. Whatever was needful to the warmth and comfort of the inmates were not lacking and books, of a kind too as are seen in the best libraries, were there in plenty.

It was Belle's intention then, as stated by herself in after years, to live for herself and her family, and to keep within the bounds of the law. With her culture and refinement she could not well associate with those who might be considered her neighbors, living within a radius of ten or fifteen miles from Belle's home, and she did not care to. Her new husband knew but very little, if anything, of her previous reckless maneuvers, and she intended to live in the future, a quiet existence, a credit to her sex and a companion to her daughter, who soon came to be styled the "Canadian Lily," a title most appropriate.

Not long after she had become comfortably located in her nook in the mountains, Belle received a visit from Jesse James, the noted outlaw and former friend of her first husband. Belle never "went back" on her husband's friends, and she made him comfortable for the night. He was passing through the country and knew he would be welcomed by his old friend's widow. Sam Starr was away from home when the bandit came to the house. The two men had never met. Starr came home before the other left, and not liking her husband to know of her acquaintance with an outlaw, she gave a fictitious name, and not for several months did the Indian learn from her the identity of their visitor. Gradually the men she had known on the range came to learn of her location and of the handy retreat it offered them, and Belle's place came to be more or less of a rendezvous for all kinds of rough characters; a little back, and up the mountains was a cave which was fitted up into a habitable abode, and there, has many an outlaw lain in security, while the officers were hot on the trail. Gradually too, it came to be whispered among the neighbors that the new corner at "Younerer's Bend," with the pretty daughter, was a terrible woman from Texas; the reports came to Belle's ears, and with each report she began to care less for her recent good intentions, which circumstances seemed determined to destroy.

It was in such a place as this, amid surroundings of the wildest character, that Pearl was reared, growing up under the name "Pearl Starr," enjoying a life as happy as it was isolated and innocent, until she was in her fifteenth year. She readily took to the wild freedom of the wilderness and of her surroundings had no word of complaint. Like her mother, she became an expert horsewoman and as she reached her teens she became more and more beautiful, and strangely enough did not take up with the rough ways of her mother's associates, but was as charming and mild mannered a Miss as one could wish to meet. Belle used occasionally to remark to the scouts, who made her place a rendezvous, sleeping at night in the cave, up the mountain, that they need never make any change in their usual demeanor when Pearl was about as she was not of a susceptible nature and while she might not approve of all she saw or heard, yet she said nothing, and having her own ideas of right and wrong, she followed the dictates of her own conscience, not the example set by others. Of the boy, Ed, however, she could not say this, and when in after years he came to be at home for a season Belle would often warn her visitors to be careful what they said before him, as his nature was quite the reverse from his sister's. Pearl made visits to her relatives in Missouri and she succeeded altogether in gaining a liberal education, considering her surroundings.

At times Belle would break away from her rough associations and, packing her trunks with raiment suitable to civilization, would lay aside her scouting suit and hie away to the popular Eastern watering places, there to spend money lavishly and mingle freely with the wealth and culture of the nation. During such seasons the depredations of the scouts would seem to largely cease, and the times to become tame by comparison, but only for a season; with her return her reign would be resumed, and people would remark, as if by intuition: "Belle Starr is back again;" though there is not the least doubt that much of this was imaginary and that the woman was not really half as black as she was painted.

NINE MONTHS AT DETROIT

In the autumn of 1882, Belle and Sam met with their first real trouble and both were sentenced to terms in the House of Correction at Detroit, Michigan. Pearl was the possessor of a beautiful young black stallion; it became a source of no little annoyance to their neighbors (neighborhoods in those days extended over miles of territory, and for a "neighbor" to live ten to fifteen miles away was no uncommon occurrence) and finally the animal was shot, supposedly by one Andrew Crane, a white man, who had a ranche in the vicinity. Soon after, Belle with Sam and Pearl, was on a visit to the home of John West, who lived some seven miles away, back from the river on the open prairie, his ranche adjoining that of Crane. West was a Cherokee Indian and the two families, the Wests and the Starrs, were on a very friendly footing and frequent visitors, Mrs. West being of a refined and lovable disposition and a favorite of Belle's. During the day in question, as West, his wife and little boy, with their guests, were sitting in the shade of a tree, a fine young horse was seen feeding on Crane's ranche nearby, and West remarked to Sam:

"You ought to go and take that colt to pay for the one Crane killed."

An ex-deputy United States marshal, named Childs, who was standing near, was preparing to leave the country and he soon after caught the horse spoken of by West and rode it away. A few days later, when Crane began searching for his property, West took fright and fearing, in his terror of the Federal Court at Fort Smith, that he might be accused of horse stealing, he went before a United States commissioner and swore to a complaint charging Belle Starr and Sam Starr with the larceny of the horse. He also attempted to make his little boy swear to having seen them take the horse but received the answer:

"Pa, you know they didn't; you know Childs rode him off."

Sam Starr had never suffered the ignominy of arrest and when he and Belle learned of the nature of the warrant, never doubting they could establish their innocence, they gave themselves up. They were indicted by the grand jury at Fort Smith and their trial commenced February 15, 1883. Belle had meanwhile begun to fear the outcome and not being willing that Pearl should be called to testify in court, had sent her to visit with an old friend, at Oswego, Kansas, whom Pearl designated by the title, "Mamma Mac;" fearing that if the officers learned of her whereabouts they might in some way compel her attendance she arranged that when writing to her, she should address to "Miss Pearl Younger." Various suggestions, untenable ones, have been offered as to why she should have chosen the name of "Younger," as an alias, but it is not the first time on record where a mature woman has held the male companions of her earlier years in kindly remembrance, and given evidence thereof in this manner.

At the trial, District Attorney Clayton fought hard for conviction, as was his custom, and when Sam Starr was on the stand, and later, in his plea to the jury, he took occasion to refer to the illiteracy of the Indian in a way that Belle considered altogether uncalled for, and that caused her cheeks to blush with mingled feelings of anger and mortification. Of this, reference will be made later. The husband and wife were convicted of larceny and on February 19, 1883, Judge Parker sentenced them to one year in the house of correction at Detroit, Michigan, with the opportunity for release, after nine months, on account of good behavior, under the prison rules.

A touching letter written to Pearl just before they were removed to Detroit is here given, as it conveys better than anything else the natural refinement of the woman and shows the strength of the maternal instinct within her as well as her pride of family. The letter was mailed at Fort Smith and, an unusual proceeding with her, was signed with her full name. The envelope bears address as follows:

"Miss Pearl Younger,

Oswego,

(My baby) Kansas."

It is said that every letter she ever addressed to Pearl bore the words' "my baby," in parenthesis at the left of the superscription. The letter aforementioned is given herewith:

Pandemonium, Feb.—, 1883,

Baby Pearl,

My Dear Little One:—It is useless to attempt to conceal my trouble from you and though you are nothing but a child I have confidence that my darling will bear with fortitude what I now write.

I shall be away from you a few months baby, and have only this consolation to offer you, that never again will I be placed in such humiliating circumstances and that in the future your little tender heart shall never more ache, or a blush called to your cheek on your mother's account. Sam and I were tried here, John West the main witness against us. We were found guilty and sentenced to nine months at the house of correction, Detroit, Michigan, for which place we start in the morning. Now Pearl there is a vast difference in that place and a penitentiary; you must bear that in mind, and not think of mamma being shut up in a gloomy prison. It is said to be one of the finest institutions in the United States, surrounded by beautiful grounds, with fountains and everything nice. There I can have my education renewed, and I stand sadly in need of it. Sam will have to attend school and I think it the best thing ever happened for him, and now you must not be unhappy and brood over our absence. It won't take the time long to glide by and as we come home we will get you and then we will have such a nice time.

We will get your horse up and I will break him and you can ride John while I am gentling Loco. We will have Eddie with us and will be as gay and happy as the birds we claim at home. Now baby you can either stay with grandma or your Mamma Me, just as you like and do the best you can until I come back, which won't be long. Tell Eddie that he can go down home with us and have a good time hunting and though I wish not to deprive Marion and ma of him for any length of time yet I must keep him a while. Love to ma and Marion.

Uncle Tom* has stood by me nobly in our trouble, done everything that one could do. Now baby I will write to you often. You must write to your grandma but don't tell her of this; and to your Aunt Ellen, Mama Me., but to no one else. Remember, I don't care who writes to you, you must not answer. I say this because I do not want you to correspond with anyone in the Indian Territory, my baby, my sweet little one, and you must mind me. Except auntie; if you wish to hear from me auntie will let you know. If you should write me ma would find out where I am and Pearl, you must never let her know. Her head is overburdened with care now and therefore you must keep this carefully guarded from her.

Destroy this letter as soon as read. As I told you before, if you wish to stay a while with your Mama Me., I am willing. But you must devote your time to your studies. Bye bye, sweet baby mine.

(Copied from the original.) BELLE Starr.

At Detroit Belle won many friends by her vivacity and her refined and gentle demeanor. When first she was ushered into the presence of the warden, who had heard many tales of the terrible Belle Starr, she was ordered to follow and was conducted to the chair bottoming department; as they passed through a room where were stacked a large number of frames ready to be given bottoms of splint or cane, the warden said: "Take a chair." Belle replied, innocently, and in her sweetest tones: "No, thank you; I don't care for a seat; I had much rather stand."

After the warden had explained to her, using a much milder tone, that he had meant for her to pick up a chair frame and carry it to the work room wither* they were going, she laughed a silvery tinkle and said that she had never known an invitation to take a chair construed in that way before.

Belle soon gained favor with the matron and her assistants and with the warden himself. Her style of dress had always been a V-shaped bodice quite décolleté, but as this was not to be thought of in a prison, the matron, with many misgivings and with evident hesitation, explained that the beautiful but offending garment must give place to one of severer cut. After the first month of her servitude Belle was given the freedom of the place, scarcely any tasks being assigned to her, but poor Sam, who knew not how to charm by his individuality, was compelled to put in the regulation hours at labor.

Discovering that Belle was possessed of fine perception and of a good flow of language, the warden offered to suspend the rules in her case and permit her the untrammeled use of pen, ink and paper in return for her promise to write a book during her term of imprisonment, upon what she saw and learned concerning the jail and its inmates. The book was never published for evident reasons, but to her friends in later years Belle expressed her regrets that she had not retained the manuscript and turned it over to a publisher, remarking that it would have taken the world greatly by surprise. Letters still in existence written to her by the matron of the institution after her return to the Indian Territory, are proof of the strong hold she gained upon the hearts of the prison officials, and only makes the wonder greater, that such a woman should have been in truth a bandit.

Before their release, Ed Reed, who was never known by the name of Starr, grew tired of his hum-drum school days, and he ran away from the home of his grand-parents in Missouri, going to the Indian Territory, and there his mother found him on her return from Detroit.

DEATH OF JOHN MIDDLETON

During the succeeding year Belle Starr and Sam were given relief from court notoriety, and if any acts of theirs were unlawful they were either skillful or fortunate in evading the officers. In the summer that Pearl attained her sixteenth birthday, 1885, Belle was again accused, unjustly, of horse stealing, and this is the opening to a tale which includes a notorious character, John Middleton, whose parents resided about three miles west of Paris, Logan county, Arkansas, near Lower Short Mountain, and whose mother, Mrs. Nancy Middleton, was an aunt of Jim Reed, Belle Starr's first husband, Pearl's father. Lee Reed, an elder brother of Jim, with four motherless daughters, the youngest being twelve years old, lived in the same neighborhood less than a mile from the Middleton home. John Middleton, at the time of the occurrences about to be related, which cost him his life and caused Belle Starr to be indicted more than a year later for horse stealing, was twenty-seven years old and an outlaw. Some years previous he had committed light offenses against the Arkansas state laws in Logan and Scott counties, and later, when the Scott county court house at Waldron was burned, young Middleton was charged with incendiarism. He adroitly eluded arrest and going to Texas, made the serious mistake, it was claimed, of stealing one or more horses and was finally captured and placed in jail in Paris, Lamar county, Texas; in August, 1884, he escaped from jail and fled to the Indian Territory. In November following he again appropriated, d horse, the property of another, and rode to Paris, Texas, and to the home of J. H. Black, sheriff of Lamar county, on the night of November 16,. and, calling Black to the door, shot him in cold blood. It was claimed by friends of the murdered officer that Middleton was employed to do this job by ex-sheriff Cook, of Paris, whom Black had defeated at the polls, and Cook and one of his former deputies were arrested and lodged in jail at Sherman, charged with being accomplices in the murder.

After killing Black, Middleton returned to the Indian Territory, and going to the home of his cousin, became a "real scout;" a charge of sufficient importance to insure his being hanged if caught was now placed against him, and the retreat at "Younger's Bend" was the one spot on earth that seemed safest. Here he rendezvoused and during the following winter and spring was said to have added others to his already long list of crimes—being charged with horse stealing, robbery and arson. About Christmas, 1884, Deputy Sheriffs Jack Duncan and J. H. Millsaps, of Lamar county, Texas, started on his trail, and as they reached the locality of "Younger's Bend" they made the acquaintance of John G. West, previously noted in this chapter, who had risen to the dignity of Indian policeman and had now become Belle's relentless enemy, and guided by him they proceeded to the nook in the mountains and made several unsuccessful attempts to locate the murderer of their former chief. Their tenacity, however, forced Middleton to keep up an uncomfortable dodging and in the meantime Sam Starr, between whom and the young murderer there had sprung up a close friendship, had been charged with burglarizing a United States post-office, in company with Felix Griffin (both were finally indicted by the Federal grand jury at Fort Smith* October 16, 1886), and he had decided to go to New Mexico and scout during the summer. Belle, too, decided to take a season away from her accustomed haunts, and renting her farming land she prepared to take a trip to the springs, near Chick-ala, Arkansas, where resided Pete. Marshal and family, old friends of Belle's.; her route would take them by the home of her brother-in-law, Lee Reed, where she would leave Pearl to visit with her cousins for a few weeks. Middleton was only too willing to leave the country where he was being so closely followed by the Texas officers, and he prepared to "go along" and make a visit at the home of his mother. The Texas authorities had, previous to this time, offered a reward of $300 for Middleton's capture, and Deputy Sheriff Duncan had offered a reward of $500, on his own account.

On May 3, 1885, Belle and Pearl packed up, and accompanied by a boy named Cook, who had been employed by Belle at various odd jobs, who served as driver, started in a "prairie schooner" for the trip to Arkansas. Their route to Fort Smith was by way of Whitefield, to which place they were accompanied by Sam Starr and Middleton, and where they camped for the night. The favorite riding horses of Belle and Pearl were tied at the rear of the wagon; and it had been arranged that Middleton, who feared to be seen in Fort Smith, should make a circuit, riding Pearl's horse, fitted with a saddle which-he had procured of Belle. This saddle was of peculiar make, was known to everyone in that country as the "Belle Starr" saddle. It was destined to be the means of her being charged later with larceny. Some trivial act of Middleton's caused a falling out between him and his pretty cousin, and Pearl refused the loan of her horse. The next morning, as the little company were at breakfast, a white ranchman named Fayette Barnette (who had married a Choctaw woman, a sister of Jim King and known as the widow Brooken), who was out, apparently, looking after his stock, approached the camp, and, dismounting, stopped to converse with Belle. Learning that Middleton was in need of a horse, he offered one for sale, and going with Middleton out upon the range, they caught a sorrel mare about fifteen hands high, branded "31" on the neck, and a half circle, or "rafter A," on shoulder. The animal was without shoes, and its right eye was blind. The purpose of this minute description will appear later, for this was the horse which Belle Starr was afterwards charged with stealing. It was the property of A. G. McCarty, a near-by ranchman, but of this fact the victims were not aware, and after catching the animal it was turned over to Middleton, who paid Barnette $50 in gold coin, and after placing on its back the "Belle Starr" saddle, rode away to his death. Three days later, on Thursday, May 7, at the point of Poteau Mountain, on Poteau River, twenty-five miles above Fort Smith, a stray horse, which had evidently swam from the opposite side, was found by H. Tallay, of Pocola, Choctaw Nation, quietly grazing, still bridled, on its back the "Belle Starr" saddle, and on the saddle a belt containing a 45-calibre revolver and several cartridges. In the belief that its rider had been drowned, a search was instituted, and on the following Monday, about 200 yards down the river from where the tracks showed the horse had entered the water, was found the dead body of a man. Around the body was a belt filled with cartridges and bearing two 45-calibre pistols. Other articles found on the body were: A silver watch, $1 I in silver coin and a $10 bank note, two pocket knives, comb, etc. The body was that of a young man of heavy build, light complexion, heavy moustache, dressed in dark cassimere pantaloons and vest, and dress shirt. The remains were badly decomposed and the face had been mutilated by buzzards. The body was buried by its finder, and a description of the horse and of the man it had drowned were sent to O. D. Weldon, of Fort Smith, then reporter for the Elevator, and by him a dispatch was sent to the St c Louis Globe-Democrat relating the discovery.

Unconscious of the sad fate of their reckless relative, Belle and Pearl had proceeded on their trip to Logan County, and the latter was left to visit with her cousins, while the mother continued to Chickala, intending to return after a month. They had separated from Middleton on Wednesday, May 6, five miles from where he was that night drowned. By some shrewd maneuver, Deputy Sheriff Duncan had learned of Belle's intended (rip to the vicinity of Dardanelle, and, supposing that Middleton would meet her there (believing that they were man and mistress eloping from a discarded husband), he went by rail to Little Rock, stationing Milsaps at Dardanelle to await the arrival of the pair. They saw the Fort Smith dispatch to the St. Louis paper, and rightly surmising that the dead man was the outlaw they were chasing, they wired John West, and the three men met at Fort Smith, where they were joined by Mr. Weldon, and the quartette proceeded to where the body had been buried, exhumed the remains and identified the body. About the neck was a string of beads made from dried snake rattles, the property of Belle Starr. A. G. McCarty, owner of the horse, also saw the published description of the estray, and going to Pocola, he identified his property. On the following Monday, May 18, the two Texas officers and John West proceeded to Dardanelle, and from there to where Belle Starr was camped at the

Springs. West served a warrant on young Cook, charging a misdemeanor. They also proposed to break open a trunk belonging to Belle, thinking to secure incriminating letters written by Middleton. Belle grasped a pistol in each hand, and coolly reminded them that if they broke open the trunk their souls would go speeding to the place of torment. The trunk was not opened. Belle had already been warned of the death of Middleton by a brother of the latter, and on learning from the officers that the horse Middleton rode was the property of McCarty, she at once thought of the saddle, and knowing that a charge of larceny would be trumped up against her on that account, she started to return, with the purpose in view of recovering the saddle and preventing it being used against her.

THE YOUTHFUL SLEUTHS

After finding the dead body of the man they sought, the Texas officers gave out the story that Middleton and Belle Starr had been on a horse-thieving raid down in Carden's Bottoms, their intention no doubt being to claim that they had chased him to the place where he was drowned, and during a fight had killed him—this with a view to securing the $300 reward. The report of the alleged raid reached the ears of people residing in Logan County, but not so the news of the bandit's death. Pearl had, in the meantime, been enjoying her visit at the home of her cousins as only a vivacious and innocent maiden can. She had attended dances in the neighborhood and was regarded by the rustic youths as the sweetest girl on earth. Her ability as a horsewoman was regarded as something wonderful and every boy in the neighborhood was her champion. One of these, whom Pearl fancied more than any, was Johnny Hazlett, twenty-one years old, now a staid man of family, resident of Fort Smith. He was full of ambition and hearing of the fabulous sums offered for the arrest of their neighbor, he, with Plarrison Popham and Aus Beecham, decided to try a hand at securing the reward. Hazlett learned from Pearl about the time she expected her mother's return, and going down the military road, toward Paris, he met Belle and the Cook boy, and rode with them to the Reed home, where Pearl was visiting. Under the pretense of seeking merely the company of the girls, but with the purpose of learning of the time when the bandit might be expected home, he stayed about until he was advised by the elder Reed to leave. Meeting his companions in the bold plan he informed them that he believed Middleton would be home the following night, Monday, and at an appointed hour the three bandit catchers went to the Middleton home; they left their horses in charge of one of their number, a quarter of a mile from the house, the others ambushing near the house to await the coming of the man who, cold in death, had been buried for more than two weeks. After several hours their hearts began quaking with fear at the very audacity of their intentions, which were nothing less than to kill the bandit, Middleton, at his first appearance, and at last they gave it up and returned to their homes. It was weeks before they learned that they had ambushed for a dead man.

BELLE AND THE TENDERFEET

As soon as Belle had returned to her home in the Cherokee Nation, one of her first acts was to secure possession of the saddle which had been used by Middleton on the stolen horse he had purchased. The story of its being found, however, gradually leaked out and reached the ears of one or more of Belle's enemies, and in due time she was again indicted for larceny. The story connected with her arrest on this charge is entertaining, to say the least. It was in midsummer, 1886. Sam Starr, who was still scouting, was at home. The shades of evening had gathered, and as he sat by the fire, Belle was berating him soundly for his carelessness in not keeping to safer quarters. Finally, she declared that she did not care if the officers did get him, she hoped they would, and Sam indifferently echoed the wish, saying:

"If they want me, let them come and get me; I don't care."

At that moment Pearl, who had been outside, entered and told them that a posse of officers had just appeared in front of and a short distance away from the house. Sam rose quietly, reached for his Winchester, and while Belle turned down the light he slipped from the door and around the house into the bush unobserved by the officers. In a few minutes a knock was heard at the door and in came Deputy Marshal Tyner Hughes and his posse, each of them showing evident signs of nervousness, indicative of the fear they felt at the arrival at the place where their task was to be performed. The mother and daughter sat unconcernedly by the fireplace—no Sam was to be seen. Belle joked them about their chattering teeth and the condition of their clothing, showing, as she asserted, that they had crawled to the house on their hands and knees, and asked their mission, and being shown the warrant in the horse stealing case, she consented to accompany the officers to Fort Smith. Pearl saddled her pony and accompanied her mother a matter of ten miles, and thereby, doubtless, prevented her step-father, or "Uncle Sam" as she always called him, from committing murder. For several miles of the journey Sam kept abreast of the party and near enough for his rifle to kill seeking for a favorable opportunity to lay low his enemies; every time he would attain proper range either his wife or Pearl would unconsciously move between him and the officer he sought to destroy; he at last gave up the attempt and returned to his home.

After traversing half the way to Fort Smith, the camp of the posse was reached and the officers prepared for a night's rest; Pearl had returned home and Belle was provided with accommodations at a house occupied by white people. Supper was prepared, and during the meal and until the hour for retiring the one chosen theme for conversation seemed to be the notorious Belle Starr. Belle heard of herself accused of daring acts and of blood-curdling crimes of which she had never dreamed, much less performed. As for Belle Starr in person, she made an excellent impression upon her hostess, as she did with everyone when she so desired. It became tiresome, however, to hear herself discussed, even if she was, like a German prince, traveling incognito, and in the morning, before breakfast had been prepared in the farmhouse, she walked the short distance to the officer's camp and finding Deputy Hughes' pistol, which he had left carelessly in the pocket of a coat he was not wearing, she appropriated it and with a grim smile returned to the house, the weapon hidden by the folds of a long cloak. At the breakfast table the conversation again turned to the notorious female outlaw and after a few moments of silence Belle turned to her host and enquired if he or any of his family had ever seen Belle Starr, this terrible woman they had told her so much about. He promptly answered in the negative. This family had but recently come from one of the Eastern States and they were, as usual, ready to believe and repeat as truth every impossible story they had ever heard regarding Belle Starr; Belle had marked them for "tenderfeet" and she proposed to have a little sport. At his answer, Belle sprang to her feet, displayed her revolver, assumed a tragic air and a hoarse voice, and said:

"Well, you have told me so much about Belle Starr, I'll just introduce her to you: I am the notorious Belle Starr!"

She might have gone farther but Deputy Hughes appearing just at that moment claimed his revolver and quiet was restored, the hostess declaring, as soon as she had recovered from her shock:

"Well, if you are Belle Starr, you are a lady, and I hope you will stop at my house every time you pass."

Belle did stop there many times after that and she numbered that family of "tenderfeet" among her best friends. Belle was tried on the larceny charge and acquitted, September 30, 1886, largely through the assistance of Fayette Barnett and his brother. They even paid Belle's attorney fees, fearing that Belle, if convicted, would turn the tables and prove the sale of the stolen mare to Middleton by the real thief. Barnett,

I am informed, afterwards deserted his Choctaw wife and going to New Mexico made a fortune in the liquor traffic.

THE. STAGE ROBBERY

It was during that season that Belle gave the exhibition of a wild west performance at the Sebastian County Fair Grounds. Judge Parker, always a public spirited man, requested her to arrange and take the leading part in a mock stage coach robbery; he offered himself as one of the passengers to be robbed. Belle consented and the affair was carried out to the satisfaction of the large crowd who came to the fair, in response to the widely advertised "stage robbery," and whose coming added to the profits of the association. One of the occupants of the stage was a flashily dressed young man, who had insisted that he be given a part in the performance. When Belle overhauled the coach and flung open the door, she ordered the young man to hand over his watch; he wore a heavy chain on his vest front; in vain did he beg to be excused of conforming to the play in so realistic a manner, Belle seized the chain and drew from his pocket— nothing but the swivel. The young man blushed a rosy red and leaving the coach he disappeared in the crowd.

Belle had sought to have District Attorney Clayton, also, as a member of the stage party but some accident prevented his taking part. A year or more later, after she had become friendly to him, having employed him to transact some legal business, she informed him that had he been an occupant of that stage coach she would have killed him; she intended having in her pistol one cartridge, not a blank, in order that she might avenge the attorney's ridicule of her husband's illiteracy.

Another amusing incident attending the fair was one in which A. A. Powe, the small of stature and bespectacled editor of the now defunct Fort Smith livening Call. Powe was a "would be" politician, but he was unpopular. While he was standing in a dense crowd, watching the races, some sports picked him up and threw him astride the horse on which Belle Starr was seated; she was equal to the occasion and putting spurs to her steed she dashed upon the track at full speed, making the circuit twice, while Editor Powe clung to her for dear life, dropping his hat and nearly losing his spectacles.

SAM STARR'S CAPTURE AND DEATH

Meanwhile a posse of officers had attacked Sam Starr and several others; a number of shots were fired from both sides and Sam fell wounded in the head, his horse being shot from under him and Sam was thought to be mortally wounded. Leaving four of their number to guard Sam and another wounded man the rest of the posse returned to camp with several prisoners. Watching a favorable opportunity, Sam slipped upon the officers unobserved, appropriated a rifle and backed away while he held them at bay and harmless to his interests by his steady and persistent aim, and so made good his escape. Later, on the advice of his wife, he gave himself up. He was arraigned with Felix Griffin on the post-office charge, November 17, 1886 and trial of the case was postponed to March 7, 1887. On the occasion of his arraignment, Belle and Pearl were among the witnesses who expected to go on the stand in his defense. After the case had been set over and his bond had been fixed the party started for home. At Whitefield, where they stopped for the night, a dance was in progress. Of course there were intoxicants present and quarrels were numerous. In the crowd was a member of the posse who had unhorsed Sam a month or so before. A discussion arose over the question as to who killed Sam's horse and the other boasted.

"I killed your horse."

In the quarrel that ensued Sam was killed and Belle was once more a widow. When the case against him was called up in court, his demise was announced and on the twentieth day of May following the death of his co-partner in the case, Griffin, was announced to the court and the case was then marked "abandoned."

THE TURNING POINT IN PEARL STARR'S LIFE

In the meantime, "Baby Pearl" had become a woman; had met the fate which should influence, to a great degree, her entire future. As she had neared her fifteenth year her mother had often said to her: "Never marry a poor man. The man you marry must have $25,000." Pearl feared her mother yet loved her, and-made it her rule to "always obey mamma," but her natural girlish inclinations led her to seek the acquaintance of young men of her age and she had many admirers among youths of irreproachable character. One of these Pearl conceived a special liking for and during some of her mother's raids, when she would be away from home for days together, Pearl would allow him to call at their home, and after a happy hour spent in the usual lover's conversation, she would saddle her pony and go with him for a ride; they enjoyed each other's' company as only a pure maiden and a high model youth can do. The friendship between them ripened into something more lasting, unobserved by her mother, and when, finally, in August, 1885, following the death of Middleton, the young swain asked Belle's permission to make Pearl his wife, Belle was taken by surprise but immediately entered a refusal saying, as she had so often told her daughter, that the man Pearl should marry must have at least property to the amount of $25,000.

She spoke with such certain determination that the youth went away with a heavy heart remarking, "Well, Mrs. Starr, you know I will never have one-tenth of that sum," Not knowing to what extent this little love affair had reached, Belle sent Pearl on a visit to her friends, the Marshall's, at Chickalah, Arkansas. Pearl was delighted at thought of the trip, expecting to return in a few weeks, but Belle kept her there for several months. Belle had a "cunning hand" and could imitate penmanship to a creditable degree; fearing that Pearl's absence would not be sufficient to wean the youthful lovers, she wrote what purported to be a letter written by Pearl to the young man and enclosed in a letter to herself, under date of early winter. She then sent for the youth and gave him the letter. It was a series of farewells and contained this sentence:

"I was married last Thursday to a rich man who has lots of stock and $25,000 in the bank: so you see I have got that money just as mama said. PEARL."

The innocent boy believed the letter was from the hand of his loved one and he believed its contents. He went away with a pain in his heart at the thought that the girl, he believed so pure, could, forget his love so soon, could sell herself for riches.

"Many a heart is caught at the rebound;" and it is not strange that he turned to a girl of his acquaintance, who had long before set her cap for him, and when Pearl returned a few weeks later it was much to her chagrin, as well as her disappointment, that she learned of his recent marriage. Her maiden's heart was piqued that her boy love could forget her so soon. She had received several letters from him when first she went on her visit, full of love and yearning for her return. Pearl had refrained from answering any of these letters, in obedience to her mother's command, and finally, just before the time of Belle's forged letter, his letters to Pearl had ceased.

Pearl met the young man several times, but still thinking of how quickly his pretended love had cooled, she passed him by in cold silence, a stranger. Hein turn discovered that Pearl was not married and he persisted in his attentions until finally, about the middle of July, 1886, at a picnic, he met her face to face, seized her hand, and before she could break away, had forced a part of the truth upon her, and her assertion that he had quickly forgotten his lover's vows in her absence resulted in both coming to a clear understanding of the mother's duplicity which had resulted in separating two loving hearts.

The two met again a few days later, in the seclusion of a leafy nook, for a "last talk." They lived over the past; the unloved wife was forgotten; certainly it would have been better had they never met again, but who can account for the acts of disunited lovers suddenly brought together? There was so much to tell; and then, with the story told and fully understood, Pearl discovered that not only had her mother thwarted her plans for happiness, but she had accomplished it by trickery and deception. It created a feeling of abandon in the girl which portended ill for her. It was now too late to undo her mother's work; the man she loved was bound to another, and when at last the youth offered to seek a legal separation on Pearl's account and his own, Pearl nobly refused to listen; in that respect she was the stronger of the two. Her love had been of the kind that makes its possessor better and more womanly, and she would not stain it by allowing its object to heap dishonor upon his own head and wrong upon that of the innocent instrument of their separation. In another respect she was the weaker because of her very womanliness, and the love in the heart of her companion, because of its having been unjustly restrained, had now become like a heated furnace in its intensity and was of the kind that knows no restraint—no shame, and at last, just as they were about to separate, he to go to one whom he did not love, she to commune with her lonely heart, the tempter became master of each and ****** who can wonder that she yielded? Condemn the seducer if you will, but not the seduced; no, not the seduced, until you have been placed in exactly her condition, with all the attendant circumstances, and proved strong to resist.

A noted French writer has said: "Many women are counted virtuous who never have been tempted." Until we have been tempted, and successfully resisted, we are not competent to criticise the fallen.

It was not long before Pearl discovered that she was *enceinte*, and she was filled with serious foreboding. She feared that if her mother discovered her condition she would at once suspect the author of her ruin and that she would lose no time in killing him. She was a woman now, though not yet 17 years old, with all a woman's passions, and though she knew her love was dead to her, she would not see a hair of his head injured.

Pearl continued at home, and during the summer, because of being called several times as a witness at the Federal court at Fort Smith, and from the sale of several horses that she had been allowed to hold in her own name, she had accumulated, by the beginning of the following year, a sum amounting to $200. By artifices best known to those of her sex, the girl kept her secret to herself, only disclosing it to a girl slightly her senior, Mable Harrison, whom Belle had given a home for several years past, and who was Pearl's companion.

It was Pearl's intention to steal from home and with the money at her command go away among entire strangers, never to communicate with her mother again. She had received an offer of marriage from a wealthy Fort Smith liveryman, who met her in the summer of 1886 while she was in attendance at court, but she was too true to accept his offer without informing him of her condition, and of that she had not the slightest intention, fearing it could only result in scorn being heaped upon her.

THE TRUTH DISCOVERED

At Whitefield was a store conducted by a white man named Kraft, who had been almost as a father to Pearl, who had given her her first red dress as a child and had in many ways endeared himself both to the girl and her mother. One evening early in February, 1887, he called at the little home in the mountains; while he and Belle indulged in a friendly chat, Pearl and Mable were absent on an errand, and Belle proposed to procure a sheet, cover her head and play the ghost. Her visitor warned her against the plan, as it might have a serious effect upon her daughter, to which Belle replied:

"Pshaw! Pearl would not be frightened if she saw a real ghost, let alone a make-believe."

"Is it possible," asked the merchant, "that you have not yet discovered that Pearl is in a delicate condition?"

In an instant Belle was like a thousand furies. She understood only too well the insinuation, and surmising that Kraft might be the author of her daughter's ruin, since he knew of it first of all, she began to berate him, but was met by a prompt and straightforward denial. Just then Pearl and Mable entered the house and went at once to their room, but in the one glance she gave her mother she had discovered a look she had never seen before; as the two girls prepared to retire Pearl said to the other:

11 Mamma knows something!"

A moment later Belle called to her, and with trembling heart she re-entered the room. "That look" was still on her mother's face as she asked:

"Pearl, is it true that you are in trouble? And who is responsible for this?" at the same time clenching tightly the handle of a revolver that lay on a table by her side.

Pearl hesitated. "Mamma, I have deceived you once, but I never will again; but—"

"Tell me who it is," she demanded.

Again she hesitated. "No, mamma; not even if you were to kill me. I will never tell anybody."

At this the trembling old merchant ran to her, crying:

"Save me, Pearl! save me!"

Pearl turned to her mother in astonishment.

"Him? Mamma, Mr. Kraft has been like a father to me; you know he has. No, it is not him."

Belle saw it was useless to insist. She discovered for the first time that Pearl was no longer a child. For several days she studied on a plan, but said nothing. Pearl accompanied her to Fort Smith, and there the girl again met the infatuated liveryman. He urged his suit, and Pearl told him all. He was surprised, but he did not give her up. He accompanied mother and daughter to their home. From the privacy of her room Pearl heard the others calmly discussing a plan for her to meet a noted Fort Smith physician. The arrangement completed, the lover departed, and Pearl at once sought her mother.

"Mamma, I have heard all, and I will never consent; I am afraid.

Belle at once declared that the only alternative was for her to leave home, adding: "You must never bring the child into my presence.

Pearl, with tightly compressed lips, replied:

"Mamma, I'll go, and you will never see me again."

Early the next morning Pearl mounted her horse and proceeded to Fort Smith. She left the animal at the stable owned by her suitor, and then she met him and told him she was going away forever. He at first demurred, and then asked her to place the child in a St. Louis foundling asylum and then return and marry him. Pearl would not promise. Another brief consultation, and a span was harnessed and the pair drove to an adjoining county, where a quiet marriage ceremony was performed; and the next train north bore Pearl to the home of her grandparents in Missouri. There she found her grandmother preparing for a trip to Siloam Spring, Ark., for the benefit of her health. Pearl accompanied her, and there, in April, 1887, Pearl became the mother of a pretty girl baby, which she named "Flossie."

Her husband had given her the best span in his stables as a marriage gift, and he regularly forwarded to her their full earnings.

A month after the baby was born he visited her at Rich Hill (wither Pearl and her grandmother had returned), and renewed his plea that the baby be placed in an asylum in St. Louis. Pearl loved her baby, and refused to give it up. Her husband left her with money; and after a few weeks he again visited her, pleading with her to give up the infant and return to gladden his home in Fort Smith.

Pearl finally suggested that she might consent to give the baby to an aunt residing in the Osage Nation, in the Indian, Territory, and the husband gave her $300 to defray traveling expenses and leave means for the little one's support, after which Pearl was to return to him. He accompanied her on board the train, and as he sat on the arm of the seat, looking-into her eyes, he said:

"Pearl, you do not intend to come back to me."

Pearl hugged her baby closer and smiled.

"I will give you three months," he said. "If, in that time, you do not return, I will seek a legal separation and marry a girl who loves me, but who can never fill my heart. If you do not come back to me, I will try and make her a good husband—will try to make her happy."

Pearl assured him she would return, but she hugged her baby closer.

Pearl proceeded to the Osage Agency, and resided with a sister of her father for a year. Her husband kept his word, and married a girl he did not love. Belle had told Pearl that as long as she kept her child she never wanted to hear from her, and on leaving her grandmother's home she left instructions that if her mother wrote to inquire concerning her, they were to reply that she had left for some place unknown. Six months, later Belle's heart began to yearn for "Baby Pearl," and she addressed a letter to Rich Hill, receiving an answer as above. Again she wrote, saying she must hear from Pearl or she would go insane. In answer to this second appeal she was given Pearl's address, and a week later Pearl received by express a package of dress goods, laces, ribbons, and other dainty articles dear to the feminine heart. The package was accompanied by a letter full of love to "Baby Pearl," but this strange woman strongly admonished that none of the finery must ever adorn the form of the despised Flossie, declaring that if her commands, were disobeyed she would haunt the one who dared so to do, after her death; that she would seek vengeance, even at the muzzle of her pistol, while yet living.

Pearl's aunt frowned over the peremptory order, and urged Pearl to use some of the goods with which to dress the pretty baby. Pearl shook her head.

"I deceived mamma once," she said. "I never will again."

The aunt surreptitiously made a baby dress from a piece of the goods, and trimmed it with the ribbons and lace. When Pearl saw it she removed the beautiful garment and burned it, saying:

"Baby shall not wear any of those things in disobedience to mamma's wishes, if she has to go naked; I deceived mamma once."

When her baby was a little past a year old, Pearl removed to Wichita, Kansas, and found a home with a sister of her father, of whom Belle had not heard in years, and who was supposed to be dead She again left instructions that her mother should not be informed of her whereabouts, but should be told that she had left for parts unknown. In October, 1888, when Flossie was eighteen months old, Pearl's brother, Ed Reed, was shot during a quarrel, receiving a serious wound. His life was despaired of. Belle sought for Pearl's whereabouts, but failed. In despair, she forwarded $20 to the grandmother at Rich Hill, stating that if Pearl wanted to see her brother before he died she must come at once; she must leave her baby behind, but she could return to it later. The money and the message was sent to Pearl at Wichita, and leaving her baby in care of her aunt, she started for home. She was received with open arms by this strange mother. Ed recovered, but Belle would not allow Pearl to leave her. A few months later and Belle Starr, "Queen of the Prairie," mistress of the ranche at "Younger's Bend," was numbered with the dead.

BELLE STARR MURDERED

As her life had been a tumultuous one so was her death; there is something awful to contemplate in the thought of a woman dying "with her boots on," but who could expect that other than natural results should follow; that a human being be it man or woman, whose whole life, nearly, had been one of reckless daring, whose every act had been that of a tartar, should at last meet with mortal violence; should die by an assassin's hand. It was on her forty-third birthday, February 3, 1889, that the notorious Belle Starr's earthly career was ended.

About fourteen months previous, a neighbor, one Edgar Watson, had removed from Florida. Mrs. Watson was a woman of unlimited education, highly cultured and possessed of a natural refinement. Set down in the wilderness, surrounded by uneducated people, she was attracted to Belle, as unlike the others, and the two women soon became fast friends. In a moment of confidence she had entrusted Belle with her husband's secret, he had fled from Florida to avoid arrest for a murder he had committed; Belle, of course, confided the secret to Pearl. Early in the year just given, Watson had sought to lease a portion of Belle's landed possessions, but she had conceived a dislike for him on account of his having taken a letter, from the post-office, addressed to her and she declined to deal with him and entered into a contract with another man to raise a crop upon the land wanted by Watson, upon learning which, the latter advised Belle's tenant to break the contract, assuring him that he would be greatly annoyed by numerous visits of Federal officers if he were to remove to Belle Starr's land, and so worked upon him that the contract was broken. Belle heard of this, and during a visit to her place Watson was met in the yard by Belle and soundly she berated him for having interfered in her business affairs; she added with scorn:

"I don't suppose the United States officers would trouble you but the Florida officers might."

Watson flushed and went away. Pearl, sitting in the house, had overheard the conversation and she chided her mother for being so careless as to allow Watson to know she was in possession of his terrible secret, but Belle laughed and forgot the circumstance.

Since the death of Sam Starr, his cousin, Jim Starr, alias Jim July, had made his home with Belle and Pearl. He was under indictment at the Fort Smith Court for horse stealing; h$ had been under bond for several years and by some means had managed to secure a continuance from term to term of court. On the morning of Saturday, February 2, 1889, he started for Fort Smith, to appear in answer to the old charge, and was accompanied by Belle to San Bois, Choctaw Nation, twenty-nine miles from the Canadian River. There they stopped for the night and on Sunday morning July proceeded to Fort Smith and Belle started for home. She arrived at the house of Jack Rose, two miles from home, at 3 o'clock p. m., and stopped for dinner. Several men were in the yard, Edgar Watson being one of the number.

A few minutes after Belle entered the house Watson left abruptly, going to his home, 150 yards away. Belle remained for a half hour, then continued her journey, riding along a road leading around Watson's field to a point where it intersected an old road that had been fenced off, near a corner of another field, 150 yards from Watson's house. Inside the fence, at the corner of this field, stood the assassin whose bullets took the life of Belle Starr. As there was no brush or other means of hiding she must have seen him as she passed, and a moment later she was shot in the back; four buckshot took effect, three in the center of the back and one in the neck. She was knocked from her horse and her slayer climbed the fence and shot her a second time with a heavy charge of turkey shot as she lay on her back in the mud, the charge taking effect in the face, neck and one arm. A few minutes later, Milo Hoyt came riding along the road and discovering the body at a short distance, approached no farther but immediately turned back to go and inform Pearl of her mother's condition, but Belle's horse, freed of its rider, had proceeded home and Pearl, knowing that something unusual had happened, started out to investigate. She met Hoyt and was guided to the spot and found her mother in the throes of death; Belle spoke one or two words, gasped and died. Neighbors gathered and the body was carried to the mountain home, a mile away.

When Belle's horse reached home, Pearl had just returned from a ride; she had passed the home of John West and Mrs.

West had called to her: "I want you to tell your mamma I must see her as soon as possible; I must tell her something." "Can I carry the message?" asked Pearl." No, no, child, I must see your mamma. I can't tell it to you." Whether the woman, who was a kind friend of belle's, knew of the attempt sooner or later to be made upon her life will never be known.

Jim July heard of the killing and securing another continuance of his case he hastened home on Monday and assisted in trailing the murderer. Tracks led from Watson's house to the place of the killing and were plainly visible on the inside of the fence nearly opposite where Belle fell, as well as where the murderer had jumped over the fence and to the side of the road where he stood when the second shot was fired; from there the tracks led in a round-about way to Watson's house.

Suspicion could point to none other than Watson; he attended Belle Starr's funeral on Wednesday, and that evening he was arrested by July and turned over to the

Federal officers. Watson was given a hearing before United States Commissioner Brizzolara and on account of insufficient evidence to bind him over to the grand jury the case was continued and two weeks later he was released. He was afterwards convicted in the Crawford County Circuit Court, at Van Buren, as a horse thief and sentenced to a term of fifteen years at Little Rock; later he escaped and was killed.

There were some who had another theory for the killing and who, for a time, believed that Belle Starr s assassin was none other than her own son, Ed Reed, who was then nearing his eighteenth birthday. The grounds on which this theory was based were as follows:

Belle had a fine black horse which she prized very highly. Old deputy marshals will recognize the animal. Shortly before the killing Ed had asked permission to ride the horse to a dance several miles away. His request was denied and he stole the animal from its stable after dark and did not return until just before daybreak the next morning. Belle awoke at his return and on rising she went to the stable and discovered that her favorite had been badly mistreated and ill cared for. She grasped her quirt (a small riding whip of braided strips of leather, much in use on the plains) and stalked to the house and into the room where Ed lay in bed asleep, and gave him an unmerciful whipping. His punishment greatly angered the boy, and he left home and was not seen for two weeks; it was said that he threatened his mother's life in return for the chastisement, and there was talk of his arrest and trial by an Indian court, but the matter finally quieted and he was not arrested.

Since Pearl's return from Wichita she had received several letters from her aunt regarding her baby, and acting on the aunt's advice she had allowed the child to be legally adopted by a wealthy family, and after her mother's death she decided that the best interests of her little one demanded that she allow it to grow up in ignorance of its parentage, though means were provided by which she could hear concerning it at stated intervals. The child is now past 12 years old; she is happy with her foster parents whom she believes to be hers by birth, and she is evolving into an excellent musician.

AX UNHAPPY MARRIAGE

Two years after her mother's death Pearl married Will Harrison, a brother of her foster sister, Mable Harrison, and for a time she tried to live happily at Tamaha, in the Choctaw Nation, but their temperaments clashed, frequent quarrels occurred and at last Pearl deserted him.

About this time her brother, Ed, met with serious difficulty. He had always been of a different turn than Pearl. With him kindness or human sympathy had little influence, though he had a marked fondness for his sister, a redeeming trait. From the age of fourteen years he had been subject to the evil influences prevailing in the Indian Territory, and he fell as if by nature, an easy prey to whatever temptations crossed his path. He evinced a fondness for intoxicants and thus lie-became at an early age a "boot-legger," and after several encounters with the officers and many narrow escapes from death he was at last landed in the Fort Smith jail, convicted and sentenced to seven years in the penitentiary at Columbus, Ohio, for horse stealing.

After Pearl's separation from her husband, Harrison, it is probable that her conduct was not always the most circumspect and she began gliding towards the pace that kills, and with her brother's removal to the penitentiary she entered a house of nameless reputation in Fort Smith, for the purpose, as she said, of procuring money with which to secure his release, intending, in the event of failure, to return to the walks of respectability.

With her natural spirit of independence she soon sickened at the variety of company she was forced to mingle with, and taking advantage of an opportunity that offered, she leased a building in the "bad lands" and became herself mistress of a "boarding house" such as she had been an inmate of for three months. She accumulated money rapidly and was soon able to employ attorneys in her brother's behalf. Col. Ben T. DuVal and W. M. Cravens were retained and their best efforts were put forth, and at last, after he had served several years of his sentence, Judge Parker and District Attorney Clayton, knowing of the example set by his mother and the evil influences that surrounded him, which had made him a criminal, recommended to the President of the United States that a pardon be granted in his case, which was accordingly done, and he returned to Fort Smith and soon after was sworn in as a deputy marshal of Judge Parker's court.

When he visited his sister and discovered her vocation he was overwhelmed with sorrow, but Pearl reasoned: "There are only us two now; everybody knows the conditions under which we have been placed; a change now would not help matters, and if you cannot bear your sister's disgrace I will provide you with money and you can go far away where I am not known."

THEIR FATE AGAINST THEM

Ed served as a deputy marshal for about three years, making, with little exception, an excellent officer. The desperate characters wish whom he had trained, and who knew his antecedents, took exception to his being empowered with authority" by the criminal court, and his pathway among the criminal classes in the Indian Territory, after it had become generally known that he had been made a deputy, was fraught with much danger, even more than usually fell to the lot of an officer of the court: but he was fearless in discharge of his duty' and much

BELIT STAKE S SOX

Ea. Keen. valuable work was performed by him. Among those who opposed his authority were Dick and Zeke Crittenden, brothers, and ex-Deputy United States Marshals, previously' noted in this work. On the afternoon of Thursday, October 24, 1895, the two brothers were in Wagoner, Indian Territory, and both became influenced by intoxicants. They were well-behaved men when sober, but were quarrelsome and dangerous when in their cups. On this day they were obstreperous and had started out to "paint the town red;" they had fired their pistols promiscuously and had slightly wounded a man named Burns, proprietor of the principal restaurant of the place, the bullet cutting

ED REED'S INDIAN WIFE

Mrs. Jennie Reed, nee Cochrane. his scalp. The city marshal attempted to arrest them and called on Reed for assistance. The brothers had followed Reed about a good portion of the day with undue persistence, had become very annoying in their carousals, but Reed had paid very little attention to them as he did not wish to exceed his authority. When they had shot the restaurant keeper however he decided his time had come to act, and soon after he met Zeke Crittenden coming up the street on foot and ordered him to surrender his pistol; he was answered by a shot, at which Reed drew his pistol and fired, killing the other instantly. Dick Crittenden was then in the custody of the city marshal at the other end of town. He soon learned of his brother being killed and he immediately rode away in the direction of where he fell, and when within about six feet of the place he saw Reed on the opposite side of the street and opened fire. Reed did not return the fire but ordered him to "drop" his gun. No heed was taken and Reed began to fire, shooting three times. The first shot was ineffective, but the second struck Crittenden in the side, driving a cartridge from his belt into the body, where it exploded, making a terrible wound; the victim of his own bullet died the next morning at 3 o'clock. Reed was fully exonerated by the citizens of Wagoner and by the court.

Still later he, too, seems to have begun to feel too much his own importance, or because of too free use of whiskey, and becoming reckless he one day in November, 1896, drove two men, the proprietors, from a saloon; they returned later and killed him.

Several months prior to his death he had married a pretty little half Cherokee school teacher, Miss Jennie Cochran. She was a good wife, and while they lived together their home was a happy one. After his death the wife returned to her former home at Claremore, where she still resides.

As for Pearl, she continued in charge of her house until 1897, when, partly from being urged by an inmate of her place, (a beautiful girl of excellent breeding, who seemed strangely out of place amid such surroundings) she built a house in the eastern part of the city, a highly respected locality, to which she removed, taking the girl with her. Pearl afterwards married, in October 1897. She loved her husband and was true to him. In the summer of 1898, he was stricken with typhoid fever and on September 13, he succumbed to the disease, leaving Pearl disconsolate but with the care of a baby boy, three weeks old.

Thus is chronicled the romance of Belle Starr and her issue, leaving Pearl and her son the only living acknowledged representatives, of a family whose antecedents were the best, but against whom fate seemed to have decreed.

SAVED BY HER GRANDMOTHER'S PRAYERS

Before closing this chapter I wish to relate briefly, the history of the girl who was largely instrumental in inducing Pearl to give up her house in "shady row" and build in a respectable portion of the city. The name given "Myrtle Pemberton," is not that of her father, it being withheld for the sake of the family, which is one of the best known and most highly respected in Kentucky, but it justly belongs to her as being the name of another prominent family closely akin, residing also in the blue grass state.

She was born December 4, 1876; her home was at Horse Cave, Kentucky, though she was born at San Antonio, Texas, wither her mother had gone to visit her husband, who spent several months in the vicinity on business. On the day that Myrtle was born her highly refined and cultured mother died, and for that reason (none other is known) her father always hated the child, his own flesh and blood.

Six years after he had, with broken heart, laid his wife away, he married again and the step-mother drove from their home, Myrtle, her brother a year older, and their aged grandmother, the mother of their father. The boy went to Texarkana, Arkansas, secured a place with the Iron Mountain railroad company, as call boy and worked his way, by degrees, to appointment as conductor of a passenger train; on the day the appointment was made he was killed, while coupling cars. From the time of his first pay day until he married he divided his salary, giving half to Myrtle, keeping her in school till she was 12 years old. She was her grandmother's constant companion and when driven from her father's house they had gone to the home of one of her uncle's and later had removed to Texarkana, and were given a home by still another son of the grandmother.

The latter was deeply religious and she taught Myrtle the right side of life from her infancy but the girl was of keen perception; her father was a professed Christian as was the step-mother, and, influenced by their unchristian like treatment of her and hers, she developed traits of infidelity.

When Myrtle was 14 years old her brother married; with female intuition Myrtle discovered that his bride cared only for the money he could provide her with and the latter took a keen dislike for her. At this point she too had an opportunity to marry, and in April following, she became the wife of a gambler, on account of whose brutal treatment she left him twelve days after her wedding day. She secured employment in a hotel and saved money with which to procure a divorce; she gave it to a lawyer who chanced to be a friend of the gambler husband and the divorce was not granted. He tried to kill her on the street by shooting at her; he missed and was arrested on a charge of assault with intent to kill but was acquitted. Myrtle's employer operated a hotel at Little Rock; he sent her there and brought a girl from Little Rock to take her

378

place. At Little Rock the girl managed to secure a divorce, but her ex-husband followed her there, persisted in his annoyance and circulated stories derogatory to her character. At last the girl, as she was about to lose her situation, gave up in despair and entered a house of infamy.

She was beautiful of face and figure, as well as of gentle and quiet demeanor, and she soon attracted the attention of a young man of wealth and station, who took her away as his mistress. Six months later the young man decided to marry; his bride was a pure young woman of excellent parentage; on the day that she became his wife, Myrtle left his home, and unbeknown to the new corner, gave up to her the place she had occupied for half a year.

I ask the reader for a logical answer to this question: In the sight of God and manly men, which had the better right at his hearthstone?

Myrtle left the city, went to Fort Smith and became a boarder at the house conducted by Pearl Starr. Dissipation proved not to her nature and she was strongly advised, by her physician, to give up the life she was trying to lead. She did so and when Pearl married she again went at honest labor, in Fort Smith, and soon after went to a town of several thousand inhabitants, in Eastern Arkansas, secured a position in a hotel, won a place in the hearts of the landlord and his wife and came to be regarded by them as a daughter, and later, with the full consent of the parents, who had learned to idolize the girl, she became their son's promised wife.

In the spring of 1898, before her engagement as above, Myrtle decided to visit the home of her childhood. Several years before, she had received a letter announcing that her grandmother, (who had returned to Kentucky after Myrtle's marriage) was dead. It was untrue, and the first person Myrtle met as she ascended the steps of the vine covered porch, made dear by childhood's recollections, was the aged grandmother, past eighty years old; she came tottering and throwing herself into Myrtle's arms, cried:

"Myrtle, my baby! They told me I would never see her again, but I prayed to God and I knew He would not let me die till I had seen my baby; now Lord take me;" and the good old soul expired in the girl's arms. It was a strange scene and it had a marked effect upon Myrtle, who stayed at home long enough to attend to the little details of her grandmother's burial, following instructions she had received when but a child not six year's old.

For one short week Myrtle enjoyed the scenes she loved so well, but the story of her recent past had preceded her home coming and one day the heartless step mother, member of a Christian church, realizing the sweet nature of the girl and fearing she might win a way to the heart of her father, and thus come in for a share of his property, to the disparagement of the younger brood of children, sneeringly referred to Myrtle's shady record and vehemently declared that "such women should all be burned at the stake;" a beautiful example of Christian (?) character.

Myrtle returned to Arkansas. She was well-nigh heartbroken, but that fragile article seemed to mend itself by becoming stony. Her friends at the hotel were as loving as ever, and soon after she engaged to marry the son. It is doubtless true that but for the memory of her sainted grandmother, and the gentle influences thus thrown out to guard and guide her footsteps, she might have gone from the home scenes to rapid destruction, and the untoward and cruel influence exerted by the step-mother seemed accentuated a few months later, when a traveling man entered the hotel diningroom, was attracted by the girl's singular beauty, and the next moment he knew that he had met her—at a Fort Smith bagnio—two years before.

Of course he had to tell of it. There are not enough of America's fairest and choicest girls going to destruction every year; he must strike the blow that should precipitate headlong one who was striving against odds to maintain a life of respectability, to outlive the mistakes of youth.

Myrtle's best friend, the mistress of the hotel, (would to heaven there were more women like her) refused to believe the story, declaring that even if it should prove to be true, Myrtle was a good girl and she should have a home with her as long as she lived. But Myrtle had learned before this what power for harm lay in the tongue of the scandal monger; she realized that any at time another traveling man might come that way, one who had visited (with no detriment to himself of course) the bawdy-house where she had been an inmate, and choking back a sob for the things that might have been, the poor girl deliberately packed her trunk and set about preparations to return to Fort Smith and again enter one of the gilded palaces she had learned to hate.

At the depot she met the young man, who, a few months before, had pleaded with such tenderness for her hand in marriage; to him she made a full confession of her past life, before she had known him, and awaited his answer.

He carelessly replied, while unable to meet her honest and steadfast gaze that she need not go away on that account.

With bated breath and fluttering heart, the poor girl listened and waited for him to proceed. O, would he ask her to remain and become his wife, to share his heart and home, in spite of the whole world; she felt she had no right to ask or even expect it, but would he?

But no. His next words, his tone, his manner towards her, the hot flush in his face and the unwonted fire in his eye, told only too plainly what was in his mind; he would have her stay but not as his wife, to accept an honored position where calumny could not strike, and a blush of shame mantled the cheek of the girl who was even then on her way to a house of infamy and she escaped from the gaping crowd by entering a coach and was hidden from view.

At the bagnio in Fort Smith she appeared as gay as the gayest and none would have thought to see her that:

"E'er she had a virtuous thought,

Nor ever had a care but during her first week of "returning giddiness," in a spirit reverie, she composed the sweetly solemn poem here given, and named it "Fallen." It was a true history of her life, blending with her present ennobling thoughts.

The good influences of her aged grandmother's prayers were at work. Try as she would, she could not throw off the yoke. She took to drink and nearly ruined her health. Her physician warned her, and she was afraid to die, or she might not have heeded the warning.

There came a young man of keen perception; a student of human nature. He met her quite by accident and watched her narrowly. He saw that she was beautiful, and further, that nature had intended her for a place far above the inmates and patrons of a bawdy house. He made a quiet investigation, learned of her antecedents, learned that the girl loved to work, that she was an excellent seamstress, and that she made all her own clothing—even when plying her present vocation. His sympathy was arrested. He talked kindly to her and her heart went out to him. He married the beautiful creature and provided a home for her.

"A dangerous experiment," do you say?

Ah! who can tell? Let us fondly hope that the influence that inspired the tender sentiment enwreathed in the beautiful lines she has given us, together with that of the many earnest prayers of the dear old grandmother, may continue a means of saving grace, and that she may, sometime, be welcomed by the angels "as a sister, as one of precious worth," and be tendered her rightful place by the side of her sainted mother, who died that she might be born.

Jake Harless and Bright Harless were white men, brothers, the former about twenty-six years old and the latter nineteen. Lizzie Harless, their aunt and wife of the deceased Dick Harless, uncle of Jake and Bright, who were charged with his murder; all Jived in a thickly wooded country about five miles from Siloam Springs, Arkansas, on the east bank of the Illinois River, a beautiful, clear stream in the Cherokee Nation.

They were farmers. The uncle and his wife, Lizzie Harless, resided about 400 yards from Jake and Bright, who lived with their parents. As to what their relations were for years previous to the killing I am unable to say, except so far as appeared at the trial. They were respected people, with considerable property. The father of the two boys, for his second wife, had married a Cherokee woman, giving him a right in the

Nation, and he had a good farm with a goodly amount of personal property. The farm occupied by both families took in a long stretch up and down this little river, including the rich alluvial bottoms, the finest possible corn land.

It was claimed by' the prosecution in the case, and there was much evidence tending to prove, that Lizzie Harless (who was much younger than her husband, the deceased uncle, and was about the age of defendant Jake Harless) was intimate with Jake, and various facts and circumstances came out tending to show that this intimacy had existed for a long time and was the basis for the motive of the killing of the uncle, Dick Harless.

At the time of the killing Jake had a sore foot, it having been cut with an axe; this foot was bandaged while the other foot went unshod.

The uncle, Dick Harless, on a pleasant afternoon in the fall of 1889, was about three-quarters of a mile from his home and the home of the defendants at work with a scythe, cutting weeds from the fence corners around a corn field. He was alone. It seems he had grown tired, had gone to a nearby pond and procured a drink of water, and was sitting on the fence at rest, and was doubtless thinking of the future, of the coming winter and of the larder well filled for the sustenance of himself and wife.

While thus occupied, at peace with all the world, an assassin crept up from the rear, hidden by the fence and the standing corn, and fired a bullet across the corner of the field, it was claimed, from the victim's own gun, which had been furnished him by the wife of the latter. The bullet in its course left its mark—a hole in a blade from one of the stalks of corn—and striking the old man Harless low in the back passed through his body, coming out at the base of the stomach, a few inches to the left. He lived only a few hours.

His shouts for assistance brought the defendant, Bright Harless, from the woods, two hundred yards away, armed with a gun; it was claimed that he was there in ambush, while his brother, Jake, crept from the house through the fields, under cover of some scattering timber and concealed by the corn, found his way to the place from where the fatal shot was fired, after which he escaped unobserved.

Bright Harless gave the alarm and was joined by the others and the old man was carried to the house. In a few days the brothers, with Lizzie Harless, were arrested and conveyed to-Fayetteville, Arkansas, for examination by the commissioner and held to answer to an indictment by the grand jury. They employed Thomas H. Barnes and J. Warren Reed, the law firm of Barnes & Reed, to make their defense. The case came on for trial in the spring of 1890; it was a hard fought battle and resulted in a "hung" jury.

The defendants stayed in jail for a number of months. Their attorneys strengthened their testimony; the case was again tried. It was one of the hardest fought battles, at that time, in the history of the court. Mr. Reed had taken notes of the speech made by Prosecuting Attorney Clayton at the first trial, and at the second trial forestalled his argument by telling the jury just what he would say, disconcerting the prosecutor and weakening his argument. Mr. Reed here won one of his early victories. His clients were acquitted.

DECLARED INSANE

Isaac Youtsler was a white man about forty-five years old, unmarried, a native of Illinois. He was a highly educated man and was much of an artist in portrait and scenic painting. He early took to traveling westward and was interested in silver mines in Colorado. He was a person of peculiar disposition, in other words, he was sometimes called a crank. During some of his hallucinations he would be classed as a lunatic.

In his Western rambles he found his way to Joplin, Missouri, and in the spring of 1894 he was the owner of a team, wagon, hack, some fine guns and other articles of personal property. He was staying about a man by the name of Irwin Williams. From some cause, Williams preferred a petty charge against Youtsler and caused him to be locked in jail at Joplin^

While Youtsler was in jail, his property was gathered up by Williams, who took it, and accompanied by a beautiful woman who claimed to be his wife and her little daughter, about twelve years old, went into the Cherokee Nation, near Kansas post-office, claiming to have made the trip for the benefit of his health and for the purpose of hunting game; he set up house-keeping in a poor, wretched log tenement in the center of a few acres of cleared land.

Youtsler was soon after discharged from jail and learning; of the mysterious disappearance of Williams with his personal) effects, he followed, breathing vengeance and threatening the-annihilation of Williams to every man he met. Several days-later, he appeared at the log hut occupied by Williams, in the Cherokee Nation, but the proof produced at the trial showed that while he had been threatening to kill Williams as soon as he found him, yet as soon as they met they became reconciled and friendly and went into a partnership preparing for a crop and commenced to clear land. Matters continued friendly, and Youtsler and Williams traveled about the country together on various errands, and all was apparently smooth until about three weeks later when, one Sunday morning, Youtsler took his double-barrel shotgun and started out to kill a wild turkey to-supply the family with meat. Soon after Youtsler left the house Williams started out about the place on some errand. Directly, the report of a gun was heard, about 300 yards from the house, in the brush. A half hour or so later Youtsler returned to the house and asked Mrs. Williams for the axe; on being told where the instrument was he replied that he did not need it. Going to another part of the house he procured a loaded cartridge, charged with buckshot, returned to the. direction from whence the sound of the shooting had come, and soon after another shot was heard. In a short time he returned to the house and told the woman he had killed her husband; had shot him accidentally while firing at quail.

Mrs. Williams accompanied him to the place where the body lay and they conveyed it to the house, then alarmed the neighbors who soon appeared. Examination discovered two^ sizes of shot in the body.

As the neighbors gathered he would conduct them, one or two at a time, to the place where Williams was killed, and tried to explain how he had done the killing by accident while shooting at birds, but his explanations were so clumsy, his actions so strange, that all the circumstances, together with the many threats he had previously made against the life of Williams, indicated that a terrible crime had been committed, that he had purposely lured his victim to the brush on that calm and beautiful Sabbath morning, and after filling his body full of fine shot, his greed for vengeance not satiated, he had gone to the house for an axe with which to complete his work, then changed his mind and procured a charge of larger shot with which Williams was finally dispatched. Believing this, they notified the officers, and Youtsler was arrested and conveyed to the Fort Smith jail.

It was observed, among other things, that Youtsler's conduct was strange. Some suggested that possibly he was of unsound mind, but there was nothing certain on which to base the conclusion. He was soon indicted for murder, was arraigned before the court, and being unable to employ counsel, the court appointed J. Warren Reed to defend him. Mr. Reed investigated his case, gathered sufficient facts to make it doubtful whether he was sufficiently sane to be placed upon trial, and in this condition he layed in jail about two years. Mr. Reed urged for him that he was insane, while the officers of the court claimed that he was of sound mind, but was playing insanity to cover his crime.

This apparent mental defect continued during the two years, though at intervals he would exhibit the highest degree of intelligence, make fine speeches, argue logically and reason correctly. Mr. Reed made a deep study of his case, and argued that he was a victim of the same class of insanity as was claimed for Deustrow, the noted St. Louis murderer; that he reasoned logically but that he never saw things as they really were.

By a thorough preparation of his case and, when his trial came on in the fall of 1897, by an able defense, Mr. Reed succeeded in clearing Youtsler of the charge of murder on the ground of insanity, the jury finding in their verdict that he was mentally unsound.

Youtsler was sent to the United States Insane Asylum at Washington, D. C., where he subsequently recovered his sanity and was discharged as cured,

A CASE OF CIRCUMSTANTIAL EVIDENCE

A. H. Craig was a white man, about forty years old. He had emigrated from Texas and settled in the Indian country, at Braggs Station, on the Arkansas Valley Railroad, in 1873. He was an energetic, upright business man, and he accumulated considerable property. About the year 1890 he married a Miss Ratliff, daughter of a farmer residing near Braggs; she was half Cherokee and half white; a very amiable woman, beautiful in features and possessed of good education. To-them two children were born. Mr. Craig was a merchant; he ran a general merchandise store at Braggs and was also a farmer.

Thomas R. Madden was a wealthy white man who had lived for many years in the Territory and had married an. Indian woman, a cousin of Mrs. Craig, thus securing an Indian right; he, too, was the proprietor of a large general merchandise store at Braggs, situated across the railroad track from, and facing the store of Mr. Craig. Until about one year prior to the killing of Thomas R. Madden, hereafter detailed, Craig and Madden had been intimate acquaintances and friends.

One Sunday morning, April 19, 1896, the little town of Braggs, a place of 300 population, was the scene of a terrible homicide. Thomas R. Madden, who lived about 500-yards north of his store, near the railroad track, rose from his slumbers, on the morning of the day which was to be his last; he was that day killed in front of his store, about noon, by Mose Miller, a Cherokee Indian, about nineteen years old. The proof showed that the Miller family, consisting of the father and several sons, among them Mose, had for several years been having trouble with Madden. Many threats had passed from both sides; Madden had caused one of the brothers to be sent to the penitentiary for stealing his cattle, and it was expected by Madden's friends at any time to hear of a shooting affray between Madden and Mose Miller.

A few months before the killing of Madden, a terrible quarrel had been engaged in by Madden and Craig, growing out of Madden's jealously of Craig on his wife's account, he claiming that during his absence from home, on a business trip to Kansas Ci ty, Craig had entered his house and made improper proposals to his wife. At this time bitter threats were made and six-shooters were brandished, but by the aid of friends serious conflict was prevented.

Craig was arrested the next day after the murder, charged with being an accessory to the killing of Madden. It was claimed by the prosecution that Mose Miller, being a bitter enemy of Madden's, was ready to take his life at any opportunity, and that being a willing tool he was procured, counseled and advised by Craig and provided with a weapon with which to kill Madden, and that Mose Miller performed the killing in pursuance of a conspiracy between himself and Craig.

The proof at the trial showed that on Saturday, the day before the killing, Mose Miller had been brought to Braggs by the Indian officers, charged with having committed an assault, and Craig and two other persons having signed his bond he was discharged, and he stayed all night at Craig's home; and the next morning after breakfast Mose Miller and Craig's boy, about thirteen years old, went up town, a distance of about a quarter of a mile, and loafed about the stores and the post-office. Miller was armed with a six-shooter concealed about his person, which, it was claimed by the prosecution, had been furnished him by Craig to kill Madden. This, however, was disputed, and denied by Craig.

Madden was informed that morning that Mose Miller was in town, loafing about as if looking for him, and he was advised to stay at home and thereby avoid a personal conflict. At this, Madden remarked to his stepson:

"I have two good guns; let's go and get them and go down and fight it out."

He proceeded in the direction of his store, going by a back way to prevent being seen on the principal street. Calling the assistance of his brother, John, who lived back of the store, they entered the store and arranged several loaded guns near the front door. Looking from the window they saw Miller walking listlessly up and down the street with his hands in his. pockets. Tom Madden remarked to his brother that he believed Miller was lying in wait with the intention of waylaying and killing him and he wanted to go out and try and "talk him out" of his design. The brother advised against this, but Tom Madden insisted.

It was claimed by the prosecution that as Miller passed the store again, Madden opened the door, stepped out and began a friendly conversation. Miller replied with few words, then turned, drew his pistol, shot Madden through the body, killing him instantly, and fled, and as he ran fired back several times. John Madden immediately ran out with his gun and fired several shots in the direction of the fleeing Miller, who escaped, uninjured, ran between two buildings out to the fields and circled around to Craig's house. It was claimed that an hour later Craig and Miller saddled their horses and rode rapidly away, for the purpose, as Craig claimed, of surrendering Miller to the sheriff (whom they did not find). The government claimed that Craig was aiding Miller to escape.

It was claimed by the defense that Tom Madden stepped out of his store with a gun and after a few words with Mose Miller, fired at him; that Miller turned and drew his pistol and fired in self-defense, killing Madden, and that Madden fell, dropping his gun; that John Madden rushed out of the store door, picked up the gun, fired a few shots at the fleeing Miller, and fired two shots at the defendant Craig, who at this point was crossing the street from the post-office to his store, about 120 yards away. A number of eye witnesses testified to each of these different statements, diametrically opposed, each to the other.

It was claimed by the prosecution that during the previous night, while Miller was staying at Craig's house, they formed a conspiracy and laid plans to kill Madden; that Miller had gone up town the next morning and looked about the streets seeking an opportunity to do the work; that a little later Craig had gone to his store and to the post-office, locating himself, conveniently, at the latter place that he might render Miller assistance if necessary, and that on hearing the shot he immediately started from the post-office and looking down the street saw Madden lying dead and shouted: "Hurrah for you,

Mose!" then continued to his place of business, secured a Winchester and coming out ask d who had shot at him, saying:" Show me the man and I'll shoot his head off."

The defendant denied all conspiracy, denied the shouting noted above, denied assisting the man to escape, stating that he had honestly tried to turn him over to the sheriff, who was sick in bed at the time and that the deputy sheriff, to whom they were referred, was away from home and could not be found.

The case was prosecuted by Thomas Markham, of Muscogee, employed by Madden's widow to conduct the case against Craig. The defense was represented by the law firm of Barnes & Melette, of Fort Smith, There were about thirty witnesses, and the trial lasted two days and resulted in a disagreement by the jury, the case being held to the next term of court.

In the meantime, one of Craig's attorneys—Mr. Barnes—was appointed United States District Attorney, and was thereby disqualified. Craig then employed J. Warren Reed and William M. Cravens, of Fort Smith, and they took the case through two subsequent trials.

At the next term of court the case was tried again; the number of witnesses on both sides had increased, and now numbered about seventy. This trial was a hard-fought case, lasting seven days, and it, too, resulted in a "hung" jury, and was again set over to the following term.

In the meantime, Mr. Reed, determined to win the case and clear Craig, made a trip to Braggs, investigated the premises about the scene of the killing, made a large plat showing the location of the several stores, houses, and the post-office with the streets and whatever alleys entered into the evidence for use before the jury, developed further evidence in the case, and showed the falsity of some of the claims made by the prosecution.

The third and last trial came on in March, 1898. Upwards of eighty witnesses were sworn. The trial lasted eight days. It was strongly contested by both sides, and resulted in a verdict of acquittal. Able speeches were made by all the attorneys in the case; six hours were occupied in the arguments, and when the verdict was announced it was a high compliment to the skill and ability, of the matchless J. Warren Reed and his associate counsel, Mr. Cravens.

A GREENLEAF MOUNTAIN ROMANCE

Mose Miller had been jointly indicted with Craig for the murder of Madden, but scarce any effort was made to secure his arrest, and for nearly three years he enjoyed the reputation of being a refugee from justice.

Within a dozen miles of the scene of his crime, amid the fastnesses of the Greenleaf mountains, where nature had so bountifully provided him with opportunities for concealment, he was comparatively safe, surrounded as he was by his friends, members of his tribe, who inhabited the scattered settlements among the hills and canyons, and during the time he remained at large he led an easy, careless existence, never coming in contact with the outside world except by his own desire.

Nearly three years he spent in the midst of these surroundings, baffling the skill and daring of the Federal officers in their efforts to capture him, his friends warning him of any impending danger and keeping him informed of the movements of any suspicious stranger who might appear in the neighborhood, giving him opportunity to seek one of his many safe and impregnable retreats.

During the time that Mose Miller was thus a fugitive from outraged justice he was indicted for another murder, and was charged with numerous other crimes, among the latter being the killing of Red Cloud Brown, son of Deputy United States

Marshal John Brown, of Vian, Indian Territory, though it was always claimed by those conversant with his surroundings that he had no hand in this murder. He was not devoid of social pleasures, for he had friends everywhere among the denizens of the hills. Miller was of a jovial disposition, possessed of a naturally friendly mien, and was fond of the gentle sex, and the women residing in the vicinity of his stronghold, almost to a unit, admired him for his reckless bravery.

Finally, a large reward was offered by the government for his capture; yet, during the summer and autumn of 1898, he made numerous trips to Braggs, the scene of his crime of nearly three years before. He would ride leisurely into town, proceed from store to store, trading as suited his fancy, and at his pleasure ride away unmolested. He was sometimes followed to the mountains by officers who, returning, told wonderful stories of a cave in the mountains, where Miller had prepared a barricade, fitted up with a formidable arsenal, a veritable Gibraltar, from where it was alleged he could successfully resist an armed force of many men.

This condition could not last always, however, and Miller's collapse was destined to come from an unexpected source. Among Miller's many feminine admirers was a young and beautiful Cherokee maiden, of good education, pleasing manners, and carriage stately as a queen, who had learned to love the outlaw with true devotion, and he, with his vanity tickled by her openly expressed admiration, professed to reciprocate the attachment. He fondled her love until he grew tired of wooing and his manner toward her began cooling; a little later she learned he had found another sweetheart and her love turned to hate.

Knowing that since the offer of rewards for his capture the officers were becoming bolder and more in earnest in their endeavors to capture him, she decided to assist them to that end.

A high social affair was preparing in the neighborhood on the night of December 13, 1898, in honor of Miller, and she knew that he and his latest love would be present; on account of the outlaw's important social connections the affair was attended by a crowd of both sexes; liquor flowed freely and the spirits of the dancers soared high, but among the company none were as gay as Miller, who, not aware of it, was attending his last dance, and meanwhile his every movement was closely watched by the zealous eyes of his discarded inamorata.

Miller drank heavily; he carried a huge six-shooter in a holster by his side, while his waist was encircled with a belt filled with cartridges, and he felt perfectly safe among his friends.

The mistreated maiden laid her plans well. She had arranged with Deputy Marshal Brown to assist him and his posse in capturing Miller, but she knew the officers would hesitate about attempting to arrest him in an open fight and besides she wanted no opportunity given her quondam lover to shed' the blood of those who were to assist her in gaining revenge. She knew Miller would drink himself to stupor; as the evening wore away, she sent for the officers, who, in accordance with her plans, were secreted nearby. They came and peered in at the windows, watching the outlaw in the glory of his last revelry, but calmly they waited for the time, so near, when they could effect his capture without giving him an opportunity to commit another crime.

The revelry increased and the fun grew more boisterous but just before the dawn of another day Miller's conviviality turned to inebriety and his friends, all unconscious of his danger, carried him to a house nearby and laid him on a bed to sleep away the effects of his potations, little dreaming that with his wakening he would find himself bound, hand and foot.

The opportunity promised to the officers had arrived; they entered the house, and ere his befogged intellect could comprehend the situation he was securely shackled, and on the following afternoon he was conveyed to the Federal jail at

Muscogee, there to languish, while reflecting upon the uncertainties of the life of even the most reckless of outlaws—even in the homes of his friend—while awaiting trial, conviction and punishment for his crimes.

Back in the Greenleaf mountains were his friends, still steadfast; both his girls too, were there, the one sorrowing over the fate of her lost lover and the ending of her romance, the other glorying in her revenge upon him for his desertion of her. The

389

homely frolics were re-enacted; on the Christmas eve, two weeks after his capture, a rousing dance was given, in the same neighborhood, and gallons of fire-water were disposed of, but Mose Miller was absent. He had enjoyed his last frolic and his scouting among the fastnesses of the Greenleaf mountains had ceased.

THE CASE OF JESS MILLER

Jess Miller was a young white man, about 20 years old. He lived about four miles north of Hampton, in the Cherokee Nation. His wife was a beautiful Cherokee girl. Miller was a son of the noted marksman, Dr. "Winchester" Miller. They were farmers in liberal circumstances. Jess was of good character, and had never been charged with any offense. This was his first and was the result of bad associations, an exemplification of the time worn fable related of "poor dog Tray."

For some time a protracted meeting had been in progress in young Miller's neighborhood, and on the night of the killing about to be narrated, the victim, Will Hall, with Jess Miller, Nelson Benge and one "Dave," an Indian, attended the meeting. The services were being conducted by an evangelist, who had that day baptized several candidates for admission to the church. Before the services were ended, Hall, Miller, Benge and "Dave," conceived the idea of going after whiskey, and after imbibing freely, Benge and Hall made a bet on a horse race, the stakes being $5 and a saddle on one side and a horse on the other. Before the race, Benge expressed a desire to withdraw the stakes but Hall was holding the money and refused to give it up. Benge being intoxicated became very-boisterous and exasperated and shot Hall with a pistol, jumped on to the body, tramped it with his feet, and again shot him as he lay upon the ground, then mounted his horse and made the animal jump over the corpse.

Just before the shooting, Jess Miller's horse had taken fright and he had chased it several miles, hence was not present at the killing. Right away afterwards, Miller, Nelson Benge and "Dave" were arrested and because of the two latter being Indians, they were given in charge to the Indian courts. Miller was taken to Fort Smith for trial, was indicted, was put on trial for his life, and his father employed J. Warren Reed and C. J. Frederick to conduct the defense. The case was stoutly combatted, and Mr. Reed again distinguished himself by acquitting his client.

A SOUTH M'ALLNER HORROR

South McAllister is the center of the coal mining district of the Choctaw Nation, where the miners congregate. While the sale of intoxicating liquors is forbidden by law, yet by the aid of "boot-leggers" those who are lovers of ardent spirits can always find enough to satisfy their cravings.

On a beautiful Saturday night in the spring of 1895, a colored boarding house on one of the principal streets was made the scene of blood-shed and terror. At the saloon, boarding house and business place of one Jim Smith, a colored man, who also ran a barber shop, was gathered a motley crowd of whites, Indians and colored of

390

both sexes, imbibing freely of hard cider, discussing the events of the week just past, telling stories, dancing, singing and screeching; pandemonium reigned supreme until near midnight. While these scenes were in progress, one William Messick, between whom and William Glover and Rufus Brown some extreme unpleasantness had sprung up that night, started out with a girl on his arm for home. As he stepped from the door Robert Glover shot him with a pistol, killing him instantly, and it was claimed that Rufus Brown knocked down another man with a rock with the intention of killing him. However, this proposition relating to Brown was denied and became the bone of contention at the trial, the prosecution claiming that Brown knocked the man down with murderous intent, in compliance with an agreement previously made with Glover.

Glover escaped that night and was not apprehended. Brown was arrested the next day, charged with the murder of Messick, through a conspiracy with Glover, and given an examining trial before the United States commissioner, held to answer an indictment by the grand jury and was indicted at the next term; his mother, who was a wealthy Choctaw negress, employed J. Warren Reed to defend her son. The case came up for trial in the spring of 1897. There were a great many witnesses, and after a long and hard fought contest, the case was given to the jury, but no agreement was reached

The case passed two terms of the court and came up for trial a second time in March, 1898. At this trial there was a baker's dozen of new witnesses, and the case was more hotly contested than before. It resulted in an acquittal. Brown was released after lying in jail over three years, and another plume was placed in the cap of his counsel, J. Warren Reed.

ECHOES OE THE PAST

In the Fort Smith *Weekly Elevator* of September 23, 1898, appeared the following item, under the caption, "Arrested in Kansas City," which is self explanatory:

"Bob Glover, who was charged with being implicated in the murder of John Messick in Jim Smith's hop ale joint in South McAllister in 1895, was arrested last week in Kansas City. Rufus Brown, who was indicted jointly with Glover for Messick's murder, was tried for the offense in the court here several years ago and acquitted."

Glover was conveyed to South McAllister too late for trial at the December, 1898, term of court, and he was placed in jail to await trial at the May term; 1899.

Glover had. been indicted jointly with Brown by the Federal grand jury in the Western District of Arkansas, before the establishment of the Federal criminal courts in the Indian Territory, and the question might arise: "Why should not he, too* be tried at Fort Smith." The language of the act of congress vesting exclusive original jurisdiction of all offenses against Federal laws in the Indian Territory in the newly established Federal courts in the Indian Territory after September, 1896, excepted only such cases as the Federal courts at Paris, Texas* Fort Smith, Arkansas and Fort

Scott, Kansas, may have already acquired jurisdiction of (see 1895, March 1, U. S. Stat. L, 53d Cong., sess. Ill, vol. 28, chap. 145, p. 633, § 9), and the courts hold that to have acquired jurisdiction, in the meaning of the statute, the said courts must have had, prior to the specific date, custody of the defendant. Hence, as Glover, though indicted by the Federal court at Fort Smith, prior to September 1, 1896, yet was not apprehended and placed in custody by said court, its jurisdiction had never attached in Glover's case.

THE DALTON GANG

A STORY OF TRUSTED DEPUTY MARSHALS WHO TURNED TO RUFFIANISM

Prominent among the Indian Territory desperadoes, during a period of about a year previous to the time of their last raid, October 5, 1892, was the Dalton gang, composed, at the time of its dissolution, of Bob Dalton, the leader, a smooth-faced boy of 22, Gratton Dalton, 31, Emmet Dalton, 20 years old, the best shot and possessed of the greatest amount of reckless bravery of the three, and Bill Powers, alias Tom Evans, and Richard Broad well, the two latter being of the class with which the Indian Territory abounded, who were ready at all times to follow a determined leader into almost any kind of crime.

On the day last noted, at Coffeyville, Kan., during an attempt of the gang to rob two banks in the full light of day, they were met by a determined lot of citizens, and all were shot dead but Emmet Dalton, who was badly wounded, and was subsequently given a life term of imprisonment. A brief history of the family from which sprung the three bandits who gained so unenviable a reputation in so short a time, will be interesting, as showing the easy stages from good citizenship to outlawry:

They were from among thirteen children, nine sons and four daughters, whose parents were Lewis and Adaline Dalton. One son and one daughter died in infancy. The elder Dalton was a Kentuckian, born in 1824. He served as a fifer under General Taylor during the Mexican war, and at the close of hostilities returned to his native town, and in 1850 he moved west, settling near Independence, Mo. Here he wooed and won Miss Adaline Lee Younger. They were married in 1851. The bride was one year younger than her husband, and was a native of Cass County, Mo., although she had grown to womanhood in Jackson County, near Independence, her parents having removed there when she was a child.

Mr. and Mrs. Dalton were respectable people, and were not of the class from which one would expect desperadoes to come. In 1860 they settled near Lawrence, Kan., and later they removed to Montgomery County, in which the fair city of Coffeyville is situated. Here the father died suddenly in 1890, at the home of a friend near Dearing, and his body was buried in the Robbins cemetery west of Coffeyville. His one passion was for fast horses, and it may be that their imitating their father in becoming expert horsemen was the means by which the three sons cultivated the company which resulted in their becoming criminals.

In 1889, when the Oklahoma Territory was opened for settlement, Mrs. Dalton secured two good claims near Kingfisher, and there she now resides with her three eldest sons, Charles, Henry and Littleton. Near them also lives William Dalton, another son, who was born in 1863, went to Montana in 1881, then to California, where he married, and returned to Oklahoma in 1891. The daughters, Eva, Leona, Nannie and Simon (the first being the wife of John Whipple), also reside in the same neighborhood, the unmarried daughters, like the unmarried sons, living with their mother, who is a pleasant old lady—not such a woman as one would pick out as a mother of outlaws. The sons are peaceable, industrious farmers.

The first member of the Dalton family to meet with a violent death was Franklin, better known as Frank. He became a deputy United States marshal, and gained the reputation of being a brave and efficient officer, being recognized as a terror to evil-doers in the Indian Territory. In 1887, while attempting to arrest some horse thieves and whisky peddlers in the Indian Territory, near Fort Smith, Frank and his posse became engaged in a hand to hand fight, and the former was killed.

Gratton, the elder of the three who afterwards became outlaws, was born near Lawrence, Kan., in 1861. In 1880 he moved to California, but soon returned, and after the death of his brother, Frank, he was given a commission as deputy United States marshal. He received a bullet wound in the left forearm in 1888, while with his posse he was attempting to arrest a noted Indian desperado. He was afterwards made a deputy United States marshal for the Federal court at Muscogee. During the first part of his services he conducted himself as a model officer, but later he and his brothers, Robert and Emmet, were charged with crooked transactions, and they finally overstepped the bounds of official decency to the extent of stealing and running away a herd of horses, which they sold in Kansas.

Robert, who became the leader of the noted Dalton gang, was born in Cass County, Missouri, in 1870. He served as a member of the posses of his brothers, Frank and. Gratton, while they were deputy marshals, and was with Frank in the fight which cost him his life. He was afterwards made deputy United States marshal for the courts at Wichita, Kan., and Fort Smith, and was also, for a short time, chief of police of the Osage Nation. He was known as a crack shot, and knew no fear.

Emmet Dalton, the youngest member of the gang, was born in Cass County, Missouri, in 1872. He lived quietly at home until the death of his father, when he unexpectedly launched out in his career of crime, which was destined, however, to be of short duration, and he soon rivaled his brother, Bob, in the ready use of his gun and his coolness while under fire.

Very soon after the theft of horses noted above, Gratton and Emmet Dalton fled to California, and. there, early in 1891, they were accused of a daring but unsuccessful attempt to rob an express train in Tulare County. The robbers were driven off by the bravery and rapid shooting of the messenger, but during the fight the fireman was killed by a bullet fired by one of the robbers, and Gratton, William and Emmet Dalton were charged with murder and attempted train robbery. Gratton and William were arrested on the charge; William was acquitted and Gratton was sentenced to twenty years in the penitentiary. Before his removal he escaped from the county jail. Emmet Dalton escaped being arrested for his complicity in the California train robbery, and at the time of their death, in 1892, at Coffeyville, an offer of $6,000 by the Southern Pacific Railroad Company for the arrest and delivery of Gratton and Emmet Dalton was still standing.

A few months after the escape of Gratton Dalton from the jail in California the brothers seem to have returned to their old stamping ground, where as United States officers they had been the means of apprehending criminals, and themselves entered upon a career of crime.

On the ninth of May, 1891, three masked men stopped a Santa Fe train at Wharton, Oklahoma Territory, and robbed the express car of a large amount of valuables. The bandits escaped, but from the lucid descriptions given of them by the trainmen and passengers, it was generally believed that the work was done by the Daltons. A little more than a year later, June 1, 1892, a Santa Fe train, south bound, was held up and robbed at Red Rock, in the Cherokee Strip. This, too, was believed to be the work of the Daltons, and the name became a terror to all whose business or daily vocations compelled them to travel across the Indian Territory. In the following month, near Adair, on the Missouri, Kansas & Texas Railway, a north bound passenger train was held up and robbed at 9 o'clock in the evening. This act was the most audacious and daring of any in the career of the Daltons up to that time. A large force of armed railroad detectives and Indian police were on the train, and a hot fire was poured upon them, but the robbers succeeded in carrying away all the valuable contents of the mail and express cars and escaped unharmed, though several of the police, as well as a number of the passengers, were wounded and a physician who resided near Adair was killed. Gratton and Bob Dalton were positively recognized as members of the gang of outlaws who performed the bloody work, and officers were at once put upon their trail. These they eluded, however, and they succeeded in keeping out of the clutches of the law until they finally planned and partially executed the bold task of robbing two banks in broad daylight in a city of over three thousand inhabitants, where they were well-known to the majority of the citizens. This, the last raid of the Daltons, was in line with the proud boast of Bob Dalton that they would eclipse anything ever accomplished by the James boys, but, thanks to the courage of the citizens of the town where they resided, the scheme was the one disastrous attempt of their lives and resulted in the tragic death of two of the Daltons and of two of their accomplices, and the capture, badly wounded, Emmet Dalton, the youngest of the outfit. A brief history of this last act in their career of crime closes the chapter.

THE LAST RAID OF THE DALTONS

It occurred on the fifth day of October, 1892. Those who have experienced October in Southern Kansas can imagine the clear sky, the balmy, bracing atmosphere, and the general beauty of the day in which all nature seemed to rejoice at existence. No firmament was ever quite so blue, and the slight tendency to frost the night previous had left the air spicy and keen, putting zest into the movements of the toilers as they prepared for their daily tasks, and as the sun ascended it shone upon a scene of peace and splendor, in marked contrast to those enacted in the early history of the state, which had given it the title of "bleeding," now termed by common consent, "Sunny Kansas."

The morning wore away and five men were discovered entering the beautiful little City of Coffeyville, by one of the principal thoroughfares. It was 9:30 o'clock, and the people were as usual astir. Several who were on the sidewalks or driving on the streets observed the party, mounted on thoroughbreds, richly companioned. Their saddles were "Mexican," new, with trappings glistening in the sunlight. The customary hair covered pockets hung from either side of each and behind the riders were their slickers in compact rolls, ready to be donned in case of a sudden storm, giving them the appearance of travelers on a long journey, while some concluded they were a deputy marshal and possee, not at all an unusual sight in Coffeyville and therefore no occasion for alarm. No weapons were visible, such as the men carried, including their Winchesters being concealed from view by their closely buttoned coats. Their broad brimmed black hats drawn down well in front helped to conceal their features and besides, the leader of the party, which the reader has already recognized as Bob Dalton, bore a heavy false mustache and goatee, black in color, disguising him well; Emmet Dalton wore a heavy black beard and Gratton's face was covered with a long, scraggly beard and mustache. Broadwell and Powers, the other members of the gang, were without disguises.

The party continued at a slow trot along the principal street, the three Daltons abreast in front, until they reached within a block of the public square, when they wheeled to the right and rode south half a block, then suddenly turned to the left and disappeared in an alley, and dismounting, tied their animals at the rear of the lot occupied by and within thirty feet of the residence of Police Judge Munn, then continued afoot along the alley until they reached the principal business street. In the city were many farmers who had come early to dispose of produce or to make purchases, and as the five robbers emerged from the alley and crossed the street, a local merchant who was standing in front of his store discovered them, and his keen eye penetrated their disguises. He watched them after they crossed over, and as he saw Grat Dalton, Powers and Broadwell enter the Condon & Company Bank, while Bob and Emmet Dalton ran across the street again to the First National Bank, he realized the awful status of affairs, and saw in advance the bloodshed that must soon follow. He saw Grat Dalton through the window of the first named bank, pointing his Winchester at the cashier's head, and turning towards the open doorway of his store, shouted, "The bank is being robbed." At the same time, other men who saw Bob and Emmet Dalton entering the First National Bank, followed closely, and witnessed the first act in the "hold-up" there. Instantly a call to arms resounded from various points along the street and what followed in detail can be better imagined than briefly described.

Shots fired by enraged citizens through the windows of the banks at the robbers narrowly missed killing some of the bank's' officers, but nothing daunted, the robbers proceeded calmly to place the currency, gold and silver to the amount of thousands of dollars, from the banks' stores, in the large sacks they had brought with them for the purpose. The time occupied was much less than that it takes to tell it, but by the time

396

the booty had been secured, many Winchesters had been secured from the nearby hardware stores and as the outlaws attempted to leave with their booty they were met with withering broadsides, that caused the two younger Daltons in the First National Bank, to change their tactics and escape by a rear door into an alley, fighting as they ran.

Meanwhile Grat Dalton and his companions, one of them wounded in the arm, had emerged by the door they had entered and made a dash for the alley where their horses were tied. Within less than fifteen minutes from the time the five robbers entered the two banks, four of their number had been shot dead and the fifth, Emmet Dalton had surrendered, with a bullet wound through the right arm and another through the left hip. He might have escaped as he had succeeded in mounting his horse, but he had boldly ridden to where his brother lay dying, and reaching down tried to raise him to a place behind and while thus engaged was struck in the back with the contents of a double barrelled shot gun, causing him to reel and fall to the ground.

Broadwell reached his horse and tried to escape, but just as he mounted, a charge from a shot gun and another from a Winchester struck his body; bleeding profusely he clung to the animal as it dashed out over the road by which they had entered the city. His dead body was found, a little later, lying by the roadside in the outskirts, and his horse was recovered near where he fell. Two of the bandit's horses were killed by the bullets as were a span of horses attached to an oil tank, that had been driven into the alley just as the robbers emerged therefrom on their way to the scenes of the robbery, but the one saddest of all features in connection with the affair, was the killing, by the bandits, of four brave citizens, Lucius M. Baldwin, George B. Cubine, Charles Brown and City Marshal Charles T. Connelly, and the serious wounding of Charles T. Grump, Thomas G. Ayers, and T. A. Reynolds.

Indescribable scenes of sorrow, following soon after the last shot of the twelve minutes firing, denoted the dearly bought victory for the citizens. Mourning relatives weeping over their dead loved ones made a picture most pathetic and long to be remembered. Threats of lynching the one unslain bandit, were freely made but wiser counsels prevailed and naught was done to smirch the fair reputation of the city.

The bodies of the dead bandits were picked up and carried to the jail and a guard was placed over them until the arrival of Mrs. Dalton, the mother, two of the sons, William and Ben, and the married sister, Mrs. Whipple, who came on to Coffeyville as soon as they heard of the death of Bob and Gratton, and they remained with the wounded Emmet until his removal to the jail at Independence.

When quiet had been restored it was found that over $11,000 had been taken by the robbers from the First National Bank and over $20,000 from the Condon Bank; of the latter, $20 was lost in the struggle. Citizens who were honorably mentioned for their bravery during the light were: John J. Hokloehr, Henry H. Isham, Charles T. Gump, T. A. Reynolds, Louis A. Dietz, Carey Seamen, M. X. Anderson, Parker L.

Williams, Charles K. Smith and others. Of the courageous men who risked their lives to protect the property of their neighbors, a local writer with ready pen, David Stewart Elliott, in speaking of the events of that sad day, said: "They are noble and brilliant examples of that courage that makes the world better and purer because of its possessors having lived in it. Their nerve was of the kind that actuates the lives of heroes and elevates the standard of manhood."

Of the bandits and what is sometimes termed their bravery, this same gifted writer says: "Their boasted bravery was of the kind that is manufactured for a specific object, born of a spirit of desperation and pampered into undue proportions for illegitimate purpose. Under the ordinary circumstances of everyday life, should a display of true courage become necessary for the advancement of a notable object, such as they had would be found wanting."

Let me add: It is the kind of bravery that causes its possessor to be loudly bombastic when he "gets the drop" and knows his opponent is at his mercy; the kind that causes him to cringe in absolute terror and cry for quarter the moment he, from lack of ammunition or from other cause, can no longer deal out death to the enemy. Such men lack even the stoicism in the face of danger that is possessed by the untutored American Indian, and their much boasted bravery is in truth but the most abject cowardice.

A LIFE SKETCH OF THE NOTED OUTLAW, HILL COOK

Of all the bandits who roamed the plains and mountains of the Indian Territory, none, with the exception of his early associate, Cherokee Bill, won such notoriety over the length and breadth of the United States as William Tuttle Cook, known to fame as "Bill Cook," the leader of the most desperate and dangerous gang that ever operated in the Indian country.

There was this difference between" The Two Bills," who started upon the shady road to ruin about the same time, in the spring of 1894; that while Cherokee Bill had apparently but little or no regard for human life, seeming rather to revel in human gore, and was as "game" a man as ever rode the plains, the other was never a "slayer of men," but confined his operations more to conducting robberies; in fact, Bill Cook was never regarded, by those who knew him best, as a "game man," and though enough times he placed his life in jeopardy it was generally on occasions when forced to the wall, rather than from a desire to shed human blood.

Personally, he was not an aggressive appearing man, having rather the mien of a very ordinary cowboy, and the close observer of him would wonder that the government was ever compelled to use such extreme measures to bring him to a state of docility; yet he accomplished what the Fort Smith Chamber of Commerce could not—forced the railroad company operating between Fort Smith and Coffeyville, Kan., to run a day train between the two cities, as it became unsafe for valuable express matter, or even passengers, to travel over the route at night, and the depredations committed by Bill Cook and his gang (or' that were charged to them) from June, 1894, and during the six months following, in the territory contiguous to Fort Gibson, Wagoner, Muscogee, and in all the towns along the Missouri Pacific Railroad as far west as the Kansas line, gained for him a national reputation, and came near causing the national government to call out detachments of the regular army to bring the bandits under subjection, and resulted, finally, in rewards being offered for his capture by the government and the railroad and express companies, aggregating several thousand dollars. All this, too, before he had arrived at the age of 21 years. He was 5 feet 9 inches high, of light complexion and hair, light-blue eyes, a mild manner, and showed scarcely any trace of Indian blood.

His name became a byword for all that was brave, daring and disreputable; yet, like the notorious Sam Bass, of Texas fame, he never robbed a poor man, except of a horse or of food, when compelled by personal safety on account of being closely pressed by the officers to have the same on short notice. He was not an inveterate horse thief, either, for, as he valued his life too highly to become a murderer and thus place his neck in a halter, so, too, he took little chances of inviting pursuers to his own lynching by violating the unwritten law of the plains, except, as stated, when immediate personal safety demanded. Of a truth, Bill Cook was intended by nature for a worthy citizen. He was largely the victim of circumstances, and when at last he had "gone too far to get out,"-his desire seems to have been to gain a reputation which he was, after all, in no wise anxious to earn.

Bill Cook's father was James Cook, a Southern man, who fought in the Federal army. After the close of the civil war he settled in the Cherokee Nation, four miles north of Fort Gibson, and married a quarter-blood Cherokee woman, widow of one Mat Morton. Here Bill Cook was born December 19, 1873, and four years later his brother, Jim Cook, was given birth. In the spring of 1878 the father died, and the mother rented the farm and removed to a point in Arkansas near Fort Smith, and after a year or more returned to the old home and married a half-Cherokee Indian. In 1880 the mother sold their home, and with her family (consisting of the two sons and a daughter, who afterwards became Mrs. Lou Hardin, of Fort Gibson) lived for a year in Fort Gibson, that her children might have opportunity to attend school. From there they removed to Fourteen-Mile Creek, where the mother died.

The step-father soon made away with all of his dead wife's property, and a cousin came out and took the children, and after a year placed the two boys in the Cherokee Orphan School at Tahlequah, but they were not allowed long to remain, as they had no order from the Board of Education. By this time Bill Cook was 14 years old, and becoming tired of his surroundings, he went to the Creek Nation and found employment with F. A. Sawyer, becoming an excellent "corn hand." From there he went to a cattle ranch, where for two years he associated with reckless men—his seniors—who told him he could not be a "cow-puncher" unless he learned to shoot, drink whiskey and play cards. He became a famous "cow-puncher," and spent all his earnings for whisky, and so drifted into selling whisky to the Indians, thus placing himself under the ban of the law, and in 1892 he fled, to avoid arrest, to New Mexico, and worked for a time on a cattle ranch at Puerto De Lina.

He returned after a few months and fell in love with a girl, pretty Martha Pittman, residing with her parents near Tahlequah. The girl loved him devotedly, and he at one time intended to marry her; the girl's father objected to the match, and Bill was arrested on the old whiskey selling charge, was convicted at Fort Smith and sentenced to lay in jail forty days. He served out his term and returned to the Cherokee Nation, intending to marry Miss Pittman and settle down. He decided he did not have enough money then, and he either never obtained "enough" or he never came to the point where he was ready to "settle down." The girl continued to love him even after he became an outlaw, but, to use her own words, he proved himself unworthy of her by dragging her name down with himself, and she learned to hate as earnestly as she had ever loved him. She finally became the wife of Henry Golding, a steady-going upright citizen, with whom she is still living in the Cherokee Nation.

Little thought had Bill Cook, when he walked from the Federal jail at Fort Smith, at the close of his forty day term, of ever becoming an outlaw. In 1893 we find him employed as a posse, assisting United States deputy marshals of the Fort Smith court, in their work in the Indian Territory. J. E. Kelly, the founder of Kellyville, Creek

Nation, mentioned in the Cherokee Bill story, tells of Bill Cook coming to his store, at Kellyville, in the fall of 1893, as posse for Deputy Marshal Bill Smith, who was in search of Lon Gordon, wanted on a whiskey charge. It appears that Gordon, who was a lad of 20 years, "had grown a little tough" and during the previous spring had shot a hole in Marshal Smith's hat brim, while Smith was trying to arrest him, Mr. Kelly continues thus:

"Smith was not anxious to crowd Gordon; he told me he did not want to 'drive him into the wild bunch' and he said if Gordon would surrender he would help him out of his trouble. I helped to effect a meeting between Smith and Gordon, which took place that evening. Smith laid off his gun and went to meet Gordon in his shirt sleeves. Smith was 'dead game' and did not want any advantage. He made Gordon a proposition which the latter accepted; he went with Smith to Fort Smith and 'beat the case.' Smith proved his friend and tried hard to put Gordon on the road to success. Gordon seemed for certain to have reformed but in the summer of 1894, he joined Bill Cook's gang; he helped to rob the Chandler, Oklahoma bank and was killed at Sapulpa, on Thursday, August 2, with Henry Munson, by the Creek Light Horse, while resisting arrest. He was a 'dead game' fellow and died fighting. He was a fine specimen of physical manhood and was fine looking. He was uneducated and I think that accounts for his career."

In the spring of 1894, Jim Cook was charged with stealing horses and he went to the Creek Nation and scouted, his brother Bill scouting also on his account. In June of that year they in company with Crawford Goldsby, as related in the chapter devoted to the career of Cherokee Bill, went to "Half Way House" on Fourteen Mile Creek, for the purpose of drawing their "strip" money, and here, at the home of Effie Crittenden, occurred the famous fight with the officers in which Sequoyah Houston lost his life. The story of this fight is given at greater length in the story of Cherokee Bill.

From that moment, Bill Cook was an outlaw, and like many another bandit, after making his first mistake, his only chance for liberty was in keeping out of the range of the officers, or in making a desperate fight should they chance to cross his path. During the balance of the summer many bold robberies were committed in the Cherokee and Creek Nations and nearly all were charged to the Bill Cook gang, but there is little doubt that not half of them did Bill Cook have any hand or interest in, neither is there the least doubt that the robberies committed by Bill Cook and the lawless characters under him, were many and daring People throughout the scope of country in which Cook operated, became aroused and co-operated with the officers of the Cherokee authorities, and aided the deputy marshals and the Indian Police in their endeavors to encompass the gang or drive its members from the country. The columns of the local press and of the great eastern dailies teemed with the exploits of "Bill Cook the famous outlaw," and the conditions developed writers with rare powers of descriptive and—'tis true-—fiction as well.

On October 21, 1894, Chief Marshal Crump, for the Western Judicial District of Arkansas, issued an order, offering rewards of $250, each, for the several members of the Cook gang. In the meantime Cook began operating farther west, the more thickly settled portions of the Indian Territory, becoming "too hot," for him. The robbery at Lenapah, on November 9, when Earnest Melton lost his life, and the robbery of the train on the Missouri, Kansas & Texas railroad, at Blackstone switch, once more aroused the people and caused the officers to double their energies at capture, and the Indian Territory correspondents of the eastern dailies increased their earnings several fold. Late in December, of that year. Cook, with his gang, encountered the Texas Rangers, near Wichita Falls, Texas, and Jess Snider, Will Farris and Thurman Baldwin, alias "Skeeter," were captured and conveyed to Fort Smith. They pleaded guilty to having participated in the robbery of McDermott's store and the post-office at Red Fork. Snider and Farris were each sentenced to twenty years imprisonment and "Skeeter" (who was 27 years old, a native of Ohio) was given a sentence of thirty years. They were all conducted to Detroit, in company with about twenty other convicted felons, among whom were Elmer Lucas and Curtis Daysen, also members of the Cook gang, who had been previously convicted and sentenced—Lucas to fifteen years imprisonment and Daysen to ten years.

About this time, Bill Cook began to realize fully that his acts of outlawry had placed him in a perilous position and he sickened of his "profession;" knowing that he could not much longer safely remain in the Indian Territory, that scores of officers were on his track and like the hunted cur, it was only a question of time until he too would be run down and be given a long penitentiary sentence, for his misdeeds, he left the country, going west, with the firm intention of going to Mexico, and there, on foreign soil, under an assumed name, to give up the life he had led for the past few months and become once more an honest man.

An incident tending to show that Cook was not naturally a dangerous man—was not by nature "game"—is related by J. E. Kelly, noted above, an eye witness to the scene. The story is given in his own language:

"One day Hill Cook, Cherokee Bill and Elmer Lucas were sitting on my store porch. Jesse Allen, George Baker and some other Uchce Indians had been out searching for the thief of a saddle and some horses, stolen the night previous. As I returned from dinner, Allen and Baker were seen approaching at a little distance and Cook asked me if it didn't look 'a little smoky around the edges.' I told him I thought not, and he asked: 'What is Jesse Allen up to? I replied that I did not think he was after him; he then looked at Cherokee Bill and said: 'Say, by—, we'll hold him up.' I at once advised him not to interfere with Allen and told him I had heard the Indian say if Bill Cook left his stock alone he would not bother him. Allen, though an Uchee, was as white as any man; he is well-known through the Indian Territory as a terror to horse and cattle thieves. He is as 'game' as any man that ever walked—a quiet, mild-tempered fellow, who could not run if he wanted to. Cook evidently wanted to work a bluff on Allen. As the two men approached closer Cook declared he would halt him. I argued with him to no avail. Allen was busily engaged in conversing with his companion and did not observe Cook and the others. When he had approached a point within fifty yards of the store, Cook, Cherokee Bill and Lucas stepped from the porch, Winchesters in hand.

"'Hold up, there!' yelled Cook, half presenting his gun.

"Allen was taken a little off his guard; he wheeled his horse across the road and his left hand went to the scabbard for his Winchester. It appeared to have been but one motion. He had turned his horse and snatched his gun quicker than the eye could follow, and as he brought his weapon to position, Cook yelled:

"'Hold on; we want to talk to you; we don't want to fight.'

Jesse cleared his throat and said: 'It looks like you fellows wanted to fight.' The five men then talked the matter over and separated without difficulty. Bill failed, on that occasion, to add to his reputation as a bad man; he simply lacked the nerve.

On January 11, 1895, Bill Cook was arrested by Sheriffs T. D. Love, of Burden County, Texas, and C. C. Perry, of Cheves County, New Mexico, at the sod house of an isolated cattle ranche on the Great Plains, a few miles from old Fort Sumner in New Mexico. A few weeks before, Sheriff Love had run across a camp of two strangers and had taken particular notice of the men. Two days later, he received a dispatch from Capt. McDonald, of the Texas Rangers, giving a description of Bill Cook and telling him to look out for him, as he was headed in the direction of Burden County. Cook and his gang had been met by a band of Rangers at Wichita Falls, as previously stated, and Cook, with Jim Turner, had escaped after a desperate fight, and it was then that he determined, once for all, to leave the country and go to Mexico.

The description in the dispatch to Sheriff Love tallied with that of the two men he had seen; the officer at once went to the camp and found it deserted. Sending a deputy back to Capt. McDonald to notify him of the course taken by the bandits, Love took to the trail alone and followed a chase that led him over 500 miles before he finally overtook his man. Much of the trail was over high, dry prairie without roads and travel was necessarily slow. In the first 400 miles Cook had stopped at but two ranches and a few small camps. The Rangers, during their fight, had secured Cook's rifle and his 38-calibre Winchester, the latter having been plundered from McDermott's store* during the raid already mentioned, and at one of the ranches he had given a cowboy a lot of 38-calibre cartridges, saying he had no use for them as he had no gun.

*This Winchester was afterwards returned to McDermott by the Texas officers and by the owner was presented to the editors of the Fort Smith Elevator.—note in original

At both ranches Cook gave the name of John Mayfield. At Four Lakes Love lost the trail and went back and finally, after again picking it up, he found where Cook's horse had cast a shoe, and in coming loose one of the nails of the shoe had broken off a piece of the hoof. This was good fortune for the officer as it enabled him to follow the trail in the public roads to near Roswell. Cook had one day the start of the sleuth-like Sheriff and he gained another on account of the officer's temporary loss of the trail. On the sixth day of January, Cook stopped at a ranche a few miles from Roswell and placed one of his horses in a pasture, saying he would return for it in a few days. It afterwards developed that Rill and lint Turner had unintentionally become separated, soon after leaving the camp where they were first seen by Sheriff Love, and expecting Jim to follow, Cook waited at Roswell one day and then proceeded, not knowing he was being trailed by the officers, leaving the extra horse for his pal to pick up, that he might exchange his jaded mount for a fresh horse. By stealing a horse occasionally' he could undoubtedly have outstripped the officers, but not knowing that he was followed the necessity" of such a course did not appear to him, and he also knew that were he to be°-in stealing horses he would soon have the whole country' full of men hunting at his heels.

At Roswell, Cook said his name was John Williams, and here he passed several of the Texas Rangers who had come on by rail; they failed to recognize him and Cook continued on his western course. Love identified the horse as one he had seen at the camp and it was closely watched but no one called for it. In company with Sheriff Perry, Love continued the chase to a small settlement called "The Cedars," thirty miles from Roswell, and from there the trail led across the Capitan, the roughest portion of all New Mexico.

THE CAPTURE

Late on January 10, the officers followed the bandit's trail in the direction of Yates' ranche, but stopped at the house of Mitner Gray, and by means of strategy they succeeded in bringing Yates to their place of rendezvous, ostensibly to treat a sick horse. Yates readily informed them that Cook was at his place and promising to have the outlaw up early the next morning to assist in feeding the stock, conducted them to a place where they could lay in wait for his appearance. Cook knew every foot of the country, having rode that section a few years before as a cowboy, and could easily have escaped had he known the close proximity of the officers. The latter laid in ambush as directed by Yates, and the next morning as he proceeded to feed his horse the bandit walked by their hiding place, within three feet of them, his first knowledge of their near presence being when he suddenly discovered two Winchesters pointing in his face. His hands went up promptly and that was the end of Bill Cook's days as a fugitive. He had no guns and the pistol the officers found in his bed he gave to Love, with the remark, "I don't suppose I will need it again."

He first denied his identity, but when confronted with the officers' knowledge of his affairs he confessed fully, and told of his family relations and of his early life, much as is given in the opening of this chapter. He proved to be a very tractable prisoner and the trip to Fort Smith, of Cook and his two cap-tors, accompanied by Sheriff Y. D. McMurray, of Mitchell County, Texas, was without incident, except that at Fort Worth,. Texas, 1,500 people were gathered at the depot to gaze at the famous scout.

The party arrived at Fort Smith late Saturday night, but, notwithstanding the hour, a considerable crowd was present. The curious followed to the Federal jail and Cook was placed in the cell with Henry Starr. On the following day the jail was visited by over 1,500 people, all eager to take a; look at the man who, in a few months had risen from obscurity to national, though unenviable, fame. But the majority were surprised when the awkward-looking cowboy was pointed out to them; they had expected to see a regular brigand in appearance, such as is described in cheap novels.

"That Bill Cook?" was the expression often heard; "why, he doesn't look like a bad man."

On Tuesday morning, following, Cook was taken to the court house for arraignment. The prison van was not running and Bill was obliged to walk the four intervening blocks.

As he was going up on the elevator he was asked if he was going to call on Judge Parker.

"Oh, yes," he replied, "the judge has a little business with me, but I think we'll make it all right."

Cook was arraigned on twelve counts, charging robbery. He entered a plea of not guilty, but at his trial he made no defense except on two counts, and on February 12, 1895, he was sentenced to a term of forty-five years at Albany, New York.

His attorneys were J. Warren Reed and Thomas H. Barnes. The case against their client was so clear they could do very little for him.

At the time, and since, it was believed by many that a ten years sentence would have been sufficient, also, that if again given his liberty after a few years of penal servitude he would make a good citizen. His prison record is excellent. Before being taken from Fort Smith he expressed deep regret at the course he had run, and said he was glad his career as a bandit was at an end. There is no doubt in the minds of many that a few years more of servitude will fully satisfy the ends of justice, and that within that time a pardon should be granted him.

THE OUTLAW JIM FRENCH

THE LAST OF THE NOTORIOUS COOK GANG

With a view to showing to the reader more explicitly than I have already done, the character and condition, in the Indian Territory at the time Judge Parker sat upon the bench, I deem it advisable to give a brief history of Catoosa, in the Cherokee Nation, a village station on a branch of the "Frisco" railroad running from Monett, Missouri, to Sapulpa, Creek Nation.

It was here that Jim French, at one time a companion of Belle Starr, and later a member of the notorious Cook gang, was slain. Of the bandits composing this gang I have already given the history of the justice meted to Cherokee Bill, Henry Starr, Bill Cook, and several lesser lights; Verdegris Kid and Tom Sanders were killed at Braggs, while attempting to rob Madden's store, in 1895, and Jake Lewis, who was assisting in the enterprise, was wounded and was attended by Clarence Goldsby, brother of the boy whom he had whipped, the said whipping being the alleged cause of Crawford Goldsby becoming, finally, an outlaw.

There remained Jim French, and his departure from earth will be included with the following brief history of Catoosa:

The casual visitor to Catoosa, a village in proportions but a city by charter right, would hardly believe from present appearances that it was, only a few years ago, one of the most desperate towns in the Indian Territory. Catoosa has a red record. Blood has flowed in her streets like water, but with the advent of Mayor Thomas M. Reynolds, a native of Texas county, Missouri, much was done to change the state of affairs that existed for years.

The town of Catoosa is beautifully situated. South of the little city the densely wooded bottoms of the Spunky River stretch as far as the eye can reach; to the westward the vast Creek pastures open their gates to hundreds of thousands of cattle; while northward the prairie rolls its broad expanse to the lime rock bluffs that terminate at Round Mountain, on the bank of Bird Creek, famous for big bass and jack salmon. More peaceful or picturesque surroundings could not be desired than those which environ the erstwhile crimson city of Catoosa, while in the vicinity live some of the prettiest Indian girls ever seen. Instead of the howl of the besotted ruffian, the roar of big six-shooters, or the death yell of knifed or pistoled victims, one hears the notes of the parlor organ and the voice of song. Business and social life move on with only an occasional friction to mar the harmony of existence on the brink of the bottom lands of the Virdigris.

Tulsa was a bad town, Claremore had its bad men and saw many bloody encounters, but Catoosa, the smallest of them all, can boast of lawlessness in the past that certainly puts all in the shade.

406

One night, in the autumn oi 1895, the big general store of Reynolds is: Co. was attacked. Jim French and a stripling forced two citizens to break in the windows oi the store and then entered. They discovered that there was a back office separate from the store and decided that that was the place most likely to contain the cash they were after. French went around to a side window of the little office and his partner to the door that enters from the passageway between the office and the store. The two citizens might easily have aroused the town, but so fearful were they of the bandit, French, that they decided their lives depended on saying nothing.

French could command a view of the interior of the office from his position at the west window. He discovered Colonel Irwin, the manager, sitting at a desk on the east side, with his back to the window. He raised his Winchester to shoot when his keen eye caught sight of the muzzle of a double-barreled shotgun. The gun was in the hands of the night watchman, who was seated in a rocking-chair facing the door. French's companion grew restless and sent a ball from his Winchester crashing through the door. The missile just missed the night watchman. Like a flash Irwin sprang to the door, pulled it wide open, himself behind it. The watchman's shotgun roared and the bandit at the door fell forward on the sill with the roof of his head gone. There was a crash at the window and Jim trench's Winchester pushed through the pane. The watchman swung round and fired, but missed his aim, the charge landing in the window frame, where the deep scar can still be seen. French's aim was true, however, and a 45-calibre bullet from his gun passed through the loins of Colonel Irwin. The latter fell with a groan, and French bounded in the door with a yell. The watchman had dodged behind a dresser in the northwest corner of the room, but French made him come out.

"You killed my partner, you cheap hireling. Help me put Irwin on the bed; I don't want to hurt him anymore," was the command of French.

The two men placed the mortally wounded man on the bed, which was in the northeast corner of the room.

"Now, help me bring in my partner, and I'll attend to you, G—d d—n you," said the cool and reckless French.

The body of the young bandit was brought into the office and laid upon the floor. The face was literally shot away. It was a ghastly sight, but French's nerve was as steady and his voice as cold and calm as a windless winter day.

"Now," he said, grimly, after viewing the remains, "you coyote, I'm going to kill you."

In vain did the watchman protest that he had no weapon. French let his Winchester rest at his left side and drew his murderous-looking 45. As he was pulling down on the helpless watchman the dying manager of the store raised himself with one arm, pulled a big revolver from under the pillow and blazed away twice in rapid succession. Both bullets passed through the bandit's neck, just below the ears. He staggered but did not fall. He dropped his guns, and. with the blood spouting from his wounds, rushed out and away to Spunky' Creek. A crowd took after the desperado, and he was run down into a little old Indian hut not far from town. He was in a dying condition, but the watchman gave him a settler (rom the double barrel Remington which had laid low his partner in crime. Irwin died the next day, and the famous old shot gun with its two notches is now the property of Col Reynolds. He uses it on all his hunting expeditions, and would not part with it for a fortune.

REMINISCENT OE CATOOSA

The last bad man whose light went out in Catoosa, was Bill Voss, a desperado of local reputation. He rode in from the brush one day and turned his gun loose on animate and inanimate things. His six-shooter cut deep scars in the depot building, which was already marred and splintered by the sportive missiles of the bad men, Voss took a shot at everything and every place; at last he rode in front of the post-office, which was in Reynolds & Co.'s store, and deliberately sent bullet after bullet into the front door. He then rode down toward the depot, yelling and firing his weapon, when a young clerk in the big store waltzed out with a Winchester and sent a 45 chunk of lead through the bandit's heart. Voss fell from his horse and lay where he dropped for some time. Finally several old, fat hogs that were nosing around for choice morsels, came across the prostrate bandit. They lapped up the blood, and were just attacking the dead man's anatomy, when Clark, a car repairer for the "Frisco," came on the scene and drove the porkers away. Clark then got a branch from a nearby tree, laid it over the face of the dead ruffian to keep the flies off and to hide from view the ghastly stare of the sightless eyes. He then took a seat on a pile of logs nearby and protected the body until the coroner's arrival.

While Clark was on watch a companion of Voss' rode up in great excitement and dismounted. He whipped out his big gun and declared himself.

"That's my old pard, Voss. I kin tell by his boots. D—d if I don't kill somebody for doin' that job," and the new arrival wildly swung his big weapon and howled defiance to the whole town.

"Look here, my friend," said Clark in a mild and conciliatory tone, "you had better put that gun up, or you'll get what that fellow did who lies under the brush there. They have got Winchesters trained on you right now, and if you don't put up that six-shooter at once the coroner will have a pair of stiffs to sit on when he arrives."

The big bushwhacker looked cautiously around, tucking the weapon in the holster at the same time.

D'ye reckon they'll do me, pard?" asked the bandit.

"Sure thing," replied Clark.

"Well, I'm goin' to have Bill's belt, 'cause he told me to take it when he dropped from under the hat," and the big man stooped down as if to unbuckle the cartridge-holder.

"Don t touch that," cautioned Clark. 'If you remove anything from that body before the coroner views it you'll go up the road for life."

"D'ye reckon, pardr" said the crestfallen bandit, as he slowly arose.

"Sure," replied Clark.

"Wall, pardner, guess I'll take your advice. You look like er good fellow. I'll jist get on the horse an' go out scoutin' again. Poor old Bill."

The big lank specimen of the Verdigris bottom bandit then mounted his horse, put the spurs to the beast, and dashed away, leaning low over the pommel for fear someone might take a shot at him.

A STORY OF BORDER RUFFIANISM

Charles Myers, the game little conductor, who ran for years on the "Frisco" to Sapulpa, related to me many startling incidents of Catoosa and other towns.

'I was compelled to witness a most shocking murder in Catoosa," he said. "Our train was blocked by a freight wreck, and I spent several hours in the devil-may-care-town. The usual music of the six-shooter was heard in the main street. The 'corn-shellers' were busy. A gang was riding up and down, whooping and shooting at the bunches of corn ears hung up in front of the stores where feed was sold. Riding at full speed, half a dozen men, one behind the other, each would take a shot at the innocent insignia of the corn dealer. Up and down the street the gang rode, and fired until nothing remained of the big bunches of corn but the husks, which had been drawn back for the purpose of hanging up the ears. Kernels of corn were scattered for thirty yards each way, while the vagrant hogs leisurely sauntered along, picking them up.

"Everybody seemed to enjoy the exhibition of marksmanship until some of the bad men had too much whisky in their stomachs; then the comedy began to shift toward the tragedy. It came sooner than was expected. A man came dashing up the street from the direction of Spunky Creek bottoms. With a yell, one of the revellers started for the new arrival, who had pulled up in front of the post-office and dismounted. Immediately the 'corn-sheller' began shooting at the man, who was wrapping his lariat around the horizontal hitching-post. The party attacked pulled his gun, and soon unhorsed the bad man and his load of whisky with a well-aimed shot. No sooner had the man struck the ground than he bounded to his feet, and began pumping the lead at his intended victim. One of his shots cut a deep furrow across the scalp, another one passed through his right shoulder. The victim of the assault staggered forward and grappled with his assailant, his gun having fallen from his hand when the bullet entered his shoulder; he was practically helpless in the hands of the ruffian burning up with alcohol. The 'corn-sheller' grasped his victim by the hair, pushed his

409

head back over the hitching-rail, drew his murderous looking knife and deliberately cat the poor devil's head off and stuck it upon a post. The murderer then picked up his own and his victim's gun, and started yelling down the street, shooting as he went; but before he reached the Lone Star Hotel John Reynold's gun cracked, and the side partner of Verdigris Kid fell forward with a curse. He was not more than forty feet from the headless trunk of his victim."

Jim French was the son of Tom French, who died in 1890. He was a well-to-do citizen of Fort Gibson; he was regarded as one of the best of men by his friends, but was recognized as a dangerous enemy. Jim's mother died when he was a child. The boy inherited the nerve of his father but failed to achieve his better traits. His tragic ending is a warning to young men. He evidently realized his position when too late, as evidenced by two sentences written on the back of a letter found in his pocket:

"It is hard to live in hell and then go to hell, but it looks like such a fate is in store for me."

"A fool never knows nothing until it is too late; so, boys, beware, and look before you leap. J. K. FRENCH."

THE WONDERFUL, CRIMINAL AND DARING CAREER OF BOB ROGERS

Bob Rogers was the son of white parents. He was of the "criminal intruder class" and it is possible that he committed a greater number of crimes, large and small, than any other desperate character in the Indian Territory considering the short space of his reign. It was not long; none of the Territory desperadoes lasted very long, as time is counted in civilization, but the time of any of them was altogether too long for the comfort and peace of mind of all who were not bandits from choice.

Rogers was born in Washington County, Arkansas, in 1873. His mother died when he was a boy of thirteen years leaving, besides Bob and her husband, several small children from four to ten years old. A year later, in 1874, the father sold the farm, upon which he had thus far raised his family, for $5,000 and invested his all in eighty yoke of oxen, 300 head of stock cattle, several span of horses, wagons, implements, etc., and moved to the Indian Territory, prepared to start in as a wealthy farmer. He settled in the Cherokee Nation, twenty miles south of Coffeyville, Kansas, on the Verdegris River and seven miles east of Lenapah, married a Cherokee woman and fenced in a claim. On this he erected a box house and outbuildings, in one of the most favorable spots for resisting the cold north winds, for which that country is noted in winter, that could be imagined. On the land which he enclosed, the center of a beautiful prairie that extended for miles in either direction, was a mound, doubtless a relic of the unknown race designated "Mound Builders," who may have inhabited portions of America before the flood, and the results of whose labors have been styled by one writer "The Mounds of the Mississippi Valley." Many of these mounds dot the stretch of country reposing between the Rocky Mountains and the Allegheny's, and from some of them very valuable relics have been taken.

The mound upon the Rogers inclosure was of peculiar construction, was in the shape of a horseshoe, with the outward part, or "toe," pointing to the north. The mound was upwards of seventy-five feet high and on the inner side the decline was very abrupt, the base striking the level not more than twenty yards away from the center; on the outer sides the mound sloped away for perhaps 200 yards, making the descent very gradual. A more congenial location for a winter home, or a more favorable one for the uses to which it was afterwards placed, it would be hard to find. The land embraced several acres, and at the extreme back portion, close under the "toe," Rogers built his house and proceeded to gather wealth. For some reason, after he had become well settled, having by' his marriage gained the right of title under Indian laws to all the land he would enclose (provided he kept at a distance of one-fourth of a mile from any other enclosure), he began to grow tired of his squaw wife and in 1893 forced a separation.

In that same year, in the month of April, Bob Rogers, then twenty years old, started out on the scout; sixty days later his brother, Sam, started out and in November another brother, Jim, only fourteen years old, made a dash to swell the list of bandits.

Jim with another boy younger than himself met a big negro in the road. He was named Hayden and weighed 300 pounds. He was postmaster and merchant at Hayden, a cross-roads named for himself, and carried a small stock of groceries, tobacco, etc. When the negro found himself confronted by a chit of a boy with a dangerous looking revolver in his hands, he said:

"I'm a mighty big man and you're a little devil, but I'll have to give up," and turned over $20 and a quantity of tobacco. This occurred on Lightning Creek, near Chelsea.

The youthful highwaymen were quickly followed by several armed men, who got within close range and opening fire shot down the horse ridden by the youngest of the pair. Jim Rogers at once slipped from the saddle and while the other boy held his horse he dropped down in the tall grass and with a few well directed shots drove back the advancing party.

Previous to the spring of 1893 this had been a very peaceful neighborhood, settled largely by industrious farmers, who had not yet learned to cope with dare devils who valued not their own lives.

The father of young Rogers heard of the affair and overtaking them the next day, after they had robbed a store at Coody's Bluff, six miles from Nowata, on the Missouri Pacific Railroad, owned by a man named Armstrong. By talking with his son, the father succeeded in getting their weapons and then took the boys to Fort Smith and both were sent to reform schools in different States, the Rogers boy going to an institution of that nature in Kansas.

The second boy, Sam, ran for a year and was shot and crippled while committing a bold robbery, in August, 1894; he was captured and conveyed to Fort Smith and sentenced to three years of penitentiary life. When their terms were completed both Jim and Sam Rogers concluded that sober citizenship was the better course and both returned to their father's home where they now peaceably reside

Bob Rogers' first crime was as a horse thief. With the assistance of George Preston he drove away a dozen or more horses belonging to Bill Martin, a neighbor, and disposed of them for cash in Arkansas. Preston soon after became frightened at his own boldness, tented the consequences of his crime and left the country: he has not been heard of since. Bob Rogers continued in the evil way, made no secret of his avocation, organized bands of his own, robbed banks and trains, stole horses and cattle, and made his father's house in the horseshoe mound his rendezvous or relied on the old man to bring him provisions when stationed for a while in the vicinity when for certain reasons he dared not show up at home.

For the first two years after he went on the scout he confined his depredations principally to thievery. With his gang he would round up a bunch of horses or cattle and then employ a cowboy to take them to the nearest shipping point and go with them to Kansas City, make a sale and return with the money received, and it was noticeable that his father always had a supply of fine horses about the place. In the summer of 1895, Bob organized a gang and robbed a train at Adair, on the Missouri, Kansas & Texas railroad, twenty miles from Vinita. He shot off the fireman's lower jaw and secured a few hundred dollars booty.

Soon after he, with others, robbed the Mound Valley Bank at Mound Valley, Labett county, Kansas, and a deputy United States Marshal named Jackson went out from Fort Smith to search for the leader. He met Rogers near Coffeyville, and the bandit rode up to him and inquired: "Jackson, what are you doing up in this country?" The deputy replied that he was riding about, attending to his duties. Rogers covered him with his pistols, compelled him to give up his arms, advised him to go back to Fort Smith and stay there, then returned to his home and proudly exhibited to his neighbors the guns he had taken from the United States marshal.

I have space here to speak of only a few of the more than one hundred robberies committed by Rogers, but such as are told will suffice to show the desperate character of the famous boy bandit.

HE BETRAYS HIS COMPANIONS

It was in January, 1895, that he "gave his pals away." Deputy Marshals Jackson and Heck Bruner arranged with him to assist in the capture of four desperadoes he was associated with, for which they were to pay him $1,400. Each of the four had prices set upon their heads, and one of them "Dynamite Jack," was wanted by Colorado authorities, and they had offered a standing reward of $1,400 for his capture or his death. The officers furnished Rogers with a quantity of whiskey and chloroform. The gang met at Rogers' home that night, and the four mentioned were given the drugged liquor. They soon became drowsy and went to bed. Bob and his father remained 'below stairs, and when Jackson, Bruner and two other officers came to the house, they were conducted to the chamber. They at once opened fire on the bandits, killing Jack and one of the others, and wounding a third so that he died at Vinita while being taken to Fort Smith. The fourth awoke in time to surrender; he was taken to Fort Smith and given a long penitentiary sentence. Bob Rogers and his father were taken to Fort Smith at the same time, but within three days they were back. On that occasion Judge Parker told Bob:

"This is the fourth time you have been before me; if you are brought here again death will be the penalty."

For a few months after this warning, Bob was satisfied with petty larceny and crimes of a less degree than robbery or murder, until the train robbery noted above and the Mound Valley bank robbery, but on the night of December 24, 1895, he planned and with three others robbed a train at Seminole switch, a small station on the Missouri Pacific railroad, where was located a small store and post-office. For some reason they failed even with the assistance of dynamite to gain entrance to the express car, so had to be content with rifling the mail, after which Rogers and another went through the coaches and compelled the passengers to give up their watches, jewelry and pocket knives. The passengers, especially of the weaker sex, were terribly frightened, with the exception of a large Cherokee woman and a little girl only ten years old, who, with her mother, was returning from a short trip. This mother and child were near neighbors of Rogers, senior, but they had never seen the bandit, and the mother nearly fainted as he and his pal entered the car. The daughter calmed her fears, assuring her there was no danger, and both she and the Cherokee woman were complimented next day by Bob, when, happening to be told by his neighbor that it was his wife who was so terribly frightened, he said:

"Well, your little girl is the bravest little woman I ever saw; and the Cherokee, she sassed us back."

A number of costly overcoats they also appropriated and whenever they found a man with a cheap or well-worn overcoat they, with pocket knives, cut them into shreds. They secured about $750 in cash, besides the other plunder. The next morning about 10 o'clock, Rogers rode into the neighborhood where his father lived, twelve miles from the scene of the holdup and as he pissed by the home of his nearest neighbor, above mentioned, he was asked, "Bob did you hear of the train robbery at Seminole last night.'"

"By G—d, I reckon so," he replied, "I helped do it."

He said that they didn't get much, "only $700 or $800, and some watches and jewelry," then drawing a handsome gold watch from his pocket he said, "Here's the conductor's watch, a'int she a daisy? And I got this too," he added, pointing to a fine beaver overcoat that rested on the pommel of his saddle. The neighbor with his eyes open wide with astonishment, said.

"I should think you would be afraid of being caught."

"By G—d I'll fight'em," said Bob.

Evidently the officers were aware of this for no attempt was ever made to apprehend him for this act.

Under the circumstances it is possible that Rogers might have continued unmolested longer than he did, had he confined his depredations to burglaries, and have kept clear of horse and cattle stealing, for the officers had come to have a wholesome dread of an encounter with him and as long as no reward was offered for his capture, no desperate efforts were made in that direction, but the continued spiriting away of stock from nearby ranches, begat the secret enmity of his neighbors and in the early part of 1896, an association was organized under a Kansas charter called the "Anti Horse Thief Association," with 102 members made up largely from among Rogers' neighbors, and under the leadership of Deputy United States Marshal Jim Mayes, whose home was within one-half mile of the "house in the horse shoe."

Having laid their plans, the members of the association awaited their opportunity. In Rogers' house lived Charlie Collier and his wife, both in the employ of the elder

Rogers, Mrs. Collier being housekeeper. Just at sundown on the afternoon of March 13, 1896, a signal was sent up, by prearrangement, from a place of rendezvous, a few hundred yards north of the "horse shoe," informing the members of the association that Bob Rogers and a pal, a half-breed Indian, had come home for the night.

They had come from an extended trip of some weeks, each riding a fine specimen of horse flesh and Bob leading another, a peculiarity of his. It is stated as a curious fact that after he took to the plains he was never seen without two horses. Someone asked him why he always led a second horse. "By G—d" he replied, "I may need him some time."

Soon after they entered his father's house, Bob's companion said to him, "I not stay here. I go your sister's house (Mrs. John Daniels, a married sister of the bandit, lived about a mile away), so if there be trouble they won't get both of us."

Whether this was only a case of ordinary precaution often practiced or whether by aid of his semi-savage instincts, he intuitively felt that Bob was that moment nearing his doom can only be conjectured. Bob had always found a safe shelter beneath his father's roof; by what strange hypothesis did the Indian imagine it was not a safe place now?

The night was a memorable one in more ways than one. The weather was bitter cold. It had been bright and balmy for a week previous, but during the night of the twelfth, a freezing north wind, known in that section as a "norther," had come wheeling over the prairies, and all day the "zephyrs" had raged across the plains, chilling to the marrow all animal creation.

Just at midnight on the day of Bob's return, twelve determined looking men, under Marshal Mayes, all heavily armed, gathered at the place from which the signal had been given, tied their horses in a little clump of tree bordering a dry creek bed and seeking shelter as best they could, awaited the proper hour, conversing the while in low but earnest tones, discussing plans of attack. There was not a coward in the lot; each man knew why he was there. All had counted the danger they were about to encounter; each was ready to brave shot and shell, that their otherwise peaceful community might be cleared of a desperate and dangerous parasite.

THE TERRIBLE FIGHT OPENS

At 4 o'clock, Marshal Mayes rose to his feet and said, "Boys are you ready?" For answer each of the dozen grasped his Winchester and stood erect. Not a word was uttered. Silently they followed their leader, going direct to the top of the mound below which, enshrouded in the inky darkness, lay the little box house which sheltered the man whose crimes were at last to be avenged.

The men halted. Below all was still as the grave, save the soughing of the tempest as it swept across the prairies chilling them through and through. Rogers senior was the possessor of two vicious dogs. It had been expected by the avengers that these animals would discover their presence and by loud barks and howls, warn the bandit of his danger. Strangely enough the expected did not occur, and nothing was seen nor heard of the beasts that night. Noiselessly, the steep descent was made, and in a moment the house was surrounded. Still no sound came from within.

The building was one and a half stories in height, had two rooms below and one above, and the upper room was provided with one "half" window on the north side, two on the south, and a window at each end. The interior was lined with heavy paper, covered with canvass. While the men crouched low, their rifles bearing upon the various chances of escape, Marshal Mayes went to the door at the south side of the house and knocked.

Mrs. Collier, who slept in the first story with her husband, heard the rapping and said:

"Who's there?"

Collier was deaf and did not awake. Mayes knocked again.

"Who's there?" again shouted Mrs. Collier.

"Jim Mayes."

"What's wanted?" she shouted in return.

It was believed by members of the assaulting party that the woman suspected danger, and that her loud answers were for the purpose of arousing Rogers and his father, who were in the loft asleep. It matters not her intention—the object, either intended or otherwise, was attained, and during the colloquy her husband and the others awoke.

"Open the door,' demanded Mayes.

Collier arose, undid the fastenings, and the instant the door was opened eight men crowded into the room, the rest of the party laying on the outside, according to the plans agreed upon, each with his rifle pointing at a side or an end of the building.

In a few moments Rogers, senior, came down the stairway and Mayes said:

"Light a lamp."

The order was obeyed, and as its rays fell upon the faces of the visitors and reflected the polished barrels of their weapons, the father asked in faltering tones, but with a show of bravery:

"My God, men! what do you want?"

"We want that dastardly son of yours," replied Mayes; then shouted to Bob, telling him to come down.

A determined refusal was the only answer, and three of the men—W. C. McDaniels, Phil Williams and C. E. Smith—volunteered to go up after him, while Collier and his wife, frightened out of their wits, bolted from the house into the awful cold, clad only in. their night clothes, the woman carrying her 5-year-old daughter, and ran a mile to the house of a neighbor, the husband being the first to reach shelter.

Despite the warning of the others, the three men named, McDaniels in the lead and with Smith in the rear, ascended the stairway, compelling the father to go ahead with the lamp. As the latter reached the top and stepped to one side, Rogers was seen standing about eight feet away with pistols drawn.

"Hands up!" ordered McDaniels, and for answer Bob fired.

The bullet struck McDaniels below the heart, and passing through his body, came out just below the right shoulder blade and passed over the head of Williams.

McDaniels fell forward dead, and as the others pressed forward another shot rang out, and Bob's second bullet struck Williams's left wrist, as it was raised to shoot, passed out near the elbow and cut away one-half of his moustache. The shot staggered him, and falling back against Smith, both were precipitated to the foot of the stairway. As they came tumbling down the others became excited, and with loud execrations they began shooting upwards through the floor. About fifty shots were thus fired. One of them, the very first, it is claimed, cut the big toe from the right foot of Rogers, senior. After Smith and Williams fell backward down the stairway, Bob had rushed forward and removed the well-filled cartridge belt from the dead body of McDaniels, put away his own weapons and fired, with the dead man's Winchester, two or three shots downward through the floor, then remained quiet, doubtless with a view to saving ammunition till a time when he could use it more effectively, or for the purpose of leading the attacking party to believe he had been killed. Had they come to this conclusion and again entered the chamber, others would have been murdered.

They were not deceived, however, and as none cared to ascend the stairway a second time, they all went outside, and from all points opened up a hot and continuous fire upon the upper part of the building.

After a few minutes, Will Collier, a brother of Charlie Collier, who was on friendly terms with Bob, was sent in to confer with the desperado and ask him if he would give up.

Rogers replied, "You tell them that after I'm killed I will give up."

The messenger returned and all hands commenced shooting into the house as before. Three times was young Collier sent in to urge Bob to surrender, and the last time Bob had come down stairs, still without a scratch; it was a wonder he was alive. Some 300 or more bullets had been fired into the chamber, the inch boards offering almost no resistance. Some of the rafters supporting the roof, which were in dimensions three by four inches, were nearly cut in twain and scarce a square foot I of the outside of the upper story, but had a bullet hole. How Bob ever escaped being riddled is a mystery that will never be solved. Where he could have lain and avoided the terrible onslaught none can tell.

Alter he came down he shouted out to Mayes, "If you will let me bring my gun I will come out."

Mayes answered, "All right, if you will come out with the muzzle down."

By this time dawn was approaching; in the cast the sky was just beginning to show a gray or leaden color. It was still too dark, however, to see objects plainly, especially for one just emerging from a lighted room.

In front of the house, about ten yards from the door ran a fence, and at about the same distance south it turned and ran north until it reached the foot of the incline. Outside of this fence, south of the open space in front of the house, was a pile of poles behind which several of the gunners were in ambush, and directly in front of the house, outside the fence, was a sudden descent of two feet or more, and right here was a pile of rails behind which were several others of the attacking party, every one of them with their guns trained on the door. Mayes stood in the open about twenty feet from the fence and between the fence and the pile of rails.

Bob opened the door and peered around; he could see no one. He held McDaniels' Winchester with the muzzle pointed downward, but his finger was on the trigger. He advanced a few steps, then descried Mayes, and cautiously walked to the fence; he asked:

"Have you got a warrant for me?"

"No, but I'll take you anyway."

At this Rogers started to step backwards as if to turn and run or that he might have room to raise his gun, fire and run, and Mayes gave the word, "Fire."

Instantly the rifles roared, and Rogers, with a groan, fell forward; the shooting continued, some of the gunners firing four or five times in what only seemed as many seconds, and when the smoke cleared away and the body was picked up, it was a sight such as was never seen before.

It was shot through and through; the body had been pierced by twenty-two 38-caliber bullets and two charges of buckshot. The latter from the weapon in the hands of the marshal, had struck the breast and right shoulder perforating both, some of the buckshot going entirely through the body. In the center of the breast was a terrible hole, made by a bullet from Bill Dilly's 52-90 rifle; in the back where the slug had come through was a hole even larger than the one in front. Was ever a human body so terribly riddled?

Strange as it may seem, the excitement had been so great that none had watched the absence of McDaniels, nor that he had not been with them while the shooting was going on from the outside. Now that Rogers was dead the members began to look about and ascertain if any were injured. Then someone asked:

"Where is McDaniels?"

The men looked at each other, and one of them remarked that he had headed the brave dash for the chamber. He was the president of the association, was a wealthy bachelor, and was held in the highest esteem. The house was quickly entered, and there where he had fallen, with his belt and weapon gone, was his body, stark and stiff and partially frozen.

About the chamber was a direful sight, every pane in the five windows as well as portions of several of the sash were shot away; splinters strewed the floor; the bed was riddled and the covers were like sieves; a stove pipe which ran up through the center of the room was pierced in more than a score of places.

With a shudder at the thought of the night's awful work, his comrades lifted the form of McDaniels and conveyed it to his home a little over a mile away where the dead man had resided with his bachelor brother.

The father of the bandit, the last few years of whose life had been so turbulent, and whose end was so shocking, at once sent a man to Coffeyville and in the afternoon a costly casket was placed in the house and the body prepared for decent burial.

Before the casket was closed the father went to its side and looking down upon the features which bore no mark of the recent battle said, "They've killed my boy but he died brave."

News of the shooting and of the death of Bob Rogers traveled rapidly and before noon, crowds began to arrive at the house. Some there who came from miles away, all moved by the common impulse of human curiosity, and it was after night fall before the last of them went away. Thus perished a man whose bravery amounted to recklessness, who was skilled in cunning, vast in resources, and who might have become a useful citizen had he but regarded the rights of others and held a proper esteem for law and order; his own actions changed his fellow creatures to foes and he was shot down like a hunted cur, with scarce a mourner, and was buried without eulogy other than this.

"He died brave, with his face to the enemy."

419

Among the great events that characterized the criminal history of the Indian Territory, was the Bland-McElroy case.

Dr. John C. W. Bland, was a white man, about 35 years old, who had emigrated from the states, found his way to the Indian Territory and married a Creek woman, giving him the right to hold land in common with the members of the Creek tribe. At the time of the trouble here narrated, he had located several farms, had several tenants and was following his profession as a medical practitioner; he resided on a farm near Cimarron river, near the scene of the tragedy, hereafter described.

George McElroy was a white man, about the age of Dr. Bland. His father lived at Tulsa, in the Creek Nation. His stepmother was a sister of Bruce Miller, later referred to in this narrative. George also had married a Creek woman, giving him likewise citizenship in the Creek Nation. He at this time, was living some seven miles from the home of Dr. Bland, and not far from the Arkansas river he had several ranches and farms upon which his tenants resided.

It was a beautiful country where these men lived. The soil was a rich alluvial deposit lying between the Arkansas and Cimarron rivers, about twenty miles east of the Oklahoma line. They had come to the country in an early day, and had almost the first choice, with the exception of a large and valuable tract lying between the Bland and McElroy claims, which had been located, before their advent, by Bruce and El Miller, white men and step-brothers of George McElroy. They were tenants of Daniel Drew, a Creek Indian.

Testimony adduced at the trial, showed that for several years, a feud had existed between the Millers and McElroy, and that Dr. Bland was the friend and ally of the latter. It was shown that the Millers had received numerous offers for the purchase of their interests in the land, and that these propositions were traced to Bland and McElroy, who sought to get them out of the country, for the purpose, it was claimed, of obtaining for themselves the fine body of land occupied by them under the license granted by Drew.

Henry and Charles Houk, father and son, were white men, and were tenants in that country, unlicensed, and without rights and were employed, alternately by Bland, McElroy and others as laborers. Tom Stufflebean was also white, probably 35 years old, living at Tulsa, and had been at one time a deputy United States marshal; he too was without property or tights in the Creek Nation.

The testimony indicated that a conspiracy existed, amounting to an alliance, consisting of Bland, McElroy and their friends; banded together against the Millers, and that they had circulated base reports charging the Millers with harboring outlaws and of complicity in various unlawful acts, It was stated on the stand that during the previous six years, Bruce Miller had been arrested seven times and El Miller twice, charged with introducing whiskey, receiving stolen property, and various other crimes; that in every case where arrests were made it was on charges made directly or indirectly by Bland and McElroy, for the purpose of annoyance, and that every charge was exploded on examination before the United States Commissioner; neither Bruce nor El Miller were ever tried before a jury on any charge whatever.

In April, 1894, Bruce and El Miller with their families, were living in log houses built upon their leased land, about one-half mile apart. With the latter lived also Mrs. Elizabeth Miller, their mother, and with Bruce Miller lived Lawrence Baldinger, an inoffensive German boy, known as "Dutch John," who worked as a farmhand, and Sam Patch, an honest, hard-working man, about forty-five years old. Just before the middle of the month the Millers received information from some source, causing them to believe that an assault was to be made upon the home of Bruce Miller by Bland, McElroy and their allies, and Bruce, with his family and "Dutch John," on the evening of April 15, left his home and proceeded across the fields to the home of his brother for the night.

Early the next morning "Dutch John" started out and when about forty yards away from the house he was shot by a volley from the trees and rocks by a gang of men who, it was supposed, had watched the house during the night. He fell, mortally wounded. Later, when it became apparent that the mob intended remaining in ambush during the day, Mrs. Elizabeth Miller went out and covered the dead body with a blanket to protect it from the rays of the sun and from flies, and while thus employed, she was fired on, one of the bullets passing through her clothing, wounding her arm. Still, later. Bruce Miller was fired upon, a bullet cutting the waistband of his trousers. Another bullet struck his son, Sherman Miller, a boy six years old, inflicting a bloody wound in the shoulder. Several bullets pierced the house; the trees around showed the marks of the conflict. One bullet hole was found where a slug had gone through the house and into the bed of a wagon; this bullet was supposed to have been fired by Dr. Bland because of the fact that he was the possessor of a gun carrying the largest bullets of any in that part of the country; its cartridges were near six inches in length. Another bullet cut a wagon spoke in two, and altogether, the scene presented the appearance of a battle ground.

Sam Patch, who was employed by Bruce Miller, was found by the mob, after the battle commenced, while attending to his work. They arrested him and kept him with them the entire day. On the stand he identified Dr. Bland, McElroy, the Houks and Stufflebean as being members of the gang who held him under arrest, and he said that there were about eighteen persons in the mob. During the day Bruce Miller's house and stable were burned. Patch described the scene, explaining how the burning was accomplished; he said that they gathered combustible material and piling it against the buildings, set it on fire.

Mrs. Elizabeth Miller identified several of the men, and Mrs. Bruce Miller identified one of them as being the man who was with the mob that day riding a gray horse, which was seen by other witnesses and was known by all the people in the vicinity to be the gray horse that George McElroy always rode. A number of witnesses testified that immediately after the burning of the house and stable Bland and McElroy admitted that they were there, members of the mob, and that they attempted to justify themselves by claiming that the Millers were outlaws, a menace to their neighbors, and that it was right to attempt to drive them from the country.

During a heavy storm on the night following the above described crimes, the Millers escaped without being observed by the mob and two weeks later, on the first day of May, El Miller's house and contents, together with his stable, were entirely destroyed by fire. Early in June, Bland, McElroy, the Houks, Stufflebean, Frank Sennitt and several other men were arrested and taken to Fort Smith and the six named were held to answer to the grand jury, charged with the murder of "Dutch John," with assaulting with intent to kill Elizabeth Miller and Sherman Miller and with burning the Miller homes. The examination before the commissioner was concluded, July 14, and the men were released on bond, pending action by the grand jury, on July 28. They were indicted in August and soon after Sennitt, who was a white man and lived at Sennitt Post-office, in the Creek Nation, was killed at a Shawnee dance. After the indictment the five principals above named, were again released on bonds of $5,000 each. Their trial for the murder of "Dutch John" came on in March, 1895. There were many witnesses and it was a long and tedious trial. The defense was conducted by the firm of Barnes & Mellette and William M. Cravens, of Fort Smith, the prosecution by Assistant District Attorney, J. B. McDonough and the criminal lawyer, J. Warren Reed. The trial continued eight days. The court allowed six hours to each side for argument. The jury deliberated several hours, returning a verdict of acquittal. Soon after the trial, Bruce Miller, who was the chief prosecuting witness, was assassinated at Ingalls, Oklahoma, shot through the open window of a saloon, by unknown persons, after night.

Before the next term of court Bland, McIilroy, the Houks and Stufflebean were arrested on the old indictments, charging them with assault with intent to kill on two counts, and with arson on two counts, and they gave bond. These indictments all pertained to acts performed at the time of the killing of "Dutch John," and the witnesses were necessarily the same in all the cases. The government had procured additional testimony, and this trial commenced Monday morning, September 8, 1895, and continued four days.

The case was marked by a peculiar interest, and it was indeed a peculiar case. More witnesses were present to testify than at any case in years; those who were sworn numbered 150. When, on Tuesday afternoon, the witnesses for the government were called up to be sworn, every person outside the railing on the north side of the aisle arose. The next moment an equal number of persons seated on the south side of the aisle arose and took the oath as witnesses for the defense. It was then seen and appreciated for the first time, perhaps, by the twelve men chosen as jurors what an important case they had been called upon to decide.

The evidence was puzzling. That for the government charged that Bland and McElroy had persecuted the Millers in an endeavor to force them to leave the country that they might possess the valuable land leased by them from Drew, and that this was the motive for the assault on the home of El Miller on the morning of April 16, 1894, at which "Dutch John" was killed. It charged, also, that instead of Bruce Miller having been arrested thirteen times, as had been claimed, he had never been arrested but seven times, and then on warrants sworn out at the behest of Bland and McElroy, not for crimes committed, but because they were determined to harass the Millers continually and make it so disagreeable for them that they would finally leave the country and allow them to gain possession of the land they coveted. The government testimony also tended to prove that the many charges against the Millers of receiving stolen property and harboring bandits, were false; and that it was the defendants who had harbored law-breakers, and who were a constant menace to all law-abiding citizens; while the Millers were at all times law-abiding, and their only offense was the holding of leases on land that Bland and McElroy determined to possess.

The defense attempted to introduce a large mass of evidence tending to show that the Millers were a desperate class of outlaws, and that they harbored such characters as Bill Doolin and Bill Dalton, with their gangs, and were a terror to the community in which they resided; but Judge Parker refused to admit the evidence, on the grounds that it mattered not what their previous character may have been, there was nothing in that which could in any way justify the assault, the killing or the burning; he stated that if they were bad people and violated the law, they could be arrested and tried in the courts; there was no authority for a mob to assault them, burn their property nor destroy their lives; there was no justification for mob violence in this land, where courts are open and all are presumed to receive justice.

This considerably narrowed the testimony for defense. They then confined their evidence to proving an alibi, their testimony tending to show that Bland and McElroy were not at the killing of "Dutch John" and the burning of Bruce Miller's property, which occurred early in the morning, but that they arrived at the scene after o'clock of that day, with other persons, who came there as sight-seers.

All of the defendants took advantage of the privileges granted by law and refrained from testifying in the case, and in the minds of the jury it may or may not have reflected against them, that they urged a plea to which they were unwilling to testify.

From the opening of the trial, the government made a strong case. Witness after witness was placed on the stand and many were the incidents related, some of them of a nature to cause the spectators to wonder if such things could occur in a civilized community.

The defense was equally strong. Throughout the trial the impression was sought to be made upon the jury that although the defendants may have joined in the crimes alleged, they were justified, because of the bad character of the persons upon whom the attacks were made. Sympathy for the men on trial was very strong in Fort Smith, where they were well-known and had it been necessary for them to furnish bonds of untold amount, it could have been easily accomplished. The same attorneys were pitted on this case as at the previous trial and never did attorneys work harder for their clients than Cravens, Barnes and Mellette. Three hours were given to each side for argument and the three attorneys for defense took an hour each.

They were overmatched by J, Warren Reed, who was employed to conduct the prosecution. Assistant District Attorney McDonough remained on the case during the examination, but he took no part in the closing argument. Mr. Reed occupied an hour in outlining the points upon which he relied for conviction. Confident of his ability to bring the minds of the jurors to the point that they might say they were satisfied "beyond a reasonable doubt," he laid down the bars, and so to speak, challenged those upon the other side to a combat upon the issues. He reviewed the evidence in a purely logical manner, anticipating coming attacks and meeting them with argumentative attacks.

It was his final and closing argument, however, that proved the masterpiece of that legal battle. It was this that called forth the admiration and chained the attention of those who heard it. From six minutes past 9 o'clock in the morning of Thursday until an hour before noon, there rolled from his lips gems of oratory seldom equaled. The last hour especially sparkled for everyone save the five defendants and the attorneys representing them. The defense which earlier in the case was made to appear as the stoutest fabric was torn to shreds. Their walls of vindication were rent asunder and as the able lawyer took his seat those who had heretofore predicted the acquittal of the defendants were all but ready to admit that they were doomed to conviction.

The charge by the court was regarded by many as the most impressive ever delivered by him. He became so over wrought that nature gave out; he broke down and was obliged to rest before completing; he finished at 3 o'clock, and thirty minutes after the twelve men filed into court, after the announcement by a bailiff, that a verdict had been reached. The five defendants were seated a short distance behind the places they had occupied during the trial; they looked up expectantly. They had been ill at ease but sought to maintain a confident air. The foreman handed up the indictment with the verdict written thereon, amid perfect silence; when the word "guilty" was spoken, an ashen pallor overspread the countenances of the defendants. From that moment they were under guard and as soon as the court room could be cleared they were conducted to the jail, where quarters were at once provided for them, on the lower floor; four prisoners, Frank and Henry Smith, Andy Crittenden and Ben Howell, were transferred to the second tier of cells in order that there might be room for the quintet in "Murderer's Row."

Attorney Mellette at once filed a motion for new trial. On October 19, the motion was overruled and Judge Parker passed sentence upon the defendants. Among other things Judge Parker said:

"The crime of which you have been convicted was one of the blackest on the pages of crime It was so foul and brutal, that it should cause every law-abiding man to shudder. Since your first trial, when you were tried for the murder of an inoffensive German boy, and, I think unjustly, and improperly acquitted, three innocent human lives have been taken and all were important witnesses against you. It is clear to my mind, that your associates are guilty of these crimes. I am glad that so few crimes of this character are committed within the jurisdiction of this court and I give warning now, that every one within this jurisdiction, who engages in mob violence, may expect to suffer the consequences, as long as I am on the bench."

The sentence imposed against Bland and McElroy was twelve years each in the penitentiary, and the other three were given nine years each. Notice of appeal was at once served and under a previous order by Justice White, of the Supreme Bench, Judge Parker fixed their bonds at $10,000 each, which was given and a. writ of error was taken to the Supreme Court of the United States.

Shortly after the conviction, "Date" Miller (an elder brother of Bruce and El Miller), with his aged wife and. young son, Dorsey, important witnesses for the government, against McElroy and Bland, were assassinated after night, in their own home, by persons unknown. It appeared that the assailants rode to the house, shot them in their beds, through a window and departed quietly. Still later, one. Dr. Beggs, who lived across-the line of the Creek Nation, in Oklahoma, an important witness for the prosecution, and who testified that one of the-defendants, on the; day after the murder-of "Dutch John," confessed to being on the ground, boasting of it, was killed by an unknown assassin, after night; shot through a window or door while in his home. The killing of Bruce Miller, "Date" Miller and his family and Dr. Beggs so frightened the other important government witnesses that they scattered and left the country, making their whereabouts unknown.

In the early part of 1897, the Supreme Court, passing upon the case, reversed it and granted a new trial. When the case came on again, many of the witnesses being dead, and a number of the other important ones having left the country, the prosecuting attorney not being able to go to trial, *noll prossed* the case, and thus ended one of the most noted criminal cases of the Fort Smith court.

Another case which caused not a little attention, and which was destined to become one of the noted cases before the Federal court, was that of Jim Mills, a half-breed Cherokee Indian, charged with the crime of rape upon the person of Mrs. Florence Hendricks, on the night of December 7, 1894. The complainant was the wife of James Hendricks; they were united in marriage at Halltown, Missouri, eighteen miles from Mount Vernon, in 1885, and at the time this crime was alleged to have been committed four children had been born to them. They lived a few years at Monett, Missouri, and then, a few months before the time noted, had removed to near Claremore, in the Cherokee Nation, and early in November (1894) they had moved into a house belonging to a young half-breed Cherokee named Joe Maxwell, having received permission from another white man who had formerly rented the house, but who had moved his family elsewhere without the knowledge of Maxwell.

On the night in question, which was described as being "bright and moonlight," about 8 o'clock, as the Hendricks family had retired, there came a shout from without from a stranger, who claimed that he had lost his way. There was a conflict of evidence at the trial regarding what followed, that produced by the government being briefly as follows; it shows the husband, James Hendricks, to have been much of a craven.

According to the government witnesses Hendricks, after the second shout, raised up from the bed on the floor where he and his wife were prepared to sleep, and while yet resting on his knees, gave the desired directions. The stranger, who proved to be James Mills, ordered him to come out and show him the way, and as the horseman was within three feet of the door, and as the order was made more peremptory by a Winchester which he "threw down" on Hendricks, the latter obeyed in spite of his wife's objections. Without waiting to dress, he went into the open air clothed only in his under clothing. Mills then marched Hendricks away about ten yards and threatened to kill him, saying, "I am Henry Starr, the notorious train robber, you gave me away to the officers and I'm going to kill you." Hendricks cried out; "For God's sake don't kill me." As her husband left the house, Mrs. Hendricks had risen from the bed and stood by the partly opened door, watching the proceedings, and as she heard the words above noted, she ran to her husband's side, clad as was he, in only her night clothes.

Mills then ordered them both to proceed to the high road several hundred yards away, several times threatening to kill them, and when they arrived at the road he sent the husband off down the road, threatening death if he did not obey. Then, after he was out of sight, he threw the trembling woman to the ground and ravished her again and again, threatening to blow her brains out if she made an outcry. According to Mrs. Hendricks' testimony he continued his abuse for near three hours, then, forcing a polluting kiss upon her lips, mounted his horse and rode away. The woman, as soon as she was released, hastened back to her home, where she could hear her baby crying, and after making sure all was well with her children, started out again in search of her husband. She met him almost at the door. He had marched away, quaking in every joint, leaving his wife to the mercy of Mills, and had not dared stop until a turn in the road had placed him out of their sight. Then he had walked up and down, up and down, a space about fifty yards in length, as he described it, in a frenzy of fear, walking to keep warm, and too much of a coward to return, until finally, after about three hours, he had seen Mills riding off across the prairie away from his house;, then he hurried back, arriving soon after his wife, it being about 11 o'clock.

The occurrence above narrated was on Friday night, and on the following Sunday Hendricks plucked up courage to go to Claremore, ten miles away, to lay a complaint before a deputy United States marshal residing there. Learning that the officer had been killed about an hour before he reached town, he returned, and on Wednesday he went to Fort Smith and filed a complaint before one of the United States commissioners in the Federal court.

A warrant for Mills was at once issued and placed in the hands of an officer, but for some reason Mills was not arrested for about a year. One of the United States deputy marshals into whose possession the warrant passed, showed the paper to Mills with the remark: "I don't want to serve it, Jim; let someone else attend to it." Although fully aware of the charge against him Mills made no attempt to escape, and he continued to stay about his home near Foyil until the warrant was served, when he was lodged in the Federal jail at Fort Smith.

Mills from the outset had denied his guilt, although admitting that he called at the house, as stated by the complainants. He had been "out with the boys" that night and had been drinking, else he never would have done so foolish an act as to force a stranger from his bed at night. Strong drink was the cause of his being charged with a serious crime, placing his life in jeopardy.

Mills was the owner of several horses, and he at once employed Attorneys Buckley and Jamison to defend him, giving them a mortgage on his stock to secure the required fee. They examined the case and decided that the only proper defense was to set up an alibi. They therefore prepared an application naming witnesses by which it was alleged Mills could prove that he was elsewhere than at the place where the crime he was charged with was claimed to have been committed, at the time alleged; and, acting on the instructions of his legal advisers, Mills made oath to the statements set up in the application, in accordance with the usual custom. Later on, just before the time set for the trial, his attorneys had opportunity to personally examine the witnesses they had summoned, and finding that they had made a mistake, and that the claim for alibi could not be sustained, they decided the case to be hopeless, and abandoned their client, and so reported to the court.

Judge Parker then brought Mills into court and informed him that his attorneys had refused to defend him. Mills having no further property, was thus unable to employ counsel, and was thrown upon the mercy of the court, whose duty it was to appoint an attorney to defend him.* Judge Parker asked Mills if he had any choice of attorneys, and he selected J. Warren Reed, who was thereupon appointed. Mr. Reed was busy in his office and knew nothing of the case, the circumstances surrounding it nor the character of testimony it had been attempted to establish. He at once took charge of the case, secured a continuance of a few days, and when the trial came on he made a strong fight, combating the testimony produced by the government, and his cross-examination of the prosecutrix [sic] was the most searching ever heard in that court. The statement under oath in the defendant's application for witnesses relative to his absence from the scene of the alleged crime at the time alleged, was used against him quite effectively, and Mills was convicted. On the first day of April, 1896, he was given the death sentence, June 23 being named as his last on earth. Mr. Reed took the usual writ of error to the Supreme Court, and a new trial was granted.

In the meantime he had made a further investigation of the case and obtained strong testimony for defense. He sent to Halltown, Lawrence County, Missouri, and secured evidence concerning the previous reputation for chastity and for truth of Florence Hendricks. At the first trial he had discovered in the person of Joe Maxwell, brought to court as a government witness, but not placed on the stand, a valuable witness for rebuttal of the main story set up by the prosecution. He obtained permission from the prosecution to interview Maxwell, and sent for him to come to his office. The witness ignored the summons, knowing that Mr. Reed was conducting the defense, and fearing that he would get into trouble with the court. Mr. Reed finally went to Maxwell's boarding place, told him he had permission from the district attorney, and at last discovered why the witness had not been sworn by the prosecution, learning from him the following facts:

On the night on which the crime was claimed to have been committed, and a short time before the arrival of Mills at the house occupied by Hendricks and his family, Maxwell had come to the house for the purpose of looking after his rents, not knowing that his former lessee had removed therefrom, and discovering then, for the first time, that his property was occupied by strangers. After a short conversation with Hendricks, Maxwell was induced to remain for the night, and when Mills arrived he had retired to an improvised bed in the one room 'which the house provided.

When Mills, somewhat in a state of hilarity, rode up to the house and called Hendricks out, Maxwell knew the voice, and as he had not long before had a slight difficulty with Mills while both were partially intoxicated, he deemed it prudent to keep quiet and not allow Mills to know of his presence. Maxwell had a Winchester rifle, and he feared that should Mills become aware of his being in the vicinity he might, in his drunken state, provoke him to use the weapon, resulting in serious trouble to himself. Now comes the statement in rebuttal to the harrowing story told on the stand by the prosecutrix and her husband, Jim Hendricks, showing the improbability of their sworn statements. Maxwell stated that, after Hendricks went from the house in obedience to Mills' command, all was quiet for a few moments until he heard Hendricks cry out: "For God's sake don't shoot!" At this the wife hastily left the house, going to her husband, who was talking with Mills, in plain sight from the house and less than fifty yards away. When the woman left, Maxwell arose, donned his apparel, and for a few moments watched the trio from the door. After a short parley', which was spoken in tones too low for hint to distinguish the words, he saw Mills start to ride off across the prairie and saw the husband and wife start back, walking toward the house. Maxwell's suspicions became aroused, and as Hendrix was a stranger to him he began to fear that some scheme to do him personal harm had been planned by the three, during the short conversation he had but partially overheard, and fearing that Mills' riding away was only a pretext to deceive him, and that if he returned to his bed in the house Mills might come later and attack him in his sleep, decided to quit the vicinity, and so left the house, disappearing just before Hendricks and his wife returned to it.

The second trial came on in March, 1898, before Judge John H. Rogers, who had been appointed to the bench after Judge Parker's death. After a hard fought battle, of three days' duration, the case was given to the jury, and when two-days had been consumed in deliberation, it was reported that no agreement could be reached, there being six for acquittal, and six for conviction. The jury was therefore discharged and the case remanded for trial at the following June term of court.

When the time arrived the government was not ready for trial. Mr. Reed had secured a witness who was ready to testify that he had seen Hendricks and his wife in a "Prairie schooner," removing from their recent habitation and that they told him they were going to their former haunts in Southwest Missouri, as they feared to go on the stand and repeat their former testimony. Mr. Reed was therefore not surprised when the prosecution entered a continuance to the October term of court. In due time the day for the trial came and both sides reported ready. Hendricks and his wife were on hand to repeat the old story (with some unfortunate and very evident variations), pocket their fees and return to Missouri, unmindful of the human life they were attempting to swear away,

Mr. Reed was primed for defense and stood ready to meet whatever obstacle might be thrown in his way. He had never lost a case of this kind and he told his friends, some of whom feared the outcome, that he was going to save Mills' life at this term of court. Since the first trial, Mills had been paid a small sum of money, as his portion of the fund paid by the government for the "Cherokee Strip," and he had given his attorney $150; all but about ten dollars of this, Mr. Reed had expended in securing the reversal of the former verdict by the Supreme Court, yet he appeared as anxious to win as if he had been guaranteed a large fee.

The trial opened. The prosecution was conducted by District Attorney, J. K. Barnes and his assistant, F. A. You-mans. They made a vigorous fight and were as vigorously combated by the defense; the trial lasted nearly a week. Mr. Reed was handicapped, by reason of Judge Rogers ruling out certain testimony that had been allowed by

Judge Parker; particularly was this true, of testimony regarding the profits in the case Hendricks had spoken of, as shown at the first trial.

The testimony for both sides was finished on Friday afternoon, October 21, and the argument by counsel closed at 5:15 o'clock. Judge Rogers then charged the jury, occupying half an hour.' When the jury filed into court at the opening hour, the next morning, they announced ready to report, and their verdict of acquittal was promptly given, and Jim Mills, the last longtime prisoner at the old jail, walked forth a free man.

The Fort Smith News Record of Sunday morning, October 23, reported the trial in a column article, one paragraph of which was as follows:

"With the acquittal by the jury of James Mills, the Cherokee, charged with the crime of criminal assault, there passes away the last of the famous Indian Territory cases handed down' by the death of Judge Parker to his successor, Judge Rogers. * * * The third trial of this famous case, which has just been completed, was the most viciously fought of the three. Mr. Reed depended very little upon the witnesses for defense. He assaulted the government witnesses in cross examination, and to the surprise of many, wholly destroyed positions which were thought to be impregnable. In his address to the jury, Mr. Reed was concise, logical, keeping the minds of the jury fixed upon the discrepancies in the testimony for the prosecution. He tore down what the government had built up, and the lengthened faces of the jurors betokened how true to the mark Reed's logic and argument had been fired. His whole effort was a combination of facts, logically presented and clothed in rich word raiment."

JUDGE PARKER ON SELF-DEFENSE

THE DAVENPORT CASE

Perhaps the most frequent plea of the murderer before the bar, when the evidence is so strong as to admit of no possibility of its denial on an absolute plea of not guilty, is that of self-defense, the defendant setting up the claim that the killing was done under such circumstances as to be justifiable under the great common law that is recognized everywhere as the first of nature, that of the protection and I preservation of self. That this recognition is often abused and that many guilty men have escaped punishment upon a craftily sustained plea, claiming justification on the ground stated, there can be no doubt, nor of the further fact that many times has the plea been allowed to stand practically unchallenged when a more minute adherence to the real intent of the law of self-defense by the judge and jury would have resulted in conviction instead of acquittal.

Upon the conditions governing what constitutes self-defense, Judge Parker took what was considered by many as a strong position and he was reversed by the Supreme Court of the United States in several instances on account of his charge to the jury in cases where murder was charged and in which self-defense was the principal claim alleged by the respondent. There were some, however, broad enough to understand that the cloak of a Supreme Judge but covers mortal clay, who maintained that there were sinister and hidden motives in many of the reversals of verdicts given from Judge Parker's court, and who believed that as between the verdict and the opinion reversing it there was more logic in the former. However that may be a history of the court where Judge Parker presided for near a quarter of a century would be incomplete without an abstract from one of his memorable charges to the petit jury, on the law of self-defense, since it was one of his strongest points, and a special feature of the court and the man.

The extract here given is taken from the charge delivered by Judge Parker, June 3, 1895, in the celebrated Davenport case, wherein James Davenport was charged with the murder of William Goforth, in the Cherokee Nation.

STORY OF THE CRIME

Davenport was a fine looking white man, a good lawyer, and previous to his killing of Goforth had been considered a good citizen. His crime was the result, not of a naturally bad disposition, but of a fiery and unmanageable temper, the monster that has led so many young men into serious difficulty. Davenport had many friends in Fort Smith. He had married a handsome Cherokee girl, a member of the Ross family; they resided near Vinita, in the Cherokee Nation. William Goforth, his victim, was living on land leased from Davenport, and on the day of the killing, the latter had driven to the house occupied by the former to consult about a business matter relating-to the land in question. A dispute arose and the lie was passed, at which Davenport drew his pistol and fired, but without inflicting injury. Goforth sprang at him as he fired and Davenport shot again, missing his mark a second time. Goforth then grasped the weapon and in the struggle that ensued, Davenport secured the pistol and struck Goforth with it, knocking him down and, as the latter lay on his side making an effort to rise, he received the fatal shot.

Davenport was indicted for murder by the Federal grand jury at Fort Smith. His attorneys were George B. Dennison, of Muscogee (a former law partner of Davenport), Major G. W. Bruce, of Conway, Arkansas, and Thomas H. Barnes, of Fort Smith. At the trial his dark haired wife sat at his side, but, with remarkable stoicism, she retained complete composure, exhibiting no signs of the conflict which was raging in her breast. The defense claimed that Davenport believed he was acting in self-defense; that Goforth, as he grappled with Davenport, placed his right hand to his hip-pocket, as if to draw a weapon, placing the defendant's life in danger. It was also claimed that at the time of the struggle, a man named Miller stood behind Goforth with a hatchet, intending to assist Goforth to perform some great bodily injury upon the defendant.

The jury, on due deliberation, returned a verdict of manslaughter and Davenport was sentenced to seven years imprisonment at Albany, New York. His attorneys took a writ of error to the Supreme Court, a new trial was granted and on October 16, 1897, he was acquitted.

THE CHARGE

In charging the jury empaneled at the first trial, Judge Parker spoke, without prepared notes, from twenty minutes before 2 o'clock p. m., closing at five minutes past four, occupying two hours and twenty-five minutes. As usual, he spoke very rapidly, and the stenographer's report made fifty-five pages of closely typewritten matter. Judge Parker devoted considerable time to the questions, "willful killing," "malice aforethought," "premeditation" and "manslaughter," and after debating upon the case under consideration as applied to these propositions, took up the consideration of "The Law of Self-defense:"

"Now, it is claimed by the defendant in this case that what he did he had right to do, that he acted in the defensive and not in the aggressive, that he had a right to kill William Goforth. If he had that right of course he must get it under the law, for none of us have any rights outside the law. * * * If this right of self-defense existed in this case for the defendant he has" it from the law, and we must know whether he has it or not; by the only means at hand, the application of the facts relating to the case in the light of the evidence presented to us. If the right does not exist, then there is crime, and it falls under the head of one of the other of the definitions I have given you.

"Now, there are two propositions that make up this law regarding self-defense. There are many subordinate ones which enter into them. * * * The law says that if at the time the person was slain there was a certain condition existing, and if was one that could not be avoided except by the other doing what he did, he had a right to do as he did. We are to note the character of that condition. * * * The jaw says that if a man who is in the lawful pursuit of his business is attacked by another—in a violent way—'under such circumstances which denote an intention to take away his life, or to do him some serious bodily harm, he may lawfully kill his assailant, *provided he use all the means in his power otherwise* to save his life or prevent the intended harm, such as retreating as far as he can ox disabling his adversary without killing him, if it be in his power.' You see the duties that rest upon him. All the time that he is seeking to protect this great right that belongs to him, there is never a moment when this duty leaves him. The duty of using less violence than that which produces death, the duty of disabling his adversary if it be in his power, without killing him, having due regard to his own safety, the duty of getting out of the way of the deadly danger, if he can do so with due regard to his own safety. Why is that duty? In the first place, because if he can save a human life his duty to society calls him to do so. In the second place, his duty to himself calls upon him to exercise caution and care because if he recklessly engages in a deadly conflict when he could avoid it or otherwise protect himself, he may be slain, he may be the one to fall a victim. The duty to himself, his self-interests, the protection of his own life, compels him to avoid a resort to this dernier remedy if he can safely do so.

"But more than this must exist, as this law tells you. In the first place, under this law, at the time the defendant slew William Goforth, he must have been doing what he had a right to do; he must have been in the lawful pursuit of his business, and when he was so situated was attacked by Goforth in such a way as to denote a purpose by Goforth to take away his life or do him some enormous bodily harm. * * *

Now, the nature of the resistance must have regard to the nature of the offense about to be committed. If one is attempting to commit an ordinary assault or battery upon me, or attack me because I cut down his timber as a trespasser merely, I might justify beating him so as to make him desist, yet if I make use of a deadly weapon and slay him I will not stand justified in the eyes of the law. ' You are to see whether at the time of the killing the deceased had the means at hand to execute a deadly purpose upon the defendant, or whether he, at that time, was actually engaged in the purpose of executing that deadly purpose, or about to do it, and then, whether or not, under the circumstances, the defendant could have avoided that condition otherwise than by slaying him, or whether he could have avoided it by the exercise of less violence than he exercised, and in that way have paralyzed or destroyed the danger. Now, that is the first proposition. It is the one which contemplates a state of real danger or actual danger, or deadly danger, or danger of great violence to the person, that might result in maiming or in the taking of life. That is the kind of danger it is required to be. Under this proposition it must be actual. It must be real. It must be then and there impending and about to fall, so near thereto as that the defendant could not avoid it. If it was danger that might come in the future, and the defend ant could avoid it, he must do so. It contemplates a state of danger existing at the time, because this law is called the law of necessity. It is a law that is in the hands of the citizen from the necessity of the case. If that necessity does not exist, then the law is not available to him.

"But there is another proposition that is found in this law which is called the law of apparent danger. It is sometimes grossly misconceived; it is sometimes misapplied. It is sometimes believed by the jury to be a principle of law which says that if a man thought he had a right to kill under the circumstances, he could kill. If that were the law no provision of the law on the face of this earth would be more dangerous to innocent life. Such a provision of law would be more dangerous than the deadly Winchester or the death-dealing revolver in the hands of an angry, vicious man. A principle of that kind in the minds of the reckless, the wanton and the wicked, would destroy all the power of the law in this land for the protection of human life, because if you could ever find a man who would say that he did not think that he had a right to kill when he was arrested for that killing, and upon trial for it, it would be something unheard of, it would be something beyond conception, something that could not take place, something that never would take place. Hence you see the very absurdity of a proposition of that kind when you come to contemplate that the highest and the only purpose of the law is protection, protection of innocent life, protection of all the rights that belong to the citizen under circumstances where the citizen has not forfeited the rights by his misconduct. Such a law would mean a destruction of all rights, especially the right of life. There is no such provision of law. The conception in the mind of the man alone cannot determine the state of case that would give him the right to slay. There must be in existence such facts as would give a reasonable man, situated as he was, the right to believe that there was deadly danger to him, or that there was danger of great violence being inflicted on his person. And that reasonable man's conception of that state of case must grow out of some overt act of violence or apparent violence being done by the person who was slain, at the time he was slain, because we are unable to draw an inference as to what was the condition unless we can see it shadowed forth by external acts, overt acts, to know whether or not the person had the ground for an honest conception of that condition. We must look at the facts upon which he acted, and judge of that state of case for ourselves, and make our own conclusion upon this state of facts. Now, what must be these facts? I read you the rule, and then I will read you the illustration of it, which, to my mind, clearly and emphatically, and in the most satisfactory way, tells what is meant by this law of apparent danger, and what must exist before it can be invoked. Not a bare conception of danger in the mind of slayer, not a bare conception that he, under the circumstances, must take human life, but there must be something 'in the nature of an attack,' says the law. Let me read it to you:

"'When, from the nature of the attack, there is reasonable ground to believe that there is a design to destroy life, or commit any felony upon the person, the killing of the assailant will be excusable homicide, although it should appear afterwards that felony was intended.'

"Now, let us read that again and then take the case and illustrate it: 'When, from the nature of the attack—' that Goforth, in this case, was doing some act at the time he was slain which was apparently of a character that would result in the death of the defendant, there would then be reasonable grounds to believe that Goforth had a design upon his person that might result in his death, or in maiming him. You are to take these facts to see whether he had reasonable grounds for such a belief, or whether his assertion at this time when he is upon trial for that act is a mere pretense to shield him from the consequences of the act. You are the final arbiters in passing upon the question as to whether at the time of the killing there was that in existence that did give him the right to kill, that gave him the right to slay Goforth. Now, let us take the illustration, reading from the case of Evans vs. The State, a case passed upon by the Supreme Court of Mississippi; the Chief Justice, in passing upon this question, says:

"'To shoot down another on sight, and who at the time is making no hostile demonstration, dangerous to life and limb, and especially if not prepared and armed so to do, is in law— murder. It is murder because the law tolerates no justification and accepts no excuse for the destruction of human life on the plea of self-defense, except the death of the adversary was necessary, or apparently so, to save his own life or his person from great bodily injury and there shall be imminent danger of such design being accomplished.' The danger to life or great personal injury must be imminent, present at the time of the killing, really or apparently, and so urgent that there is no reasonable mode of escape except to take life. When we use the term 'apparent,' 'apparent danger,' we mean such overt, actual demonstration by conducts and acts of a design to take life, or do some great personal injury, as would make the killing apparently necessary to self-preservation.

"Now comes the illustration:

"'As if A, who had threatened the life of B, presented a gun at him in shooting posture, and within range, B might well anticipate the fire, and if he should kill A he would be justified, although it should turn out afterwards that the gun was not loaded and it was only intended to frighten him.'

"There was an act done which was apparently dangerous to life in execution of a threat. This serves to illustrate what is meant by apparent danger. Now, suppose he had not drawn any gun; that he had no gun and could not therefore use a gun. He had no deadly weapon, and he therefore could not use any. Then the state of case does not exist and cannot, under the law which creates a conception of apparent danger, because, as you have been, told again and again. by is law, there must be a reasonable conclusion formed from the nature of the attack; the attack must be of a character to give the person who is shot down the present opportunity to slay the man who shoots him, and he who thus shoots under such circumstances can safely act upon appearances, provided there is that in existence which creates a state of case that would lead a reasonable man to believe there was deadly danger; not that the man flung epithets or words of denunciation or abuse at the defendant, because that (creates no state of apparent danger; it does not create a state of case where it could be said that a person acted upon bare fear even, but it must be a state of case growing out of that which is an attack, or apparent attack, made by Goforth at the time, and an attack, too, not to inflict slight injury, but an attack where there is a purpose to inflict deadly violence or to create a state of deadly fear to the defendant, and that he was then and there, really or apparently, engaged in the execution of it, and that the defendant could not get out of the way of it by the exercise of reasonable prudence and reasonable care on his part having due regard for his own safety, nor could he turn it aside by executing an act of less violence in its character upon Goforth. If either of these propositions I have named exist, he had no right to slay, he had no right to kill Goforth. And you are to go to this evidence in the case; you are to see just what part of it is true as reflecting the true condition that existed at the time of the killing, and you are to see whether either of these conditions did exist.

"There are certain things that deprive a man of this right of self-defense, notwithstanding his adversary may be really or apparently doing that which, had he not done the thing that which deprives him of the right, would give him the right to slay. If he is deprived of the right of self-defense by his own wrongful conduct, by his own wrongful actions, he cannot invoke it, no matter what the conduct of the other may be.

"Now, what are these things, the commission of which* by us, deprive us of the right of self-defense, in slaying or doing great bodily harm, in the case of a deadly or apparently deadly attack? I am going to enumerate them to you briefly: A man commences an assault or battery upon another. It is important in this case to see who it was that commenced the assault. If these two men had words and one flung words at the other, words of denunciation, words of abuse, that did not give either the right to assault the other, even by the commission of a simple assault; and if because of the use of those words before Goforth attempted any violent demonstration the defendant committed an assault upon him, deadly or otherwise, and during the affray that ensued the defendant drew his weapon, or fired it, having it already drawn, and killed Goforth with it, the defendant is deprived of the right of self-defense under the circumstances, no matter what Goforth was doing. The defendant is deprived of that right because he would have no right to commence such an attack as that under the circumstances. Again:

"Attacking another with a deadly weapon.'

"This really would embrace the proposition I have already given you, because if he struck him with his pistol, and if it be true that Goforth made a movement towards him for the purpose of preventing him from using the pistol upon him, when he had drawn the pistol when the lie passed between them, and he struck him on the head with it, that would be a deadly assault; that would be the use of a deadly weapon in such a way as to jeopardize life, and that would be a deadly assault upon him, if it was under the circumstances I have enumerated, and it would be a case where he was wrongfully making an assault and he would not have the right to stand upon the defensive, because under such circumstances from that time Goforth would have the right to stand upon the defensive.

"'Going to the place where the person (afterwards slain) is, with a deadly weapon for the purpose of provoking a difficulty with the intent of having an affray,'

"If a man does that he does a wrong, because he has no right to hunt up an adversary for the purpose of slaying him. He can arm himself, he can go about his business, he can carry arms (carrying arms in this case by the defendant was in violation of the law of the Cherokee Nation, but that fact is of no importance in this case), but if it is apparent from the fact that he armed himself to have a deadly conflict with the deceased, that he hunted him up for that purpose, he is deprived of the right of self-defense, no matter what Goforth may have done.

Using provoking language or resorting to other device in order to get another to commence an assault so as to have a pretext for taking his life.

"That is the only kind of a case where the use of words are of importance as effecting the case. If a man uses them to provoke another so far that he will make a violent demonstration, and when he is making that demonstration he shoots him, he is deprived of the right of self-defense because he used the words for that purpose."

After devoting considerable time to various propositions concerning "threats," "the crime of manslaughter," "the credibility of witnesses," "impeachment," "reasonable doubt," and as to what is meant by the term "reasonable doubt," Judge Parker spoke briefly upon certain propositions of law offered by the defendant, and after reviewing the case, as related to Goforth and the defendant, he concluded with:

"I am now about to submit this case to your hands. I hope you will have strength of character with intelligence and ability to see, first, what the law is in this case that is applicable to the truth of it, and when you have determined that you will pronounce your findings without fear, without favor and without affection. There is one thing the law contemplates, and that is, that all men stand upon the same plane before it. If this defendant has committed a crime, he must answer for it as all other men must answer for it by that law. If he has not committed any crime he is entitled to the law's protection; he stands before us just like any other citizen, entitled to the same rights, and no more; he is on the same plane with us, entitled to a full, fair and impartial trial. If the consequences of that trial go against him, it is his misfortune. If they go in his favor, that is a vindication of the late equally with the case where guilt may be found by the jury. William Goforth, stranger though he may have been in that country, is as much entitled to the full power of this protecting agency called the law as you are, or I. He stands in this court today with his memory to be vindicated if he was in the right, and with the power of the law to be vindicated if his life was stolen from him by crime. The law treats all persons as equals, and when it puts in your hands the solemn duty of enforcing its provisions it says to you, in a voice that cannot be mistaken, that you must heed its mandate, you must do your duty as citizens, as men, as jurors, vindicating its power, its dignity and its supremacy.

"Gentlemen, you will take the case. You will calmly, deliberately and faithfully, as becomes honest men, consider the evidence, search for the truth, find what it is, though it may require diligence, great labor, great pains and great intelligence upon your part. Apply justly and fairly these rules of law given you to enable you to search for the truth, and when you have found it, apply that principal of the law which fits the case and which is, therefore, applicable to it.

"You will retire to make up your verdict."

THE CHEROKEE PAYMENT

One of the most noteworthy events in the ever changing history of the Five Civilized Tribes of Indians in the Indian Territory, perhaps the most important of any in the history of the Cherokee Nation, was the distribution, per capita, among the members of the Cherokee tribe, in the summer of 1894, of $6,640,000, known as the "Strip Money."

This payment was the result of an Act of Congress, approved March 3, 1893 (U. S. St. at L., 52d Cong., Sess. I1, vol. 27, chap. 207, p. 640, § 10), appropriating $8,300,000 (to be drawn by the Secretary of the Interior and paid out as here designated), "and so much in addition as may be necessary to pay the Cherokee Indians for all right, title, interest and claims which the said nation of Indians may have in and to certain lands described and specified in an agreement concluded between David H. Jerome, Alfred M. Wilson and Warren G. Sayre, duly appointed commissioners on the part of the United States, and Elias C. Boudinot, Joseph C. Scales, George Downing, Roach Young, Thomas Smith, William Triplet and Joseph Smallwood, duly appointed commissioners on the part of the Cherokee Indians in the Indian Territory, on December 19, 1890, bounded on the west by the one hundredth degree of west longitude; on the north by the State of Kansas; on the east by the ninety-sixth degree of west longitude, and on the south by the Creek Nation, the Territory of Oklahoma and the Cheyenne and Arapahoe reservation, created and defined by Executive order dated August 10, 1869; said lands being commonly known as the 'Cherokee Outlet.' Said agreement is hereby ratified."

The agreement above noted was ratified by the Cherokee Nation by a written agreement dated May 17, 1893, and was the act closing the gigantic deal by which the "Cherokee Strip" was sold by the Cherokee Indian Tribe to the United States.

On August 19, 1893, the President issued a proclamation declaring the "Strip open to settlers at I J o clock noon on Saturday, September 16, 1893.

It is not my purpose here to describe the scenes enacted on that memorable Saturday, morning and afternoon. when thousands of men—and *women*—whose feet for years had itched to tread the "public domain" on whose broad acres their covetous eyes had lingered greedily, longing, waiting for the time when the 'Cherokee Strip" should be opened to actual settlers, which actual settlers could and then would be citizens, not aliens nor "intruders" in the land in which rested their home:—were finally permitted to "settle the wilderness in a day;" neither will I describe at length the almost unbroken line of humanity that extended for miles along the boundaries of the "Strip," within the allotted space 106 feet wide all along the lines separating the coveted holdings from States, territories and reservations, each and every person in the motley throng "with best foot forward," each eager to gain even the slightest advantage over his or her neighbor in the grand rush for a homestead or a town lot, in many cases long ago selected, and, as it seemed to some of them, the last earthly chance to secure a spot of ground in fee simple, a home. Grizzled veterans of the plains stood shoulder to shoulder with blooming young tender feet" from Eastern cities; gray haired widows and charming and energetic young women, more energetic than wise, perhaps, with a determined pressure of the lips that proved how deeply in earnest they were, crowded for frontage against horny-handed sons of the rural districts, old and young, while hard by were white canopied wagons, "prairie schooners" and vehicles of every description loaded with household utensils and farming implements, the tow-headed youngsters, peeping from between and beneath the covers, betokening families, large and small; a heterogeneous mass of humanity of all kinds and conditions, likewise of beasts of burden and draft, men, women and children, mounted and on foot, armed and unarmed, all waiting for the signal that should grant them, at last, the right to stake a spot of God's green earth they could call their own. Cities sprang up in a day, and where was then but a raw prairie as bare as in the day of antiquity, today stand flourishing towns and cities; broad acres fenced and in a high state of cultivation cover the plains where, but a few years ago the herds of the syndicate stockmen with the attendant boisterous cowboys, held full control. The object of this chapter is to relate some of the scenes attending the payment by "Uncle Sam" to the Indians of the greater portion of the indebtedness incurred in purchasing this magnificent tract for use of his children.

On Wednesday, May 30, 1894, Treasurer E. E. Starr, the accredited paymaster for the Cherokee government, passed through Fort Smith, having in his possession $1,000,000 in coin and paper money, with which to commence the payment to the individual members of the Cherokee tribe of their shares of the great amount about to be distributed. He proceeded to Fort Gibson with a strong guard, and thence to Tahlequah, where on Monday, June 4, the distribution commenced. Captain Cochrane, with a guard of fifty picked men, well-armed, were stationed about the treasurer's office to keep perfect order and protect the treasurer's funds against the crowds of sharpers and tricksters who had gathered and who mingled with the beneficiaries, intent on gathering in a portion of the money being paid out, by some means or other, and by unfair means, where others failed. During the previous week, Chief Harris, of the Cherokee tribe, had addressed the following letter to his people:

TO THE CHEROKEE PEOPLE

"I deem it advisable, under existing circumstances, to call your attention to the attendant dangers and the melancholy aspect of the present per capita distribution now going on in your midst; and to the necessary caution, on your part, in your intercourse and dealings with the hundreds of adventurers, sharps and tricksters now in the country for dishonorable purposes. Never before in the history of our nation have there been such inducements for the assembling of bad characters, intent upon any manner of gain. I would therefore warn you against all such persons on account of the troubles they may get you into and the bad reputation they will give our nation. The good Lord knows that we have to answer for enough bad characters in our own country, under ordinary circumstances, regardless of the flood that is pouring in from the adjacent states. Not only for their presence with us are we blamed, but for the crimes they commit, and by reason of them and their crimes we are threatened with political extinction and subject to the tender mercies of those who are encompassing our ruin.

"I would also warn you against indulgence in any kind of intoxicating drinks. The too free use of these has been the prime cause of all the bloodshed in our country, and of our moral and political unfitness for self-government, as alleged against us.

"The sum of money, to be distributed among you, is the largest at any time in the history of our nation, and may be the last. Therefore in all earnestness and desire for your future welfare, permit me to advise you to make best of it by putting your means into good farms; your own interest and that of your families demand this of you.

"It is said, the history of a nation is the history of its wars, but less of war and more of the cession of lands to the United States is ours, until by actual count the number of acres is less than six millions. The money now being distributed is for the sale of lands, and presents the melancholy fact that they are the last we have to part with unless it be our homes The limit has been reached at last, as we have now barely enough of land for the occupancy or the need of our own people.

"The past should be no concern of ours now. In the future, whatever may be our present condition, is where lie the duties we owe ourselves and people. Let us begin in the present in their performance, not forgetting at any time that much of our happiness and prosperity depends upon ourselves."

Your fellow citizen,

C. J. Harris,

Principal Chief.

From the time of the ratification of the agreement, selling the "Strip" to the United States, after it was known that millions in cash were sooner or later certain to be paid out to the Indian Citizens of the Cherokee Nation, far sighted merchants, agents and all classes of men having goods to sell, from thread and calico to household utensils, furniture and agricultural implements, had "worked" the Cherokee Nation, assiduously, urging the Indians to buy on credit or as it was termed, "on the strip," in anticipation of the money they would receive when the time of the "payment" should arrive. Thousands of dollars' worth of goods were thus disposed of on the credit plan, often at ruinous prices, and many homely habitations were graced with high grade musical instruments, sewing machines, etc., the salesmen depending entirely upon the honesty of the people and their promise to pay, whenever they should receive their "strip" money. Horses and cattle and all kinds of personal property were sold on time upon a similar basis, and with the advent of the treasurer with his millions came collectors by the score, even by the hundreds, armed with stacks of bills, ready to collect, each his quota, from the first money in sight. To the credit of the full blood

Indians, be it said, that of the merchants and others, who had "sold on the strip," scarce one failed to collect every dollar he had been promised.

In the first two days at Tahlequah, Treasurer Starr paid out over $300,000. The amount received by each individual Indian was $265.70 ($1,000,000 of the nearly $7,000,000 being reserved for general purposes), and it was paid in either gold, green backs or checks, as preferred. Hundred dollar bills were as common as silver dollars and many of those who drew their money, after paying their debts, to the ubiquitous collector, tucked the balance snugly away for future use.

An auction house, opened for the occasion, did a heavy business. Thousands of horses were sold during the week and the dealers found a ready market. Merry-go-rounds, with their wheezy automaton music, and dance halls in plenty were running twenty hours of the twenty-four. An opera troupe, too, and a circus, were on the scene and both played to crowded houses making money for their owner. Boarding houses and hotels, did a "land office" business, and notwithstanding the presence of the United States deputy marshals, there was much whiskey sold at fancy prices. Gamblers were on hand in large numbers and several heavy games of poker were indulged in, $1,500 and $2,000 "jack-pots" being frequent. "Chuck-a-luck" and other "skin" games were run openly and the manipulators secured a liberal share in the "strip" money. On the night of June 15, Dr. C. C. Savage was robbed of $225. Two men entered his room at a hotel and took the money from him by force, making their escape through a rear window.

During the second week, a woman played a shrewd trick on Treasurer Starr, securing $2,200, to which she had not the shadow of a claim and escaped without exciting suspicion. She had represented herself the mother of several children, whose names were on the rolls, and which, together with their ages, she gave correctly; later the real mother of the family put in an appearance and the amount was paid a second time.

Among the money makers present were a few usurers, responsible business men, who bought claims, discounting usually, $10.70 per share; those who thus disposed of their claims by private sale, at a loss of four per cent, did so that they might not be seen in possession of money by their creditors. The transactions were legitimate but much dissatisfaction was expressed by the army of collectors, who attempted to suppress the traffic, they finally succeeded in discouraging it to the extent of inducing the treasurer to pay the orders held by the usurers on the last day of the payment.

THE TRAGEDY

Two deaths occurred on Saturday, June 9, on the road to Fort Gibson. On schedule time the stage left Tahlequah for Fort Gibson, with seven passengers, driven by Bill Newsome, a deputy marshal, formerly a resident of Sebastian County, Arkansas. Levi Sanders, a young Cherokee Indian, very drunk, sat on the box by the driver. As the stage reached the Seminary reserve, about one and a half miles from the outskirts of

Tahlequah, Sanders drew a pistol and ordered Newsome to stop; the order was obeyed and the Indian next demanded of the passengers that they line themselves by the roadside and one of their number was compelled to search the pockets of his companions. A gold watch and $70 in money was secured and pocketed, when Sanders observed one of the passengers, Courtney S. Kenny, a young man from Decatur, Wise County, Texas, standing a little back of the others in the line and with an oath he placed the muzzle of his pistol against Kenny's back, shoving him forward, at the same time pulling the trigger, the bullet passing through the fleshy part of the body and making exit just above the heart, failing to cause death by a narrow margin. At the crack of the pistol the terror stricken passengers scattered and Sanders dashed into the bush and after proceeding a short distance he met Milo Willey, with whom he exchanged several shots, one of them cutting a hole in the side of Willey's hat. Taking possession of Willey's horse he mounted and rode rapidly toward Tahlequah and when near the city he met Felix Duncan and his mother, Mrs. Nancy Duncan, in a wagon. He ordered them to stop and at once fired, the bullet, supposed to have been intended for the son, striking the mother in the breast, killing her instantly. Duncan had a new Winchester in the wagon and seizing the weapon he returned the fire, killing Sanders' horse. The Indian sprang from the dead animal and attempted to escape but was brought down by the unerring rifle in the hands of Duncan, who continued to fire until five bullets were deposited in the body. Mrs. Duncan was a sister of Watt Starr, a judge in the Cherokee Nation, and an aunt of Henry Starr, the noted train robber; she was highly esteemed by a large circle of acquaintances among the best of the Cherokee citizens. This affair caused the people who were compelled to travel the road between Fort Gibson and Tahlequah to be very nervous while en route and the slightest rustle of the bushes was sufficient to cause the boldest passenger to turn pale with fright.

The horde of gamblers, with all manner of schemes to trap the unwary and lure dollars from their pockets, became so much in evidence during the first week of the payment that an order was issued by Chief Harris for the purpose of putting a stop to all kinds of gambling. Its effect was conjectural.

The payment at Tahlequah, for the Tahlequah and Going Snake Districts, finally closed on Saturday, June 16, and Treasurer Starr, heavily guarded, proceeded to Vinita and on June 20 he commenced distributing the funds due the citizens of the Delaware and Cooweescoowee Districts. Here, again, the scenes at Tahlequah were mainly repeated. Stores, merry-go-rounds, lemonade stands and other catch-penny devices paid into the city treasury $200 per day in licenses. Hotels, boarding houses and lunch stands had all the business they could accommodate. No games of chance of any character were allowed to run openly, all gambling being confined to private rooms. Horse races every afternoon at the fairgrounds drew large crowds, as did the circus and theatricals. Hectors and attorneys were on hand and fees for professional services long ago rendered were collected aggregating many thousands of dollars.

The payment at Vinita closed on Saturday, June 30, and on July 3, the Treasurer was on the ground at Clare more, and a good day's work performed. No money was paid out on July Fourth, the national holiday, but on the fifth it was resumed and continued during the week It was a lively six days for the little city, but the officers were equal to the emergency and no serious disturbances occurred.

At Fort Gibson the scenes previously enacted were repeated. The payment opened on Thursday, July 12 and closed a week later. The crowd here was larger than during any previous occasion. On July 20 a crowd numbering thousands Hocked to Webbers Falls and during Saturday and Sunday the town and surrounding forest were fairly alive with visitors, waiting for the distribution of funds, which commenced at nine o'clock on Monday morning, July 22. Good order generally prevailed, though there was some few cases of reckless shooting and several robberies reported. These were believed to be false claims, put forth by the alleged victims as a means of avoiding the payment of just debts. The payment at Webbers Falls continued four days and the Treasurer with his assistants and guards removed to Flint, forty miles from Webbers Falls, to be in readiness for the opening on Monday morning, July 30, the crowds following. At this place very little whiskey was sold. Several cases of pint and half pint flasks of the liquid were captured by the officers and destroyed and but few drunken men were seen. Senter Peyton's Comedy Company played to full houses during the stay of the paying officers.

On Monday morning, August 13, Treasurer Starr threw open the doors at Sequoyah Court House for the commencement of the payment to citizens of the district. For a week previous the people had been gathering and on the first day of the payment fully five thousand were present. And what a crowd it was! All kinds of business were represented; the hot tamale man and the Mexican chili vender cried their wares alongside the more pretentious dispensers of ham and eggs, fried chicken and—the great American dessert—the toothsome pie, while the lemonade and soda pop man regaled parched humanity fort ten cents or a nickel at the choice of the purchaser. Booths were everywhere; eating booths, lemonade and taffy candy booths, barber stalls in plenty, "hot catfish and ice cream" booths, musical instruments of every description, cheap jewelry' by the ton, dry goods and clothing booths, sleeping tents, where the weary could secure the use of a fairly good bed for twenty five cents; gambling tents, where those so inclined could play almost any kind of game that suited their fancy, and the ever present merry-go-round, which never failed to catch the young and old, the rich and the poor alike. Horse traders were in ample evidence and auction sales of horses every day met many sales. The camp was laid off regularly, in streets, and water wagons were continually passing up and down, selling water by the barrel. The best of order was maintained and everybody seemed in good spirits. Only a few hours each day were consumed in paying claims, the paying officers spending the rest of the time in the shade of the trees. In spite of the torrid heat the Peyton shows had crowded houses each night. Hundreds of Fort Smith people were present; without a murmur they made the eight mile ride over rocky roads, after

444

leaving the train at Muldrow, coming singly and in pairs, by dozens and in droves. Some were called there by business interests but more out of mere curiosity. The stifling heat failed to curb the interest of the sightseer and truly it was a sight of a lifetime. Notwithstanding the immense crowds, the payment at Sequoyah was the quietest of any, and was the only one where a robbery or hold up of some kind was not reported. The payment here closed on Saturday, August 18 and opened again on Wednesday, August 22, at Saline Court House, twenty miles east of Pryor Creek, off the Missouri, Kansas & Texas Railroad. This was the eighth and last of the Cherokee payments, and the crowds in attendance were as large if not larger than at any of the others. More drinking, too, was indulged in; Jamaica ginger and whiskey from Prohibition Kansas were to be had in any quantity desired, and there was more drunkenness, by far, than at any of the other places. More than half of the money distributed at this payment was paid out Tuesday, August 28, the last day, to those who held orders from persons whose claims they had purchased. From Saline Court House the Treasurer removed to Tahlequah, where he was stationed for a time, paying such as had failed to draw their money at the payments in their respective districts, numbering near 200 persons, and with the last penny paid, the last sale of Cherokee lands passed into history.

FIRST EXECUTION UNDER FEDERAL JURISDICTION

The first execution in the Indian Territory under the laws of the United States, occurred at Muscogee, on July 1, 1898, when Henry Whitefield and K. B. Brooks, two negroes, suffered the death penalty for murders committed in the Northern Judicial District of the Indian Territory, after the removal of the jurisdiction of the Indian Territory from the United States District and Circuit Courts for the Western District of Arkansas.

Henry Whitefield, alias Charles Perkins, one of the two negroes hanged at Muscogee, on the date named, was a native of Tennessee, and was said to be 55 years old. He was convicted under the name of Charles Perkins and that was the only name by which he was known to the officers until just before he was executed. When he first went to the Indian Territory, he worked for the Missouri. Kansas & Texas Railroad Company, and was known as Charles Jones; afterwards he located at Wagoner and assumed the name, Charles Perkins. Two days before the day set for the execution, he wrote to his brother at Pulaski, Tennessee, addressing him as William Whitefield, told him of his difficulty and his approaching dissolution and bade him good bye.

The crime for which Whitefield was hanged was committed in Wagoner, December 2, 1897. On that day he went to the home of Nancy Adkins (colored), who lived with her mother and employed her time as a laundress. Several persons were at the house, among them being George Miller. Perkins was infatuated with the young colored woman and he had frequently visited her, but something had occurred to ruffle their friendship and after a few minutes he began abusing her on account of whatever had come between them, and, at last, Miller interfered in behalf of the girl, telling Perkins his treatment of her was unjust, at which Perkins cursed Miller and left the house, crossed the street, then returned to the gate and called to the girl, who refused to go to him. Just then another man entered the house and told her she was wanted by Perkins; she arose, went to the door and told him to go away. He replied:

"I'll kill Miller before he leaves," then went a short distance and laid in ambush for several hours, and finally went away. A few hours later, as Miller was on his way home, he was halted by Perkins who said:

"Now I said I was going to kill you and I am going to do it."

Miller attempted to grapple with his assailant, who was reaching for a weapon, but the other was too quick; he shot Miller twice in the body, causing instant death. He immediately left the city but was soon afterwards captured by Deputy United States Marshal LeFlore, of the central judicial district, at Atoka, who took him to Muscogee, where he was tried April 2, 1898, before Judge John R. Thomas, convicted of murder and sentenced to be hanged. He was defended by attorney W. H. Twine.

K. B. Brooks, who was executed in company with Henry Whitefield, was a native of Clarkston, Texas; he was raised in Paris, of the same state, where his father and one sister resided at the time of his execution. His crime was as dastardly as was ever committed within the jurisdiction of any court. Left by the father of three little girls, as their sole protector he betrayed his trust and forced the eldest to disgrace and almost death; he might better have murdered the child.

Brooks was an employe of a white man named Coombs, at Hudson, in the Indian Territory. Coombs was the father of three motherless daughters, Lulu, aged 16 years, Cora, aged 11 years, Ida, a baby of five years. On the morning of October 28, 1897, Mr. Coombs started on a business trip to Coffeyville, Kansas, leaving his children at home. When bed-time came the little ones retired together in one room. Sometime during the night the negro entered the house and proceeded into the room where the children were sleeping. His coming aroused the eldest girl and she called to her sister, Cora, to light the lamp, at which Brooks fell on her bed and attempted to ravish her. She pushed him away and began to scream and was knocked unconscious by a club in the hands of the negro. At the first scream from her sister little Cora hastily scrambled from her bed and, catching up the baby, ran from the house and hid behind a tree. Seeing that his victim was unconscious and noting the absence of the other children, Brooks went on a search of them, fearing they would alarm the neighbors, but, failing to find them, he returned to the house, found that Lulu had recovered sufficiently to steal away, and he found her a few yards from the house in a half dazed condition; here he again raised his club and struck her on the front part of the head, breaking the club in three pieces and almost killing her. As she fell in a swoon the brute ravished the child, then fled, leaving his victim in a horrible state.

In the meantime little Cora had carried the baby sister to the home of the nearest neighbor, a mile and a half away, through the darkness, clad only in her little white nightgown, tearing her tender feet on the rough, frozen ground, and awakening Mr. Hicks and his family, acquainted them with the terrible facts. They hastened to the scene and found the poor girl back in the house, lying on her bed in a dreadful plight. A physician was called and an examination showed the child's condition to be precarious. The alarm was at once given, and on the next day a posse, composed of every man and boy in the vicinity, scoured the country for Brooks, and they would doubtless have made quick work of dealing justice had they found him.

After satisfying his mad passions, Brooks had gone to the home of Moore Gibson, about three miles distant, and, after borrowing a blanket, went to the barn and calmly slept till morning, then went to Gibson's house and ate breakfast; as he entered the dining room his host saw blood on one of his hands, and in reply to a question he said he had slapped Lulu Coombs' face. After breakfast he went to Lenapah and from there to Bartlesville and into the Osage Nation, intending to leave the country. He was followed by Deputy Marshal Ledbetter, who trailed him with all the tenacity of a blood hound for nearly a week, finally overtaking and arresting him.

A preliminary examination was held by United States Commissioner Jackson, who committed him to jail. Later he was indicted and was tried before Judge Thomas and found guilty of the crime of rape, April 28, 1898.

Brooks was defended by Koogler & Watkins, and like the attorney in the Perkins case, they did all in their power to save their client's neck, but the evidence was too clear, and the verdict was given within a few minutes after the jury retired.

Both the condemned men appeared to realize the awful fate awaiting them, especially during the last week, after the death-watch was put on, and the sounds of the carpenters outside constructing the scaffold, from which they were full)aware they would swing, at times unnerved them. They went to the gallows, however, denying their guilt, and Brooks talked for five minutes, protesting his innocence, and declaring that he was the victim of oppression in a land of strangers. The trap was sprung at 9:32 o'clock a. m.; the execution was witnessed by Marshal Bennett, Jailor Lubbes, Turnkey James Wilkerson (formerly of Fort Smith), Judge Barker (a guard, ex-judge of a Cherokee court), who sprung the trap, two colored preachers and five physicians.

After death, the bodies were placed in coffins and returned to the Colored Baptist Church in Muscogee, where funeral services were held, alter which interment was given in the colored cemetery near the city.

1896 Interview with Judge Parker, courtesy of the National Park Service

Ada Patterson was a female reporter for the St. Louis *Republic*, and was in Fort Smith to cover the end of the court's Indian Territory jurisdiction on September 1, 1896. This interview, done at the Parker Residence that day, provides some of the judge's most famous quotations.

It is important to note that the article contains some minor factual errors, most especially in regards to the men put to death on the gallows. Her numbers are incorrect, as well as many of the names of the condemned.

Judge Isaac C. Parker

—

AN INTERVIEW WITH THE DISTINGUISHED JURIST BY A ST. LOUIS CORRESPONDENT,

—

Who Believes the Indian Territory Has Lost Its Best Friend.

—

St. Louis Republic, 6th inst.

The scepter departed from a judicial Judah last Tuesday. With the relinquishment of Judge I.C. Parker's authority over the Indian Territory that torn and bleeding southland lost at once its best friend and its reputed foe.

Congress believed that it acted wisely when, on March 1, 1895, it passed a law providing that after September 1, 1896, the criminal jurisdiction of the United States Court at Fort Smith, Ark., over the Indian country should cease. It is a matter of grave doubt in many minds whether the national legislature did not make a grievous mistake in so doing. Multitudinous memorials and petitions representing that view were sent to congress during the last session, but the labor for the repeal of the law was lost, and the experiment of the administration of justice in the border country by local courts in under way. It was initiated in a portentous manner, the public celebration of the event in McAlester and other settlements of the so-called emancipated land.

"There be some talk of hangin' Judge Parker in effigy over that," said an irate Arkansan. "They'd better be careful or we'll go over and hang a few of them before breakfast." This man shared in the esteem in which the Judge, so much maligned and misunderstood abroad, is held in his home city.

He is the gentlest of men, this alleged sternest of judges. He is courtly of manner and kind of voice and face, the man who has passed the death sentence upon more criminals than has any other judge in the land. The features that have in them the horror of the Medusa to desperadoes are benevolent to all other human-kind.

THE MOST MISREPRESENTED OF MEN

"I am the most misunderstood and misrepresented of men," said the Judge on the day of the passing of his scepter. "Misrepresented because misunderstood. But not withstanding that, we are proud of the record of the court at Fort Smith. We believe we have checked a flood of crime. We believe, too, that it was suicidal to remove the protection of a strong court from the Indian Territory."

He was supported by pillows on a bed that has been one of pain to him for two months when he talked to me of this passing of his power that day. Even in his pitiable physical weakness it was evident that it was a magnificent constitution with which disease had grappled and upon which she is trying her dreaded tactics of slow "wearing out." Judge Parker's frame is that of a powerful man, one who has rejoiced in a superabundance of vigor, a vitality evidenced in health by sunny spirits and a laugh that is infectious. He has a great breadth of shoulders and a noble chest development. Eight weeks of suffering have not greatly reduced the color that contrasts with his snowy hair and beard makes more pronounced. His blue eyes still have much of the fire of health. It is in the strong, nervous hands that the ravages of illness are shown the most.

"I have not been sick for forty-five years," he told me, and said the physician had told him this visitation of weakness was the result of overwork. "Dropsy and an affection of the heart" is the way the good-natured town gossips describe it.

Judge Parker was born in Belmont county, Ohio, in 1838. In 1859 he came to Missouri and engaged in the practice of law in St. Joseph. The following year he was elected city attorney and in 1864 was chosen as prosecuting attorney of that district. He was president of the first Stephen A. Douglas club organized in this State, but at the opening of the war espoused Republican principles. He was elected a presidential elector in 1864 and assisted in casting the vote of the State for Lincoln. In 1868 he was made Judge of the Twelfth Judicial Circuit of Missouri and in 1870 was elected to congress from the St. Joseph District. He was re-elected to that office in 1872 and during his second term was appointed a member of the Committee on Territories, of which James A. Garfield was chairman. This committee graduated a President of the United States; a Vice-President, William Wheeler; a Postmaster-General, Hale of Maine, who declined that appointment under Grant; Mr. Tyner, who accepted that appointment, and a United States Judge, the man who has made himself loved by the law-abiding and hated by the law-breaking class by his valiant stand for law and order in the ruffian-infested Territory. In 1875 Judge Parker was appointed Chief Justice of Utah and it is probable that his forceful personality would have made a deep impression upon the peculiar passing conditions of the territory beyond the Rockies. But two weeks afterwards President Grant withdrew this appointment and, and at the instance of Senators Dorsey and Clayton, ended the fierce Brooks-Baxter war that made the country side along Arkansas the abode of terror by establishing the strange precedent of appointing a Judge from another State, and his appointee, Kinman of Massachusetts, failing of confirmation by the senate, choosing Judge Parker for that difficult post. It was in May. 1875, that he assumed charge of the court that had just been removed from Van Buren to Fort Smith. The man who wielded the chief judicial power of Western Arkansas and the region extending to Colorado was the youngest judge on the bench.

"I did not expect to stay here more than a year or two when I came," said the Judge. "The President had said to me, 'Stay a year or so and get things started,' but I am still here, as you see."

ABOLISH CAPITAL PUNISHMENT—PROVIDED

"Yes, and it was the greatest mistake of your life," said Mrs. Parker, a dark-eyed, gray-haired matron, still handsome, if no longer young. She leaned above the pillows and waved a palm leaf fan. "It has broken you down," she said to him tenderly, and then to me, "He is only fifty-eight, but he looks like a very old man."

"No, Mary, not a mistake, for we have been enabled to arrest the floodtide of crime here, as we would not have had an opportunity to do elsewhere," said the Judge.

"Under ordinary circumstances I don't believe in capital punishment," said Mrs. Parker, sinking into the big rocking chair and ceasing her loving labor of wielding the fan while she adjusted the rebellious folds of her pretty white wrapper. "The first novel I ever read was Eugene Aram, and that convinced me that as a rule capital punishment is wrong, but my husband has had to deal with extra-ordinary cases and conditions."

Judge Parker turned restively upon his pillows and made a remarkable statement for one who had condemned well-nigh two hundred men to the gallows.

"I favor the abolition of capital punishment, too," and smilingly noting the effect of this surprisingly noting the effect of this surprising statement upon his listeners he continued, "provided, (there was remarkable stress upon the word provided) that there is a certainty of punishment, whatever that punishment may be. In the uncertainty of punishment following crime lies the weakness of our 'halting crime.'"

He grew wonderfully earnest as he talked, and one could see that the ruling passion of his life held sway. He sat erect, spurning the pillows upon which he had lately leaned. His color grew deeper and his kind, blue eyes grew darker and sterner.

THE BENCH INDIFFERENT AND CARELESS

"The trouble is with the bench," he said, "and behind it a maudlin sentimentality that forgets and condones a crime upon which the blood stains have dried. The bench is indifferent and careless. The avarice, which is the curse of this age, has so poisoned the people that civil law for the protection of property concerns it more than the criminal law which protects life. 'Which is of greater value, your house or your life!'

451

asks the bench, and the people by their attitude in specific instances answers: 'My house.' Small wonder that the bench comes to take the same view and adjudges accordingly.

"The fault does not lie with juries. The persons who constitute them are usually honest men. We have had as fine juries at Fort Smith as could be found in the land. They have never failed me. Juried are willing to do their duty, but they must be led. They must know that the judge wants the enforcement of the law.

I NEVER HUNG A MAN

"People have said to me 'You are the judge who has hung so many men,' and I always answer: 'It is not I who has hung them. I never hung a man. It is the law.'

"The good ladies who carry flowers and jellies to criminals mean well. There is no doubt of that. But what mistaken goodness! Back of the sentimentality are the motives of sincere pity and charity, sadly misdirected. They see the convict alone, perhaps chained in his cell. They forget the crime he perpetrated and the family he made husbandless and fatherless by his assassin work."

The vehemence of his speech had exhausted the Judge. He sank back upon his pillows and closed his eyes.

A sweet-faced old lady came in at that moment. "My daughter, Susie, sent you these," she said, laying some yellow blossoms on the table, where stood a bowl of red and white roses and sweet geranium leaves and about which were massed other bright-hued flowers, all the gifts of loving hands and hearts. "Bless the child!" said the Judge, with the smile that made his face as pleasing as a lovely woman's. The visitor chatted a moment about the weather, deplored the fact that there had been no rain since May 17 and that the roses were blighted somewhat, water them as they might, was glad to see that the Judge was improving and hurried away.

Judge Parker sat up again, but this time he did not disdain the friendly support of the pillows.

"Crime is fearfully upon the increase," he said. "Do you know that in the past five years 43,900 persons, more than there are in the regular army, have been murdered in this country? Parallel with these have been 723 legal executions and 1,118 lynchings. Think of an average of 7,317 murders a year. Last year, 10,500 persons were killed. That is at the rate of 875 a month, while five years ago there were but 4,200. There is a doubling of the murder rate in five years."

These were appalling statements, but the Judge repeated them with the familiarity with which he would greet an acquaintance.

"This fearful condition does not exist because laws are defective. We have the most magnificent legal system in the world. The bench is not alive to its responsibilities. Courts of justice look to the shadow in the shape of technicalities instead of the substance in the form of crime. Everyone knows, too, that corrupt methods are used to defeat the administration of law.

"This is d dangerous condition. The government cannot survive a demoralized people, swayed and dominated by the man of crime. We must have a remedy. Thinking persons are realizing this, but they are wrongfully looking toward the abolition of the jury system as a relief from these evils. I believe this is wrong. Not a jot or tittle of the dignity of the right of trial by jury should be abated. I told you that juries should be led. They have a right to expect that, and if guided they will render that justice that is the greatest pillar of society.

WOULD REMODEL APPELLATE COURTS

"I told you I had been misrepresented. The press has put me in the attitude of opposing the courts of appeals. I would remodel them, but I would not dream of destroying them. I would like to see organized in the States and in the nation courts of criminal appeals, made up of judges learned in criminal law and desirous of its speedy enforcement. To these courts I would like to see sent full records of the trials and would have the case passed upon according to its merits as soon as possible. I would have brushed aside all technicalities that do not affect the guilt or innocence of the accused. I would that the law would provide against the reversal of cases unless innocence was manifest. The establishment of such courts would restore the public confidence in the law and its administrators. The party convicted should of course have the right of having his case reviewed upon writ of error, but it should be passed upon according to its merits."

Have you noticed what a metamorphosis a man undergoes when he is talking of that which has a more absorbing interest than anything else in life, more especially if this be an idea? He may talk with a modicum of enthusiasm about his wife, his family or his sweetheart, but they are, in a way, known quantities, and are in reserve, but when he is wedded to that elusive, intangible thing, an idea, and to that extent most men are bigamists, how he glows and flashes and beams with fervor! When he talks of that sacred something he is like one inspired, and, if scoffers do pronounce that something a hobby or a hallucination, he is none the less touched by the divine fire of eloquence when he talks of it. Fortunate is the man whose inspirer of his deepest interest is a dignified aim. Such a man is Judge Parker, and when he had outlined this plan of his one could but be in a glow of admiration for the man and the measure.

"You are two [sic] tired to talk more now, Mr. Parker," said his wife, but he had much more to say, and his eager interest gave him an artificial strength. He toyed unconsciously with the bedspread, and his face was alight with energy as he went on.

"People have said that I am cruel," he said, "but they do not understand how I am situated.

DEMONS IN HUMAN FORM

"The Territory was set apart for the Indians in 1828. The government at that time promised them protection. That promise has always been ignored. The only protection that has been afforded them is through the courts. To us who have been located on this borderland has fallen the task of acting as protectors. The Territory has always been infested by a class of the refuse of humanity to whom I have given the name of 'criminal intruders.' They are refugees from justice from the States and have left behind them often more tangible records than the mere reputation for vice. They have perpetrated several murders, perhaps, and then come to the new country with a tigerish appetite for blood, whetted by their previous experience. Often they come from a race of criminals, and it is with their foul heredity, as well as their thirst acquired for crime, we have to contend. For many years it was with the ruffians of this immense tract of 74,000 square miles, extending to the Colorado line, I had to cope. Criminals were brought to Fort Smith, where they could be tried by a disinterested jury, which the conditions made impossible in the Territory. They were brutes, or demons rather in human form. Their crimes were deliberately planned and fiendishly executed. Robbery was the chief incentive, and the victims were usually men with whom the murderers traveled on long, lonely rides across the plains.

"Cruel they have said I am, but they forget the utterly hardened character of the men I dealt with. They forget that in my court jurisdiction alone sixty-five deputy marshals were murdered in the discharge of their duty. Wilson, who was connected with the Starr gang, was one of the men whom I sentenced to death. It did not appear to me to be an act of cruelty to sentence that fellow to hang by the neck until he was dead.

"My first term was a portent of what was to follow. Eighteen murder cases came before me for trial. Thirteen were convicted. One of the men I sentenced to death was a half-breed named Sam Foy [sic]. He had murdered and robbed a character known in that region as 'The Barefooted School Teacher.' The young school teacher had been seen to handle a roll of bills, and Foy [sic] shot him and obtained possession of them. He hid the body of the victim in the mountains, and no trace of the young man was discovered till years afterward, when an Indian boy found the skeleton in a secluded spot. There was a fly-leaf of a teacher's manual among the bleaching bones, and on this, strange to say, was still legible the name of the murdered youth.

"Another of those early cases was that of a young physician and his wife from Chattanooga, who began their married life in a little home in the Arbuckle Mountains. Two negroes, who haunted the neighborhood, waylaid the doctor and tied him to a tree, leaving him there to starve. They went to the little home among the fir trees where the young wife was anxiously awaiting the return of her husband, and told her that he had fallen from a boulder high up among the mountains and had broken a leg. They would guide her to him. She went with them and went to her death, for they killed her and threw her into an old well sixty feet deep. Months afterward a searching party found the poor girl's burial place, their attention being attracted by a piece of her dress which had caught upon the rocks in her fall. Her skeleton was found in what

454

had become a den of rattlesnakes. It was a strange chain of circumstances which led to the conviction of one of the murderers. One of them had boasted to his brothers of the double crime and they kept the secret until the fellow was murdered by his partner in the fearful crime. The brothers captured Bully Johnson, the remaining criminal, and he was brought to justice.

"A desperado who murdered a camper and followed the murdered man's little son into the brushwood and killed him even while the little fellow was begging for mercy was one of the men whom I sentenced to death. The half-breed brute told the story himself. 'I killed big white and little white man," he said.

"John Pointer was another. He killed two fellows who had left Eureka Springs with him for a wagon trip across the Territory. With an ax he clove the head of one while he was mixing a pan of dough and the other, who was a lame boy, he struck down in the woods, whither he had pursued him.

INDIAN RACE NOT CRIMINAL

The sick man was pale and exhausted when the earnest recital came to an end. His wife bent above him and plied the fan steadily and soothingly.

"It is this class of men that has come before him," said she; "What could be done?"

"Nothing less than the Judge has done," I answered.

"Don't understand that what I say about these ruffians is directed against the Indians," Judge Parker said, after a little. "Twenty-one years' experience with them has taught me that they are a religiously inclined, law-abiding, authority-respecting people. The Indian Race is not one of criminals. There have been sporadic cases of crime among them, it is true, but as a people they are good citizens.

"A right administration of justice means the abolition of mob violence, which is the result of neglect by judge or jury. During my twenty-one years there have been but three mobs in my jurisdiction, If people expect justice they prefer that the court should mete it. A man arrested the murderer of his son and brought him four hundred miles to me for trial."

DIFFERENCES WITH THE SUPREME COURT

Judge Parker smiled when the conversation turned upon his differences with the United States supreme court. "The justices are men from the civil walks," he said, "and it is not surprising that they are liable to err in criminal cases Our chief point of difference was in the case of a man whom I denied bail, and whom the supreme court maintained should be granted bail. Upon my refusal the court declared its intention to issue a writ of mandamus compelling me to give him his temporary liberty. It never did, however. My chief controversy was with the department of justice last winter. That was a stormy one. My letters on the subject were published in The Republic.

"People have generalized in regard to my administration. They have called me a heartless man, a blood-thirsty man, but no one has pointed to a specific case of undue severity. They are given to saying, 'Judge Parker is too rigid,' but they do not point to any one case and say, 'He was too severe in this,' or 'He should have been more lenient in that.'

"I have ever had the single aim of justice in view. No judge who is influenced by any other consideration is fit for the bench. 'Do equal and exact justice,' is my motto, and I have often said to the grand jury, 'Permit no innocent man to be punished, but let no guilty man escape.'

THE GOVERNMENT'S FEARFUL BLUNDER

"The government has committed a fearful blunder in depriving the Indian Territory of the moral force of a strong federal court, where disinterested juried remote from the scene of the crime can be secured."

The Judge has said all he cared to upon the subject so near his heart. He dismissed it with a gracious wave of the hand, and passed from one subject to another, touching each with the ease and charm of a finished conversationalist.

He thinks the disposition of certain judges to engage actively in politics is reprehensible. "In my twenty-one years of judgeship, I attended but one political meeting, and that was when we drifted into a Democratic street meeting," he said. "I have another motto for my court, 'No politics shall enter here.' I resigned judicial position when I became a candidate for congress."

HANNA AND JONES PLAY CRACK LOO

Referring to the political situation, Judge Parker remarked, dryly, that it reminded him of "a game of crack loo with Jones throwing silver and Hanna gold dollars."

When I bade him good-by, this still vigorous invalid, the judge whose warm heart is controlled by his keen mental vision and unerring sense of justice, he said: "Don't think me too much of a pessimist. I believe better times are coming. The fact that men like Taylor and Duestrow of Missouri and Durrant of San Francisco are being convicted is a good omen."

I tarried a little in the large, cool parlor down stairs before taking my leave. Some neighbors had called to make inquiries about the Judge's welfare, and they lingered to exchange a pleasant word or two with the mistress of the hospitable home. Their son, James, a handsome youth who will leave shortly for his second year at Ann Arbor, stood on the veranda and a patriarchal Newfoundland dog and another that looked as though one of its remote ancestors might have been a setter frolicked about him in clumsy fashion.

The house that has been the home of this just judge and his family for the past fifteen years is a large brick structure with a curiously homelike look about it and is in the heart of a six-lot tract that, while not unkempt, has enough irregularities in its

456

surface and enough variety in shrubbery and trees to make it picturesque in the extreme. There is a mellowed look about everything within and without the house to show that every object has the added charm of association. Charles C. Parker, the older son, is engaged in the practice of law in this city and when he leaves his duties for a few days at the old homestead the family circle if four is complete. Mrs. Parker's maiden name was O'Toole. She comes of a Kentucky family. Her brother, Captain William O'Toole, formerly of the Regular Army, is the Registrar of the Land Office at Seattle. She is related, on the maternal side, to the Hickman family of Columbia, Mo.

HIS WAS A PERPETUAL COURT.

Judge Parker's life at Fort Smith has been a busy one. He has presided over what was practically a perpetual court, for its vacations are hardly more than nominal. The sessions lasted "from 8 a.m. till dark," as an old citizen of Fort Smith assured me.

The official records from 1875 to March, 1895, show that 13, 490 criminal cases have been listed on the docket. Of this number 9,454 persons, or about 70 per cent, of those tried, were either convicted by a jury or entered pleas of guilty. There were 344 of these criminals tried for capital offenses and 151 convicted. Of those convicted 76 had been executed, one was killed while attempting to escape, four have died in jail, two were pardoned and the sentences of the remaining 68 were commuted by the President to terms of imprisonment ranging from 10 years to a lifetime.

It was a gruesome array of criminals that passed before Judge Parker in a horrid phantom of more than two decades. Among those who paid the death penalty were David Evans, John Whittington, Edmund Campbell, James Moore, Smoker Mankiller, Samuel Foy, Aaron Wilson, Isham Seeley, Gibson Ishtonbee, Office McGee, Osey Sanders, William Leach, John Nalley, Sinker Wilson, Samuel Peters, John Postoak, James Diggs, William Elliott, Henry Stewart, Geo. W. Padgett, William Brown, Patrick McGowan, Amos Manley, Abler Manley, Edward Folsom, Robert Massey, Wm. H. Finch, Tualisto, Martin Joseph, Thos. L. Thompson, John Davis, Jack Womankiller, James Arcine, William Parchmeal, Joseph Jackson, James Wasson, Calvin James, Kit Ross, Lincoln Sprole, James Lamb, Albert Odell, John T. Echols, Patrick McCarty, John Stephens, Silas Hampton, Seaborn Kalijah, George Moss, Jack Crow, Own D. Hill, Gus Bogle, Richard Smith, Henry W. Miller, James Mills, Malachi Allen, Wm. Walker, Jack Spaniard, George Tobler, Harris Austin, John Billy, Thos. Willes, Sam Goins, Jimmison Burris, Jefferson Jones, John Stansberry, Bood Crumpton, Shepard Busby, John Pointer, Lewis Holder and Crawford Goldsby, alias Cherokee Bill.

Frank Butler, who was under sentence of death, was killed while trying to escape, and Jackson Marshal, William Hamilton, Kyman Hamilton, and Gibson Partridge died in jail.

As reported in the Fort Smith *Elevator*, September 18, 1896.

ADDENDA

William Meadows, George Brashears, John Jacobs and Frank Collins, convicted of murder, were afterwards pardoned, the last two named in February and March, respectively, 1899.

Ex-Deputy United States Marshal J. H. Mershon, prominently mentioned in this work, became insane in 1898, at his home in Denison, Texas, and was placed in an asylum at Terrell, where he died of heart failure, April 16, 1899. His age was past sixty years. His body was conveyed to Fort Smith for burial.

"Kid" Wilson and Frank Cheney were adjudged insane and were placed in an asylum at Washington, D. C.

Emmet Dalton, serving a life sentence in the penitentiary at Lansing, Kansas, is foreman of the tailoring department.

THE RUBBISH REMOVED

The statement near the top of page 77, relative to the use made of the basement beneath the old court room in what is now the hospital building, was true at the time the matter was given to the printer; the basement has since been cleared of all rubbish, and only "the old, high-panneled desk" remains of the relics referred to.

ERRATA

On page 28, center of page, read: "The fort was garrisoned with a small force of two companies under command of Captain Sturgis, and on April 25, 1861, was captured by a detachment of Arkansas State troops under Col. Solon Borland.

Page 286, sub-head, read: "convicted in spite of bribery."

THE END

BIG BYTE BOOKS is your source for great lost history!

Made in the USA
Las Vegas, NV
21 January 2024

84666875R00270